Java™ Developer's Guide with XML and JSP

by Bill Brogden, Chris Minnick
464 pages ISBN 0-7821-2827-0 US $49.99

Your Java programming knowledge will go a long way toward building an effective e-commerce site. XML is the missing piece, and *Java Developer's Guide to E-Commerce with XML and JSP* gives you expert instruction in the techniques that unite these closely aligned technologies. Covering the latest Servlet and JSP APIs and the current XML standard, this book guides you through all the steps required to build and implement a cohesive, dynamic, and profitable site.

Java™ Developer's Guide to Servlets and JSP

by Bill Brogden
432 page ISBN 0-7821-2809-2 US $49.99

See what Java brings to Web site development. Are you ready to put your Java programming knowledge to work building a dynamic, database-driven Web site? *Java Developer's Guide to Servlets and JSP* gives you exactly what you need: expert instruction in the techniques for constructing a powerful enterprise site from custom servlets and Java Server Pages. Covering the latest APIs, this book is your introduction to technologies that will fundamentally change your approach to Web site development.

Mastering XML™, Premium Edition

by Chuck White, Liam Quin, Linda Burman
1,200 pages ISBN 0-7821-2847-5 US $49.99

Perhaps no other web standard is having as great an impact as XML. The reason? XML is all about structuring data so that you can use it the way you need—getting it into and out of databases and displaying it on any browser, including wireless devices. *Mastering XML Premium Edition* gives you everything you need to leverage the power of XML: Structure data for seamless multi-platform processing, create links that point to multiple documents, and dynamically incorporate data in the linking page. You will also learn about the evolving standards, new vocabularies for vertical markets, and the way XML is being used in real enterprises.

XML COMPLETE

SYBEX®

SAN FRANCISCO ▸ PARIS ▸ DÜSSELDORF ▸ SOEST ▸ LONDON

Associate Publisher: Richard Mills

Acquisitions and Developmental Editor: Tom Cirtin

Compilation Editor: Chuck White

Editors: Pat Coleman, Jeff Gammon, Pete Gaughan, Susan Hobbs, Gene Redding, Liz Welch

Production Editor: Jennifer Campbell

Technical Editors: Gregory A. Beamer, Ashok Hanumanth, Charlie Hornberger, Darlene Khasrowpour, Adrian W. Kingsley-Hughes, Piroz Mohseni, Todd Stauffer, John Zukowski

Book Designer: Maureen Forys, Happenstance Type-O-Rama

Graphic Illustrator: Tony Jonick

Electronic Publishing Specialists: Judy Fung, Jill Niles

Proofreaders: Laurie O'Connell, Yariv Rabinovitch

Indexer: Ted Laux

Cover Designer: Design Site

Cover Photographer: Jeffrey Coolidge/ImageBank

Library of Congress Card Number: 2001094593

ISBN: 0-7821-4033-5

Manufactured in the United States of America

10 9 8 7 6 5 4 3 2 1

ACKNOWLEDGMENTS

This book incorporates the work of many people, inside and outside Sybex.

Richard Mills and Tom Cirtin defined the book's overall structure and contents. Chuck White offered his technical expertise in adapting the material for publication in this book.

A large team of editors, developmental editors, production editors, and technical editors helped to put together the various books from which *XML Complete* was compiled: Raquel Baker, Tom Cirtin, and Denise Santoro Lincoln handled developmental tasks. Elizabeth Campbell, Pat Coleman, Jeff Gammon, Pete Gaughan, Susan Hobbs, Leslie E. H. Light, Gene Redding, Colleen Strand, and Nathan Whiteside all contributed to editing or production editing. And Gregory A. Beamer, Ashok Hanumanth, Charlie Hornberger, Darlene Khasrowpour, Adrian W. Kingsley-Hughes, Piroz Mohseni, Todd Stauffer, and John Zukowski provided technical edits.

Thanks to Liz Welch for her hard work in editing the book. Chuck White deserves particular thanks for making sure all of the material in this book was up-to-date and organized, and flowed in a seamless manner.

The *XML Complete* production team of electronic desktop specialists Judy Fung and Jill Niles, production editor Jennifer Campbell, and proofreaders Laurie O'Connell and Yariv Rabinovitch worked with speed and accuracy to turn the manuscript files and illustrations into the handsome book you're now reading. Rachel Boyce, Liz Paulus, Dan Schiff, and Erica Yee also helped in various ways to keep the project moving.

Finally, our most important thanks go to the contributors who agreed to have their work excerpted into *XML Complete*: Kurt Cagle, Bill Brogden, Chelsea Valentine, Mary Burmeister, Chuck White, Liam Quin, and Martin C. Brown. Without their efforts, this book would not exist.

CONTENTS AT A GLANCE

Appendices

CONTENTS

Part III ▶ Working with XHTML   243

Part V ▸ E-Commerce Solutions with XML and JSP

Appendices

Appendix A   Extensible Markup Language (XML) 1.0 (Second Edition)   803

Appendix B   XML Schema Elements   865

INTRODUCTION

XML Complete is a one-of-a-kind computer book—valuable both for the breadth of its content and for its low price. This thousand-page compilation of information from some of the very best Sybex books provides comprehensive coverage of the hottest topics in XML programming today. This book, unique in the computer book world, was created with several goals in mind:

- ▶ To offer a thorough guide covering all the aspects of XML programming at an affordable price

- ▶ To acquaint you with some of our best authors—their writing styles and teaching skills, and the level of expertise they bring to their books—so you can easily find a match for your interests as you delve deeper into XML

XML Complete is an essential reference for XML developers, or aspiring XML developers, who want to broaden their understanding of this powerful language. This book covers a wide spectrum of XML technologies and vocabularies. Some of the key topics include

- ▶ XML Schema

- ▶ The Document Object Model (DOM)

- ▶ XML Processing using Perl, Python, and other open source implementations

- ▶ SOAP and XML-RPC

- ▶ The servlet/JSP/XML architecture

- ▶ XHTML

- ▶ XSLT

The book also contains introductory chapters on basic XML development. Even if you are familiar with the core syntax of XML, you'll find these chapters to be a handy reference. They cover element and attribute creation, DTDs, and entities. If you've read other computer "how-to" books, you've seen that there are many possible approaches to the task of showing how to use software effectively. The books from which *XML Complete* was compiled represent a range of the approaches to teaching that Sybex and its authors have developed—from the specific *Developer's Guide* style to the wide-ranging, thoroughly detailed *Mastering* style.

These books also address readers at different levels of computer experience. As you read through various chapters of this book, you'll see which approach works best for you. You'll also see what these books have in common: a commitment to clarity, accuracy, and practicality.

You'll find in these pages ample evidence of the expertise of Sybex's authors. Unlike publishers who produce "books by committee," Sybex authors are encouraged to write in individual voices that reflect their own experience with the software at hand and with the evolution of today's personal computers. Nearly every book represented here is the work of a single writer or a pair of close collaborators, and you are getting the benefit of each author's direct experience.

In adapting the various source materials for inclusion in *XML Complete*, the compiler preserved these individual voices and perspectives. Chapters were edited only to minimize duplication and update or add cross-references, so that you can easily follow a topic across chapters. A few sections were also edited for length so that other important information could be included.

Who Can Benefit from This Book?

XML Complete is designed to meet the needs of any developer who wants a complete reference to building XML applications, particularly those scaled for the Internet. The contents and index will guide you to the subjects you're looking for.

NOTE
Readers will also find all of the sample code from this book on the Sybex website, www.sybex.com.

How This Book Is Organized

XML Complete has five parts, consisting of twenty-four chapters, and three appendices.

NOTE
Readers will find a fourth appendix, the DOM Appendix, on the Sybex website at www.sybex.com. Simply search for *XML Complete*—you'll find a link to the appendix on the book's page.

Part I: XML Fundamentals   These first four chapters cover the core essentials of XML: Document creation, the creation of elements and attributes, and the understanding and creation of entities.

Part II: XML Data Design   These four chapters study the design of XML data and structure. The first chapter considers basic design principles, and the next three chapters get into the specifics of data design using DTDs and schemas.

Part III: Working with XHTML   These three chapters cover XHTML, which is the official new version of HTML as an XML vocabulary.

Part IV: XML Scripting and Processing   These ten chapters will demonstrate how to harness the true power of XML using such long-established scripting languages as Perl, Python, and TCL, as well as some newer languages like PHP. This section also covers XSLT, which makes it possible to transform XML documents into different markup and vocabularies.

Part V: E-Commerce Solutions with XML and JSP   The last three chapters cover e-commerce applications in a Java environment using JavaServer Pages (JSP).

A Few Typographical Conventions

When a Windows operation requires a series of choices from menus or dialog boxes, the ➤ symbol is used to guide you through the instructions, like this: "Select Programs ➤ Accessories ➤ System Tools ➤ System Information." The items the ➤ symbol separates may be menu names, toolbar icons, check boxes, or other elements of the Windows interface—any place you can make a selection.

This typeface is used to identify Internet URLs and code, and **boldface type** is used whenever you need to type something into a text box.

You'll find these types of special notes throughout the book:

TIP

You'll see a lot of these—quicker and smarter ways to accomplish a task, which the authors have based on many years of experience working with XML.

NOTE

You'll see these Notes, too. They usually represent alternate ways to accomplish a task or some additional information that needs to be highlighted.

WARNING

In a few places you'll see a Warning like this one. When you see a warning, do pay attention to it.

YOU'LL ALSO SEE "SIDEBAR" BOXES LIKE THIS

These boxed sections provide added explanation of special topics that are noted briefly in the surrounding discussion, but that you may want to explore separately. Each sidebar has a heading that announces the topic, so you can quickly decide whether it's something you need to know about.

For More Information...

See the Sybex website, www.sybex.com, to learn more about all of the books that went into *XML Complete*. On the site's Catalog page, you'll find links to any book you're interested in. Also, be sure to check the Sybex site for late-breaking developments about the sample code and applications.

We hope you enjoy this book and find it useful. Good luck in your XML programming endeavors!

PART I
XML Fundamentals

Chapter 1
CREATING XML DOCUMENTS

The eXtensible Markup Language (XML) is a text- and data-formatting language that, like HTML, has a tag-based syntax. At first glance, in fact, it looks a lot like HTML, but it's capable of doing much more: Not only can you prescribe text styles, but the power of XML comes from its capability to define data types for cross-platform communication. Furthermore, XML's *extensibility* enables you to create your own tags for developing applications for specific needs.

The basis of XML is the XML document. In its most essential form, it is a text file with the .xml extension that contains text, data, and the XML tags. XML does no data processing, however; for that, you need to employ an XML processor, or *parser*. Parsers are compiled applications developed in any number of programming languages, such as C or Java. Parsers come in many flavors, and sometimes are embedded in other applications, such as Internet Explorer 5 (IE 5) and above. But first, you need to learn how to create a basic XML document.

The simplest XML documents can be created using a text editor and just a few short lines of code. The most complex

Adapted from *Mastering™ XML, Premium Edition*, by Chuck White, Liam Quin, and Linda Burman
ISBN 0-7821-2847-5   1,155 pages $49.99

XML documents, however, could not possibly be developed without the help of powerful software. In fact, many XML documents are extracted from a database or through other processes.

This doesn't, however, preclude your understanding the intricacies of XML. The contrary is probably true, because the more that is hidden from you, the harder it is to understand what is happening under the hood.

This chapter explores how to build an XML document. First, we'll begin with a simple XML document. Next, we'll take you through the basic syntax of XML. Then, we'll break an XML document into its components. We'll look briefly at namespaces, and then we'll help you understand how to choose which rule-based system to use—document type definitions (DTDs) or schemas. Finally, we'll build another simple XML document, with enough added complexity to get you ready for the rest of the book.

CREATING AN XML DOCUMENT

Writing your first XML document is so easy, we're going to dive right in and write one. We're even going to write a simple style sheet to get you to see it in a Web browser.

NOTE
You'll need IE 5 or above or Netscape 6 or above to view this example.

This basic XML document contains one element, called `Basic`. This is really the essence of XML: the ability to define your own meaning and structure to a document. So open your favorite text editor and type the contents of Listing 1.1, beginning with `<?xml version="1.0"?>`.

Listing 1.1: A Basic XML Document

```
<?xml version="1.0"?>
<?xml-stylesheet type="text/xsl" href="Basic.xsl"?>
<Basic>Hello World</Basic>
```

Next, save the file as `HelloWorld.xml`. If you are using Notepad in Windows, in the Save As dialog box be sure to select All Files from the Save As Type drop-down list. If you don't, Notepad will save the file with a .txt extension, and you may not be able to open the document in an XML processor. You can also wrap the filename in quotes as an alternative. If you are on a Macintosh, be sure to save the file with an .xml extension. Most Macintosh programs default to saving files without an extension of any kind, so you will need to account for this.

Next, let's develop a simple style sheet so we can view the file in a browser. This isn't necessary, because XML parsers, including the one that comes with IE 5, will parse the document and reveal its structure. But we want to give you something here that looks familiar, and most people have by now seen a simple Web page.

The next step then is to create our simple style sheet. Type the contents of Listing 1.2, beginning with <?xml version="1.0" ?>.

Listing 1.2: A Basic XSL(T) Document

```
<?xml version="1.0" ?>
<xsl:stylesheet version="1.0"
      xmlns:xsl="http://www.w3.org/1999/XSL
➡/Transform">
<!- xmlns:xsl="http://www.w3.org/TR/WD-xsl" for
most versions of Internet Explorer 5 ->
        <xsl:template match="/">
          <html>
            <head>
              <title>A Basic Stylesheet
              </title>
            </head>
            <body>
              <xsl:value-of select="/"/>
            </body>
          </html>
        </xsl:template>
</xsl:stylesheet>
```

Next, save this file as Basic.xsl in the same directory or folder as HelloWorld.xml. The browser will need to be able to access it in order to view HelloWorld.xml.

If you have Netscape 6, you can choose Open File from the File menu and navigate to the directory in which you saved HelloWorld.xml. Open the file in Netscape, and the screen shown in Figure 1.1 should appear on your desktop.

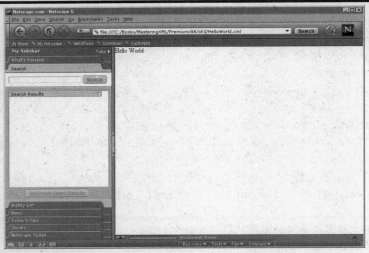

FIGURE 1.1: The file Basic.xml as rendered by Netscape 6

NOTE

You don't need to build a style sheet in Netscape. Netscape will render the document using built-in style sheets based on Cascading Style Sheets (CSS), which is a style sheet language used by some Web browsers.

If you have IE 5, choose File ➢ Open to navigate to HelloWorld.xml. You may need to swap the portion of the XSL code that reads xmlns:xsl="http://www.w3.org/1999/XSL/Transform" for the commented code that reads xmlns:xsl="http://www.w3.org/TR/WD-xsl" and resave Basic.xsl if IE 5 doesn't seem to render anything. Just replace one with the other doing a copy and paste. There's no need to change the code between the <!-- and --> comment tags. (See the "Miscellaneous Statements" section later in this chapter for more information about using comments.) If you found that step necessary, refresh your browser after resaving Basic.xsl. The page should now display, looking like the screen in Figure 1.2.

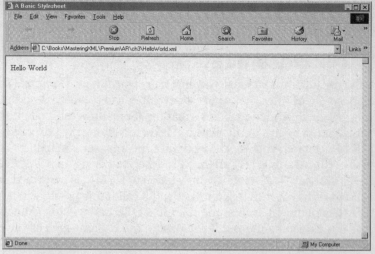

FIGURE 1.2: The file HelloWorld.xml as rendered by Internet Explorer 5

Two Kinds of "Legal" XML

XML parsers read two types of XML documents that can, if not marked up properly, generate errors: *well-formed* and *valid*. A well-formed document is syntactically correct but isn't necessarily valid against a DTD. A valid document has been validated against a DTD.

Well-Formed XML Documents

A well-formed XML document satisfies the production rules described in the XML specification, which is defined at www.w3.org/TR/REC-xml and in Appendix A of this book. These rules are discussed in this chapter. An XML parser will always generate errors if it encounters an XML document that is not well formed and will never make any adjustments to try to compensate for the offending document. This is very different from an HTML browser, which will generally allow for syntax mistakes in HTML code and render a document as best it can.

A well-formed document consists of character data and markup. The markup separates the content (character data) of a document from its start tags, end tags, empty element tags, entity references, character references, comments, CDATA section delimiters, document type declarations, and processing instructions. You'll learn what each of these are as this chapter progresses.

Valid XML Documents

A valid document is validated against a *document type definition (DTD)*, which is a set of rules that you as a developer can create to describe the semantics of an XML document's markup. Semantics tell a computer what meaning to give to the markup. Browsers know the purpose behind an HTML element such as <H1> because the browser is somehow made aware of the meaning. (HTML itself is described using an SGML DTD, and XHTML, an XML-conformant version of HTML, is described using an XML DTD.) An XML parser that isn't a validating parser will not check the document against the rules in a DTD and will not generate any errors if the document doesn't conform to the DTD, as long as the document is at least well formed. A validating parser will examine the XML document to see if it matches the rules as declared by the DTD with which it is associated. If the document doesn't match the rules perfectly, it isn't a conforming document, and the parser will generate an error, even if the document is otherwise a well-formed document.

UNDERSTANDING GENERAL SYNTAX

The general syntax of an XML document is dictated by a set of rules defined by a document created by the W3C (World Wide Web Consortium). This document is called the XML 1.0 Specification, and it consists of a grammar-based set of production rules that are based on a formal notation called the Extended Backus-Naur Form (EBNF), which is used to formalize the syntax of a computer language, in addition to explicit rules that extend beyond the EBNF production rules and which must also be adhered to. EBNF is designed to be read by a machine, so at first glance it can be quite a mysterious-looking beast, but it's actually no worse than getting through a DTD. It just looks different from what you might be used to seeing.

We've eliminated EBNF entirely from the mix in this chapter and spelled out the grammatical rules of XML entirely in plain English (or, if you're reading a translated version of this book, in your own language). If you want to see the actual EBNF-based specifications, take a look at Appendix A. We also provide a guide to EBNF in Appendix A to make interpreting its syntax easier.

The Basic Rules

You need to understand a few basic rules of syntax before diving into the rest of the structure of XML documents. These rules are absolute. When we say, for example, that you need to put quotes around attribute values, we don't mean sometimes, or with the possible exception of another event, but *always*. This is one of XML's strengths. Getting used to this depends on your background. If you come from a SQL background, you'll find XML rather intuitive. If your background is HTML, the constraints may initially frustrate you. Eventually, though, you'll find that just as a database constraint is your best friend, so are the constraints in XML, and you'll learn to love them.

Case Sensitivity in XML

XML is case sensitive. This is the first rule we'll cover, and it bears repeating: XML is case sensitive. If a rule in a DTD defines an element called foo, you can't call it FOO when you use that element in your document. In addition, the element's start tag must exactly match the end tag: <foo></foo>, not <foo></FOO>. Any variation from that rule will generate an error.

A real-world example: XHTML, which is the newest version of HTML and which conforms to an XML DTD, requires, by definition, that all its elements be lowercase. There was not a small amount of wrangling over this, but the W3C group that authored the specification needed to make a decision one way or the other. If they had gone the other direction, a large group of folks who prefer lowercase would have put up substantial resistance. Either way, the W3C group in charge of XHTML was going to make people unhappy. They could also have defined both lower- and uppercase rules, but that would have made the DTD twice as big and would have made extending the spec more unwieldy.

Start and End Tags

All start tags must have end tags. End tags, without exception, must always follow start tags in XML. An end tag can appear immediately after the name of the element if the element doesn't contain content, but it must appear. The following elements have both start and end tags:

```
<Basic>Hello World</Basic>

<Basic/>

<Basic></Basic>
```

As you can see, you can create an empty element tag in two ways. By convention, most developers use the first empty element example (<Basic/>). Many developers also prefer to add a space between the tag name and the / character, which keeps it consistent with XHTML.

Start Tag Consistency

The start tag that begins a document instance must end it. This is the same thing as saying that all XML documents must contain a root element (also referred to as the document element in the Document Object Model, or DOM, which is a set of interfaces that allow you to manage an XML document programmatically). The root element is always the first element in a document instance, and a root element must contain all other elements, if any exist. The following, then, will generate an error:

```
<Basic/>
<Next></Next>
```

The following is correct:

```
<Basic>
<Next></Next>
</Basic>
```

NOTE

The root element is not the same as the *root* of the document, sometimes referred to as a *root node* in applications such as XSLT. The root of the document begins with the first character an XML processor encounters when parsing an XML document and ends at the last character.

Proper Nesting of Elements

Elements must be properly nested. Elements can't stand alone in a document (unless there is only one element, the root element). All of them need to be contained within a hierarchy of elements that begins with the root element.

The easiest way to understand this concept is to simply get into one valuable habit when marking up an XML document: When you create a start tag for an element, immediately create the end tag. Another element can exist within an element, but each element's start tag must have a corresponding end tag before another element's start tag begins.

Think of plastic storage containers in your kitchen. If you have a lot of them, you probably store some of them together, one inside another. The largest one contains the next largest one, and that one contains the next largest size, and so on. XML doesn't care how big your element is, but like with the storage containers in your kitchen, you can't place part of one element inside one element and another part inside another element. If you have three elements total in your XML document, the root element must contain the other two:

```
<Basic>
    <Next type="the next one">
        <onemore>some content</onemore>
    </Next>
</Basic>
```

This markup would be wrong if the elements weren't nested properly. The following will generate an error:

```
<Basic>
    <onemore>

        <Next type="the next one">some content
    </onemore>
        </Next>
</Basic>
```

The preceding code contains an example of an element with another element as content and an element with character data as content. You could also have an empty element mixed in:

```
<Basic>
    <onemore>

        <Next type="the next one">some content
            <br />and some more</onemore>
        </Next>
</Basic>
```

We included the extra space in the <br> element in deference to HTML browsers, which can have trouble with an empty <br> element without the space (
) but can handle it otherwise.

Reserved Markup Characters

The open angle bracket (<) and ampersand (&) are reserved for markup.
Element tags must begin with the < character, and entities and character
references in a document instance must begin with the & character, which
means that if you use either of these characters for any other purpose,
you'll generate an error. When an XML parser encounters the < character,
it assumes an element or other markup statement is about to start. If it
doesn't find the characters it is expecting next, an XML name followed
directly by a right angle bracket (>), or a comment or processing instruction, it generates an error. Similarly, when an XML parser encounters an
& character, it assumes it has encountered an entity. There are five predefined entities in XML:

   <   Generates the < character in character data.

   >   Generates the > character in character data.

   &   Generates the & character in character data.

   '   Generates the ' character in character data.

   "   Generates the " character in character data.

If the characters following the & character don't consist of characters
that help to build one of the preceding list of entities, the parser will
assume the entity was defined in the DTD or is a character reference. If
the parser doesn't find that definition or the proper character reference,
it will generate an error.

Character references are similar in appearance to entity references,
but, depending on encoding, they don't need to be declared and they
refer to specific characters (such as accented letters) using a special numbering system called Unicode. You can find a chart of character references
in Chapter 4, "Understanding and Creating Entities."

Using predefined entities in place of the <, >, &, ', and " characters is
called *escaping* a character. This just means you are guaranteeing their
safety so that you actually do end up with the characters you're hoping
for. Notice the greater-than character (>). Always escape this character
even if you're pretty sure there is no less-than character (<).

Examine the following lines of code to see if you can identify the legal
and illegal uses of the < and & characters. We'll identify the correct
answers by referencing the code's line numbers in the paragraphs that
follow.

```
1.  <!ENTITY rights "&#169;">
2.  <fragment>&rights;2001 Chuck White</fragment>
3.  <&fragment>foo</&fragment>
4.  <fragment>foo & foo</fragment>
5.  <fragment>1 < 2 </fragment>
6.  <fragment>&replacement;  &more</fragment>
7.  <fragment>&replacement;  &more;</fragment>
8.  <fragment>
    The <> operator must be escaped
    </fragment>
9.  <fragment>
    I was hoping I could create this "null" element:
    </></fragment>
10. <fragment>
    Maybe it will work if I add a space:
    < /></fragment>
11. <fragment>
    I was hoping I could create
    this "null" element: <![CDATA[</>]]>
    </fragment>
```

Line 1 correctly uses an entity reference declaration in a DTD document. The declaration says, "Replace the entity `rights` with the copyright symbol (the © character reference)."

Line 2 correctly uses the declared entity within the document instance. If output to text using an XSLT transformation, the result would look like this: `2001 Chuck White`.

Line 3 is incorrect. It will generate an XML parser error that says something like "A name was started with an invalid character."

Line 4 is also incorrect, because you can't use the & character as part of element content when it's not following the rules we've described here. You'll get an error message similar to "White space is not allowed at this location."

You'll receive the same message if you try to parse Line 5. That's because the parser expects the < character to be a start tag.

Line 6 would have been legal if both ENTITY declarations were made in the DTD, but the author left off the semicolon at the end of the second entity, which would generate an error.

Line 7 is correct. It's a corrected version of Line 6 (assuming there is a corresponding ENTITY declaration).

Lines 8, 9, and 10 will not work either, because they are all incorrect uses of the start tag character.

Line 11 corrects Line 9 by using a CDATA section to escape the characters into raw text so that the parser does not attempt to interpret them as markup.

XML Declaration Priority

If you are using an XML declaration, it must come first. The XML declaration simply declares that a document is an XML document and describes its version. It is optional, but if you use it (and by convention you should unless you're working with a document fragment for inclusion in another XML document), it must, unequivocally, be the first statement in an XML document:

```
<?xml version="1.0"?>
```

The XML declaration is part of the document prolog, as you will discover later, and not part of the document instance (the main body of the document that holds the data you're working with). It has no bearing on the ordering or nesting of elements and is, in fact, not an element itself. Therefore, it is not subject to the rule that dictates that a root element must contain all other elements. This is *not* an exception to any rules; it is part of the rules. Because an XML declaration does not qualify as an element, it is not subject to the rules to which elements must adhere. It is also not a processing instruction, although it looks like one. A processing instruction hands off instructions to another application. An XML declaration doesn't do that.

Quotation Marks for Attribute Values

Attribute values must be enclosed in quotation marks. In HTML, attribute values don't have to be in quotes for a browser to render a document. Not so for XML. Leave off the quotes, and an XML parser is *required* to generate an error. Whether you use single or double quotes is up to you, but be consistent at each end of the attribute value. It's okay to nest one type of quote, such as single quotes, inside another set of a different type of quotes, such as double quotes. The following are examples of attribute values in each kind of quotes:

```
<foo myatt="1.0">
<foo myatt='1.0'>
```

Characters, Markup, and Tags

To create an XML document, you should also have an understanding of markup and character data. Each of these can be categorized as one of the following:

- ▶ Part of a name token
- ▶ A white space character
- ▶ A member of a literal string
- ▶ Markup

These are explained in the following sections.

XML Names and Name Tokens

XML *names* are important because so many parts of an XML document are bound by the rules associated with them. An XML name describes the rules that declare how an XML name can be defined. A *name token* is any mix of name characters. XML names consist of name tokens, but there are some restrictions, as noted in the following rules. There is a distinction between name tokens and XML names. Name tokens aren't used only in XML names. They can also be used to identify the data type of an attribute and to define the syntax for enumerated values in attributes (values that are declared as the only acceptable values by a DTD). The rules are as follows:

- ▶ An XML name may begin with an underscore or a letter.
- ▶ XML names can contain letters, digits, periods, hyphens, underscores, and colons.
- ▶ XML names can contain combining characters (a letter with a mark attached to it, such as the combination of an accent mark that appears directly over a letter), and extending characters (which aren't letters but rather alphabetic symbols that some languages use and that act like letters in many ways). Extending characters are not an English language phenomenon.

- ▶ XML names cannot contain any punctuation marks other than periods, colons, or hyphens.

- ▶ XML names cannot contain white space.

- ▶ XML names cannot begin with a number (or more correctly expressed, a digit), but can contain digits (yes to `<element5>`, no `<5element>` o).

- ▶ Name tokens adhere to the same rules as XML names, except that they *can* begin with a number.

- ▶ Both XML names and name tokens are case sensitive.

Examine the following lines of code to see if you can identify the legal and illegal uses of XML names. We'll identify the correct answers by referencing the code's line numbers in the paragraphs that follow.

```
1.  <fragment></fragment>
2.  <fragment5></fragment5>
3.  <5fragment5></5fragment5>
4.  <fivefragment5></fivefragment5>
5.  <five,fragment5></five,fragment5>
6.  <five;fragment5></five;fragment5>
7.  <five_fragment5></five_fragment5>
8.  <five_fragment5:frag5></five_fragment5:frag5>
9.  <!fragment></!fragment>
10. <[fragment]></![fragment]>
11. <xmlFoo/>
```

Lines 1 and 2 are correct.

Line 3 will generate an error that states an element began with an invalid character.

Line 4 is correct.

Lines 5 and 6 contain invalid characters.

Line 7 fixes Lines 5 and 6 by using a legal underscore character.

Line 8 will generate an error that says something like " Reference to undeclared namespace prefix: `five_fragment5`." Namespaces are covered at the end of this chapter.

Line 9 will generate an error that complains that a declaration has an invalid name.

Line 10 will generate an error that complains that an element began with an invalid character.

Line 11 is incorrect, because it starts with xml, which cannot start XML names; however, it will not generate an error.

White Space Characters

White space has different meanings in different applications, whether it be print media, code development, or HTML. The term *white space* here designates such characters as line feeds, tabs, carriage returns, and non-breaking spaces outside XML markup, which are always preserved. For example, when the following fragment of code is output into text via an XSLT transform, the space is preserved (unless steps are taken to override the default XSLT mechanism):

```
<?xml version="1.0"?>

<fragment>foo                foo



   foo</fragment>
```

The preceding fragment, when transformed into text, looks like this:

```
foo                foo



foo
```

You'll get the same kind of result if you place the white space in an attribute value. So the following is perfectly acceptable, and when output, the spaces will be preserved:

```
<fragment x="1  2         5 "/>
```

However (and you'll see the logic here), if you add a space to the frag-ment element, you'll have a mess on your hands. The parser will expect an equal sign after *ment*:

```
<frag ment x="1  2         5 "/>
```

You can probably see why just by examining the code. When a white space appears within an element, that element name ends. Thus, the following works fine:

```
<fragment    ></fragment>
```

That's because as soon as the XML parser encounters the white space in the XML element name, it is satisfied that, in this case, the name is `fragment`, and it moves on to the next order of business.

Having said all that, if you were to load the above text into an HTML browser, the browser would "normalize" the text so that the spaces disappear to the point where there is no more than one space between words, and no line breaks (unless you include markup to quash this behavior). So if you are used to HTML's treatment of white space, be aware that XML acts differently.

Literal Strings

Literal strings are quoted strings that don't contain other quoted strings. They manage the content of internal entities, attribute values, and external identifiers. There are three kinds of literal strings:

▶ Literal strings that define entity values. These can consist of any character except the % and & characters, unless they are starting an entity reference within the literal string (in other words, the literal string that defines your entity reference can itself contain an entity reference). So `"Today &amp; Tomorrow"` is okay as part of your literal string entity reference, but `"Today & Tomorrow"` will generate an error.

▶ Literal strings that define attribute values, such as the following: `<fragment x="1"/>`.

▶ System literals that define URIs (Uniform Resource Identifiers), such as those found in entity definitions: `<!ENTITY foofrag SYSTEM "foo.txt">`.

Examine the following lines of code to see if you can identify the legal and illegal uses of string literals. We'll identify the correct answers by referencing the code's line numbers in the paragraphs that follow.

```
1.   <fragment x="y">"<markup/>"</fragment>
2.   <fragment x="1+2, 'x/3'=1, '5"/>
3.   <!ENTITY foofrag SYSTEM "foo">
4.   <!ENTITY foofrag SYSTEM "foo.txt">
5.   <!ENTITY foofrag  "foo">
```

```
6.  <fragment >"Excellent," said Holmes, "That's why she
    cried, 'Liar!'"</fragment>
```

Line 1 is fine. It consists of a simple string literal used as content within an element.

Line 2 may look like a lot of funny business is going on, but it's really okay. All the quotes within the double quotes are single quotes. The only bad thing that can really happen is when a non-XML parser encounters such a beast and is expecting a terminated string. But the XML parser itself doesn't care about such things. It only cares that literal strings be encapsulated within a pair of double quotes.

Line 3 is a mini-brain teaser. Technically, it is okay, but because it's a system literal, the parser will expect to be able to locate the named URI.

Assuming the entity is a text file, Line 4 is a much better bet. It could also be that the author of the DTD meant the entity to merely be the string, foo, in which case Line 5 is the correct syntax.

Line 6 is a good example of why it's important to be able to include single quotes within double quotes. This is an acceptable use of string literals.

Markup

Markup is notation that provides information to an XML parser on how to parse, or read, an XML document; which parts of a document to skip; and which parts of a document to hand off to another application. Based on that information, a parser, as part of its parsing routine, looks to see if the document is well formed. If a DTD is associated with the document, the parser will, if it is a validating parser (in other words, if it actually possesses the ability to test for it), test the document to see if it is valid. If the document fails either a well-formedness test or a validity test, the parser will return an error.

The kind of markup you encounter depends on the type of nodes, or components, of an XML document you encounter. The markup for a processing instruction is different from the markup for an element, an entity, or a comment.

As mentioned at the beginning of the chapter, the following characters or group of characters all form markup: start tags, end tags, empty element tags, entity references, character references, comments, CDATA section delimiters, document type declarations, and processing instructions.

The Components of an XML Document

XML doesn't require two documents in order to accomplish something. But starting off this way does force you into thinking the way you will need to in the long term when managing XML development.

XML documents consist of two or more main document entities: the document prolog, the document instance, and, optionally, any processing instructions you might have. The prolog is like an introductory notation that gives instructions to a processor about how to handle the main part of the document, which is the document instance. Processing instructions can appear arbitrarily within either the document prolog or the document instance—it's up to you. They are for sending instructions to another processing application beyond the realm of the XML parser.

The Document Prolog

All XML documents start with a prolog, even if there is nothing in the prolog. Generally, there is something, because a prolog contributes mightily to a processing environment's capabilities and removes default processing routines that may not be wanted. A document prolog consists of the following, in the order shown:

1. An optional XML declaration

2. Zero or more miscellaneous statements

3. An optional document type declaration

4. Zero or more miscellaneous statements

The order of these is important. If you stray from the order specified, your XML parser will generate an error message.

NOTE

XML parsers are not allowed by the specification to "fix" errors in your code. All they are allowed to do is generate a message that reports the error to you.

The XML Declaration

The XML declaration is the first thing you usually will see in an XML document (the only exception is if there is nothing in the prolog). It consists of a left angle bracket, followed by a question mark character, and, with no spaces, the following three characters: xml. The simplest XML declaration looks like this:

```
<?xml version="1.0"?>
```

The declaration consists of, in the order shown, the following:

1. This specific string <?xml

2. A required statement defining the version of XML used by the document instance

3. An optional declaration defining the encoding

4. An optional declaration describing whether the XML document is a standalone document

5. An optional white space character

6. The string value, ?>

Here is an example of a complete XML declaration:

```
<?xml version="1.0" encoding="UTF-8"
standalone="yes"?>
```

Many people mistake some of the statements in an XML declaration for attributes, and some XML editing applications even describe them as such in their graphical user interfaces (GUIs), but they're not attributes. An XML declaration, like the rest of the document prolog, has its own rules of syntax, quite separate from the document rules that govern a document instance. In addition, many people mistake XML declarations for a processing instruction.

XML Version Declaration   There is only one version of XML: 1.0. When creating an XML version declaration, you can use single or double quotes (as long as the opening and closing quotes are either both single or both double), and you can include a white space character on either side or both sides of the = operator. The following is a legal XML declaration:

```
<?xml version = '1.0' ?>
```

Naturally, there may be versions of XML in the future. So by convention, almost everyone now includes the version information in their XML declaration so they won't need to worry about backward-compatibility issues.

Encoding Declaration   This is especially useful for dealing with non-Western languages. Generally, if you are an English speaker, your operating system uses a 7-bit ASCII encoding, which is a subset of UTF-8 (a Unicode encoding), which in turn is the default encoding scheme in XML parsers.

Standalone Declaration   The standalone declaration indicates whether the document has any links that make it a complete document. You can use single or double quotes (as long as the opening and closing quotes are either both single or both double).

The following is an XML prolog with an encoding declaration and a standalone declaration. The order is important. And remember, even though they look like attribute value pairs, these declarations are not attribute value pairs and need to be in the order shown:

```
<?xml version = "1.0"
encoding="UTF-8" standalone="yes" ?>
```

Miscellaneous Statements

Miscellaneous statements can include comments, which are notations describing the purpose of one or more aspects of the document and which are completely ignored by the parser because they are designed strictly for human consumption. They can also include white space and processing instructions.

Comments are simple to create in XML. They always start with the <!-- characters and end with the --> characters. The parser always ignores everything in between. The following is an example of a comment:

```
<!-- this is a comment. Anything can go here -->
```

The following comment is also acceptable, even though it contains characters that would generate errors in other circumstances:

```
<!-- <1 & anything else : ;  -->
```

Document Type Declaration

The document type declaration declares which document type definition (DTD) is associated with the document instance. If the DTD is embedded within the document as a whole, its declarative statements follow. If the

DTD is linked, the declaration contains link information that tells the XML parser where to find the DTD.

Let's take a look at both embedded and linked document type declarations. Listing 1.3 shows an embedded document type declaration, and Listing 1.4 shows a linked document type definition.

Listing 1.3: Embedded Document Type Declaration

```
<?xml version = "1.0"
encoding="UTF-8" standalone="yes" ?>
<!DOCTYPE fragment
[ <!ELEMENT fragment (#PCDATA)>
<!ENTITY foofrag  "said Holmes, ">
]>
<fragment >"Excellent," &foofrag;
"That's why she cried, 'Liar!'"</fragment>
```

Listing 1.4: Linked Document Type Definition

```
<?xml version = "1.0"
encoding="UTF-8" standalone="yes" ?>
<!DOCTYPE fragment SYSTEM "fragment.dtd">
<fragment >"Excellent," &foofrag;
"That's why she cried, 'Liar!'"</fragment>
```

If you don't specify an absolute URI in Listing 1.4, your parser will need some other way of locating the DTD. Generally this means it exists in the same directory or a named directory relative to the root of the XML document.

The Document Instance

The document *instance* is the main part of an XML document that follows the prolog. It contains the content of the XML document, or the data. The name *instance* may be familiar to those of you with programming backgrounds who understand class hierarchies. The document is an instance of the class defined by a DTD. If there is no DTD, the instance consists of an undefined class. If you don't have a programming background, think of a DTD as a set of rules. The document instance contains data described as a set that follows the rules set out in the DTD, which may or may not be embedded in the document. The document instance can be broken into a number of subcomponents, or entities. The entire root element is one such entity. Entities can be broken down further so that individual elements and groups of elements can be considered entities, which you can, if you want, separate out of the document and link to the document instance using ENTITY declarations in your DTD.

Elements

Elements consist of three character-level components: the start tag, the end tag, and the content, if there is any. The names of elements must follow the production rules of XML names. Not all elements have content, and there is no rule that says they must.

More details of element construction can be found in Chapter 2, "Understanding and Creating Elements."

Start Tags   Start tags begin with a <. This is called a left angle bracket. They must be followed by an XML name.

XML Names   After creating the start tag, you name your element using an XML name. As we mentioned earlier, XML names may begin with an underscore, a letter, or a colon. They can contain letters, digits, periods, hyphens, underscores, colons, combining characters (a letter with a mark attached to it, such as an accent mark or a macron), and extending characters (which aren't letters but rather alphabetic symbols that some languages use and that act like letters in many ways).

XML names can never begin with numbers, periods, or hyphens.

WARNING

If you use a colon in an XML element—as in <foo:Element/>—most XML developers will immediately assume you are working with XML namespaces. General convention, but not the XML standard, demands that you reserve the colon for use with namespaces. And the standard itself is specific about what the intent of the colon is (namespace). Of course, the rebel in you may want to go against the grain of conventional thinking and use colons for purposes other than namespaces, but you'll run into enough resistance that you may decide to take up another cause. Most parsers will not validate a document that uses a colon in an XML name without a declared namespace.

End Tags   End tags (also called closing tags) begin with a </ and end with a > . Their names must correspond exactly to the names of the beginning tags of the element description. If a start tag begins and an end tag with a different name of any kind follows, even if only the case is different, no element exists, and the XML parser will generate an error. This is okay:

```
<Basic>Hello World!<anElement/></Basic>
```

The fragment `<anElement/>` is not an end tag and so does not violate the rule. It is a complete element tag set (it's an empty element with a start and closing tag). You can include a full element tag set within another element before closing an element tag. The full element tag set is said to be *nested* and is considered part of the element's content. The following will generate an error:

```
<Basic>Hello World!</basic>
```

Element Content   The content is whatever lies between the start tag and the end tag. The following example is that of an element with content:

```
<foo:anotherEmpty>Data here</foo:anotherEmpty>
```

So is this:

```
<foo:anotherEmpty>Data here
<foo:empty/>
</foo:anotherEmpty>
```

Empty Elements   An element does not have to have content. If you've seen an HTML `<hr>` element, you have seen an empty element at work. Translated to XML, the `<hr>` element would look like this: `<hr/>`. Even better would be the following, especially if you're worried about browser compatibility issues: `<hr />`.

If there is no content, the element is said to be an *empty element*. The following is an example of an empty element:

```
<empty/>
<foo:anotherEmpty></foo:anotherEmpty>
```

There is nothing wrong with writing out the entire start and end tag set of an empty element, although it does go against current convention somewhat, which tends to favor empty elements written as a single tag set rather than as a pair:

```
<foo:empty><foo:empty/>
```

The Root Element   The document instance consists of the root element. Every other element must be contained within a root element. `Basic.xml` consisted of one element, which happened to be the root element. If we add another element, that element *must* be contained within the root element:

```
<Basic>Hello World
<child>This is a child element</child>
</Basic>
```

In the preceding document fragment, the code highlighted in bold text consists of a child of the root element and the child's contents. The child element and its contents form the child of the root element.

When an XML processor encounters an element, it knows nothing about its semantics, which means it doesn't understand the *purpose* of the element. It doesn't care if you place a baby picture, or simply another element, within the child element to define it. You need to provide a way to give meaning to each element you create. Throughout this book you'll discover hundreds of ways to do this, which is one reason XML is so glorious.

Is It a Tag, or Is It an Element?   Now that you've seen start and end tags and defined element content, it's useful to understand what a tag *isn't*. The following is not a tag:

```
<tagreference>This is not a tag</tagreference>
```

The preceding line of code represents an element, not a tag. A tag is a specific instance of markup that helps define an element. The preceding line consists of a start tag containing a generic identifier (<tagreference>), followed by some element content (This is not a tag), followed by an end tag (</tagreference>). Because we've determined it's not a tag, take another look at the preceding line of code and think about what it *is*. The combination of all the markup (the start tag and the end tag) and the element's content is the element. Think of a tag as a markup instance. Think of an element as the whole of all the parts—the tag, zero or more attributes, plus any content (if any content) in the element.

Building a Tree   You can keep adding to the document instance until an entire *tree* of elements forms. XML trees consist of elements and element content, like a flow chart in descending order that begins with a parent element, which is the topmost element. The parent element in turn contains *child* elements. Child elements are so called because they are next in line on the descendant tree. These children may themselves have children, and so on. The tree is built from this hierarchical pattern. Some XML implementations, such as XSLT, consist of trees that consist of more than elements and element content, which means that attributes and namespaces can be part of the tree. The DOM (which, as we explained earlier, is a set of interfaces for accessing XML trees programmatically) is another example of an implementation that uses a more granular approach to this definition of a tree.

For the purposes of Listing 1.5, however, let's keep the concept of a tree as simple as we can and limit it to elements and their content. Listing 1.6 later in this chapter shows a longer document that consists of several child elements that themselves consist of siblings.

Listing 1.5: Children and Siblings Create a Tree

```xml
<?xml version="1.0"?>
<Basic>Hello World
    <child type="siblingOfChildElement">
This is a child element</child>
    <child
 type="siblingOfChildElement">
This is another child element</child>
    <child type="siblingOfChildElement">
        <grandChild>
        This is a grandchild of the root element
            <greatGrandChild>This is a great
            grandchild of the root element
            </greatGrandChild>
        </grandChild>
    </child>
</Basic>
```

You can see we've discarded one part of our prolog—the XSL style sheet processing instruction. That way we can open the document in IE 5 and see the tree. By clicking the + and – symbols on the browser document window in IE 5, we can collapse and expand the tree. This is not a functionality of XML. This is done by a combination of CSS and Dynamic HTML within the scope of a default rendering object inherent to all instances of IE 5. By creating your own style sheet, you override this default mechanism in IE 5.

Figure 1.3 shows a truncated, but still well formed, version of this file before the tree is expanded. Figure 1.4 shows the same file with the tree expanded when the user clicks the + symbol. It uses empty elements to represent the child elements. You can see how XML's containerlike methodology works and how the different elements branch off to make a tree-like structure.

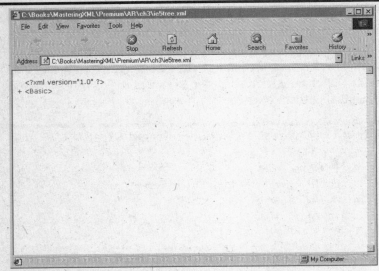

FIGURE 1.3: The tree collapsed in Internet Explorer 5

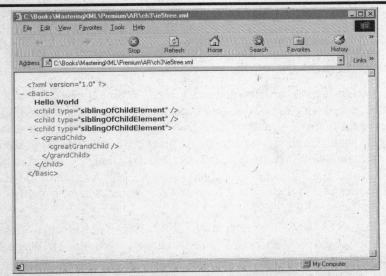

FIGURE 1.4 The tree expanded in Internet Explorer 5

Accessing the Document Tree   In the world of object-oriented programming, everything in an XML document is a node. Start tags, end tags, empty element tags, entity references, character references, comments, CDATA section delimiters, document type declarations, and processing instructions are all nodes, as is any one contiguous string of character data. Even the document itself is a node, which contains all the other nodes.

We won't go too in-depth here about all this, because plenty of space in this book is devoted to some XML-related programming concepts. It's worth pointing out, though, that a document tree can be accessed programmatically in one of two ways: through an event-based system or by the process of indexing the tree into memory and accessing the hierarchy. An event-based process, such as SAX, considers each node instance an event.

You can also navigate the tree of an XML document programmatically using the DOM. Each object of the hierarchy is indexed in memory and accessed by an object-oriented program, such as Java, or through JavaScript or another scripting language.

Is It Well Formed?   Examine the following lines of code to see if you can identify which of these elements are well formed and which aren't. We'll identify the correct answers by referencing the code's line numbers in the paragraphs that follow.

```
1.    <fragment ><foo/>"Excellent," said Holmes. "That's why
      she cried, 'Liar!'"</fragment>

2.    <fragment foo="foo1" >
      <foo></foo><foo/>
      </fragment>

3.    <fragment><fragchild></fragment>

4.    <fragment><fragchild/></fragment>

5.    <fragment><fragchild<frag/></fragment>

6.    <fragment><fragchild/>frag></fragment>

7.    <fragment><fragchild/>frag&gt;</fragment>

8.    <fragment><fragchild/>frag<</fragment>

9.    <fragment><fragchild/>

          <!- comment ->frag

      </fragment>

10.   <fragment><fragchild/><STOP!/></fragment>
```

```
11.   <fragment><fragchild/><STOP?/></fragment>
```

Line 1 is okay. You can include character data with other elements in element content if you want, as long as you're not validating against a DTD that prohibits this.

Line 2 is also well formed. It contains two empty elements within a parent container.

Line 3 would be okay if the author had closed the fragchild element.

Line 4 is how Line 3 should look.

Line 5 is wrong. It contains a start tag before the end of the XML name. A parser will complain about an invalid XML name.

You might get away with Line 6, but you should always escape > characters, just to be safe.

Line 7 is better.

Line 8 is guaranteed to generate an error, because the < character will always be interpreted as a start tag by an XML processor.

Line 9 is well formed. It contains an element with content and a comment.

Lines 10 and 11 are not well formed. They each contain an invalid character in the element's name.

Attributes

Attributes are like modifiers. They describe certain properties of elements. They consist of attribute value pairs—the name of the attribute, followed by an equal sign, followed by the value of the attribute. The attribute must have a value:

```
<fragment foo="foo1" >
<foo/>"Excellent," said Holmes.
"That's why she cried, 'Liar!'"
</fragment>
```

Chapter 3, "Understanding and Creating Attributes," explores attribute notation in detail.

Examine the following lines of code to see if you can identify which of these attributes are well formed and which aren't. We'll identify the correct answers by referencing the code's line numbers in the subsequent list.

```
1.   <foo myatt="Pete's Place">
2.   <foo myatt="Pete's' Place">
```

```
3.  <foo test="'false'">
4.  <foo myatt='false">
5.  <foo myatt=false>
6.  <foo myatt='false'>
7.  <foo myatt="false">
8.  <AttachExpression
    Expression="&lt;A HREF=orderView3.asp?Order_ID=
➡[[Order_ID]]&gt;{{Order_ID}}&lt;/A&gt;"/>
9.  <FormatDate Format="%b %d, %Y"/>
```

Line 1 won't generate an error as long as the attribute type defined in an associated DTD is not a tokenized type even though there is a single quote nested within the double quotes. You should, however, use an apostrophe entity to represent the apostrophe (') here to avoid confusing the parser.

Line 2 is acceptable (though probably not the author's intent) and is an example of how a typo could actually be interpreted by the parser as a value.

Line 3 is also correct and demonstrates how nesting a string within a value can prove useful when trying to differentiate between a string value and some predefined data typed-value test.

Line 4 is a fairly obvious; we opened the attribute value with a single quote but closed with a double quote, so the statement will generate an error.

Line 5 is also easy because we left off the quotes, so an error will be generated.

Line 6 is fine, because we started with a single quote and ended with a single quote.

Line 7 is also fine, because we started with a double quote and ended with a double quote.

Line 8 also works, despite the heavy use of special characters, since none of them violate the rules that govern the use of attribute value types. This last one was tricky. You'll learn more about attribute value types in Chapter 3, but this is a good example of how you can combine XML with programming techniques to handle parameter passing.

Line 9 is well formed. The characters within the attribute values are CDATA, which allows for a wide range of values.

CDATA Sections

A CDATA section is an especially wonderful little markup unit that programmers will turn to often as their salvation for dealing with operators that conflict with XML rules. CDATA sections contain nothing but character data, no matter what their contents look like. They can contain the < and the & literal values. This means if you use them in a CDATA section, you don't need to escape them. A CDATA section has the funkiest syntax in all of XML, but it's worth the trouble.

If you're a JavaScript or Java developer, you can place all your JavaScript in a CDATA section, as is, without worrying about escaping the < and the & characters. The syntax for CDATA sections looks like this:

```
<![CDATA[content here]]>
```

A typical example, using Java, might look something like this:

```
<?xml version = "1.0"
encoding="UTF-8" standalone="yes" ?>
<fragment>
    <![CDATA[
    (while i <= 8)
    sum += i++;
    )]]>
</fragment>
```

Using CDATA sections provides clear advantages, and it's a good idea to use them whenever there's even a threat of a character that might be construed as XML markup by a processor.

Processing Instructions

Processing instructions consist of the following, in the exact order of their appearance in this list:

1. The string <?

2. The name of the processing instruction target, which can be any XML name unless the string is XML in either uppercase or lowercase (which would confuse the parser)

3. Optional white space characters

4. Any additional, and optional, characters (this is fairly open-ended because you might be passing parameter lists off to an external processor, although you can't use `?>`, because the processor will think you're closing the instruction statement)

Remember that an XML declaration is not a processing instruction. An example of processing instructions is our reference to a style sheet processor at the beginning of this chapter. It bears repeating here:

```
<?xml-stylesheet type="text/xsl" href="basic.xsl"?>
```

You can use processing instructions for a variety of reasons, most of which have to do with extending the reach of the XML parser that is controlling the XML document you are working with. One simple example is for letting Web spiders know whether or not you want a page indexed:

```
<?robots index="no" follow="yes"?>
```

An XML processor itself does not do anything with instructions other than hand them to other processors.

Comments

Comments, like processing instructions, can appear in either the prolog or the document instance. Comments can't be read by machines—they are for people, so anything contained within a comment will not be parsed, including elements.

Comments are a good way to debug code. Debugging, or finding out what is wrong with your code, can be an art in any computer language, and comments have long been a way to isolate potential problem code chunks.

You need to keep a few rules in mind when using comments. If you've used them in HTML, they'll seem intuitive. If not, they're still rather simple:

▶ Comments begin with the string `<!--` and must always close with this string: `-->`.

▶ The parser ignores everything between the `<!--` and `-->`.

▶ Nothing can precede an XML declaration in an XML document, and comments are no exception.

▶ As in HTML, comments cannot be nested within a tag that defines an element name. The following will generate an error:
```
<tag <!-- this is not a well-formed comment -->.
```

▶ Once you've started a comment, you can't use the — characters together until you've decided to close your comment. Additionally, this means there is no such thing as a comment within a comment.

INTRODUCTION TO NAMESPACES

If you build an XML document and define an element named sound, what happens if it needs to interact with another document that contains an element named sound, but has a meaning that is different from the same element in your document? You have a *collision* of elements. You need to find a means of dealing with the different ways elements work together when they have the same names. After all, you can't run around the world trying to make sure nobody uses *your* element name with a different meaning.

The answer is namespaces. You can create an attribute, either global or local in scope, that uniquely identifies your element through a URI. A URI is not the same as a URL (Uniform Resource Locator). A URI is a string that identifies a Web resource. It doesn't necessarily point to anything, even though it can.

NOTE

If you're a regular reader of the XML-Dev list, you'll know that there is a vocal contingent that would say, "Namespaces are not the answer!" However, namespaces are a part of XML today and have taken on considerable significance.

By identifying a namespace, you can create elements that are unique to that namespace and thus will be sure to have the meaning you intended.

Namespaces are created via an attribute that describes the namespace within which an element's definition resides. When a namespace is declared, a prefix is associated with each element bound to that namespace. The namespace is itself bound to a URI. A processing application that understands the set of rules for that namespace can then be used to process the data according to the rules set forth within the scope of that particular namespace. Let's look at a hypothetical example to explain how a namespace works.

A Hypothetical Namespace Application

Let's say you want to create a special set of elements that describe some specific functions of your company, a financial institution. To keep this simple, let's further say that there is only one element, called bankrupt. Well, bankrupt can mean different things to different people. There's out-of-money bankrupt. There's also morally bankrupt. But even within the scope of financial bankruptcy, there's a significant difference between the kind of bankruptcy most people experience and the kind a big company experiences. Further, some institutions may have their own specific definitions of bankruptcy, at least in the eyes of determining creditworthiness.

Therefore, your IT department has decided to take the bold step of defining its own internal vocabulary and binding it to a namespace. To do this, you've made your URI as unique as you think it can be (to avoid colliding with other similar vocabularies) by using your company's domain name as the binding entity. So, assuming your company is named Top Company, your URI for the application's namespace might be http://www.topcompany.com/bankrupt/2001. This URI does not necessarily point to anything. It merely acts as an identifier. Next, you need to be sure that your XML parser can understand that namespace. Unfortunately, since the namespace is created by your company, you'll probably need to build the processor yourself, because your XML parser *can't* understand the elements defined by that namespace.

So what does a namespace look like? First, you need to declare the namespace itself. This is accomplished by attaching an xmlns attribute to the element or elements bound to the namespace:

```
<?xml version="1.0"?>
<bk:bankrupt
xmlns:bk = "http://www.topcompany.com/bankrupt/2001"
>
```

From that point on, you can use the namespace and its bound element any way you want within the scope of the definitions you choose. It doesn't matter that there is no physical presence of your rules on the site listed in the declared namespace attribute. What *does* matter is that the processor used to parse those elements *understands* what those elements mean. Therefore, someone has to build the processor.

XSL and XSLT are two common namespace-driven XML lingoes. Unfortunately, XSL and XSLT stumbled out of the gate a bit when

Microsoft hurried out an XSL processor that used a namespace that was bound to an early, pre-standard version of the language. When the language became standardized, the namespace URI changed (it had to, because its rules changed, and the new rules would have been in conflict with the old if the namespace was the same). This caused considerable hair pulling, but it was a classic example of namespace use and the importance of understanding its use.

Namespaces can be scoped across more than one element, of course, and even across entire documents.

WHAT'S A NAMESPACE?

An XML namespace is a way of "qualifying" a set of elements and attributes. It's a way of mixing elements from multiple DTDs, or multiple sets of names, in a single document, and of saying which elements and attributes came from which set of names.

XML namespaces are used for three main reasons: intermixing vocabularies, intermixing document fragments, and establishing reserved names.

You use a namespace declaration to associate a URI reference with one or more XML elements, as a prefix to disambiguate them from each other. Then if two elements have the same name but different URI prefixes, they are considered to be different.

For example, consider this document fragment:

```
<myElement
    xmlns:foo="http://www.mydomain.com/foo.xsd"
    xmlns:fooFo="http://www.mydomain.com/fooFo.xsd"
>
<p>This is a p element that denotes a paragraph</p>
<foo:p>This is a "foo:p" element.
The "foo:p" element has a completely different pur-
pose than the "p" element.
</foo:p>
<fooFo:p>And this element has yet another completely
different purpose than either the "p" element or the
"foo" element.</fooFo:p>
```

We may need different definitions for what amounts to the same element name, p. So we append a prefix to each p element carrying a different meaning than the original, define what that prefix means by referencing it to a schema (which carries all the rules associated with that prefix), then append that same prefix when using it in the

CONTINUED ➡

document instance. So, according to a fictional foo schema referenced by the first namespace declaration in bold, the foo:p element does not represent a paragraph, but, perhaps, a proposal. It
all depends on what the schema's intent is. You hope it's a well-
defined schema.

You'll also see namespaces used in major XML vocabularies, like
XSLT. The key in that case is that the processor must have instructions on how to handle the namespace. The URIs being pointed to
don't necessarily exist in some physical space, like a URL does. A
URI is an identifier, identifying for a processor which vocabulary is
being used and which version of that vocabulary is being used. A
processor either understands this vocabulary or it doesn't. If it
doesn't, the element remains essentially meaningless.

CHOOSING BETWEEN A DTD AND A SCHEMA

Up to this point we've focused our attention on creating XML documents
based on DTDs. However, a significant portion of this book is devoted to
another validation scheme for XML documents: *schemas*. Schemas, like
DTDs, define the structure and semantics of an XML document, but in a
more verbose way, using XML to define the rules and allowing for a richer
set of data types to do so.

Schemas are an important enough development in XML that we've
devoted two chapters to the topic. The first, Chapter 7, "An Introduction
to Schemas," is a basic introduction. The second, Chapter 8, "Writing
XML Schemas," delves more comprehensively into how to create them.

Many in the XML community believe that the DTD will not survive as a
rules mechanism. Although this is extremely unlikely, especially considering that the core standards used to develop the schema vocabularies themselves are written using DTDs, it does point to their increasing value. This
value stems largely from the rich data typing they provide, which means
their elements can be more easily mapped against existing databases.

A schema definition is created by following a set of rules defined by
the W3C that specifies how schemas should be set up. Schemas are
defined within the framework of XML. An XML file is created that

describes exactly how to define all the elements in a document instance that conforms to a specific schema. This is similar to the function of DTDs. The main differences are that DTDs have a special syntax that looks different from the kind of syntax used in document instances and that DTDs have limited data typing capabilities.

A portion of a schema is shown in Listing 1.6. This schema has been truncated (all but one element definition has been taken out) for space purposes. By looking at the elements, you can probably figure out what is going on to some degree. The sequence and purpose of each element is defined in the schema document. When validated against a processor that validates against schemas, the XML document instance is matched to the definitions created in the schema. The XML document instance doesn't need to be a file. It can be a streaming instance passed from one server to another server as a message (which, in XML, is still considered a document). There are no specific rules about the physical nature of the XML document instance when using schemas. The only thing that matters is whether the document instance is valid against that schema.

Listing 1.6: Using a Schema to Define an Element

```
<schema xmlns="http://www.w3.org/2000/10/XMLSchema">
    <element name="lillybook">
        <annotation>
            <documentation>documentation
            </documentation>
        </annotation>
        <complexType>
        <sequence>
            <element ref="Title"/>
            <element ref="Author"/>
            <element ref="Abstract"/>
            <element ref="Chapter"/>
        </sequence>
        <attribute name="ref"
         type="string" use="required"/>
            <attribute name="id" type="string"
             use="required"/>
        </complexType>
    </element>
<!- additional schema elements here ->
</schema>
```

Deciding whether to choose DTD or schema validation for your XML development depends on a number of factors (and remember, you are not required to use). Ask yourself a few questions:

▶ Who's using the XML document? If it's for a massive audience, a DTD is usually the answer. If it's a more specific group, and you have confidence that the applications available to your target can process schema-based XML, choose schemas.

▶ Are you extracting data from a database? Most database vendors are leaning heavily toward schemas because of their data typing capabilities. This means that you can define integers, and even dates, in your schemas, thereby binding your elements to stronger data types that more closely resemble the real data in your database.

▶ Are you exchanging information with partners? If you are, schemas may be a good answer for managing the dialogue between two or more organizations.

If you're interested in immediately pursuing the advantages schemas offer, read through Chapter 7, "An Introduction to Schemas," for a more comprehensive look at how they work.

BUILDING A COMPLETE XML DOCUMENT

This chapter has carefully reviewed each component of an XML document. Now, it's time to put your newfound knowledge to the test by examining a complete document. The document in Listing 1.7 demonstrates how easy it is to make a simple XML document with a minimal amount of effort (and a minimal DTD). Your XML documents in production environments are sure to be considerably more complex. As you continue with this book, your ability to create and work with such documents will grow.

Listing 1.7: A Complete XML Document

```
<?xml version="1.0" encoding="UTF-8"?>

<!DOCTYPE lillybook SYSTEM "lillybookv3.dtd">
<lillybook id="FreedomsDream"
xmlns:xlink="http://www.w3.org/1999/xlink">
   <Title>Freedom's Dream</Title>
```

```
<Author>
    <FirstName>Chuck</FirstName>
    <LastName>White</LastName>
</Author>
<Abstract copyright="2001, Chuck White">
    <Paragraph>Descriptive narration for
    interactive short story "Freedom's Dream"
    </Paragraph>
</Abstract>
<Chapter>
    <ChapterTitle>One</ChapterTitle>
        <score source="chapter_1Score"/>
            <Section classification="multimedia"
             level="one">
                <SectionTitle>PartOne</SectionTitle>
        <Paragraph>Had it been a dream, Antron Crimea's memory
of the clenched fist piercing the sky of a tumultuous, thun-
dering crowd would have been bearable solitude. As it was
though, the reality brought him to another place, to a dis-
tance only something like a dream could take him.</Paragraph>
        <Paragraph>"The crowd forgot everything," is how
Antron described the situation to his psychiatrist,
<characterLink id="chesapeake" xlink:title="Chesapeake Alert"
xlink:href="Chesapeake.xml"
xlink:label="ChesapeakeAlert">Chesapeake
Alert</characterLink>. Antron remembered the rhythm, the
pulse, everything. After all this time the energy of the
crowd still seemed to reverberate through his
head.</Paragraph>
        <Paragraph>Chesapeake Alert was nothing but a large
bulbous mass of jelly-like flesh; a brain plopped down on an
empty, expensive slice of carpet. And though he had no legit-
imate locomotive capabilities of his own, he was aware of the
movements of a billion others.</Paragraph>
        <Paragraph>Antron's hundred legs crawled around what
was left of the carpet in the kind of pace unknown to you or
me. His earlier confusion had long ago been dissolved by the
righteous events of what he had seen during the course of
events Billy Freedom had ignited</Paragraph>
        <Paragraph>"Sometimes betrayal is a necessity," said
Chesapeake. "Startling. And expensive. It must be weighed
carefully."</Paragraph>
    </Section>
```

```
        </Chapter>
    </lillybook>
```

You can download the DTD for Listing 1.7 at www.tumeric.net/ projects/books/complete/support/ch01_toc.asp. The file is named lillybookv3.dtd. At this point in your XML development, you should focus most on the structure of the document. Notice the way each element is nested within another and that there is one root element.

The document begins with an XML declaration. There is no processing instruction for this document, but if we wanted to develop a style sheet or transformation for it, we would want to add a processing instruction to handle it. Next comes the DTD, which is external. After that, the document instance is parsed, beginning with the root element, lillybook.

You will also notice a number of other important attributes about the document, such as the consistent case use among elements and the fact that all the attribute values appear in quotes without any exceptions.

TIP

If you are creating a common type of document, such as an online book, you should really look to see if someone else has already created a publicly available DTD before setting out to create your own like we have here.

As you examine Listing 1.7, try to take everything you've learned into account and see if you can identify some of our main points about how to create XML documents. As you progress throughout the book, any mysteries remaining about Listing 1.7 will gradually clear. Let yourself explore the basic syntax. There are many more mysteries ready to be disclosed to you as the next several chapters unfold.

SUMMARY

In this chapter we introduced some of the basic concepts and constructs of XML documents. You now have an understanding of all the syntax requirements you'll need to create your first XML document.

In the next chapter, we'll explore how to create elements, which are one of the core entities in all XML documents.

Chapter 2

UNDERSTANDING AND CREATING ELEMENTS

One of the chief characteristics of XML's extensibility is the power for you to create your own elements. Elements, the central building blocks of HTML markup, have a long tradition. An HTML element, such as the body element, might contain a number of other elements, such as a number of paragraph elements (the p element) or several link elements (the a element).

In HTML, you must use elements that the target browser will recognize. In other words, you can't make up elements as you go along. If you create markup that looks like the following, the browser will ignore it:

```
<FAKEELEMENT>Here is some content</FAKEELEMENT>
```

Nothing bad will necessarily happen, but if you hope to achieve something by creating the element and the browser ignores it, your efforts are wasted.

Adapted from *Mastering™ XML, Premium Edition*, by Chuck White, Liam Quin, and Linda Burman

ISBN 0-7821-2847-5   1,155 pages $49.99

NOTE

Technically, you *can* create elements for use in Microsoft Internet Explorer 4 (IE 4) and 5 (IE 5), the latter of which handles XML. This exception is beyond the scope of this chapter, but you still need to tell the browser what to do with these new elements, generally through a scripting language such as JScript, a Microsoft-specific implementation of JavaScript.

What is possible with the power to create your own elements? Although, in theory, only your imagination and the resources of your development team limit you, several uses come quickly to mind:

▶ In publishing environments, you can use elements to manage wide varieties of information. Such information might track author names, book titles, ISBN numbers, colophons, synopses, and just about anything else you might think of that is relevant to the publishing world.

▶ Accounting and other business departments might use custom elements to map relational databases to XML documents. Imagine, for example, a database of products. Each product name in the database could be assigned an element name automatically by specialized software that converts database tables into XML documents. By assigning each Product ID in the database an ID attribute within each element, you can manipulate the document in any number of ways, creating endless possibilities for you and your customers.

▶ The scientific community is already making substantial use of XML by creating shared DTDs within specific scientific fields for a vast range of purposes. The Chemical Markup Language (CML) is one example of a vocabulary that has taken XML's element-creation power and refined it for use in practical ways.

▶ Component messaging, which consists of transferring programmatic code (sometimes referred to as remote procedure calling) between disparate systems or processing ordering and invoicing routines, is already playing a big role in B2B (business-to-business) transactions. Examples include the Simple Object Access Protocol (SOAP), used for procedure calls over HTTP, and BizTalk, a messaging API developed by Microsoft.

► You could even develop elements for home use that track recipes, bank accounts, your rotisserie baseball leagues, birthdays, and any number of other personal needs.

The list of possible uses for elements is endless. You can probably think of some of your own right now. In this chapter you'll master the art of creating elements and learn how they are accessed with scripting and programming languages. Specifically, you'll learn what an element is, how to create your first element, the fundamental rules associated with creating XML elements, the role of elements in the Document Object Model (DOM), and how to validate XML elements against a document type definition (DTD).

WHAT IS AN ELEMENT?

An *element* is a component of a document. Elements can be made up of other elements, other types of data, or a descriptive representation that tells the XML parsing application about a resource that exists elsewhere than within the document itself.

Elements can consist of content. Their purpose is generally to organize the structure of a document. An easy way to think about how this works is a book chapter outline in a technical publication. A chapter outline usually consists of several top-level headings. Within each top-level heading are subheads. Sometimes, these subheads have their own subheads. It would be silly to have a subhead outside the scope of a level-one head, because it would interrupt the flow of the text within the document.

XML elements work in much the same way as a chapter outline. They must combine to create a document with good structure in order to work properly. As XML usage has grown, people have found that creating well-structured XML documents is a true art. You'll discover that there is a good reason for XML's nesting requirements (you'll be examining those requirements later in the chapter), as you can probably guess by thinking about how a chapter outline is structured.

A simple XML element based on a typical chapter would have as its root element the information that tells the reader a new chapter has begun:

```
<CHAPTER>
<!- SOME CONTENT GOES HERE ->
</CHAPTER>
```

As you can see, the CHAPTER element is fairly generic. An element should begin by describing its contents in the broadest possible terms and then drill down to reveal more information. Which chapter is it? This markup tells you more:

```
<CHAPTER>
<CHAPTERNUMBER>Five</CHAPTERNUMBER>
    <CHAPTERTITLE> Understanding Computers
    </CHAPTERTITLE>
    <LEVELONEHEAD>Computers Aren't
    as Smart as They Look
    </LEVELONEHEAD>
</CHAPTER>
```

You can think of each of these elements as containers. All XML documents have a central container, within which resides every other container. This container is the *root element*. Keep the following four rules in mind when dealing with root elements:

- ▶ An XML document contains only one root element.

- ▶ Following any opening declarative statements, the root element is always the first element in an XML document.

- ▶ The root element's closing tag is never followed by another element's closing tag.

- ▶ Like any other element, the opening and closing tags must agree in case.

You can see, then, why it would be folly to name the first element of the fictitious book XML document CHAPTERTITLE. You would not want to include the actual content of the chapter within that element, which you would need to do if it had been named as your root element. You'll learn more about the role of a root element in a document's hierarchy later in this chapter.

STRUCTURING ELEMENT TAGS

Now that we've gone over the basics, let's move into the actual structure of elements. One rule that must be hardwired into your consciousness is this: All elements in XML documents must contain both an opening and a closing tag. There are no exceptions to this rule, and any violation of this rule will, unequivocally, result in a parsing error. In the HTML world, many browsers forgive markup errors and inconsistencies fairly readily. An HTML parser will often simply try its best to parse invalid markup. This is not so with an XML parser. An XML parser will typically generate some type of error message when it encounters malformed markup. Some parsers, such as IE 5 and up, will even tell you where the error occurred, as shown in Figure 2.1.

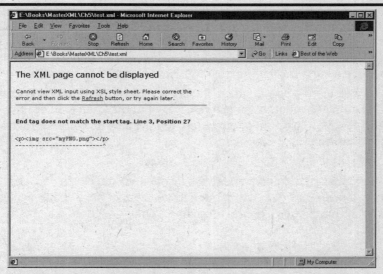

FIGURE 2.1: Internet Explorer 5 generates helpful error messages such as this one, which is generated because the element was not closed.

Understanding the Difference between Tags and Elements

To understand the structure of an element and eventually how to create an element, you first must understand the difference between a tag and an element. You've already seen what an element looks like. A tag helps create the markup for an element—it's inherently part of the element. These tags provide a descriptive framework for the element. Let's take apart the following example:

```
<p>p</p>
```

The < and > symbols are called *delimiters* and are used to separate tags from a document's character data.

TIP

In programming practice, delimiters can take various forms, as long as they are used to separate data. For example, a simple database table might use commas as delimiters, and 1, 2, 3, 4, 5, 6 could be considered a record in a database.

These delimiters also separate tags from an element's *generic identifier* (in this case, the p encased between the two delimiters: <p>). The generic identifier is also called the element name. If you put the delimiters together with the generic identifier, you have part of a tag. The <p> in this example is an opening tag. In order for it to be part of a valid XML tag, it must have a closing tag: </p>. To avoid confusing a tag with an element, just remember that a tag is the markup that is used to identify the element.

An element's opening and closing tags can take one of two forms, depending on whether an element has content. If an element has content, it should have an opening tag, followed by its content, followed by its closing tag:

```
<myelement>some content</myelement>
```

An element with no content has its opening and closing tag all within its two delimiters (you'll find out why an element might have no content later in this chapter). So the preceding element, without content, would look like this:

```
<myelement/>
```

The important thing to remember when considering empty elements is the closing backslash. If you leave it off, the XML document won't parse. It is also legal to write the closing tag after the opening tag, with no content between the two, like this:

```
<myelement></myelement>
```

Remember that XML is not like HTML, and therefore XML parsers won't even try to parse markup that isn't well formed. They'll just give up. Most pages on the World Wide Web today will not parse if browsers that follow such strict conformance guidelines open them. Therefore, it is best to pay heed to XML conformance issues early in your XML development career.

Following the Basic Rules

Now that you've learned the difference between tags and elements, and before we move into actually creating elements, we need to look at a few important rules associated with creating elements in XML. Remembering and applying these rules will go a long way toward producing error-free XML documents. In fact, breaking any of these rules will result in a parsing error:

► Use case consistently when referring to the same element. For example, `<TITLE>` is not the same as `<title>`, ever.

► Always enclose any attribute value in single or double quotation marks. The following would be acceptable in an HTML document: `<img width = 10>`. It is not acceptable in XML. Instead, you must include quotation marks: `<img width = "10"/>` (and a closing tag if the element is empty).

► All elements must consist of opening (`<`) and closing (`>`) tags. Thus, depending on whether you are using content, the element should look like `<myelement>mycontent</myelement>` or `<myelement/>` or `<myelement></myelement>`.

► All elements must be nested within one root element, and the XML document must have the root element's closing tag as the final closing tag of the document, because the root element contains every element within the document. You'll learn more about that in the next section.

► Element names must consist of XML name tokens (discussed in Chapter 3, "Understanding and Creating Attributes") and cannot begin with any variation of XML, digits, hyphens, or a period, although these can appear after the first character in the name.

That's it. There are not many rules to follow, and they're logical. That's one of the beauties of XML. It consists of a remarkably logical set of rules that make few demands on your interpretive powers. What's more, you'll never hear another argument about whether it's better to include quotes around attributes (because you don't have a choice) or whether to close a paragraph tag (all tags must close). The reason for this is that XML is all about data, and so it must be used accordingly, and its rules must have a logical structure.

CREATING YOUR FIRST ELEMENTS

As you learned earlier, there are two kinds of elements—those with content and those without. Often, the way you create an element in XML documents will be dictated either by a DTD or by a schema. Chapter 6, "Creating Your Own DTD," and Chapter 7, "An Introduction to XML Schemas," introduce you to DTDs and schemas. It's important to understand these chapters because even if you never write your own DTD, you'll often need to read one. You can't build robust XML documents if some kind of DTD or schema isn't used; you'll never get beyond static, text-only pages without a schema or DTD.

If an element does not have a corresponding element-type declaration within a DTD, it may result in an invalid document. This depends on whether the XML document containing the element has a DTD associated with it.

TIP
You can use an internal DTD to provide declarations about elements that are not handled in external DTDs, or for those occasions when you are working without any DTD at all. Sometimes, in the early phases of XML application development, you may find yourself starting off handling your declarations in an internal DTD and then transferring them to an external document when everything seems to be in order.

This section concentrates on developing elements without relying on a DTD. That way, you can concentrate on the structure of elements and the few rules that must be followed in order to end up with a well-formed XML document (described in the section "Writing Well-Formed Documents" later in this chapter).

Using Content Models

Most often, XML element content is guided by *content models*. Content models are declarative statements in DTDs that govern the kind of content an element can possess. These declarative statements can include information about the following:

▶ The nesting rules of each element—in other words, which elements, if any, an element can have as content, and the order in which they must appear. A DTD content model might, for example, forbid the order element from containing a product element.

▶ The number of times one element can be nested within another.

Content models are just one facet of a DTD you'll come to know as you create elements that follow a formal DTD. Content models fall under a larger group of four types of content that a DTD will dictate to you if you are writing a DTD-compliant XML document. The following types of content can be used in an element:

- ► EMPTY
- ► ANY
- ► Mixed
- ► Elements

Chapter 3 goes into more detail about how DTDs will affect your document creation. Specifically, you'll see the importance that attributes play in document creation. You will also learn more about content models in Chapter 6.

Creating Elements without Content

An *empty* element doesn't contain any content or data. An element might be empty for any number of reasons. It might contain only properties (represented by attributes) that reference other files or help characterize what the element is about.

The HTML element img is an example of an empty element. The newest flavor of HTML, XHTML, is an HTML specification using an XML DTD. Because XHTML is based on XML, you need to remember to use closing tags when developing empty elements.

As all elements in XML must have an opening tag and a closing tag, it is easy, if you're familiar with HTML, to guess where the opening tag in the img element must be. But what about the closing tag? You place the closing tag just after the generic identifier that names the element (in this case, img), as follows:

```
<img src="myhome.png" />
```

Adding a space before the closing slash mark is not required, so a home-grown element not expected for delivery to HTML browsers would look like this:

```
<media src="myhome.mp3"/>
```

To ensure proper rendering in browsers that don't read XML, however, add the space after any attribute value and before the closing slash mark. You could also simply create two separate sets of tags, like so:

```
<img src="myhome.png"></img>
```

Comparing HTML and XML Empty Tags   XML rules are simple and, as you'll discover, quite logical. Unlike HTML, XML is not plagued by inconsistencies. For example, there are no exceptions to the rule that all elements must have opening and closing tags. Empty elements are not an exception to this rule; they are just handled a bit differently from the way that elements with content are handled. For example, the following snippet of code will generate an error in IE 5:

```
<?xml version="1.0"?>
<body>
<p><img src="myPNG.png"></p>
</body>
```

In fact, as you saw in Figure 2.1, IE 5 generates an error message that actually helps you debug the application with this simple message: "End tag does not match the start tag. Line 3, Position 27." This message tells you two things:

▶ Not every browser refers to opening and closing tags in the same way.

▶ You must use closing tags, even with empty elements.

Chapter 11, "Converting HTML to XHTML," goes into much more detail about how to convert HTML documents to XML. The point here is to emphasize the importance of closing the empty tags, whether they are from legacy HTML files or new XML documents.

TIP

If you use HTML markup as XML, such as within the XHTML namespace, you might find yourself in a bit of a quandary when attempting to use the br element. You could use
</br>, but then the browser will interpret it as if you had created your markup like so:

. This gives you two line breaks when you most likely wanted one. The reason for this is that early browsers didn't recognize the closing tag for the break element and did not foresee the advent of XML. The workaround is to use the abbreviated version: <br />. It is absolutely vital to include that extra space preceding the closing slash mark when writing markup for older browser versions. Including the extra space is a good habit to get into for all such abbreviated elements.

Determining Empty Element Structure   An empty element can consist of no more than the name of an element, which is referred to as an element-type name or a generic identifier. So at its simplest, an empty element looks like this:

```
<anEmptyElement/>
```

Most likely, your empty elements will have some kind of attribute attached, but this is not required. An attribute is that part of an element that describes the element's properties. Expanding on the previous example, you might have the following:

```
<anEmptyElement reason="none"/>
```

Generally, you'll find empty elements in documents that are bound to some kind of DTD or schema. There's not much use for empty elements if a parser doesn't have a set of declarations from which to interpret their meaning from a scanned document.

Creating Elements with Content

On numerous occasions you'll want to include content in your element. In its simplest form, the markup for an XML element consists of an opening and closing tag, as well as the generic identifier describing the element name. Adding content to such a typical element looks like this:

```
<title>My Favorite Book</title>
```

You can also create an element with other elements as content:

```
<title>
    <chaptertitle>The Blank Look
    </chaptertitle>
</title>
```

Or you can create an element with an entity as content:

```
<title>&chaptertitle;</title>
```

These previous lines of codes are examples of the content model at work. You'll remember that the content model consists of four types of content: EMPTY, ANY, mixed, and elements. Of these, the last three types are used to specify the kinds of content used by an element when the element is not empty.

TIP

When you develop XML code using a text editor, the easiest way to guarantee that you nest elements properly is to input both the opening and closing element tags, like so: `<tag></tag>`. You can then input your content: `<tag>content</tag>`. This works if an element has content, but not for empty elements, which appear like this: `<tag/>`.

Creating Elements with *ANY* Content   An element declaration in a DTD may allow either an element or parsed character data as element content. This gives the document creator more leeway in creating the element, but it can lead to a loss of structure. A DTD containing such a declaration would include a line that looks like this:

```
<!ELEMENT MYELEMENT ANY>
```

You'll likely not run across this kind of declaration often in a DTD, and if you do, the chances are that the author of the DTD will recover control over document structure by defining a strict series of attributes for the element.

Creating Elements with Mixed Content   A DTD author might limit the structure a bit more than with an ANY declaration by allowing for mixed content. By allowing for mixed content, the DTD author will permit an element to consist of a mix of other elements and parsed character data. This is much like the ANY content model, but it's different because in this scenario the DTD author may specify which elements are allowed. There is no specific DTD declaration for mixed content. Mixed content is a generic term used to define the type of content an element declaration defines in its declarations.

Take the following example, which displays mixed content. This declaration, using the mixed-content model, is one you'll see frequently.

```
<!ELEMENT MYELEMENT (#PCDATA)>
```

This declaration tells the document author that the element MYELE-MENT can contain mixed content of any XML-compliant parsed character data. The #PCDATA type means parsed character data and can contain any amount of parsed character data, including none at all. When you're thinking about mixed-content models using parsed character data, take into account these two important considerations:

▶ Although the elements do not need to actually contain any character data (because the #PCDATA declaration allows for zero or more characters), the elements do need to appear in the document.

► PCDATA-type content is always part of a mixed-content model, even if no other kind of content is involved, such as other elements.

The DTD author can go a step further by declaring that in addition to parsed character data, it is okay to include a few other specific elements, in any order:

```
<!ELEMENT MYELEMENT (#PCDATA)
| MYOTHERELEMENT | ANOTHERELEMENT>
```

In the preceding line of code, the elements MYOTHERELEMENT and ANOTHERELEMENT can appear within the element MYELEMENT in any order. All three of the following lines of code are valid according to this content-model declaration:

```
<MYELEMENT>Here is
    <MYOTHERLEMENT>another way
    </MYOTHERELEMENT>
    <ANOTHERELEMENT>.
    </ANOTHERELEMENT>
</MYELEMENT>


<MYELEMENT>
    <ANOTHERELEMENT>
        <MYOTHERLEMENT>Here
        </MYOTHERELEMENT>
    </ANOTHERELEMENT>is another way.
</MYELEMENT>


<MYELEMENT>
    <MYOTHERLEMENT> Here is another way.
    </MYOTHERELEMENT>
    <ANOTHERELEMENT>Shall we add some
more character data just
for fun?
    </ANOTHERELEMENT>
</MYELEMENT>
```

The | operator is used to separate content-model options in the element's declaration. The options can occur in any sequence, which is unlike the content model that follows: the elements content model.

Creating Elements with Elements as Content   The elements content model could be called the child-content model, because this model dictates that any element content must contain another element. Because XML has stringent nesting rules, by necessity these elements must be descendants of the containing element. The elements contained in this content model must appear in the sequence specified. The sequence is specified in the DTD in a comma-delimited list:

```
<!ELEMENT MYELEMENT (MYCHILD, YOURCHILD, HERCHILD)>
```

In the preceding line of code, the element MYELEMENT must have the following nesting order:

```
<MYELEMENT>
<MYCHILD/>
    <YOURCHILD/>
    <HERCHILD/>
</MYELEMENT>
```

In this example, the MYCHILD, HERCHILD, and YOURCHILD elements are empty. However, these elements will also be defined by the same DTD that declared the MYELEMENT element and so would need to follow whatever content model was declared for those elements. They may or may not have been declared empty, but assume in this case, for the sake of clarity, that they were.

Summarizing the Content Model

To enhance your ability to view a DTD and determine how to develop an element according to the rules of that DTD, look at Table 2.1, which lists the content types you'll find in a typical DTD. Don't worry much about the syntax you see in Table 2.1 just yet. As you learn to write a DTD in upcoming chapters, reading one will come as a matter of course.

TABLE 2.1: Content Types Used in DTD

CONTENT TYPE	DESCRIPTION	DTD SYNTAX
EMPTY	The DTD is telling you that no content is allowed. Empty elements can have attributes, however.	`<!ELEMENT myelement EMPTY>`
ANY	The DTD allows any kind of content in an element.	`<!ELEMENT myelement ANY>`

TABLE 2.1 continued: Content Types Used in DTD

CONTENT TYPE	DESCRIPTION	DTD SYNTAX
Mixed	The DTD allows you to mix content so that character data and other elements can coexist within the element.	text-only: `<!ELEMENT myelement (#PCDATA)>`text and element content:`<!ELEMENT myelement (#PCDATA | elementName | elementName)*>`
Elements	This part of the DTD governs content models and dictates that specific elements must be nested within an element in a specific way (see the preceding discussion).	`<!ELEMENT myelement (mysubelement| yoursubelement)>`

When you learn to read a DTD, you'll make decisions about element content based on the declarations you see within the DTD, like those in the far-right column of Table 2.1. These declarations will act as rules that provide direction for placing different types of content. As XML matures, XML editing software will likely validate your documents on the fly as you write them. In the meantime, you need to do it yourself, and to do so you need to be able to read a DTD. In the next chapter, you'll learn that there's much more to element content than what you see in Table 2.1, because element attributes also have a separate set of content rules that can be applied through a DTD.

Understanding Nesting and Hierarchy

As important as all the syntactical aspects you've learned are, probably no rules of element creation are more important than the rules about *nesting*. Nesting refers to the way a group of elements reside within the structure of a document. Document elements in XML all have one thing in common, no matter what: *All document elements within the same document instance share one root, or parent, element.* This is true regardless of whether you're using a content model, and no content model is allowed to change that rule. The root element is always the first element in an XML document and always contains every other element in the document, which makes it easy to recognize an XML document. Take a look at the following snippet:

```
<book>
    <title>Mastering XML</title>
    <publisher>Sybex</publisher>
</book>
```

Notice how the two elements, title and publisher, are contained, or nested, within the book element. This is a hierarchy of elements, which is based on an old concept in computer science of nodes and abstract data that you'll be looking at in the next section.

Nesting properly is a fairly simple process, and you'll quickly find yourself able to detect mistakes. See if you can tell what is wrong with the following code:

```
<?xml version="1.0"?>
<book>
    <title>Mastering XML</title>
</book>
    <publisher>Sybex</publisher>
```

Can you tell which of the elements in the preceding lines of code is the root element? In other words, which element contains all the other elements? There isn't a root element, so, assuming the preceding lines of code represent the entire document, the document is not well formed and will generate a parsing error.

Understanding Nodes

The hierarchy of elements is based on the concept of *nodes* and abstract data structures. Nodes play a big role in the DOM, which plays a big role in the use of dynamic XML, so it helps to know something about their history. Nodes are an essential part of understanding the hierarchy at the root of XML documents (no pun intended).

NOTE

The Document Object Model (DOM) is a set of interfaces that helps developers to programmatically manage XML nodes. It is discussed in detail in Chapter 13, "Modeling the XML Document Object."

Nodes describe information about the data structures that are common to today's programming languages. Computer scientists consider these descriptions abstract because they can be applied across a variety of computer languages, such as C, Pascal, and Java. In XML, these data structures are called *trees*. Computer languages might call them something else, such as lists or collections. Whatever they are called, each individual instance of data within that tree (or list or collection) that gets processed is a node.

Generally, any time you have an abstract data structure, it must be traversed in a specific, definable way. This is an important concept in XML, particularly when considering some of the more complex tasks associated with scripting involving the DOM. When you use the DOM, you traverse the nodes of an XML document tree following a specific pattern, a hierarchical one defined by parents, children, and siblings. It's important to understand nodes because as you progress in your mastery of XML, you'll likely encounter them often. It is easy to assume that a node object is by definition an element, but that is not the case. A node can be an element attribute or even the text content of an element. In other words, it is any instance of data within a document tree that gets processed.

About Parents and Children

The hierarchy of XML is based on the way elements are nested. But it is also based on the relationship of each node in the tree, which, as you now know, means that each instance of data has a relationship with the others. Because XML is structured as a parental hierarchy, the relationships of nodes are based on each element's position in relation to the root element. The root element of an XML document is always considered the parent of any other object that immediately follows its position in the document. If another child is nested within the root element's child, that element is a child of the first child. If an element has two subelements that are not nested within each other, they are siblings.

This notion of parents and children is prevalent within the DOM. It can be confusing, too, because most documentation referring to the structure of XML documents refers to trees, leaves, and branches. Rather than getting bogged down by the semantics, try to keep in mind these general ideas:

▶ All XML documents begin at the root level with a root node followed by a root element. The root node represents the document itself. You won't be worrying about the root node in this chapter, which focuses on the hierarchical relationship among elements.

▶ The root element is referred to in a scripting or programming environment as a documentElement. This is its representation in the DOM. The key programmatic constructs of DOM properties are properties and methods, which are inherited by the root element's descendants.

▶ Any other elements that exist must be contained within the root element.

▶ The first element contained within the root element is considered a child of the root element. If there is more than one child element and the second child element is not nested within the first child element, those child elements are both children of the parent and siblings.

▶ The child element of the root element may itself contain elements. If so, those elements, also called *subelements*, are children of the child.

▶ Elements containing subelements are called *branches*, and elements without any subelements are called *leaves*. They have no child elements of their own.

Diagramming the Hierarchy   You can diagram the entire hierarchy of a document. For example, to get at the element childBChild_1 in Figure 2.2 (using JScript in IE 5), you would write the following line of script:

```
myXMLdoc.documentElement.childNodes.item(1)
➡.childNodes.item(0)
```

In the preceding line of code, myXMLdoc is the name of the XML document, in this case accessed by a unique identifier using the ID attribute within another document. One document can access another, and once it does, you refer to it often by its ID in the top level of a script (although you can access nodes in other ways, which you can learn about in Chapter 13). Such references are made from the top level down, beginning with the document, moving on to the root element, and then moving to the root element's child.

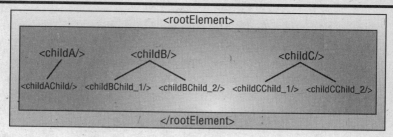

FIGURE 2.2: Looking at XML element hierarchy

If you look at Figure 2.2, you can get a better handle on how it all works. In the diagram, you can see that every element in the document myXML.xml is contained within the root element (called rootElement). This root element contains three children: childA, childB, and childC. Each of these child elements of the root element also has children. Note, however, that we did not name these children in a way that implied they were grandchildren of the root element. The reason is that the direct relationship between elements ends with the first child. This is an important consideration because if you use a scripting language, such as ECMAScript, to manipulate an XML document, you will traverse the tree one node at a time.

NOTE

ECMAScript is the newest standard for JavaScript. ECMAScript has taken on a new name to reflect a more standardized methodology. The first version of ECMAScript is equivalent to JavaScript as implemented in Netscape Navigator 3. Version 2 of ECMAScript is roughly equivalent to JavaScript 1.3, and Version 3 of ECMAScript is roughly equivalent to JavaScript 1.4. Any flavors you may encounter of JavaScript beyond that, such as the JScript implementations found in IE 4 and IE 5, are extensions to that model and not standardized in any way, at least not yet.

Understanding Dot Syntax   Don't be too concerned if the preceding line of code is completely unfamiliar. A few things are worth mentioning about it from a purely illustrative standpoint. Notice, for example, the dot syntax that is used. The dots are used in much the same way as slashes and backslashes are used to name a path within a computer's directory structure or when accessing a Web site. myXML represents the actual XML document (also called the root node). The next node in the hierarchy is the root element, represented by the documentElement property. The documentElement property is part of the document interface within the official DOM as specified by the W3C (World Wide Web Consortium). The first childNodes property refers to the childB element, and the second childNodesproperty refers to the childBchild_1 element. Listing 2.1 shows how the entire document looks as a complete XML file.

Listing 2.1: Understanding How to Traverse a Document Tree Using Dot Syntax

```xml
<?xml version="1.0"?>
<rootElement>
      <childA>
            <childAChild/>
      </childA>
      <childB>
            <childBChild_1/>
            <childBChild_2/>
      </childB>
      <childC>
            <childCChild_1/>
            <childCChild_2/>
      </childC>
</rootElement>
```

Matching the Document Hierarchy to the DOM   If you're confused about the relationship between Listing 2.1 and the line of script it's associated with, look at Figure 2.3. The diagram in Figure 2.3 matches the hierarchy as used in script with the actual XML document. Don't get too hung up right now on grasping the way the script works. The idea is to keep in mind the importance of hierarchy and nested elements, not only as they pertain to the structure of an XML document, but also as they pertain to the scripting languages that manipulate their data.

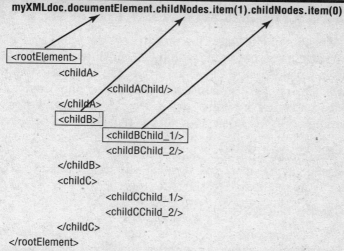

FIGURE 2.3: Matching elements with their corresponding DOM objects

Each node in an XML document can be accessed in script by traversing the XML document tree using the parent-child hierarchy. You can't get to a node without first accessing the topmost element in the tree (unless you're working with document fragments, but that's beyond the scope of this discussion). This is the same hierarchy that has been used since the introduction of JavaScript. The document model used in the earliest implementations has been made more robust for XML, but the concept is the same.

If you're familiar with scripting, you'll find accessing XML nodes (elements and their attributes and content) a breeze. If you're not familiar with scripting, and all this seems a bit perplexing, be aware that scripting will be covered in richer detail in Part IV of this book, "XML Scripting and Processing."

For now, focus on understanding the role of elements relative to one another and why it is so important to nest them properly. In our view, it's not quite enough to properly nest elements because the XML specification says you must. It is also important to understand why this logical structure exists in the first place. One reason is the way an XML document structure is traversed using the DOM, and the DOM's interface with scripting and programming languages such as Java and C++.

The Role of Elements in the DOM

The DOM is a set of interfaces that provides programming access to the nodes of a document, beginning with the document's root node, in a language-independent way. The DOM is a recommendation from the W3C (www.w3.org/TR/REC-DOM-Level-1/) that is supported in IE 5, Netscape 6, and other browsers, such as Opera. Additionally, it is receiving wide support in the Java community as a viable interface between Java and XML. You can also use a number of other languages to access the DOM and work with XML. Some of the computer and scripting languages you might consider while working with the DOM and XML may include, but are not limited to, the following:

- ► ECMAScript (JavaScript)
- ► JScript (Microsoft's implementation of JavaScript, which contains numerous extensions to the original specs)
- ► Java
- ► Visual Basic
- ► VBScript (a scripting language used primarily for IE 5–specific Web pages and Active Server Pages)
- ► Python
- ► UserTalk (a scripting language used by UserLand's Frontier)
- ► Perl
- ► C
- ► C++

Thinking about Objects

An element is made accessible to scripting languages such as JavaScript and object-oriented programming languages such as Java because every element is also an object.

An element doesn't need to contain any data to be considered a legitimate object. The img element is a good example of a familiar element from HTML that doesn't contain any data. Rather, it contains properties in the form of attributes such as src, which describes where the object is located. An image's actual data is contained in a separate file that is referred to via the src attribute. The img element, or object, always remains the same, but it can contain different properties, and these properties can be changed on the fly through scripts.

Try inputting the following code within an HTML file:

```
<img src = " " />
```

If you load this HTML file into a browser, you'll get a broken-image icon. That's because you're dealing with an object that has properties that mean nothing to the browser. In fact, its properties refer to a resource that contains no data. It's still an object, though, and thus, it is also an element. You might want to change the src attribute value to something that makes sense to a browser, such as src="http://www.myplace.com/home.gif". This is why the DOM is so important to XML. The DOM consists of object interfaces and their properties, which you can manipulate with script.

Objects have become extremely important in the computer world. By manipulating them in script, you can turn static Web pages into dynamic Web pages. To better understand how an element can be considered an object, review the following tag:

```
<p style="font-family:serif">This is a paragraph</p>
```

The p element consists of a number of parts that help describe it as an object. This element consists of data made up of a string ("This is a paragraph"). *String* is computer-talk for a series of one or more text characters. This element also consists of an attribute, style, which has the value font-family:serif assigned to it.

Within the DOM, the most commonly used interface is the element interface. Table 2.2 shows the various properties and methods associated with it. The element interface contains properties and methods that make it possible to access an element's attributes. From a technical perspective, an attribute isn't a child of anything. Therefore, the developers of the DOM built a series of interfaces within the DOM that contain properties and methods that developers can use to access element attributes. Table 2.2 contains only one such interface: the element interface. There are actually several other interfaces, but they're beyond the scope of this chapter. If you're not familiar with scripting or programming, Table 2.2 may not mean much to you. We've included it here as both an aid for programmers and a way to show nonprogrammers how the DOM is used to access elements and change their properties on the fly.

TABLE 2.2: The Element Interface in the DOM

ATTRIBUTE	DESCRIPTION
tagName	This interface attribute can be used as an element object property to retrieve the name of a specified element.

METHOD	DESCRIPTION
getAttribute (*name*)	This interface method can be used to return a string value containing the name of an attribute.
removeAttribute (*name*)	This interface method makes it possible to dynamically remove an attribute from an element.
setAttribute (*name, value*)	This interface method makes it possible to dynamically add an attribute to an element. The value in the parameter is a string value, so the method needs to be used carefully because any markup set by the method will be interpreted as literal text, not as markup. As you progress in your XML development, you'll learn how to escape specific characters, as they are set by programming methods or by other processing mechanisms.
getAttributeNode (*name*)	This interface method makes it possible to retrieve a specific attribute, which is named in the parameter.
getElementsByTagNam (name)	This interface method can be used to retrieve the names of all the elements that are descendants of the element the method is being operated on and that have the name given in the parameter.
normalize()	This interface method makes it possible to combine an element's text nodes in one normalized form to make it easier to manage the saving of documents.
removeAttributeNode (*oldAttribute*)	This interface method can be used to remove an attribute from an element's attribute list, by naming the attribute you want to remove in the list method's parameters.
setAttributeNode (*newAttribute*)	This interface method makes it possible to add an attribute to an element's attribute list.

WRITING WELL-FORMED DOCUMENTS

Now that you know all the rules about creating elements and how they fit into the document, we are going to look at ways to ensure that your documents are well formed. We'll also take a look at how to manage your element content through validation. There's a difference between these two:

▶ A well-formed document is a document that follows the core rules of XML.

▶ A valid document is a document that follows the core rules of XML *and* adheres to a DTD or a schema assigned to that document.

Before you tackle document creation using a DTD, it might be worthwhile to review some of the concepts of what makes a well-formed document. To do that, let's look at common problems that new XML developers can encounter.

Common Markup Problems

Once you get the hang of it, it's usually easy to see why some elements are well formed and some are not. Let's look at a few elements with some markup problems, keeping in mind that you're looking at elements not bound to any DTD or schema. A DTD or schema might require an element to consist of specific attributes or data types. In those cases, even though an element consists of well-formed markup, the markup may result in a document that isn't valid, because it didn't adhere to the declarations in the associated DTD or schema. Tackling DTD markup, however, adds another layer of complexity that you will want to address. DTD markup is covered in Chapter 6. For now, just think about why the elements that follow are well formed or not.

Improperly Nested Elements

If you've developed a lot of HTML, you've probably picked up some bad habits, none of which are likely to be your fault. Including a br element within a p element is pretty much second nature for an HTML code developer:

```
<p>January.<br>February</p>
```

In the XML world, two things are wrong with the preceding markup. It all revolves around the br element not having a closing tag, which means that an XML parser will not parse the document. Instead, you'll get an error message like this that will probably indicate that the parser was expecting an end tag: "Expected </br>."

This problem is easily corrected by simply adding a closing tag to the empty element:

```
<p>January.<br />February</p>
```

Notice the extra space before the slash mark? This prevents non-XML browsers from misinterpreting or ignoring the element. Using a minimized tag syntax is preferable to the longer
</br>, which is perfectly legitimate XML but will produce unpredictable results in HTML browsers. Although this may seem to be strictly an XHTML issue, using minimized tag syntax is becoming the convention in all kinds of XML, if only for its brevity.

Next, look at the following code snippet to see if you can spot what is wrong:

```
<analysis><type>psychological</analysis>
</type>
```

The problem with this one is that there is no hierarchy, because the elements are not nested. This code snippet will generate an error like this: "Expected </type>." The type element needs to be fully formed within a parent element. The following is correct:

```
<analysis><type>psychological</type></analysis>
```

Improper Case Agreement

You can easily make a markup mistake because you entered an opening tag of an element in one case (for example, all lowercase) and the closing tag in another (for example, all uppercase):

```
<title>Mastering XML</TITLE>
```

This code snippet will also generate an error. The parser will likely tell you it expected a closing tag for the title element. The following is the obvious solution:

```
<title>Mastering XML</title>
```

No Root Element

Imagine the following is a complete XML document (minus the prolog):

```
<book><title>Mastering XML</title></book>
<publisher>Sybex</publisher>
```

The problem here is that there is no root element. The first element in an XML document must always have its closing tag at the end of the document, and every other element in the document must be a child of that root element. The following fixes the document:

```
<book><title>Mastering XML</title>
<publisher>Sybex</publisher>
</book>
```

No CDATA Sections When Using < or Other XML Characters

The code in Listing 2.2 is a bit more of a brainteaser than the previous examples of bad markup. Take a close look at it and see if you can find the error. Hint: The offending markup occurs within the <SQL> tag.

Listing 2.2: Detecting an Error in Tag Markup

```
?xml version="1.0"?>
<!DOCTYPE Grid SYSTEM "AspGrid.dtd">
<Grid CanDelete="False"
MethodGet="False" MaxRows="6">
    <SQL>
    SELECT
        OCL.IO_ID,
        Orders.Order_ID,
        Orders.Client_ID,
        OCL.Publication_ID,
        OCL.IOKeywords,
        OCL.RunDate,
        OCL.IOProcessed,
        OCL.IOLineage,
        OCL.IOConfirmation,
        OCL.IOAudit FROM Orders
    INNER JOIN OCL ON
        Orders.Order_ID = OCL.Order_ID
```

```
WHERE
    (OCL.IOAdType <> 'Web'
AND
    OCL.IOAdType <> 'Collateral'
AND
    Orders.WasInvoiced <> '1'
AND
    Orders.ToBeInvoiced <> '1'
AND
    (OCL.RunDate >='10/09/00'
AND OCL.RunDate <= '12/30/00')>
ORDER BY
OCL.IO_ID
    </SQL>
    <Cols Index="IO_ID">
        <ReadOnly>True</ReadOnly>
    </Cols>
    <Cols Index="Order_ID">
    <Caption>Order Number</Caption>
    <ReadOnly>True</ReadOnly>
    </Cols>
</Grid>
```

The problem was that the developer wanted to include an SQL query but was flummoxed by the conflict between XML markup rules and very common SQL syntax. Without reproducing the entire code, the correct markup for the <SQL> tag should look like Listing 2.3.

Listing 2.3: Correcting an Error in Tag Markup by Using a CDATA Section

```
<SQL>
    SELECT
        OCL.IO_ID,
        Orders.Order_ID,
        Orders.Client_ID,
        OCL.Publication_ID,
        OCL.IOKeywords,
        OCL.RunDate,
        OCL.IOProcessed,
        OCL.IOLineage,
        OCL.IOConfirmation,
        OCL.IOAudit
    FROM
```

```
         Orders
INNER JOIN OCL ON
    Orders.Order_ID = OCL.Order_ID
WHERE
    <![CDATA[(OCL.IOAdType <> 'Web'
AND
    OCL.IOAdType <> 'Collateral'
AND
    Orders.WasInvoiced <> '1'
AND
  Orders.ToBeInvoiced <> '1'
AND
    (OCL.RunDate >='10/09/00'
AND OCL.RunDate <= '12/30/00'))]]>
    ORDER BY OCL.IO_ID
</SQL>
```

The key is the CDATA section, which allows you to use the < and > characters so that the XML parser does not interpret them as representing markup. After all, the parser needs to rely on the consistency claimed by XML that < and > are *always* used to create markup statements. Obviously, at times this conflicts with our need to be able to use these kinds of symbols for other reasons, such as operators in SQL or scripting/programming language statements.

CDATA sections can occur anywhere that character data is allowed by the XML specification. A CDATA section is an escape mechanism that protects the parser from XML markup characters that need to be used for non-XML use, such as the SQL code in the previous example. The syntax for CDATA sections goes like this:

```
<![CDATA[ somecontent ]]>
```

This device is extremely useful, and often necessary, for managing code in your XML document that is itself not XML, such as SQL, JavaScript, and Perl, among others. It may look weird, but you should get comfortable with it if you plan to embed any kind of business logic into an XML document.

Managing Data Content within Elements

As you have learned, elements can take content composed of other elements or specific data represented by text characters. Elements can also have extra information attached to them through attributes. You can manage element content in two ways: through DTD validation and through the use of a schema.

Using DTD Validation

Early in this chapter we mentioned four specific types of content models to which elements can adhere. These four types of content models are dictated through the use of a DTD. You'll recall that these four types are the EMPTY, ANY, mixed, and elements content models.

A DTD as a separate document is called an external DTD. It needs to be declared in the prolog of an XML document if that XML document is to be validated against it. You can also make your declarations within the XML document itself. These declarations are called an internal DTD. You learn how to create a DTD in Chapter 6.

When you're creating XML document elements that are validated against a DTD, ensure that the elements follow the rules specified by the DTD, whether that DTD is internal or external. If there is no DTD, the elements only need to be well formed within the XML vocabulary.

But a document that does not have an associated DTD or schema is not valid. This may seem like a confusing statement, so let's examine it. After all, saying a document is not valid seems like a strong statement. It implies that the document is no good and that it has no validity within the XML environment, which is not the case. When a document is not valid, it just means that no DTD or schema is available against which to validate it. There are, in other words, no rules for the document to follow. The document might still be perfectly well-formed XML, which means that an XML parser should parse it. A DTD provides document authors with a chance to maintain a set of rules that XML documents should follow. Using a DTD (or a schema) will make it easier to maintain consistency of structure, but there is no requirement that an XML document be valid or, in other words, follow a set of rules according to some DTD that is out there or that you create. A document can also be well formed, but invalid, if it is written against a DTD but doesn't correctly adhere to the DTD's declarations.

What you have learned in this chapter regarding when and how to recognize the various parts of the content model should serve you well as you embark on the mission of creating your own DTD. Chapter 6 provides greater detail on how to develop and interpret a DTD.

Validating against Schemas

Another area that has grown as XML matures is the validation of XML documents against schemas. Schemas are XML documents that contain content-type definitions, much like a DTD does. An XML document that wants to validate against a schema generally uses what is called a *namespace*. The namespace provides a mechanism through which the XML processor handling the XML document that is being validated knows about the schema being used for validation.

There have been several proposals before the W3C regarding schema specifications. Each has focused on a specific aspect of document creation. Among the types being considered have been the following:

- Document Content Description for XML (DCD)
- Schema for Object-Oriented XML (SQX)
- Document Definition Markup Language (DDML) Specification, Version 1
- XML Data

The W3C narrowed its focus somewhat to three candidate recommendations on schemas and finally came up with three different recommendations. The first focuses on structure, the second on data types. The first is called XML Schema Part 1: Structures, which you can find at www.w3.org/TR/xmlschema-1/. The second, called XML Schema Part 2: Datatypes, can be found at www.w3.org/TR/xmlschema-2/. The recommendation that focuses on schema structure describes the syntax and elements that are allowed when creating schemas. There is a DTD that must be adhered to.

The third recommendation is actually a primer that provides a comprehensive overview of schemas as defined by the W3C. This can be found at www.w3.org/TR/xmlschema-0/.

The recommendation that focuses on data types concentrates on the types of data that are allowed. This is where the difference between DTDs and schemas really comes into play. Schemas allow for a much larger set of data types than DTDs allow. You can specify integers and other numbers, dates, and Booleans (true-false data types). They make mapping from databases much easier, because the data typing is more closely aligned with what you might encounter in a relational database. To validate against these schemas, you need to declare a namespace and then adhere to that namespace declaration when using the elements that are validated against the schema.

Schemas are validated against a document when the document gains access in some way to the validating schema. The current recommendation does not specify how a document must gain access, but generally documents will use namespaces to do so. The only requirement is that a schema must be identified by a Uniform Resource Identifier (URI). This is not the same as the more familiar URL. A URI acts as an identifying mechanism that doesn't require a physical presence on a network. The following is an example of a namespace that declares the use of Microsoft's schema that works in IE 5 and above:

```
<MYROOTELEMENT
xmlns="mySchema: theValidatingSchema.xml">
    <MOREELEMENTS>
    ...<!- More content here ->
    </MOREELEMENTS>
</MYROOTELEMENT>
```

IE 5 and higher recognize schemas, but early versions of Internet Explorer won't recognize those written using the current W3C recommendations. Microsoft developed its own set of schema elements long before the final W3C recommendation was finished. These made it possible to develop schemas that are then used to validate documents and access the rich data types afforded to content authors who chose to use them instead of a DTD. Microsoft has since issued versions of its MSXML parser that supports the new standard. This parser can be installed side by side with any older versions of the parser for backward compatibility.

You can also generally include the namespace prefix with the element name. This is a good idea especially if you are using multiple schemas. Consider the following code snippet:

```
<MYROOTELEMENT
xmlns:schema1="http://www.mydomain.com/schemas/
➡schema1.xsd"
xmlns:schema2="http://www.mydomain.com/schemas/
➡schema2.xsd"
xmlns:schema3="http://www.mydomain.com/schemas/
➡schema3.xsd">
    <schema1:CHILDELEMENT>
```

```
    some content here
    </schema1:CHILDELEMENT>
    <schema2:CHILDELEMENT>
    some content here
    </schema2:CHILDELEMENT>
    <schema3:CHILDELEMENT>
    some content here
  </schema3:CHILDELEMENT>
  </MYROOTELEMENT>
```

The preceding lines of code create a way to access what seems to be one element (CHILDELEMENT) in three ways. Because the prefixes schema1:, schema2:, and schema3: were added, they in fact create three different elements. However, CHILDELEMENT may have originated with one definition. Schemas might then evolve to handle that same element differently, depending on the circumstances. Perhaps CHILDELEMENT referenced the same object from three different vendors. Substitute car for CHILDELE-MENT, and the three prefixes for GM (GM:car), Ford (Ford:car) and Honda (Honda:car), and you can see why namespaces and schemas might come in handy. You might build a generalized DTD to handle cars and then create a more specific schema for each make of car, which has the same general properties (or attributes) but also has many vendor-specific features.

The xsd extension of the URI in the preceding code refers to each schema. This follows the convention of the W3C's recommendations.

One drawback to schemas is that in order for an XML processor to validate against a schema, it needs an instruction set built into the parsing software. An example of a schema-aware XML processor is IE 5. IE 5 knows about the element types made possible through the XML Data schema. The XML Data schema allows you to create your own schema for more robust data types than the XML specification allows, thus making it possible to use integers, floats, and other numeric entities within elements and their attributes. That's the strength of schemas: They allow a more open model than DTD validation. The real question over time will be whether schemas become vehicles for software vendors to continue creating compatibility woes over the Web or whether schemas rally around their promise of providing access to rich data types.

Getting an Element from a Database

The XML world has changed considerably since the first edition of the XML specification was published by the W3C. One of those changes has been the way XML has been embraced by database professionals who like its ability to pass data from one database to another. It isn't a surprise that XML was immediately recognized as the excellent data-transport mechanism that it is. What *has* taken some by surprise is just how thoroughly many database programmers have become evangelists for the technology and how quickly tools have begun to appear to assist programmers in extracting data from databases into an XML format.

One reason this extraction process is important is the burgeoning world of B2B on the Web. B2B requires that you exchange data with your partners. But, generally, you can't just sniff around other peoples' databases. And legacy data exchange formats such as EDI (Electronic Data Interchange) are cumbersome, expensive, and don't port well to the Web.

Major databases are even beginning to incorporate XML into their basic query engines. We'll look at one example of this in the next several sections as we explore the way Microsoft's SQL Server 2000 has built XML queries into its version of the Transact-SQL language.

Using SQL Server 2000 to Generate XML Elements

Let's take a quick look at an example of data extraction within the simplest of scenarios. How do you convert rows in a table to XML elements?

Consider the ubiquitous SQL Server and Access database Northwind, in which you'll find two tables, one called `Order Details` and one called `Products`. Let's now take a simple SQL `Select` statement. If you don't know SQL, don't worry; it's an intuitive enough language that even a novice can figure out what is going on in this statement:

```
SELECT
    OrderID,
    [Order Details].ProductID,
    ProductName
FROM
```

```
    [Order Details]
INNER JOIN
Products
ON
    [Order Details].ProductID = Products.ProductID
WHERE ProductName LIKE '%Manj%'
```

This query requests order information about a product whose name contains the string Manj. The result of this query looks like this:

```
OrderID     ProductID   ProductName
------      ------      ------------

10249       14          Tofu
10249       51          Manjimup Dried Apples
```

Because the query is searching for order numbers (among other things), other products are likely to show up, which is fine for now. Next, watch what happens when we use SQL Server 2000's FOR XML clause, which is an extension to the ANSI SQL standard that Microsoft added specifically to return queries formatted as XML. First, in Listing 2.4, we add the clause to our original query:

Listing 2.4: Using the *For XML* Clause Using Transact-SQL in SQL Server 2000

```
SELECT
    OrderID,
    [Order Details].ProductID,
    ProductName
FROM
    [Order Details]
INNER JOIN
    Products
ON
    [Order Details].ProductID = Products.ProductID
WHERE
    OrderID=10249
FOR XML AUTO /* this adds the clause we need
to return XML */
```

Immediately, you may wonder about that space between `Order` and `Details` in the FROM clause. After all, you can't make well-formed elements with white space in the element name. You have several choices, including mapping these elements to column names yourself, but that's for later chapters. Here, we'll take the easy way out and let SQL Server 2000 handle the chore for us (that's what the AUTO keyword does in the FOR XML AUTO clause). The new result looks like this:

```
<Order_x0020_Details OrderID="10249" ProductID="14">
<Products ProductName="Tofu"/>
</Order_x0020_Details>
<Order_x0020_Details OrderID="10249" ProductID="51">
<Products ProductName="Manjimup Dried Apples"/>
</Order_x0020_Details>
```

SQL Server 2000 converted the order field in the database into an order element in the preceding lines of code (see Figure 2.4). Thanks to the flexibility of XML, you're not confined to sorting your data in any one way. Using a scripting or programming language or XSLT (a transformation language for XML), you can filter data and records in just about any manner you choose, just as you can with SQL. In fact, you may want to return all your data for some reason in SQL and then write XSLT templates to different audiences that display different parts of the results.

You can see from the preceding code that elements can take different kinds of content. The order element, for example, contains other elements. The product element has an ID attribute attached to it and contains descriptive text for its value.

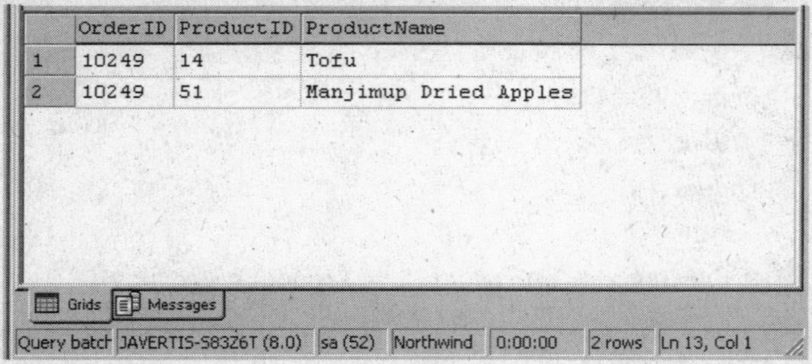

	OrderID	ProductID	ProductName
1	10249	14	Tofu
2	10249	51	Manjimup Dried Apples

Grids · Messages

Query batch JAVERTIS-S83Z6T (8.0) · sa (52) · Northwind · 0:00:00 · 2 rows · Ln 13, Col 1

FIGURE 2.4: A small result set in grid view from Microsoft SQL Server 2000

Mapping Elements

The bottom line on getting elements from a database is that somehow you have to map them from tables into XML files. Luckily, there's a lot of software out there that can help you do that. Unfortunately, much of it defaults the mapping into something like a <row> or <rowset> element as the root element. The reason we say this is unfortunate is that this is often not what you'll want. However, this method does offer a glimpse into how the process works.

The strategy is simple. Databases typically have a set of tables, but these tables don't have the kind of hierarchies associated with XML. In other words, there is no "root" column in a database.

Most automated mapping systems have a default mechanism that creates a root element called <row> or <rowset>. Many also let you decide how to choose a root element. The mapping software then plugs the data into the XML elements that map out to the database.

Begin with an SQL Query

Let's take an SQL query and watch the various mapping permutations that can take place among different software environments. Listing 2.5 shows our first, a standard query, which we will then use within a mapping scenario. Listing 2.6 shows the query results.

Listing 2.5: Simple SQL Query

```
SELECT
    OCL.IO_ID,
    OCL.Order_ID,
    OCL.Publication_ID
FROM OCL
INNER JOIN
    Orders ON Orders.Order_ID = OCL.Order_ID
WHERE Client_ID LIKE 'Cadence%'
AND    OCL.RunDate >='10/14/00'
AND    OCL.RunDate <='11/01/00'
```

Listing 2.6: Results from Listing 2.5

IO_ID	Order_ID	Publication_ID
58534	31090	JMOJOBS.COM
58538	31090	JOBTRAK

```
58227      30997      BOSTON
58226      30997      SJMN/CCT
58533      31090      DICE
58229      30997      NAPA
58266      30997      SJMN
58267      30997      PORTLAND
58268      30997      PORTLAND
58105      30958      CM FLYER-COLOR
58106      30958      CM FLYER-COLOR
57666      30796      DIVERSITY CAREERS
```

(12 row(s) affected)

Mapping Your Data

Next, we'll take a look at how one mapping tool, called Schemer, from Tennozan, LLC, maps the data into XML elements. Keep in mind that this mapping tool, like most, allows you to define your own mapping definitions.

Building the Schema Definition   First, the program generates a schema that conforms to the Microsoft schema definitions. This is shown in Listing 2.7. This is an internal schema, meaning that its definition exists within the document itself, rather than outside the document with a reference in the document instance. This is accomplished by establishing xml as the root element with two child elements. The first child element, shown in Listing 2.7, is the s:Schema element. We will look at the second child element next.

Listing 2.7: Schema Generated from SQL Query

```
<xml xmlns:s="uuid:BDC6E3F0-6DA3-11d1-A2A3-
➥00AA00C14882"
    xmlns:dt="uuid:C2F41010-65B3-11d1-A29F-
➥00AA00C14882"
➥xmlns:rs="urn:schemas-microsoft-com:rowset"
    xmlns:z="#RowsetSchema">
<s:Schema id="RowsetSchema">
<s:ElementType name="row"
content="eltOnly"
rs:CommandTimeout="30">
<s:AttributeType name="IO_ID"
rs:number="1">
```

```
<s:datatype dt:type="int" dt:maxLength="4"
rs:precision="10" rs:fixedlength="true"
rs:maybenull="false" />
</s:AttributeType>
<s:AttributeType name="Order_ID"
rs:number="2" rs:writeunknown="true">
<s:datatype dt:type="int" dt:maxLength="4"
rs:precision="10" rs:fixedlength="true"
rs:maybenull="false" />
...
</s:ElementType>
</s:Schema>
```

The actual schema is quite a bit longer than we are showing in List-ing 2.7. We've truncated it to save space. However, you can find the entire document (and, of course, its schema) on the CD. The file is called `schemerXMLExport.xml`.

Mapping to Elements   Mapping software such as Schemer then maps the elements from the database to a combination of elements and attributes that match the schema definition. Listing 2.8 shows a trun-cated version of the result. Remember, we're still looking at the SQL query we saw in Listing 2.5. Now, however, it's been mapped to a group of XML elements (or, more precisely, one main database element with a number of attributes attached).

Listing 2.8: Results from a Schema-Based Data Extraction

```
- <rs:data>
  <z:row IO_ID="58534" Order_ID="31090"
Publication_ID="JMOJOBS.COM" c3="31090" />
  <z:row IO_ID="58538" Order_ID="31090"
Publication_ID="JOBTRAK" c3="31090" />
  <z:row IO_ID="58227" Order_ID="30997"
Publication_ID="BOSTON" c3="30997" />
  <z:row IO_ID="58226" Order_ID="30997"
Publication_ID="SJMN/CCT" c3="30997" />
  <z:row IO_ID="58533" Order_ID="31090"
Publication_ID="DICE" c3="31090" />
  <z:row IO_ID="58229" Order_ID="30997"
Publication_ID="NAPA" c3="30997" />
  <z:row IO_ID="58266" Order_ID="30997"
Publication_ID="SJMN" c3="30997" />
  <z:row IO_ID="58267" Order_ID="30997"
```

```
          Publication_ID="PORTLAND" c3="30997" />
            <z:row IO_ID="58268" Order_ID="30997"
          Publication_ID="PORTLAND" c3="30997" />
            <z:row IO_ID="58105" Order_ID="30958"
          Publication_ID="CM FLYER-COLOR" c3="30958" />
            <z:row IO_ID="58106" Order_ID="30958"
          Publication_ID="CM FLYER-COLOR" c3="30958" />
            <z:row IO_ID="57666" Order_ID="30796"
          Publication_ID="DIVERSITY CAREERS" c3="30796" />
          </rs:data>
```

Previously, we demonstrated how the mapping software created a root element, xml, which contains two child elements. The first child element contained the schema definition. The second child element, z:row, does to an XML element. The z in z:row is a namespace prefix and is necessary because you're validating against a schema using a specific namespace. For more on namespaces, see *Mastering XML, Premium Edition* (Sybex, 2001), Chapter 11, "Understanding Namespaces: Core Standard."

Think about it for a moment and you'll see how much sense this makes. When you examine the z:row element in Listing 2.5, you'll see that it is mapped to the results of the original SQL query that you saw in Listing 2.2. You could actually do this yourself with a text editor, although with even a rather small data set you wouldn't have time for much else. Luckily, of course, there are software programs to help you.

TIP

To get a firm grasp on the hierarchy of the XML file that was generated for this example, we suggest you look at the file in its entirety. You can find it at www.tumeric.net/projects/books/complete/support/ch01_toc.asp. It is called schemerXMLExport.xml.

This idea of creating a <rowset> element for each row works, but once you begin to work in collaborative environments, especially with B2B applications, you'll soon yearn for a more robust approach.

SUMMARY

In this chapter, you learned how to create an element. Overall, you'll probably find that elements are fairly simple to develop. We can make elements even more robust by adding attributes to them. The next chapter, "Understanding and Creating Attributes," will explore how to create attributes and add them to your XML elements.

Chapter 3
UNDERSTANDING AND CREATING ATTRIBUTES

I f you're familiar with HTML, you've seen attributes many, many times, even if you've given them little thought. The nature of HTML is such that you can use an attribute without thinking much about it. You don't need to understand that much about the syntax involved, or even, for that matter, if it's correct. Browsers tend to simply ignore attributes that aren't structured properly. Attributes play a key role in XML development, just as they do in HTML.

If you're not familiar with HTML, the definition of an attribute is still easy. An attribute in XML is the part of an element that contains additional information about an element. Conceptually, if you're an object-oriented programmer, you'll find that attributes map out to properties. If you're a desktop

Adapted from *Mastering™ XML, Premium Edition*, by Chuck White, Liam Quin, and Linda Burman
ISBN 0-7821-2847-5   1,155 pages $49.99

publisher, attributes are like the changes you apply to style sheets to change font colors (the color is a property, or attribute, of a font) or the size of a text box. If you're a writer, an attribute is like an adjective. A house might be considered an element. To describe it, you might use an adjective, or attribute, like big.

This chapter explores the key concepts behind attributes, helps you understand the syntax behind attribute development, and shows you how to manage attribute types, particularly their relationship to a DTD.

WHAT IS AN ATTRIBUTE?

Attributes consist of name-value pairs and an equals sign (=) operator.

One example of an HTML attribute is the src attribute. The src attribute belongs to the img element, which exists in just about every Web page. In HTML, an src attribute within an img element looks something like this:

```
<img src = "http://www.mySite.com/myGif.gif">
```

The src attribute in the line of code acts as a modifier to the img element. The most obvious difference between XML and HTML is that an XML processor doesn't by itself know what to do with the element (keep in mind, too, that the preceding line of code would not be well-formed XML markup, because it lacks a closing tag).

Attribute rules are a bit like grammar. A *cat* is nice, but a *big, fancy, fluffy, splendiferous* cat is nicer. The adjectives *big, fancy, fluffy,* and *splendiferous* are all modifiers; they help give the noun (cat) attributes. Whether or not you agree that these kinds of cats are indeed nicer, you most likely will agree that the description is more specific than just *cat*.

So, as mentioned previously, an attribute in XML is the part of an element that contains additional information about an element. Attributes are especially useful for managing the kinds of content that you encountered in Chapter 2, "Understanding and Creating Elements." You'll remember that elements consist of four kinds of content with various combinations of other elements and character data. Attributes break these kinds of content down further and allow you to specify how they are managed.

Attributes can consist of 10 specific types of content. When a DTD is being followed or written, attributes are said to be one of these 10 types.

Any attribute value must consist of one of the following types of attributes available to an XML document:

- CDATA
- ENTITY
- ENTITIES
- Enumeration
- ID
- IDREF
- IDREFS
- NMTOKEN
- NMTOKENS
- NOTATION

Generally, although much of this nomenclature may be new to you, if you've worked with HTML you'll be comfortable with the various types of content involved with XML. If your programming background doesn't include HTML, you'll still be comfortable, because XML structure borrows heavily from a number of different programming concepts. Strings, for example, are mapped to the CDATA data type and are used by almost all modern object-based programming languages. Name tokens are similar to the naming constructs used for variable declarations in many programming languages.

NOTE

Wondering about the difference between CDATA and #PCDATA? #PCDATA is *parsed character data*. The # character is used so that #PCDATA could never be mistaken in a DTD element declaration as a name, because the # character can't be used in an element name. Parsed character data is a reference from SGML that in XML means that the XML processor will read a document's text and search for telltale markers that indicate markup—particularly the < and & characters. CDATA is *character data*. A CDATA attribute contains PCDATA, but the parser strips all entity values. This means that the attribute values < and & will be returned by the processor as < and &, respectively. But don't confuse CDATA with a CDATA section. A CDATA section allows you to delimit a specific chunk of code and tell the XML parser explicitly not to parse that code. For example, this CDATA section is valid: <![CDATA[x <> 0]]>. However, x<>0 would fail as element content when validated as parsed character data.

Entities should also prove to be a reasonably easy concept to grasp. If you've used img elements or used < to represent the < character in HTML, you'll certainly be comfortable with entities. If you haven't used HTML but you've worked with objects, you'll also be comfortable working with entities. If you've never worked with any kind of computer programming, for now think of entities as placeholders that act as shortcuts to larger pieces of information. XML allows a much broader scope of objects to be used in an XML file than HTML has traditionally made room for, hence the use of entities. The surprising thing about the way XML makes room for so many different kinds of content is how efficiently it does so. A key reason for this efficiency is the way attributes can be used to manage many different things.

UNDERSTANDING ATTRIBUTE SYNTAX

One of the joys of XML is its lack of a massive set of rules of syntax, and nowhere is this more apparent than with attributes. All you really need to keep in mind are these few simple conventions:

- ▶ Within the tag containing an element name and any of that element's attributes, the element name comes first.

- ▶ An element attribute's value must always be in either double or single quotes. No exceptions. However, an attribute value in double quotes can contain a value in single quotes, and vice versa.

- ▶ As with elements, you must use case consistently when referring to an attribute matched against a declaration. For example, <TITLE fiction="yes"> is never the same as <TITLE FICTION="yes">.

The following code shows what a typical attribute looks like. As with most XML document fragments, you'll usually be writing against a DTD or schema, but don't worry about that yet:

```
<BOOK type = "digital">
<TITLE fixed = 'yes'>Freedom's Dream</TITLE>
<REVIEW comments = "entertaining and clever"/>
</BOOK>
```

In the preceding lines of code, there are two attributes. The first, type, belongs to the BOOK element, and the second, fixed, belongs to the TITLE element. If the attributes in the preceding lines of code were written without quotes, an XML parser could not parse the containing document because the containing document would not be well formed.

You can also mix double quotes and single quotes. Be sure to use ASCII apostrophe and quotes, rather than "smart quotes" (such as those created in word processing programs and desktop publishing software for stylistic reasons), which map out to different character values in Unicode. A situation when you might encounter single and double quotes and when the distinction between attribute values can be important is within the context of XSL (Extensible Style Sheet Language):

```
<xsl:if test="false">
<!- really means that the test is false ->
<xsl:if test="'false'">
<!- false is a string value, not a Boolean.
The test is for the actual string value 'false' ->
```

UNDERSTANDING ATTRIBUTE TYPES

Attributes and their content types are managed most easily through a DTD or schema. If you're not using a DTD or schema to develop attributes and are just assigning arbitrary names and values, things will become more difficult as you build bigger and more complex documents. Even if you're using an XML document strictly as a document for holding data (in which case you may think you don't particularly need a DTD), you'll find that, essentially, attributes don't really mean much without a DTD to communicate their meaning to applications and external definitions. You'll learn how to create a DTD in Chapter 6, "Creating Your Own DTD."

NOTE

One notable exception to the preceding statement is projects that use XSLT to transform XML documents into other formats, such as HTML or XHTML. You can accomplish quite a bit with XSLT without a DTD for the source document.

Without a DTD or schema, you generally won't be able to do as much with your document. You also won't be able to add objects like binary files to your document, because you need to declare your entities in the DTD attribute lists (which you'll learn about in Chapter 4, "Understanding and Creating Entities"). Of course, you can easily add images and objects using XHTML to develop XML-compliant HTML. You can also view the latest W3C (World Wide Web Consortium) recommendations at www.w3.org/TR/xhtml1/.

NOTE

Using attributes in schemas have some special requirements. You should read Chapter 8, "Writing XML Schemas," to learn these. You may also want to check out www.w3.org/TR/xmlschema-0/ for the W3C's primer on schemas. The relevant W3C recommendations on schemas can be found at www.w3.org/TR/xmlschema-1/ and www.w3.org/TR/xmlschema-2/. These standardized schema vocabularies provide richer options for data types, such as dates and integers, than DTDs offer. You can also view the Microsoft proposal—which early versions of Internet Explorer (IE) 5 conform to—at www.w3c.org/TR/1998/NOTE-XML-data-0105/. Note that the W3C recommendations are the direction standards are going, not the Microsoft proposal. In fact, Microsoft itself is vowing ultimate conformance with the newest schema recommendations, although managing Microsoft namespace and versioning issues can be detrimental to one's mental health.

Learning about Attribute Lists

When you encounter a DTD, you'll see element declarations followed by what are called attribute lists. Within a DTD you'll be able to recognize an attribute list easily enough through the ATTLIST keyword. A typical attribute list in a DTD might look something like Listing 3.1.

Listing 3.1: An Attribute List in a DTD

```
<!ELEMENT lillybook (Character*, Title,
Author+, Copyright?, Abstract?, Preface?, Chapter+)>
<!ATTLIST lillybook
    type (fiction | nonfiction) "fiction"
    datadriven (yes | no) "no"
    xmlns:xlink CDATA #FIXED
    "http://www.w3.org/1999/xlink"
    xlink:type (extended | simple) "simple"
    xlink:href CDATA #IMPLIED
    xlink:title CDATA #IMPLIED
    xlink:label NMTOKEN #IMPLIED
    xlink:actuate (onLoad | onRequest |
    other | none)
```

```
#IMPLIED id ID #REQUIRED
>
```

You may not be familiar with DTD declarations yet, so let's review what is happening in the preceding lines of code. The first line declares the element and the content it can contain. Because it happens to be the root element, it contains a group of additional child elements. It is the next line you'll be most interested in as you're reading DTD requirements on attributes. When validating an XML document against this declaration, you must provide the attribute list declarations that determine what constraints, if any, the validating DTD has on the attributes you want to use in an element.

The !ATTLIST references first the element to which it applies. An element's attribute list can be as long as the DTD author wants it to be. In the preceding example, the !ATTLIST declaration is for the lillybook element, and it describes several attributes. One of the preceding declarations says that an attribute is fixed (through the use of the #FIXED keyword), which means the XML document must use the declared value:

```
xmlns:xlink CDATA #FIXED

"http://www.w3.org/1999/xlink"
```

This helps us to declare a namespace in the actual document instance so that we can reserve for future use features of the XLink language, an XML linking language. Because you can't use XLink without namespaces, this is critical. The fact that there isn't much support out there yet for XLink doesn't need to constrain us in its use. For now—and you'll see this in use in Chapter 12, "Transforming XML: Introducing XSLT"—we can map linking attributes and/or elements to HTML elements that we know will work. At the same time, now that the XLink specification is beginning to settle down, we can plan ahead a bit by including its syntax for future use.

NOTE

In a real production environment, if you want to take advantage of an XML vocabulary that has little practical processor support now but seems likely to have more in the future, you should simply account for it in a DTD and not worry about including it in an XML document instance.

An attribute list in a DTD consists of three parts: The first part is the name, the second part is a type, and the third part is something called the default.

Using Default Attribute Values

As you develop attributes, you may be constrained by a DTD that governs their use. One such constraint involves *default* values for attributes. A default value is the value given to an attribute when the document author (as opposed to the DTD author) declines to specify a value by leaving the attribute off an element's tag. It should be noted that an attribute value of " " is not in conformance with a DTD attribute list declaration unless the declaration somehow specifies this as an acceptable value. To leave an attribute out of a tag, you simply do not include it in the tag, but remember, you can do that only if the attribute is not required.

Recognizing Default Values   You can recognize a default attribute by looking at the attribute list declaration in a DTD. The general syntax within a DTD for an attribute value looks like this:

```
<!ATTLIST MYElement MyAttribute Type default_value>
```

Remember the order of the parts within attribute list declarations, because they will always occur in the same order. In the following line of code, the default value is paperback:

```
<!ATTLIST BOOK BINDING CDATA "paperback">
```

This means that if a document writer includes a BOOK element in an XML document and they leave off the attribute, BOOK would automatically be a paperback, as far as the XML document is concerned. Consider the following line of code:

```
<BOOK>Mastering XML</BOOK>
```

Based on the attribute list declaration that preceded this line of code, *Mastering XML* would be a paperback, because paperback was named as the default value of the BINDING attribute, though the XML document author didn't include the attribute value paperback when building the element tag.

Using the *#IMPLIED* Keyword   Another default type is indicated by the #IMPLIED keyword. This keyword can cause some confusion. An

#IMPLIED keyword shows up in a DTD when the author wants to make it known that an attribute is allowable for a particular element but that it doesn't need to be there. Such an occasion exists when you see an attribute list declaration that looks something like this:

```
<!ATTLIST BOOK BINDING CDATA #IMPLIED>
```

Technically, what happens here is that an XML parser will pass a blank value to the processing XML application, which may or may not enter its own default value. Here's an example of how a validated document might use the preceding declaration:

```
<Book binding="hard cover">The rest of the XML document goes
here</Book>
```

Using the *#REQUIRED* Keyword   Sometimes a DTD author will want an element to have a required attribute. Consider a DTD for a book. Most book-like documents have elements that follow a general outlining scheme. These are based on levels of headlines, similar to the H1, H2, H3, H4, H5, and H6 elements in HTML. If each descending head level is nested within a parent that is one level higher up in the sequencing order, it's easy to expand and collapse the outline. So it might be helpful to generate a requirement for a description of levels in headline elements.

You'll know an attribute is required because the attribute list declaration will contain a keyword named #REQUIRED. This occurs in the default part of an attribute list declaration. The following line of code demonstrates what an attribute list containing a requirement looks like. The following declaration merely says that the level attribute must be used within the Section element or any document instance associated with the DTD will be invalid:

```
<!ATTLIST Section
    classification (multimedia | print |
link) "multimedia"
    level (one | two | three | four | five
    | six | seven | eight | nine | ten | eleven
    | twelve | thirteen | fourteen | fifteen
    | sixteen | seventeen | eighteen | nineteen
    | twenty) #REQUIRED
    id ID #IMPLIED
>
```

A document fragment validated against the preceding line of code might look like this:

```
<Section classification="multimedia"
level="one">
    <SectionTitle>PartOne</SectionTitle>
    <Paragraph xlink:label="myNToken">
    I write silly stories.
    </Paragraph>
</Section>
```

Using XSLT, a transformation language, you could then output headline sizes based on the parent-child relationship of a Section element to a SectionTitle element. Section elements with attribute-level values of 1 could be output at the biggest font sizes, and Section elements with level values of 20 could be output at the smallest font sizes. This provides you as an author with a much more cohesive system of governance over style. You can change your style sheets at any time, while your core data stays the same.

Using the *#FIXED* Keyword   This keyword does exactly what it sounds like it does. It "fixes" the value of an attribute to your definition, without leaving the author of the XML document instance any options for changing it. Consider the attribute list declaration in Listing 3.2.

Listing 3.2: Using the *FIXED* Attribute Type

```
<!ATTLIST lillybook
    type (fiction | nonfiction) "fiction"
    datadriven (yes | no) "no"
    xmlns:xlink CDATA #FIXED
"http://www.w3.org/1999/xlink"
    xlink:type (extended | simple) "simple"
    xlink:href CDATA #IMPLIED
    xlink:title CDATA #IMPLIED
    xlink:label NMTOKEN #IMPLIED
    xlink:actuate (onLoad | onRequest |
other | none) #IMPLIED
    id ID #REQUIRED
```

```
>
```

The XML author is constrained to one value and one value only for the xlink attribute:

```
<lillybook id="FreedomsDream"
xmlns:xlink="http://www.w3.org/1999/xlink">
... </lillybook>
```

If a document author doesn't include the attribute, the value is assumed by the parser to be the default value specified in the DTD.

Managing Attribute Types

The 10 attribute types listed in this chapter fall into three general categories:

Enumerated types   Enumerated types are attribute values named specifically within the DTD (either as optional choices or as a reference to a notation named elsewhere in the document).

String types   String types consist of any kind of character data not parsed by the XML processor.

Tokenized types   Tokens are basically XML data types that provide a way for naming and identifying node instances.

You can see how to categorize the 10 attribute types in Table 3.1.

TABLE 3.1: Attribute Type Categories

String Types	Tokenized Types	Enumerated Types
CDATA	ENTITY	NOTATION
	ENTITIES	Enumeration
	ID	
	IDREFS	
	IDREF	
	NMTOKEN	
	NMTOKENS	

Before getting into the specifics of the various attribute types you might encounter in a DTD, you'll want to understand one important concept within XML: normalization.

About Normalization

Normalization is used to manage white space effectively. You've encountered it if you've ever put in more than one space between words in an HTML document and seen that only one space shows up. This is the standard way XML handles white space. It helps to think of normalization as a process that strips out extra white space and attaches character and entity references appropriately, depending on the circumstances.

In XML, white space consists of specific characters created, in keyboard lingo, by the following keystrokes: Enter, Tab, and spacebar. If you followed the normal rules of white space use, then you'd end up with lots of problems in your markup. That's because you sometimes need to hit the carriage return or use a tab to make your code cleaner and easier to read. If XML parsers didn't collapse that white space, you can imagine how hard it would be to create your attribute values:

```
type="this is different

than this"
```

This code snippet would probably have a different meaning than this one:

```
type="this is different than this"
```

As a result, the following is resolved by a parser:

```
type="    this is        different than this"
```

It becomes this:

```
type="this is different than this"
```

This is because the parser will strip space between quote marks in attribute values and their containing values *and limit the number of spaces in the value to one space*. New lines created by carriage returns are also stripped down to one space.

Using the *xml:space* Attribute   Generally, parsers collapse multiple white space characters the same way HTML parsers do, but you can control it with a special attribute called xsl:space. This special attribute is actually built into the XML specification. It's an Enumeration attribute type, with two possible values: default and preserve. The default value will just tell the XML parser to treat white space how it treats white space natively, whereas the preserve value tells the processor explicitly to preserve the white space. A typical example of it looks like this:

```
xml:space (default | preserve) "preserve"
```

Then, if you are including a stanza from a poem or a song and include the preserve value in the xml:space attribute, the white space is preserved:

```
<stanza xml:space="preserve">
        It flows this way
and then that.
                  It flows that away
and that's that.</stanza>
```

CDATA

CDATA is the easiest attribute value to understand. It's used to indicate that an attribute value can consist only of character data that won't be interpreted as markup. A typical CDATA attribute value looks like this:

```
<Abstract copyright="2001, Chuck White">
      <Paragraph>Descriptive narration for
   interactive short story "Freedom's Dream"
   </Paragraph>
</Abstract>
```

The CDATA keyword in a DTD indicates that any string of non-markup characters is legal when you create your attributes in the XML document instance. A typical attribute list declaration for character data (CDATA) looks like this:

```
<!ATTLIST BOOK CHAPTER CDATA #REQUIRED>
```

The preceding line of code indicates that the CHAPTER attribute is required within the BOOK element and that it can take any character data.

Therefore, if you create an attribute value pair from the previous attribute declaration, you might have something like this:

```
<BOOK CHAPTER="Chapter One"/>
```

In fact, thanks to the #REQUIRED keyword, you definitely need to include the CHAPTER attribute while developing a BOOK element, although what value you include is up to you, as long as it is legal XML character data.

You can use the following entity references in place of markup when you need markup in attribute values. The XML processor strips out the entity references and returns them as the following markup:

▶ < can be replaced with < or <

▶ > can be replaced with > or >

> ▶ " can be replaced with " or "

> ▶ ' can be replaced with ' or '

> ▶ & can be replaced with & or &

There is a stricter form of character data type in attribute values that can be the source of some confusion. NMTOKEN, Enumerated, and ID (and their similarly named cousins) attribute types all require what are called XML names and can't be defined using the looser restrictions of CDATA.

This same restriction does extend to CDATA if you are specifying a list of attributes as your attribute defaults. However, XML is excellent in its lack of exceptions regarding rules, and this area exemplifies the point. When you need to specify more than one default value, the attribute type is no longer considered a CDATA type. It is an Enumeration, which has its own set of rules (see the section on Enumeration for more detail). Later on in this section, you'll see that one way to refer to binary files (such as images) is to use ENTITY or NOTATION attribute types. However, neither solution is particularly useful in production environments, because there is limited XML processor support for these methods of managing external entities. A more gratifying procedure would be to use CDATA attribute types and MIME (Multipurpose Internet Mail Extensions) types (MIME types describe incoming data streams to Web servers and don't by definition actually have anything specifically to do with XML). So you might want to try something like Listing 3.3.

Listing 3.3: Using CDATA Attribute Types and MIME Types Incorrectly

```
<!ELEMENT graphic (#PCDATA)>
<!ATTLIST graphic
   src CDATA #REQUIRED
   title CDATA #IMPLIED
   id ID #IMPLIED
   type (image/gif | image/jpeg) "image/gif"
>
<!- why doesn't this work? ->
```

The preceding code doesn't work because you are restricted to XML names. The reason for this is that as soon as you "enumerate" options for attribute values, your data is no longer a CDATA attribute type, even though you might think it should be. As stated, your attribute type, because you have decided to present a list of options to your XML document writer, is now an Enumeration (which has a stricter definition of allowable characters). To accommodate this situation, it's best to leave it open-ended and revert back to CDATA. In the case of binary files, this is a good idea anyway, because additional MIME types may appear on the scene at any time. Listing 3.4 is our corrected attribute list.

Part i

Listing 3.4: Using CDATA Attribute Types and MIME Types Correctly

```
<!ELEMENT graphic (#PCDATA)>
<!ATTLIST graphic
    src CDATA #REQUIRED
    title CDATA #IMPLIED
    id ID #IMPLIED
    type CDATA "image/gif"
>
```

The type attribute defaults to image/gif, but we can put another value in there if we choose. Because it isn't an Enumerated attribute type but a CDATA attribute type, the limitations on the kinds of characters we can use are not as constraining.

ENTITY

The ENTITY attribute type is used to indicate that the attribute value will represent an external entity in the document, which when referenced by that document will match the name of the attribute value. A typical ENTITY attribute value looks like this:

```
<ChapterTitle>One</ChapterTitle>
        <score source="chapter_1Score"/>
```

Note that this document fragment alone is nonconforming (there is no root element).

Understanding ENTITY Attribute Types   You can manage objects with ENTITY attribute types. If you're familiar with HTML, you probably have used the img element, which helps you work with graphic objects. Entities work in a slightly similar way.

Like HTML objects, entities within the scope of attribute types are generally referenced through a Uniform Resource Identifier (URI). They are different than HTML objects, however, because they require that you declare their presence in a DTD. Typically, the DTD syntax for an ENTITY attribute type will look something like this:

```
<!ATTLIST MYELEMENT
    source ENTITY #IMPLIED >
```

Be aware that you can't use entities without declaring them in an internal or external DTD. Entities are parsed according to either a style sheet or how the parsing application typically processes the type of file referred to by the entity. You'll recognize an entity type within an attribute list when you see it in a line of code like the following:

```
<!ATTLIST score
    source ENTITY #IMPLIED
>
```

In order for your XML parser to know where to send the file (it won't do anything with it itself), you need to give it some guidance with another declaration:

```
<!NOTATION mp3 SYSTEM
    "C:\Program Files\Real\RealPlayer\realplay.exe">
```

This associates all MP3 documents with a helper application.

Then, you would include it in the markup of the XML document instance like so:

```
<score source="chapter_1Score"/>
```

Note that there is no trailing & character or trailing ; character when representing an entity in an attribute value.

Using Entities Example   Let's look at the preceding descriptions more closely. You've already seen the DTD declaration for the root element lillybook, which is the root element of an online interactive book. Now let's look at the declaration for the score element (see Listing 3.5).

Listing 3.5: ENTITY Attribute Type Declaration in a DTD

```
<!ATTLIST score
    source ENTITY #IMPLIED
    src CDATA #IMPLIED
    title CDATA #IMPLIED
    id ID #IMPLIED
>
<!NOTATION mp3 SYSTEM
    "C:\Program Files\Real\RealPlayer\realplay.exe">
```

```
<!ENTITY chapter_1Score
SYSTEM "chapter1.mp3"  NDATA mp3>
```

Note that neither the NOTATION declaration nor the ENTITY declaration are part of the ATTLIST declaration, nor do they need to be in any particular order within the DTD—they just need to be there somewhere. We've followed the ATTLIST declaration with them just for ease of reference.

Now, let's look at the chapter we've added (minus a large number of extraneous paragraphs) in the XML document instance that is getting validated against the DTD. Listing 3.6, if the parser bothers to pass off the information that a music file is available to another application (and it isn't required to do so), will play a nice little piece of music associated with the chapter.

Listing 3.6: Using an ENTITY Attribute Type in the Attribute Value Incorrectly

```
<Chapter>
      <ChapterTitle>One</ChapterTitle>
      <score source="&chapter_1Score;"/>
      <Section classification="multimedia"
level="one">
          <SectionTitle>PartOne</SectionTitle>
          <Paragraph xlink:label="AntronCrimea">Had
  it been a dream, Antron Crimea's memory of
  the clenched fist piercing the sky of
  a tumultuous, thundering crowd would
  have been bearable solitude. As it
  was though, the reality brought him
  to another place, to a distance only
  something like a dream could take him.
</Paragraph>
          <Paragraph>Our story continues.
</Paragraph>
      </Section>
</Chapter>
```

Did we catch you napping? Or did you see the mistake in our reference to the chapter_1Score entity? Don't feel bad if you didn't catch it, because it's easy to forget that entity references in attribute values don't contain the beginning & and trailing ; characters that you'll expect if you have any experience with entities. So the corrected fragment looks like Listing 3.7.

Listing 3.7: Using an ENTITY Attribute Type in the Attribute Value Correctly

```
<ChapterTitle>One</ChapterTitle>
    <score source="chapter_1Score"/>
        <Section classification="multimedia"
    level="one">
        <SectionTitle>PartOne</SectionTitle>
        <Paragraph
            xlink:label="AntronCrimea">
            Had it been a dream, Antron
            Crimea's memory of the
            clenched fist piercing the
            sky of a tumultuous,
            thundering crowd would
            have been bearable solitude.
            As it was though, the reality
            brought him to another place,
            to a distance only something
            like a dream could take him.
            </Paragraph>
            <Paragraph>Our story continues.
            </Paragraph>
    </Section>
    </Chapter>
```

This is important, because many desktop editing applications will punch in the value incorrectly when inserting into an attribute value by incorporating the beginning ampersand (&) and trailing semicolon (;).

TIP

XML has matured nicely, but most processors won't do anything with external parsed entities like we've just described. The XML specification allows them to pass the information off to a handler application (in the example's case, RealPlayer), but there is no *requirement* that it do so. Therefore, it's generally better to use a parser's (or its host application's) inherent capabilities (actually, a parser won't have such inherent capabilities, but its process for passing these capabilities to another application may seem invisible to you). You know that IE will pass multimedia URIs using its own helper applications, so it's best to make reference to them using a source string in an attribute, such as src=http://www.myimages.com/image.jpg and MIME types associated with HTTP.

ENTITIES

The ENTITIES attribute type is the same as ENTITY, except you can name more than one and separate them by white space in a list.

```
<ChapterTitle>One</ChapterTitle>
    <score
    source="chapter_1Score chapter_2Score "/>
```

Note that this document fragment alone is nonconforming (there is no root element). The Entities themselves would need separate declarations within the DTD.

Enumeration

This is a generic term meaning that a DTD author can declare an enumerated list of values that the attribute value in a validated document must match. Consider the following DTD fragment:

```
<!ELEMENT Player (%Players;)>
<!ATTLIST Player
   id ID #REQUIRED
   type (pitcher | leftFielder | rightFielder
| centerFielder | thirdBaseman | shortStop
| secondBaseman | firstBaseman | catcher)
#REQUIRED
>
```

In order for a document fragment to be validated against the preceding code, you would need to have, in addition to matching element values, an attribute value that matches the enumerated attribute values in the declaration:

```
<Player id="p0001" type="pitcher">
    <Name>Billy Freedom</Name>
    <Team>Chicago Cubs</Team>
</Player>
```

Generally, a default value chosen from one of the options is provided in a DTD, though in this case it doesn't make much sense, so the #REQUIRED default value is used here in its place.

Be careful, though, because enumerated values must be name tokens, which means they can't start with a number. So this won't work:

```
<Player id="p0001" type="001_pitcher">
```

```
      <Name>Billy Freedom</Name>
      <Team>Chicago Cubs</Team>
   </Player>
```

Be aware that Enumeration is not an XML keyword, like the other attribute types in this section. It merely describes the type of data. You provide the specifics.

WARNING

Enumerated types must be XML names. XML names must begin with a letter or underscore, never a number (sorry about that, database developers), followed by any combination of underscores, digits, hyphens, periods, and letters, and absolutely no white space. Colons are allowed, but if you use them, everyone will think you're using them for namespaces.

ID

These are used to establish a unique identifier for an element. If there is more than one ID with the same value, the parser will throw an error. The value must be an XML name. This can be a problem in database work, because XML names can't start with numbers. Not many people are doing database work with DTDs, though, because of a larger variety of issues (such as data typing):

```
<Player id="p0001" type="pitcher">
      <Name>Billy Freedom</Name>
      <Team>Chicago Cubs</Team>
   </Player>
```

WARNING

ID, IDREF, and IDREFS attribute types must be qualified XML names. Just a reminder: XML names must begin with a letter or underscore, never a number, followed by any combination of underscores, digits, hyphens, periods, and letters, and absolutely no white space. Colons are allowed, but they are better reserved for namespaces. Remember to use space delimiters. (It might be intuitive to use commas to separate the members of the list.)

IDREF

IDREF is used to allow an element to reference an ID that has been named for another element. See the next section to see how it works.

IDREFS

This is a list of white space–delimited ID references. Given the following player information, you can refer to an identified player later on in the document. So given two players, to refer to one of them you need access to the id attribute.

```
<Player id="p0001" type="pitcher">
      <Name>Billy Freedom</Name>
   </Player>
<Player id="p0002" type="pitcher">
      <Name>Fuji Pyjama</Name>
   </Player>
```

Then, within another element, you can refer to the player Billy Freedom by accessing the list of IDREFS within the document:

```
<description>
      <play type="strikeout" player="p0001 p0002"
id="play0001"/>
   </description>
```

Remember to use space delimiters (it might be intuitive to use commas to separate the members of the list). Note, too, our intentional use of the attribute named id. Many attributes using the ID attribute type will be named id, but there is no requirement that this be so. However, such nomenclature is becoming standard by convention, even though it is certainly not part of any *formal* standard. If you see an attribute named id, you can have a high degree of confidence that it will be an ID attribute type, but there is no guarantee.

Using ID and IDREF(S)   Many databases have fields labeled ID, where information such as customer numbers and/or key values is stored. Unique identifiers make it easy to access elements as objects, which is an important consideration when developing scripts. The reason this is such a fundamental process to the world of scripts and object-oriented programming languages like Java is that the unique identifier, by allowing access to individual elements as unique objects, makes it easy to transform those objects. (See Part IV, "XML Scripting and Processing," for extensive coverage of object-oriented programming and XML.)

Consider one of the Web's most basic and popular script mechanisms: the image rollover. An image rollover is accomplished by loading an array, or set, of images into a document so that the browser is aware of them when the document has loaded. Then, a specific img element is targeted as the rollover. When an onmouseover event occurs as a result of a user's mouse pointer hovering over an image (just before clicking), the image changes because the img element's src attribute value has changed. In an HTML document, a single line of script causes this action:

```
Img001.src = "myNewImage.gif"
```

The ID attribute value in the preceding line of code is Img001. Here, it might help to look at the corresponding HTML:

```
<img id="Img001" src="someDomain/myNewImage.gif">
<!- Remember, if this was XML-compliant
HTML, there would be a closing slash
before that last bracket ->
```

This value identifies a specific img element as the element that should be changed (when called to action by an event such as onmouseover and its associated function). Figure 3.1 and Figure 3.2 show how this works.

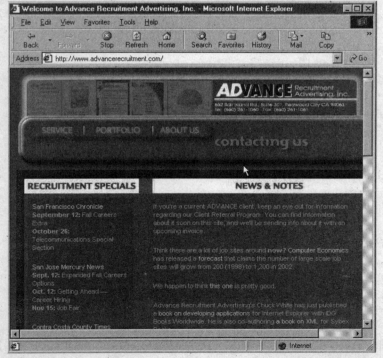

FIGURE 3.1: An image rollover—here just prior to the onmouseover event

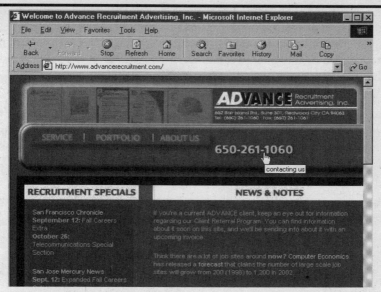

FIGURE 3.2: An image rollover—here just after the onmouseover event

IDs are also an integral part of many database tables. A DTD mapped out from a database table will often include an attribute named id or ID for certain kinds of elements (like those used in customer databases) and declare that attribute to be an ID type. ID attribute types act as unique identifiers, meaning any reference to an element's ID must be a reference to that element. This means that an element is thus uniquely identified. IDREF and IDREFS attribute values must point to a corresponding ID value. That, in fact, is what IDREF values do. They point to a unique ID previously referred to in a document. If you see an ID declaration in an attribute for a declared element, you know that the element must possess a unique identifier in order for the document to be valid against the DTD. Here's an example of an ID attribute declaration within a DTD:

```
<!ELEMENT MyElement (#PCDATA)>

<!ATTLIST MyElement myID ID #REQUIRED>
```

The corresponding attribute in an XML document instance might then look like this:

```
<MyElement myID="p:109912">
```

Then, you might want to simply refer to that ID using an IDREF attribute. The declaration would look something like this:

```
<!ATTLIST MyRefElement myIDref IDREF #REQUIRED>
```

The attribute that appears in the XML document would refer to an ID. Consider an e-commerce site and you can quickly figure out how this might come into play. You might want to reference this ID in a shopping cart. So you simply refer to it like so, using, of course, the rules supplied in the DTD:

```
<MyRefElement myIDref=" p:109912">
```

Two elements cannot have the same unique identifier. If they did, they wouldn't be unique. But IDREF attribute values allow you to refer to an ID. You might want to refer to more than one, in which case you'll use an IDREFS attribute value, assuming a declaration was made in a DTD:

```
<!ATTLIST MyRefElement myIDrefs IDREFS #REQUIRED>
```

Then, in your XML document instance, the actual attribute value pair might look like this:

```
<MYELEMENT_ MyRefElement myIDrefs="
p:109912 p:109913">
```

This way, you can add as many references to the unique identifier as you want.

TIP

If you work with databases, your first thought of ID and IDREF may focus on using them to manage key values. Because they accept only XML names (no numbers), mapping to these attributes can be a chore. Generally, if your database contains integer-based identifiers, you'll want to prefix your integers. Prefixing is a good practice anyway, because ID values that are used as primary keys in databases are not guaranteed to be unique throughout a database if the generated XML document contains data from different tables. This means you'll need to attach the attribute values to a namespace to guarantee their ultimate uniqueness and avoid collisions when bringing in database data into an XML document.

NMTOKEN

A token is the means by which XML provides a way to name a node instance. This can be achieved in different ways, and some node-naming procedures are more specific than others. Some tokenized types will be used in situations that require unique qualifiers. In those cases, you would use ID and IDREF attributes. Other occasions will warrant an identifier that focuses on providing a naming scheme, in which case you might use the NMTOKEN attribute type. Still other occasions will require the naming of entities.

Name tokens are qualified strings that have limits on what kind of character data they can contain. If there is only one allowable NMTO-KEN attribute type, the NMTOKEN keyword is used, and if more than one is allowed, the NMTOKENS keyword is used. Name tokens are restricted to letters, numbers, and the following special characters:. (a period), - (a hyphen), _ (an underscore), and : (a colon).

So, although the NMTOKEN attribute type is similar to CDATA, the character usage is limited to qualified XML names. The most important aspect is that they can't start with numbers. This is okay:

```
<Player myNmTokenAtt="p0001" type="pitcher"/>
```

This is not:

```
<Player myNmTokenAtt="0001" type="pitcher"/>
```

You might wonder why you'd want to consider using this attribute type instead of the much simpler CDATA attribute type. The reason is succinct: Sometimes you're validating not only against DTDs, but against programming languages as well. Because NMTOKEN maps out well to languages like Java, you can rely on these data types not to foul up your Java code.

Using NMTOKEN might also come into play when you're working with database information and can be one way to manage conformance issues (like when you know your database administrator doesn't allow white space in column names).

NMTOKENS

These are simply white space–delimited lists of NMTOKEN values.

```
<Player myNmTokenAtt="p0001 p0002" type="pitcher"/>
```

You won't see this too often. It works the same way as NMTOKEN.

NOTATION

A NOTATION declares that an element will be referenced to a NOTATION declared elsewhere in a document. This *notation declaration* assists helper applications to process unparsed entities. The information isn't as much for the XML parser as it is for outside applications that must recognize and work with the entity being called. You won't want to work with these much unless you have a clear idea of how to tie everything together. One way to do that is to work with entities, which is covered in the next chapter. Unparsed entities rely on notation declarations to identify them so that the application processing the XML document knows what kind of entity is being used and what to do with it. The use of the system identifier (SYSTEM-in the notation declaration) is required, and it must be a URI.

You can also include non-XML markup such as PostScript (an output language used in the printing industry that can be expressed in text files) or RTF (Rich Text Format) in an element's contents, and hope that the XML processor will pass it on to a helper application. The chances are great that it won't, because support for this is not a high priority for most XML processor developers, and there is no requirement that the XML processor actually must pass along the information to an external processing agent.

When reviewing the following example, keep in mind that several different aspects of this attribute type need to be managed.

The first step is to be sure the DTD contains a NOTATION declaration defining how the parser should treat the data. In this case, let's assume that we can get to a PUBLIC PostScript specification:

```
<!NOTATION eps PUBLIC "PostScript Level 3">
```

And here's the attribute declaration (along with the element declaration):

```
<!ELEMENT graphic (#PCDATA)>
<!ATTLIST graphic
   src CDATA #REQUIRED
   title CDATA #IMPLIED
   id ID #IMPLIED
   filetype NOTATION (eps | png) #REQUIRED
>
```

Notice the two choices you have for the filetype attribute? Each of those choices must have a NOTATION declaration, or the validating parser will return an error, something along the lines of this:

```
Declaration 'filetype' contains reference to
undefined notation 'png'. Line 104, Position 34
```

It doesn't matter that you didn't actually refer to the png file type in the XML file that is being validated. If the DTD didn't include a NOTATION declaration for that attribute value, the whole document blows up in your face. The entire group of NOTATION declarations for the preceding code, then, should look like this, one for each attribute value that is declared:

```
<!NOTATION eps PUBLIC "PostScript Level 3">
```

```
<!NOTATION png PUBLIC "PNG (Portable Network Graphics)
Specification, Version 1.2">
```

Then, when the XML document instance is created, the document fragment should look like Listing 3.8.

Listing 3.8: A Document Fragment Using NOTATION

```
<SectionTitle>
            <graphic src="images/bbbar.eps"
filetype="eps">
userdict /Adobe_level2_AI5 26 dict dup begin
put
/packedarray where not
{
TONS MORE POSTSCRIPT CODE HERE – snipped
    {
     end
    } if
    } bind def
mark...
</graphic>
</SectionTitle>
```

Note that the src attribute has nothing to do with the NOTATION attribute type filetype. We've added that so that we can reference it in a style sheet.

TIP

Generally, with code like you see in Listing 3.8, it's safer to use a CDATA section as part of the element content so that characters that would normally be parsed from an XML parser will be used for their purpose, which is for making the underlying code (in this case PostScript) work.

If you develop attributes with notation values, be very sure they have been declared in the DTD appropriately using both a NOTATION declaration and a NOTATION attribute declaration. In the next chapter you'll discover another caveat to working with unparsed entities (and their associated notations) is that processors are not obligated to handle them. This means they don't need to pass them off to another application, even if you name that application in your NOTATION declaration.

You can also use them to refer to literal notations that are publicly available or made available privately (perhaps through a corporate intranet) so that specific formatting rules can be handed off in certain situations. You might, for example, want to specify the way a date is formatted, using an internationally accepted encoding.

The use of NOTATION attribute types is really rather rare. Generally, developers are finding other ways to manage non-XML data, such as through the use of entities or MIME types.

PUTTING IT ALL TOGETHER

In the last two chapters, you learned the basics about elements, attributes, and the kinds of content they can deliver. The samples included in the following sections are intentionally basic. The key to understanding them is to try to understand how the XML document follows the DTD element and attribute list declarations.

Example 1: A Simple XML Application

First, let's take a look at how the various topics we've covered in this chapter fit together. To do that, we'll examine a DTD and see how to put together an XML file based on the rules from that DTD.

Taking a Look at a DTD

We're not going to cover every kind of element and attribute content type here. Rather, we'll demonstrate the basics of how to read the DTD so that you can put together a valid XML file. Listing 3.9 shows a DTD for a classified ad system.

Listing 3.9: A Simple DTD—*output.dtd*

```
<!ELEMENT AD (NEWSPAPER, (INCOLUMN | DISPLAY))>
<!ENTITY ADTEXT SYSTEM "adText.txt">
<!ATTLIST AD id ID #REQUIRED>
<!ELEMENT NEWSPAPER (#PCDATA)>
<!ELEMENT INCOLUMN (INCOLUMNSIZE, INCOLUMNCONTENT)>
<!ELEMENT INCOLUMNSIZE (#PCDATA)>
<!ELEMENT INCOLUMNCONTENT (#PCDATA)>
<!ATTLIST INCOLUMNSIZE lines NMTOKEN #REQUIRED>
<!ATTLIST INCOLUMNSIZE width (1 | 2 | 3 | 4 | 5
 | 6 | 7) #REQUIRED>
<!ELEMENT DISPLAY (DISPLAYSIZE, DISPLAYCONTENT)>
```

```
<!ELEMENT DISPLAYSIZE (#PCDATA)>
<!ELEMENT DISPLAYCONTENT (#PCDATA)>
<!ATTLIST DISPLAYSIZE lines NMTOKEN #REQUIRED>
<!ATTLIST DISPLAYSIZE width (1 | 2 | 3 | 4 | 5
| 6 | 7) #REQUIRED>
```

A DTD will always lead off with the root element. The filename for this DTD is output.dtd. The root node of the XML document that is validated against the DTD is the XML document instance. In other words, if the name of the file that uses this DTD is myXML.xml, then that is the document instance, and thus, the root node. Remember that the root node is not the same as the root element. The root element is AD, which means any other element that exists within the document must be nested within AD. Furthermore, this particular declaration for the root element states that it must include two elements: NEWSPAPER and either INCOLUMN or DISPLAY. You'll learn more about goodies such as occurrence indicators in Chapter 6, but for now, refer to the simple chart in Table 3.2 to explore them. They provide an opportunity for DTD authors to lay down specific guidelines about when and how often an element may occur.

TABLE 3.2: DTD Occurrence Indicators

SYMBOL	OCCURRENCE DESCRIPTION
|	Represents or, which means one or another named element may occur.
,	A delimiter that separates required elements.
?	An indicator that allows a named element but does not require the named element, and which allows no more than one instance of that named element.
*	An indicator that allows any number of occurrences, including 0, of a named element.
+	An indicator that requires the named element to occur at least once or as often as the document creator wishes, as long as the minimum requirement of one appearance is met.
()	These symbols group elements that are placed within them.

As you can see in Listing 3.9, the AD element must have the NEWSPAPER element, and, because a comma follows the NEWSPAPER in the DTD declaration, you know that more elements are required. These elements are grouped together by the () symbols, but the elements within these symbols, INCOLUMN and DISPLAY, are separated by the | symbol. This means that, as the XML document author, you have a choice between those two elements, but you must use one of them because they are grouped together and appear after the comma. The line of code referenced from Listing 3.9 is as follows:

```
<!ELEMENT AD (NEWSPAPER, (INCOLUMN | DISPLAY))>
```

The next item you'll notice in Listing 3.9 is an entity declaration. Forget that for now, because you'll be taking a closer look at this same listing, and this entity, in Chapter 4.

After the entity declaration, you find an attribute list declaration for the AD element. See if you can tell what is going on in that declaration based on what you read in the previous sections:

```
<!ATTLIST AD id ID #REQUIRED>
```

In this example, the DTD is written for an advertising agency that wants to be able to output classified advertisement text and easily sort the advertisements by ID number for use within an invoicing and confirmation database. The DTD author decided to make the ID attribute a requirement within the AD element. Thanks to the content model XML offers, the author was even able to insist that the ID attribute content act as a unique identifier. This makes it easier to process the document as a content-management system, and it also allows for easy integration into invoicing and job-tracking systems.

The next element, NEWSPAPER, is a simple declaration that states it can contain any parsed character data. Note that if the DTD author does include a declaration for the NEWSPAPER element, the DTD will fail:

```
<!ELEMENT NEWSPAPER (#PCDATA)>
```

If you are in the situation where a DTD author hands you a DTD that includes element declarations that contain other elements, make sure that the declarations are made for the elements later in the DTD, or you'll have problems.

TIP

XML editing software tools that take some of the tedium out of the process are emerging. SoftQuad's XMetal, for example, generates an error when you try to create a new XML document matched against a malformed DTD. The software even specifies the location and type of error in the DTD. This saves you the trouble of starting a document that is being written against an improperly designed DTD. An evaluation version of XMetal is available at www.xmetal.com.

The next line of code in Listing 3.9 is a declaration for one of the two kinds of elements that can be a child of the AD element. Let's take a look at this line:

```
<!ELEMENT INCOLUMN (INCOLUMNSIZE, INCOLUMNCONTENT)>
```

The preceding line of code indicates that two elements must reside within the INCOLUMN element. The next four lines of code declare these elements and their attributes:

```
<!ELEMENT INCOLUMNSIZE (#PCDATA)>
<!ELEMENT INCOLUMNCONTENT (#PCDATA)>
<!ATTLIST INCOLUMNSIZE lines NMTOKEN #REQUIRED>
<!ATTLIST INCOLUMNSIZE width (1 | 2 | 3 | 4 | 5
| 6 | 7) #REQUIRED>
```

Notice the NMTOKEN keyword in the INCOLUMNSIZE element's lines attribute list declaration? As we mentioned in an earlier section, the NMTOKEN keyword limits you to certain kinds of characters (letters, digits, dashes, underscores, periods, or colons). The second attribute list declaration for the INCOLUMNSIZE element describes the width of the newspaper ad in number of columns. Because the newspapers used for this DTD have no more than seven columns, the specific value options are listed. One of these values must be used, and the attribute, like the lines attribute, must be included with the element. The rest of the declarations follow patterns similar to those just described.

NOTE

What if you are working with possible values that are much more numerable, say 500 of them? Would you have to write the code with all of the numbers (1 | 2 | 3 | 4 | 5...499 | 500) or is there an abbreviated format? That kind of constraint would need to be handled programmatically through the use of a CDATA section in an entity. Other developers might handle it differently. For example, you could create a simple entity and put it in a different file, then make the attribute type an ENTITY instead of enumerated values, but that entity would have to list each number. The short answer is that there is no shortcut or abbreviated format for handling very large numbers of enumerated values.

Writing against a DTD

This brings us to the XML document itself, which is written against the DTD. Judging from the DTD, you know that the first element will be the AD element. Take a look at Listing 3.10 to see how the document looks.

Listing 3.10: Validating against a Simple DTD

```
<?xml version="1.0" encoding="UTF-8"?>
<!DOCTYPE AD SYSTEM "output.dtd">
<AD id="ad001">
<NEWSPAPER>San Francisco Chronicle</NEWSPAPER>
    <INCOLUMN>
    <INCOLUMNSIZE lines="50" width="1">
    </INCOLUMNSIZE>
    <INCOLUMNCONTENT>&ADTEXT;</INCOLUMNCONTENT>
    </INCOLUMN>
</AD>
```

Figure 3.3 shows how this document looks as parsed by IE 5. Notice that the entity &ADTEXT; is replaced by some actual text in the browser window. Don't worry yet about how this works; you'll learn more about it in Chapter 4. For now, focus on how the document in Listing 3.10 adheres to the DTD. Because the DTD is found on a local machine, the keyword SYSTEM is used to access the URI. Sometimes, you'll see the keyword PUBLIC used here, which makes it a public identifier. This is not a sufficient mechanism if you are looking for any kind of portability, because it refers to a specific identifier. This identifier may or may not be stored in a way that can actually be accessed by the document. The rules contained by the DTD may even be stored by a processing application. Whatever the case, they're used primarily by previously established SGML documents for compatibility with XML.

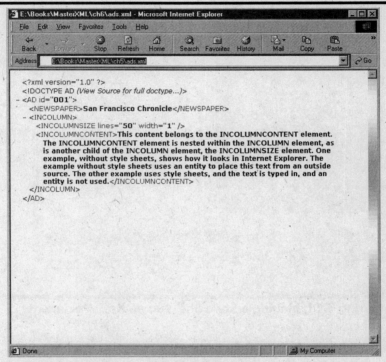

FIGURE 3.3 An XML document rendered in IE 5

Figure 3.4 shows the same document with one line of code added: a link to a style sheet. You can use Cascading Style Sheets (CSS) to present elements in XML-aware applications such as IE 5. Notice where the link to the style sheet is and the way the entity is replaced with actual text in Listing 3.11.

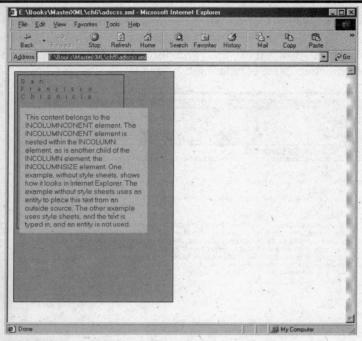

FIGURE 3.4: An XML document with a linked style sheet

Listing 3.11: Linking a Style Sheet to an XML Document

```
<?xml version="1.0"?>
<?xml-stylesheet href="adcss.css" type="text/css"?>
<!DOCTYPE AD SYSTEM "output.dtd">
<AD id="ad001">
  <NEWSPAPER>San Francisco Chronicle</NEWSPAPER>
<INCOLUMN>
        <INCOLUMNSIZE lines="50" width="1" />
        <INCOLUMNCONTENT>This content belongs
to the INCOLUMNCONTENT element. The
INCOLUMNCONTENT element is nested within
the INCOLUMN element, as is another child
of the INCOLUMN element, the INCOLUMNSIZE
element. One example, without style sheets,
shows how it looks in Internet Explorer.
The example without style sheets uses an
entity to place this text from an outside
```

```
source. The other example uses style sheets,
and the text is typed in, and an entity is
not used.
    </INCOLUMNCONTENT>
    </INCOLUMN>
  </AD>
```

We included the link to the style sheet to demonstrate the nesting concept in a more visual manner. The outside border represents the root element AD, which contains two other elements NEWSPAPER and INCOLUMN (remember from your DTD that you could have chosen DISPLAY instead). You can see from Figure 3.4 that because INCOLUMN is not nested within NEWSPAPER, the borders for the NEWSPAPER element fall beyond the borders of the INCOLUMN element. Both elements, however, fall within the root element's borders.

Example 2: A More Complex XML Application

The second example is a bit more complex. Actually, you will be revisiting this example often in the book, and each time you will see an added layer of complexity. The truth is, at this point, the application is still really quite simple.

Taking a Look at a DTD

This DTD incorporates much of what we've seen so far regarding attribute default values and attribute types. The DTD is the beginning stages of a comprehensive DTD for an online interactive short story (see Listing 3.12). Ultimately, the story will involve a large number of characters, scenes, timelines, and so forth. For now, it's just a shell. As the book progresses, we'll add to it, refine it, fix our mistakes, and eventually, conclude that it will always be a work in progress.

Listing 3.12 Another Simple DTD (lillybookv2.dtd)

```
<!ELEMENT lillybook
(Character*, Title, Author+, Copyright?,
    Abstract?, Preface?, Chapter+)>
<!ATTLIST lillybook
    type (fiction | nonfiction) "fiction"
    datadriven (yes | no) "no"
    xmlns:xlink CDATA #FIXED
```

```
            "http://www.w3.org/1999/xlink"
            xlink:type (extended | simple) "simple"
            xlink:href CDATA #IMPLIED
            xlink:title CDATA #IMPLIED
            xlink:label NMTOKEN #IMPLIED
            xlink:actuate (onLoad | onRequest | other
            | none) #IMPLIED
            id ID #REQUIRED
        >
        <!ELEMENT Character (#PCDATA | Description)*>
        <!ATTLIST Character
            id ID #REQUIRED
            Name CDATA #IMPLIED
            DroneClass CDATA #IMPLIED
            chipset CDATA #IMPLIED
            maxOrganicMemory CDATA #IMPLIED
            LifeCycle CDATA #IMPLIED
            memoryCapacity CDATA #IMPLIED
        >
        <!ELEMENT Description (Paragraph+)>
        <!ELEMENT Title (#PCDATA | graphic | score)*>
        <!ATTLIST Title
            id ID #IMPLIED
        >
        <!ELEMENT Author (FirstName, LastName)>
        <!ATTLIST Author
            id ID #IMPLIED
        >
        <!ELEMENT Copyright (#PCDATA)>
        <!ATTLIST Copyright
            id ID #IMPLIED
        >
        <!ELEMENT Abstract (Paragraph)+>
        <!ATTLIST Abstract
            id ID #IMPLIED
            copyright CDATA #IMPLIED
            xmlns:xlink CDATA #FIXED
            "http://www.w3.org/1999[/xlink"
            xlink:type (extended | simple) "simple"
            xlink:href CDATA #IMPLIED
            xlink:title CDATA #IMPLIED
            xlink:label NMTOKEN #IMPLIED
```

```
      xlink:actuate (onLoad | onRequest | other
| none) #IMPLIED
>
<!ELEMENT Preface (Paragraph)+>
<!ATTLIST Preface
    id ID #IMPLIED
>
<!ELEMENT Chapter (ChapterTitle, (Paragraph |
Section | graphic | score)*)>
<!ELEMENT Section (SectionTitle, (Paragraph | graphic |
 score)*)>
<!ATTLIST Section
        classification (multimedia | print | link)
        "multimedia"

    level (one | two | three | four | five | six | seven |
    eight | nine | ten | eleven | twelve | thirteen |
   fourteen | fifteen | sixteen | seventeen | eighteen |
    nineteen | twenty) #REQUIRED
    id ID #IMPLIED
>
<!ELEMENT ChapterTitle (#PCDATA | graphic | score)*>
<!ATTLIST ChapterTitle
    id ID #IMPLIED
>
<!ELEMENT SectionTitle (#PCDATA | graphic | score)*>
<!ATTLIST SectionTitle
    title CDATA #IMPLIED
    id ID #IMPLIED
>
<!ELEMENT Paragraph (#PCDATA | characterLink
| graphic)*>
<!ATTLIST Paragraph
    xmlns:xlink CDATA #FIXED
"http://www.w3.org/1999/xlink"
    xlink:type (extended | simple) "simple"
    xlink:href CDATA #IMPLIED
    xlink:title CDATA #IMPLIED
    xlink:label NMTOKEN #IMPLIED
    xlink:actuate (onLoad | onRequest |
    other | none) #IMPLIED
    id ID #IMPLIED
```

```
        title CDATA #IMPLIED
>
<!ELEMENT characterLink (#PCDATA)>
<!-- this is designed as a descriptive link
using xlink, rather than a representation within
the construct of the story -->
]
<!ATTLIST characterLink
    xmlns:xlink CDATA #FIXED
"http://www.w3.org/1999/xlink"
    xlink:type (extended | simple) "simple"
    xlink:href CDATA #IMPLIED
    xlink:title CDATA #IMPLIED
    xlink:label NMTOKEN #IMPLIED
    xlink:actuate (onLoad | onRequest |
other | none) #IMPLIED
    id ID #IMPLIED
    name CDATA #IMPLIED
>
<!ELEMENT FirstName (#PCDATA)>
<!ATTLIST FirstName
    id ID #IMPLIED
>
<!ELEMENT LastName (#PCDATA)>
<!ATTLIST LastName
    id ID #IMPLIED
>
<!ELEMENT extended ANY>
<!ELEMENT graphic (#PCDATA)>
<!ATTLIST graphic
    src CDATA #REQUIRED
    title CDATA #IMPLIED
    id ID #IMPLIED
    filetype NOTATION (eps | png) #REQUIRED
>
<!ELEMENT score (#PCDATA)>
<!ATTLIST score
    source ENTITY #IMPLIED
    src CDATA #IMPLIED
    title CDATA #IMPLIED
    id ID #IMPLIED
>
```

```
<!ENTITY chapter_1Score SYSTEM
"chapter1.mp3"  NDATA mp3>
<!ENTITY chapter_2Score SYSTEM
"chapter1.mp3"  NDATA mp3>
<!ENTITY chapter_3Score SYSTEM
"chapter1.mp3"  NDATA mp3>
<!ENTITY chapter_4Score SYSTEM
"chapter1.mp3"  NDATA mp3>
<!ENTITY chapter_5Score SYSTEM
"chapter1.mp3"  NDATA mp3>
<!NOTATION mp3 SYSTEM
"C:\Program Files\Real\RealPlayer\realplay.exe">
<!NOTATION eps PUBLIC "PostScript Level 3">
<!NOTATION png PUBLIC "PNG (Portable Network Graphics)
      Specification, Version 1.2">
```

Analyzing the Document

Let's break some of the more relevant aspects of Listing 3.12 down piece by piece, then show each XML document fragment associated with the portion of the DTD we are describing.

```
<!ELEMENT lillybook (Character*, Title,
    Author+, Copyright?,
Abstract?, Preface?, Chapter+)>
<!ATTLIST lillybook
    type (fiction | nonfiction) "fiction"
    datadriven (yes | no) "no"
    xmlns:xlink CDATA #FIXED
"http://www.w3.org/1999/xlink"
    xlink:type (extended | simple) "simple"
    xlink:href CDATA #IMPLIED
    xlink:title CDATA #IMPLIED
    xlink:label NMTOKEN #IMPLIED
    xlink:actuate (onLoad | onRequest |
other | none) #IMPLIED
    id ID #REQUIRED
>
```

As you can see in the preceding lines, because so many attributes carry default values of #IMPLIED, we've chosen to not use any attribute values where we didn't have to. Of course, two attribute conditions were dictated to us by the DTD. The id attribute was required, and the xlink attribute was fixed:

```
<lillybook id="FreedomsDream"
    xmlns:xlink="http://www.w3.org/1999/xlink">
```

The next snippet from our DTD is not even applicable, because we didn't use the Character element in our XML document and weren't required to by the DTD. But we have a feeling we'll be using it later.

```
<!ELEMENT Character (#PCDATA | Description)*>
<!ATTLIST Character
    id ID #REQUIRED
    Name CDATA #IMPLIED
    DroneClass CDATA #IMPLIED
    chipset CDATA #IMPLIED
    maxOrganicMemory CDATA #IMPLIED
    LifeCycle CDATA #IMPLIED
    memoryCapacity CDATA #IMPLIED
>
```

Another interesting element is the Abstract element. Most of its attributes are dictated by another realm, the XLink specification. We included XLink attributes in anticipation of *future* XLink-conforming parsers. For now, we'll handle linking in a different way, such as through the use of XSLT to create HTML links from the XLink attributes defined in this document (not shown here). Note that although we don't use any XLink attributes in this section, we will use them on another element (which of course will have to have its own XLink attribute list declarations associated with it). Here is the relevant declaration for the Abstract element:

```
<!ELEMENT Abstract (Paragraph)+>
<!ATTLIST Abstract
    id ID #IMPLIED
    copyright CDATA #IMPLIED
    xmlns:xlink CDATA #FIXED
    "http://www.w3.org/1999/xlink"
```

```
    xlink:type (extended | simple) "simple"
    xlink:href CDATA #IMPLIED
    xlink:title CDATA #IMPLIED
    xlink:label NMTOKEN #IMPLIED
    xlink:actuate (onLoad | onRequest |
other | none) #IMPLIED
>
```

And here is the XML document fragment validating against it:

```
    <Abstract copyright="2001, Chuck White">
      <Paragraph>Descriptive narration for interactive
short story "Freedom's Dream"
</Paragraph>
    </Abstract>
```

The `characterLink` element is very similar, but it has a very different purpose, which is to provide a link to a more comprehensive description of a character:

```
<!ELEMENT characterLink (#PCDATA)>
<!-- this is designed as a descriptive link
using xlink, rather than a
representation within the construct
of the story -->
<!ATTLIST characterLink
    xmlns:xlink CDATA #FIXED
    "http://www.w3.org/1999/xlink"
    xlink:type (extended | simple) "simple"
    xlink:href CDATA #IMPLIED
    xlink:title CDATA #IMPLIED
    xlink:label NMTOKEN #IMPLIED
    xlink:actuate (onLoad | onRequest | other
    | none) #IMPLIED
    id ID #IMPLIED
    name CDATA #IMPLIED
>
```

Part i

Once again, we'll need to create an XSLT style sheet to actually activate the link. The next element is very significant. It's the paragraph element. One of the optional child elements is the characterLink element:

```
<!ELEMENT Paragraph (#PCDATA | characterLink
| graphic)*>
<!ATTLIST Paragraph
    xmlns:xlink CDATA #FIXED
    "http://www.w3.org/1999/xlink"
    xlink:type (extended | simple) "simple"
    xlink:href CDATA #IMPLIED
    xlink:title CDATA #IMPLIED
    xlink:label NMTOKEN #IMPLIED
    xlink:actuate (onLoad | onRequest | other
| none) #IMPLIED
    id ID #IMPLIED
    title CDATA #IMPLIED
>
```

Note that the paragraph element itself is contained within the Section element, the declaration for which we'll skip:

```
<Section classification="multimedia" level="one">
    <SectionTitle>PartOne</SectionTitle>
    <Paragraph>Snipped to save space!</Paragraph>
    <Paragraph>"The crowd forgot everything,"
      is how Antron described the situation to
      his psychiatrist,
    <characterLink id="chesapeake"
      xlink:title="Chesapeake Alert"
      xlink:href="Chesapeake.xml"
      xlink:label="ChesapeakeAlert">
      Chesapeake Alert
      </characterLink>.
      Antron remembered the rhythm,
      the pulse, everything.
      After all this time the energy
```

```
      of the crowd still
      seemed to reverberate through his head.
    </Paragraph>
    <Paragraph> Snipped to save space!
    </Paragraph>
    <Paragraph>
     Snipped to save space!
    </Paragraph>
    <Paragraph Snipped to save space!
    </Paragraph>
  </Section>
```

Notice the characterLink element in bold. Later on, we'll probably want to map this out to an HTML linking element using XSLT.

Finally, you'll want to see the two elements we use for managing binary files. Actually, when the DTD is complete, we'll most likely reference the binary files in other ways, because there is little support from production-level XML parsers for external entity management, and using NOTATION this way is not really being done at this time.

```
<!ELEMENT graphic (#PCDATA)>
<!ATTLIST graphic
    src CDATA #REQUIRED
    title CDATA #IMPLIED
    id ID #IMPLIED
    filetype NOTATION (eps | png) #REQUIRED
>
<!ELEMENT score (#PCDATA)>
<!ATTLIST score
    source ENTITY #IMPLIED
    src CDATA #IMPLIED
    title CDATA #IMPLIED
    id ID #IMPLIED
>
```

We won't go into the whole process again, but it's useful to remind you that you need corresponding NOTATION declarations in the DTD when using ENTITY or NOTATION attribute types.

You can view the XML document in its entirety at
www.tumeric.net/projects/books/complete/support/ch01_toc.asp
. The document is called FreedomsDream002.xml. You can also download
the entire DTD from that same location. This document is called lilly-
bookv2.dtd. A better way to manage the graphic question can be found in
a separate DTD named lillybookv3.dtd.

SUMMARY

This chapter took a closer look at attributes and how to interpret DTD so
that you can write valid documents. The truth is, anyone can master the
simple art of writing the simplest attribute. All you need to do is remember those quote marks. The real skill will come in interpreting how DTD
attribute lists describe the rules you must follow. We hope this chapter
has provided some insight into the matter.

In the next chapter, we'll look at entities. Entities are powerful, easy-
to-use mechanisms that allows for complex data and document management. We'll finish up that chapter with a further look at a DTD and how
an XML document follows the declarative rules to manage validity.

Chapter 4

UNDERSTANDING AND CREATING ENTITIES

I f you've developed HTML-based Web pages, you probably have used entities quite often, even if you've done most of your development with WYSIWYG editors. If you use the < symbol in a WYSIWYG editor and look at the source code, you'll find that the actual HTML code used to represent the < looks like this:

<

This is an example of an entity. The < symbol needs to be represented as an entity, because the parser would confuse < symbols with < tags. For example, if an HTML document contains HTML code examples, entities provide a simple way to represent HTML tags without confusing the parser.

According to the XML specification, XML documents consist of a set of storage units. These storage units are called *entities*.

Adapted from *Mastering XML™, Premium Edition*, by Chuck White, Liam Quin, and Linda Burman

ISBN 0-7821-2847-5   1,155 pages $49.99

XML uses a few of the same entities as HTML to represent markup that should not be parsed by XML syntax rules. However, XML considerably extends the power of entities because you can define them just as easily as you can define elements. This means that entities can consist of a broad range of objects. These objects can include just about any programming-based object that comes to mind, including binary graphics, word processing files, or multimedia applets. This chapter will look at entities and guide you through the process of understanding and creating them. Specifically, we'll examine the following:

- ▶ What entities are
- ▶ When to use entities
- ▶ The different types of entities available to XML authors
- ▶ How to use internal and external entities
- ▶ How to use parameter and general entities
- ▶ How to be sure your entity markup is legal
- ▶ The use of system and public identifiers
- ▶ Ways of harnessing the power of entities by learning from examples that demonstrate how entities are defined in a document type definition (DTD) for referencing in a document instance

LEARNING THE BASICS ABOUT ENTITIES

The *document entity* is the most important entity in an XML document and is actually one of only two kinds of entities that are allowed to exist without having a name assigned to them (the other kind of unnamed entity is the external DTD subset). This entity is the first thing the XML processor encounters when parsing a document. It is also referred to as the document root, and it provides programmatic access to the rest of the document. The reason the document entity is important is that, at the end of the day, it's the only thing the XML specification requires an XML parser to read.

WARNING

This should not be mistaken for the root *element* of a document, which is the first element in an XML document and contains any other elements that exist.

This chapter is more concerned with two specific types of entities: general entities and parameter entities. The HTML entities described in this chapter's opening paragraphs are a type of general entity called predefined entities. Entities can be used as a kind of shorthand that allows you to embed blocks of text or even entire documents and files into an XML document. This makes updating documents across networks very easy. Entities also allow you to represent special characters like markup. You can even use entities in a DTD to cut down on the amount of code.

Within the scope of general entities and parameter entities are four other types of entities, which can be considered subsets of general and parameter entities:

Internal entities These are entity references that refer to entities whose definitions can be found entirely *within* a document's DTD.

External entities These are entity references that refer to entities whose definitions can be found outside of a document.

Parsed entities These are entities that the XML processor can and will parse.

Unparsed entities These are entities that are not parsed by the XML processor, but instead are handed off to another application for processing and are often described by binary mechanisms, such as those in image files.

Using Entities

Have you ever run a mail-merge function in a word processing program? In a mail merge, you develop a database of names and addresses and bind them to a word processing document with some markup. The markup tells the word processor where in the word processing document the address information from the database should go. If you've used mail merges, you've seen the concept of entities at work. Instead of character data, such as an address block, XML allows a wide variety of data to be used as an entity.

Entities operate on a similar principle to mail-merge functions in the sense that an entity acts as a replacement mechanism. That's why entities are such great shorthand for XML documents. Some of the uses for entities include the following:

- Denoting special markup, such as the > and < tags.

- Managing binary files and other data not native to XML.

- Reducing the code in a DTD by bundling declarations into entities.

- Offering richer multilanguage support.

- Repeating frequently used names in a way that guarantees consistency in spelling and use.

- Providing for easier updates. By using entities in your markup for items you know will be changed later—such as sports scores or software version changes—you greatly improve dynamic document automation.

- Managing multiple file links and interaction.

Making Sure Your Entity Markup Is Legal

Entity syntax rules vary depending on the kind of entity you are using, but like everything else in XML, they're pretty straightforward. When you use an entity within an XML document, you must follow five rules:

- The entity must be declared in the DTD. If you're creating an XML document that is not being validated against a DTD or schema, you need to create enough of a DTD yourself within the XML document to at least declare the entity that you are using. The exceptions to this rule are the predefined entities of XML, but there are only five of them, so they're easy to remember (you'll visit these a bit later), although many people recommend you declare these also.

- A general entity referenced within an XML document must be surrounded by the ampersand (&) on one end and the semicolon (;) at the other (&myEntity;).

- The name of an entity must begin with a letter or underscore (_) but can contain letters, underscores, whole numbers, colons, periods, and/or hyphens.

▶ An entity declaration cannot consist of markup that begins in the entity declaration and ends outside of it.

▶ A parameter entity must be declared with a preceding percent sign (%) with a white space before and after the percent sign, and it must be referenced by a percent sign with no trailing white space. A typical parameter entity declaration looks like this:
`<!ENTITY % myParameterEntity "myElement">`.

UNDERSTANDING GENERAL ENTITIES

The jargon and semantics involving XML can be overwhelming, and one example of this is entities. There are external general parsed entities and external general unparsed entities, as well as parameter entities and internal general entities. This all can get pretty confusing. Our advice is to keep it simple and focus on the two kinds of entities, general entities and parameter entities, that have a clear difference in usage. The underlying concepts are the same in that they both act as a kind of shortcut.

General entities are easier to describe by what they are not than what they are: If it's not a parameter entity, then it's a general entity. Parameter entities can appear only in a DTD. General entities appear in the main XML document (called the *document instance*) that begins with the root element. It's actually more accurate to say that the entity *reference* appears in the document instance, whereas the entity definition is found in the DTD. In fact, you can't create an entity reference within a document instance without validating it against a declaration made in either an internal or external DTD or schema.

We'll explore general entities by reviewing four different kinds:

Predefined entities These are entities defined by the XML specification for managing what might normally be considered markup so that you can represent "markup" symbols without the parser mistaking them for actual XML markup.

Character references These are character sets that represent specific characters in a given character set, which makes it possible, for example, to add special symbols using a specific markup.

Entity references   These refer to a declaration made within a document and can be parsed by the XML processor.

Unparsed entities   These are entities that are not parsed by the XML processor and, instead, need to be passed off to another application.

Using Predefined Entities

XML has several predefined, or built-in, entities that can be invoked without any special declarations. The simplest kinds of general entities, they are the only kinds that require no declarations within a DTD or schema. These predefined entities are listed in Table 4.1.

TABLE 4.1: Predefined XML Entities

ENTITY NAME	CHARACTER REFERENCE	CORRESPONDING CHARACTER
&lt;	&#60;	<
&gt;	&#62;	>
&apos;	&#39;	'
&quote;	&#34;	"
&amp;	&#38;	&

The predefined entities in Table 4.1 are not really so much shortcuts as they are a means for preventing the XML processor from throwing an error or refusing to parse your XML document. If you look at the symbols in Table 4.1, you can see that they are symbols that might often be encountered in XML markup, and thus act as a means for representing these characters when you don't want them interpreted as markup. Using an entity from Table 4.1, you could write the following line of code, without worrying about DTD validation. See Figure 4.1 to see how this is rendered in Internet Explorer 5 (IE 5).

```
<MYELEMENT>1 &lt; 2.</MYELEMENT>
```

These are the easiest kinds of entities to use. But they don't offer much beyond a few very simple, specific tasks. XML provides a method for declaring entities in a DTD for reference later in your document instance.

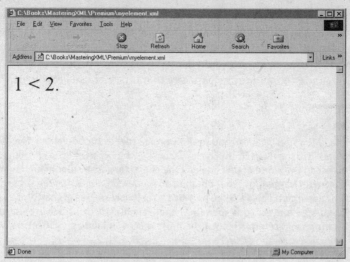

FIGURE 4.1: A predefined entity rendered in IE 5

Generally, you are best off using the entity names in an XML document. If you are seeking compatibility with legacy SGML documents, you should declare them using the character reference in the document's DTD. This is an example of a typical predefined entity declaration in a DTD:

```
<!ENTITY lt "&;#60;>
```

XML processors, however, are required by the XML specification to recognize these entities whether they are declared or not. It's when you're working with SGML applications that declaring them makes sense.

Working with Character References

You can include special kinds of references within your XML documents with *character references*. Character references are similar in look to entity references, but they refer to specific characters (such as accented letters) using a special numbering system called Unicode and don't need to be declared. Unicode is an encoding system that maps character data across the world's language boundaries. You can use a character reference in your XML document as long as you know the corresponding Unicode reference, but some developers might choose to create an entity reference to it in your DTD so that others know what you're trying to do.

The default character set for XML is the ISO-Latin-1 character set, which is what most English-speaking and Western European developers will use. There are numerous other character sets that can be included, but they need to be declared in the DTD. If you use ISO-Latin-1, you don't need to declare either the character set or the character references from that set. However, there are many languages of the world, and attempts are being made to include the capacity to manage these languages.

NOTE

The XML 1 specification requires XML processors to support character references mapped to the ISO/IEC 10646 character set, which is a Unicode encoding. To gain access to the world of Unicode and the character sets available for non–Western European languages, visit charts.unicode.org/Unicode.charts/normal/ Unicode.html. This Web site provides an extensive series of charts for a variety of languages, and the corresponding hexadecimal code to include in entity and declarations and references. For the most recent Unicode specification, visit www .unicode.org/unicode/reports/tr8.html.

The ISO-Latin-1 character set includes most of the ASCII set of characters. ASCII is an acronym for American Standard Code for Information Interchange and is the basis for most computer character sets prior to the introduction of Unicode. When you choose the Save As Text option in an application, the vast majority of English-based applications create an ASCII file rather than a binary file. Even programs that save text files in Unicode will usually make that choice clear to the user. An ASCII file is saved character by character, which means that the decimal number 83 represents the letter S. To refer to this specific number in XML, you need to add the & and ; characters. This means the full XML character reference is &83;. Unfortunately, despite the rather authoritative-sounding nature of the ASCII name, it is not a rigid standard, and it is subject to some unpleasant vagaries. Still, it's a key part of understanding how text-encoding functions work.

You use a character reference using ASCII or IS0-Latin-1 (which includes non-control ASCII characters) in XML by looking in Table 4.2 for the character you want to include in the XML file and then wrapping it in the ampersand (&) and semicolon (;).

TABLE 4.2: ASCII and ISO-Latin-1 Character Sets

CHARACTER REFERENCE	CHARACTER EXPLANATION	CHARACTER REFERENCE	CHARACTER	CHARACTER EXPLANATION
0	Null character	111	o	
1	Start of heading	112	p	
2	Start of text	113	q	
3	End of text	114	r	
4	End of transmission	115	s	
5	Enquiry	116	t	
6	Acknowledge	117	u	
7	Terminal bell	118	v	
8	Backpace (non-destructive)	119	w	
9	Horizontal tab (move to next tab position)	120	x	
10	Line feed	121	y	
11	Vertical tab	122	z	
12	Form feed	123	{	
13	Carriage return	124	l	
14	Shift out	125	}	
15	Shift in	126	~	Tilde
		160		Non-breaking space
16	Data link escape	161	i	Inverted exclamation
17	Device Control 1, normally XON	162	¢	Cent sign
18	Device Control 2	163	£	Pound sterling
19	Device Control 3, normally XOFF	164	¤	General currency sign
20	Device Control 4	165	¥	Yen sign
21	Negative acknowledge	166	¦	Broken vertical bar
22	Synchronous idle	167	§	Section sign
23	End transmission block	168	¨	Umlaut (dieresis)
24	Cancel line	169	©	Copyright

TABLE 4.2 continued: ASCII and ISO-Latin-1 Character Sets

CHARACTER REFERENCE	CHARACTER EXPLANATION	CHARACTER REFERENCE	CHARACTER	CHARACTER EXPLANATION
25	End of medium	170	ª	Feminine ordinal
26	Substitute	171	«	Left angle quote, opening guillemet
27	Escape	172	¬	
28	File separator	173		Soft hyphen
29	Group separator	174	®	Registered trademark
30	Record separator	175	¯	Macron accent
31	Unit separator	176	°	Degree sign
32	Space	177	±	Plus or minus
33	!	178	2	Superscript two
34	"	179	3	Superscript three
35	#	180	´	Acute accent
36	$	181	µ	Micro sign
37	%	182	¶	Paragraph sign
38	&	183	·	Middle dot
39	'	184	¸	Cedilla
40	(	185	1	Superscript one
41	)	186	º	Masculine ordinal
42	*	187	>>	Right angle quote, closing guillemet
43	+	188	¼	One-fourth fraction
44	,	189	½	One-half fraction
45	-	190	¾	Three-fourths fraction
46	.	191	¿	Inverted question mark
47	/	192	À	Capital A, grave accent ("À")
48	0	193	Á	Capital A, acute accent ("Á")
49	1	194	Â	Capital A, circumflex accent ("Â")

TABLE 4.2 continued: ASCII and ISO-Latin-1 Character Sets

Character Reference	Character Explanation	Character Reference	Character	Character Explanation
50	2	195	Ã	Capital *A*, tilde ("Ã")
51	3	196	Ä	Capital *A*, dieresis or umlaut mark ("Ä")
52	4	197	Å	Capital *A*, ring ("Å")
53	5	198	Æ	Capital *AE*, diphthong (ligature) ("Æ")
54	6	199	Ç	Capital *C*, cedilla ("Ç")
55	7	200	È	Capital *E*, grave accent ("È")
56	8	201	É	Capital *E*, acute accent ("É")
57	9	202	Ê	Capital *E*, circumflex accent ("Ê")
58	:	203	Ë	Capital *E*, dieresis or umlaut mark ("Ë")
59	;	204	Ì	Capital *I*, grave accent ("Ì")
60	<	205	Í	Capital *I*, acute accent ("Í")
61	=	206	Î	Capital *I*, circumflex accent ("Î")
62	>	207	Ï	Capital *I*, dieresis or umlaut mark ("Ï")
63	?	208	Ð	Capital *Eth*, Icelandic ("Ð")
64	@	209	Ñ	Capital *N*, tilde ("Ñ")
65	A	210	Ò	Capital *O*, grave accent ("Ò")
66	B	211	Ó	Capital *O*, acute accent ("Ó")

TABLE 4.2 continued: ASCII and ISO-Latin-1 Character Sets

CHARACTER REFERENCE	CHARACTER EXPLANATION	CHARACTER REFERENCE	CHARACTER	CHARACTER EXPLANATION
67	C	212	Ô	Capital O, circumflex accent ("Ô")
68	D	213	Õ	Capital O, tilde ("Õ")
69	E	214	Ö	Capital O, dieresis or umlaut mark ("Ö")
70	F	215	x	Multiply sign
71	G	216	Ø	Capital O, slash ("Ø")
72	H	217	Ù	Capital U, grave accent ("Ù")
73	I	218	Ú	Capital U, acute accent ("Ú")
74	J	219	Û	Capital U, circumflex accent ("Û")
75	K	220	Ü	Capital U, dieresis or umlaut mark ("Ü")
76	L	221	Ý	Capital Y, acute accent ("Ý")
77	M	222	Þ	Capital THORN, Icelandic ("Þ")
78	N	223	ß	Small sharp s, German (sz ligature) ("ß")
79	O	224	à	Small a, grave accent ("à")
80	P	225	á	Small a, acute accent ("á")
81	Q	226	â	Small a, circumflex accent ("â")
82	R	227	ã	Small a, tilde ("ã")
83	S	228	ä	Small a, dieresis or umlaut mark ("ä")
84	T	229	å	Small a, ring ("å")

TABLE 4.2 continued: ASCII and ISO-Latin-1 Character Sets

CHARACTER REFERENCE	CHARACTER EXPLANATION	CHARACTER REFERENCE	CHARACTER	CHARACTER EXPLANATION
85	U	230	æ	Small *ae*, diphthong (ligature) ("æ")
86	V	231	ç	Small *c*, cedilla ("ç")
87	W	232	è	Small *e*, grave accent ("è")
88	X	233	é	Small *e*, acute accent ("é")
89	Y	234	ê	Small *e*, circumflex accent ("ê")
90	Z	235	ë	Small *e*, dieresis or umlaut mark ("ë")
91	[	236	ì	Small *i*, grave accent ("ì")
92	\	237	í	Small *i*, acute accent ("í")
93	]	238	î	Small *i*, circumflex accent ("î")
94	^	239	ï	Small *i*, dieresis or umlaut mark ("ï")
95	_	240	ð	Small *eth*, Icelandic ("ð")
96	`	241	ñ	Small *n*, tilde ("ñ")
97	a	242	ò	Small *o*, grave accent ("ò")
98	b	243	ó	Small *o*, acute accent ("ó")
99	c	244	ô	Small *o*, circumflex accent ("ô")
100	d	245	õ	Small *o*, tilde ("õ")
101	e	246	ö	Small *o*, dieresis or umlaut mark ("ö")
102	f	247	÷	Division sign
103	g	248	ø	Small *o*, slash ("ø")

TABLE 4.2 continued: ASCII and ISO-Latin-1 Character Sets

CHARACTER REFERENCE	CHARACTER EXPLANATION	CHARACTER REFERENCE	CHARACTER	CHARACTER EXPLANATION
104	h	249	ù	Small *u*, grave accent ("ù")
105	i	250	ú	Small *u*, acute accent ("ú")
106	j	251	û	Small *u*, circumflex accent ("û")
107	k	252	ü	Small *u*, dieresis or umlaut mark ("ü")
108	l	253	ý	Small *y*, acute accent ("ý")
109	m	254	þ	Small *thorn*, Icelandic ("þ")
110	n	255	ÿ	Small *y*, dieresis or umlaut mark ("ÿ")

Let's look at a specific example of a character reference to see how handy they can be. In Listings 4.1–4.6, we are including characters from the ISO-Latin-1 character set. There are three groups of listings appearing in pairs. The first listing of each pair is an XSLT style sheet that renders an XML document (you could use any XML document as its source because it's a generic style sheet). In each case, we've bolded the character reference to show first the character reference, then the replacement text as it would be rendered if you were using XSLT to transform a document into HTML. You can learn more about the inner workings of XSLT in Chapter 12, "Transforming XML: Introducing XSLT."

Listing 4.1: Generating an @ Sign with a Character Reference Using XSLT

```
<xsl:stylesheet
xmlns:xsl="http://www.w3.org/1999/XSL/Transform"
version="1.0">
   <xsl:output indent="yes"/>
   <xsl:template match="/">
      <html>
         <head>
            <title>Contact Info</title>
```

```
            </head>
          <body
           style="font-size:12px;
                  font-family: Verdana, Arial, Helvetica;">
           contact me at chuckw&#64;javertising.com
          </body>
        </html>
      </xsl:template>
  </xsl:stylesheet>
```

Listing 4.2: The Result of a Tree Generated by XSLT after Interpreting a Character Reference

```
<html>
    <head>
      <META http-equiv="Content-Type"
            content="text/html; charset=UTF-16">
      <title>Contact Info</title></head>
    <body
     style="font-size:12px;
            font-family: Verdana, Arial, Helvetica;">
     contact me at chuckw@javertising.com
    </body>
</html>
```

Listing 4.3: Generating an Æ-Combined Character with a Character Reference Using XSLT

```
<xsl:stylesheet
 xmlns:xsl="http://www.w3.org/1999/XSL/Transform"
 version="1.0">
   <xsl:output indent="yes"/>
   <xsl:template match="/">
     <html>
        <head>
           <title>Contact Info</title>
        </head>
        <body
         style="font-size:12px;
                font-family: Verdana, Arial,
                Helvetica;">
         I have an ancestor who was the
         king of a small English province.
         His name was &#198;thelred.
```

```
        </body>
      </html>
    </xsl:template>
  </xsl:stylesheet>
```

Listing 4.4: The Result of a Tree Generated by XSLT after Interpreting a Character Reference

```
<html>
  <head>
    <META http-equiv="Content-Type"
     content="text/html; charset=UTF-16">
    <title>Contact Info</title>
  </head>
  <body style="font-size:12px;
        font-family: Verdana, Arial, Helvetica;">
    I have an ancestor who was the king of a
    small English province. His name was Æthelred.
  </body>
</html>
```

Listing 4.5: Generating a © Sign with a Character Reference Using XSLT

```
<xsl:stylesheet
 xmlns:xsl="http://www.w3.org/1999/XSL/Transform"
 version="1.0">
  <xsl:output indent="yes"/>
  <xsl:template match="/">
    <html>
      <head>
        <title>Contact Info</title></head>
      <body style="font-size:12px;
            font-family: Verdana, Arial,
            Helvetica;">
        &#169;2001 Sybex, Inc.
      </body>
    </html>
  </xsl:template>
</xsl:stylesheet>
```

Listing 4.6: The Result of a Tree Generated by XSLT after Interpreting a Character Reference

```
<html>
```

```
<head>
   <META http-equiv="Content-Type"
         content="text/html; charset=UTF-16">
   <title>Contact Info</title>
</head>
<body style="font-size:12px;
             font-family: Verdana, Arial,
             Helvetica;">
 ©2001 Sybex, Inc.
</body>
</html>
```

In these listings, each character reference was replaced with a specific character. As tools mature, you can expect to find tables similar to Table 4.1 built into XML editing applications.

Using Parsed Entities

Another kind of entity reference is those that refer to a declaration made within a document and that can be parsed by the XML processor. These are called *parsed entities*, which some people refer to as *text entities* because their definitions are represented as a string of text within quotation marks in the validating DTD. For example, consider the following lines of code:

```
<!ENTITY ADTEXT "This content belongs to the INCOLUMNCONTENT
element. The INCOLUMNCONTENT element is nested within the
INCOLUMN element, as is another child of the INCOLUMN
element, the INCOLUMNSIZE element. One example, without style
sheets, shows how it looks in Internet Explorer. The example
without style sheets uses an entity to place this text from
an outside source. The other example uses style sheets, and
the text is typed in, and an entity is not used.">
```

The preceding line of code may look familiar from the previous chapter on attributes, where you learned that one of the valid attribute types was ENTITY. The preceding lines of code are an example of an internal, parsed entity declaration. Such a lengthy declaration is also a good example of why external entity references are convenient (but not as well supported). The XML processor will parse this entity when it is referred to in the XML document instance:

```
<MYELEMENT>&ADTEXT;</MYELEMENT>
```

When the XML document is processed, the entity &ADTEXT; is replaced by the definition that is contained between the quotation marks (see Figure 4.2). If an entity can be used in such a way, it is considered a parsed entity. Either an entity is parsed or it is not parsed. The processor will pass on an unparsed entity to another application for processing.

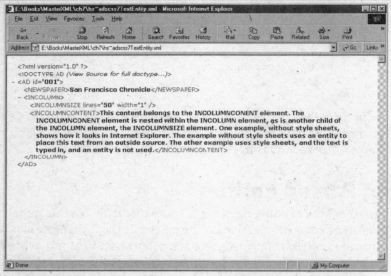

FIGURE 4.2:   The entity reference is replaced by the actual defining text.

Imagine, now, that the text in the entity declaration changes for some reason. Perhaps a new version of software has come out and the descriptions change. Or, in our case, some general silliness ensues. Thus the preceding example becomes:

```
<!ENTITY ADTEXT "This content has been completely changed in
    accordance to Best Practices, because it was best to do so.">
```

Figure 4.3 shows the result of this change. These kinds of changes become even more significant when external DTDs are used instead of internal DTDs, because global changes could be made to multiple documents: one edit, many changes.

NOTE

Note that Figures 4.2 and 4.3 shows a tree representation of the XML document, which is how IE 5 renders XML documents not attached to style sheets. Technically, however, IE 5 uses a default XSL style sheet to render the tree if a style sheet is not named for the XML document that is parsed by IE 5's XML processor.

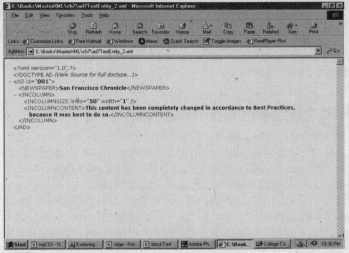

FIGURE 4.3 The XML processor interprets changes in entity definitions.

Often, an entity or character reference will be used in an ENTITY declaration. Listing 4.7 declares a copyright entity named rights by using the ISO-Latin decimal number that maps to that letter.

Listing 4.7: Using a Character Reference to Declare an Entity

```
<?xml version="1.0"?>
<!DOCTYPE fragment [
<!ELEMENT fragment (#PCDATA)>
<!ENTITY rights "&#169;">
]>
<fragment>&rights;2001 Chuck White</fragment>
```

Using the XSLT document in Listing 4.8, you can transform the document into a text document and get the results you would expect. To learn how to create XSLT documents, refer to Chapter 12.

Listing 4.8: Using XSLT to Output a Parsed Entity

```
<xsl:stylesheet
 xmlns:xsl="http://www.w3.org/1999/XSL/Transform"
version="1.0">
    <xsl:output method="text"/>
    <xsl:template match="/">
    <xsl:apply-templates /></xsl:template>
```

```
    <xsl:template match="fragment">
    <xsl:apply-templates/></xsl:template>
</xsl:stylesheet>
```

The results of applying the XSLT transform look like this:

```
©2001 Chuck White
```

Managing Unparsed Entities

Whereas parsed entities can be referenced within an element, an *unparsed entity* must appear as an attribute value. An unparsed entity, as its name implies, is not parsed by the XML processor. Processors need to know what to do with these entities, so the instructions must be laid out in the DTD. These instructions appear in the form of an ENTITY declaration that includes the file type of the entity the processor can expect. In addition, the DTD is required to include a NOTATION declaration that indicates to the processor what software will be handling the request.

The interesting thing about such NOTATION declarations is that the processor doesn't really care too much about it. If an invalid path is declared as part of the notation, the XML parser simply moves on to the next order of business. Consider the following line of code:

```
<!ENTITY ADGRAPHIC SYSTEM "border.png" NDATA PNG>
<!NOTATION PNG SYSTEM "MYGRAPHICSPROGRAM.EXE">
```

Without getting too bogged down by the intricacies of DTD authoring (which are covered thoroughly in Chapter 6, "Creating Your Own DTD"), think about the ENTITY declaration in the preceding lines of code as being part of a larger DTD. The ENTITY declaration is declared using, first, the ENTITY keyword, then the name of the entity (ADGRAPHIC in the preceding example). NDATA is an identifier and PNG is the file type. The NDATA keyword and a value indicating the file type (PNG in this case) are required.

Next, you see the NOTATION declaration. This declaration simply tells the XML processor where it can find a program to which it can pass along the information. The XML processor can choose to process the information itself if it wants to, but the DTD author needs to give the XML processor the choice. In other words, the DTD author must include the name (and path) of the software that should process the binary. Figure 4.4 shows what happens when the XML processor in IE 5 doesn't encounter the NOTATION element in an XML document's DTD.

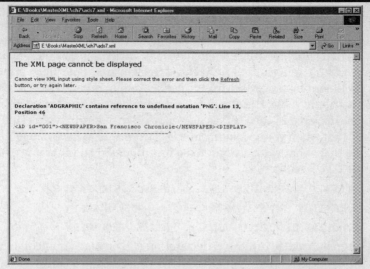

FIGURE 4.4   IE 5 will protest if you don't include a NOTATION declaration for an unparsed entity.

There is no requirement whatsoever that an XML processor actually process an unparsed entity, but it can if it wants. This is true even if that unparsed entity is an external XML document. The main thing to remember about unparsed entities, because they are often binaries of some kind (like images, music, and even Excel or Word documents), is that you're not really looking for a way to render them within an XML browser. Really, there is no such thing as an XML browser. XML, after all, is not a presentation markup language. An XML processor doesn't care what you do with the image or multimedia entity described in your XML document.

The processor is concerned with helping to manage your entities, making them searchable and easy to update, adding structure to the whole process of document creation, and passing along the entity reference to a processing application that can handle it. This doesn't mean that no errors will be generated when the entity is processed, but if you encounter an error message and are certain it's related to an unparsed entity, the message is likely being generated by the application that is handling the entity, not the XML processor. This is an important consideration when diagnosing problems associated with XML documents and their entities.

An unparsed entity is not referenced in the document instance the same way as other entity references—with a beginning & character and ending ; character. In the earlier example, in order to reference the ADGRAPHIC entity, you need to include it as an attribute value. Unparsed entities aren't, and can't be, referenced in elements. They must appear in the document instance as attribute values, and in order to be referenced as an attribute value, the attribute that references the unparsed entity must be declared in the DTD as able to work with entity types. This means that when you're looking at a DTD, it needs to have one more line of code than what you encountered a bit earlier. So add that line of code to your DTD as follows:

```
<!ENTITY ADGRAPHIC SYSTEM "border.png" NDATA PNG>

<!NOTATION PNG SYSTEM "MYGRAPHICSPROGRAM.EXE">

<!ATTLIST DISPLAYCONTENT src ENTITY #REQUIRED>
```

Generally, such an attribute declaration will be made immediately after the element declaration to which it belongs, although there is no requirement for this (though this has become a convention that most XML developers follow). For the time being, let's assume that an element declaration was made for an element named DISPLAYCONTENT a bit earlier in the DTD. The attribute list declaration for the DISPLAYCONTENT element states that there is an src attribute and that the attribute type is an entity. Now all you need to do is name the entity as the value of the attribute in the DISPLAYCONTENT element's src attribute as follows:

```
<DISPLAYCONTENT src="ADGRAPHIC"/></DISPLAY>
```

Notice that when you include the entity as an attribute value, there is no preceding & and no ending ; character surrounding the entity. You're not restricted to using binary graphics as the entity file format. You can use any number of file formats. The only limitation is the ability of the XML processor to pass it on to an application that can do something with the entity.

Using Internal and External Entities

Not only is every entity either parsed or unparsed, but every entity is also either internal or external. These are not mutually exclusive concepts. For instance, you can have an external parsed entity or an external unparsed entity.

An internal entity is one that is defined locally within a DTD, such as the earlier example, which is repeated as follows:

```
<!ENTITY ADTEXT SYSTEM "This content belongs to the INCOLUMN-
CONTENT element. The INCOLUMNCONTENT element is nested within
the INCOLUMN element, as is another child of the INCOLUMN
element, the INCOLUMNSIZE element. One example, without style
sheets, shows how it looks in Internet Explorer. The example
without style sheets uses an entity to place this text from
an outside source. The other example uses style sheets, and
the text is typed in, and an entity is not used.">
```

Generally, you want to avoid writing long definitions, like the previous, in your DTD. You also may want to develop a system by which it's easier to manage a large group of entities. One way to do this is with external entities. For instance, in the preceding example, you could include a string of text within the quotation marks in a separate text file, call it adText.txt, and then refer to that file in a Uniform Resource Identifier (URI) in the DTD entity declaration as follows:

```
<!ENTITY ADTEXT SYSTEM "adText.txt">
```

The preceding line of code accomplishes the same thing as the lines of code before it, but makes for a more compact DTD. The end result in the document instance, however, will be the same. When the entity reference is made in the document instance, the actual rendering of the document displays the replacement text contained in the file adText.txt. The result is the same screen that you saw in Figure 4.2.

Let's examine the line of code a bit more closely.

```
<!ENTITY ADTEXT SYSTEM "adText.txt">
```

The code, which is an entity declaration within a DTD, begins with the keyword ENTITY. The next word, ADTEXT, is the name of the entity. The keyword SYSTEM is called an *external identifier*, which can take the value of either SYSTEM (*system identifier*) or PUBLIC (*public identifier*). The external identifier SYSTEM refers to a URI. In the preceding example, "adText.txt" is a relative URI and could just as easily been an absolute URI such as "http://www.myDomain.com/adText.txt".

Generally you'll see the public identifier for entities either with built-in processor support or with some other kind of special retrieval mechanism. They're designed for intranet or extranet use—or any kind of a situation where the entity is common knowledge among the systems accessing its use. (You'll learn more about public identifiers and system identifiers in Chapter 6.)

You've already seen an unparsed external entity when the use of the ADGRAPHIC entity was demonstrated a bit earlier in the chapter. You can't have an unparsed internal entity because XML rules forbid it. To include an unparsed internal entity, you'd have to include the actual code in the definition that lies between the quote marks in the entity declaration, which isn't particularly realistic.

To review the syntactical difference between internal and external entities, keep the following in mind:

- ▶ Internal entities are declared without any external identifiers (the SYSTEM or PUBLIC keywords) in the DTD.

- ▶ External entities must be declared with an external identifier (the SYSTEM or PUBLIC keywords) in the DTD.

- ▶ External unparsed entities must have the NDATA keyword included in their DTD declarations.

- ▶ External unparsed entities must have a NOTATION declaration indicating to the XML processor what application should handle the entity.

HARNESSING THE POWER OF ENTITIES

Now that you've had a chance to look at entities from a conceptual standpoint, it's time to see how they work in the guts of an XML document. If you're uncomfortable with all the DTD jargon, you may want to read Chapter 6, which will provide a good grasp of DTD development. Unfortunately, in the meantime it's not really possible to discuss entities without at least taking a glimpse into their DTD syntax.

We'll focus our practical examination of general entities by looking more closely at two kinds of general entities—parsed and unparsed—and provide an example of how to recognize them in a DTD and then apply them to an XML document instance.

Developing General Entities

We'll start by taking a look at an XML document with its DTD included (this is called an *internal DTD*) to make it easier to see how entities are referenced. Take a look at Listing 4.9 and see if you can track down the entities in the listing's internal DTD. The DTD starts with the [character and ends with the] character. What follows that is the document instance, which is the main part of the XML document that you would have if you split Listing 4.9 into two listings, one with the DTD and one with the document instance.

Listing 4.9: Incorporating Entities into an XML Document Using an Internal DTD

```xml
<?xml version="1.0"?>
<!DOCTYPE AD [
<!ELEMENT AD (NEWSPAPER, (DISPLAY*, INCOLUMN))>
<!ENTITY ADTEXT_1 "Check out this entity:">
<!ENTITY ADTEXT_2 SYSTEM "adText.txt">
<!ATTLIST AD id ID #REQUIRED>
<!ELEMENT NEWSPAPER (#PCDATA)>
<!ELEMENT INCOLUMN (INCOLUMNSIZE, INCOLUMNCONTENT)>
<!ELEMENT INCOLUMNSIZE (#PCDATA)>
<!ELEMENT INCOLUMNCONTENT (#PCDATA)>
<!ATTLIST INCOLUMNSIZE lines NMTOKEN #REQUIRED>
<!ATTLIST INCOLUMNSIZE width (1 | 2 | 3 | 4
 | 5 | 6 | 7) #REQUIRED>
<!ELEMENT DISPLAY (DISPLAYSIZE, DISPLAYCONTENT)>
<!ELEMENT DISPLAYSIZE (#PCDATA)>
<!ELEMENT DISPLAYCONTENT (#PCDATA)>
<!NOTATION PNG SYSTEM
"D:\Program Files\Photoshop 4.0 LE\Photosle.exe">
<!- The processor does not actually
care where the program that executes the binary
lies, although the binary won't
run if the path isn't set correctly ->
<!ATTLIST DISPLAYCONTENT src ENTITY #REQUIRED>
<!ENTITY ADGRAPHIC SYSTEM "border.png" NDATA PNG>
<!ATTLIST DISPLAYSIZE lines NMTOKEN #REQUIRED>
<!ATTLIST DISPLAYSIZE width (1 | 2 | 3 | 4
 | 5 | 6 | 7) #REQUIRED>
]>
<AD id="a001">
    <NEWSPAPER>San Francisco Chronicle</NEWSPAPER>
    <DISPLAY>
        <DISPLAYSIZE lines="636" width="2"/>

        <DISPLAYCONTENT src="ADGRAPHIC"/>
```

```
    </DISPLAY>
    <INCOLUMN>
        <INCOLUMNSIZE lines="2" width = "2"/>
        <INCOLUMNCONTENT>&ADTEXT_1; &ADTEXT_2;
        </INCOLUMNCONTENT>
    </INCOLUMN>
 </AD>
```

Did you find the entity declaration ADTEXT_1 in the DTD in Listing 4.9? You can see that a string of text defines the ADTEXT_1 entity. Note that no external system or public identifier was used. The reason for this is that if you use an external identifier, the processor will attempt to find an external entity. But the first entity is an internal parsed entity consisting only of a string. So you leave out the identifier and simply define the entity with the string between quotes. If you use an external identifier with a parsed entity, the XML processor will return an error like this when you load the XML document:

```
Error while parsing entity 'ADTEXT_1'. Could not load 'Check
out this entity:'. The system cannot locate the resource
specified. Line 25, Position 1
```

The reason for this error is that the system or public identifier tells the processor to look for that string of text as a URI.

Now take another look at Listing 4.9 and see if you can find the next entity. This one is called ADTEXT_2. Notice how this entity is defined with the system identifier, which tells you you're dealing with an external entity. Now it makes sense for the XML processor to look for something external, in this case a text file named adText.txt.

Next, you should find an external entity called ADGRAPHIC, which is defined by a relative URI. The graphic is called border.png. The .png extension refers to the Portable Network Graphics (PNG) format, which is a graphic format somewhat akin to a high-powered GIF file (lots of color and transparency options). So the processor will look for the graphic and pass it on to another application for processing.

Now that you've located the three entity declarations in the internal DTD of Listing 4.1, it's time to see how they're referenced in the document instance. Remember that entities are referenced in different parts of the document instance, depending on their type:

▶ Parsed entities—either internal or external—such as those similar to the ADTEXT_1 and ADTEXT_2 entities are referenced exclusively in elements.

▶ Unparsed entities are referenced exclusively through an element's attribute.

In Listing 4.9 you can track down the first entity, ADTEXT_1, and see that it is referenced using the following notation: &ADTEXT_1;. The give-away is the ampersand (&) and semicolon (;) on either side of the entity name. When the XML processor encounters &ADTEXT_1;, it replaces the entity reference with the actual text used to define the entity (see Figure 4.5). The same holds true for the next entity, &ADTEXT_2;, which is also a parsed entity. The last entity, ADGRAPHIC, is referred to as a value for the src attribute in the DISPLAYCONTENT element. The rules of XML state that in order to use an unparsed entity in this way, not only must you declare the entity in the DTD, but you must declare that the attribute whose value will consist of the entity be declared as being an ENTITY type in the DTD. In the example in Listing 4.1, the following line of code accomplishes this in the internal DTD:

```
<!ATTLIST DISPLAYCONTENT src ENTITY #REQUIRED>
```

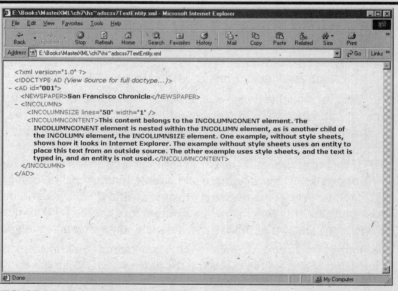

FIGURE 4.5 The &ADTEXT_1; entity is replaced by a text file when displayed in IE 5.

NOTE

The examples used here are for the humble beginnings of a hypothetical markup language for newspaper advertising. For a more robust, and real-world, example of a classified advertising DTD, see www.zedak.com/admarkup. The URL points to a system being developed by *The New York Times* and the Zedak Corporation for newspapers wanting to incorporate XML markup into older, more traditional classified advertising markup systems. The DTD is being considered as a standard by the Newspaper Association of America, and a portion of it appears in the next example.

USING PARAMETER ENTITIES

You'll actually encounter *parameter entities* in more detail in Chapter 6, because they are used exclusively in DTDs. You should become familiar with parameter entities now, if only to begin the process of keeping the syntactical differences between parameter and general entities clear in your head.

Parameter entities accomplish the same thing as other entities that act as shortcuts. Using parameter entities, you can include element and attribute list declarations as groups and refer to them easily as single entities. You can even include an entire DTD in a parameter entity.

You can probably imagine, even if your knowledge of DTD development is still in an early stage, that quite a bit of time can be saved by using parameter entities in a DTD. Of course, it can be difficult to hard-code an XML document in a text editor if you have to validate it against a DTD that uses other DTDs, but in the long term that shouldn't be a major problem. This is because text editors that make developing against DTDs much easier are beginning to appear, and these tools will help you develop elements that follow the rules set forth in the DTD and, in turn, reduce the amount of time you spend manually searching through DTDs.

Parameter entities distinguish themselves from general entities by the inclusion of one simple character, the percent sign (%), in the entity declaration:

```
<!ENTITY % myParameterEntity
 "myElement | myElement2 | myElement3">
```

Notice that there is nothing else on either side of the percent sign. When a parameter entity is referenced, you simply place the percent sign next to the entity that is being referenced followed by a semicolon:

```
<!ELEMENT ANELEMENT

(%myParameterEntity; |anotherElement)*>
```

A parameter entity is referenced only through another declaration within the DTD, never within the document instance. So you won't see anything like this:

```
<MYELEMENT>%anIllegalParameterEntity</MYELEMENT>
```

Actually, that's not entirely true. You may see something like the preceding line of code, but it won't mean anything as far as entities are concerned. An XML processor would simply parse the preceding code as it would any other character data.

A parameter entity can be defined with any valid DTD markup. This makes it very useful for large groups of entity declarations. You could catalog those entity declarations as part of a separate DTD, or within a text file, and include them using an external identifier like a system identifier or public identifier, like so:

```
<!ENTITY % myParameterEntity

"http://www.myDomain.com/someEntities.txt">
```

The preceding line of code is an example of an external parameter entity. You could use such a parameter entity to manage large amounts of language encoding, for cataloging a library of images, or for e-commerce purposes. There are no limits.

TIP

Be kind to others. As your parameter entity references grow and the complexity of your DTDs increases, comment on the code you use to develop the parameter entities in your DTD as well.

Developing Parameter Entities

Parameter entity development is a bit beyond the scope of this chapter, because you haven't yet learned how to develop DTDs, but it's worthwhile to have a look at how they work in a real-world scenario. You can read Chapter 6 for a more thorough review of parameter entities. Listing 4.10 shows a portion of a DTD that manages a classified ad system for *The New York Times*.

Listing 4.10: Portions of a Classified Advertisement System for *The New York Times*

```
<!-- Copyright 1998, The New York Times.-->


<!--                          AD TEXT-->
<!ENTITY % inline
  "#PCDATA|font|glyph|image|keyword|mailbox|margin">
<!ENTITY % spacer "space|tab">
<!ENTITY % flow    "center|left|line|right">
<!ELEMENT text    (%inline;|%flow;|reply)*>
<!ELEMENT center  (%inline;|reply)*>
<!ELEMENT font    (%inline;|%flow;|reply)*>
<!ATTLIST font
            size (agate|5|6|10|12|13|14|18|24|30|31|
          36|48|60|72) "agate">
<!ELEMENT glyph   EMPTY>
<!ATTLIST glyph
            name (en|em|thin|figure|dash|open|close|
          1-8|3-8|5-8|7-8|1-4
          |3-4|1-3|2-3|1-2) #REQUIRED
>
<!ELEMENT keyword (#PCDATA)>
<!ATTLIST keyword
          format  CDATA      ""
          name    CDATA      #REQUIRED
          punct   CDATA      ""
          scale   CDATA      ""
>
<!ELEMENT left    (%inline;|reply)*>
<!ELEMENT line    (%inline;|%spacer;|reply)*>
```

Listing 4.10 shows a small portion of a much larger DTD. Without getting too hung up on the all the semantics of this DTD, see if you can find the way parameter entities are used. Let's go through that process step by step.

First, you can see an entity declaration early on in the listing for an inline entity. The code for this first entity declaration looks like this in Listing 4.10:

```
<!ENTITY % inline
  "#PCDATA|font|glyph|image|keyword|mailbox|margin">
```

Notice the use of the percent sign (%), which tells the XML parser that the associated entity is a parameter entity. Also, notice that there's a space separating the percent sign from any other content. This is important, because it tells the XML processor that the entity is being declared and defined, not referenced. The declaration states that any element declared with the `inline` entity as part of its definition (either required or optional) would thus also consist of either PCDATA, or the font, glyph, image, keyword, mailbox, or margin elements.

To better understand this, take a look at an instance where the `inline` entity is actually used. You'll note that the `text` element declaration includes the `inline` entity in its definition:

```
<!ELEMENT text    (%inline;|%flow;|reply)*>
```

As you can see, the `inline` entity is used as part of the `text` element's definition, along with another entity and the `reply` element. This means that the `text` element could contain the `font` element, because the `font` element is declared in the `inline` definition. Unto itself `inline` is not an element; it's an entity and acts as a shortcut to gather a bunch of other declarations together for a more compact DTD.

SUMMARY

As you've seen in this chapter, entities can be a powerful tool. They provide a convenient mechanism for managing large amounts of content. You can use them to protect your XML content from being interpreted as markup or for adding multilingual capability to your document. You can also use them as powerful shortcuts that can cut endless hours of coding. Databases may use them extensively to manage large catalogs of images, legal documents, technical specifications, and the like.

The next chapter will examine how to design your documents. XML, after you get comfortable with it, is not as complicated as it first seems. But designing documents for XML is an art unto itself. The next chapter will offer some insight into the XML document design process.

PART ii
XML DATA DESIGN

Chapter 5
XML DESIGN PRINCIPLES

X ML provides a mechanism for the interchange of structured content on the Web. This structured content is tagged in XML with tag sets that are designed to serve a particular function and convey a particular meaning either to a human or to a software application. For example, some tag sets merely provide an extension of HTML to code content that provides specialized metadata to facilitate advanced search and retrieval techniques. Other tag sets are much more sophisticated and actually provide a direct map to database fields. What makes an XML tag design appropriate? How do you decide where to begin and how to design the right tag set? This chapter will help you select a design approach, write a functional specification, recruit your design team, and develop your own XML tag set using structure charts as a design aid.

Adapted from *Mastering XML™, Premium Edition*, by Chuck White, Liam Quin, and Linda Burman

ISBN 0-7821-2847-5   1,155 pages $49.99

SELECTING A DESIGN METHODOLOGY

Before you begin your tag set design, it is important to select the appropriate methodology. The methodology you choose primarily depends on the type of XML creation environment because this is where tags are first entered. The following are the three main sources of XML data:

- ▶ Software designed to automatically tag XML data from structured sources such as databases
- ▶ Editors who update existing tagged XML data sources
- ▶ Authors who create original material and tag that data in XML as they write

If software automatically tags XML data, a highly complex tag set can be used with little impact on staff or schedules because the program does the tagging. If you are updating and supplementing existing data, the number of tags and ease of use is a concern, but not a critical one. The number of tags and their ease of use is most critical when an author must "tag" data in XML as text is created. In this case, the usability of the tag design is paramount, and the design approach you select for your project will be influenced by which XML source is at the heart of your design.

TIP
Selecting nomenclature that is familiar to authors and editors is a major factor in usability. XML designers assign tag names. XML tag names do not have to be complex; simple, easy-to-understand tag names are best!

Depending on your XML authoring environment, you can select one of the following XML design approaches:

Chief Engineer   A single designer creates the design.

Facilitated Team   A project team assisted by an XML design expert creates the design.

Informed Partnership   An XML design expert with guidance from a project team creates the design.

We describe these three approaches in detail in the following sections and discuss both their advantages and their disadvantages.

The Chief Engineer Approach

The *chief engineer approach* is based on employing the expertise of a chief engineer to create the XML design, typically in the form of an XML document type definition (DTD) or schema. The chief engineer may be an internal staff resource or an outside XML design consultant. In this approach, an XML designer, or a chief engineer, gathers both requirements and data samples and then develops a tag design that meets the project requirements. Typically, the chief engineer documents the XML design and may even present a review of the new XML tag set and its proposed usage to the implementation and/or authoring staff. Often the chief engineer hands the XML design off to an internal user, technology group, or integration group that will use the design as the basis for developing their XML system.

A group of independent XML consultants have formed the International Digital Enterprise Alliance Independent Consultants Cooperative. Their purpose is to provide services for members and to support user-driven standards activities. You'll find their home page at www.idealliance.org/icc/, which is shown in Figure 5.1.

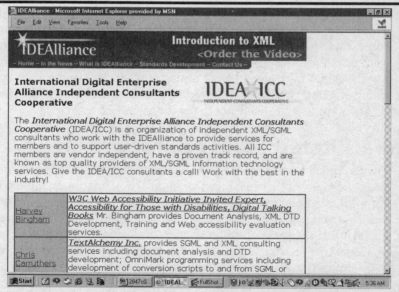

FIGURE 5.1 Independent XML design consultants do not represent or sell specific products.

Advantages

The chief engineer approach has several advantages. First, if the XML consultant assuming the role of chief engineer is the expert that he or she purports to be, the XML design will be elegant. That is, you should not find beginner errors in the design. Perhaps the greatest benefit is that the DTD will be developed with little impact on the resources of your organization. If you are looking at the bottom line in terms of development dollars only, this approach provides a high-quality solution and incurs the least overall cost.

Disadvantages

Perhaps the biggest disadvantage of the chief engineer approach is the lack of participation by eventual stakeholders and users in creating the XML design. When document-type designs are handled "offline," the project sponsors typically do not clearly understand the design decisions and why they are the best decisions. Likewise, end users typically do not participate or participate little when the chief engineer approach is employed. The chief engineer approach has little negative impact when the XML data is tagged automatically because it is extracted from a structured database.

However, handing editors or authors a de facto tagging scheme, to which they must conform, can be disastrous. The support and buy-in of end users in a direct XML editing/authoring environment is key. If end users don't own the development process, they may revolt. Revolt can run the gamut from a very slow learning and adoption curve to end users simply walking away from the project. In such environments, the chief engineer approach is likely not the best choice.

The Facilitated Team Approach

The *facilitated team approach* to XML design represents the exact opposite philosophy of the chief engineer approach. Using the facilitated team approach methodology, the XML designer serves as a facilitator to a project team and begins by identifying all stakeholders. This group typically includes technology staff, editorial staff, production staff, trainers, and representatives from management. The facilitator works with the group to introduce the principles of XML modeling and to guide the team through the development of each and every model. The designer must continually balance design decisions made by the team, based on their knowledge of the data, with solid XML design practices. Design participants become owners of the XML design and understand the design decisions.

Advantages

Clearly, developing an XML design utilizing the facilitated team approach takes more time and internal organization resources than does the chief engineer approach. Depending on the complexity of the data or the document being modeled, a design session may run from several days to several weeks and will require the involvement not only of the XML design expert, but of the project staff as well. However, the XML expertise gained by the staff and the design that results from user-centric development may be worth the increased expense. When using the facilitated team approach, it is important to deploy the XML design throughout the organization using the same approach.

Disadvantages

The facilitated team approach may require a greater commitment of organizational resources than are justified by the benefits or return on investment for the project. This approach has more value when authors and editors are directly involved in XML tagging. It has little positive impact in the automated XML tagging environment and therefore may not be the best design methodology for that environment.

TIP
Before committing to a facilitated team approach, be sure that you have the necessary corporate resources as well as development time.

The Informed Partnership Approach

Using the *informed partnership approach*, an organization employs an XML designer to help define project specifications. As in the facilitated team approach, the designer involves all stakeholders and leads the process of defining initial requirements, followed by a brief design session. Rather than work through every detail of the design, the team defines general data models for certain data constructs, and then the designer completes these objects at a later time.

Following the initial team design sessions, the designer continues to work on and take responsibility for refining the document model as well as creating and validating an XML DTD or schema offline. The designer continues to hold review meetings with project staff along the way to maintain close communication. During the final stakeholders' meeting, all project members review the DTD and sign off on it. Using this methodology, all participants become owners of the DTD just as they do using the facilitated team approach. Stakeholders understand the design decisions and can help foster adoption of the design.

Advantages

The informed partnership approach works well to provide the insight and consensus that is required to ensure ease of use when XML tagging must be done by authors or editors, and it does not impose undue burden on corporate resources. It also is appropriate when translating a structured database design into data that will be automatically tagged in XML because staff will understand the design decisions and be able to support the design as it evolves over time. This approach provides significant design benefits, minimizes the cost in staff resources, and decreases development time.

Disadvantages

Although less expensive than the facilitated team approach, the informed partnership approach will be more costly and take more time than the chief engineer approach. You must carefully weigh the costs and benefits when deciding if XML will be created by automatic tagging.

THE FUNCTIONAL SPECIFICATION

Imagine that you have just hired a new programmer. You want the programmer to design and write a JavaScript or a C++ program. You would never tell the programmer to just write the program without giving instructions about what the program must do. In fact, the thought of writing a script or program without a clear specification of intended functionality is ridiculous.

Creating an XML design is similar to designing any kind of software. An XML design is developed to facilitate encoding data in such a way that it can be processed to provide required functionality. Developing a clear specification of the functionality of the XML design is the starting point for creating XML designs.

NOTE
The functional specification need not be lengthy, although it can be. The basis of functional specification is simply a set of statements about the expected functionality of the XML-tagged data.

Examples of statements from a functional specification include the following:

▶ The tag set will support three levels of indexing.

- ▶ The tag set will enable searching on both part and model numbers.

- ▶ The tag set will support production of both the print and online format.

- ▶ The tag set will adopt the nomenclature found in the SPEEDE/Express industry data standard.

- ▶ The tag set must conform to the requirements set forth by the SAE J2008 Standard for the interchange of automotive service information.

- ▶ The tag set must identify a security classification for each procedure, illustration, and technical overview.

The functional specification that you develop will be used as your guide to creating an XML design. The resulting XML tag set should support all requirements in your functional specification.

TIP

Be careful not to introduce a level of complexity in your tagging that is not required by the end users of the data. A common error is to design a tagging scheme that is more complex than the project actually requires, which places undue burden on application software developers, as well as on authors and editors.

When your design is complete, evaluate it against the specified functional requirements for XML data to ensure that it meets all your requirements. Requirements can change during the design process. Changes to your functional specification are acceptable, but document them so that the final design and functional specification match.

DESIGN MEETINGS

If you are using either the facilitated team approach or the informed partnership approach, you will work with a team to create your XML design. Although some members of the team may understand XML, many may not, so it is important to begin your design meetings with a kickoff session. At this session, introduce the members of the team to one another and highlight their individual areas of expertise. Explain basic XML concepts, including elements and attributes, in a brief opening tutorial so that all team members share at least the same nomenclature if not the same level of understanding. It is also helpful to review the business requirements that are driving the XML design project so that all team members understand both the necessity and the goals of the project.

Following the XML tutorial, review the functional specification for the design. The team should discuss the functionality and update it if they discover any shortcomings. Often, team representatives each bring functional requirements that provide benefits to their particular area within the organization. Each viewpoint is valuable and should be reflected in the final design. As you might guess, negotiation and compromises are often required.

TIP

It is often a good idea to hold an off-site design session. Doing so prevents interruptions and reduces the chance that critical personnel will be pulled away to solve day-to-day work problems. It also sends a message that the XML design session is important to the organization.

DOCUMENT ANALYSIS

By this point, you have selected your design methodology and design tools. You have also selected your design team and gathered any relevant specifications and data samples. You are now ready to begin the work of data analysis. So where do you start?

The next step in the process is called *document analysis, data analysis*, or *data modeling*. All three terms mean basically the same thing. You need to look at your existing data, understand the relationships among the various parts of that data, and create some kind of model or graphical representation of those relationships. These models or charts can be as simple as an outline in a word processing document or as elaborate as a flowchart produced by a specialized software tool.

Using Structure Charts

While working with your team, remember that you are working primarily with subject-matter experts. These people understand the data that your team is modeling, but they are not XML experts, and they may have little experience with the general idea of data modeling.

Experience shows that steering clear of XML syntax and using a graphical approach to representing your data is a much more comfortable starting point for the team's subject-matter experts. This approach enables both the designer and the team to concentrate on data modeling rather than getting hung up on the details of syntax.

Originally, the only way to record the structure of your XML design was through a formal schema called a DTD. XML designs are now formalized with either an XML DTD or a newer form of XML schema. Either choice provides definition, constraints, and relationships for the data objects that make up the design. The difference is that an XML DTD is created using the rules of syntax that XML inherited from SGML. XML schemas are designed to describe the same information that a DTD contains but using the syntax of XML itself. For more information on XML schemas, see Chapter 7, "An Introduction to XML Schemas," and Chapter 8, "Writing XML Schemas."

When using structure charts to represent the creation and flow of data, adopt a clear syntax for representing the structures and relationships that will later be translated into the final XML design. For example, you must have a way to show that an element is made up of subelements. You must also have a way to show how often an element may occur and whether an element or subelement is optional or required. The chart of elements, subelements, and their relationships is sometimes called a *content model*.

A popular tool that allows for graphically creating and analyzing content models or structure charts that end up as XML schemas and DTDs is XML Authority, from Extensibility. Figure 5.2 shows how this software displays a chunk of financial information.

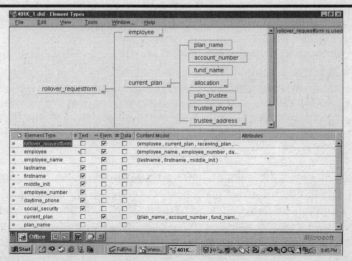

FIGURE 5.2: XML Authority graphically displays the content model of a proposed financial application.

NOTE

You can create structure charts or content models using flip charts, overhead transparencies, or even colored sticky notes. Software tools such as Visio, which are designed specifically for this purpose, are also available.

Using Reference DTDs, Schemas, or Vocabularies

In the early days of document-data modeling, every model was unique. But since document data modeling began in the early 1980s, experts in many disciplines have conducted extensive data modeling efforts, bringing the best minds and most experienced subject-matter experts into play.

Today, numerous efforts are under way to support Web-based business-to-business electronic commerce by creating XML DTDs, schemas, or tag sets for specific industries or for common business or industry practices, such as billing or purchasing. These models and examples have been developed to make data interchange between companies and organizations more efficient.

Several organizations have taken on the task of coordinating the publication and exchange of XML-based resources. One such effort is the BizTalk initiative sponsored by Microsoft and others. Groups such as CommerceNet and RosettaNet and companies such as CommerceOne or Ariba have created other XML-based e-resource exchanges.

NOTE

For the latest information on groups and companies offering schemas and other resources, see the XML Catalog maintained by XML.org at www.xml.org/xmlorg_registry/index.shtml. Also, Microsoft's BizTalk initiative is profiled in *Mastering XML, Premium Edition* (Sybex, 2001), Chapter 27, "Microsoft .NET and XML."

When you begin your own data design, start by examining existing data models to determine if a good base, or reference model, already exists for the type of data you want to tag in XML. Starting from a reference DTD or industry schema enables you to take advantage of design, development, testing, and documentation done by others. Application software may already be available for the standard you choose. This will save you and your organization time and money.

Formal SGML and XML reference DTDs have been developed for more than 16 industries. From manufacturing and telecommunications, to airlines and railways; from the Department of Defense, to automotive and heavy trucking; from computer systems to electronics; from pharmaceutical to medical and legal; from newspapers to multimedia, entertainment, and commercial publishing, cross-industry groups have built industry-specific tag designs.

NOTE

Several vertical industries developed reference DTDs for use by all organizations within that industry. This means that many people within a particular industry have contributed structures to the DTD. A reference DTD tends to have more elements and options than a DTD that has been developed for specific use within any of the contributing organizations.

To find the right reference model, you might look in your industry. The "standard" DTD or schema in your industry is usually a good starting point. It may have many of the data structures that you have in your own documents. It also may share a nomenclature that is specific to your industry. You may even have legislative or business requirements to conform to the industry standard model. If there is no specific industry-standard DTD, you may find an existing general-purpose DTD or schema that you can enrich for your own purposes. Table 5.1 shows a number of existing DTDs that you may find useful.

TABLE 5.1: Reference DTDs by Discipline

REFERENCE DTD	USE OR DISCIPLINE
MIL38784B (CALS)	Military Specification; technical documentation.
ATA Spec 2100	Specification for Airframe/Engine Documentation.
SAE J2008	Specification for documentation of Vehicle Service Information; some use for other service information as well.
HL7	Health Level 7; for use in the medical community for charting and diagnosis.
SIF	Schools Interoperability Framework; defines the interchange objects in the K–12 school software interoperability environment. Based on SPEEDE/Express data structures.
TCIF	Telecommunications Industry Forum standard; defines major structures that compose a data sheet.
TEI	The Text Encoding Initiative is a book-oriented structure for documents. It has additional features to support software documentation.

Part ii

TABLE 5.1 continued: Reference DTDs by Discipline

REFERENCE DTD	USE OR DISCIPLINE
DocBook	Specification for software documentation; some use for hardware as well.
ISO 12083	Electronic Manuscript Standard; used for journals, articles, serials, and books. Some use for magazine articles as well.

If you find a reference DTD to use as the basis for your XML design, you must decide whether to use it as is or to modify it. The advantage of using a reference DTD as it was written is that you can also use off-the-shelf applications that were written for that DTD. This will save you development time and cost. On the other hand, the reference DTD may contain many structures that you do not need and that writers and editors will not use. These structures will most likely be confusing to your authors if you do not take the time to eliminate them.

If you decide to modify the reference DTD you have selected, begin by reviewing the DTD and deleting any structures that you do not use in your documents. For example, the DocBook DTD contains a number of very specific content elements such as MouseButton, ReturnValue, UserInput, Literal, Command, Key, and Function. You may not need writers to identify each of these kinds of data in order to meet your functional requirements. Rather than asking writers to tag data to this level of granularity, you may choose to delete these specific content elements from the reference DTD. Deleting elements from a reference DTD is often called *pruning*.

Next, review your documentation samples and the functional requirements for the project against the reference DTD to determine if the reference DTD meets all the requirements. Suppose that you want to search on ModelNumber but ModelNumber is not an element in the reference DTD. You must add the new element ModelNumber to the DTD so that it can serve the intended business function.

TIP

Some reference DTDs are available only in SGML. If you want to use an SGML DTD as your reference DTD, you must first convert it to an XML DTD. This process includes removing all inclusions, exclusions, and connectors. Once the reference DTD is a valid XML DTD, you can begin the process of pruning the DTD and adding your own unique extensions.

In addition to using a complete industry-standard DTD or a published XML schema as the basis for an XML design, you can use new XML vocabularies as the basis for your own team or your project's design. An XML vocabulary is an XML tag set. Because well-formed XML does not require a complete DTD or schema, an XML vocabulary may simply be a set of tag definitions upon which you can base the tag names in your design.

You can find XML vocabularies wherever you would find DTDs or schemas—industry associations, XML groups, or e-commerce partnerships such as BizTalk, CommerceNet, or RosettaNet.

Modeling an Existing Database

Another way you can find a structure to use as a starting point for your XML design analysis is to model an existing database. Both Oracle 8i and Microsoft SQL Server 2000 have utilities that allow an experienced database administrator to convert the table, record, and field structures used in an existing database into well-formed XML.

The documentation for Oracle's XML-SQL Utility provides this example of a SQL query: `select * from scott.emp`. This in turn yields the XML fragment shown in Listing 5.1.

Listing 5.1: An XML Fragment Generated from a SQL Database

```
<?xml version='1.0'?>
<ROWSET>
    <ROW num="1">
      <EMPNO>7369</EMPNO>
    <ENAME>Smith</ENAME>
    <JOB>CLERK</JOB>
    <MGR>7902</MGR>
    <HIREDATE>12/17/1980 0:0:0</HIREDATE>
    <SAL>800</SAL>
    <DEPTNO>20</DEPTNO>
  </ROW>
  <!- additional rows ... ->
</ROWSET>
```

Any XML derived in this way from an existing database can then be converted into an XML schema and graphically displayed by a program such as XML Authority, as shown in Figure 5.3.

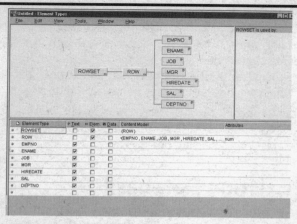

FIGURE 5.3: An XML fragment from a SQL database can be converted to an XML schema or DTD.

This process of looking at existing data models is not a shortcut and doesn't eliminate the need for an XML design process, but it can be a useful starting point to examine the relationships between information sets already being used by your company or organization.

Basic Design Decisions

Before you begin document analysis, make some conscious design decisions. Making design decisions up front can speed the overall process of analysis. In addition, if you have a clear design philosophy, the resulting XML design will be consistent and much more usable.

NOTE

Basic XML design decisions must be made no matter which design approach you selected. The approach (chief engineer, facilitated team, or informed partnership) does not dictate actual XML design decisions.

Content-Based Model versus Structure-Based Model

The first decision you are likely to face will come as you model high-level elements, the major logical divisions of the XML design. Let's suppose you are modeling a service manual composed of the following sections:

▶ Introduction

- ▶ Operation
- ▶ Electronic Parts
- ▶ Mechanical Parts
- ▶ Hydraulic Parts
- ▶ Troubleshooting
- ▶ Wiring Diagrams

You are immediately faced with two choices for modeling the service manual. You can model the manual based on content or based on generic structures that make up the manual.

You can model based on its content as follows:

```
<!ELEMENT ServiceManual (Introduction, Operation,
ElectricParts, MechanicalParts, HydraulicParts,
Troubleshooting, Wiring)>
```

When you model the manual based on content, you can immediately zero in on the content that you want to retrieve or reuse by the element type. However, you create numerous tags for your authors and editors to learn. You also create a prescriptive environment with this sort of model. You cannot alter the order of the content types that make up the manual, nor can you add new content types to the manual without changing the XML DTD.

You can model the service manual based on generic structures as follows:

```
<!ELEMENT ServiceManual (Section+)>
```

Here you have a design with fewer tags for authors and editors to learn. You also have a much more flexible, general-purpose model. You can change the order of the sections and even add new sections without updating the XML DTD. However, to locate specific content in a service manual tagged to this model, you would need to search on section titles.

The choice here must be guided by the functional specification for the project as well as by the method of tagging. If tagging is applied automatically by a program (perhaps during a database extract process), the number and specificity of the tags is of little concern. If your functional specification indicates a highly controlled authoring environment (authors/editors) or that there is some end requirement for data in sections to be specifically identified, the content approach is warranted.

NOTE

In either case, making this design decision before beginning the data analysis and development of the XML design can be most helpful.

Rigid Model versus Flexible Model

Another design decision involves the rigidity or flexibility of the model. In XML, you must precisely enumerate all possible ordering of elements in your DTD. You cannot list elements and specify that they can occur in any order, but you can specify options for any element in a model and provide alternatives.

NOTE

XML does not allow for the AND connector (&) as does ISO 8879 (SGML). This occurrence specification has been dropped from the XML subset of SGML.

In the service manual example, the content-based model is rigid; it specifies elements that must occur in an exact sequence. You could add flexibility to that model by making the elements optional. This would allow you to specify the order but not mandate the presence of each and every element:

```
<!ELEMENT ServiceManual (Introduction?, Operation?,
ElectricParts?, MechanicalParts?, HydraulicParts?,
Troubleshooting?, Wiring?)>
```

Another way you could add flexibility to this model is to create a repeating OR group. In this way, writers can select only the sections that are appropriate, in the order they determine is best:

```
<!ELEMENT ServiceManual (Introduction, (Operation |
ElectricParts | MechanicalParts | HydraulicParts |
Troubleshooting | Wiring)*>
```

In this model, a writer can include two Operation sections. Nothing in XML says to select one of each of these in any order, which was the function of the AND connector in SGML.

The selection that the XML designer makes must be based on both the functional specification and the tagging mechanism. Again, if data is being automatically tagged (from a database), specifying a prescribed element order is sensible. If authors and editors are involved, and if data is subject to variability, a more flexible approach makes good sense.

Inline Content versus Metadata

The functional requirement to identify content for purposes of retrieval or reuse requires you to choose how the content will be tagged to facilitate retrieval. In some cases, it makes sense to identify the content inline as data is authored. In other cases, it is more reasonable to identify metadata or keywords at the beginning of the document or for major logical document structures.

Suppose, for example, you are creating a design for the documentation of a specific kind of hardware (such as an engine or a gasoline pump). Technical writers and engineers will author the data. It is critical that part numbers and model numbers are identified within each procedure. If you are working in an environment in which writers use XML editing software, it is not unreasonable to expect them to identify the content as they author each paragraph:

```
<!ELEMENT Para (#PCDATA | PartNbr | ModelNbr )*    >
```

If, on the other hand, the writers are not using an XML-aware editing tool, identifying inline content becomes much more difficult. In such an environment, some tagging could be automated based on scanning text for key words. The limits of automated tagging should be your guide in designing inline content tags.

Even in the XML-aware editing environment, identifying each model and part number within a paragraph may be too burdensome for the engineers and technical writers. If you judge this to be the case, you can move the specification of content to a higher level of the XML design. In fact, in many cases it is placed at the document level. At this level, content identification is considered metadata; it is really *data about the data* within the document:

```
<!ELEMENT ServiceManual
(ModelNbrs,PartNbrs,Introduction,(Section)+ )>
```

If you decide to include XML tags to identify content, either inline or as metadata, be sure that the content tags in your XML design provide the functionality required in your initial specification. You must account for all business requirements in your design, but don't get carried away and place an undue content tagging burden on authors and editors.

Recursive versus Specified

Many times you will find that certain structures repeat within themselves. For example, you might have a list within a list. Or you might have subprocedures within a major procedure. Or you might have subsections within a section. How you model these cases is a basic design decision. Making that decision before you create the model will lead to consistency across the models you create.

One way to model structures that repeat within themselves is to simply model them in that way:

```
<!ELEMENT list (item | list)+
```

This is called a *recursive* model. A recursive model is elegant. It enables elements to nest inside each other infinitely. There is no real concern that you would exceed the nesting level for lists with such a model. It is often difficult to develop software that will handle an infinite level of nesting. In addition, allowing many levels of nesting often confuses writers who lose track of which level they are authoring.

TIP

Ask yourself, "Can my authors keep track of the level of writing when each element that is nested has the same tag name?" (for example, <list>. . . <list>. . .<list>. . .).

An alternative to creating a recursive model is to specify the level of nesting and to clearly indicate the nesting level in the tag name:

```
<!ELEMENT List (item | List2)+   >
<!ELEMENT List2 (item | List3)+   >
<!ELEMENT List3 (item)+  >
```

In this model, there are only three levels of lists. With this sort of model, it is much easier to configure XML software, and writers always know the level at which they are writing. The downside is that it is possible to exceed the nesting level. In that case, you will need to update the DTD to allow an additional level of lists, and you will need to reconfigure all related XML software as well.

TIP

The standard HTML heading tags (H1, H2, H3, H4, H5, and H6) have numbers that may seem to indicate levels of headings. But the HTML DTD is not designed in nested levels as discussed here. The numbers in these tag names simply indicate the relative "size" of the heading format and do not imply level of nesting!

What about Exclusions?

In some cases, you can develop a general model that works almost everywhere. For example, let's consider the following model for a paragraph. It allows for text entry as well as identification of part numbers, model numbers, internal cross references, and footnotes:

```
<!ELEMENT Para (#PCDATA | PartNbr | ModelNbr | Ftnote |
IntXref )*    >
```

Now suppose you model a footnote. In a footnote you want to allow paragraphs and lists. But you do not want to allow a footnote within a footnote, so you create the following model:

```
<ELEMENT Ftnote (Para | List1)+ >
```

In XML there is no easy way to exclude the footnotes that are allowed within a paragraph (see the paragraph model) when the paragraph occurs within a footnote. Handling situations like this requires making a basic design decision and using it consistently throughout the design.

NOTE

Handling exclusions is the most difficult decision facing industry-standard organizations that want to convert their SGML DTD to XML DTD. You can see how this was handled by ISO 12083 (Electronic Manuscript Standard) by referring to www.xmlxperts.com/12083.htm.

You can take one of two approaches. The first is to simply leave the model as it is shown earlier. The philosophy here is that a writer or an editor would never put a footnote inside a footnote and that you must trust them to use good judgment.

The second approach is to create a special paragraph model for the footnote that does not allow a footnote. Because you cannot have two elements with identical names in an XML design, you must give the paragraph in the footnote a unique name.

```
<!ELEMENT Ftnote.Para (#PCDATA | PartNbr | ModelNbr | IntXref
)  *   >
<ELEMENT Ftnote (Ftnote.Para | List1)+ >
```

Although creating special elements provides a great deal of control over our XML models, it also adds a great number of tags for authors and editors to use. This is often not an easy choice to make.

Modeling High-Level Structures

Once you have formalized the design approach, you are ready to begin by modeling high-level structures. The process of document analysis is basically a top-down approach in which you begin to divide the document into logical units beginning with one *root element*. All other elements must nest within the root element. Figures 5.4, 5.5, and 5.6 show examples of high-level structures modeled in the HTML, ISO 12083, and SAE J2008 reference DTD. You will find one root element at the highest level and then several other high-level elements that indicate the logical units that nest within the root element.

FIGURE 5.4:   HTML DTD high-level structures

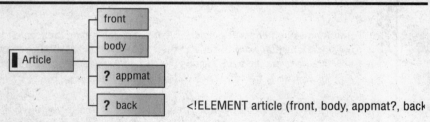

FIGURE 5.5:   ISO 12083 article DTD high-level structures

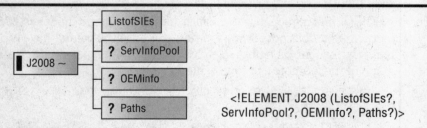

FIGURE 5.6:   SAE J2008 DTD high-level structures

Creating Building-Block Elements

After you model high-level structures, you are at the text level of the document. Here you enter text using familiar structures such as titles, paragraphs, lists, and tables. Many designers call these the *text building-block elements*. Typical text building-block elements include headings and titles, paragraphs, procedures, different kinds of lists, footnotes, cross references, tables, figures, and graphics.

You can borrow text building-block elements from a reference DTD, even if you cannot borrow the high-level document structures. Again, the advantage of borrowing models from a reference DTD is that the work has already been done, tested, and documented. Even borrowing models at this level can save you time and money.

TIP

Although the HTML DTD is not particularly useful in situations when defining a hierarchical structure or specific content tagging is required, using text building-block elements from HTML may make sense because so many people already know these elements.

Using Element Classes

Some text building-block elements can be grouped into element classes. For example, one class of building-block elements consists of those elements that identify inline content. A second class is composed of elements that define paragraphs. A third class is composed of elements that make up phrases. The advantage of creating an element class is that you can define the class once and then use the entire class (group of elements) wherever appropriate. To form element classes you use *parameter entities* in your XML design. The following example shows the definition and use of a parameter entity called %chardat (character data) in the SAE J2008. First, all the elements that can appear at the character level are grouped and given a parameter entity name (chardat). This group is then used, or called, when writing an element definition.

```
<!ENTITY % chardat
 "Emph| Sub |Sup |Ftnote |Intxref |Figureref |
  Tableref | Diagref |Extxref | Symbol" >
<!ELEMENT Title  - - (#PCDATA | %chardat;)*>
<!ELEMENT SubTitle  - - (#PCDATA | %chardat;)*>
```

You can also design classes of attributes using the parameter entity mechanism. For example, you could design an attribute set called %ids to be used in any attribute list that has the ID/IDREF attributes. You could also design an attribute set called %meta that is made up of metadata attributes to be used with many element types.

XML USABILITY

When your XML design is complete, it is time to review the design to determine its usability. This is a time to make edits that will significantly improve implementation, training, and use of the design.

Begin by reviewing the tag names (generic identifiers). If authors or editors will be doing the tagging, review the tag names with them. Here are a couple of important questions to ask:

- ▸ Are the tag names intuitive?
- ▸ Would any change in nomenclature make this tag set more user friendly?

If the answer to the second question is yes, make the changes now.

TIP

If you are using an industry-standard DTD in order to interchange with others or to meet legal/contractual requirements, you have little control over the tag names. Creating a mapping table from current or accepted names to the standard tag names will be a useful addition to the documentation you create for the tag set.

Next, examine the capitalization of tag names, how the tags are constructed, and how abbreviations are used. Consistency is critical to the usability of the tag set.

The tag set on the left side of the following list adheres to consistent capitalization rules (XML tags are case sensitive). The tag set on the right side does not.

<ServiceManual>	<Servicemanual>
<Section>	<section>
<Title>	<title>
<WiringDiagram>	<Wiringdiagram>

The tag set on the left side of the following list is consistent in the way tag names are constructed. The tags set on the right is not consistent:

<service.manual>	<ServiceManual>
<section>	<Section>
<title>	<Title>
<wiring.diagram>	<Wiring.diagram>

<ftnote.para>   <ftnotepara>

WARNING

Never use a colon (:) in a tag name. The colon is reserved to indicate the *namespace* of the tag and has a special meaning to XML processors.

The tag set on the left side of the following list uses standardized abbreviations. The one on the right side does not. Review the tags in your design, and make sure that abbreviations are standardized wherever they are used.

<ServiceManual>   <ServiceManl>

<PartNbr>   <PartNumber>

<ModelNbr>   <ModNbr>

<ChapterNbr>   <ChapNum>

Next, examine the tag set for consistency in design. The design for elements in a class should be parallel. This means that similar elements should have similar designs for both the elements and attributes.

This example shows three kinds of lists. Note the similar design.

```
<!ELEMENT alphalist (item,item+) >
<!ELEMENT numlist (item, item+)  >
<!ELEMENT bullist (item, item+)  >
```

In the following example, the lists do not have a similar design. This can be confusing to writers and tends to compromise the usability of the different kinds of list tags.

```
<!ELEMENT alphalist (item,item+) >
<!ELEMENT numlist (numitem+)     >
<!ELEMENT bullist (bul,item)+    >
```

A final consideration that affects the usability of the tag set is the sheer number of tags. A large number of tags affects usability the most when authors or editors are responsible for tagging data, but it can also affect the complexity of programs designed to apply tags automatically. Count the number of tags in your design and see if you can use a generalized structure in place of unique structures (which require more tags). If possible, replace specific structures with general-use structures. This may not be an option for high-level elements but is often easy for text building-block elements.

Look back to the example of the three list types. Why are there three list types? If it is so that the formatting of each list type will be different, you could combine the lists into one model and differentiate the formatting by using a type or role attribute. Be sure to constrain the number of types so that you limit the possibilities for both the end user and the software developer. Using this approach, you can consolidate the three list models into this model:

```
<!ELEMENT list (item, item+)>
<!ATTLIST list   type (bul | alpha | num) "bul" >
```

Now Throw Your Schema Away!

Throughout this chapter we have discussed the principles of XML design. We have consistently discussed that the outcome of the XML design process is an XML DTD or schema. Now you may wonder why we talk in these terms when one of the attractive features of XML is its well-formedness and the fact that XML does not require a DTD.

The XML specification clearly allows for two levels of conformance— valid and well-formed. *Well-formed* means that the data coded in XML is properly nested and that all entities are declared. *Valid* XML is not only well formed, but also has a DTD and conforms to the constraints expressed within the DTD.

XML is designed so that data coded in XML is self-describing by virtue of being well formed. As such, XML without a DTD can be processed. This provides you with extraordinarily flexible data-delivery capabilities. You can, for example, sort and filter information to deliver well-formed and personalized XML information sets on the Web.

Delivery of well-formed XML does not mean that a schema was not used when the data was created. It simply means that the DTD is not required for this use of the data. An XML DTD can be used when validity is important, such as during the authoring process. At other times, such as when viewing the data, the constraints imposed by a DTD are not required and may, in fact, slow processing.

Summary

Now that you know how to select a design approach, write a functional specification, and recruit your design team, you're ready to move on to the next step: learning how to actually write the DTD. The next chapter will carefully guide you through that process.

Chapter 6

CREATING YOUR OWN DTD

As you have seen, XML has the power both to describe existing information and to create new information. A large part of the success of XML is the result of how it helps you place restrictions on what documents can contain. A purchase order must not contain a bibliography, and you would not normally expect bank account information in a recipe for gingerbread. Content is restricted in this way for two reasons: first, to help people who are creating documents by enforcing a set of guidelines, and second, to simplify any subsequent processing of documents by eliminating surprises. When information is structured in predictable ways, software can be simpler and hence more reliable and cheaper.

XML provides two mechanisms for controlling content: using a document type definition (DTD), as described in this chapter, or using an XML schema, as described in Chapter 7, "An Introduction to XML Schemas." An XML document that has been checked against a DTD successfully is said to have been *validated*.

Adapted from *Mastering™ XML, Premium Edition*, by Chuck White, Liam Quin, and Linda Burman
ISBN 0-7821-2847-5   1,155 pages $49.99

In this chapter, you can learn about when to write your own DTD and when to use DTDs that others have written, about the process of writing a DTD, and finally the actual syntax that you will use to create a DTD. Even if you do not plan to use DTDs in your projects, you may find the first three sections useful reading.

WHEN TO CREATE YOUR OWN DTD

DTDs already exist for almost every imaginable sort of information, including newspaper articles, transcriptions of medieval plays, press releases, and bird-watching trip reports. You should look closely at these existing DTDs. Even if you don't find one that is suitable for your own use, you can choose to use part of an existing DTD and build on it, or to learn from its mistakes and move on.

There are a number of compelling reasons for using an industry-standard DTD:

- ▶ Other people have already solved difficult problems; for example, how to represent cross-references to a bibliography or how to mark up a purchase order.

- ▶ Other people in your industry may already be familiar with the standard DTDs, so hiring and training become easier.

- ▶ You can exchange information with other people; that is, you can make your documents available, and you can also use the documents of others.

- ▶ A program written to work with one DTD might or might not work with documents using a different DTD. General XML tools work with any DTD, but applications using XML may have specific requirements. When you write your own DTD, you may make it more difficult to use other people's software. Look for available software that depends on a relevant DTD or a DTD fragment such as OASIS (Organization for the Advancement of Structured Information Standards) tables or MathML (Mathematical Markup Language).

- ▶ If you need style sheets for printing your XML documents or software (perhaps using XSLT) to convert the documents to another format such as HTML or RTF, you may well find available free documents that you could use immediately if you used the appropriate

DTD. For example, a lot of software uses the DocBook DTD, a popular document-centric DTD. (For more information on DocBook, go to www.oasis-open.org/docbook/, or see *Mastering XML, Premium Edition* (Sybex, 2001), Chapter 24, "Producing Documents Using DocBook.")

▶ Off-the-shelf XML tools such as editors, formatters, and even databases may support industry-standard DTDs.

If you decide not to create your own DTD, you should still follow the steps outlined in the "Processes and People" section in this chapter to ensure that everyone involved agrees to use the DTD you select.

If you do create a DTD of your own, consider making it public so that others can build on your work and perhaps even contribute software or ideas. You can get a lot of publicity and visibility for your organization within your industry in this way and make valuable contacts, all for a relatively small cost. The experiences of others can also help you avoid costly mistakes.

In the next section, we'll give you an overview of the controls available in a DTD. You might want to compare this section with the corresponding section in the next chapter when you're deciding whether to create a schema or a DTD.

THE BUILDING BLOCKS

A DTD consists of two parts. The first part contains a set of declarations of elements, entities, and so forth, and it is called the *document type declaration*. The second part of a DTD includes documentation and conventions that specify how your documents are processed. Documentation is an integral part of the markup process. It's no good defining a pnUPkg5 element without telling people when and how to use it, what it represents, and how to handle the element in software.

The following are the most important declarations that you will use in writing a document type declaration:

Element declarations   These are statements that say, for example, that a chapter contains a title followed by one or more paragraphs, interspersed with illustrations. You can specify which elements can contain text, but you can't specify anything about that text. For example, a date element could contain the text "In the third year of the reign of Edward II, king of this land," or it could even be empty. If you need to control textual content, you must use an XML schema either instead of or together with a DTD. Element declarations are the most important part of most DTDs, after the documentation and examples.

General entity declarations   You use general entity declarations to define general "boilerplate" text items or references to special symbols such as paragraph markers. A general entity can refer to any external resource that you can address with a URL, such as a file or even a database query. You can also supply the replacement content for an entity in the declaration.

Comments   Comments are simply notes to other human readers of the DTD itself and do not affect the XML documents that use the DTD. You'll find examples of comments throughout this chapter. Comments are only allowed *between* declarations, not inside them.

Conditional sections   It is possible to construct a DTD whose behavior depends on a marker in the XML document itself. For example, users could set a flag to enable the use of cross-references. Some DTDs make extensive use of this feature to support a wide range of document types with a single DTD file, which is easier to maintain than many separate files.

Parameter entities   Parameter entities are used with conditional sections to customize DTDs; they also contain code snippets that you can reuse in your DTD. For example, wherever general printed text can appear in a document, you might allow any combination of emphasis, cross-references, inline images, superscripts, and subscripts; you could achieve this in a DTD with a parameter entity.

PROCESSES AND PEOPLE

Designing a DTD isn't just a matter of syntax. It's about getting a group of people to agree to use a particular markup for their documents so that they can be more productive. In the next few sections, we'll describe the process for writing a good DTD.

Getting the Right People Involved

Identify everyone who will create, use, or process the information and discuss with them whether they should be actively involved or merely monitor the process. If people are fully involved from the outset, they will understand exactly how they will benefit and the costs involved.

NOTE

Be careful to establish who has *editorial authority* over the content or structure of the information at each stage. These people will need to support your DTD-writing process, and the DTD will need to help them in their work.

Milestones

The more people you involve, the more important it is to have a clear schedule. Often the individual steps are more important than the actual dates, although it rarely seems so at the time. Some of the usual milestones include a date by which you'll have some marked-up samples agreed on; a date to have a draft DTD prepared; a review period; and final sign-off from all parties involved. As soon as you start using the DTD in production, you'll need to change it. In the next section, we'll describe how to control change requests, but you should probably build an initial trial period into your schedule.

Change Requests

Make clear to people that once you finish the design of your document architecture, changes may be expensive. One way to do this is with a formal change request procedure, which can also become a record of why each change was made and for whom.

Correcting design defects in a DTD is cheap before the DTD is finished. If you find errors after you create documents that use it, you may need to go back and correct the documents. If you share the DTD and documents with other departments or organizations, you will need a formal change request procedure, and everyone involved will have to update their copies of the DTD. As a result, when you find yourself making design decisions that differ from other industry-standard DTDs, consider carefully whether your needs are justified.

Part ii

Make sure that every copy of your DTD or any fragment of it includes a version number. This is especially important for printed copies!

It is worth investing in a revision control system for managing changes. If you are the only person changing the files, a free system such as the Revision Control System (RCS) will work well; it's included in most Linux and Unix systems and is widely available for free, including ports to Microsoft Windows. If a group of people will be making changes, you might want to set up a client/server system such as the Concurrent Versions System (CVS) (also available for free; see www.cvshome.org) or to invest in a commercial system. At an absolute minimum, put the DTD files up on a Web server, even if it's internal only to your department.

TIP

If you make it easier for people to get an updated copy than to change their own copy, you will find fewer incompatible versions floating around.

Making the First Draft

When you first start writing a DTD, it's often helpful to involve an external industry consultant for a few days. Arrange a meeting room where you'll be undisturbed for a day or two, and include representatives from authoring, editing, publishing, archiving, programming, and any other departments or groups that will be involved. Be sure to include people who work with the documents daily.

A useful exercise is to give everyone a copy of a few sample documents. The first document should be short, a page or two at most. Ask the participants to use colored pens to mark every piece of information that they think has to be marked up separately, whether because it's printed as a separate paragraph that has special formatting, because a database query needs to find it, or because it's somehow intellectually unsatisfying to leave it unmarked. Compare the results, and discuss the differences in people's marks. Try to be inclusive: If someone marks something, it's probably worth marking up.

An XML publishing system can usually generate list numbers and bullets; such *generated text* should be marked up only if it's irregular (that is, if a computer couldn't easily get it right otherwise). Page numbers, running heads, and decorations around chapter headings are also usually generated automatically.

After identifying the most important items, try to name them. If you can all generally agree on names, that's a sign you're moving in the right direction. If there are disagreements, note them and move on. When you have names for most items, go back and investigate the more difficult items. If not everyone can see how to handle all the items, consider seeking external advice.

At this point, you'll be close to a DTD for the single documents you've examined. Most experienced XML consultants will be more than willing (for a fee!) to review your DTD and help you progress to later drafts. Making the first step yourself (even if a consultant is present) is much cheaper, and, more important, taking the time to do the work yourself means that you will end up with a result that better fits your needs.

You can then meet with the people who will be working with the markup and help reassure them that all this XML stuff really is going to make their lives easier.

Beyond the First Draft

The best way to reach a final DTD depends on your organization and the uses you envision. The rest of this chapter is about the actual syntax of DTDs and how to write them and lay them out. It's possible for you to write a complete DTD using this chapter alone, but you should be looking at other DTDs and talking to other XML users to make sure that you don't reinvent square wheels. Think of this chapter as a springboard as you dive into the deep but beautiful waters.

ELEMENTS AND ATTRIBUTES

In Chapter 2, "Understanding and Creating Elements," you saw how to use elements in an XML document. Elements are the most important part of any XML document, and element declarations are the most important part of a DTD. The following sections show you how to declare XML elements and attributes.

XML Names

XML elements, attributes, and entities all have names. A name in XML must start with a letter or an underscore (_) and then can be followed by zero or more letters, digits, Unicode combining characters and extenders, periods (.), minus signs (-), and underscores (_). There is no length limit. Letters can include accents.

XML names may include a single colon (:) anywhere, including at the start; the XML Namespace Specification defines the meaning of this. (You can read about namespaces in *Mastering XML, Premium Edition* (Sybex, 2001), Chapter 11, "Understanding Namespaces: Core Standard.") Here are some examples of valid names:

Paragraph	veryLongNameThatIsHardToType
Part-number	p12-z46-9-12.html
sock.color	ElNiño
mf825	resumé
p	

The following names are *not* allowed:

Part number (names can't include spaces)

2001inventory (names can't start with a digit)

-12.5 (names can't start with a minus sign)

main::print (names can't include more than one colon)

All XML names, including names of elements and attributes, are *case sensitive*. Accents on letters are also significant: rôle and role are different names, as are boy, BOY, and Boy, and café, CAFÉ, and CAFE.

It is a good idea to lowercase your element names or to use Initial Capitals. Don't use ALLCAPS, because CAPS ARE HARD TO READ and lowercase letters are easier to type, and because people are used to the idea that words in capital letters are not case sensitive.

Some people capitalize the first letter of an element name that's used for a chapter or other "container" element and lowercase the first letter of a name that can hold text, but this is too fussy if you are creating documents in a text editor that doesn't insert the element names automatically.

If you have names made up of multiple words, such as a part number, choose a convention early on; a minus sign works well, with part-number being easy to read. If the names will need to be translated into a computer programming language such as Perl or Java or an object-oriented interface such as CORBA, use mixed capital; for example, PartNumber, because a minus sign isn't allowed in a name in most programming languages.

If you have names that represent an object and a property, such as a person's sock color, you might want a mixed convention, with a period separating the object name and the property name: `table-waiter` `.sock-color` or `TableWaiter.SockColor`.

Declaring Elements

When you use a DTD, you provide a list of every XML element that can appear in your documents, what each element can contain, and which attributes it can have.

TIP

See the sidebar, "Namespaces and DTDs," later in this chapter for some important restrictions on XML DTDs.

An element declaration looks a bit like this:

```
<!ELEMENT cat
    (eat|sleep|purr)*
>
```

This declaration begins with `<!`. All XML declarations start in this way. The word `ELEMENT` shows that we're about to declare an element. This word must appear in capital letters exactly as shown, with no space before it. Next is the name of the element being declared, in this case, `cat`. Following is a list of other elements allowed inside this one. This is the *content model* of the `cat` element. Content models are described in the next section. The declaration ends with a `>` on a line by itself.

You don't have to lay out an element declaration like that. You can put it all on one line if you like:

```
<!ELEMENT cat (eat|sleep|purr)*>
```

However, your DTD will be much easier to read and maintain if you use the layout suggested previously.

Element Content Models

An *element content model* specifies what an element is allowed to contain. For example, a chapter might be required to start with a title and then to have at least one paragraph. You could express that in a content model like this:

```
title, paragraph+
```

That would appear in an element declaration like this:

```
<!ELEMENT Chapter
     (title, paragraph+)
  >
```

The comma after `title` means "followed by." The plus sign after `paragraph` means "one or more." This is really a sort of pattern. The XML processor reads your DTD and stores all the element declarations in memory. It then tries to match the elements in the input document with these content models. If the input doesn't match, the processor signals an error and halts.

To match an element in a document against a content model, simply start at the left of the content model and look at one item at a time. Say a document contained the following:

```
<Chapter><paragraph>hello</paragraph></Chapter>
```

If you tried to validate the document against a DTD containing the earlier declaration for `Chapter`, you'd get an error. The content model for `Chapter` must start with a `title` element, and our document doesn't have one.

Content models are built of particles. A *particle* is the name of an element, optionally followed by an occurrence indicator. An *occurrence indicator* can be an asterisk (*) to mean "zero or more"; a question mark to mean "zero or one (optional)"; or a plus sign to mean "one or more." In the following example, a team must contain at least one player but could contain any number of players, even tens of thousands:

```
<!ELEMENT team
     (player+)
  >
```

You can combine lists of particles with a *connector* between each of them. The connector can be either a comma or a vertical bar. The comma means "followed by," so in the following example, a figure must contain an image followed by a caption:

```
<!ELEMENT figure
     (image, caption)
  >
```

The vertical bar means "or," so one or the other must follow. In the following example, a `measure` element must contain a pint, a gallon, or an ell:

```
<!ELEMENT measure
```

```
(pint|gallon|ell)
>
```

You can build quite complex content models in this way. The following is an example of a simple visiting card database:

```
<!ELEMENT onePerson
    (name, address+, birthday?, email*, shoe-size?)
>
```

This example says that a `onePerson` element must contain a `name` element, followed by one or more `address` elements, then an optional `birthday` element, maybe some email elements, and finally an optional `shoe-size` element.

You can build more complex content models too. Wherever you have an element name, you can also have an entire content particle in parentheses. In the following example, you can have either a suite or an apartment after `street`, or because of the `?`, you can have neither and go straight from street to city.

```
<!ELEMENT USAaddress
    (number, street, (suite | apartment)?,
 city, state, zip)
>
```

Textual Content

Eventually you want to stop using elements and write some text. That's done with the oddly named #PCDATA keyword. You can use #PCDATA by itself or at the start of a content model, and that content model must be a list of choices followed by an *, meaning that everything is optional:

```
<!ELEMENT name
    (#PCDATA)
>
<!ELEMENT paragraph
    (#PCDATA|emphasis|footnote)*
>
```

It's generally best to use the asterisk form, even if the choice contains no other elements:

```
<!ELEMENT part-number
```

```
    (#PCDATA)*
>
```

This example makes it really clear that *text is always optional in XML.*

Special Content Models

There are two special forms of content model: EMPTY and ANY.

An element declared EMPTY has no content:

```
<!ELEMENT br
    EMPTY
>
```

The br element appears in a document either as <br /> or as
</br>.

An element declared as ANY can contain any combination of text and elements, but all the elements must be mentioned in the DTD. Thus, you can write a DTD that's halfway between simple well-formed XML (with no element declarations) and fully valid XML with all the content models specified. Doing so can be useful when you're developing and testing a DTD.

Printing Element Declarations

If you are making a printed copy of a DTD, it's useful to put the element name in bold and to indent the content model by four spaces. Leave a blank line after the content model.

The bold element names are much easier to see when people are scanning a printout for a definition, and using four spaces (a traditional spacing in programming) is enough to show structure without making items march too far to the left of the page to be easily read.

```
<!ELEMENT boy
    (noise|dirt|trouble|cuteness)+
>
<!ELEMENT pizza
    (cheese+,
(pepperoni|anchovy|onion|pepper|chicken|potato)*
>
```

NAMESPACES AND DTDS

There are some difficulties with combining XML DTDs and namespaces:

The XML namespace mechanism allows you to use a *default namespace*, which means that you can use names such as y:Simon and Simon interchangeably, if y: is the default namespace prefix. But y:Simon and Simon are two entirely different element names as far as XML validation with a DTD is concerned. Therefore, if you are using a DTD and namespaces, you will need to be careful to ensure that element names always appear exactly as they are declared in your DTD, including the namespace prefix.

A common use of namespaces is to allow a "sprinkling" of elements from different DTDs in one document. To achieve this, you need to make a single master DTD that declares all the elements together with their content models. For many uses, that turns out to be impractical, and you're left with not using validation. You may want to consider using schemas if these problems affect you.

Declaring Attributes

An element declaration associates an element name with a content model but says nothing about attributes. You declare attributes with an attribute list declaration. The general form is

```
<!ATTLIST name
    stuff
>
```

The stuff inside (not a formal term!) is a list of attribute declarations, like this:

```
attName type occurrence
```

The attribute types are explained in more detail later in this chapter. The occurrence part specifies whether the attribute is optional or required and, if optional, whether it has a default attribute value. You should place an attribute list declaration immediately after the element declaration for the same element. You'll learn more about declaring attributes in the next section, but let's look at an example first:

```
<!ELEMENT boy
```

```
            (#PCDATA)*
    >


    <!ATTLIST boy
        age CDATA #REQUIRED
        mother  CDATA #IMPLIED
        gender (male|female) "male"
    >
```

In this example, the element boy can have two attributes: age and mother. It also specifies that *every* boy element must have an age supplied and that the age must be a whole number. A boy might also know the name of his mother, so we make that optional, and we allow the boy to identify either as male or as female, defaulting to male.

The following is an example of an employee element in a document:

```
<employee age="38" department="dispatch">
Leslie
</employee>
```

TIP

A better design would use a date of birth, not an age, because birth date doesn't change with time. Storing a person's age means that your documents get out-of-date. Even if you store only the year, it's still better to store constant information and to derive the changing part (the age) in software.

Attribute Types

As you saw in Chapter 3, "Understanding and Creating Attributes," XML attributes cannot contain elements. Refer to that chapter for more detail about attribute types. Following are short summaries of the most important types.

CDATA   A simple string; the value can contain entity references and character references, such as & and & but no other markup.

Example: <Company name="Hat & Sock Trading Company Inc." />

Use an attribute if there is no short list of fixed values.

ID   You can give an element a unique identifier; an element can have only one attribute of type ID, and the value must be an XML name (as described earlier). You should normally use ID as both the name and the value of the attribute so that non-validating XML processors can recognize it and to make it easier for human users. An ID attribute must be either #REQUIRED or #IMPLIED; that is, it cannot have a default value.

IDREF   Use an IDREF attribute to refer to another element. The value in this attribute must be *exactly* the same as the value in the ID attribute of the other element. You should normally use IDREF as both the name and the value of the attribute, so that nonvalidating XML processors can recognize it and to make it easier for human users. The variant IDREFS declares an attribute that contains a list of IDs separated by spaces.

NMTOKEN   An attribute of type MNTOKEN can contain only a single XML name; it's similar to an ID or IDREF except that it has no special meaning. Because you can't include an apostrophe or space, MNTOKEN is not useful in practice. The variant NMTOKENS declares an attribute that contains a list of names separated by spaces.

Entity   The value of an attribute of type ENTITY is the name of an *unparsed entity* you have declared. This is sometimes used as a way to refer to graphics image files. The variant ENTITIES declares an attribute that contains a list of names separated by spaces.

Enumeration   An attribute can also be declared to have one of a list of values; this is the commonest form after CDATA. We'll discuss enumerated attributes in a later section in this chapter.

NOTATION   You must declare an attribute of this type to allow a list of declared notations. We discuss notations in a later section in this chapter; for now, all you need to know is that this is a possible attribute type. This type of entity value is rarely used.

Enumerated Attribute Values

An *enumeration* is simply a list of possible values. An enumerated attribute declaration looks like this:

```
<!ATTLIST sock
```

```
        fabric (wool|nylon|acrylic|cotton) #REQUIRED
>
```

This example specifies that a sock element has to have a fabric attribute whose value is one of the items listed. If you have kevlon socks, you're out of luck, because that's not a listed value. Because that's a common situation, here is a workaround:

```
<!ATTLIST sock
    fabric (wool|nylon|acrylic|cotton|other)
#REQUIRED fabric.other CDATA #IMPLIED
>
```

You would probably want a user interface that enabled users to enter only a value for fabric.other if other was selected as a fabric type. The values are all case sensitive. You'll see in the next section how to give a default value too.

Attribute Default Values

You can declare attributes to have any of the following default values:

#REQUIRED   This isn't really a default at all. It says that the value must always be specified.

#IMPLIED   This means that if the attribute is not used, there is no default value.

#FIXED   This must be followed by an attribute value and says that the attribute always has this value. This value is useful for DTD versions and also for "architectural forms," a concept from the SGML community.

"string"   A literal string can be used for the default value; it must be a legal value, of course. Here are some examples:

```
<!ATTLIST document
    author CDATA #REQUIRED
    editorName CDATA #IMPLIED
    dtdVersion CDATA #FIXED "1.3"
    documentVersion CDATA #REQUIRED
    documentState (initial|draft|review|published)
"draft" language CDATA "en"
>
```

WARNING

A nonvalidating XML processor does not have to read the DTD and, therefore, cannot always supply default attribute values.

Every XML element has a number of predeclared attributes, including xml:space and xml:lang; it is not necessary to declare these yourself.

When to Use Attributes

You might be wondering when to design a DTD with attributes and when to use elements. Let's look at the employee example again, perhaps with a few more details:

```
<!ELEMENT employee
    (#PCDATA)*
>


<!ATTLIST boy
    DateOfBirth CDATA #REQUIRED
    Department CDATA #IMPLIED
    EyeColor CDATA #REQUIRED
    Gender (male|female) "male"
    FavoriteSaying CDATA #IMPLIED
>
```

Now, we can agree that date of birth is a property of a person; that is, it's something about the person. It's an *attribute* of a person, as is eye color. But a favorite saying is something that a person might *have*; it's not a property. Probably it should be a subelement. You probably also agree that the saying might need extra markup such as emphasis elements. Because attributes can't contain other markup, the saying should certainly be an element.

Once we introduce elements into the content model of the employee, we'll need somewhere to store the name. It'll also be easier to add other textual fields such as a description. Here is a rewritten example:

```
<!ELEMENT employee
    (Name, Department, FavoriteSaying?, Description?)
>
```

```
<!ATTLIST employee
    DateOfBirth CDATA #REQUIRED
    EyeColor CDATA #REQUIRED
    Gender (male|female) "male"
>
```

The new elements (Name, Department, and so forth) need to be declared too, of course.

NOTE

In practice, this doesn't illustrate the best way to store information about an employee. Department should be an enumeration or a number so that someone can't enter it as **dispatch** instead of **despatch**; in some countries there may also be laws about storing personal information about employees.

Printing Attribute Declarations

Just as with element declarations, it's best to use simple formatting for attribute declarations. Some people like to align the attribute types vertically, like an addition sum, but this makes the DTD harder to read, despite looking tidier. That's because it forces the types farther from the attribute names, increasing the chance that someone will misread the DTD.

Keep the attribute declarations near the corresponding element declarations. It helps to put the element name in bold; you might want to boldface attribute names too, although that's not really necessary. Try to split long content models and enumerations at logical points.

```
<!ELEMENT employee
    (
        Name,
        Department,
        FavoriteSaying?,
        Description?
    )
>

<!ATTLIST employee
    DateOfBirth CDATA #REQUIRED
```

```
EyeColor CDATA #REQUIRED
Gender (male|female) "male"
>
```

GENERAL ENTITIES

A *general entity* is a name that stands for a piece of document content. (Refer to Chapter 4 for more detail about using and creating entities.) A general entity can be declared more than once, in which case the first declaration is used. (See the section on the DOCTYPE declaration, later in this chapter, for how to use this process to override entity values in your documents.)

There are two types of general entities:

▶ An internal general entity has a declaration that includes a value.

▶ An external general entity has a declaration that names a file or other resource containing the value.

Internal General Entities

You declare an *internal general entity* like this:

```
<!ENTITY moon

    "Buzz Moonkitty LoveyDovey BonkBonk"

>
```

You can use the following in a document to save typing:

```
Our cat's full name is &moon; although we just call
her Moon.
```

General entities can be used inside entity values and also inside attribute values:

```
<!ENTITY server

    "www.holoweb.net"

>
<!ENTITY homepage.liam

    "http://&server;/~liam/"

>
. . .
<IMG SRC="&homepage.liam;" />
```

External General Entities

An *external general entity* is simply a general entity whose value is stored separately:

```
<!ENTITY bibliography
    SYSTEM "bibliography.xml"
>
```

The content of the `bibliography.xml` file must be well-formed XML. You use an external general entity wherever you could put the corresponding content:

```
<chapter> . . . </chapter>
&bibliography;
&appendixA;
```

PARAMETER ENTITIES

You can use *parameter entities* to reuse parts of your DTD. This is similar to the way that you can use general entities to substitute for fixed or boilerplate content. A parameter entity has an extra percent sign in its declaration and is otherwise just like a general entity:

```
<!ENTITY % useHappiness
    "INCLUDE"
>
<!ENTITY % bibliography
    SYSTEM "bibliography.dtd"
>
<!-* now include the file: *->
%bibliography;
```

Parameter entities can only be used to substitute whole tokens or whole declarations. You can't define half a word in one parameter entity and the other half in another, for example. To encourage this, outside of strings, parameter entities are expanded with an extra space at the start and end. (See the section "The Document Type Declaration and the Internal Subset" later in this chapter for more restrictions.)

The following sections show examples of some common uses of parameter entities.

Running Text

You'll probably have a lot of elements that can contain text. You might start by allowing only #PCDATA, but soon you'll want emphasis too. After a while, perhaps you'll need superscripts and subscripts, and you'll have to go back and edit all the content models in your DTD that mention #PCDATA.

If you make a mistake, you might end up with one particular element (bookTitle, for example) that doesn't allow superscripts (for example). Later, long after you have left the company, people might have built software that "knows" that book titles can have emphasis but not superscripts. And then one day along comes a book called $e = mc^2$ *and Other Famous Equations*, and people realize that superscript was left out by mistake, not deliberately.

You can easily avoid this sort of error. Wherever you have plain, normal running text, use a parameter entity:

```
<!ENTITY %RunningText

    "#PCDATA|emphasis"

>

. . .

<!ELEMENT BookTitle

    (%RunningText;)*

>

<!ELEMEMT PartDescription

    (%RunningText; | PartNumber)*

>
```

The PartDescription declaration shows how you can add other elements to the running text. You should also use this technique for blocks (paragraphs, lists, and so forth), perhaps using a %paragraphs; or %blocks; parameter entity.

Using Parameter Entities in Conditional Sections

The *conditional section* is a powerful feature of XML DTDs. You can arrange for optional modules in a DTD to be included or not, as needed. A conditional section has a somewhat disconcerting syntax:

```
<![INCLUDE[
```

```
    anything here

]]>
```

If you change the word INCLUDE to IGNORE, the contents of the conditional section are ignored.

WARNING

Conditional sections can appear only in external DTD files, not in the document type declaration internal subset. See the section "The Document Type Declaration and the Internal Subset" later in this chapter for an English translation of this restriction!

You can use a parameter entity to control a conditional section. In the following example, the bibliography DTD is only included if the useBibliography parameter entity is set to INCLUDE:

```
<!ENTITY % useBibliography

    "IGNORE"

>

<![%useBibliography;[

    <!ENTITY bibfile %

        SYSTEM "bibliography.xml"

    >

    %bibfile;

]]>
```

You can nest one conditional section inside another, but if any of them has the keyword IGNORE, all conditional sections nested inside are ignored, irrespective of their keywords.

NOTE

There is no way to include the string]]> inside a conditional section. If you have to do this, you might want to use a Unicode zero-width nonbreaking space inside the string.

See the section "The Document Type Declaration and the Internal Subset" later in this chapter for ways to make conditional sections much more useful.

Printing Entity Declarations

The same general principles as for other declarations apply:

```
<!ENTITY bibliography
    SYSTEM "bibliography.xml"
>


<!ENTITY address
    "

        <line>12, The Maltings</line>
        <line>Mudbury-on-Sludge</line>
        <line>Slimeshire</line>

    "

>
```

UNPARSED ENTITIES AND NOTATIONS

An unparsed entity is an external file or resource, such as an image, that isn't XML. An unparsed entity has an associated *notation*, such as image/JPEG. You saw some examples of unparsed entities in Chapter 4.

The theory is that you can say that this object is a JPEG image and point to it. Unfortunately, that's not how the Web works. An HTTP server is free to give you a file of any format—the client simply has to accept what it receives. In a closed environment, however, this XML facility may be useful.

Declaring a Notation

A notation declaration is fairly simple and can take either of the following two forms:

```
<!NOTATION JPEG
    SYSTEM "meaningless URL"
>
<!NOTATION JPEG
    PUBLIC "meaningless string" "meaningless URL"
>
```

Probably the best compromise is to use a SYSTEM identifier that's a semicolon-separated list of MIME media types, such as `text/html` or `image/PNG`. As elsewhere in XML, the PUBLIC identifier has no well-defined meaning.

Notations are used in three places in XML: with unparsed entities, in notation attributes, and with processing instructions.

Unparsed Entities

Where a parsed general entity has its value expanded in-place in the document, an *unparsed entity* is only referred to. The assumption is that it is not well-formed XML, so there's no point trying to read it. Listing 6.1 gives an example of such a declaration.

Listing 6.1: An Unparsed Entity Declaration

```
<!--* First, we'll declare a notation to use. You only
declare each notation once.
*-->
<!NOTATION JPEG SYSTEM "image/jpeg">

 <!--* Now declare an entity that is stored in that notation:
    *-->
<!ENTITY sock-picture
    SYSTEM "http://www.holoweb.net/~liam/sock.jpg"
    NDATA JPEG
>
```

If you actually fetch this picture (it's rather uninteresting), you'll see that it is indeed a JPEG image. But it could equally well be a piece of text saying that the image is unavailable, and in that case it would have a MIME media type of text/html.

Notation Attributes

A *notation attribute* implies that the content of the given element, in addition to being well-formed XML, also happens to be in the specified notation.

```
<!ATTLIST employee-picture
    format NOTATION (JPEG|GIF|PNG) #REQUIRED
>
```

Of course, if the content of the element were really a JPEG image, it would be binary and might contain < or even characters not allowed in a Unicode document. So you would need to add a second attribute to specify the content encoding, for example, base64 from MIME. This facility is not widely implemented, and there is no standard way to specify a content encoding.

An XML processing instruction starts with the name of a *target*, such as

```
<?troff .pp?>
```

The target must be declared as a notation; in this example, the name troff would be so declared.

COMMENTS

You can place comments anywhere you like—before, between, and after declarations. Comments look like this:

```
<!-- This is a short comment. -->


<!--* This is a multiline comment.
    * If you put four spaces at the start of
    * continuation lines, the asterisks will all
    * line up, and it's easy to spot an error.
    *-->
```

The asterisks (*) in the longer example are optional, but if you use them, they make it immediately obvious that the large block is a comment.

Some people like to have a template for comments at the start of each file and sometimes at the start of each element declaration. If you do this, don't go overboard. If you include too much detail, finding the important information becomes difficult. Use a revision management system to track changes, or put a change history at the end of a file. At the start, say what the file is for, who can use it, where to get it, and where to submit changes. Before an element declaration, state the purpose of the element being defined, perhaps in a single short sentence.

Comments are no substitute for separate detailed documentation with examples.

WARNING
Comments cannot contain two minus signs in a row.

Part ii

Printing Comments

If you use a variable-width typeface, set the spacing so that the asterisks make a clean vertical line in a multiline comment. Be careful that your formatter doesn't turn -- into a dash. Microsoft Word in particular likes to turn the end of a comment (-->) into an arrow (→); you can disable this in the "autocorrection" preferences in most versions. It helps to use a fixed-width font for most of the DTD and a variable-width italic font for the text of comments:

```
<!--* This DTD was written by Liam Quin <liam@holoweb.net> for
     * representing etymologies transcribed from Nathan Bailey's
     * 1737 Universal Etymological Dictionary.
     *
     * The latest version is available on request.
     * This is version 3.17.
     *
     * This DTD is in the Public Domain and may be reused
     * freely in whole or part without need for permission
     * or payment.
     *
     *-->
```

THE DOCUMENT TYPE DECLARATION AND THE INTERNAL SUBSET

Every XML document starts with an XML declaration followed by an optional document type declaration. You use the document type declaration to link a document to its DTD; the document type declaration also lets you override some of the definitions in the DTD if you want.

Listing 6.2 is a short sample XML document complete with a document type declaration:

Listing 6.2: A Sample XML Instance with Document Type Declaration

```
<?xml version="1.0"?>
<!DOCTYPE love SYSTEM "love.dtd">
<love><happiness /><smile /><hug /></love>
```

This sample uses an external DTD in a file called `love.dtd`. If the document in the example was downloaded from `http://www.xxx/docs/sample.xml`, the DTD file will be `http://www.xxx/docs/love.dtd`. The SYSTEM identifier is a relative URL, not a filename. The DTD file might look like Listing 6.3.

Listing 6.3: DTD for a Sample Instance

```
<?xml version="1.0"?>
<!ELMENT love
    (happiness|smile|hug)*
>
<!ELEMENT happiness EMPTY>
<!ELEMENT smile EMPTY>
<!ELEMENT hug EMPTY>
```

The document type declaration can also include element declarations, using an *internal subset*. The internal subset is called internal because it's inside the document, not in an external file, and it's called a subset because it's not the whole DTD, only a part of it. The internal subset lives inside a pair of square brackets:

```
<?xml version="1.0"?>
<!DOCTYPE message SYSTEM "love.dtd" [
    <!ELEMENT message
        (#PCDATA)*
    >
    <!ATTLIST message
        to CDATA #REQUIRED
        from CDATA #REQUIRED
        subject CDATA #REQUIRED
    >
]>
<message
    to="all staff"
    from="bigwig"
    subject="Inappropriate clothing"
>
```

```
It has come to my attention that some staff
have been wearing inappropriate clothing.
This must stop. Clothing is not to be worn
in the office.
```

```
</message>
```

Restrictions on the Internal Subset

You cannot use conditional sections in the internal subset. In addition, you should avoid using parameter entities. They are allowed, but a nonvalidating parser has to stop reading the internal subset if it finds a parameter entity.

The following two snippets are equivalent, except that the second defines an extra parameter entity:

```
<!DOCTYPE boy SYSTEM "student.dtd">
```

and

```
<!DOCTYPE boy [
    <!ENTITY % theDTD SYSTEM "student.dtd">
    %theDTD;
]>
```

Because the parameter entity to include the external DTD is the last thing in the internal subset, it doesn't matter that a nonvalidating XML processor might stop reading the subset at that point. The first form is preferred, even though both forms have the same effect, for several reasons. The first form makes clear that student.dtd is the main DTD for the document; some software might also use that as a hook for attaching styles. It also involves less syntax.

Public Identifiers

A *public identifier* in SGML (as opposed to XML) is intended to be a formal string that refers to a published document that's guaranteed not to change. In XML, no formal meaning is assigned to a public identifier, but if you are using old SGML software you may find that it has support for looking up the value of a public identifier in an external file, called a catalog, and returning a system identifier.

You can use a public identifier to link a document to its DTD, but even if you do, you must provide a valid system identifier. Most people, therefore, prefer to avoid public identifiers. Here is an example:

```
<?xml version="1.0"?>
<!DOCTYPE article PUBLIC "-//QUIN//DTD
  Etymology v3.12//EN" "etymology.dtd">
<article>
 . . .
</article>
```

Again, it must be emphasized that public identifiers are informational only. The system identifier (`etymology.dtd` in this fictional example) must always be used to fetch the DTD.

You can include public identifiers anywhere a system identifier is used, including in external entity declarations. Public identifiers are literal strings and cannot contain any markup, so there is no way to escape a double quote in one, and entities are not expanded.

Overriding Entities in the Internal Subset

If an entity is declared more than once, the first definition is used. The external DTD is read *after* the internal subset. If your DTD defines a parameter entity useBibliography as having the value IGNORE, you could override that in your document:

```
<!DOCTYPE article SYSTEM "article.dtd" [
    <!ENTITY % useBibliography "INCLUDE">
]>
```

Now when the DTD is read, the useBibliography entity will already be defined, so that in the following fragment, the file bib.dtd will be used:

```
<!ENTITY % useBibliography "IGNORE">
<![%useBibliography;[
<!--* this section is only used if the document instance
      * set useBibliography to INCLUDE     *-->
    <!ENTITY % extfile.bib "bib.dtd">
    %extfile.bib;
]]>
```

Adding Attribute Declarations in the Internal Subset

If you have more than one list of attribute declarations for an element, the lists are merged. If an attribute was already defined, as with entities, the earliest definition is used. If your document regularly adds attributes, ask yourself if there is an inadequacy in your DTD design. There might or might not be, but it's a possibility.

TOOLS FOR UNDERSTANDING AND BUILDING DTDs

Some commercial tools for building and analyzing DTDs are available. You can find Near & Far Designer (originally produced by Microstar) at www.opentext.com. This tool is popular, but it is no substitute for understanding the DTD itself.

There are a number of open source tools; go to Robin Cover's pages at www.oasis-open.org/cover/ for a good listing.

RCS can be obtained from any GNU archive; there may be a Windows port at www.Cygnus.com (this is actually a link for www.redhat.com). CVS is also widely used, and you can find this and other revision control tools by searching at www.freshmeat.net.

SUMMARY

This chapter has covered a lot of ground. Designing your own DTD isn't just about syntax; it's about understanding information and about working with people. You need to look at DTDs other people have written and to talk to other XML users. The next chapter will introduce you to another way of defining the content of XML documents: using XML schemas.

Chapter 7

AN INTRODUCTION TO XML SCHEMAS

X ML schemas are a more powerful alternative to the document type definition (DTD) that you read about in the previous chapter. You use schemas to constrain the element structure of XML documents and to limit the textual content, something a DTD cannot do. In this chapter, you'll get an overview of what schemas can do, and you'll learn about using schemas that other people have written. Chapter 8, "Writing XML Schemas," shows you how to write your own schemas.

Schemas are specified in three W3C (World Wide Web Consortium) publications: a primer, the schema syntax, and a data types document. You can read the W3C's current specifications for XML schemas by visiting www.w3.org/XML/Schema and following the links; the exact locations may have changed after this book was printed, but the XML schema page there will still work. At this Web site, there are also pointers to examples and to tools you can use. (You can find a reference to XML schema elements in Appendix B, "XML Schema Reference.")

Adapted from *Mastering™ XML, Premium Edition*, by Chuck White, Liam Quin, and Linda Burman
ISBN 0-7821-2847-5   1,155 pages $49.99

WHAT IS AN XML SCHEMA?

An *XML schema* defines a class of XML documents by providing constraints on both structure and content. You use a schema to specify which elements are allowed in your documents, the attributes they may have, and what they may contain. An XML schema is similar to a DTD, but an XML schema is more powerful because it also lets you specify the text content of elements. For example, you can specify that a `DateOfBirth` element must contain a valid date or that `NumberIn-Stock` must contain a whole number. If you have worked with relational databases, an XML schema will feel comfortable, because it's in many ways similar to a database schema.

When you use a schema in practice, you apply it to a well-formed XML; this process may result in an augmented document. For example, you might include default values. This process is called *schema validation*, and the schema processor will tell you whether the document does in fact conform to the schema—that is, whether the document is valid. Schema validation goes further than DTD validation, because the schema can impose more constraints on the document than a DTD can.

NOTE
The version of W3C XML schema dated May 2001 builds on the XML Infoset (explained later in this chapter), and as a result, some implementations may require a DTD and a schema. In addition, XML schemas cannot describe general entities.

An XML schema is itself an XML document, so you can use standard XML tools to create and edit it. You will see a short example later in this chapter.

WHEN TO USE XML SCHEMAS

If you have just read Chapter 6, "Creating Your Own DTDs," you might be wondering when to use a DTD, when to use an XML schema, when to use both, and when to use neither! The following sections will help you choose.

Features Specific to a DTD

Only a very few DTD features are not supported by an XML schema. The most significant is that an XML schema knows nothing of XML entities. You cannot declare an entity in an XML schema, and you cannot specify where an entity is used.

The most important other aspect of a DTD is that support for DTDs is required by the XML 1 specification in all validating XML parsers. At the very least, *every* XML parser must understand the internal document type subset—that is, the place at the start of an XML document that can contain declarations. A DTD will give you the most validation in current tools, but as support for XML schema validation becomes more widespread, this may change.

Features Specific to an XML Schema

Whereas a DTD specifies validity in terms of elements, an XML schema specifies validity in terms of elements, XML namespaces, and typed data such as integers, dates, and strings. This approach is at a much higher level than that of a DTD.

Some of the more important features available with an XML schema and not in a DTD are as follows:

Text content   You can specify which text content is allowed in any given context, not simply *whether* text is allowed. A DTD can't even force you to include one or more characters: #PCDATA always matches zero or more characters.

Typed data   In addition to specifying that text content must be present, you can specify that it must conform to a certain *type*, such as a whole number, a date, a name, or a sequence of uppercase letters. This is particularly important to applications using relational databases with XML, an important application for XML schemas.

Text patterns   You can use patterns (strictly speaking, Perl-like *regular expressions*) that the data must match. For example, a U.S. zip code must contain five or more numeric digits, and a Canadian postal code must contain two alphanumeric groups separated by a space (M6E 3J5).

WARNING

Don't be too constraining with your text patterns. Many Canadians are familiar with trying to order online from a U.S. Web site that lets you choose a country but then requires a "valid zip code" and won't accept a postal code.

Complex content models   Both DTDs and XML schemas let you specify a content model for each element, to specify what it can contain. The XML schema content models are more powerful, allowing you to specify, for example, that this element must contain exactly one of each of *these* elements but in any order.

Derived types   Whereas a DTD can specify only what an element *contains*, an XML schema can specify what an element *is*. For example, you can define a data type called `OvenTemperature` in your XML schema and specify that an XML element of that type contains a whole number such as 325, with an attribute to specify whether it's in Celsius or Fahrenheit.

TIP

A recipe will often give a range of temperatures or suggest a "hot oven." You might want to require that authors use exact numbers, but sometimes it's useful to be vague. In this example, you might allow a choice of an `OvenTemperature` or an `ApproximateTemperature`.

Documentation   A DTD does not specify a standard location for documentation about individual elements or for metadata such as the author's name. An XML schema can store such items, and more, in the `documentation` element.

Namespaces   XML schemas have built-in awareness of namespaces. If you mix elements from multiple namespaces or if you use default namespaces, DTDs cannot easily validate your documents; use a schema. XML schemas provide a much more intellectually satisfying way to describe XML documents. They are more nearly complete, and they are easier to maintain because they are easier to understand.

Unfortunately, little of today's software understands an XML schema. Until we have a tool to generate a minimal DTD from an XML schema, you may be forced to use a DTD simply for backward compatibility. XML Spy (`www.xmlspy.com`), an XML environment for Microsoft Windows, has experimental support for W3C XML schemas and can convert to DTDs.

When to Use Both a DTD and an XML Schema

The XML schema specification builds on the XML Information Set Specification (www.w3.org/TR/xml-infoset/), informally known as the *Infoset*. The Infoset describes the result of processing an XML document as if a DTD had been used. As a result, some XML schema software may actually require a DTD. You might also want both a DTD and an XML schema if you have to use a mixture of software, some of which doesn't support XML schema validation.

Whenever you keep information in two places, you risk changing one and not the other. In the database world, this leads to what are called *integrity errors*. If you use both a DTD and an XML schema, consider generating one from the other, perhaps using Perl or XSLT.

When to Use Neither a DTD nor an XML Schema

Some people really do want to use a *primordial soup* of elements, mixing from different DTDs or namespaces seemingly at will. Others are describing existing documents and do not want additional constraints. Some applications can't afford the efficiency overhead of validation.

You might find an XML schema to be a useful repository for the elements you use, even if you don't use it for validation or if you use it to validate only random samples.

When the University of Waterloo team was converting the *Oxford English Dictionary* to SGML, they discovered far too many different test cases to analyze all of them properly. Consequently, their approach was to create a DTD that had "ANY" for all content models—it listed which elements were known and little else. The team found this useful, but the term "Waterloo DTD" has since been used somewhat disparagingly to refer to any DTD that performs an incomplete analysis. Even such a simple DTD is better than no DTD in most cases, because you can use it to check for typing mistakes in your element names!

Upgrading from a DTD to an XML Schema

The W3C provides a Perl script that you can use to convert a DTD into an XML schema. This script is just a starting point. The idea is that you use it once and then edit the resulting schema, but it will save you a lot of tedious typing. You can find this script, the documentation, and the source at www.w3.org/2000/04/schema_hack/.

If you go through the careful process described in Chapter 6 to write your DTD, you will need to ensure that you involve all of the appropriate people as you construct your XML schema. It's also important that you don't invalidate any existing documents if you add constraints—or, if you do, to identify the documents and fix them! Also take the time to add documentation or to convert comments from the original DTD to documentation elements where appropriate. XML never *forces* you to use a DTD or an XML schema, but both are useful tools and are key to successfully deploying XML in most situations.

A SHORT EXAMPLE

You've heard a lot about XML schemas, so let's look at one. Listing 7.1 shows a simple example DTD, and Listing 7.2 shows a fragment from a corresponding schema, so you can compare them. Notice first that the DTD is smaller than the schema. It's a more concise notation.

A recipe is defined to contain a title and then a body; the title must contain at least one index item so that the index in the back of the book can be constructed. The index items in this rather simplistic model appear in the recipe title exactly as they appear in the back of the book. In the 1782 edition of the book that the author used for the example, these terms are printed in capital letters in the recipe titles.

The DTD cannot force a title to contain at least one index item. It can *allow* one or more index items but cannot *require* them. The schema in Listing 7.2 specifies that a title must contain at least one index item, however, thus enforcing the restriction.

Notice also how the DTD uses a comment between the declarations for title and indexItem to describe the restriction; you cannot include comments inside declaration in XML DTDs. The XML schema has an annotation inside the element definition for title, and you can easily imagine an interactive XML editor that could display such annotations. Listing 7.3 shows a short document that is valid both with the schema and with the DTD.

Listing 7.1: A Short DTD

```
<!ELEMENT recipe
    (title, body)
```

```
>
<!ATTLIST recipe
    page #CDATA #REQUIRED
>

<!ELEMENT title
    (#PCDATA|indexItem)*
>

<!--* An indexItem appears at least once in every title *-->
<!ELEMENT indexItem
    (#PCDATA)*
>
<!ELEMENT body
    (#PCDATA)*
>
```

Listing 7.2: A Sample XML Schema (fragment)

```
<element name="recipe">
    <complexType content="elementOnly">
        <element ref="title"/>
        <element ref="body"/>
        <attribute
            name="page"
            type="integer"
            use="required" />
    </complexType>
</element>

<element name="title">
    <type content="mixed">
        <annotation>
            <documentation>

                The recipe title always contains at
                least one indexItem; they are printed
                in Caps/small-caps in
                the 1782 edition of the book.

            </documentation>
        </annotation>
        <element ref="indexItem" minOccurs="1"/>
```

```
        </type>
     </element>

     <elememt name="indexItem" type="string" />

     <element name="body" type="string" />
```

Listing 7.3 A Sample Document

```
<?xml version="1.0"?>
<recipe page="286">
<title>To fry <indexItem>CELERY</indexitem>
</title>
     <body>
       Boil your celery as for a ragout, then cut it
       and dip it in batter, fry it a light brown
       in hog's-lard; Put it on a plate,
       and pour melted butter
       upon it.

     </body>
</recipe>
```

LINKING A SCHEMA AND A DOCUMENT

To connect an XML schema to a document, you use one of two attributes that are defined in a namespace published by the W3C:

```
<recipe
     xmlns:xsi=
  "http://www.w3.org/2001/XMLSchema-instance"
   xsi:schemaLocation="recipe.schema">

   . . .

</recipe>
```

or

```
<recipe
     xmlns:xsi=
  "http://www.w3.org/2000/10/XMLSchema-instance"
```

```
    xsi:nonamespaceSchemaLocation="recipe.schema">
. . .

</recipe>
```

WARNING

Be careful to capitalize these attributes correctly; like all XML attributes, they are case-sensitive!

You can include URLs for multiple XML schemas in the attribute values, separating them with white space:

```
<recipe
    xmlns:xsi=
"http://www.w3.org/2001/XMLSchema-instance"
    xsi:nonamespaceSchemaLocation=
 "recipe.schema ../metadata.schema">
. . .

</recipe>
```

The URLs here are *relative*, but they could just as well be complete. In fact, the XML Schema Recommendation (www.w3.org/TR/xmlschema-1/ #schema-loc) specifies that these URLs are each a "namespace URI," and a recent amendment to the namespace URI deprecates the use of relative URLs. In practice, however, you can probably expect an XML schema processor to download your schema from either an absolute or a relative URL.

```
<recipe
    xmlns:xsi=
"http://www.w3.org/2000/10/XMLSchema-instance"
    xsi:nonamespaceSchemaLocation="
        http://www.holoweb.net/~liam/old-books/
➡raffald/recipe.schema
        http://www.holoweb.net/~liam/old-books/_
➡/metadata.schema">
. . .

</recipe>
```

Summary

The purpose of a schema is to specify the elements that are allowed in your documents, the attributes they can have, and what they can contain. An XML schema is more powerful than a DTD because a schema enables you to specify the *text content* of elements.

This chapter compares DTDs to schemas, shows you when to use schemas, and demonstrates converting a DTD to a schema. It also explains how to link a schema to a document. The next chapter builds on this by teaching you how to create your own schemas.

Chapter 8
WRITING XML SCHEMAS

You've seen how to write a document type definition (DTD) in Chapter 6, "Creating Your Own DTD," and you had a brief look at schemas in Chapter 7, "An Introduction to XML Schemas." Now we'll go into a lot more detail and show you how to write your own schema.

Adapted from *Mastering™ XML, Premium Edition*, by Chuck White, Liam Quin, and Linda Burman
ISBN 0-7821-2847-5   1,155 pages $49.99

TIP

If you're not sure what a schema is, or what it's for, review Chapter 7 before diving into this chapter.

SCHEMA VARIATIONS

Three main kinds of schemas were in use at the time of writing:

- ▶ W3C XML
- ▶ Microsoft XML
- ▶ RELAX

We'll discuss each of these in the following sections, and then we'll look at each in more detail. We'll spend the most time on the W3C XML Schema because it's the most important.

The W3C XML Schema

The W3C XML Schema specification is the most widely used XML schema today, and this specification is divided into three parts:

- ▶ XML Schema Part 0: Primer (`www.w3.org/TR/xmlschema-0`), which is not a "normative" document. In other words, implementations don't have to verify that they conform with this part.

- ▶ XML Schema Part 1: Structures (`www.w3.org/TR/xmlschema-1`), which defines the basic syntax of XML schemas.

- ▶ XML Schema Part 2: Datatypes (`www.w3.org/TR/xmlschema-2`), which defines facilities for specifying data types on elements and attributes.

The schema version used in this book is from the W3C Recommendation dated May 2, 2001. Before writing your own XML schema, check the URLs we've provided here for a later version or amendments to the current recommendation.

The Microsoft XML Schema

The oldest schema is Microsoft's XML Schema, called XML Data Reduced (XDR). Microsoft's XML Schema was used in the initial version of SOAP (Simple Object Access Protocol) and is supported by some Microsoft tools, including the Microsoft XML parser for Internet Explorer, MSXML. You can read about Microsoft's XML Schema at `http://msdn.microsoft.com/library/default.asp?url=/library/en-us/xmlsdk30/htm/xmconrepresentingthexmlschemaasadtd.asp`; it has largely been eclipsed by the W3C XML Schema. Microsoft has a tool to convert an XDR schema to W3C XML at `http://msdn.microsoft.com/downloads/default.asp?URL=/code/sample.asp?url=/msdn-files/027/001/539/msdncompositedoc.xml`.

The RELAX Schema

RELAX (REgular LAnguage description for XML) is a Japanese national standard, and you may find it a useful bridge to the W3C XML Schema if you're currently using XML DTDs. It's at `www.xml.gr.jp/relax`.

THE W3C XML SCHEMA

A W3C XML Schema is an XML document whose elements describe the structure of documents that conform to that schema. You use a schema to specify which elements are allowed where and their attributes and content. Unlike a DTD, a schema can also specify which textual content is allowed in an element or attribute, as well as describe the data type for the element.

A schema defines elements and attributes, just as a DTD does. It also defines the possible content of an element or attribute. You define content by associating a *type* with an element or attribute. A type can be one of those built into the XML Schema specification, such as `integer` (a whole number), or it can be one you make up, such as `telephoneNumber` or `properNoun`.

Let's start by looking at an example, and then we'll discuss it piece by piece. Listing 8.1 shows a schema for a simple recipe, which has a title and then a flowing body of text with embedded ingredient elements. Listing 8.2 shows a sample document that validates against this schema; notice the `xsi:noNamespaceSchemaLocation` attribute that says how to find the schema.

Listing 8.1: A Sample Schema

```xml
<?xml version="1.0" encoding="UTF-8"?>
<xsd:schema
    xmlns:xsd="http://www.w3.org/2001/XMLSchema"
    elementFormDefault="qualified">

    <xsd:element name="Recipe">
    <xsd:annotation>
      <xsd:documentation>
        A Recipe from the 1782 English Housekeeper book
      </xsd:documentation>
    </xsd:annotation>
    <xsd:complexType>
      <xsd:sequence>
        <xsd:element ref="title"/>
        <xsd:element ref="Body"/>
      </xsd:sequence>
    </xsd:complexType>
  </xsd:element>

  <xsd:element name="title" type="xsd:string">
    <xsd:annotation>
      <xsd:documentation>The title of a recipe
      </xsd:documentation>
    </xsd:annotation>
  </xsd:element>

  <xsd:element name="Body">
    <xsd:annotation>
      <xsd:documentation>container for the content
      </xsd:documentation>
    </xsd:annotation>
    <xsd:complexType mixed="true">
      <xsd:choice>
        <xsd:element ref="ingredient" minOccurs="0"
        maxOccurs="unbounded"/>
                </xsd:choice>
    </xsd:complexType>
  </xsd:element>

  <xsd:element name="ingredient" type="xsd:string">
```

```
    <xsd:annotation>
      <xsd:documentation>A single ingredient
      </xsd:documentation>
    </xsd:annotation>
  </xsd:element>
</xsd:schema>
```

Listing 8.2: OxfordJohn.xml Linked to the Schema

```
<?xml version="1.0" standalone="yes"?>
<Recipe
    xmlns:xsi="http://www.w3.org/2001/
    ➥XMLSchema-instance"
    xsi:noNamespaceSchemaLocation="recipe.xsd">
  <title>Oxford John</title>
  <Body>
    TAKE a stale leg of
        <ingredient>mutton</ingredient>,
    cut it in as thin collops as you possibly
    can, take out all the fat sinews, season
    them with <ingredient>mace</ingredient>,
    <ingredient>pepper</ingredient>, and
    <ingredient>salt</ingredient>,
    strew among them a little shred
    <ingredient>parsley</ingredient>,
    <ingredient>thyme</ingredient>,
    and two or three
    <ingredient>shalot</ingredient>s,
    put a good lump of
    <ingredient>butter</ingredient>
    into a stew-pan; when
    it is hot put in all your collops,
    keep stirring them with a wooden
    spoon till they are three parts done,
    then add half a pint of
    <ingredient>gravy</ingredient>, a little
    <ingredient>juice of lemon</ingredient>,
    thicken it a little with
    <ingredient>flour</ingredient> and
    <ingredient>butter</ingredient>,
    let them simmer four or five minutes
    and they will be quite enough, if you
    let them boil, or have them
```

```
ready before you want them,
they will grow hard: serve them up hot, with
<ingredient>fried bread</ingredient>
cut in dices, over and round them.
</Body>
</Recipe>
```

This example starts with the xml declaration (because a schema is an XML file), followed by the main schema element:

```
<?xml version="1.0" encoding="UTF-8"?>
<xsd:schema
    xmlns:xsd="http://www.w3.org/2001/XMLSchema"
    elementFormDefault="qualified">


    . . .


</xsd:schema>
```

The schema element associates the namespace prefix xsd (XML Structure Definitions) with the URI that's been assigned to the W3C XML Schema as of the time of writing this book. A schema-aware processor can process any elements given that prefix. You could also use a default namespace if you prefer:

```
<schema
    xmlns="http://www.w3.org/2001/XMLSchema"
    elementFormDefault="qualified">


    . . .


</schema>
```

Some people find the version with the explicit prefix more readable, and because the most widely used tool for creating schemas (XML Spy at www.xmlspy.com) includes them, we've retained them.

Within the schema element is a sequence of declarative elements. The first of these declares an element called Recipe:

```
<xsd:element name="Recipe">
<xsd:annotation>
  <xsd:documentation>
```

```
    A Recipe from the 1782 English Housekeeper book
  </xsd:documentation>
 </xsd:annotation>
 <xsd:complexType>
  <xsd:sequence>
   <xsd:element ref="title"/>
   <xsd:element ref="Body"/>
  </xsd:sequence>
 </xsd:complexType>
</xsd:element>
```

This says that any document using this schema can include an element called Recipe. It then goes on to describe that element:

- ► The element represents a recipe from the 1782 *English House-keeper* book.

- ► The element must contain a sequence: first a title element and then a Body element.

Already we've done something that a DTD cannot: We have associated a short description with the element. An XML editor might use this description in an "insert Element" menu, for example. Here is a DTD version (placing the annotation in a comment, which is the best we can do):

```
<!--* Recipe: A Recipe from the 1782 English Housekeeper book
*-->
<!ELEMENT Recipe
   (title, Body)
>
```

After defining Recipe, we move on to title:

```
<xsd:element name="title" type="xsd:string">
 <xsd:annotation>
  <xsd:documentation>The title of a recipe
  </xsd:documentation>
 </xsd:annotation>
</xsd:element>
```

A title contains a simple string: it's given a type of xsd:string, which simply means that the title must contain character data, and not elements. You can see the full list of types built into the XML schema in Appendix B, "XML Schema Reference."

Next let's look at Body, because (as bodies usually are) it's slightly more interesting:

```xsd
<xsd:element name="Body">
  <xsd:annotation>
    <xsd:documentation>container for the content
    </xsd:documentation>
  </xsd:annotation>
  <xsd:complexType mixed="true">
    <xsd:choice>
      <xsd:element ref="ingredient"
        minOccurs="0" maxOccurs="unbounded"/>
    </xsd:choice>
  </xsd:complexType>
</xsd:element>
```

You can see that a Body element has its mixed attribute set to true, which means that Body has mixed content: text and elements. The only element actually allowed in the mixture is ingredient, and there can be any number of those. The minimum is zero, and the maximum is unbounded, meaning more than you can count.

In a DTD, you might write the following:

```
<!-* Body: container for the content *->
<!ELEMENT Body
   (#PCDATA|ingredient)*
>
```

Finally, the ingredient element is a simple string:

```xsd
<xsd:element name="ingredient" type="xsd:string">
  <xsd:annotation>
    <xsd:documentation>A single ingredient
    </xsd:documentation>
  </xsd:annotation>
</xsd:element>
```

Now we've looked at a complete example. The following sections show you the various components in more detail and introduce you to defining your own types above and beyond `string`, `integer`, and friends.

WARNING

The XML Specification uses the term "element type" to refer to the *name* of an element. In the W3C XML Schema, the *type* of an element is not the same as its XML *element type* but refers instead to what it can *contain*.

Declaring Elements

We've seen examples of declaring elements in the previous section; it's time to get a little more formal. The `xsd:element` element looks like this, in a DTD:

```
<!ELEMENT element
(
    annotation?,
    (complexType | simpleType)?,
    (unique | key | keyref)*
)
>
```

NOTE

The DTD in the specification uses parameter entities for all the element names so that you can declare them with a namespace prefix. For clarity, we've expanded them to get element names here.

The annotation is intended for human use; you could put elements of your own inside it too, using a different namespace. Some people place documentation in DocBook or HTML there.

We then move to the *type* of the element, which can be either complex or simple. A *complex type* contains other elements, and a *simple type* doesn't. If the type is built in, you use the `type` attribute to the element `element`. If it's a type you've defined yourself elsewhere, you can refer to it in the same way. Otherwise, you can define a type for this element right here, using `simpleType` if the element you're defining can't contain subelements. If it might contain subelements, you use `complexType`.

The `unique`, `key`, and `keyref` elements establish database-style relational properties. You can say, for example, that the content of an element must be unique, that an element's value is to be used as an index key for searching, or that the value must appear in another element defined as a key.

In a DTD, elements are generally declared along with their attributes and content models, but before we get into attributes, we need to explain more about types.

Types Explained

Consider a DTD representing an XML view of a database of employee records. The records include contact information, such as a `homePhone` and `postalCode` or `ZIPcode` elements. Now, a DTD lets us declare an element called `homePhone`, but a schema goes one step further: we can say that a `homePhone`, a `workPhone`, and a `cellPhone` are all examples of telephone numbers, wherever they occur. This gives us a number of benefits:

▶ We can define the content of a telephone number in one place so that if we need to refine our definition, we have to change it in only one place.

▶ Because the definitions are all the same, users of the schema won't be frustrated, for example, by being able to enter an area code in one place but not another.

▶ Anyone reading the schema will immediately understand that `cellNumber` is about telephones and not about prisons. The type name helps people understand the meaning of the markup.

▶ We can use software to find all telephone numbers for a given person, without having to list them explicitly. This explicit knowledge representation lets us build smarter applications in a standard way.

Let's look at how to go about defining a type and at how to represent that type in an XML schema.

A Telephone Number Type

Let's define a telephone number. Now, if you live in North America, you probably think of a telephone number as something like this:

```
416-555-1212
```

In this case, 416 indicates a city, 555 indicates an area within the city, and 1212 is a person's number. You also know that you have to put the digit 1 in front of that number when you dial it (unless you're in an area that uses 10-digit dialing).

We could model this telephone number as a regular expression:

```
(long-distance-prefix? area-code)? local-code number
```

Using the regular expressions defined by the W3C Schema data types specification, we can write this as a pattern, in which \d represents a single digit:

```
((1-)?\d\d\d-)?\d\d\d-\d\d\d
```

Two problems are associated with this definition:

► It's difficult to read.

► It's wrong.

The definition is difficult to read, but perhaps not too difficult if you're familiar with regular expressions. The real problem comes when we try to write the telephone number:

```
416-555-1212 extension 409, or, if busy, ext. 410
```

The first part matches what we expect, but we need to add room for an extension.

Now we are starting to add structure under a telephone number, and we might want to consider subelements:

```
<workNumber>
  <areacode>416</areacode>
  <exchange>555</exchange>
  <number>1212</number>
  <extension>409, or, if busy, ext. 410</extension>
</workNumber>
```

Marking up these subelements might be a hassle, but now a program can find all users with the same area code and perhaps even check that data against a database of cities. How far you go with this depends on your application and on the use cases you have developed.

Unfortunately, our sample markup still won't work when we have someone from another country. In the following example, the first number is for the UK, and the second is for Australia:

```
+44 (0)151 342 00192
```

Part ii

```
+61 2 9144 2483
```

The + sign at the start means to dial your "international prefix," usually 011 if you are dialing from the United States. You might not have many overseas customers or employees, but one day an employee will go on vacation to Wales or you'll get *one* customer, and suddenly you'll need to deal with the situation. If you rarely need to do so, you might simply allow an exception element:

```
<workNumber>
  <exception>+61 2 9144 2483</exception>
</workNumber>
```

You'll never be able to keep up with the possible formats for all countries, so you might as well give up and say string for this one.

Finally, if you have a lot of international numbers, you may need something more structured:

```
<workNumber>
    <countryCode>61</countryCode>
    <countryNumber>2 9144 2483</countryNumber>
</workNumber>
```

A few months ago, a Canadian friend was unable to purchase a ticket over the Internet from a major airline because he had to have a "valid zip code." The database programmer had defined a zip code as a sequence of digits, and although the booking software asked for my friend's country, province, and city, it still wanted his zip code and M5A 3C7, which is a Canadian postal code, didn't cut it. When he tried entering 00000 for his zip code, the database checked against his credit card account, found that didn't match, and refused the transaction.

WARNING

Whenever you are designing types, you have to consider all the exceptions. You can't say, "Most values are like this, so this is all I will allow," because then you've failed to represent the data you have.

If we were writing a DTD, we'd have written the content model and moved on at this point; with a schema, we have freedom to choose between subelements and regular expressions, freedom to choose the *granularity* at which we control the data.

Telephone Numbers in a Schema

Now that we've done some initial analysis, let's try to represent this telephone number type in a schema. In this example, we use either a U.S.-style number or an international number, so we'll start with a choice. Each branch of the choice is a sequence. Figure 8.1 shows one way we could encode the schema, as shown by XML Spy (www.xmlspy.com), and Listing 8.3 shows the corresponding text.

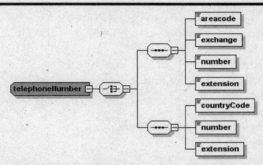

FIGURE 8.1: The W3C XML Schema data type definition for telephone number (graphical)

Listing 8.3: W3C XML Schema Data Type Definition for Telephone Number (Textual)

```
<xsd:complexType name="telephoneNumber">
    <xsd:choice>
      <xsd:sequence>
        <xsd:element name="areacode">
          <xsd:simpleType>
            <xsd:restriction base="xsd:integer">
              <xsd:maxInclusive value="999"/>
            </xsd:restriction>
          </xsd:simpleType>
        </xsd:element>
        <xsd:element name="exchange">
          <xsd:simpleType>
            <xsd:restriction base="xsd:integer">
              <xsd:maxInclusive value="999"/>
            </xsd:restriction>
          </xsd:simpleType>
        </xsd:element>
```

Part ii

```
<xsd:element name="number">
  <xsd:simpleType>
    <xsd:restriction base="xsd:integer">
      <xsd:maxInclusive value="999"/>
    </xsd:restriction>
  </xsd:simpleType>
</xsd:element>
<xsd:element name="extension">
  <xsd:simpleType>
    <xsd:restriction base="xsd:integer">
      <xsd:maxInclusive value="999"/>
    </xsd:restriction>
  </xsd:simpleType>
</xsd:element>
</xsd:sequence>
<xsd:sequence>
  <xsd:element name="countryCode"
  type="xsd:string"/>
  <xsd:element name="number"
   type="xsd:string"/>
  <xsd:element name="extension"
   type="xsd:string"/>
</xsd:sequence>
</xsd:choice>
</xsd:complexType>
```

Although the XML markup is rather fearsome at first, it's actually rather simple. The values for U.S. telephone numbers are integers with a maximum of 999; probably we could have set a minimum of 100 too. Each number has two definitions. In other words, an element can have a different content depending on where it occurs. This is a major departure from validation with an XML DTD and is considerably more powerful.

You'd use this type by putting it in your XML schema at the top level, as a child of schema, and then referring to it:

```
<xsd:element name="homePhone"
type= "telephoneNumber"/>
```

Now you can refer to that data type wherever you need it, which is what we started out wanting to do. But the actual act of creating the complex type is still a mystery, because we haven't shown you all the possibilities.

Using Patterns

We mentioned earlier that you can use *patterns*, or *regular expressions*, to constrain the contents of an element. This is a powerful feature of the W3C XML Schema specification, and it's worth taking some time to understand it.

The idea is that all content of the element must match the pattern. For example, the pattern "\d" matches a single digit, so the following fragment from a schema specifies that an areacode element's content must have three digits:

```
<xsd:element name="areacode">
  <xsd:simpleType>
    <xsd:restriction base="xsd:string">
      <xsd:pattern value="\d\d\d"/>
    </xsd:restriction>
  </xsd:simpleType>
</xsd:element>
```

A valid instance of this element would be <areacode>301</areacode>.

You can make up your own patterns using the following simple building blocks:

Letters and numbers   represent themselves. Given <xsd:pattern value="hello"/>, the element's content must be exactly the string hello.

a|b|c   matches exactly one of a, b, or c. You can use any pattern instead of a, b, or c, and you can have any number of "|" characters (pronounced *or).

(a)   is the same as a; you use the brackets for grouping, as you'll see.

.   (the period) matches any single character except a newline (\n) or carriage return (\r). b.y matches boy, bay, b}y, b y, and so on.

a?   matches either a or nothing. The pattern wine?d matches both wind and winded, so an element e with that pattern as a constraint could have content either <e>winded</e> or <e>wind</e>.The pattern (dis)?comfort matches either comfort or discomfort.

a* matches zero or more of a. The pattern (tick|tock)* for e would allow <e></e>, <e>tick</e>, <e><tickticktock- tickticktock</e>, and so on.

a+ is like a* but is one or more, not zero or more.

a{2,5} matches aa, aaa, aaaa, and aaaaa. If you leave off the second number, a{2,} matches two or more a's. The form a{17} requires exactly 17 a's. You must always give the first snumber, but a{0,2} would match zero, one, or two a's.

[w-z] matches the single character w, x, y, or z; [aeiouy] matches a vowel, and [0-9] matches a digit. Hence, f[ieo]+t matches fit, feet, and foot (and also fiiit, foet, foioioet, and so on).

[^aeiouy0-9] matches anything *except* what would be matched by [aeiouy0-9].

NOTE
Since the XML character set is Unicode, a negated character class such as [^aeiouy] matches an awful lot of characters, including Chinese, Indian, and Klingon scripts!

\\, \[, \{, \}, \] match the corresponding special characters, so where 3+5 matches 35, 335, 3335, and so on, 3\+5 matches only 3+5. You can use \ in front of \ [ ] { } ( ) * . ^ -

\r, \n, \t The sequences \r, \n, and \t match carriage return (), newline (
), and tab (&#8;) respectively.

As if that weren't enough, you can also match some *character properties.* This includes \d for a digit, \p{Sc} for a currency symbol, and many others.

You can build fairly complex patterns, with patience and care, but remember to comment them carefully! Pity those who come after you (most likely you in a month's time!).

RELAX SCHEMAS

RELAX schemas are an interesting bridge between DTDs and W3C XML Schemas. RELAX takes a somewhat different approach from that of other schema languages and defines *interfaces*. An interface is rather like a Java class description, and in fact it's possible to generate Java classes directly from RELAX schemas.

RELAX is in two parts:

▶ Core

▶ Namespace

The Core handles elements in a single namespace and their attributes; it uses the data types from W3C XML Schema Part 2. Namespace specifies how to combine multiple RELAX modules so as to handle multiple namespaces.

Listing 8.4 shows a RELAX module for our recipe example. The module is terse and clear.

Listing 8.4: RELAX Module for Poetry Example

```
<module
      moduleVersion="1.2"
      relaxCoreVersion="1.0"
      targetNamespace=""
      xmlns="http://www.xml.gr.jp/xmlns/relaxCore">
<interface>
  <export label="Recipe"/>
</interface>
<elementRule role="Recipe">
  <sequence>
    <ref label="title"/>
    <ref label="Body/>
  </sequence>
</elementRule>

<elementRule role="Body">
  <mixed>
    <ref label="ingredient" occurs="*"/>
  </mixed>
</elementRule>

<elementRule role="title" type="string"/>

<elementRule role="ingredient" type="string"/>
```

```
        <tag name="Recipe"/>
        <tag name="Body"/>
        <tag name="title"/>
        <tag name="ingredient"/>
    </module>
```

SUMMARY

This chapter has introduced you to writing W3C XML Schemas and has mentioned some other schema specifications. It's not been possible to show all the features of XML schemas by any means. That would take several chapters. But perhaps now the W3C specifications will make sense to you, especially the Primer. You can also get started with products such as XML Spy or XML Authority from TIBCO, both of which can convert between different schema types.

In the next part of this book you'll learn about XHTML, an XML-compliant version of HTML that is now considered by the W3C to be the new HTML standard.

PART iii
WORKING WITH XHTML

Chapter 9
XHTML Structure and Form

When the World Wide Web Consortium (W3C) made the move from HTML to XHTML, structure and form moved into the spotlight. As Web developers, most of us never *really* paid attention to structure. Some of us knew that DOCTYPE declarations existed, but few of us actually used them. We knew that there were a few required elements, but if we accidentally missed one, no harm, no foul. The time of lazy markup is over!

The usual reaction to this idea is outrage, and if not outrage, a little groaning and moaning. However, we're convinced that after you read this chapter, you'll agree with us. Not only will XHTML's strict rules make it easier for you to troubleshoot problems, but they will also make it easier for you to learn the language.

Adapted from *Mastering™ XHTML*, by Ed Tittel, Chelsea Valentine, Lucinda Dykes, and Mary Burmeister

ISBN 0-7821-2820-3   1,056 pages $39.99

A WELL-FORMED DOCUMENT

The concept of a "well-formed" document is not new; however, it's central to XHTML and therefore is the first item we discuss. As you may know, XHTML is an application of XML—which means that it adheres to requirements defined by the XML specification. XML defines two types of constraints for documents:

Well-formedness constraints   Every XML document must follow a small handful of XML syntax and document rules. These rules are easy to follow and are a requirement for any XML, and therefore, XHTML document.

Validity constraints   Most validity constraints are optional constraints that deal with associating a document type definition (DTD). If you include a DTD, the DTD defines rules for your elements and attributes. The document must then adhere to these rules.

All XHTML documents must be *well formed*. This means that all XHTML documents must follow XML's syntax and document rules. There aren't that many of them, and if you're familiar with HTML, you already have a head start. In the following section, we cover each and every well-formedness constraint.

TIP

Throughout this chapter, we refer to "XML" rules and requirements. Because XHTML is an application of XML, it too must follow these rules. We want to be as technically accurate as we can, and technically, the syntax rules are defined by the XML specification.

XML Rules

The rules to which XML documents must adhere make it easier to create tools to parse the documents. These rules also make XML easy to work with. The rules are simple, and some of them will be familiar if you've worked with HTML. We define XML's rules in two categories:

▶ XML syntax rules are the rules that define basic syntax requirements.

▶ XML document rules are the rules that govern basic document requirements.

XML Syntax Rules

Many of the syntax rules required for every XHTML document are stricter than those required for HTML documents. For this reason, each rule in this section is accompanied by an HTML example using HTML syntax and an XHTML example following the rules defined by each section. For example:

```
HTML:  <p>This is a paragraph.

XHTML: <p>This is a paragraph.</p>
```

In the previous example, the XHTML syntax is correct, whereas the HTML example is not considered well-formed XHTML and should not be parsed by a parser. This is not to say that a browser won't parse, interpret, and render the ill-formed markup. In most cases, browsers don't parse XHTML as XHTML, but rather as HTML. This is not expected to remain this way. Eventually, browsers will parse XHTML as XML. However, for the time being, you might want to use a stand-alone parser to check your documents for errors before uploading them to your server. See the section "Parser's Response" later in this chapter for more on parsers.

Close All Elements   All elements must be balanced with an opening and closing tag. This is not the case according to HTML, in which several elements are defined with optional closing tags, such as the p element.

```
HTML:  <p>This is a paragraph.

XHTML: <p>This is a paragraph.</p>
```

The XHTML example defines opening and closing tags that contain character data (its content). The HTML example defines an opening tag that marks the beginning of a paragraph. The only way the processor infers that the paragraph is closed in HTML is if it encounters an opening block-level element, such as another p element. The opening of another block-level element suggests that the previous block-level element is closed. This leaves element relationships a tad open-ended, and to make the distinction clearer, XHTML requires that all elements must be terminated (closed).

Empty Elements Must Be Terminated   If you already know HTML, you're probably wondering what you do with the img and br elements. Both of these elements need to be closed, but because they're empty elements, they follow a different syntax. Empty elements accept attributes but do not contain character data. For example, the following markup defines an element that contains character data (the character data is defined in bold):

```
<p>This is a paragraph.</p>
```

An empty element, on the other hand, looks like this:

```
<img src="logo.gif" alt="Corporate Logo" />
```

The img element doesn't contain any character data. Instead, it uses attributes to define its functionality. According to the img element defined in the preceding markup, the source file of the image can be found using "logo.gif" as a relative Uniform Resource Locator (URL), and the alternative text, Corporate Logo, is displayed when a user agent can't interpret images or while the image is loading.

Empty elements must also be terminated, and according to XML syntax rules, you have two options:

▶ Terminate the tag with a space and a slash, as follows:

```
<img src="logo.gif" alt="Corporate Logo" />
```

▶ Add a closing tag, as follows:

```
<img src="logo.gif" alt="Corporate Logo"></img>
```

The first option saves space and time, and logically makes a little more sense. You can use either syntax, but we suggest (and most developers use) the first option, rather than the latter.

According to HTML, you didn't need to terminate empty elements. XHTML is a tad different:

```
HTML:  <img src="logo.gif" alt="Corporate Logo">
XHTML: <img src="logo.gif" alt="Corporate Logo" />
```

WARNING

According to the XML specification, most white space within a tag is not significant. For example: `<img src="logo.gif" alt="Logo"/>` is the same as `<img src="logo.gif" alt="Logo" />`. In the second example, you should notice white space between the closing quotation mark (") and the forward slash (/). However, older browsers have problems interpreting the first example because there is no white space separating these items. If you add a space before the /, you can ensure that most older browsers will interpret the empty element without any problems.

Quote All Attribute Values   Another XHTML rule is that all attribute values be delimited with quotation marks. HTML allows several attribute values to be defined without quotation marks—although the specification recommends that they always be used.

This rule is easy enough.

```
HTML:  <table align=center>
XHTML: <table align="center">
```

The HTML example does not contain quotation marks, and the XHTML example does.

TIP

In many HTML examples, you're likely to see the attribute value in uppercase (CENTER). Most attribute *values* are not case sensitive. In this chapter, we generally use lowercase to define attribute values, for readability.

All Attributes Must Have Values   One of the trickier XML rules is that all attributes must have values. At first glance, this may seem to be an easy rule to grasp, but there's a trick or two you have to master when applying it to XHTML. For most attributes, it's fairly straightforward. For example:

```
<table align="center">
```

In this case, the align attribute has to have a value to tell the processor just how to align the table. But what do you do with Booleans that are used as stand-alone attributes? The HTML vocabulary defines a handful of stand-alone attributes that when present, turn the function on; when they're absent, the function is assumed to be off. For example:

```
<input disabled>
```

In this case, the disabled attribute is present and the input form control is disabled. If you added other attributes, the element would look something like the following:

```
<input disabled name="pet" value="cat">
```

Because this element is empty, we need to terminate it:

```
<input disabled name="pet" value="cat" />
```

(Note that we added white space before the trailing slash.) Although the preceding attribute syntax is fine according to HTML, it's not well formed according to XHTML, because all attributes must have values.

The problem is that these stand-alone attributes do not have any predefined values, and therefore, a value is not really needed. However, according to XML's rules, it must have a value, so a workaround was created. You set the attribute equal to itself:

```
<input disabled="disabled" name="pet" value="cat" />
```

This workaround is perfect because legacy browsers won't have problems with these attributes and the syntax is still well-formed XHTML.

```
HTML:  <dl compact>
XHTML: <dl compact="compact">
```

XML Is Case Sensitive   The rule that XML is case sensitive can also be defined as a validation constraint; however, we define it here because it's a primary concern to proper syntax. XML is case sensitive, which means that however the elements and attributes are named in the associated DTD is how you have to use them.

The XHTML DTDs define elements and attributes in lowercase, so we too have to adhere to it. This is a sticky point for many HTML developers who are used to writing their markup in uppercase. Most developers don't want to change, and many of them want to know why they have to. There's no compelling reason that the DTDs defined all elements and attributes in lowercase, but because it was done that way, you have to abide by those rules in your XHTML documents:

```
HTML:  <TABLE>...</TABLE>
XHTML: <table>...</table>
```

TIP
If you choose to not use a DTD, XML still requires that the opening and closing tag match. For example, <P> is not the same as <p>.

Nesting Is Important   The concept of nesting is central to document structure. Nesting defines where an element can occur. For example, the following markup defines a title element that is nested with the head element:

```
<head>
    <title>Document title</title>
</head>
```

This may seem straightforward; however, there are cases where people make mistakes. For example, can you spot the mistake in the following markup?

```
<p>You can bold a <b>word</p></b>
```

The problem is that the tags are overlapping; no one element is nested within the other. The golden rule is "what you open first, you close last." To correct this syntax, you would write:

```
<p>You can bold a <b>word</b></p>
```

Notice how the b element is nested completely within the p element.

```
HTML:   <p>You can bold a <b>word</p></b>
XHTML:  <p>You can bold a <b>word</b></p>
```

TIP

When referring to an element that is nested within another element, we call the nested element a *child* of the container element; the container is the *parent* element. Throughout this chapter we refer to nested elements as "children of a parent element."

XML Document Rules

If you thought the syntax rules were a snap to understand, you'll be delighted to read this section. There are only a few document rules that govern a well-formed XML document. We also define a few optional rules that we recommend you follow, but they're not necessary.

Required Root Element   All XML documents must have at least one root element. This is a simple rule really. Without at least one root element, there's no content. The root element must contain all other elements on the page. In XHTML, the root element is the html element. You're probably thinking, "Why didn't they change root element from html to xhtml?" That's because XHTML uses the same vocabulary as HTML, which makes it easier for parsers, authoring tools, and developers to work with XHTML.

Optional XML Declaration   The XML specification defines an optional XML declaration. The declaration uses the syntax of an XML processing instruction, but it's not one. The XML declaration announces to both developers and processors that the current document adheres to the XML specification. The declaration can accept three attributes: ver-sion, encoding, and standalone. The syntax is as follows:

```
<?xml version="1.0" encoding="UTF-8" standalone="no"?>
```

Please note that xml is lowercase and there is no white space separat-ing the < or > from the ?.

So far, there's only one version of the XML specification, and because the XML declaration is optional, you could leave it off entirely. After all, every XML document is currently an XML 1 document, so <?xml version="1.0"?> is not really necessary. However, it's unlikely that the XML specification will *never* evolve; XML documents will at some point be declaring themselves with <?xml version="9.0"?>. If you use the XML declaration to begin with, current and future proces-sors will unequivocally know how to handle your document.

TIP

A second edition of XML has been released, but it only corrected minor mis-takes in the 1.0 specification and did not represent any content-related changes to the standard. Its formal title is XML 1.0 (Second Edition).

If you're creating an XML document, you must include an XML decla-ration. However, if you're creating XHTML documents, you should use caution when adding the XML declaration. A few legacy browsers have problems interpreting the XML declaration. If you choose to leave it off, your document must be UTF-8 or UTF-16 encoded (UTF-8 is the default encoding type). In this case, you might want to include information about the character set using the http-equiv="Content-Type" conven-tion in a meta element.

WARNING

Do not include the XML declaration if your users are accessing the Web with non-XML-aware user agents (browsers). Most older versions of browsers (Inter-net Explorer 5 and earlier and Netscape 4.7 and earlier) are not XML-aware and will have trouble processing the XML declaration.

If you do include the XML declaration, there are two rules you *must* follow:

▶ It must be the first item in your document.

▶ It must begin on the first line, and in the first character position (no preceding white space).

Optional *DOCTYPE* Declaration   In the next few sections, we cover DTDs. DTDs are optional; however, if you use a DTD, you need to reference it within a DOCTYPE declaration. The use of DTDs is optional according to XML. XHTML takes a departure on this rule and requires the use of a DTD.

TIP

For a document to be a strictly conforming XHTML document, it must reference (and adhere to) one of the three XHTML DTDs. This rule is defined by the XHTML specification and is not a requirement according to the XML specification. See the section "Referencing the Three Flavors of XHTML" later in this chapter.

Parser's Response

A *parser* is a program used in conjunction with other applications. A parser prepares your document for other programs and checks for well-formedness to ensure that your document follows all of the syntax requirements. One of the first things a parser does is check that the XML document is well formed. If it's not, it reports an error message and fails to display the document.

This is most definitely not the case with HTML processors. If you break an HTML rule, the processor seems to look the other way and display your document the best it can. With XML, however, you find a stronger reliance on syntax rules and the parsers uphold this idea. If you break one of the well-formedness rules, your document will not render.

The error messages you receive are quite wonderful because most of them (they differ from parser to parser) let you know the line and position where the error occurs, and they will even define the mistake. This makes troubleshooting potential problems much easier. Figure 9.1 shows a typical error message presented by Microsoft Internet Explorer.

Part iii

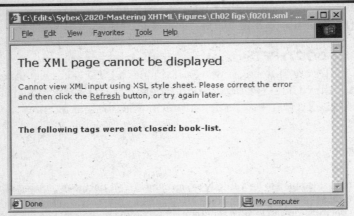

FIGURE 9.1:   An error message in Internet Explorer

A parser's response to XHTML is a little different. Ideally, the parser would verify that the XHTML document is indeed well formed; however, most parsers that are used by browsers produce error messages for XHTML documents. Because most browsers actually view XHTML as HTML, it treats the documents as HTML.

If you want to check your XHTML document for well-formedness, you have to find a non-validating parser other than the ones found in the major browsers. We recommend using the W3C's online validator to check both for well-formedness and validity.

In the future, we expect that browsers will provide better support for XHTML parsers; however, that's up to the browser vendors.

NON-VALIDATING VERSUS VALIDATING PARSERS

Essentially, there are two different types of parsers that can parse an XML document: a non-validating parser and a validating parser. A *non-validating parser* only evaluates a document against XML's well-formedness constraints. Issues of validity are not considered. A *validating parser* checks both for well-formedness and validity. For a document to be valid, you have to reference and adhere to a DTD.

The W3C offers an online HTML validating parser that validates both HTML and XHTML documents. You can upload your XHTML document, cut and paste it into a text box, or (if your page is already

CONTINUED ➡

online) enter the URL. We should warn you that the error messages it presents take some getting used to. For example:

▶ "Error: Missing DOCTYPE declaration at start of document" means that the document does not reference a DTD, and therefore, the document cannot be validated.

▶ "Error: Required attribute "ALT" not specified" means that a required attribute (the `alt` attribute, in this case) is missing.

▶ "Error: End tag for "A" omitted; possible causes include a missing end tag, improper nesting of elements, or use of an element where it is not allowed" means that a closing tag is missing. There are many reasons the validator cannot locate the closing tag:

  ▶ The elements might be incorrectly nested; therefore, the end tag is defined later in the document.

  ▶ The end tag is missing altogether.

  ▶ It's an empty element that is not terminated correctly. (In this case, the a element requires a closing tag, so we can rule out this possibility.)

The validator states the exact line and position of the error, so you don't have to blindly search through the entire document trying to locate the mistakes.

You can try out the W3C's validator at `http://validator.w3.org`.

VALIDITY

A document is considered *valid* if it adheres to all the rules defined by an associated DTD. According to the XML standard, adhering to a DTD is optional. In other words, an XML document is not required to be valid.

The XHTML standard, on the other hand, says that not only must an XHTML document be well formed, it must also be valid. This means that all XHTML documents must adhere to an XHTML DTD.

Outside of it being a requirement, there are many advantages gained by referencing a DTD. The most important of these is troubleshooting. A DTD defines the rules for your markup. For example, the DTD defines element and attribute names, where elements can occur within the document, and where attributes can occur. When creating an XHTML document by hand, you'll undoubtedly make mistakes. If you choose not to use a DTD, you'll have to comb the document with your eyes to find all your mistakes. However, if you use a DTD, you can use a validator to locate them.

DTDs as Applied to XHTML

In Chapter 6, "Creating Your Own DTD," we covered the basics of how to construct a DTD. In this section, we'll review those principles as they apply to XHTML.

In the XHTML DTD, there's a declaration that requires every document to contain the html element, and requires that the html element contain two child elements: head and body. Therefore, the declaration requires the following:

```
<html>
    <head>...</head>
    <body>...</body>
</html>
```

TIP

The previous example is a simplified version of an XHTML document and should only be used to illustrate a point. We intentionally left out some required components. For a complete example of an XHTML document, please visit the end of this chapter.

Simply put, a DTD defines rules for elements and attributes, and these rules can be checked by a validating parser. If a document fails to abide by the DTD's rules, it will produce an error message that tells you where you made mistakes.

The Heart of an XHTML DTD

The heart of a DTD consists of declarations. Four types of declarations are defined.

TIP

For each declaration example, we've simplified actual XHTML element declarations to make it easier on the eyes. Our examples do not represent the complete declaration for a given element or attribute. Most XHTML DTD declarations use entities, and the syntax can become rather complex. If you're interested in seeing the real thing, feel free to visit www.w3.org/TR/xhtml1/ DTD/xhtml1-transitional.dtd.

Element type declarations   Define element names and content models. Each content model defines the type of content an element can contain. For example, it could state that an element can only contain data, or that an element can only contain the head and body elements as children—for example:

```
<!ELEMENT html (head, body)>
```

Attribute list declarations   Define attribute names and the elements they can modify. Each attribute list declaration also defines default values and data types. For example, in XHTML, the img element is required to accept both the alt and src attributes, and the height and width attributes are optional. Here's an example:

```
<!ELEMENT img EMPTY>
<!ATTLIST img src     CDATA   #REQUIRED
             alt     CDATA   #REQUIRED
             height  CDATA   #IMPLIED
             width   CDATA   #IMPLIED   >
```

Entity declarations   Define a data item and provide a way to reference that data item. Entities are used to define common data items that will be used throughout the XML document or the DTD itself. Once a data item is declared as an entity, you can reference it using an entity name, saving you time and bytes. You can reference entities from within your document or from within a DTD subset. For example, if you want to create information that you reuse a lot in a DTD subset, such as the group of heading elements, you can create an entity for those values—for example:

```
<!ENTITY % heading "H1|H2|H3|H4|H5|H6">
```

Notation declarations   Identify objects that are not to be parsed as XML. Because all text in an XML document is parsed by the XML parser (unless otherwise indicated), there must be some way to identify items that are not XML. For example, if

Part III

you want to include a GIF image, you would need a way to tell the processor to not parse the GIF image as XML. A notation declaration does just that—for example:

```
<!NOTATION gif SYSTEM "image/gif">
```

These are the only four types of declarations that you will find in a DTD. They are not as simple as they may appear. Each declaration type can take on many different forms—although these forms are not necessary for our discussion of DTDs. For more on these declarations, visit the XML specification at www.w3.org/TR/1998/REC-xml-19980210.

REFERENCING THE THREE FLAVORS OF XHTML

There are three variations of XHTML: Strict, Transitional, and Frameset. Many developers/writers refer to them as the "three flavors" of XHTML. Each variant is defined by its own DTD. As the document author, you reference which DTD the document supports. When you reference one of the DTDs, you're providing the processor with a list of elements and attributes and with the rules defining their relationships. If your document breaks one of those rules, it's not valid.

The three possible DTDs are as follows:

The Strict DTD   Allows for the XHTML elements relating to document structure, leaving out most presentational elements.

The Transitional DTD   Allows for most XHTML elements, including presentational elements.

The Frameset DTD   Allows for frame markup, and is used only when defining frameset documents.

Before we define each flavor of XHTML, you learn the basic syntax needed to reference each XHTML variant.

DOCTYPE Declarations

Lucky for us, the XHTML DTDs have already been defined, and all you have to do is learn how to reference them. A *DOCTYPE declaration* is markup that references the DTD that defines the grammar for an XML document. In the following sections, we define DOCTYPE declaration syntax and point out some ways you can use these declarations to improve troubleshooting and validation.

XHTML OPPORTUNITIES

Because XHTML is an XML application, it's extensible, and therefore you can mix XML vocabularies. For example, you can add Scalable Vector Graphics (SVG) elements to an XHTML document because both are XML vocabularies.

You can also add your own elements and attributes to your XHTML documents. If you use a DTD, you must define all elements and attributes that are used in your document. This means that you would also need to extend your XHTML DTD. To do so requires that you can read and write a DTD.

Syntax

DOCTYPE declaration syntax is not that complicated. There are a few parts to the declaration, but first you need to understand the delimiters used.

All XML declarations, including DOCTYPE declarations, begin with a less than symbol and an exclamation point (<!). The declaration is closed with just a greater-than character (>). What we have so far is:

```
<!>
```

WARNING
Note that this is not a comment tag!

All declarations use a keyword to identify their type. For DOCTYPE declarations, this keyword is DOCTYPE (all uppercase). The keyword must be added directly after the exclamation point. No white space is allowed. If you add the keyword, you have the following:

```
<!DOCTYPE>
```

You're not yet done, because after all, the DOCTYPE declaration must reference the file, and as of yet you've only identified the type of declaration. Four (or three, depending on the type of DOCTYPE declaration) other pieces of information must be added:

Type of document   This is essentially the root element.

```
<!DOCTYPE rootelement>
```

In XHTML, this must be html, in all lowercase, as follows:

```
<!DOCTYPE html>
```

Type of DTD   Identifies whether the document is using a DTD that is not publicly defined (SYSTEM) or one that is and has a public identifier available (PUBLIC).

```
<!DOCTYPE html KEYWORD>
```

For example:

```
<!DOCTYPE html PUBLIC>
```

Public identifier of the DTD   A Uniform Resource Name (URN) that is recognized as a public identifier for the DTD. A public identifier is used only if the keyword PUBLIC is used; when you do include an identifier, the syntax looks like this:

```
<!DOCTYPE rootelement KEYWORD "identifier">
```

For example:

```
<!DOCTYPE html PUBLIC "-//W3C//DTD
    XHTML 1.0 Strict//EN">
```

URL of the DTD   Defines the location of the external DTD subset (essentially, the DTD). When you've added this component, you get the following:

```
<!DOCTYPE rootelement KEYWORD "identifier" "URL">
```

For example:

```
<!DOCTYPE html PUBLIC "-//W3C//DTD
    XHTML 1.0 Strict//EN"
   "http://www.w3.org/TR/xhtml1DTD/
    ➥xhtml1-strict.dtd">
```

TIP

As an XHTML developer, if you want to use one of the three XHTML DTDs—and you should—all you have to do is add one of the three DTD declarations. For example, you would include the preceding markup as the first line of your XHTML document. In the following sections, we define how to include DTD declarations within an internal subset (within the DOCTYPE declaration itself); however, this is not necessary for using the XHTML DTDs. One of the rare reasons you would want to know how to use internal subsets is if you're creating your own declarations.

Internal versus External

In the previous section, you saw how to reference an external DTD document. However, DTDs can be defined both externally and internally. Although you're not likely to use internal declarations, if you're only using XHTML elements, there's a chance that you will want to extend your markup and add your own elements. If this is the case, you need to know all your options.

DOCTYPE declarations reference DTDs, but just where do those definitions reside? There are several options for referencing definitions:

▶ Declare all the definitions within the DOCTYPE declaration itself:

```
<!DOCTYPE rootelement [document type definitions]>
```

▶ Declare all definitions in an external document that is referenced using a SYSTEM identifier:

```
<!DOCTYPE rootelement SYSTEM "URL">
```

▶ Declare some definitions in an external document and reference them using a SYSTEM identifier, and also declare some definitions within the DOCTYPE declaration:

```
<!DOCTYPE rootelement SYSTEM
  "URL" [document type definitions]>
```

▶ Reference a PUBLIC DTD:

```
<!DOCTYPE rootelement PUBLIC "identifier" "URL">
```

▶ Reference a PUBLIC DTD, and also define some additional definitions within the DOCTYPE declaration:

```
<!DOCTYPE rootelement PUBLIC
  "identifier" "URL" [document type definitions]>
```

In each case, the declarations are either defined internally as an internal subset or externally as an external subset. The DTD is seen as a combination of all internal and external definitions. XHTML only uses an external subset for DTDs.

Referencing a System DTD

If you use the SYSTEM keyword, it must be followed by the URL that references the DTD. This URL can be an absolute or relative address, the same as when referencing any document on your server or the Web. For example, if the DTD resides in the same directory as the file that is referencing it, you could use relative addressing:

```
<!DOCTYPE classListing SYSTEM "classlisting.dtd">
```

Part iii

However, if the DTD resides on another machine, you need to provide an absolute URL to identify it:

```
<!DOCTYPE classListing SYSTEM
    "http://www.lanw.com/DTDs/classlisting.dtd">
```

XHTML DOCTYPE declarations do not use system identifiers; they use public identifiers, as described in the following section.

Referencing a Public DTD

Several common DTDs can also be referenced using a name in addition to a URL. This name, known as the *public identifier*, is a unique string that can be used to reference a DTD. If the processor recognizes the public identifier, it will translate that into the URL of the DTD. If it does not recognize the public identifier, it looks to the URL in the declaration.

For the processor to recognize, and be able to translate, a public identifier, it has to be hard-wired into the processor. The idea is that this might all change: There may eventually be public identifier repositories that allow processors to look up a public identifier and download the DTD. However, we'll have to wait for that functionality.

If you do use a public identifier, you have to use the PUBLIC keyword, followed by the public identifier and URL. This is how you reference public XHTML DTDs:

```
<!DOCTYPE html PUBLIC "-//W3C//DTD
   XHTML 1.0 Strict//EN"
    "http://www.w3.org/TR/xhtml1DTD/
      ➥xhtml1-strict.dtd">
```

XHTML DTDs

As we mentioned, there are three different variations of XHTML. Each has its own DTD. Again, the three variations are Strict, Transitional, and Frameset. They were also defined in HTML 4, so they may look familiar.

Strict DTD

The Strict DTD is not used often because it doesn't allow the deprecated markup that is sometimes necessary when older browsers are viewing documents.

WARNING

Elements and attributes that are defined as *deprecated* are not expected to be included in the next version of the XHTML specification. Most formatting elements and attributes are deprecated in favor of using Cascading Style Sheets (CSS).

The Strict DTD also assumes that you're using style sheets to format your document. This can be a problem because many older browsers don't support style sheets. If you use the Strict DTD, you have to use the following DOCTYPE declaration:

```
<!DOCTYPE html PUBLIC "-//W3C//DTD
XHTML 1.0 Strict//EN"
 "http://www.w3.org/TR/xhtml1
  ➥/DTD/xhtml1-strict.dtd">
```

You can also abbreviate the URL and define the DOCTYPE declaration as the following:

```
<!DOCTYPE html PUBLIC "-//W3C//DTD
XHTML 1.0 Strict//EN"
 "DTD/xhtml1-strict.dtd">
```

TIP

Some of you may be scratching your head wondering why you could include a relative URL to a page that isn't saved somewhere in your computer. This is a convention allowed by the W3C only for the XHTML DTDs. You cannot make a habit of using relative addresses to point to documents that do not reside on your computer.

Part iii

Transitional DTD

The XHTML Transitional DTD is based on the HTML 4.0 Transitional DTD (also known as the *loose* DTD) and supports most element and attributes except for frame-related markup. Because this DTD includes support for most deprecated elements and attributes, it's used more than any other XHTML DTD.

If you're creating an XHTML document that will be viewed in older browsers, you'll most likely need to use some of the deprecated presentational elements, such as the font and basefont elements. If you use the

Strict DTD, you cannot use these two elements—you'd have to use CSS to define presentational properties.

The syntax is similar to the Strict DOCTYPE declaration; the only difference is the public identifier and URL:

```
<!DOCTYPE html PUBLIC "-//W3C//DTD
    XHTML 1.0 Transitional//EN"
     "http://www.w3.org/TR/
        ➡xhtml1/DTD/xhtml1-transitional.dtd">
```

Frameset DTD

The XHTML Frameset DTD is based on the HTML 4.0 Frameset DTD and is used only with frameset documents. Frameset documents replace the body element with a frameset element and require the use of frame empty elements. Because a frameset requires specific elements, it gets its very own DTD.

When creating a frameset document, you'll need to use the following DOCTYPE declaration. Notice the public identifier and URL:

```
<!DOCTYPE html PUBLIC "-//W3C//DTD
    XHTML 1.0 Frameset//EN"
     "http://www.w3.org/TR/
        ➡xhtml1/DTD/xhtml1-frameset.dtd">
```

XML NAMESPACES

XML allows you to create your own elements and attributes. XML also allows developers to combine XML document types. For example, you could embed into an XHTML document elements from a document type that you created. The following would be an example of embedding your own elements into an XHTML document, but there's a possible problem; look at the bolded elements:

```
<!DOCTYPE html PUBLIC "-//W3C//DTD
    XHTML 1.0 Strict//EN"
     "http://www.w3.org/TR/xhtml1/DTD/
        ➡xhtml1-strict.dtd">
<html xmlns="http://www.w3.org/1999/xhtml">
    <head>
```

```
    <title>Working with Namespaces</title>
  </head>
  <body>
    <h1>Online Class Offerings</h1>
    <class>
      <title>Introduction to XML</title>
      <instructor>Chelsea Valentine</instructor>
    </class>
    <class>
      <title>TCP/IP for Webmasters</title>
      <instructor>Ed Tittel</instructor>
    </class>
  </body>
</html>
```

The bold lines illustrate the problem of element name conflicts. The first `title` element belongs to the XHTML document type; however, the next two `title` elements belong to our own document type. The problem arises when the processor has to decide what to do with them. How does the processor know which `title` element is which? The answer is XML namespaces.

XML namespaces allow you to use an element from one document type (such as an XML document) and embed it in another document type (such as an XHTML document). Because namespaces uniquely identify a set of elements that belongs to a given document type, they ensure that there are no element name conflicts.

The namespace in the XML recommendation document is seen as a complement to the XML specification and can be found at www.w3.org/TR/REC-xml-names. The recommendation document defines a special syntax to identify namespaces. The document defines how a collection of elements can be given unique identifiers; therefore, no matter where an element is used, you can be sure that it belongs to the namespace.

There are two ways to define a namespace:

Default namespace   Defines a namespace using the `xmlns` attribute without a prefix, and all child elements are assumed to belong to the defined namespace. XTHML uses the default namespace construct to define the XHTML namespace.

Part iii

Local namespace   Defines a namespace using the xmlns attribute with a prefix. When the prefix is attached to an element, it's assumed to belong to that namespace.

In both cases, you define a namespace using the xmlns attribute. The attribute's value is the name that identifies the namespace. A namespace name can be a Uniform Resource Identifier (URI). A URI can be a URL or a URN. Most times, you'll find URLs used. This may seem strange, but the namespace is only symbolic and does not point to a document or schema. The value should be unique.

We look at both types in the next two sections.

Default Namespaces

A *default namespace* is considered to apply to the element where it's declared and to all child elements that are not assigned to another namespace. You define the namespace as you would define an attribute: The attribute name is xmlns, and the value is the namespace name.

For example, XHTML uses the default namespace syntax to define the XHTML namespace. The xmlns attribute is defined within the html start tag and is applied to all child elements that do not have a prefix pointing to another namespace. In the following snippet of markup, the XHTML namespace is declared within the html start tag:

```
<html xmlns="http://www.w3.org/1999/xhtml">

<head>

   <title>Example Transitional XHTML Document

   </title>

</head>

<body>

   <h1>My First XHTML Document</h1>

   <p>

      <font color="#CCCC00" size="+1">

      After reading this book,

      we will become XHTML gods!

      </font>

   </p>

</body>

</html>
```

The namespace name is already defined for us, because it belongs to a public document type. If you visit the URL in the preceding code, you'll find that no content resides there. This is because it's only meant to be a symbolic unique identifier used to resolve possible element name conflicts.

If you created your own XML document, you could create your own namespace name; for example:

```
<classListing
    xmlns="http://www.lanw.com/namespace/
    ~CAonlinetraining/">
    <class>
        <title>Introduction to XML</title>
        <instructor>Chelsea Valentine</instructor>
    </class>
    <class>
        <title>TCP/IP for Webmasters</title>
        <instructor>Ed Tittel</instructor>
    </class>
</classListing>
```

In this case, we've created our own unique namespace that uses our domain name. The `classListing` element and all of its children belong to the `http://www.lanw.com/namespace/onlinetraining` namespace.

Local Namespaces

Local namespaces are similar to default namespaces; however, they add another identifier: a prefix. A local namespace can be defined anywhere within the document. In other words, you don't have to declare it within the element that it is to modify (as you do with default namespaces). In this case, you define a namespace and associate a prefix that can be used later to reference the namespace.

Local namespaces are often used when embedding document types within another document. For example, in the section "XML Namespaces," we provided an example that uses both XHTML elements and our own class elements. The XHTML elements are uniquely identified by the XHTML default namespace, but what about our class elements? Because we already have a default namespace, we will have to define a local namespace for them. In the following example, we have bolded elements to illustrate this concept:

```
<!DOCTYPE html PUBLIC "-//W3C//DTD
   XHTML 1.0 Strict//EN"
    "http://www.w3.org/TR/xhtml1/DTD/
    ➥xhtml1-strict.dtd">
<html xmlns="http://www.w3.org/1999/xhtml"
    xmlns:lanw="http://www.lanw.com/namespace/
    ➥onlinetraining">
<head>
    <title>Working with Namespaces</title>
</head>
<body>
    <h1>Online Class Offerings</h1>
    <lanw:class>
        <lanw:title>Introduction to XML
        </lanw:title>
        <lanw:instructor>Chelsea Valentine
        </lanw:instructor>
    </lanw:class>
    <lanw:class>
        <lanw:title>TCP/IP for Webmasters
        </lanw:title>
        <lanw:instructor>Ed Tittel
        </lanw:instructor>
    </lanw:class>
</body>
</html>
```

In the previous example, a local prefix is defined for the class elements:

```
xmlns:lanw="http://www.lanw.com/namespace/
➥onlinetraining"
```

The xmlns attribute is used, but notice the colon and characters that follow (:lanw). To define a local namespace, you must define a prefix that can be used as a reference later in the document. The colon separates the xmlns attribute name from the prefix. You can create your own prefix for your own document types; however, if you're using someone else's vocabulary, be sure to check and see if they have defined a prefix for you.

After you've defined the local namespace, you can reference it with the prefix. In our example, all elements identified with the prefix (`lanw`) and a colon (`:`) belong to the `http://www.lanw.com/namespace/onlinetraining` namespace. Most local namespaces are defined in the root element and then referenced when needed.

The Required XHTML Namespace

All XHTML elements and attributes belong to the XHTML namespace. Each XHTML element and attribute has its very own name—all of which belong to the same namespace. The XHTML namespace is defined as a default namespace and is a required component of an XHTML document. The `xmlns` attribute is a required attribute of the `html` element, and the `xmlns` value is fixed as `http://www.w3.org/1999/xhtml`. This makes it easy, because there's no mistaking what goes where; you should always define the XHTML namespace like so:

```
<html xmlns="http://www.w3.org/1999/xhtml">
```

Combining Namespaces

In the section "Local Namespaces," our example combined two namespaces. This is becoming a common practice. The future of XHTML is as a document structure language. Gone are the days of using XHTML as a multipurpose language for document structure, presentation, and describing metadata.

The W3C has turned its focus to creating XML applications that have dedicated tasks and that can work together. The following XML applications could be combined:

- ▶ XHTML defines document markup.

- ▶ MathML (Mathematical Markup Language) defines mathematical expressions.

- ▶ SMIL (Synchronized Multimedia Integration Language) defines synchronized multimedia tasks.

- ▶ SVG defines a scalable vector graphic language.

For example, you could add mathematical expressions to your XHTML document. The following example is defined by the XHTML specification document (we've added the bold highlighting):

```
<html xmlns="http://www.w3.org/1999/xhtml"
    xml:lang="en" lang="en">
<head>
    <title>A Math Example</title>
</head>
<body>
    <p>The following is MathML markup:</p>
    <math xmlns="http://www.w3.org/1998/
     ➥Math/MathML">
        <apply>
            <log/>
            <logbase>
                <cn> 3 </cn>
            </logbase>
            <ci> x </ci>
        </apply>
    </math>
</body>
</html>
```

There are a few ways to combine these document types. The first way, as demonstrated previously, is to define a default namespace for the root element and then redefine a default namespace for a child element. The nested default namespace is then applied to its current element and all its child elements. For example, all the elements in bold in the preceding code belong to the MathML namespace. The elements that are not in bold belong to the XHTML namespace.

The second way to combine namespaces is to define a default namespace and a local namespace in the root element. In this case, all elements that do not have a prefix belong to the default namespace, and all the elements that have a prefix belong to the associated local namespace. An example of this can found in the "Local Namespaces" section.

Finally, you can define only local namespaces and add prefixes to all the elements within the document. This is the least commonly used approach; however, there are times when you might want to use only local namespaces.

SAMPLE XHTML DOCUMENTS

In this section, we present complete XHTML document examples. Listing 9.1 shows a Strict XHTML document, Listing 9.2 shows a Transitional XHTML document, and Listing 9.3 shows a Frameset XHTML document.

Listing 9.1: A Strict XHTML Document

```
<!DOCTYPE html PUBLIC "-//W3C//DTD
  XHTML 1.0 Strict//EN"
  "http://www.w3.org/TR/xhtml1/DTD/
    ➥xhtml1-strict.dtd">
<html xmlns="http://www.w3.org/1999/xhtml">
  <head>
    <title>Example Strict XHTML Document</title>
    <link href="style.css" type="text/css"
    rel="stylesheet" />
  </head>
  <body>
    <h1>My First Strict XHTML Document</h1>
    <p>After reading this book, we will become
        XHTML gods!
    </p>
  </body>
</html>
```

Listing 9.2: A Transitional XHTML Document

```
<!DOCTYPE html PUBLIC "-//W3C//DTD
  XHTML 1.0 Transitional//EN"
  "http://www.w3.org/TR/xhtml1/DTD/
    ➥xhtml1-transitional.dtd">
<html xmlns="http://www.w3.org/1999/xhtml">
  <head>
    <title>Example Transitional XHTML Document
    </title>
  </head>
  <body>
```

Part iii

```
<h1>My First Transitional XHTML Document</h1>
<p>
   <font color="#CCCC00" size="+1">
   After reading this book, we will
   become XHTML gods!
   </font>
</p>

   </body>
</html>
```

Listing 9.3: A Frameset XHTML Document

```
<!DOCTYPE html PUBLIC "-//W3C//DTD
   XHTML 1.0 Frameset//EN"
   "http://www.w3.org/TR/xhtml1/DTD/
   ➥xhtml1-frameset.dtd">
<html xmlns="http://www.w3.org/1999/xhtml">
   <head>
     <title>Example Frameset XHTML Document</title>
   </head>
   <frameset cols="20%, *">
     <frame src="nav.html" name="navigation" />
     <frame src="index.html" name="content" />
   </frameset>
```

SUMMARY

This chapter focused on some basic XHTML concepts that must be understood to take advantage of the language. You learned how to create well-formed XHTML documents, reference DTDs, and declare and combine namespaces. The next step is to start creating your XHTML documents:

▶ See Chapter 10, "Creating Your First XHTML Document," to find out how to create your own XHTML documents.

▶ Check out Chapter 11, "Converting HTML to XHTML," for information on how to convert HTML to XHTML documents.

If you keep in mind that XHTML is an XML application and validate your documents according to one of the XHTML DTDs described in this chapter, you'll find XHTML development a simple process. The next chapter will walk you through the steps to your first XHTML document.

Chapter 10

CREATING YOUR FIRST XHTML DOCUMENT

I f you're ready to create your first XHTML document, you're in the right chapter! Here, we'll help you start a new XHTML document and save it using the appropriate file formats, demonstrate how to add document structure elements (which help browsers identify your XHTML document), and explain how to apply some common formatting elements.

Before starting this chapter, you should be familiar with elements and attributes, as well as how to apply them to your content. You were introduced to elements in Chapter 2 ("Understanding and Creating Elements") and attributes in Chapter 3 ("Understanding and Creating Attributes").

Throughout this chapter, we provide lots of code samples and figures to help guide you and to show you what your results should look like. You can substitute your own text and images if you prefer, or you can duplicate the examples in the chapter.

Adapted from *Mastering™ XHTML*, by Ed Tittel, Chelsea Valentine, Lucinda Dykes, and Mary Burmeister
ISBN 0-7821-2820-3   1,056 pages $39.99

The step-by-step instructions will work regardless of the specific content you use. After you work through this chapter, you'll have developed your first XHTML document, complete with text, headings, horizontal rules, and even some character-level formatting.

CREATING, SAVING, AND VIEWING XHTML DOCUMENTS

Exactly how you start a new XHTML document depends on which operating system and editor you're using. In general, you'll find that starting a new XHTML document is similar to starting other documents you've created. With Windows or Macintosh, you'll choose File ➤ New from within your editing program. (If you're using Unix, you'll type **vi**, **pico**, or **emacs**, and use the appropriate commands.) You'll make your new document an official XHTML document by saving it as such, which is discussed next.

Before you begin hand-coding XHTML, be aware that you should frequently save and view your work so you can see your progress. By doing so, you can make sure that things appear as you expect them to and catch mistakes within a few new lines of code. For example, we typically add a few new lines of code, save the XHTML document, then view it... then add a few more lines of code, save the document, then view it.... Exactly how often you save and view your documents depends on your preference. Chances are that at the beginning, you'll probably save it frequently.

You create an XHTML document in much the same way that you create any plain-text document. Here's the general process:

1. Open your text editor.

2. Start a new document. If you're using Windows or Macintosh, choose File ➤ New. If you're using Unix, type **vi** or **pico** to start the editor.

3. Enter the XHTML code and text you want to include. (You'll have plenty of practice in this chapter.)

TIP

We recommend that you practice using XHTML by doing the examples throughout this and other chapters.

4. Save your document. If you're using Windows or Macintosh, choose File ➤ Save or File ➤ Save As.

GUIDELINES FOR SAVING FILES

As you work your way through this chapter, keep these saving and viewing guidelines in mind:

▶ Name the file with an .htm or .html extension. Windows 3.*x* doesn't recognize four-character extensions, so you're limited to htm on that platform.

▶ If you aren't using a text-only editor such as Notepad or TeachText, verify that the file type is set to Text or ASCII (or HTML, if that's an available menu option). If you use word processing programs to create XHTML documents, save your documents as HTML, Text Only, ASCII, DOS Text, or Text With Line Breaks. The specific options *will* vary depending on the word processor you use.

▶ Use only letters, numbers, hyphens (-), underscores (_), and periods (.) in your filename. Most browsers also accept spaces in filenames; however, spaces often make creating links difficult, so it's best to avoid them.

▶ Save the document and any other documents and files associated with a particular project all in one folder. You'll find that this makes using links, images, and other advanced technologies easier.

Viewing the XHTML documents that you develop is as simple as opening them from your local hard drive in your browser. If you're working with an open XHTML document in your editor, remember to save your latest changes and then follow these steps in your browser:

1. Choose File ➤ Open, and type the local filename or browse your hard drive until you find the file you want to open. Your particular menu command might be File ➤ Open Page Or File, or Open File, but it's all the same thing.

2. Select the file and click OK to open it in your browser.

ALTERNATIVE WAYS TO OPEN FILES

Most browsers provide some clever features that can make developing XHTML files easier.

You can easily see your editing changes in a file by *reloading* it. For example, after you view a document and then save some editing changes, you can reload the document and see the latest changes. You'll probably find that clicking a button is much easier than going back through the File ➤ Open and browse sequence. Generally, you reload documents by clicking a Refresh or Reload button or by choosing a similar option from the View menu.

In addition, you can open a file by selecting it from your list of bookmarks or favorites. Creating bookmarks or favorites (which means adding a pointer to the file so you can open the file quickly) is as easy as clicking a menu option (or even just typing a keyboard shortcut) while viewing a page. Whenever you want to go back to that page, simply click the bookmark rather than choosing File ➤ Open and selecting the file. Most browsers have bookmark options; just look for a button or a menu command.

APPLYING DOCUMENT STRUCTURE ELEMENTS

After you create a new document, your first task is to include *document structure elements*, which provide browsers with information about document characteristics. For example, document structure elements identify the version of XHTML used, provide introductory information about the document, and include the title, among other similar things. Most document structure elements, although part of the XHTML document, do not appear in the browser window. Instead, these elements work behind the scenes and tell the browser which elements to include and how to display them. Although these elements do not directly produce the snazzy results you see in Web pages or help files, they are essential.

TIP

Most browsers, including Netscape Navigator and Microsoft Internet Explorer (IE), correctly display documents that do not include document structure elements. However, there's no guarantee that future versions will continue to do so or that your results will be consistent. We strongly suggest that you use the document structure elements because they're required by the XHTML specification.

All XHTML documents should include five document structure elements, nested and ordered as in the following sample markup:

```
<!DOCTYPE HTML PUBLIC
    "-//W3C//DTD XHTML 1.0 Transitional//EN"
    "http://www.w3.org/TR/xhtml1/DTD/
    ➥xhtml1-transitional.dtd">
<html xmlns="http://www.w3.org/1999/xhtml">
  <head>
    <title>Title That Summarizes the
    Document's Content</title>
  </head>
  <body>
    Mastering XHTML Document Body
  </body>
</html>
```

TIP

You can save time when creating future XHTML documents by saving document structure elements in a master document. That way, you can easily reuse them in other XHTML documents, rather than retyping them time after time. If you use an XHTML authoring program, this markup (or something similar to it) is usually the base of a new document.

The *DOCTYPE* Declaration

The DOCTYPE declaration tells browsers and validation services with which XHTML version the document complies. The XHTML 1 specification requires this nonpaired declaration, and, therefore, you should use it in all your documents. The key part of the DOCTYPE declaration is the

Part iii

document type definition (DTD), which tells browsers that the document complies with a particular XHTML version. A DTD specifies the organization that issues the specification (the World Wide Web Consortium, or W3C, in these cases) and the exact version of the specification.

Enter the DOCTYPE declaration at the top of your document, like this:

```
<!DOCTYPE html
  PUBLIC "-//W3C//DTD XHTML 1.0 Transitional//EN"
   "http://www.w3.org/TR/xhtml1/DTD/
   ➥xhtml1-transitional.dtd">
```

This example complies with the XHTML 1.0 Transitional DTD, which is the most flexible DTD. To use the XHTML 1.0 Strict DTD, you would use this code:

```
<!DOCTYPE html
  PUBLIC "-//W3C//DTD XHTML 1.0 Strict//EN"
   "http://www.w3.org/TR/xhtml1/DTD/
   ➥xhtml1-strict.dtd">
```

You can also abbreviate the URL and define the DOCTYPE declaration as the following:

```
<!DOCTYPE html PUBLIC "-//W3C//DTD
  ➥XHTML 1.0 Strict//EN"
   "DTD/xhtml1-strict.dtd">
```

As new XHTML standards evolve, you can expect this declaration to change to indicate new versions. For example, in a year or so, the DOC-TYPE declaration might look like this:

```
<!DOCTYPE xhtml PUBLIC "-//W3C//DTD
  XHTML 2.0 Transitional//EN"
   "http://www.w3.org/TR/xhtml2/DTD
   ➥/xhtml2-transitional.dtd">
```

Even after new standards appear, you don't need to revise the DOCTYPE declaration in existing documents. If your document conforms to the XHTML 1 standard, it'll conform to that standard, regardless of more recent XHTML versions.

WHICH XHTML 1 DTD SHOULD I USE?

As we explained in Chapter 9, "XHTML Structure and Form," the XHTML 1 specification comes in three varieties: Strict, Transitional, and Frameset. The Strict version prohibits everything except "pure" XHTML, and you're unlikely to use it unless you're writing XHTML documents that use no formatting elements and are relying on style sheets to make them look good. To indicate that your document complies with the Strict DTD, use the following markup:

```
<!DOCTYPE html PUBLIC "-//W3C//DTD
    XHTML 1.0 Strict//EN"
     "http://www.w3.org/TR/xhtml1/DTD/
        ➥xhtml1-strict.dtd">
```

The Transitional version is the most flexible for accommodating deprecated but still frequently used elements and attributes, including nearly all formatting elements. To indicate that your document complies with the Transitional DTD, use the following declaration:

```
<!DOCTYPE html PUBLIC "-//W3C//DTD
    XHTML 1.0 Transitional//EN"
     "http://www.w3.org/TR/xhtml1/DTD/
        ➥xhtml1-transitional.dtd">
```

The Frameset DTD is similar to the Transitional DTD, but it also supports the elements needed to use frames. To indicate that your document complies with the Frameset DTD, use the following declaration:

```
<!DOCTYPE html PUBLIC "-//W3C//DTD
    XHTML 1.0 Frameset//EN"
     "http://www.w3.org/TR/xhtml1/DTD/
        ➥xhtml1-frameset.dtd">
```

See Chapter 9 for more information on these DTDs.

The *html* Element

The html element identifies the document as either an HTML or XHTML document. To specify that it's an XHTML document, you should also add the XHTML namespace. (See Chapter 9 for more on namespaces.) The html element is necessary for older browsers that do not support the DOCTYPE declaration, and it's required by the specification. It's also helpful to people who read the XHTML markup. To use the html element along with the XHTML namespace, enter it in your document under the DOCTYPE declaration, like this:

```
<!DOCTYPE html PUBLIC "-//W3C//DTD
   XHTML 1.0 Transitional//EN"
    "http://www.w3.org/TR/xhtml1/DTD/
     ➥xhtml1-transitional.dtd">
<html xmlns="http://www.w3.org/1999/xhtml">
</html>
```

The *head* Element

Found in every XHTML document, the head element contains information about the document, including its title, scripts used, style definitions, and document descriptions. Not all browsers require this element, but most browsers expect to find any available additional information about the document within the head element. To add the head element, enter it between the html opening and closing tags, like this:

```
<!DOCTYPE html PUBLIC "-//W3C//DTD
   XHTML 1.0 Transitional//EN"
    "http://www.w3.org/TR/xhtml1/DTD/
     ➥xhtml1-transitional.dtd">
<html xmlns="http://www.w3.org/1999/xhtml">
   <head>
   </head>
</html>
```

TIP

Don't confuse this document head element, which is a structure element, with heading elements such as h1, which create heading text in a document body. We discuss heading elements later in this chapter in the "Creating Headings" section.

Additionally, the head element can contain other elements that have information for search engines and indexing programs.

The *title* Element

The title element, which the XHTML 1 specification requires, contains the document title. The title does not appear within the browser window, although it's usually visible in the browser's title bar, which has limited space. Therefore, make sure your title briefly summarizes your document's content and keep keywords at the beginning of the title. To use the title element, enter it between the opening and closing head elements, like this:

```
<!DOCTYPE html PUBLIC "-//W3C//DTD
   XHTML 1.0 Transitional//EN"
    "http://www.w3.org/TR/xhtml1/DTD/
    ➥xhtml1-transitional.dtd">
<html xmlns="http://www.w3.org/1999/xhtml">
    <head>
        <title>
            Title That Summarizes the
            Document's Content
        </title>
    </head>
</html>
```

Titles should represent the document, even if the document is taken out of context. Some good titles include the following:

▶ Sample XHTML Code

▶ Learning to Ride a Bicycle

▶ Television Viewing for Fun and Profit

Less useful titles, particularly taken out of context, include the following:

▶ Examples

▶ Chapter 2

▶ Continued

TIP

The information in the title element is also used by some search engines and indexing programs.

Part iii

WARNING

Watch out for the default titles produced by WYSIWYG editors. Always be sure to put in your own title.

The *meta* Element

The meta element is a child of the head element (that is, it can nest within head); it's also an empty element. The meta element is used to embed document meta-information. *Meta-information* contains information about the contents of the document, such as keywords, author information, and a description of the document. The primary advantage to including meta elements in your XHTML document is that these elements make it possible for search engine robots and spiders to identify, catalog, and locate the information in your document. Here's an example of some meta elements in an XHTML document:

```
<!DOCTYPE html PUBLIC "-//W3C//DTD
    XHTML 1.0 Transitional//EN"
     "http://www.w3.org/TR/xhtml1/DTD/
     ➥xhtml1-transitional.dtd">
<html xmlns="http://www.w3.org/1999/xhtml">
    <head>
        <meta name="author" content="Your name" />
        <meta name="keywords"
         content="A keyword,a keyword,a keyword" />

                    <meta name="description"
         content="This is the Home Page of
         the Web site of Your Name." />
        <title>
            Title That Summarizes the
            Document's Content
        </title>
    </head>
</html>
```

When using the meta element, remember to close it with a space and a slash before the final angle bracket (/>) because it's an empty element.

Other Children of the *head* Element

In addition to the `title` and `meta` elements, the head element may contain the following child elements:

`script`   Instructs the browser that the enclosed content is part of a scripting language such as Perl, PHP, JavaScript (also called JScript or ECMAScript), or VBScript.

`style`   Contains internal Cascading Style Sheets (CSS) information.

`link`   Defines a link. The `link` element is most commonly used to link external CSS style sheets to a document or to link the various frames that make up documents authored under the XHTML Frameset DTD.

`isindex`   Formerly used to create text controls, the `isindex` element has been deprecated in favor of the `input` element.

`base`   Defines a document's base Uniform Resource Locator (URL) using the `href` attribute. It must occur as a child of the head element and establishes a base URL for all relative references. This element is often used in conjunction with anchors to enable navigation within a single document. Another popular use of the `base` element is with a frameset where a frame is named as an attribute of the `frame` element.

TIP

A URL is a type of Uniform Resource Identifier (URI). The value of the `href` attribute can be any type of URI, such as a Uniform Resource Name (URN).

The *body* Element

The body element encloses all the elements, attributes, and information that you want a user's browser to display. Unless you're creating a framed document, almost everything else we talk about in this chapter (and the other two chapters on XHTML, Chapters 9 and 11) takes place between the body elements). To use the body element, enter it below the closing head element and above the closing `html` element, like this:

```
<!DOCTYPE html PUBLIC "-//W3C//DTD
    XHTML 1.0 Transitional//EN"
```

```
        "http://www.w3.org/TR/xhtml1/DTD/
         xhtml1-transitional.dtd">
     <html xmlns="http://www.w3.org/1999/xhtml">
        <head>
           <title>
              Title That Summarizes
              the Document's Content
           </title>
        </head>
        <body>
           All the elements, attributes,
           and information in the document
           body go here.
        </body>
     </html>
```

TIP

Throughout this chapter (and the other chapters on XHTML) we'll provide examples for you that won't include these structure elements. This doesn't mean you shouldn't include them; it just means that we're focusing on the immediate topic.

If you've been following along, save your document, view it in a browser, and compare it with Figure 10.1 to confirm that you're on the right track. The title appears in the title bar, and some text appears in the document window.

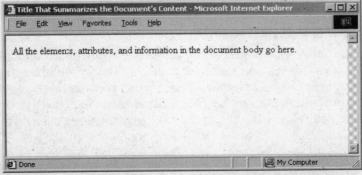

FIGURE 10.1:   Your first XHTML document, including all structure elements

TIP

Remember that you can also include the XML declaration (`<?xml version= "1.0" encoding= "UTF-8" standalone="no"?>`), but it's not required by the W3C at this time.

APPLYING BASIC ELEMENTS

After you include the structure elements, you're ready to start placing basic content in the document body. The following sections show you how to include headings, paragraphs, lists, and rules (horizontal lines). These elements constitute the basic XHTML document components and, unlike the structure elements, do appear in the browser window. Learning to apply these basic elements and attributes will prepare you to apply practically any XHTML element or attribute.

As you create your content, keep in mind that its exact appearance will vary from browser to browser. Two browsers will both display a heading bigger and bolder than body text, but the specific font, size, and emphasis will vary. In addition, users may have specific browser settings on their machine that will affect the display of the document.

About Common Attributes

In XHTML, there are several attributes that can be applied to most elements; these are known as the *common* attributes. They include:

`id="name"`   Assigns a unique name to an element within a document.

`style="style"`   Allows the author of the document to use CSS style sheets as attribute values or to define the presentation parameters for that specific element. You can use the `style` attribute with all elements except `html`, `head`, `title`, `meta`, `style`, `script`, `param`, `base`, and `basefont`.

`class="name"`   Assigns a class or a set of classes to an element. This attribute is frequently used with CSS to establish the display properties for a particular subset of elements.

`lang="language code"`   Declares the language to be applied to the element. For example, `lang="en"` declares that English is the designated language for the element.

`dir="ltr|rtl"`   Specifies the direction text should be read. This doesn't seem like an important attribute unless you remember that many of the world's languages are not read from left to right. Yes, `ltr` means "left to right" and `rtl` means "right to left," so this attribute is most useful in cases where the direction of the text is ambiguous at best and totally confusing at worst.

`title="text"`   Functions in a manner similar to the `title` element but applies only to a specific element instead of an entire document. Caveat: The attribute's behavior is not defined by the XHTML specification. Instead, the way that behavior is rendered is left up to the browser. This attribute is currently most useful on sites or documents that the author knows will be viewed by users employing IE 5 or later. The `title` attribute cannot be used with the following elements: `html`, `head`, `meta`, `title`, `script`, `param`, `base`, and `basefont`.

Deprecated Elements Abound

One of the main goals of XHTML is to separate document structure from presentation. This goal alone makes XHTML the antithesis of HTML and its "tag soup" of deprecated elements. *Deprecated elements* are elements that will be phased out of the next version of XHTML.

Although the XHTML 1.0 Transitional DTD permits the use of many of these deprecated elements, it's better to think toward the future and avoid their use altogether in favor of other elements or other options, such as CSS. Table 10.1 lists the HTML elements that have been deprecated in XHTML 1 but are still used by some authors.

NOTE
You can find information on CSS *in Mastering XML, Premium Edition* (Sybex, 2001) and *Mastering XHTML* (Sybex, 2001), which includes a Master's Reference on CSS.

TABLE 10.1: Deprecated Elements in XHTML 1

Deprecated Element	Description	Deprecated in Favor of
applet	Java applet	The object element
basefont	Base font size	CSS

TABLE 10.1 continued: Deprecated Elements in XHTML 1

DEPRECATED ELEMENT	DESCRIPTION	DEPRECATED IN FAVOR OF
center	Shorthand for div align="center"	CSS
dir	Directory list	Unordered lists (the ul element)
font	Local change to font	CSS
isindex	Single-line prompt	Using input to create text-input controls
menu	Menu list	Unordered lists (the ul element)
s or strike	Strikethrough text	CSS
u	Underlined text	CSS

When we discuss these elements in the following sections, we note that they are deprecated and give alternatives where possible.

Creating Paragraphs

One of the most common elements you'll use is the paragraph element, p, which is appropriate for regular body text. In HTML, you could use just the opening p element to mark your paragraphs. However, in XHTML, the paragraph element should be paired—use the opening element <p> where you want to start a paragraph and the closing element </p> to end the paragraph. It's easier to identify where the element begins and ends if you use both opening and closing tags.

To use the paragraph element, enter the opening and closing tags around the text you want to format as a paragraph, like this:

```
<p>
A whole paragraph goes right here.
</p>
```

TIP

It isn't necessary to type a tag's content on a separate line; <p>Paragraph goes here.</p> is also valid. We do this just to make the demonstration code easier to read.

Part iii

Figure 10.2 shows a few sample paragraphs.

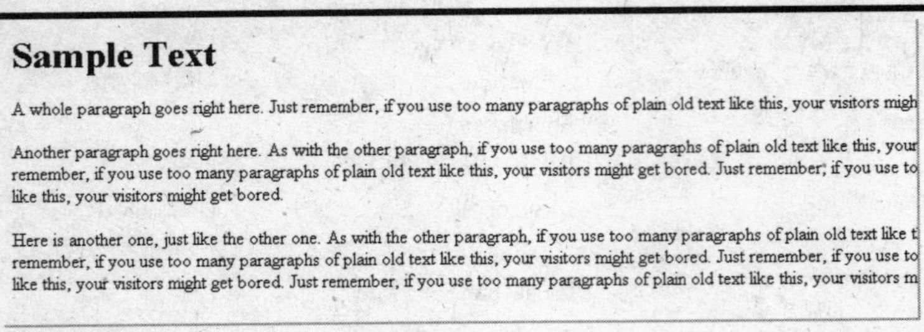

Sample Text

A whole paragraph goes right here. Just remember, if you use too many paragraphs of plain old text like this, your visitors migh

Another paragraph goes right here. As with the other paragraph, if you use too many paragraphs of plain old text like this, your remember, if you use too many paragraphs of plain old text like this, your visitors might get bored. Just remember, if you use to like this, your visitors might get bored.

Here is another one, just like the other one. As with the other paragraph, if you use too many paragraphs of plain old text like t remember, if you use too many paragraphs of plain old text like this, your visitors might get bored. Just remember, if you use to like this, your visitors might get bored. Just remember, if you use too many paragraphs of plain old text like this, your visitors m

FIGURE 10.2: Paragraph text is the most common text in XHTML documents.

The `align` attribute can also be used with the paragraph element, but it's deprecated, so we suggest using style sheets to achieve the same effect. The values of `align` are `left`, `center`, `right` or `justify`. To apply this attribute, include it in the opening paragraph element, like this:

```
<p align="center">
Paragraph of information goes here.
</p>
```

You can also apply other paragraph formats instead of the p element to achieve some slightly different paragraph formats, as explained in Table 10.2.

TABLE 10.2: Other Paragraph-Formatting Elements

ELEMENT	EFFECT
address	Used for address and contact information. Often appears in italics and is sometimes used as a footer.
blockquote	Used for formatting a quotation. Usually appears indented from both sides and with less space between lines than a regular paragraph.
pre	Effective for formatting program code or similar information (short for "preformatted"). Usually appears in a fixed-width font with ample space between words and lines.

Figure 10.3 shows how the `address` and `pre` elements appear in Internet Explorer.

Sample Text

A whole paragraph goes right here.

```
Preformatted text is pretty ugly.
You wouldn't want to read much of this.
```

Use the address element for information similar to this:
Mastering XHTML Comments
info@lanw.com

FIGURE 10.3: Special paragraph-level tags make information stand out.

Creating Headings

Headings break up large areas of text, announce topics to follow, and arrange information according to a logical hierarchy. XHTML provides six levels of headings; h1 is the largest of the headings, and h6 is the smallest. The paired tags look like this:

```
<h1>...</h1>
<h2>...</h2>
<h3>...</h3>
<h4>...</h4>
<h5>...</h5>
<h6>...</h6>
```

TIP

For most documents, limit yourself to two or three heading levels. After three heading levels, many users begin to lose track of your hierarchy. If you find that you're using several heading levels, consider reorganizing your document or dividing it into multiple documents—too many heading levels often indicates a larger organizational problem.

Here's an example of how to use the heading elements:

```
<!DOCTYPE html PUBLIC "-//W3C//DTD
  XHTML 1.0 Transitional//EN"
   "http://www.w3.org/TR/xhtml1/DTD/
    ➥xhtml1-transitional.dtd">
<html xmlns="http://www.w3.org/1999/xhtml">
```

```
<head>
    <title>Sample Headings</title>
</head>
<body>
    <h1>First Level Heading</h1>
    <h2>Second Level Heading</h2>
    <h3>Third Level Heading</h3>
</body>
</html>
```

Figure 10.4 shows how Netscape 6 displays a few heading levels.

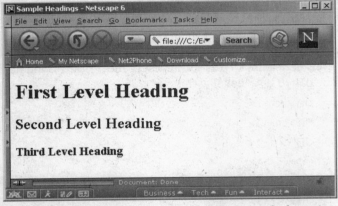

FIGURE 10.4: Heading levels provide users with a hierarchy of information.

In general, you should use heading elements only for document headings—that is, don't use heading elements for figure captions or to emphasize information within text. Why? First, you don't always know how browsers will display the heading. It might not create the visual effect you intend. Second, some indexing and editing programs use headings to generate tables of contents and other information about your document. These programs won't exclude headings from the table of contents or other information just because you used them as figure captions, for example.

By default, all browsers align headings on the left. However, most browsers support the align attribute, which also lets you right-align, center, and justify headings. To use the align attribute, include it in the heading elements, like this:

```
<h1 align="left">Left-aligned Heading</h1>
```

```
<h1 align="center">Centered Heading</h1>
<h1 align="right">Right-aligned Heading</h1>
```

Figure 10.5 shows headings aligned left, center, and right.

Left-aligned Heading

Centered Heading

Right-aligned Heading

FIGURE 10.5: Headings aligned left, center, and right

XHTML OPPORTUNITIES

The XHTML 1 specification deprecates (strongly discourages) the use of the `align` attribute. Therefore, although this attribute is still currently supported, if your users will be using current browsers, you should consider using CSS for your formatting needs.

TIP

If you're writing for a wide audience, some of whom might be using older browsers, nest the element that has the `align="center"` attribute inside a center element, to ensure that the text actually appears centered. The markup would look similar to this: `<center><h1 align="center">Centered Heading </h1></center>`

Creating Lists

Lists are great ways to provide information in a structured, easy-to-read format. They help your users easily spot information, and they draw attention to important information. A list is a good form for a procedure. Figure 10.6 shows the same content formatted as both a paragraph and a list.

> **Information in a Paragraph**
>
> Providing information in a paragraph is not nearly as effective as putting the same information in a list. By clearly chunking information into a list, you make the information easier to find, easier to read, easier to use, and more attractive.
>
> **Information in a List**
>
> Providing information in a paragraph is not nearly as effective as putting the same information in a list. By clearly chunking information into a list, you make the information:
>
> - easier to find
> - easier to read
> - easier to use
> - more attractive

FIGURE 10.6: Lists are often easier to read than paragraphs.

Lists come in two varieties: numbered (called *ordered* lists) and bulleted (called *unordered* lists). To create either kind of list, you first specify that you want information to appear as a list, and then you identify each line item in the list. Table 10.3 shows the list and line item elements.

TABLE 10.3: List and Line Item Elements

ELEMENT	EFFECT
li	Specifies a line item in either ordered or unordered lists.
ol	Specifies that the information appear as an ordered (numbered) list.
ul	Specifies that the information appear as an unordered (bulleted) list.

The following steps show you how to create a bulleted list; use the same steps to create a numbered list but use the ol element instead of the ul element.

1. Start with text you want to format as a list, such as the following:

   ```
   Lions
   Tigers
   Bears
   Oh, My!
   ```

2. Insert the ul elements around the list text.

   ```
   <ul>
   Lions
   Tigers
   Bears
   Oh, My!
   </ul>
   ```

3. Put the li opening tag and closing tag around each list item.

```
<ul>
<li>Lions</li>
<li>Tigers</li>
<li>Bears</li>
<li>Oh, My!</li>
</ul>
```

The resulting list, viewed in a browser, looks similar to that shown in Figure 10.7.

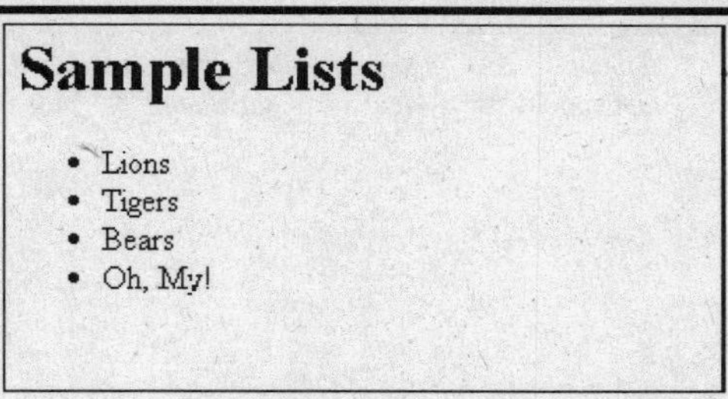

Sample Lists

- Lions
- Tigers
- Bears
- Oh, My!

FIGURE 10.7: Bulleted lists make information easy to spot on the page and can draw attention to important points.

To change your list from unordered (bulleted) to ordered (numbered), change the ul element to ol. The resulting numbered list is shown in Figure 10.8.

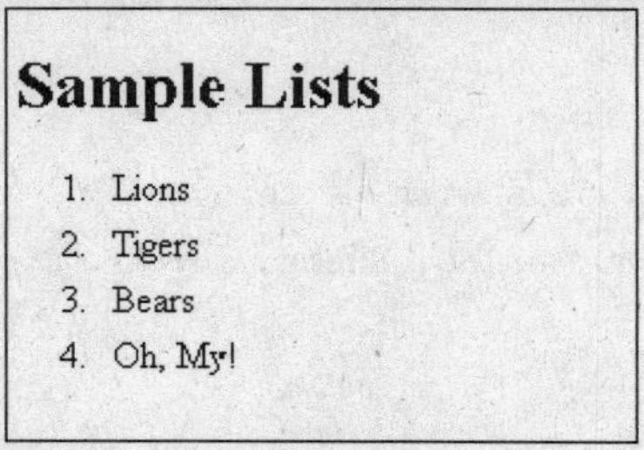

Sample Lists

1. Lions
2. Tigers
3. Bears
4. Oh, My!

FIGURE 10.8: Numbered lists provide sequential information.

TIP

Other, less commonly used and deprecated list elements include dir, to create a directory list, and menu, to create a menu list. You use these elements just as you use the ul and ol elements.

Part iii

Setting List Appearance

By default, numbered lists use arabic numerals and bulleted lists use small, round bullets. You can change the appearance of these by using the attributes listed in Table 10.4.

TABLE 10.4: List Attributes

ELEMENT	EFFECT
For numbered lists:	
type="A"	Specifies the number (or letter) with which the list should start: A, a, I, i, or 1 (default).
type="a"	
type="I"	
type="i"	
type="1"	
For bulleted lists:	
type="disc"	Specifies the bullet shape.
type="square"	
type="circle"	

To use any of these attributes, include them in the opening ol or ul tag or in the opening li tag, like this:

```
<ol type="A">
<li>Outlines use sequential lists with letters.</li>
<li>So do some (unpopular) numbering schemes for
    documentation.</li>
</ol>
```

Or like this:

```
<ul type="square">
<li>Use bullets for non-sequential items.</li>
<li>Use numbers for sequential items.</li>
</ul>
```

Or this:

```
<ul>
<li type="circle">
 Use bullets for non-sequential items.
</li>
<li type="square">
 Use different bullets for visual
    interest.
</li>
</ul>
```

Figure 10.9 shows how these attributes appear in a browser.

Sample Lists

1. Lions
2. Tigers
3. Bears
4. Oh, My!

A. Outlines use sequential lists with letters.
B. So do some (unpopular) numbering schemes for documentation.

■ Use bullets for non-sequential items.
■ Use numbers for sequential items.

○ Use bullets for non-sequential items.
■ Use different bullets for visual interest.

FIGURE 10.9: You can change the appearance of numbers and bullets using list attributes.

Part iii

TIP

You can add the `compact` attribute in opening `ol` or `ul` elements to tell browsers to display the list as compactly as possible. Generally, this setting will make little difference, because most browsers render lists this way by default. This attribute is deprecated.

TIP

The `type` attribute for unordered lists is currently supported by many (but by no means all) browsers; it is also deprecated.

More Options for Ordered Lists

Ordered lists have additional attributes that you can use to specify the first number in the list, as well as to create hierarchical information.

First, you can start a numbered list with a value other than 1 (or A, a, I, or i). Simply include the `start` attribute in the initial `ol` element, as in `<olstart="51"`, to start the list at 51. Or you can even change specific numbers within a list by using the `value` attribute in the `li` tag, as in `<li value="7">`.

TIP

Both the `start` and `value` attributes are deprecated.

To use these attributes, include them in the `ol` element, like this:

```
<ol start="51">
    <li>This is the fifty-first item.</li>
    <li>This is the fifty-second.</li>
    <li type="i" value="7">This item was renumbered to
    be the seventh, using lowercase roman numerals,
    just because we can.
    </li>

</ol>
```

Figure 10.10 shows how this code appears in a browser.

Sample Lists

1. Lions
2. Tigers
3. Bears
4. Oh, My!

A. Outlines use sequential lists with letters.
B. So do some (unpopular) numbering schemes for documentation.

   □ Use bullets for non-sequential items.
   □ Use numbers for sequential items.

   ○ Use bullets for non-sequential items.
   □ Use different bullets for visual interest.

51. This is the fifty-first item.
52. This is the fifty second.
vii. This item was renumbered to be the seventh, using lowercase roman numerals, just because we can.

FIGURE 10.10: Attributes let you customize ordered lists in several ways.

Second, you can use nested ordered lists and different `type` attributes to create outlines. The numbering continues past each lower-level section without the need to manually renumber with a `value` attribute. Here's an example of what the code looks like:

```
<ol type="I">
    <li>Top Level Item</li>
    <li>Another Top Level Item</li>
    <ol type="A">
        <li>A Second Level Item</li>
        <li>Another Second Level Item</li>
        <ol type="1">
            <li>A Third Level Item</li>
            <li>Another Third Level Item</li>
        </ol>
        <li>Another Second Level Item</li>
    </ol>
    <li>A Top Level Item</li>
</ol>
```

The results are shown in Figure 10.11.

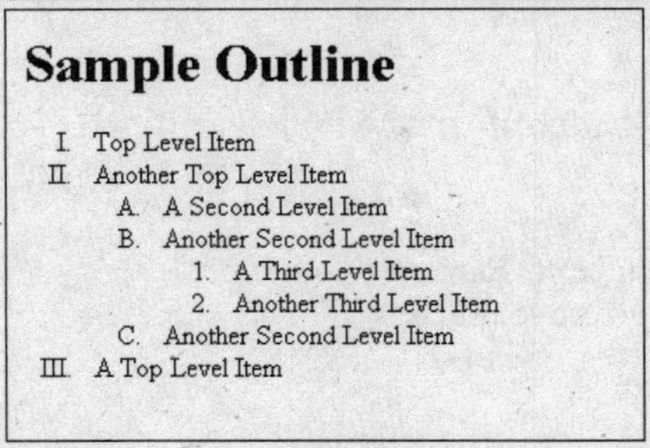

Sample Outline

   I. Top Level Item
  II. Another Top Level Item
      A. A Second Level Item
      B. Another Second Level Item
         1. A Third Level Item
         2. Another Third Level Item
      C. Another Second Level Item
 III. A Top Level Item

FIGURE 10.11: Ordered lists are even flexible enough to format outlines.

Part iii

Using Definition Lists

Finally, one special list variant, *definition lists*, can be useful for providing two levels of information. You can think of definition lists as dictionary entries—they have two levels of information: the entry and a definition.

You can use these lists to provide glossary-type information, or you can use them to provide two-level lists. Table 10.5 lists the elements and their effects.

TABLE 10.5: Definition List and Item Elements

ELEMENT	EFFECT
dl	Specifies that the information appear as a definition list.
dt	Child of dl; identifies definition terms.
dd	Child of dl; identifies definitions.

To create a definition list, as shown in Figure 10.12, follow these steps:

1. Enter the dl opening and closing tags to start the definition list.

   ```
   <dl>
   </dl>
   ```

2. Add the dt opening and closing tags around the definition terms.

   ```
   <dl>
   <dt>XHTML</dt>
   <dt>Maestro</dt>
   </dl>
   ```

3. Add the dd element to identify individual definitions.

   ```
   <dl>
   <dt>XHTML</dt>
   <dd>Extensible Hypertext Markup
       Language is used to create
      Web pages.
   </dd>
   <dt>Maestro</dt>
   <dd>An expert in some field.
       See "Readers of <i>Mastering
      XHTML</i>" for examples.
   </dd>
   </dl>
   ```

TIP

A great way to apply definition lists is in "What's New" lists—a special page that tells people what's new and exciting on your site or at your organization. Try putting the dates in the dt element (maybe with boldface and italics) and the information in the dd element.

Definition List

XHTML
> The Extensible Hypertext Markup Language is used to create Web pages.

Maestro
> An expert in some field. See "Readers of *Mastering XHTML*" for examples.

FIGURE 10.12: Definition lists are a formatting option that is useful when presenting dictionary-like information.

In addition to creating paragraphs, headings, and lists, you can apply formatting to individual letters and words. For example, you can make a word appear *italic,* **bold**, underlined, or superscript, as in e^2. You use these character-level formatting elements only within paragraph-level elements—that is, you can't put a p element within a character-level element such as b. You have to close the character-level formatting before you close the paragraph-level formatting.

Correct:

```
<p>
  <b>This is the end of a
     paragraph that also uses boldface.
  </b>
</p>
<p>This is the beginning of
    the following paragraph.
</p>
```

Incorrect:

```
<p>This text <b>is boldface.</p>
<p>As is this.</b></p>
```

Although many character-formatting elements are available, you'll probably use b (for **boldface**) and i (for *italic*) most often. Table 10.6 shows a list of the most common character-formatting elements.

TABLE 10.6: Common Character-Formatting Elements

ELEMENT	EFFECT
b	Applies boldface.
blink	A proprietary Netscape element that makes text blink; usually considered highly unprofessional.
cite	Indicates citations or references.
code	Displays program code; similar to the pre element.
em	Applies emphasis; usually displayed as italics.
i	Applies italics.
s or strike	Apply strikethrough to text; deprecated.
strong	Applies stronger emphasis; usually displayed as bold text.
sub	Formats text as subscript.
sup	Formats text as superscript.
tt	Applies a fixed-width font.
u	Applies underline; deprecated.
var	Displays variables or arguments.

To use these elements, enter them around the individual letters or words you want to emphasize, like this:

```
Making some text <b>bold</b> or <i>italic</i>
is a useful technique, more so than
<strike>strikethrough</strike> or
<blink>blinking</blink>.
```

Figure 10.13 shows some sample character formatting. The blinking word doesn't appear in this figure so you can see that it disappears.

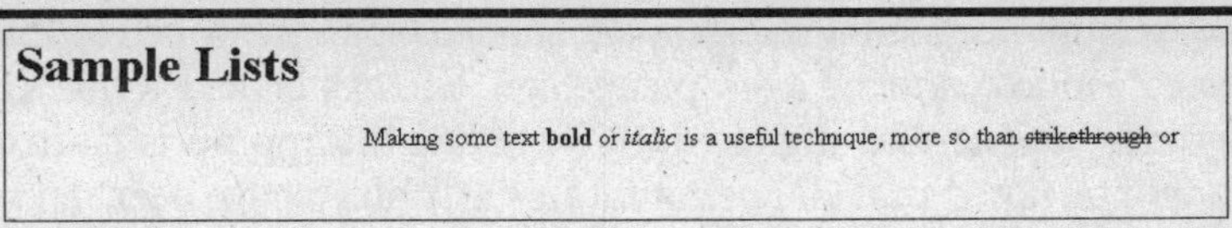

Sample Lists

Making some text **bold** or *italic* is a useful technique, more so than ~~strikethrough~~ or

FIGURE 10.13: Character formatting helps you emphasize words or letters.

TIP

Spend a few minutes trying out these character-formatting elements to see how they work and how they look in your favorite browser.

XHTML OPPORTUNITIES

The XHTML 1 specification strongly encourages using CSS for your formatting needs. Although the specification still supports many deprecated individual formatting elements, the use of CSS is the recommended way to include formatting in your XHTML documents. Using CSS, you can apply the following:

▶ Character-level formatting, such as strikethrough and underline

▶ Paragraph-level formatting, such as indents and margins

▶ Other formatting, such as background colors and images

Including Horizontal Rules

Horizontal rules are lines that break up long sections of text, indicate a shift in information, or help improve the overall document design. To use a horizontal rule, which is an empty element, include the hr element where you want the rule to appear, like this:

```
<p>Long passages of text should often be broken
    into sections with headings and,
    optionally, horizontal rules.
</p>

    <hr />
<h3>A Heading Also Breaks Up Text</h3>
<p>A new long passage can continue here.</p>
```

By default, horizontal rules appear shaded, span the width of the browser window, and are a few pixels high. You can change a rule's shading, width, height, and alignment by including the appropriate attributes. It should be noted that all horizontal rule attributes have been deprecated in favor of the use of CSS. Table 10.7 shows horizontal rule attributes.

TIP

Pixels are the little dots on your screen that produce images; `pixel` is an abbreviation for `picture element`. If your display is set to 800×600, you have 800 pixels horizontally and 600 pixels vertically.

TABLE 10.7: Attributes of the Horizontal Rule (hr) Element (All Deprecated)

ATTRIBUTE	SPECIFIES
`align="…"`	Alignment to `left`, `center`, or `right`
`noshade="noshade"`	That the rule has no shading
`size="n"`	Rule height measured in pixels
`width="n"`	Rule width (length) measured in pixels
`width="n%"`	Rule width (length) measured as a percentage of the document width

To use any of these attributes, include them in the hr element, like this:

```
<hr width="80%" size="8" />
<hr width="50%" />
<hr width="400" align="right" />
<hr noshade="noshade" align="center" width="200" />
```

Figure 10.14 shows some sample horizontal rules with height, width, alignment, and shading attributes added.

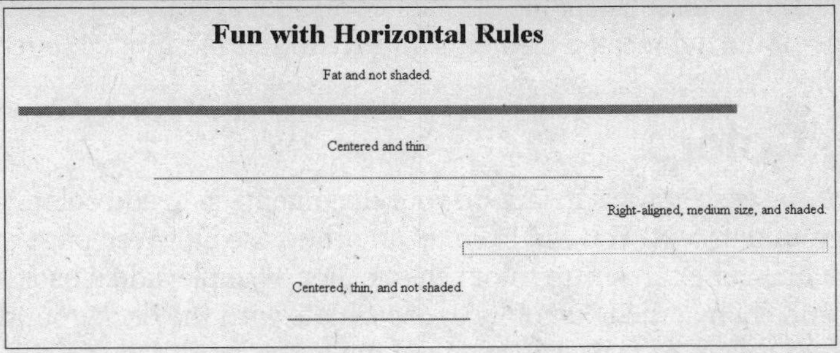

FIGURE 10.14: Horizontal rules can help separate information, improve page design, and simply add visual interest to the page.

Specifying Line Breaks

Sometimes you need to break a line in a specific place, but you don't want to start a new paragraph (with the extra spacing). For example, you might not want lines of poetry text to go all the way across the document; instead, you might want to break them into several shorter lines. You can easily break paragraph lines by inserting the empty element br where you want the lines to break, like this:

```
<p>
There was an XHTML writer<br />
Who tried to make paragraphs wider<br />
He found with a shock<br />
All the elements did mock<br />
The attempt to move that text outside-r.<br />
Mercifully Anonymous
</p>
```

INCLUDING FANCIER FORMATTING

Now that you have a firm grip on using the basic XHTML formatting options, you can dive into some of the fancier formatting effects. In the following sections, we'll show you how to add colors and specify fonts and sizes. Although most newer browsers support these effects, not all browsers do; your fancier effects might not reach all users. Also, the XHTML 1 specification deprecates many of these effects in favor of CSS.

If your users use CSS-capable browsers, you should consider using CSS instead of the deprecated elements and attributes mentioned here.

Adding Colors

One of the easiest ways to jazz up your documents is to add colors to the background or text. You can liven up an otherwise dull Web page with a splash of color or an entire color scheme. For example, add a background color and change the text colors to coordinate with the background. Or highlight a word or two with color and make the words leap off the page. Or, if you're developing a corporate site, adhere to the company's color scheme to ensure a consistent look.

The drawback to setting colors is that you really don't have control over what your users see. Users might set their browsers to display colors they like, or they might be using a text-only browser, which generally displays only black, white, and gray.

You specify colors using hexadecimal numbers, which combine proportions of red, green, and blue—called *RGB numbers*. RGB numbers use six digits, two for each proportion of red, green, and blue. As you're choosing colors, remember that not all RGB numbers display well in browsers; some colors *dither*, meaning that they appear spotty or splotchy. We recommend that you select RGB values that are appropriate for Web-page use, as listed in Table 10.8, which illustrates that each of R, G, and B can each take on the values 00, 33, 66, 99, CC, or FF—giving you 256 possible combinations. Although you'll most likely never go wrong with these "safe" colors, it's most important to use these colors in page backgrounds or in places with large patches of color, where dithering may occur if you don't use these number combinations.

TABLE 10.8: Recommended RGB Values

R	G	B
00	00	00
33	33	33
66	66	66
99	99	99
CC	CC	CC
FF	FF	FF

To create an RGB number from the values in this table, simply start with a pound sign (#) to indicate the hexadecimal system and then select one option from each column. For example, choose FF from the Red column, 00 from the Green column, and 00 from the Blue column to create the RGB number #FF0000, which has the largest possible red component but no blue and no green; it therefore appears as a pure, bright red. (Note that the color values are not case sensitive.)

Setting Background Colors

Using a *background color*, which is simply a color that fills the entire browser window, is a great way to add flair to your Web pages. By default, browsers display a white or gray background color, which may be adequate if you're developing pages for an intranet site where flashy elements aren't essential. However, if you're developing a public or personal site, you'll probably want to make your site more interesting and visually appealing. For example, if you're developing a public corporate Web site, you might want to use your company's standard colors—ones that appear on letterhead, logos, or marketing materials. Or you might want to use your favorite color if you're developing a personal site. In either case, using a background color can improve the overall page appearance and help develop a theme among pages.

As you'll see in the following section, pay careful attention to how text contrasts with the background color. If you specify a dark background color, use a light text color. Conversely, if you specify a light background color, use a dark text color. Contrast is key for ensuring that users can read information on your pages.

To specify a background color for your documents, include the bgcolor attribute in the opening body tag, like this:

```
<body bgcolor="#FFFFFF">...</body>
```

Setting Text Colors

Similar to background colors, text colors can enhance your Web pages. In particular, you can specify the color of the following:

- ▶ Body text, which appears throughout the document body
- ▶ Unvisited links, which are links not yet followed
- ▶ Active links, which are links as they're being selected
- ▶ Visited links, which are links previously followed

Changing body text is sometimes essential—for example, if you've added a background color or an image. If you've added a dark background color, the default black body text color won't adequately contrast with the background, making the text difficult or impossible to read. In this case, you'd want to change the text color to one that's lighter so that it contrasts with the background sufficiently.

Changing link colors helps keep your color scheme intact—for unvisited as well as visited links. Set the visited and unvisited links to different colors to help users know which links they've followed and which ones they haven't.

To change body text and link colors, simply add the attributes listed in Table 10.9 to the opening body tag.

TABLE 10.9: Text and Link Color Attributes (All Deprecated)

ATTRIBUTE	SETS COLOR FOR
text="…"	All text within the document, with a color name or a #RRGGBB value
alink="…"	Active links, which are the links at the time the user clicks them, with a color name or a #RRGGBB value
link="…"	Unvisited links, with a color name or a #RRGGBB value
vlink="…"	Links the user has recently followed (how recently depends on the browser settings), with a color name or a #RRGGBB value

TIP

We recommend setting all Web page colors at one time—that way, you can see how background, text, and link colors appear as a unit.

To change text and link colors, follow these steps:

1. Within the body element, add the text attribute to set the color for text within the document. This example makes the text black.

   <body text="#000000">

TIP

When setting text colors, using a "safe" color is less important for text than for backgrounds. Dithering is less apparent in small areas, such as text.

2. Add the `link` attribute to set the link color. This example uses blue (#0000FF) for the links.

    `<body text="#000000" link="#0000FF">`

3. Add the `vlink` attribute to set the color for visited links. If you set the `vlink` attribute to the same as the link, links will not change colors even after users follow them. This could be confusing, but also serves to make it look like there is always new material available. This example sets the visited link to a different shade of blue.

    `<body text="#000000" link="#0000FF" vlink="#000099">`

4. Finally, set the `alink`, or active link, color. This is the color of a link while users are clicking it and will not necessarily be visible in IE 4, depending on the viewer's settings. This example sets `alink` to red:

    `<body text="#000000" link="#0000FF" vlink="#000099" alink="#FF0000">`

TIP

Specify fonts and increase font sizes to improve readability with dark backgrounds and light-colored text.

Specifying Fonts and Font Sizes

You can use the `font` element to specify font characteristics for your document, including color, size, and typeface. However, it's worth noting that the `font` element and its attributes have been deprecated in favor of CSS. We suggest you check out the font properties in CSS and use them instead of the `font` element. Table 10.10 describes the element and attributes you'll use to set font characteristics.

TABLE 10.10: Font Characteristics (All Deprecated)

ITEM	TYPE	DESCRIPTION
font	Element	Sets font characteristics for text.
color="..."	Attribute of font element	Specifies font color in #RRGGBB numbers or with color names. This color applies only to the text surrounded by the font elements.
face="..."	Attribute of font element	Specifies possible type faces as a list, in order of preference, separated by commas—for example, "Verdana, Arial, Helvetica".
size="n"	Attribute of font element	Specifies font size on a scale of 1 through 7; the default or normal size is 10. You can also specify a *relative* size by using + or – (for example, +2).
basefont	Element	Sets the default characteristics for text that is not formatted using the font element or CSS.

As you're determining which font face to use, keep in mind that the font must be available on your users' computers for them to view the fonts you specify. For example, if you specify Technical and your users do not have it, their computers will substitute a font—possibly one you'd consider unacceptable. As a partial way of overcoming this problem, you can list multiple faces in order of preference; the machine displays the first available. For example, a list of "Comic Sans MS, Technical, Tekton, Times, Arial" will display Comic Sans MS if available, then try Technical, then Tekton, and so forth.

So, which fonts should you choose? Table 10.11 lists fonts that are commonly available on Windows, Mac, and Unix platforms.

TABLE 10.11: Commonly Available Fonts

WINDOWS	MACINTOSH	UNIX
Arial	Helvetica	Helvetica
Courier New	Courier	Courier
Times New Roman	Times	Times

TIP

You might check out Microsoft's selection of downloadable fonts (www.microsoft.com/typography/free.htm). These fonts are available to users who have specifically downloaded the fonts to their computers, or who are using IE 4 or newer, or Windows 98 or newer.

To specify font characteristics, follow these steps. You can set some or all of the characteristics used in this example.

1. Identify the text to format with the font element.

   `<font>Look at this!</font>`

2. Select a specific font using the face attribute. See Table 10.11 for a list of commonly available fonts.

   ```
   <font face="Verdana, 'Times New Roman', Times">
      Look at this!</font>
   ```

3. Change the font size using the size attribute. You set the size of text on a scale from 1 to 7; the default size is 3. Either set the size absolutely, with a number from 1 to 7, or relatively, with + or – the numbers of levels you want to change. Almost all newer browsers, and all XHTML 1–compliant browsers, support size to set font size. The only significant downside to setting the font size is that your user might already have increased or decreased the default font size, so your size change might have more of an effect than you expected.

   ```
   <font face="Technical, 'Times New Roman',
    Times" size="+2">
      Look at this!</font>
   ```

4. Add a color attribute to set the color, using a color name or a #RRGGBB value.

   ```
   <font face="Technical, 'Times New Roman',
    Times" size="+2"
      color="#FF0000">Look at this!</font>
   ```

   Figure 10.15 shows the result.

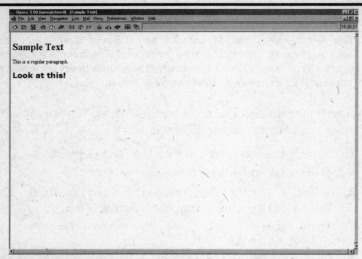

FIGURE 10.15: Setting font characteristics can spiff up your pages and help you achieve the visual effect you want.

SUMMARY

Congratulations! You've just learned to apply XHTML code, and you even learned some of the most common elements and attributes. This chapter should have been a natural transition from Chapter 9, which introduced some basic XHTML concepts.

One way to improve your XHTML development skills is to simply carve out your XHTML documents from scratch by using the principles you learned in this chapter. Another way, however, is to convert some preexisting HTML documents into XHTML. You'll find out how to do that in the next chapter.

Chapter 11

CONVERTING HTML TO XHTML

The odds are that you already have a few (or many) HTML documents lying around. It may be that you want to do what we did: Update your entire HTML site to XHTML. That doesn't mean you have to start over from scratch.

Remember that XHTML uses the same elements and attributes as HTML (with the exception of adding the XHTML namespace). This means that you don't have to change your vocabulary much; all you need to do is update your syntax. There are two ways you can do this: by hand or with the help of a tool.

Adapted from *Mastering™ XHTML*, by Ed Tittel, Chelsea Valentine, Lucinda Dykes, and Mary Burmeister
ISBN 0-7821-2820-3   1,056 pages $39.99

WHY CONVERT YOUR DOCUMENTS?

This seems to be the first question that comes out of a Web developer's mouth: "Why should I convert to XHTML?" Because the two languages use the same element set, and they should function the same in a browser, why would you want to take the time to convert them?

To understand why you would want to convert to XHTML, you have to understand where XML is coming from and going to (reread Chapter 9, "XHTML Structure and Form," if this doesn't make sense). If you still feel the conversion is not worth the time, here are just a few of the reasons you would want to convert your documents to XHTML:

- ► Because XHTML is an application of XML, an XML processor can process XHTML.

- ► XHTML can be extended to include other document models (or vocabularies), including Scalable Vector Graphics (SVG), Synchronized Multimedia Integration Language (SMIL), Mathematical Markup Language (MathML), or even your own XML vocabulary.

- ► XHTML encourages the separation of style from structure.

- ► XHTML promotes cleaner markup that will be easier for both processors and humans to read.

- ► Mobile-phone vendors selected XHTML as their markup language of choice.

- ► XHTML allows traditional HTML content developers and Web designers to continue using what they know, albeit in the framework of a more structured markup environment.

- ► Although many tool vendors have not yet caught on, most experts think it's just a matter of time before vendors big and small make mechanical validation part of their built-in editing processes.

- ► Current efforts on XHTML modularization (which breaks markup into categories and lets each category be used independently of the others in documents) and related forms of XML-based markup—for instance, the outstanding work on XForms that's currently under way—promise to give XHTML documents access to markup and capabilities that HTML does not (and will never) have. Over time, improved functionality will move the market simply because content developers will need the capabilities that other XML applications can deliver.

▶ More history and experience with XHTML and with the XHTML–XML connection are likely to demonstrate lower costs of ownership, maintenance, and development. If realized, these benefits will move the market inexorably in that direction.

▶ HTML won't be developed any further by the W3C (World Wide Web Consortium) except as new versions of XHTML; therefore, it's unlikely to be taken any further by browser vendors. (Browser vendors will most likely continue support for HTML, but they just won't develop additional support.)

CONVERTING DOCUMENTS BY HAND

If you're only updating a few documents, and you're anxious to get some XHTML practice, you might choose to convert your HTML page to XHTML by hand. To be honest, this will rarely happen. There's no need to, because there's a wonderful free tool (HTML Tidy, discussed in the "Working with Tidy" section later in this chapter) that will do it for you at the click of a button. However, it's important that you understand what the tool is doing so that you can utilize its customizable options.

To understand what the tool is doing, let's take a look at what you would have to do if your tool of choice was your fingers.

Backward Compatibility

XHTML is backward compatible with legacy browsers. Keeping in mind that XHTML uses HTML's vocabulary, the only real obstacle that would prevent XHTML from compatibility with older browsers would be syntactic conventions. Lucky for us, XML syntax is close enough to SGML (and therefore HTML) that the syntactic differences are small.

In Chapter 9, you learned all the rules your XHTML document must follow, most of which were already defined by HTML. A few additions, such as closing all elements and adhering to an empty-element syntax, are new. Whereas older browsers have very few problems processing

XHTML documents, you need to abide by a few rules to avoid any problems:

▶ When using XML's empty-element syntax, include a space before the trailing forward slash (/); for example, `<br />`.

▶ Most older browsers will render the XML declaration

```
<?xml version="1.0" encoding="UTF-8"
standalone="no"?>
```

as content, so it's best to leave it off any XHTML document that will be viewed in older browsers. If you do leave the XML declaration out of your document, the document can only use UTF-8 or UTF-16 character encoding.

▶ Use external style sheet or script documents, rather than embedding them in the head of your XHTML document. Prior to XHTML, Web developers used HTML comments to hide script and style sheet syntax from older browsers. XHTML uses XML CDATA sections to mark internal scripts and style sheet syntax. Old and new processors are likely to conflict. If you cannot use external scripts or style sheets, be sure that the internal syntax does not contain <, &,]]>,][, >, or --.

WARNING
Currently, no browsers know how to handle XML CDATA sections. However, further support for XML is very likely in the next versions of browsers.

▶ Do not add line breaks or multiple white-space characters within attribute values. Many XML developers use line breaks to aid document readability, but browsers handle white space inconsistently, and multiple white-space characters can translate into problems when rendering XHTML documents. If you're going to use white space for readability, be sure you include it only between elements.

▶ Use both the `name` and `id` attributes when referring to a fragment identifier that begins with a pound symbol (`#value`). The `name` attribute was originally used to refer to named anchors; however, HTML 4 deprecated this attribute and introduced the `id` attribute to replace it as a way to uniquely identify a given element. For future compatibility, you want to use the `id` attribute;

however, because many current and older browsers don't support this attribute, you use the name attribute as well. For example:

```
<a name="one" id="one">...</a>
```

▶ Again, for forward and backward compatibility, use both the lang and xml:lang attributes to define the language for a given element. The xml:lang attribute takes precedence over the lang attribute.

▶ Don't use more than one isindex element within the head element. The isindex element is deprecated in favor of the input element.

TIP

If you're concerned with creating XHTML documents that support backward compatibility with older browsers, be sure that you use elements that are supported by the older browsers. For example, if you use form markup in your XHTML document, Internet Explorer (IE) 2 will not recognize it because it does not support complex forms.

The Rules

As an application of XML, XHTML requires that you follow XML's syntax requirements. These syntax requirements are similar to those followed by HTML and should be easy to get a handle on. In the following sections, we briefly go over the rules one by one.

These rules are defined in detail in Chapter 9. For more information about each specific syntax rule, see Chapter 9.

Terminate all elements.   All elements must be balanced with a closing tag, or if considered empty, they should follow XML's empty-element syntax.

Use proper empty-element syntax.   Empty elements must also be terminated; however, as the document author, you have two options. You could add a closing end tag to balance the empty element; for example,
</br>. However, because adding a closing tag doesn't seem logical, a shortened syntax was also defined—adding a trailing forward slash to the opening tag; for example, <br />. If you use the empty-element syntax (<br />), you have to add a white-space character before the trailing forward slash, for backward compatibility reasons.

Part iii

Quote all attribute values.   All your attributes' values must be in quotation marks.

Give values for all attributes.   HTML allows for a handful of attributes that function as Boolean attributes, which stand alone, without a value. When one of these is present, it turns a function on. When the attribute is omitted, the function is not activated. Because XHTML follows XML's syntax rules, all attributes must have values; for example,

```
<input type="checkbox" checked="checked" />
```

Lowercase element and attribute names because XHTML is case sensitive.   The XML specification requires that XML documents obey the rules of an associated DTD, including naming conventions for elements and attributes. If the DTD defines all element and attribute names in lowercase, as developers we have to abide by that rule. Therefore, all XHTML elements and attributes must be lowercased. We also lowercase case-insensitive attribute values to be consistent.

Nest elements correctly.   Nesting elements correctly wasn't important to HTML; however, it's a strict requirement for XHTML. Because elements must be balanced with an opening tag and a closing tag, it's necessary to be careful with nesting; it establishes element hierarchy and relationships.

TIP

There's an easy way to remember your nesting principles: What you open first, you must close last. Repeat that to yourself over and over and you will never forget how to nest again.

Include a *DOCTYPE* declaration.   If you're adhering to one of the XHTML 1 DTDs, you can't use an HTML 4 DTD reference. When you're converting your document from HTML to XHTML, make sure that you're using the correct DOCTYPE declaration. For a listing of the three XHTML DTDs, see Chapter 9.

Add the XHTML namespace.   XHTML makes use of XML namespaces to help uniquely identify its collection of elements and attributes. This is especially handy if you plan on mixing (embedding) other XML vocabularies. Namespaces are covered in Chapter 9. Be sure to read more about namespaces if you haven't already. According to the XHTML specification, all XHTML documents must use the default XHTML namespace (xmlns="http://www.w3.org/1999/xhtml"). This namespace is required and must be defined within the html start tag.

Summing It Up

Listing 11.1 is not a well-formed XHTML document, and we're going to make it one.

Listing 11.1: Sloppy HTML Document

```
<HTML>
<HEAD>
<TITLE>Sloppy HTML</TITLE>
</HEAD>
<BODY>
<H1>Element Rules</H1>
<P><FONT COLOR=RED>Elements provide the structure that holds
your document together.</FONT>
<BR>
<OL COMPACT>
<LI>Close all elements.
<LI>Empty elements should follow empty-element syntax, and be
sure to add the white space for backward compatibility.
<LI>Convert all stand-alone attributes to attributes with
values.
<LI>Add quotation marks to all attribute values.
<LI>Convert all uppercase element and attribute names to
lowercase.
<LI>Use the appropriate DOCTYPE declaration.
<LI>Add the XHTML namespace to the html start tag.
<LI>Make sure you comply with any backward-compatible steps
defined in the section "Backward Compatibility."
</OL>
</BODY>
</HTML>
```

Follow these steps to make the document well formed:

1. Close all elements. Notice that the p element and none of the list item (li) elements have closing tags, so add the closing p and li tags.

```
<P><FONT COLOR=RED>Elements provide the structure that
holds your document together.</FONT></P>
<BR>
<OL COMPACT>
<LI>Close all elements.</LI>
<LI>Empty elements should follow empty-element syn-
tax.</LI>
<LI>Convert all stand-alone attributes to attributes
with values.</LI>
<LI>Add quotation marks to all attribute values.</LI>
<LI>Convert all uppercase element and attribute names to
lowercase.</LI>
<LI>Use the appropriate DOCTYPE declaration.</LI>
<LI>Add the XHTML namespace to the html start tag.</LI>
<LI>Make sure you comply with any backward-compatible
steps defined in the section "Backward
Compatibility."</LI>
</OL>
```

2. Empty elements should follow empty-element syntax, and
   be sure to add the white space for backward compatibility.
   The BR element is the only empty element in this document.
   Change it to <BR />.

3. Convert all stand-alone attributes to attributes with values.
   Change COMPACT to COMPACT=COMPACT.

4. Add quotation marks to all attribute values.

```
<P><FONT COLOR="RED">Elements provide the structure that
holds your document together.</FONT></P>
<BR>
<OL COMPACT="COMPACT">
```

5. Convert all uppercase element and attribute names (and
   attribute values) to lowercase.

```
<html>
<head>
<title>Sloppy HTML</title>
</head>
<body>
<h1>Element Rules</h1>
<p><font color="red">Elements provide the structure that
holds your document together.</font></p>
<br />
<ol compact="compact">
<li>Close all elements.</li>
```

```
<li>Empty elements should follow empty-element
syntax.</li>
<li>Convert all stand-alone attributes to attributes
with values.</li>...
```

6. Use the appropriate DOCTYPE declaration. We're going to use the Transitional DTD:

```
<!DOCTYPE html
  PUBLIC "-//W3C//DTD XHTML 1.0 Transitional//EN"
  "http://www.w3.org/TR/xhtml1/DTD/
  ➥xhtml1-transitional.dtd">
```

7. Add the XHTML namespace to the html start tag.

```
<html xmlns="http://www.w3.org/1999/xhtml">
```

8. Make sure you comply with any backward-compatible steps defined in the section "Backward Compatibility." Our document doesn't need any adjustments here.

TIP

According to the XHTML specification, you should wrap any script or style sheet syntax with XML CDATA sections to avoid conflicts with < and &, or to avoid the expansion of entities such as & or <. In theory, this would be an additional step in the conversion process. Although this would be ideal, most browsers don't recognize CDATA section syntax. To avoid browser confusion, it's recommended that you use external script and style sheets when possible.

Your resulting code should look like Listing 11.2.

Part iii

Listing 11.2: Clean XHTML Document

```
<!DOCTYPE html PUBLIC "-//W3C//DTD
  XHTML 1.0 Transitional//EN"
  "http://www.w3.org/TR/xhtml1/DTD/
  ➥xhtml1-transitional.dtd">
<html xmlns="http://www.w3.org/1999/xhtml">
  <head>
    <title>Sloppy HTML</title>
  </head>
  <body>
    <h1>Element Rules</h1>
    <p><font color="red">Elements provide the structure that
    holds your document together.</font></p>
    <br />
    <ol compact="compact">
```

```
<li>Close all elements.</li>
<li>Empty elements should follow empty-element syntax,
and be sure to add the white space for backward
compatibility.</li>
<li>Convert all stand-alone attributes to attributes
with values.</li>
<li>Add quotation marks to all attribute values.</li>
<li>Convert all uppercase element and attribute names
to lowercase.</li>
<li>Use the appropriate DOCTYPE declaration.</li>
<li>Add the XHTML namespace to the html start tag.</li>
<li>Make sure you comply with any backward-compatible
steps defined in the section "Backward Compatibility."
</li>
  </ol>
 </body>
</html>
```

WARNING

We don't suggest using the font element to define presentation. We recommend using Cascading Style Sheets (CSS) to define presentation style rules for your document. If your target audience uses IE 5.0 or higher, we recommend you opt for CSS style rules.

WORKING WITH TIDY

HTML Tidy, a tool created by David Raggett, is the answer to any Web developer's prayer. Tidy, which has been around for a while, converts HTML documents into clean XHTML in a matter of seconds. In the beginning, it was designed to clean up HTML markup. Now, Tidy is included as a plug-in with most big-time HTML editors. In addition, Tidy comes in a version you can run from the command prompt and a GUI version (TidyGUI).

You may be wondering just what Tidy can do. Well, it pretty much does everything you need it to do. For example, Tidy corrects the following:

Detects mismatched end tags   In most cases, Tidy will locate mismatched end tags and make the appropriate corrections.

Corrects incorrectly nested elements   In most cases, Tidy will correct nesting errors.

Locates misplaced elements   Tidy will alert the document author if an element is misused—for example, if the td element is nested within a form element.

Lowercases element and attribute names   Tidy will correct any uppercase element names and attribute names automatically.

Adds quotation marks to attribute values   Tidy will add double or single quotation marks around all attribute values (you can specify which).

This is not the end of what Tidy can do. In fact, you can customize Tidy to do just about anything relating to the conversion process. For example, you can control whether the modified version uses indentation for nested elements, or you can request that Tidy invoke only some, but not all, of the rules. To learn more about HTML Tidy's many, many abilities and options, visit www.w3.org/People/Raggett/Tidy.

The markup shown in Listing 11.3 is the sloppy.htm document that we'll convert to clean XHTML. The clean markup that's produced by all methods discussed in the following sections is shown in Listing 11.4.

Listing 11.3: Sloppy HTML Document

```
<HTML>
<HEAD>
<TITLE>LANWrights Online Training</TITLE>
</HEAD>
<BLOCKQUOTE><B>Note: </B>For a complete bibliography and pub-
lication information, please visit the LANWrights <A
HREF="http://www.lanw.com/books.htm">Book Nook.</BLOCK-
QUOTE></A>
<H1>LANWrights Web-based Training</H1>
<P>All classes share a similar design approach, including the
following:
<UL COMPACT TYPE=SQUARE>
<LI>A collection of stand-alone lessons equal to about 16
hours of classroom training
<LI>Online exercises, with built-in feedback on results
<LI>Online discussion group software that allows students to
interact with each other online, and access to a telephone
hotline open during regular business hours
<LI>Automated mastery tests for each lesson, including score
reporting
```

```
<LI>Individual student tracking and results reporting avail-
able 24/7
<LI>Printable access and how-to instructions for student use
<LI>Printable and/or downloadable versions of all lessons
</UL><P ALIGN=CENTER>If you are interested in hiring us to
provide online training for your company, you can visit our
<A HREF="http://www.lanw.com/training/wbt-
brochure.htm">online brochure</A>, which includes specific
information about pricing, structure, availability, and the
instructors.
</BODY>
</HTML>
```

Listing 11.4: Clean XHTML Version Produced by HTML Tidy

```
<!DOCTYPE html PUBLIC "-//W3C//DTD XHTML 1.0
Transitional//EN" "http://www.w3.org/TR/xhtml1/DTD/xhtml1-
transitional.dtd">
<html xmlns="http://www.w3.org/1999/xhtml">
<head>
<meta name="generator" content="HTML Tidy, see www.w3.org" />
<title>Sloppy HTML</title>
</head>
<body>
<blockquote><b>Note:</b> For a complete bibliography and pub-
lication information, please visit the LANWrights <a
href="http://www.lanw.com/books.htm">Book Nook.</a></block-
quote>
<h1>LANWrights Web-based Training</h1>
<p>All classes share a similar design approach, including the
following:</p>
<ul compact="compact" type="square">
<li>A collection of stand-alone lessons equal to about 16
hours of classroom training</li>
<li>Online exercises, with built-in feedback on results</li>
<li>Online discussion group software that allows students to
interact with each other online, and access to a telephone
hotline open during regular business hours</li>
<li>Automated mastery tests for each lesson, including score
reporting</li>
<li>Individual student tracking and results reporting avail-
able 24/7</li>
<li>Printable access and how-to instructions for student
use</li>
```

```
<li>Printable and/or downloadable versions of all
lessons</li>
</ul>
<p align="center">If you are interested in hiring us to pro-
vide online training for your company, you can visit our <a
href="http://www.lanw.com/training/wbt-brochure.htm">online
brochure</a>, which includes specific information about pric-
ing, structure, availability, and the instructors.</p>
</body>
</html>
```

To learn how to work with Tidy, you'll need to read the section appropriate to your computing method:

Working Via	Read This Section
Windows command prompt	"Using Tidy from the Windows Command Prompt"
Windows GUI	"Using TidyGUI" or "Using Tidy in HTML-Kit"
Macintosh	"Using Tidy on the Mac"

Using Tidy from the Windows Command Prompt

If you remember the days of DOS, you may be comfortable using Tidy as a stand-alone tool at the command prompt. Windows users who are uncomfortable working from the MS-DOS prompt should skip forward to the sections "Using TidyGUI" or "Using Tidy in HTML-Kit." Macintosh users need to jump ahead to the "Using Tidy on the Mac" section.

Before we get started with this mini tutorial, download the DOS version of HTML Tidy from the Web at www.w3.org/People/Raggett /tidy. Click the Downloading Tidy link and select tidy.exe. After you've downloaded the executable to your hard drive (maybe save it in a folder called Tidy on the C drive), you're ready to begin:

1. To fire up the DOS prompt, select Start ➤ Programs ➤ Command Prompt or MS-DOS Prompt, depending on your version of Windows. (You might need to go to Start ➤ Programs ➤ Accessories ➤ Command Prompt or MS-DOS Prompt.) A window with a black background and text, C:\>, appears (see Figure 11.1).

FIGURE 11.1: Working from the command prompt

2. Locate the `tidy.exe` file. If you saved it in its own folder, `Tidy`, you can navigate to that folder using the following command:

`cd ..\Tidy`

This command says the following:

`cd`   Tells the processor that you're changing folders. You should follow this command with a white-space character.

`..\`   Navigates up one level to the root folder.

`Tidy`   Opens the `Tidy` folder.

Once you've navigated to the `Tidy` folder, you're ready to use the tool. Tidy allows you to point to an HTML document and use commands to convert the document. To do this, you need an HTML document to work with. We use the document shown in Listing 11.3; we'll assume the document to be converted has a filename of `sloppy.htm`.

To convert your document to XHTML using Tidy, follow these steps:

1. Type the following command at the Windows command prompt:

`tidy -asxhtml -m c:\XHTML\sloppy.htm`

The above command breaks down as follows:

> `tidy`   Calls the Tidy program.
>
> `-asxhtml`   Tells Tidy to convert the HTML document to XHTML.

-m   Tells Tidy to convert the document in its current location, and therefore, modify the original document rather than saving the clean version into a separate file.

`c:\XHTML\sloppy.htm`   Defines the location of the sloppy HTML document that needs to be converted. (Substitute whatever drive, path, and folder your document is in.)

2. After you type this command, press Enter. The `sloppy.htm` document will be replaced with a cleaner XHTML version. The cleaned-up version of our sample document is shown in Listing 11.4.

Of course, there might be an instance where you want to preserve the initial HTML document and have Tidy create a new XHTML document. If this is the case, enter the following command line instead of the previous one, taking care to be sure that the entire line appears on one line (it may seem in this book that there is a return, but, but if you have a return character it has the same effect as issuing a command, which will not execute the program unless everything is actually on one line in the terminal):

```
tidy -asxhtml c:\XHTML\sloppy.htm >
  c:\XHTML\output.htm
```

The XHTML document will be saved as a separate document in the XHTML folder. You can name the document whatever you want. In this case, we've named the document `output.htm`.

Using TidyGUI

Many of you might not be inspired by the command prompt. In fact, you may want to run from it. There are also some of you who won't want to download another text editor. If you're interested in using a GUI interface for Tidy but don't want a full text editor attached, André Blavier created a version that you just might get along with.

This GUI version of Tidy is beyond easy to use. Take a look at the TidyGUI interface shown in Figure 11.2.

You simply browse for the file you want to Tidy by clicking the Browse button and then click the Tidy! button. After that, you click the Show Output button and save the Tidied output to a new document to save it as your own. To read more about this version, visit `http://perso.wanadoo.fr/ablavier/TidyGUI/`.

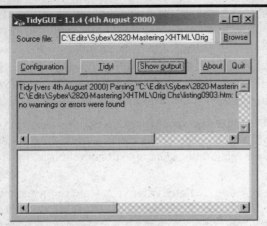

FIGURE 11.2:   The simple TidyGUI interface.

Using Tidy in HTML-Kit

Windows users who don't like to work from the command prompt can
also use HTML Tidy in a GUI interface, as a part of HTML-Kit. HTML-
Kit is a free text editor that allows you to use predefined templates for
HTML documents, and it can do anything a snazzy text editor can do.
However, in addition to helping you create HTML documents, it uses
HTML Tidy to convert HTML documents to XHTML. There's no extra
download needed; all you have to do is download HTML-Kit (from
www.chami.com/html-kit/) and Tidy comes as a part of the package.

WARNING

The download size of HTML-Kit is significantly larger than the download size of
both tidy.exe and TidyGUI.

After you've downloaded and installed HTML-Kit, open it to see what
its interface looks like. Figure 11.3 shows the main HTML-Kit interface
(with a new document open).

In the top-left corner of the window, you'll see a little broom-like icon
(the HTML Tidy icon). To convert all your documents to XHTML, you
should customize the conversion options. Select Edit ≻ Preferences and
choose the Tidy tab shown in Figure 11.4. For our purposes, make sure the

Output field says XHTML. After you customize the conversion options, you just click the HTML Tidy icon and your document's converted to XHTML.

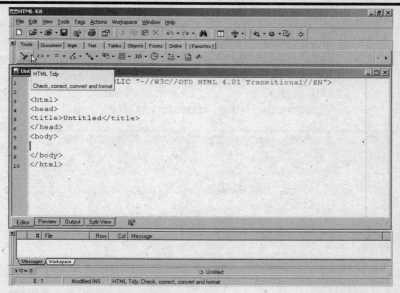

FIGURE 11.3:   HTML-Kit's interface

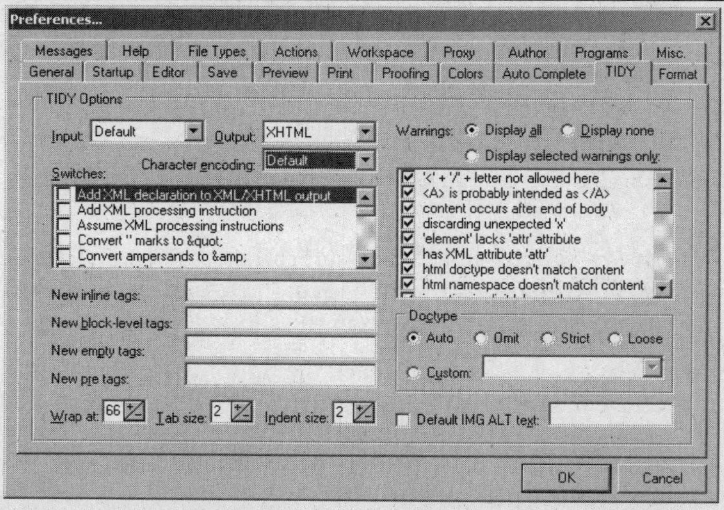

FIGURE 11.4:   The Tidy tab of the HTML-Kit Preferences

Part iii

Now, let's convert a document (for example, Listing 11.3) to XHTML using HTML-Kit. Follow these steps:

1. Select File ➤ Open File and find the document.

2. Click the HTML Tidy icon. Alternatively, you could select the down arrow next to the HTML Tidy icon shown in Figure 11.3 and select Convert To XHTML from the drop-down menu. The new output (Listing 11.4) appears on the right side of the screen, and any errors found in the document appear at the bottom of the screen (see Figure 11.5).

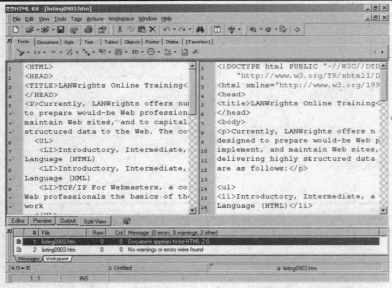

FIGURE 11.5: Tidy has cleaned up this document, all within HTML-Kit.

3. If you want to replace the old HTML document with the new XHTML document, right-click in the right window and select Copy Output To Editor from the shortcut menu.

4. Select File ➤ Save, and click the Editor tab at the bottom of the window to continue modifying your document, or just to see the XHTML in all its glory.

Using Tidy on the Mac

Tidy support for the Mac has been around for a while. There are several options for Mac users, all of which are described and available for download at the Tidy for Mac OS site:

```
www.geocities.com/SiliconValley/1057/tidy.html
```

One of the possibilities is comparable to the TidyGUI application for Windows: It's called MacTidy. In fact, TidyGUI was based on MacTidy. However, the most common way to use Tidy with the Mac is to download a plug-in for BBEdit.

TIP

BBEdit is one of the premier text editors for Macintosh Web developers and can be found at www.barebones.com.

Download the HTML Tidy plug-in from the Tidy for Mac OS page listed earlier. After you've downloaded the StuffIt file that contains the plug-in, copy the BBTidy plug-in to the `BBEdit Plug-ins` folder. After the installation is complete, you can convert your first XHTML document.

To start the conversion process, make sure you have an HTML document (Listing 11.3, for example) open in BBEdit, and then select Tools ➢ Tidy HTML, and BBEdit will begin to work its magic (see Figure 11.6). You will be presented with two documents, one that documents the errors and warning messages and one that provides the output XHTML document (Listing 11.4, for example).

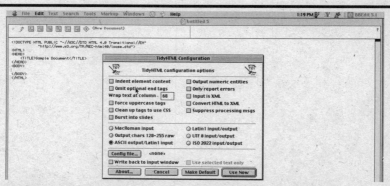

FIGURE 11.6: Selecting HTML Tidy from the BBEdit Tools menu

SUMMARY

This book has devoted three chapters to XHTML:

- ▶ Chapter 9 offered an introduction to XHTML and covered the basic differences between HTML and XHTML.

- ▶ In Chapter 10, you created your first XHTML document.

- ▶ This chapter demonstrated techniques for converting HTML to XHTML. Generally, you'll find it more convenient to use one of the tools we described to convert HTML to XHTML, especially when converting large numbers of documents. However, the conversion-by-hand process can go a long way in improving and/or developing your XHTML coding skills.

In the next chapter, "Transforming XML: Introducing XSLT," we're going to look at another way to move XML data into HTML. This involves taking any XML data with your own element definitions and transforming it into HTML, XHTML, or, in fact, almost any other text-based format you can think of.

PART IV

XML SCRIPTING AND PROCESSING

Chapter 12

TRANSFORMING XML: INTRODUCING XSLT

XSLT (Extensible Stylesheet Language Transformations) is a very powerful tool for transforming an XML document into a variety of formats by copying it into a separate tree structure. Currently, XSLT is used primarily to transform XML semantics into different formats, such as HTML, or into other formats that are used to manipulate data in some way. Despite considerable debate about semantics within the XML/XSLT development community, XSLT has moved along rapidly as a viable XML transformation language.

The nice thing about XSLT is that you can process as much or as little of an XML document as you want. With very long XML documents you may, in fact, end up with only one line actually rendered in a browser or processed by an XSLT processing agent. You'll find that there are very practical reasons for this.

Adapted from *Mastering™ XML, Premium Edition*, by Chuck White, Liam Quin, and Linda Burman

ISBN 0-7821-2847-5   1,155 PAGES $49.99

XSLT itself was also split into two different recommendations. The part that was split off, XPath, is a non-XML language that is explicitly designed to access nodes of an XML document tree.

Some of the specific concepts you'll explore here include:

▶ Fundamental XSLT concepts such as transformations and pattern matching, templates, and a review of key XSL Transformation elements

▶ How to combine Cascading Style Sheets (CSS) with XSL

▶ The basics behind the available formatting options

NOTE
This chapter makes extensive use of CSS, a style sheet standard developed by the W3C (World Wide Web Consortium) to add style and formatting to XML and HTML documents. For details on this language, go to www.w3.org/style.

DEFINING XSLT

In this book, we use XSL to paint a picture of what are, in reality, three separate languages in various stages of development at the W3C. When we refer to XSL in this book, we are referring to any one of the following languages, which can be used in various combinations for XSL development:

The XML vocabulary describing the formatting objects portion of XSL   The syntax in this book is based on the November 21, 2000, W3C Candidate Recommendation. The most current recommendation can be found at www.w3.org/TR/xsl/. If you follow the W3C links for XSL, this is where you'll end up. Formatting objects can be inserted into a result tree created by another part of XSL, called XSLT, or XSL Transformations.

XSL Transformations   This is a markup vocabulary describing the transformation part of XSL. Most of the syntax in this book is based on the November 16, 1999, Recommendation, which can be found at www.w3.org/TR/xslt.html. XSLT takes an XML document (called a *source document*) and outputs a completely different version of the document (called a *result tree*) based on a series of filters and patterns that you include within a style sheet.

The XML Path language (XPath)   Although not technically XML, XPath is a language used to address XML document fragments, which are portions of an XML document. This language is used by XSLT (and XLink) to describe the expressions and location paths (which you'll learn about later) that manage the selection of nodes for more advanced XSL transformations. The syntax in this book is based on the November 16, 1999, Recommendation on XPath, which can be found at www.w3.org/TR/xpath.html. You'll also see XPath used by SQL Server 2000 and other databases to manage queries and resulting XML trees.

NOTE

Review www.w3.org/Style/XSL/ for the most current links and the status of all the documents relating to XSL.

UNDERSTANDING TRANSFORMATIONS

An XSLT processor begins its transformation process when it reads an XSLT document, takes a set of rules defined there, and applies them to the XML document that you want to "convert" into another kind of document—the *source document*. The new document that the processor produces is called a *result tree*; it can be another XML file, an HTML file, or even a simple text file. This result tree isn't necessarily a third "file" in the traditional sense, because it may be just loaded into memory, but in the XML world, even if something is simply loaded into memory, it is considered a document.

The XSLT processor makes decisions about how to transform the XML source document based on the way you write the XSLT style sheet. You may, for example, tell the XSLT processor to transform *only* the text element (not to be confused with a text node in general) in an XML document. You can tell the processor to do this in an XSLT style sheet by employing transformation mechanisms such as *patterns*. The pattern-matching process may remind you somewhat of a mini–search engine. The process for developing patterns will look somewhat familiar to anyone who has worked with SQL, which is a common database querying

Part iv

language. The XSLT processor searches for a pattern, and a series of one or more *templates* that match these patterns, to return a result tree. For example, the following line of code is a pattern match that matches the root node of the source document:

```
<xsl:template match="/">
```

Everything that is defined within the `template` element will end up in the result tree. There may be many other elements within that template that will in turn end up as part of the result tree, or only a few, depending on the circumstances. These elements will all be, in one way or another, part of the ultimate transformation that takes place to the source document, because they will be used to either copy parts of that source document into the result document or manage those parts in some way.

Getting Started with XSLT Tools

Before you do anything, you're going to want some tools to work with so that you can try the sample code in this chapter. The tool you choose will depend on the platform you're on.

XT

XT is easy to use, but if you're not familiar with Java and the way class paths work, it can be fairly intimidating at first. XT is an XSLT processor written by James Clark, a legendary XML guru who has been developing XML and SGML applications for years. XT is available on the *Mastering XML, Premium Edition* (Sybex, 2001) companion CD-ROM or can be downloaded at www.jclark.com.

XT makes understanding the tree structure of a result document easy because the file you want to turn into a result tree is the name of the last parameter. XT creates this file after processing the first two parameters: the source document and the style sheet document. If you leave off the last parameter—the name and location of your result tree file—XT generates the file on screen. XT is a good choice if you are comfortable running Java programs.

Architag XRay XML Editor

With the Architag XRay XML Editor from Architag International (www.architag.com), you can view transformations on the fly as you write your XSLT. It lets you create a result window from a source document and an XSLT document that you specify, and reports XSLT errors to you as you alter your code.

Internet Explorer

You can also simply browse an XML file by associating the source document with an XSLT document (using the `<?xml-stylesheet>` processing instruction in the source document as described in "Creating an XSLT Document" later in this chapter) and opening the source file in Internet Explorer (IE). The huge caveat to that is that you need to be sure that IE is using the correct parser, because older versions of IE 5 contain XSLT processors that process an older, obsolete version of XSLT.

To be sure the latest XSLT processor is installed, run a Find on your Windows operating system for the `msxml3.dll` file. If you find it, you have MSXML 3.0 on your system, which is the minimal version you need to run the samples in this chapter, which conform to the newest specification (XSLT 1.0). If you don't find it, go to `http://msdn.microsoft.com/xml/` to get the latest version. The nuances behind XSLT support in IE 5 and higher can be a little tricky, but the main thing to remember is that the standard, W3C namespace works as long as the MSXML 3.0 parser can be accessed. As this book was being written, version 4.0 was in beta, and will very likely be released by the time you read this book. Luckily, the XSLT you write for version 3.0 will work in 4.0.

Xalan

The Apache Software Foundation also makes an XSLT processor, named Xalan, which can be found at `http://xml.apache.org/xalan-c/index.html`. Binaries and source code for Java and C++ are available.

Saxon

You can also download Saxon, an XSLT processor from noted XSLT expert Michael Kay, at `http://saxon.sourceforge.net/`. Kay is the author of the excellent *XSLT Programmer's Reference* (Wrox Press, 2000).

You need a Java virtual machine, preferably the Sun JDK 1.3, on your machine to run it (it is not as reliable using the Microsoft Virtual Machine). Saxon is a good choice if you want to play with some of the extensions that can be made available to XSLT.

Learning about XSLT Node Types

Besides finding some good tools to use for working with XSLT, you'll also want to understand a few basic concepts behind the architecture of how XML documents are transformed.

XML documents consist of what are called *trees*, which are examined by XSLT processors to determine how to output results. You begin with a *source tree* and end with a *result tree*. Central to the concept of trees is the concept of *nodes*, which are, in effect, data objects that can be categorized in one way or another. When talking about a tree, or an XML hierarchy, we are talking about the way an XML document's nodes are navigated, named, sorted, and output. Seven node types are used in XSLT:

Root nodes   There can be only one root node because it represents the document's root, of which, by definition (the XML spec requires a tree), there can be only one. This node represents the document itself. Its value is the same as the document node in the Document Object Model (DOM) and can be referred to in any number of ways depending on what you are reading. It's best to refer to the root node as the root node and to the root element as the *document element* (especially since it is referred to by the DOM as documentElement).

Element nodes   An element node represents an element, can include a Uniform Resource Identifier (URI) reference, and can have comment nodes and processing instruction nodes as children. The document order is determined by the order of appearance of the elements within the root node. Any entity references are expanded, character references are resolved, and a unique identifier can exist only if the XML document containing it is validated against a document type definition (DTD) that declares that element as an ID. If there is no DTD declaration, then there are no unique identifiers. The value of this node consists of all the character data within the element. If the element has children, then the character data is concatenated (think of two strings of text strung together) in document order.

Text nodes   Text nodes consist of groups of one or more instances of character data, including character data in a CDATA section. Comments and processing instruction content are not considered character data.

Attribute nodes These are nodes consisting of attributes. If a DTD includes an #IMPLIED attribute but the XML source document does not name that attribute, there is no associated node for it. There are also no attribute nodes associated with namespace declarations.

Namespace nodes Each element also has a namespace node corresponding to its namespace prefix and the default namespace prefix (such as xsl: and xmlns, respectively).

Processing instruction nodes Any processing instruction appearing in the document has a corresponding node consisting of the name, which is the target of the processing instruction, and the value, which is a string that appears after the target but doesn't include the ?> termination delimiter. A processing instruction node is not included in the processing tree.

Comment nodes A comment's *value* is that part of the comment that falls within the <!-- and --> characters. The nodes are associated with the comment's value.

As an example of a few of these types, assume the following snippet is a full document:

```
<?xml version="1.0"?>
<?xml-stylesheet type="text/xsl" href="basic.xsl"?>
<Basic><greeting>Hello World</greeting></Basic>
```

The *root node* of the XML document fragment is the whole of the document—all three lines. The *document element* is this:

```
<Basic><greeting>Hello World</greeting></Basic>
```

The first child node of the document element happens to be an *element node* (greeting). The first child node of the root node is a *processing instruction node* (the middle line of the three).

Each node has a corresponding string value that is either an inherent part of that node or can be ascertained from the value of the node's descendants. Because of the normalization rules of XML, it's possible that white space will be stripped during the transformation process. XSLT provides ways to control this, including the xsl:text element and the xsl:space attribute. Neither the processing instruction node nor the comment node is included in an XSLT processing tree.

Part iv

Learning about XSLT Formatting

The notion of separating transformation from formatting is one of the main advantages of the XSLT style sheet model. Keeping transformations separate from formatting means you can pick how to format the XML documents you are trying to transform, by choosing a namespace that your target XSLT processor understands. You can also send your result trees via your server directly to browsers as HTML documents, or some other format, including, albeit through an additional step, PDF.

Deciding on a Formatting Model

The transformation process is basically the same no matter what your result tree looks like. Even the original IE 5–based XSL Transformation syntax is similar to the W3C's standards, although syntactic differences exist that are fatal to a compatible, write-once run-anywhere approach when attempting client-side XSLT. The formatting model you choose for the result tree, however, can vary significantly. Among the possibilities:

- ▶ You can use an HTML-based formatting model, meaning you can end up with a result tree consisting of HTML markup (either XML-compliant or not).

- ▶ You can use formatting objects based on the W3C's official recommendation for XSL (also often referred to as XSLFO), which is a series of markup tags that describe a paged media similar to what you might find in print media layout programs but that can also be displayed in browsers.

- ▶ You can output the result tree as raw text or byte streams.

- ▶ You can output the result to other XML-based vocabularies, such as SVG (Scalable Vector Graphics), an emerging vector-graphics Web standard.

- ▶ Theoretically, you can probably even output the result tree as PostScript, RTF (Rich Text Format), or some other non-XML language or markup, but the difficulties encountered in doing so probably wouldn't make it worth the bother (although never underestimate the resilience of determined programmers).

Even though there is a W3C-defined standard for formatting objects, you are not bound to it, and the W3C XSLT specs have examples showing several formatting options. There are no formal official requirements or restrictions on what to use as your result tree–formatting model.

No matter what formatting model you choose, you are likely to add what are called *literal elements* to your result tree. A literal element is an element you hard-code into your output yourself, and it isn't part of the XSLT namespace. This acts as the formatting information for the data that is inserted into a result tree from the source document. The following code shows what may seem like some strange-looking syntax within a typical formatting object template:

```
<fo:block
    font-size="40pt"
    background-color="#ff6600"
    border-color="#000033"
    start-indent="12pt">
        <xsl:apply-templates
        select="advertisement/text"/>
</fo:block>
```

The fo:block element is an example of a literal result element found in templates. The XML data can't format itself; you need to give it some help. You do this by adding these literal result elements to a template in your style sheet and using it as a formatting container of sorts for the data from the XML source document. In the preceding code, the data in the text child element of the advertisement element will take on the formatting characteristics of the surrounding literal result elements. You could just as easily have used HTML as your literal result element, assuming you were working within the scope of an HTML namespace.

Comparing Formatting Output Options

A transformation can send a result tree to a formatting namespace that tells the XSLT processor how to format the result tree. Recall that one way to apply formatting is to use HTML.

Obviously, the namespace issue discussed earlier in this chapter is a large one when you're writing to a wide audience. Even though versions of IE 5 and 5.5 exist that handle the W3C's recommended namespace, there are numerous early versions of IE lurking about that don't, which will make it impossible to be sure your audience will be able to view your documents. If that sounds like a familiar lament regarding browser conformance issues, it is.

The most obvious answers are to create your result trees on the server and send out HTML from there. Any browser can then read these files. Or, use an auto-detect script to redirect browsers to the correct page.

What happens when XSLT processors output HTML? Two key operations are taking place:

▶ The XSLT processor inserts HTML literal result elements and/or a copy of a requested XML source document node into a named HTML element so that it can be rendered as HTML in a Web browser.

▶ Unless you include a namespace declaration that indicates the HTML 4 Specification (using the xmlns="http://www.w3.org/TR/REC-html40" namespace attribute/value pair), or use the xsl:output element, the HTML that is output *must* be valid XML, because the output by default is an XML result tree.

Letting Built-In Transformations Take Over

XSLT provides a default mechanism so that there is always *something* rendered when a style sheet is created. These are "built-in" and recognized by the XSLT processor (although IE 5 has its own defaults). Any template you create overrides these defaults, but they do exist and result in text being placed into a result tree.

Built-In Element Transformations

The simplest default transformation involves the way elements are handled. If you had no definitions of your own, then the XSLT processor would handle elements as if you had written the following:

```
<xsl:template match="*|/">

    <xsl:apply-templates/>

</xsl:template>
```

The preceding code covers everything, because if you translate the search pattern to English it means "any element node or the root node." The forward slash (/) always represents the root node when it is by itself.

Built-In Text and Attribute Transformations

There is also a built-in transformation for text and attributes. This transformation copies the text and attribute values from the source document to the result tree:

```
<xsl:template match="text()|@*">
    <xsl:value-of select="."/>
</xsl:template>
```

Additional Built-In Transformations

There are also built-in transformation rules for processing instructions and comment nodes. They tell the processor to go ahead and do nothing. This means that when no rule is matched, no processing instruction or comment node is created in the result tree from the source.

What Transformations Are Not

Transformations in XSLT can involve several different processes, but generally they are all centered on the notion of a special kind of addressing based on pattern matching and expressions. This is really a pretty simple concept, although the implementation of XSLT addressing can be quite complex. If you were to translate the syntax of XSLT into English, a typical addressing mechanism in XSLT at its most basic level might go something like this: "I'm looking for every Siamese cat in your database. Please return each match as you find it." You can push these types of queries into just about any direction imaginable. You won't necessarily get a response to queries of this type, but you might, and nothing really bad happens by asking. For example, figuratively speaking, you could say something like, "I'm looking for every Siamese cat in your source document that has green ears and speaks Esperanto." Chances are, you'll come up empty. XSLT lets you try, however, using the syntax that is designed for XSLT pattern matching.

You might be wondering, then, why transformations are not called "queries." The reason is that XSLT processors don't truly respond to queries, at least not in the typical sense of a database query via SQL. XSLT converts a source document into a new result tree, based on a pattern of matches you develop. Each element in the source document is matched against the matching elements in the XSLT style sheet as the source document is read; this process is known as *ordering*. The result tree is often written out as an HTML document, but it can also be written as a group of formatting objects or even plain text. In other words, the processor *transforms* a copy of an XML source into something else.

You may end up writing this new result tree to disk, or sending it off as a message in an e-commerce environment, or displaying it in a browser. The important thing to remember about the whole transformation process is that it is quite separate from the formatting process. The transformation vocabulary (specifications as implemented by the W3C) makes no demands about how your documents should be formatted or where they should go when their results are returned.

Learning about Pattern Matching and Selecting

One key tool that drives the transformation engine is pattern matching. Perhaps the easiest way to understand pattern matching is by returning to the search for Siamese cats. Let's say you have a small database of cats. If you maintained this information in XML, it might look something like Listing 12.1.

Listing 12.1: An XML Document of Cats

```
<CATS>
<SIAMESE>
<NAME>Maurice</NAME>
<NAME>Felica</NAME>
<NAME>Fred</NAME>
<NAME>Tom</NAME>
<NAME>Elroy</NAME>
<GREENEARED>Elroy</GREENEARED>
<YELLOWEARED>Tom</YELLOWEARED>
<NOEARS>Maurice</NOEARS>
</SIAMESE>
</CATS>
```

Rather than doing a search for all the cats, you can create a pattern (a template) against which each incoming element from the source XML document is matched. You could match each instance of a cat whose name was represented in the XML source file as a value for the NAME element. The following values would show up if the result were to appear in a comma-delimited text file: Maurice, Felica, Fred, Tom, and Elroy.

Understanding the Concept of Pattern Matching

Often in any search there is a process called "drilling down," which means that you want more specific information from the results you've already retrieved. Pattern matching works in a similar way. In the current matching attempt for green-eared Siamese cats who speak Esperanto, you first need a template that will match any Siamese cat whose name is in your XML source file. This is handled by specific elements that are part of the XSLT vocabulary. To create your first template, you might merely write the following line of code:

```
<xsl:template match="NAME">
```

The preceding line of code matches any element called NAME. This pattern is not particularly effective, though, if your XML document has multiple elements with NAME children. You might have a bunch of dogs (with names) in the same database, or maybe different kinds of cats other than Siamese, so you need to find a way to filter out the stuff you don't want, unless you are sure that all the properties you give to the NAME template are properties you will want all objects that match it to have. XSLT provides convenient syntax for filtering called *location paths*.

Using Location Paths

Using xsl:template match="NAME" to match Siamese cats wasn't specific enough; you need to filter out the other cats and dogs that might be in the database. You can create a *location path* to help you address your match properly. *Location paths* are a feature of the XPath language, which is used extensively by XSLT. The structure of a location path will remind you of the kind of paths you see for URLs in your Web browser. To make your addressing specific, you just traverse the XML document tree, following its structured hierarchy to your destination:

```
<xsl:template match="CATS/SIAMESE/NAME">
```

It might be natural to assume based on what you know about XML that it would be incorrect to write

```
<xsl:template match="NAME">
```

After all, you haven't included the root element. The short version isn't invalid, however, because XSLT lets you simply ask the XSLT processor to find a match against a specific element. Whatever additional information you supply is up to you (as long as it's legal syntax according to XSLT or XPath). One form of information you can add comes in the form of operators that describe an element's relation to the current node being worked from. You'll learn more about these in "Using Pattern Operators" later in the chapter.

Let's look quickly, then, at how we might access the names of all our cats. Listing 12.2 shows a simple style sheet that outputs a text document listing all the names of Siamese cats in our source document.

Listing 12.2: Finding Out Cat Names in an XSLT Document

```
<xsl:stylesheet
 xmlns:xsl="http://www.w3.org/1999/XSL/Transform"
  version="1.0">
 <xsl:output method="text"/>
 <xsl:template match="/">
    <xsl:apply-templates
     select="CATS/SIAMESE/NAME"/>
 </xsl:template>
 <xsl:template match="CATS/SIAMESE/NAME">
    <xsl:value-of select="."/>
    <xsl:text> </xsl:text>
 </xsl:template>
</xsl:stylesheet>
```

This isn't the most efficient way of achieving what we want, but it does illustrate the use of pattern matching. The result of this document is a simple text string:

```
Maurice Felica Fred Tom Elroy
```

Again, you may not always need the entire hierarchy in the template's match attribute. In a database where every entry is a Siamese cat, you would get the same result with `"NAME"` in place of `"CATS/SIAMESE/NAME">`.

Patterns and a similar but more complex addressing mechanism called *expressions* form the core of the XSL Transformation language. One thing about it that is similar to the way Web addresses work is how you drill down; going from higher level to lower along a directory structure on the Web is similar to going down through the XML source document's hierarchy. Given the Cats XML source document, you'd get no results if you wrote something like this:

```
<xsl:template match= "CATS/GREENEARED">
```

This kind of match would not be successful because the GREENEARED element is a child of the SIAMESE element, not the CATS element. A pattern-matching sequence must use a very specific procedure that strictly follows the hierarchy of an XML source document in order to be success-ful. You'll find that expressions deviate from this rule to some extent, but even complex expressions require a context from which everything else is referenced. In a nutshell, patterns must use what is called a *context node* from which XSLT processors initiate their search. A context node is the first instance of a match within a transformation element. If there is no value named in an XSLT element's match attribute, then the context node is always the root node. In the preceding example, the context node was CATS. The only way to drill down is to work with:

- ▶ The element's children
- ▶ The element's attributes
- ▶ The element's siblings (if expressions are used)
- ▶ The element's parents (if expressions are used)

TIP

Much XSLT matching will be done without the knowledge you have here. In other words, you already know there is no GREENEARED element that is a child of the CATS element. But what if you don't know whether there is or not? There are two possible solutions. (1) XSLT allows for extremely sophisticated filtering, so you might be able to accomplish a satisfactory match using more sophisti-cated patterns. (2) This is a good reason why DTDs (or schema) should be used whenever possible. A DTD will tell you whether or not such an element is per-mitted, and you can then manage your patterns based on the rules in the DTD.

These rules are managed by *location match patterns*, which guide the process of identifying the way location paths are traversed. In the example, we established our context node using the match attribute of the xsl-template element. Then we focused on getting to specific children of that element. All XSL transformations follow this basic concept. It can all get pretty complex, but just remember that no mat-ter how extravagant some XSLT code may seem, it is all based on this general matching or selecting mechanism that is designed to help you filter out specific information.

Using a More Practical Example   Consider a situation in which you want only one small portion of an XML document to be transformed. Much of an XML document may be dedicated to information that you're not interested in showing to anyone else. If you are developing for a news-paper, you may want your classified advertising to have XML constructs, but you don't want to display or send to the client such items as run dates or client names. XSLT allows you to simply choose which elements you want to display or send. We'll use the information in Listings 12.3 and 12.4 to demonstrate.

Listing 12.3: An XML Source Document for XSLT Pattern Matching

```xml
<?xml version="1.0" encoding="UTF-8"?>
<!DOCTYPE SeasonStats SYSTEM "stats.dtd">
<SeasonStats>
    <Player id="p0001">
        <Name>Billy Freedom</Name>
        <Team>Chicago Cubs</Team>
        <ERA>1.08</ERA>
        <W>28</W>
        <L>0</L>
        <Sv>0</Sv>
        <Hold>0</Hold>
        <G>28</G>
        <IP>200</IP>
        <H>28</H>
        <R>24</R>
        <ER>24</ER>
        <BB>26</BB>
        <K>297</K>
        <AVGAGAINST>.238</AVGAGAINST>
        <SUP>2.62</SUP>
    </Player>
</SeasonStats>
```

Let's assume that all we want to output is the name of the player in Listing 12.3. Quite a bit of information in the XML source document isn't pertinent to our task at hand. So we create a simple XSLT document—a style sheet—that, in effect, matches the Name element and displays its child node, which in this case is a text node containing the string "Billy Freedom". The style sheet will attempt to match only *one* element for transformation; it will create a result tree out of that element and leave the rest of the original document and elements alone.

The initial match in this case is made on the root node of the XML document, which is always the document itself (not the root *element*, as one might suspect). Listing 12.4 shows the style sheet.

NOTE

Remember this important point: The root node of the XML source document is always the document instance, which is a node. The patterns that are matched against this node are matched to the children of the root node, and do not include the node itself.

Listing 12.4: A Style Sheet Outputting a Single Node

```
<?xml version="1.0" encoding="iso-8859-1" ?>
<xsl:stylesheet
  xmlns:xsl="http://www.w3.org/1999/XSL/Transform"
    version="1.0">
    <xsl:output method="text"/>
    <xsl:template match="/">
        <xsl:apply-templates/>
    </xsl:template>
    <xsl:template match="Player">
        <xsl:apply-templates select="Name"/>
    </xsl:template>
    <xsl:template match="Name">
        <xsl:value-of select="."/>
    </xsl:template>
</xsl:stylesheet>
```

The key ingredient to this code is this fragment: `xsl:template match="Name"`. This element is used to create templates, or patterns to match. These templates, when selected by the `xsl:apply-templates` element, contain instructions on how to copy nodes from the source document into the result tree. In this case, a template was made for the source document's Name element. The `xsl:apply-templates` element processes a set of nodes defined by the `xsl:template` element (here, any Player element) and accessed by the `xsl:apply-templates select` attribute (here, any Name element within a Player).

By using no `select` attribute in the template for the root node (the first template in Listing 12.4, the one that "matches" just a slash: "/"), all of the root node's child templates are processed. Actually, we could have eliminated the root node template and ended up with the same result. If you remove these three lines of code from Listing 12.4

```
<xsl:template match="/">
    <xsl:apply-templates/>
</xsl:template>
```

you get the same result: the text string "Billy Freedom".

Understanding Selection Patterns

Pattern matching involves many possible addressing routines, and the sections that follow don't come close to covering them all. But to get a handle on the concept, it's best to take a look at the simplest transformation elements first.

The one important point is to remember the difference between *pattern matches* and *selection patterns* (generally referred to as *selections*). Selection patterns use XPath expressions to greatly expand your pattern's filtering capabilities. Pattern matches are limited to templates, numbering (XSLT has automatic numbering capabilities), and keys (which offer a kind of cross-referencing capability to XSLT).

Pattern matches are also limited in the patterns that can be constructed. You can use pattern matches only on element names, child elements, descendants, and attributes. Selection patterns, however, have the full vocabulary of XPath expressions at their disposal, so in addition to what pattern matches can accomplish, expressions give you access to parent and sibling elements.

Another big difference between pattern matches and selection patterns is that pattern matches only generate node lists, whereas selection patterns can also generate strings, numbers, and Booleans.

NOTE

The truth is, in your day-to-day XSLT development you often won't notice the semantic differences between pattern matching and selection patterns. But you'll find that this knowledge comes in handy during those occasions where you run into trouble, like generating result trees that aren't what you expect.

Using Expressions

So far you've seen how pattern matching uses a process similar to searching to make it possible for you to develop your result trees. Architecturally, the process is not quite that simple. A pattern is considered a subset of a larger group of *expressions* that are used for a variety of transformation purposes. These are expressed in the XPath language, which is a separate set of syntax rules governing XML node access.

Evaluating Expressions

Technically, an expression is a set of conditions used to determine whether a node meets some criteria. If it does, the result is one of the following four possible data types:

- ► A node set

- ► A number, which can be any floating-point number. If you flinch when you encounter mathematical terms, a floating-point number is basically a number with a decimal point in it, like 3.14 or 55.5555. Specifically, XPath numbers are allowed any IEEE double-precision 64-bit format value.

- ► A Boolean (true or false)

- ► A string (in Unicode format)

Some specific uses for expressions include:

- ► Generating text into the result tree using the xsl:value-of element's select attribute

- ► Managing conditionals to process named nodes using the test attribute in the xsl:if and xsl:when elements

- ► Processing nodes from the source tree using the xsl:apply-templates, xsl:for-each, xsl-sort, and xsl:copy-of elements

- ► Using the xsl:template element to name patterns matched to the source tree using the match attribute

- ► Managing default variables or processing values using the xsl:number, xsl:param, and xsl-variable elements

When you're evaluating an expression, you are not strictly limited to the context node. More complex expressions evaluate by referencing the context in a number of additional ways. The simplest is the context node, but there are five possible uses in all:

- ► The context node

- ► The context position and context size (always both, and the integer representing the context position is never greater than the context size)

- ► A set of XSLT functions (often referred to as a *function library*), which consists of functions built into the XSLT language and which facilitates the expression evaluation process

Part iv

▶ Variable bindings (derived from the way XSLT variable names map out to variable values)

▶ The namespace declarations in scope

Using Node Tests

Expressions can contain tests for nodes that aren't elements or attributes, such as text nodes. For example, MYELEMENT/text() will select the text node children of the MYELEMENT node. Four node tests you'll encounter are presented in Table 12.1.

TABLE 12.1: Node Tests

NODE TEST	DESCRIPTION
text()	Any text node
node()	Any type of node
comment()	Any comment node
pi()	Any processing instruction node

Using XSLT Predicates and Expression Operators

One subset of expressions, called *patterns*, is used to manage the selection process. Another subset of expressions is the *predicate*. A predicate typically extends the capability of a pattern match by filtering the pattern's selected nodes. Filtering will be explored in more detail in the section on functions, but one commonly used function returns the position of a node in a node list. The best way to understand how this works is to see it in action. Review the following XML document to find out the position of a specific node in the node list:

```
<?xml version='1.0'?>
<?xml-stylesheet type="text/xsl"
  href="position2.xsl" ?>
<nodeTester type="referral">
  <function>
```

```
        <name>position() function</name>
      </function>
      <text> The position in the node list is:</text>
    </nodeTester>
```

To find out the node list position of an element—for instance, the text element—you could develop a simple test using a predicate that takes advantage of one of XSLT's built-in functions as follows:

```
<?xml version='1.0'?>
<xsl:stylesheet
 xmlns:xsl="http://www.w3.org/1999/XSL/Transform">
    <xsl:output method="text" indent="no"/>
    <xsl:template match="nodeTester">
       <xsl:apply-templates/>
    </xsl:template>
    <xsl:template match="text"> The position in the
    node list is:
       <xsl:value-of select="position()"/>
    </xsl:template>
</xsl:stylesheet>
```

This results in the following result tree (output as text):

```
position() function

The position in the node list is: 4
```

Using Operators

There are two kinds of operators. One kind is used for managing expressions, the other for pattern matching.

Using Expression Operators

Expression operators help manage expressions within the context of a particular data type. You'll encounter them most often when using predicates and functions. The data-type operators used in expressions are shown in Table 12.2.

Part iv

TABLE 12.2: XSLT Expression Operators

OPERATOR	DESCRIPTION
+	Used with numbers for addition
–	Used with numbers for subtraction
*	Used with numbers for multiplication
=	Equal to
!=	Not equal to
< (< when used in an attribute value)	Less than
<= (<= when used in an attribute value)	Less than or equal to
>	Greater than
>=	Greater than or equal to

TIP

Later in this chapter you'll encounter a special character called a *variable reference* ($). The variable reference is not an expression operator, but rather is used as a way to reference an XSLT variable.

Some operators can also be called by name and are called *operator names*, as described in Table 12.3.

TABLE 12.3: Operator Names

OPERATOR	DESCRIPTION
and	Logical and, meaning the combination of two selections
or	Logical or, meaning one or the other selection
mod	Modulus, which takes the remainder of two divided numbers
div	Division

Using Pattern Operators

Various XSLT operators are important because they help manage patterns; in particular, they help describe the scope of patterns. Technically, they're shortcuts to more complex descriptions of XSLT patterns, but they're easy to use and make for shorter code.

The @ Operator   The @ is an attribute operator that locates the named attribute within a given element. To use it, you place the operator in front of the name of the attribute you're searching for within the search pattern string:

```
xsl:value-of select="keyword@name"
```

The preceding line of code translates in simple English as "Select the value of the name attribute of the keyword element." If you're trying to perform a pattern match for a specific attribute value, you can use brackets to set it off:

```
xsl:value-of select="keyword[@name='auto_exterior']"
```

This translates in English as "Select a name attribute of the keyword element whose value is auto_exterior."

The * Operator   The * operator mimics a wildcard, which means it can find all instances of a named node's children. It's not really a wildcard in a true programming sense, but is instead an operator for managing the syntax of abbreviated axis identifiers. Nevertheless, you will see it referred to often as a wildcard in XSLT documentation, so we'll follow that convention in the examples in this chapter.

To see this operator at work, take a look at the next two code listings. Both of them are used to format an XML source document fragment. Listing 12.5 demonstrates what happens when one element is selected within a template match pattern. (The source document is Listing 12.9, which appears later in this chapter.)

Listing 12.5: Selecting One Element

```
<?xml version='1.0'?>
<xsl:stylesheet
  xmlns:xsl="http://www.w3.org/1999/XSL/Transform"
  version="1.0">
  <xsl:template match="/">
    <HTML>
      <BODY>
```

```
                <xsl:apply-templates
                  select="advertisement/text"/>
             </BODY>
          </HTML>
      </xsl:template>
      <xsl:template match="text">
         <p style="font-family:sans-serif;
            color:#003300; font-size:12pt">
         <xsl:value-of select="*"/>
         </p>
      </xsl:template>
   </xsl:stylesheet>
```

NOTE
You'll be examining elements such as `xsl:for-each` and `xsl:value-of` **a bit later in this chapter.**

The result of this transformation looks like this:

```
<HTML>
<BODY>
<p style="font-family:sans-serif; color:#003300;
font-size:12pt"> Computers Director of Information
Technology
</p>
</BODY>
</HTML>
```

The only element that has any formatting displayed is the `advertisement` element.

You can quickly amend your document to display the `advertisement` element *and all its children* by simply adding a wildcard after a backslash:

```
<xsl:for-each select="advertisement/*">
```

If we add this feature to Listing 12.5, the style sheet looks like Listing 12.6.

Listing 12.6: Using a Wildcard

```
<?xml version='1.0'?>
<xsl:stylesheet
 xmlns:xsl="http://www.w3.org/1999/XSL/Transform"
 version="1.0">
```

```
<xsl:template match="/">
    <HTML>
        <BODY>
            <xsl:apply-templates
            select="advertisement/text/*"/>
        </BODY>
    </HTML>
</xsl:template>
<xsl:template match="text">
    <p style="font-family:sans-serif;
    color:#003300; font-size:12pt">
    <xsl:value-of select="*"/>
    </p>
</xsl:template>
</xsl:stylesheet>
```

It's the same style sheet, with that one exception of a new wildcard operator. As you can see within the xsl:value-of element, you can also use the operator by itself as an attribute value. In both uses of the wildcard operator in Listing 12.6, it is part of an abbreviated location path. Here are the results of the revised style sheet:

```
<HTML>

    <BODY>Computers Director of Information Technology Modern
    Communications is seeking a proven and dedicated IT profes-
    sional with at least 5 years experience in enterprise, sys-
    tems and network management and administration. Must have
    experience in COBOL, Y2K, PBX systems, Novell, Networking,
    and be able to manage large-scale enterprise systems.no calls
    please

    </BODY>

</HTML>
```

You can see that no filtering has been done. If you look at Listing 12.7 and look at the text element (which is a child of the advertisement element, not shown in the document fragment in Listing 12.7), you'll see that all the text was copied into the result tree, even if some of the text is contained within child elements of the text element. Note that Listing 12.7 is a document fragment that consists of only a small portion of a larger XML document, whose root is the advertisement element, not shown here. You can download the source code at www.tumeric.net/projects/books/complete/support/Chapter12/L1207.xml.

Listing 12.7. A Source Document Fragment

```
<text>
    <font size="10"><center>
        <keyword name="empl_category" punct=" ">
        Computers</keyword>
        <keyword name="empl_title"
         punct=" ">Director of Information
         Technology </keyword>
    </center></font>
    <keyword name="empl_experience">Modern
    Communications is seeking a proven and
    dedicated IT professional with at least 5
    years experience in enterprise, systems and
    network management and administration.
    </keyword>
    <keyword name="empl_skills">Must have
    experience in COBOL, Y2K, PBX
    systems, Novell, Networking, and be able to
    manage large-scale enterprise systems.
    </keyword>
    <center>
        <keyword name="phone">no calls
        please</keyword>
    </center>
</text>
```

Using / and // Operators   You can manage your pattern selection process by using a / or // operator to tell an XSLT processor how to navigate a source document's hierarchy. The forward slash (/) tells the processor where a named node lies in relation to its child or parent. The node to the left of the slash is a parent of the node on the right, and vice versa. The node on the right is a child of whatever is on the left:

```
xsl:value-of select ="PARENTELEMENT/CHILDELEMENT"
```

Another selection operator is the double forward slash (//). This is called *the recursive descent operator*, which tells the processor to search for every node named on the right of the operator that is below the node named on the left of the operator. So PARENT//CHILD would return every CHILD node under PARENT, even those with another node in between, as in PARENT/OLDERCHILD/CHILD.

By default, if there is nothing to the left of the element, the processor assumes you're searching from the root node. Thus, //MYELEMENT would result in every instance of MYELEMENT being returned. In other words, the recursive descent operator looks for all the descendants of the named node and doesn't care where in the hierarchy they are located.

The . (period), or *current context operator*, tells the processor to look for the pattern named on the right within the current context. When there is one slash following the current context operator (./), the XSLT processor searches in direct children of the current context. When the current context operator is followed by two slashes (.//), the processor searches in all children from the current context down to the bottom of the hierarchy. For example, ./TEXT would generally mean the same thing as /TEXT. However, .//TEXT would result in all TEXT elements being selected that are descendants, or below, the current context node (the current element).

The / Operator   Also called the *union operator*, the vertical bar (|) is used to allow your pattern to take an either/or search. You can use it in a match pattern, like so:

```
<xsl:apply-templates
 match="MYELEMENT | YOURELEMENT"/>
```

Using Grouping Operators   You can also use *grouping operators* to manage hierarchy navigation. The grouping operators include parentheses (), brackets [], and braces { }. Generally, brackets are used for filtering operations; they describe conditions that need to be satisfied, such as the following, where you search for a Siamese cat with yellow ears:

```
SIAMESE[EARS="YELLOW"]
```

The preceding code searches for a child element of the SIAMESE element called EARS, then drills further down by checking whether the content of EARS is YELLOW. The corresponding XML fragment would look like this:

```
<SIAMESE>
<EARS>YELLOW</EARS>
</SIAMESE>
```

CREATING AN XSLT DOCUMENT

An XSLT document uses namespaces to enable XML documents to pass transformation and formatting instructions to an XSLT processor. The style sheet can then be accessed with a processing instruction in the XML source document:

```
<?xml-stylesheet type="text/xsl"
href="myXSLdoc.xsl" ?>
```

Note the difference in the type attribute value when you are processing an XML document for display using CSS instead of XSLT:

```
<?xml-stylesheet type="text/css"
href="myXSLdoc.css" ?>
```

There is no requirement that a processing instruction be used in order to process an XML source tree with an XSLT document. XSLT processors may be able to process the document in some other way. You could, for example, provide the processor the information through parameters or within a visual editing/processing environment.

Managing XSLT Processing Instructions

The processing instruction for a style sheet can take several *pseudo attributes*. Pseudo attributes are those parts of a processing instruction that are similar to attributes in an XML element and help define the processing instruction. The same pseudo attributes are used whether you're linking an XSLT style sheet or a CSS style sheet. All but the alternate pseudo attribute behave like the HTML 4 LINK element (<LINK REL="stylesheet">); alternate indicates whether the style sheet is considered the preferred style sheet or is an alternate. The available pseudo attributes are shown in Table 12.4.

TABLE 12.4: Pseudo Attributes Used with the <?xml-stylesheet ?> Processing Instruction

PSEUDO ATTRIBUTE	REQUIRED	DESCRIPTION
href	Yes	Gives the location of the style sheet as a URI string.
type	Yes	Names the kind of style sheet being linked.
title	No	Names the style sheet.

TABLE 12.4 continued: Pseudo Attributes Used with the <?xml-stylesheet ?> Processing Instruction

PSEUDO ATTRIBUTE	REQUIRED	DESCRIPTION
media	No	Names the target media.
charset	No	Names the character set associated with the style sheet.
alternate	No	Available values are yes and no, with a default of no.

The XSLT style sheet itself is an XML document. Like with all XML documents, you can create an XSLT style sheet in any text editor. Rather than saving the file with an .xml extension, however, give it an .xsl extension.

The style sheet's elements all have a leading prefix that matches the namespace prefix declared at the beginning of the style sheet. Technically, you don't need to use the xsl: prefix you'll find throughout this chapter (you can use another as long as it binds itself to the XSLT namespace), but you should use it anyway because it's the general convention.

Using the *xsl:processing-instruction* Element

You use the xsl:processing-instruction element when you want to output a processing instruction. Any special characters occurring within the element's contents will not be escaped. A processing instruction invoking XML 1 looks like this:

```
<xsl:processing-instruction name="xml">version="1.0"

</xsl:processing-instruction>
```

This element can appear anywhere within the xsl:template element and has two attributes. The name attribute is required; possible values are any valid XML character data. The optional xml:space attribute (possible values default or preserve) is used to manage white space.

Establishing the Root Element

Like any XML document, an XSLT document must have one and only one element. The root element for an XSLT document is always the xsl:stylesheet element.

Part iv

NOTE
You can use the `xsl:transform` element in place of the `xsl:stylesheet` element—the two elements are interchangeable and are defined in precisely the same way in the XSLT DTD.

Using the *xsl:stylesheet* Element

The `xsl:stylesheet` element is always the first element you'll encounter in a style sheet. You can create a template, then apply it as needed. The `xsl:stylesheet` is where you specify any namespaces for the style sheet. If you use formatting objects, for example, you can say so within the `xsl:stylesheet` element using the `result-ns` attribute:

```
<?xml version='1.0'?>
<xsl:stylesheet
    version="1.0"
    xmlns:xsl="http://www.w3.org/1999/XSL/Transform"
    xmlns:fo="http://www.w3.org/1999/XSL/Format"
    result-ns="fo">
```

The preceding code tells the XSLT processor that it should format the result tree using formatting objects. There are other formatting procedures available to the processor. The key question will be whether or not the processor will honor your request. The extensibility of the language means that there is considerable discretion in declaring result namespaces, as long as they don't conflict with the namespace (or its prefix) assigned for your style sheet.

Managing Namespaces within the *xsl:stylesheet* Element   Early in this chapter you learned about how you can use different formatting models in your result tree. Namespaces can be confusing, especially if you're not really interested in namespaces and just want to write style sheets. Namespaces are important, however, because they manage the way XSLT and XML documents interact with one another. One way this management occurs is when you use namespaces to define the formatting model. There are several namespaces that can be used within the `xsl:stylesheet` element. Some of these define the formatting model; others provide information about the transformation process. Some of these namespaces are:

```
xmlns:xsl="http://www.w3.org/1999/XSL/Transform"
```

This is the official standard transformation namespace used as part of the W3C Recommendation. You should use this for XSLT style sheets you expect to follow the most current standards. Be aware that the only versions of IE that support it are those that use the MXSML 3.0 parser.

```
xmlns:xsl="http://www.w3.org/TR/WD-xsl"
```

This is the namespace you must use for style sheets processed by most instances of IE 5. The bad news is that most instances of IE 5 won't process style sheets with the `"http: ... Transform"` namespace mentioned above, and most processors that can render that namespace won't process IE 5–compliant style sheets. This is, of course, because early versions of IE 5 didn't use a standards-based namespace.

```
xmlns:axsl="http://www.w3.org/1999/XSL/
    ➥TransformAlias"
```

This namespace allows you to create an "alias" transformation namespace. This allows you to place XSLT elements into literal elements, without the XSLT processor actually processing them as XSLT elements. They are merely written into the result output. In your style sheet, such an element might look something like this:

```
<asxl:template match="someElement">
<!- some result elements here ->
</asxl:template>
```

Managing Result Trees with Namespaces   You can describe how you want your result formatted by including namespace attribute values within the `xsl:stylesheet` element. Note that the result namespace tells the processor what method it *should* use for transforming the source tree. The processor is not required to do so, however. In fact, the XSLT processor is not required to use *any* specific formatting vocabulary. A result namespace attribute can only offer a recommendation, or preference, for how the source tree should be transformed.

You can define the result to be formatting objects by using the following namespace:

```
xmlns:fo="http://www.w3.org/1999/XSL/Format"
```

You should use this in conjunction with the `result-ns="fo"` attribute name/value pair, but this is not a requirement. Thus, to make a fully

compliant, standards-based XSL style sheet using formatting objects, you
would use the following style sheet element:

```
<?xml version="1.0"?>
<xsl:stylesheet
    version="1.0"
    xmlns:xsl="http://www.w3.org/1999/XSL/Transform"
    xmlns:fo="http://www.w3.org/1999/XSL/Format"
    result-ns="fo">

...

</xsl:stylesheet>
```

Use this namespace to declare your result tree as being HTML
4–compliant:

```
xmlns="http://www.w3.org/TR/REC-html40"
```

This means that the XSLT processor should (but is not required to) output the result tree in a way that is compliant with HTML 4. Empty elements can thus end up in the result tree with no closing slash mark
(<br>). If you don't use this namespace, the XSLT processor will transform empty elements by including closing slash marks (<br/>), according to XML rules.

NOTE

An exception to this is when you use the xsl:output element, which also
allows you to name your result output formatting. You'll explore this element
later in this chapter.

When working with XHTML, an XML-based version of HTML under
development at the W3C, use the following namespace:

```
<xsl:stylesheet
    xmlns:xsl="http://www.w3.org/TR/xhtml1">
```

If you know your style sheet will contain only one template for the root
node, you can use a simplified form of syntax for managing HTML:

```
<html
    xmlns:xsl="http://www.w3.org/1999/XSL/Transform"
    xmlns:xsl="http://www.w3.org/TR/xhtml1"
    xsl:version="1.0">
```

The preceding code is the same as using this:

```
<xsl:stylesheet
    version="1.0"
    xmlns:xsl="http://www.w3.org/1999/XSL/Transform"
    xmlns:xsl="http://www.w3.org/TR/xhtml1">
```

You can use a processor-specific namespace, if you know the XSLT processor will support the namespace you're using in your attribute value. The following namespace is used by XT, James Clark's XSLT processor, to output raw text:

```
xmlns="java:com.jclark.xsl.sax.NXMLOutputHandler"
```

SVG is a vector-based imaging markup language in development at the W3C. This namespace declares the result to be in SVG format:

```
xmlns="http://www.w3.org/Graphics/
➥SVG/svg-19990412.dtd"
```

NOTE

The SVG DTD declared in the preceding code is a specific working draft. Any future processor that supports SVG will probably use a different namespace. This example is used for illustrative purposes only. Remember that namespaces require processor support in order to work.

As you might have surmised from this review of formatting namespaces, it's not the prefix assigned to the namespace that is important. An XSLT processor won't recognize a namespace by its prefix. It will (or won't) recognize the URI assigned to that prefix. You can write your own processor in Visual Basic, put it on your NT server so that it works with Active Server Pages (ASP), and have it output XHTML. The key for creating an XSLT-compliant program will be, aside from programming skills, making sure the processor recognizes the URI and processes the result accordingly.

Using the *xsl:exclude-result-prefixes* Attribute   This attribute is used in the `xsl:stylesheet` element for those occasions when you want to include style sheet elements in your result tree without confusing the XSLT processor. You can use the `xsl:exclude-result-prefixes` attribute in literal result elements (non-XSLT elements) to achieve the same effect. The value of this attribute in either context should contain prefixes of the namespaces you want to exclude from the processor's XSLT interpretation, separated by white space if there is more than one prefix.

Using the *xsl:namespace-alias* Element

You can use the xsl:namespace-alias element to generate result trees consisting of style sheets. To do this, first declare a namespace in the top-level element of your style sheet (the xsl:stylesheet element) in addition to the namespace you're using with the XSLT document you are creating. Then use the declared namespace with the stylesheet-prefix attribute, and set the namespace attribute in the result document to be the XSLT namespace using the result-prefix attribute. (Both of these attributes are required; no others are available.) For an example, view the namespace-alias.xsl document on the CD-ROM bundled with *Mastering XML, Premium Edition* (Sybex, 2001) using namespace-alias.xml as the source document.

Learning about *xsl:stylesheet* Child Elements and Attributes

Children of the xsl:stylesheet element (except for result child elements) are shown in Table 12.5. The child elements of these elements are also shown, thus giving you a summary of many of the elements available to you as an XSLT developer. They are based on the November 16, 1999, W3C Recommendation.

TABLE 12.5: Child Elements of the xsl:stylesheet Element, and *Their* Child Elements

ELEMENT	CHILDREN
xsl:import	None
xsl:include	None
xsl:strip-space	None
xsl:output	None
xsl:preserve-space	None
xsl:key	None
xsl:functions	None
xsl:namespace-alias	None
xsl:decimal-format	None
xsl:attribute-set	xsl:attribute, xsl:use

TABLE 12.5 continued: Child Elements of the `xsl:stylesheet` Element, and *Their* Child Elements

ELEMENT	CHILDREN
`xsl:import`	None
`xsl:variable`	`xsl:processing-instruction`, `xsl:comment`, `xsl:element`, `xsl:attribute`, `xsl:apply-templates`, `xsl:call-template`, `xsl:apply-imports`, `xsl:for-each`, `xsl:value-of`, `xsl:copy-of`, `xsl:number`, `xsl:choose`, `xsl:if`, `xsl:text`, `xsl:copy`, `xsl:variable`, `xsl:message`
`xsl:param`	`xsl:processing-instruction`, `xsl:comment`, `xsl:element`, `xsl:attribute`, `xsl:apply-templates`, `xsl:call-template`, `xsl:apply-imports`, `xsl:for-each`, `xsl:value-of`, `xsl:copy-of`, `xsl:number`, `xsl:choose`, `xsl:if`, `xsl:text`, `xsl:copy`, `xsl:variable`, `xsl:message`
`xsl:template`	`xsl:processing-instruction`, `xsl:comment`, `xsl:element`, `xsl:attribute`, `xsl:apply-templates`, `xsl:call-template`, `xsl:apply-imports`, `xsl:for-each`, `xsl:value-of`, `xsl:copy-of`, `xsl:number`, `xsl:choose`, `xsl:if`, `xsl:text`, `xsl:copy`, `xsl:variable`, `xsl:message`, any result elements

The child elements in Table 12.5 can generally appear in any order. There are two exceptions to this rule: If you use the `xsl:import` element, it must always be the first child element of the `xsl:stylesheet` element, and if you use the `xsl:output` element, it must be a top-level element (which means it must appear before any of the other elements aside from other top-level elements such as `xsl:import` and `xsl:include`). You'll learn more about these elements later in the chapter.

Table 12.6 summarizes the attributes that are available to the `xsl:stylesheet` element.

TABLE 12.6: Attributes of the `xsl:stylesheet` Element

ATTRIBUTE	REQUIRED	DESCRIPTION
`xml:space`	No	An XML attribute that tells the XSLT processor what to do with white space. Possible values are `default` and `preserve`.
`id`	No	The style sheet's unique identifier.

TABLE 12.6 continued: Attributes of the xsl:stylesheet Element

ATTRIBUTE	REQUIRED	DESCRIPTION
xmlns:xsl	Yes (but you can use a prefix other than xsl)	Declares a namespace for the style sheet; for the current specification, the DTD for XSLT indicates that this is a fixed attribute with the value of http://www.w3.org/1999/XSL/Transform.
extension-element-prefixes	No	A white space–delimited list of additional namespaces that can be used as extensions.
exclude-result-prefixes	No	A white space–delimited list of namespaces that should not be processed as XSL Transformation elements.
version	Yes	States what version of XSLT the style sheet uses.

MASTERING TEMPLATES

An XSLT template governs the way specific elements are matched and transformed. These specific elements can include the entire XML source tree or only a small portion of it. The choice is made through the use of templates. Templates are matched up against source tree elements, and formatting elements are inserted into them by another part of the style sheet.

The core process underlying the use of XSLT templates is a programming trick called *recursion*. In the programming world, recursion occurs when a function calls itself, which in some languages can be a dangerous thing if you don't include a way to stop it from calling itself (the function may just repeat forever). In XSLT, this isn't a problem. XSLT templates are able to apply themselves within their own definitions, and the action elements that apply templates (surprisingly enough, called xsl:apply-templates elements) can search recursively for templates that are defined later in the style sheet.

Understanding the Concept of Templates

On a purely tactical level (but not a technical one), templates are much like the master pages in page layout programs like QuarkXPress and Adobe PageMaker. These print-publishing software programs allow you to create a master page that you can apply to a newly created page. When you apply a master page to a page, the master page automatically inserts all its objects into the page. A similar concept works with XSLT templates. The structure of a multiple-template XSLT document looks something like this:

```
ROOT TEMPLATE
template a
template b
template c
template d
template e
template f
```

You then apply `template a`, b, c, d, e, or f (or any combination of these) to the root template using one of several processing elements, which include `xsl:apply-templates`, `xsl:for-each`, `xsl:sort`, and `xsl:copy-of`. These elements manage node processing. They don't insert any text data, which is the responsibility of the `xsl:value-of` element.

The easiest way to go about managing templates is to define each template for each node you want to process. Will an element named `myelement` have a large typeface? Then define your template for that element `myelement` by using either a formatting object with a large typeface or an HTML object with CSS styling and a large typeface type defined in the CSS. Define each node one by one until you have a series of defined templates. Then you can develop your style sheet easily by adding the template(s) as the need arises.

Using Template Elements

To understand how templates are used, let's get right into the elements that are used to manage them. In the next few sections we'll look at the two key elements: The `xsl:template` element is used to define a template, and the `xsl:apply-templates` element is used to apply it and its children. (There are other ways to add content to templates besides the `xsl:apply-templates` element, but they will be covered in later sections.)

Using the *xsl:template* Element

A template manages the way a source tree or a portion of the source tree is transformed. Generally, when you build a style sheet, you'll build a series of templates that match elements you'd like to output. The xsl:template element defines a set of rules for transforming nodes in a source document into the result tree. This is handled by the match attribute, whose value provides the pattern.

You might have an element named CATS in your XML source document (document instance). In the example that follows, the XSLT processor will search for CATS elements and insert the corresponding content into an HTML div element by copying it from the source tree:

```
<xsl:template match="CATS">
    <div>
        <xsl:apply-templates/>
    </div>
</xsl:template>
```

The preceding example is rudimentary. Most likely, you'll want to be more specific about what you want to do. As it stands now, the template processes the children of its selected node set, which is the set of nodes that matches the node specified by the xsl:template match attribute value. This means that given the XML file

```
<?xml version='1.0'?>
    <CATS>
        <SIAMESE>Sam</SIAMESE>
        <PERSIAN>Pete</PERSIAN>
    </CATS>
```

you'll end up with just this in your result:

```
<div>Sam Pete</div>
```

Table 12.7 lists the attributes available to the xsl:template element and provides a brief description of their use.

TABLE 12.7: Attributes of the xsl:template Element

ATTRIBUTE	REQUIRED	DESCRIPTION
mode	No	Identifies the processing mode and matches it against an apply-templates element that has a matching mode value.
name	No	Gives a name to the template so that it can be accessed by the apply-templates element.

TABLE 12.7 continued: Attributes of the `xsl:template` Element

ATTRIBUTE	REQUIRED	DESCRIPTION
priority	No	Used to prioritize among duplicate matches.
match	No	Identifies the node to be processed. A value of / indicates that the root node should be processed.

Using the *xsl:apply-templates* Element

This element tells the processor to process a named template (which means the children of the named template are processed) that has been defined using the `xsl:template` element. Child elements of `apply-templates` include `xsl:sort` and `xsl:with-param`.

The possible attribute values for `xsl:apply-templates` are `mode` and `select`. You'll probably use the `select` attribute most often; it tells the processor which template to return into the output. If `select` is not used, the processor will process the templates of the current node in the order of their appearance in the source document. The `mode` attribute identifies the processing mode and selects only those `template` elements that have a matching mode value.

In the example that follows, the template for the P element is applied within the same context as its description. In this case the child nodes of an XML source file's P element are applied to the result tree. It gives the result tree the following formatting instructions: "Apply all templates that match child elements of the P element from the source document and insert into the result tree as instructed by those templates."

```
<xsl:template match="P">
    <fo:block font-size="12pt">
        <xsl:apply-templates/>
    </fo:block>
</xsl:template>
```

The `xsl:apply-templates` element tells the processor to look for any other templates that match the `xsl:-templates select` attribute in the style sheet and apply them here if they match child elements of the context node. Note that in creating this template, you don't have to use the `apply-templates` element within the `xsl:template` element to make it work. You could choose to apply the template somewhere else:

```
<xsl:template match="P">
    <fo:block font-size="12pt">
    </fo:block>
</xsl:template>
<xsl:template match="DIV">
    <fo:block>
        <xsl:apply-templates select="P"/>
    </fo:block>
</xsl:template>
```

In the preceding block of code, the template is defined in one place and applied in another. In the previous lines of code, the processor will insert P children of any DIV element into the result tree.

If you use the `xsl:apply-templates` element without the `select` attribute, be aware that you may inadvertently be applying default templates. In other words, you might be inserting text nodes (or some other node), even though that is not your intent. Consider the XSLT shown in Listing 12.8.

Listing 12.8: Default Rules Using *xsl:apply-templates*

```
<?xml version='1.0'?>
<xsl:stylesheet version="1.0"
xmlns:xsl="http://www.w3.org/1999/XSL/Transform">
    <xsl:output method="text" indent="no"/>
    <xsl:template match="nodeTester">
        <xsl:apply-templates/>
    </xsl:template>
    <xsl:template match="text">
        <xsl:variable name="myPositionVariable"
         select="position()"/>
        NodeList position =
        <xsl:value-of select="$myPositionVariable"/>
    </xsl:template>
</xsl:stylesheet>
```

Now take a look at the source document in Listing 12.9.

Listing 12.9: Source Document for Listing 12.8

```
<?xml version='1.0'?>
<?xml-stylesheet type="text/xsl"
  href="Listing12_7.xsl" ?>
<nodeTester type="referral">
  <function>
      <name>position() function</name>
  </function>
  <text>This function helps find the position of
  a node in the node list.
  </text>
</nodeTester>
```

The result document that would be created by this style sheet would look like this:

```
position() function
NodeList position = 4
```

The main purpose of this exercise is to point out that because the xsl:apply-templates element is used without the select attribute in the nodeTester template, the default rules take over until they're told otherwise. As an experiment, try adding a select attribute to this xsl:apply-templates element:

```
<xsl:template match="nodeTester">
    <xsl:apply-templates select="text"/>
</xsl:template>
```

If you run the new code through your XSLT processor, you'll find that it bypasses the default rules and applies the specific templates you ask it to.

There are many variations on how to manage the way you apply a template. The main point to remember about this element is that it calls on the processor to apply any templates (if they are child elements of the source element) that appear in a given style sheet. Or, if the select attribute is used, the processor is instructed to apply all the child templates of the named template.

TIP

You've seen the xsl:for-each element a few times now. We'll go into more detail later, but for now think of it as having much the same function as the xsl:apply-templates element. The difference between them is their context. Use xsl:apply-templates when mixing content; use xsl:for-each for repeating data with the same structure. A table of baseball statistics, for example, will probably be more efficiently transformed using xsl:for-each.

Part iv

Using the *xsl:sort* Element

You can sort elements by naming a sorting pattern as children of
xsl:apply-templates and xsl:for-each elements. This prevents the
processor from processing elements in the order they appear in the document, and instead processes them according to the order named using
xsl:sort. You can use more than one xsl:sort element, but the first
appearing in the template takes order precedence over the next. The
attributes for the xsl:sort element are listed in Table 12.8.

TABLE 12.8: Attributes of the xsl:sort Element

ATTRIBUTE	REQUIRED	POSSIBLE VALUES	DESCRIPTION
order	No	ascending, descending; default is ascending	Denotes whether the sort should occur in ascending or descending order.
lang	No	Same values as xsl:lang	Describes the language used for the sort keys.
data-type	No	text, number; default is text	Specifies the data type of the strings that are being sorted.
case-order	No	tupper-first, lower-first	Signals whether upper- or lowercase strings should be ordered first.
select	No	Any node; default is .	The value of the current node denotes which node should be sorted.

Using the *xsl:copy-of* Element

You can repeatedly write a node collection in more than one place by
using the xsl:copy-of element. Its only attribute is use-attribute-
sets, an optional attribute that names any attribute sets that should be
applied if the copied node is an element.

OUTPUTTING RESULT TREES

XSLT processors send result trees out from input documents based on
the criteria you set. The processor can look at more than one document

at a time using the document() function, and can create a result tree based on more than one XSLT document.

Using the *xsl:for-each* Element

The xsl:for-each element makes it possible to get more specific with your selection patterns. Actually, the use of this element is only the tip of the iceberg in the selection process. Things can get pretty complex when managing pattern searches. Your filtering options are quite extensive, but they're easiest to understand when you start with this most basic of search patterns. When using the xsl:for-each element, you are in effect saying, "For each instance of the element I am naming, do this."

The only attribute of the xsl:for-each element is select, which identifies the node to be processed. This attribute is required.

If you examine the code that follows, you can see how specific you can get when selecting a node. The xsl:for-each element names the element you want the subsequent node test to apply to. It says, "For each text element that is a child of the advertisement element," (note the use of the backslash for an abbreviated location path) "find the first name instance of a keyword element that has a name attribute, and that name attribute must have a value of auto_year. If the search is successful, insert the value of the auto-year attribute into an HTML p element, and style it as shown by the included style attribute." Whew! That's a lot of information to take in. (You'll learn a bit more about the xsl:value-of element in the next section.)

```
<?xml version='1.0'?>
<xsl:stylesheet
 xmlns:xsl="http://www.w3.org/TR/WD-xsl">
  <xsl:template match="/">
    <html>
      <body>
        <xsl:for-each select="advertisement/text">
          <p style="font-family:sans-serif;
          color:#ff6600; font-size:100pt">
            <xsl:value-of
            select="keyword[@name='auto_year']"/>
          </p>
```

```
        </xsl:for-each>
      </body>
    </html>
  </xsl:template>
</xsl:stylesheet>
```

Generally, this element is used in place of apply-templates during those occasions when you are familiar with an XML source document's specific hierarchy. If you know there is a text element that is a child of the advertisement element, it is safe to use this element. If you don't know whether this is the case, however, it's best to use apply-templates. The xsl:for-each element is also good for repetitive tasks that involve traversing a tree in document order, especially when inserting source XML data into an HTML table.

Did you notice the namespace attribute name/value pair (xmlns:xsl="http://www.w3.org/TR/WD-xsl")? This is the namespace used by the IE 5 XSLT processor. If you use the XSLT standard namespace, the associated XML file won't show up in most versions of IE 5 (but of course can still be processed by standards-compliant XSLT processing software).

Using the *xsl:value-of* Element

This element evaluates a node and returns its value as a string into the source tree. This is an easy, convenient way to format a specific element by using an HTML style sheet from Listing 12.10.

Listing 12.10: Using the *xsl:for-each* Element

```
<?xml version='1.0'?>
<xsl:stylesheet
 xmlns:xsl="http://www.w3.org/1999/XSL/Transform"
 version="1.0">
  <xsl:output indent="yes" />
  <xsl:template match="/">
    <html>
      <body>
        <xsl:for-each
select="advertisement/contact/address/address_line">
          <span style="font-family:sans-serif;
          color:#ff6600; font-size:12pt">
            <xsl:value-of select="."/><br />
```

```
            </span>
          </xsl:for-each>
        </body>
      </html>
    </xsl:template>
  </xsl:stylesheet>
```

At this point it may be helpful to look at the XML source tree this document is transforming. What follows is a small fragment from the XML document (advertisement.xml, which can be found at www.tumeric .net/projects/books/complete/support/ch01_toc.asp):

```
<contact id="contact1">
    <name>John Smyth</name>
    <address>
        <address_line>c/o Bat Accessories, Inc.
        </address_line>
        <address_line>Hitchcock Building, 80th Floor
        </address_line>
        <address_line>1313 Mockingbird Lane
        </address_line>
        <city>New York</city>
        <state>NY</state>
        <postal>10000-1234</postal>
        <country>USA</country>
    </address>
    <phone>19085551212</phone>
    <fax>19085551213</fax>
    <email>jsymth@batacc.com</email>
    <url>http://www.batacc.com/~smyth</url>
</contact>
```

Can you tell what the XSLT style sheet is doing? Keep in mind that the XML source tree's root element is an unseen advertisement element. So the location path for reaching the text element is advertisement/ contact/address/address_line.

The XSLT processor is told that for every instance where an address_line element is found within the location path described, it should do something. See if you can tell what the XSLT processor is told to do for each instance it encounters the advertisement/ contact/address/address_line combination. Basically, the XSLT processor is told to narrow down the search—or more correctly, refine the pattern. Using your xsl:value-of element, the XSLT processor is told to look for specific elements nested within the contact element.

The xsl:value-of element has two attributes available. The mandatory select attribute identifies the node to be processed; the optional disable-output-escaping attribute disables escaping of special characters when its value is yes.

TIP

The value-of element only returns the first instance of the element that matches the selection. It's easy to make the mistake of thinking xsl:value-of will return every instance of the matching element, but that's not the case (in fact, that's what the xsl:for-each element is for).

Managing Output

XSLT does not limit you to creating only XML result trees. For instance, your result trees can be another kind of text or a sequence of bytes. Although this means that the result isn't necessarily a "tree" in the true XML sense, we will refer to output as result trees for consistency.

Using the *xsl:output* Element

You control the way your result tree is output by using the xsl:output element. This must be a top-level element, meaning that it must appear as a child of the xsl:stylesheet or xsl:transform element (these are synonymous with each other).

The type of output generated depends on what's chosen with the method attribute, which takes one of three values: html, text, or xml. If the value is html, the output is generated as HTML (the old-fashioned kind that doesn't care about case sensitivity). If the value is text, every text node is generated in document order without any escaping. If the value is xml, the output is generated as a well-formed XML general parsed entity.

An example of how to use this element is in the section describing the xsl:text element. The attributes for the xsl:output element are listed in Table 12.9.

WARNING

One caveat regarding the xsl:output element is that the XSLT processor is not required to honor your request.

TABLE 12.9: Attributes of the xsl:output Element

ATTRIBUTE	REQUIRED	POSSIBLE VALUES OR DESCRIPTION
method	No	html, text, xml, or a name with a prefix that is expanded into a URI using namespace declarations in scope on the xsl:output element (in which case, the handling of the output depends on the namespace and the processor handling the output).
version	No	Version of the XML document returned as a result tree, or if a different format, the version of that format language.
cdata-section-elements	No	A list of XML qualified names whose text node children are output as CDATA sections.
indent	No	A yes value indicates that the processor can add white space to indent the results; no indicates that it should not.
media-type	No	Names the media type (MIME type).
doctype-system	No	Names the system identifier for use in the document type declaration.
doctype-public	No	Names the public identifier for use in the document type declaration.
comit-xml-declaration	No	yes, no; specifies whether the processor should omit an XML declaration.
standalone	No	yes, no; specifies whether the processor should output a stand-alone document declaration.
encoding	No	Describes the encoding of the byte sequence (e.g., UTF-16, ISO8859-1, etc.).

Part iv

Managing Elements and Attributes

There are two XSLT elements you can use to create elements and attributes on the fly. The xsl:element is used to create elements, and the xsl:attribute is used to create attributes.

Creating Elements with the *xsl:element* Element

You can create an element using the xsl:element element. This element has a required attribute—name—that is used to provide the element's new name. The newly created element acts as a template for any children or attributes that you create with the new element. The xsl:element element is useful for several reasons. One simple application you might want to try is adding a link:

```
<xsl:element name="a">
    <xsl:attribute name="href">http://myDomain.com/
    ➥myFancy.htm
    </xsl:attribute>
    <xsl:text>This is a link</xsl:text>
</xsl:element>
```

This produces the following result fragment:

```
<a href="http://myDomain.com/myFancy.htm">
 This is a link
</a>
```

The xsl:text element (discussed later in the chapter) allows you to insert element content into your element (one nice thing about XSLT is that many of its element names are self-explanatory). There is also a namespace attribute for providing a namespace for your new element. All the attributes for this element are listed in Table 12.10.

TABLE 12.10: Attributes of the xsl:element Element

ATTRIBUTE	REQUIRED	POSSIBLE VALUES, DESCRIPTION
name	Yes	yes, no; used only when copying element nodes, this attribute references attribute sets that are named in a separate xsl:attribute-set element and is interpreted as an attribute value template (described later in this chapter).
namespace	No	Provides a namespace for the attribute and is interpreted as an attribute value template.
use-attribute-sets	No	yes, no; used only when copying element nodes, this attribute references attribute sets that are named in a separate xsl:attribute-set element and is interpreted as an attribute value template.
xml:space	No	default, preserve; used to manage white space.

Creating Attributes with the *xsl:attribute* Element

You can create an attribute using the xsl:attribute element and then nest it within the applied element. This element has a required attribute—name—that is used to provide the attribute's name. The value of the attribute is placed within the xsl:attribute element's contents. The following short example shows how to create a simple element and its associated attributes:

```
<xsl:element name="PARA">
    <xsl:attribute name="ALIGN">LEFT
    </xsl:attribute>
    <xsl:attribute name="TYPE">FOOTNOTE
    </xsl:attribute>
    Output some contents here
</xsl:element>
```

The preceding snippet of code results in the following fragment:

```
<PARA ALIGN="LEFT" TYPE="FOOTNOTE">
Output some contents here
</PARA>
```

Attributes must be created in such a way that none of the following guidelines are violated:

▶ An attribute can't be added after any of the new element's children within the tree structure.

▶ An attribute can't have a duplicate name.

▶ An attribute can only be added to an element node.

▶ An xsl:attribute element's content can contain only character data during its instantiation, and the XSLT processor should insert a closing /> tag as soon as non-attribute content is encountered.

The attributes for this element are listed in Table 12.11.

Part iv

TABLE 12.11: Attributes of the xsl:attribute Element

ATTRIBUTE	REQUIRED	POSSIBLE VALUES, DESCRIPTION
name	Yes	yes, no; used only when copying element nodes, this attribute references attribute sets that are named in a separate xsl:attribute-set element, and is interpreted as an attribute value template.
namespace	No	Provides a namespace for the attribute.
xml:space	No	default, preserve; used to manage white space.

Copying with the *xsl:copy* Element

You can copy an element from the XML source document into the result tree by using the xsl:copy element. Whether or not you copy the character data, child elements, or attributes of a node depends on how you direct the xsl:copy element. You can include the xsl:applytemplates element as a child element to include other information, such as character data and attributes.

This is different than using the xsl:value-of element, which specifically inserts text from an element into the output tree. The idea behind xsl:copy is to copy the beginning and end tags of the matched element, and optionally, its character data, children, and attributes (by using, for example, xsl:apply-templates). The syntax for this element looks like this:

```
<xsl:template match="myElement">
    <xsl:copy>
        <xsl:apply-templates select="@myElement"/>
        <xsl:apply-templates/>
    </xsl:copy>
</xsl:template>
```

In the next example, we copy an attribute/value pair in the source document to a result tree as the content of an element, rather than as an attribute/value pair, beginning with this portion of the source document:

```
<status value="accepted"></status>
```

If we want element content instead of an attribute value/pair, we can copy the attribute value node as in Listing 12.11 into the result tree.

Listing 12.11: Using the `xsl:copy` Element

```
<?xml version='1.0'?>
<xsl:stylesheet
 xmlns:xsl="http://www.w3.org/1999/XSL/Transform"
 version="1.0">
  <xsl:template match="/">
    <html>
      <body>
        <xsl:apply-templates
          select="advertisement/status"/>
      </body>
    </html>
  </xsl:template>
  <xsl:template match="status">
    <xsl:copy>
      <xsl:apply-templates select="@value"/>
      <xsl:apply-templates/>
    </xsl:copy>
  </xsl:template>
</xsl:stylesheet>
```

You can add multiple elements with an `xsl:for-each` statement. Consider the following source fragment. The parent elements of the match target (the `keyword` element) are `advertisement/text`:

```
<keyword name="auto_year" punct=" ">1997 </keyword>
<keyword name="auto_exterior"  punct=" ">
 yellow
</keyword>
<keyword name="auto_body" punct=", ">
convertible,
</keyword>
<keyword name="auto_mileage"
 format="9'k miles'" scale="1000" punct=", ">
14k miles,
</keyword>
```

Listing 12.12 shows one way to copy multiple instances of an element into the result tree.

Listing 12.12: Using xsl:copy to Copy Multiple Instances of an Element

```
<?xml version='1.0'?>
<xsl:stylesheet
xmlns:xsl="http://www.w3.org/1999/XSL/Transform"
version="1.0">
  <xsl:template match="/">
    <html>
      <body>
        <xsl:apply-templates
         select="advertisement/text/keyword"/>
      </body>
    </html>
  </xsl:template>
  <xsl:template match="keyword">
    <xsl:copy>
      <xsl:for-each select="@*">
        <xsl:copy/></xsl:for-each>
      <xsl:apply-templates/>
    </xsl:copy>
  </xsl:template>
</xsl:stylesheet>
```

When you use xsl:copy, children are not automatically copied; if you want to copy them, you need to create additional markup. The two attributes for this element—both optional—are use-attribute-sets and xml:space. The use-attribute-sets attribute has possible values of yes or no; used only when copying element nodes, this attribute references attribute sets that are named in a separate xsl:attribute-set element. The xml:space attribute, used to manage white space, can have a value of default or preserve.

Managing Text

You can use XSLT tags to manipulate the text content of your result trees, both the user-visible text (with the xsl:text element) and the programmer-visible text (with the xsl:comment element). Both elements allow you to create text, defined by including the text you want to create as the element content, to be inserted into the result tree.

Using the *xsl:text* Element

You can output the text of selected nodes by using the xsl:text element, which outputs the content within its tags. This text-generating element is helpful when you want to trim white space. It also improves the management of special characters, such as < (the character reference for the < character), or when you want to create non-XML code of some kind within a text file.

Take a look again at the xsl:output element you saw a bit earlier in this chapter, and see how both it and the xsl:text element might be useful. Given the following XML document fragment, you can construct newspaper markup that can be read by a classified advertising markup system. The target classified advertising system doesn't use XML, but that doesn't matter because you can use the xsl:output element's method attribute to output text (method="text"). The following is a fragment from a source document:

```
<text>

    <headline>Career Opportunities at Modern</headline>

    <para fontsize="agate" justify="flushleft">Modern
Communications Company is a competitive local exchange car-
rier (CLEC) focused exclusively on delivering dedicated data
to growing businesses nationwide through wholesale agreements
with service provider partners. If you would like to speak
with our recruiters in person, come see us at the WorkWorld
High Tech Career Expo in San Francisco (Hyatt Embarcadero
Pacific Concourse) on May 3rd and 4th from 10 am to 7 pm.

    </para>

</text>
```

The XSLT file is shown in Listing 12.13.

Listing 12.13: Using the xsl:text Element

```
<?xml version='1.0'?>
<xsl:stylesheet
 xmlns:xsl="http://www.w3.org/1999/XSL/Transform"
 version="1.0">
  <xsl:output method="text" indent="no"/>
  <xsl:template match='/'>
    <xsl:apply-templates
      select="advertisement/text"/>
  </xsl:template>
  <xsl:template match="text">
```

Part iv

```
            <xsl:apply-templates/>
        </xsl:template>
        <xsl:template match="headline">
            <xsl:text>\F4</xsl:text>
            <xsl:value-of select="text()"/>
        </xsl:template>
        <xsl:template match="para">
            <xsl:if test="self::para[@fontsize='agate']">
                <xsl:text>\F1</xsl:text>
                <xsl:value-of select="text()"/>
            </xsl:if>
            <xsl:if test="self::para[@justify='flushleft']">
                <xsl:text disable-output-escaping="yes">
                &lt;
                </xsl:text>
            </xsl:if>
        </xsl:template>
    </xsl:stylesheet>
```

Take note of the last xsl:text element in bold. You'll see the < character reference, which the XSLT processor returns as the less-than character (<). The target markup, which is designed for a non-XML classified newspaper advertising markup system, requires the less-than character to declare text to be flush left, but using this character can cause problems in the XML world. The combination of the xsl:output and xsl:text elements eliminates this problem. The result looks like this:

```
\F4Career Opportunities at Modern

\F1Modern Communications Company is a competitive local
exchange carrier (CLEC) focused exclusively on delivering
dedicated data to growing businesses nationwide through
wholesale agreements with service provider partners. If you
would like to speak with our recruiters in person, come see
us at the WorkWorld High Tech Career Expo in San Francisco
(Hyatt Embarcadero Pacific Concourse) on May 3rd and 4th from
10 am to 7 pm.<
```

Keep in mind that it's illegal to have an end tag without a start tag, and vice versa, so don't create this kind of markup if you are generating XML elements. Also, if you are outputting XML, you shouldn't get a < character anyway, but the character reference (<) instead. If you are generating elements that *are* well formed, you don't need to use xsl:text; you can just create the elements using the xsl:element element or literal result elements because that's what the XSLT processor expects.

TIP

White space is among the more vexing issues with XSLT, because it may or may not be stripped out of the source document or the style sheet. In addition, it's possible that white space will be added to a result tree. Generally, a text node is never stripped unless it contains nothing but white-space characters. It also won't get stripped if the text node's parent has a white space–preserving attribute or if the closest ancestor of the text node contains a preserve value in an xml:space attribute.

You can also use the xml:space attribute (despite its name, this is an attribute, not an element) in one of the xsl:text element's parent elements to preserve white space using a value of preserve. This attribute is basically the same as the xml:space attribute made available through the XML 1 specification.

The xsl:text element takes one possible attribute, the optional disable-output-escaping you saw in Listing 12.13. The default value is no. If the value is yes, character references are not escaped.

Using the *xsl:comment* Element

Traditionally, programming and markup languages have used comments to add clarity to programs, scripts, or markup. In markup languages, comments are often used to hide functionality from a processor or browser that might not understand the syntax of the functionality. Consider the way a style sheet document is added in HTML, as follows:

```
<head>
<title>My Title</title>
<style type= "text/css">
<!-
.mystyle {font-size:10px}
->
</style>
</head>
```

The style sheet in the preceding lines of code is hidden from view from lower-level browsers that can't understand style-sheet element content. Browsers that recognize the style element will ignore the comment tags (<!- and ->). XSLT comments accomplish the same thing as comments in other languages, such as HTML. Three main uses for the xsl:comment element are adding comments to an XSLT style sheet, adding a script, and debugging your code.

Using this element also makes it easier to debug XSLT documents. If you need to locate code that is generating errors, you can isolate it using the xsl:comment element. There are no attributes for this element, although you can use the XML xml:space attribute, whose values of default or preserve are used to manage white space.

Importing Document Trees

XSLT provides ways to import document trees from sources outside the document you create for output. This has the effect of creating a modular architecture. Using two elements to drive this process, the xsl:import element and the xsl:include element, you can create one main style sheet that consists of several others.

Using the *xsl:import* Element

The xsl:import element imports other style sheets into your style sheet document. When you import a style sheet, you add all the nodes and content of that style sheet to the imported style sheet document. Unlike most XSLT style sheet elements, the xsl:import element is governed by strict rules about where it can appear in the style sheet: It must always be the first child of the xsl:stylesheet element.

The xsl:import element defines the value for the element's required href attribute (there are no other attributes for xsl:import). The value of the href attribute consists of a URI where the imported style sheet is located. If the style sheet being imported is being referenced through a relative URI, the base URI is always the importing style sheet:

```
<xsl:stylesheet
  xmlns:xsl="http://www.w3.org/1999/XSL/Transform">
<xsl:import href="myimport_1.xsl"/>
```

Of course, you can also use an absolute URI:

```
<xsl:import
  href="http://www.mydomain.com/myimport_2.xsl"/>
```

If you're wondering which elements take precedence in this scenario, the rule is pretty simple: The elements in the style sheet containing the *link* to the imported style sheet take precedence over the elements *in* the imported style sheet.

Using the *xsl:apply-imports* Element

The xsl:apply-imports element is similar to the xsl:apply-templates element. The difference is that xsl:apply-imports is used to apply an imported style sheet to a template.

The rules for imported style sheets dictate that the oldest style sheet always takes precedence. You might have a style sheet with an imported style sheet, which in turn may have an imported style sheet of its own. What happens to precedence then? The result nodes simply appear in the order of appearance within the various imports. The xsl:apply-imports element cannot have other elements nested within it and is always an empty element; it also has no attributes.

Using the *xsl:include* Element

This element works the same way as the xsl:import element, except that the elements included within the included document replace the xsl:include element. Again, the only attribute is a (required) href whose value is a URI. Consider an included document that looks like this:

```
<xsl:stylesheet
 xmlns:xsl="http://www.w3.org/1999/XSL/Transform">
    <xsl:template match="MyElement">
        <MyElement1>
            <xsl:apply-templates/>
        </MyElement1>
    </xsl:template>
</xsl:stylesheet>
```

If this style sheet is named myStyleSheet_1.xsl, and you include it in another style sheet, its elements will replace the xsl:include element in memory:

```
<xsl:include href="myStyleSheet_1.xsl"/>
```

The preceding line of code becomes:

```
<xsl:template match="MyElement">
    <MyElement1><xsl:apply-templates/></MyElement1>
</xsl:template>
```

If this included style sheet contained any xsl:import elements, those elements would move into their place in the tree, right under any other xsl:import elements already there. Any imported style sheets already in place within the root template will take precedence over any imported style sheets from within an included style sheet.

Managing Numbers and Sorting

One way to add precision to generating result output and refine your matches is to use numbering elements and sorting elements.

Formatting Numbers with the *xsl:number* Element

You can number elements automatically using the xsl:number element, which rounds a numerical attribute value into an integer and then inserts the number as text into the result tree. The architecture behind this mechanism relies on the construction of a list that is based on various factors, each controlled by attribute values specified at design time. The resulting list is converted into a string and inserted into the result tree. The attributes for the xsl:number element are listed in Table 12.12.

TABLE 12.12: Attributes of the xsl:number Element

ATTRIBUTE	REQUIRED?	DESCRIPTION/POSSIBLE VALUES
level	No	Names the level of the source tree where the element applies. Three possible values: single, multiple, and any. If single, the processor counts starting with the current node and continues to count all the preceding siblings of the current node that match the pattern defined in the count attribute. If multiple, the processor constructs a list of the current node's ancestors in the order of their appearance in the document hierarchy and begins counting the preceding siblings of each member of the list. If any, the processor begins to count at the current node and includes any preceding elements that are matched to the count attribute.
count	No	The default value is the element type name of the current node. It can also have a specific value defined for it that names the element that should be counted.

TABLE 12.12 continued: Attributes of the xsl:number Element

ATTRIBUTE	REQUIRED?	DESCRIPTION/POSSIBLE VALUES
from	No	A value that names a pattern for starting the counting. When this attribute is used, the counting facilities initiated by the level attribute are begun at the element named in the from attribute (whether the count goes to preceding or ancestor elements depends on which level attribute value is named).
format	No	Allows you to choose from several numbering styles; a value of i results in lowercase roman numerals; a value of I results in uppercase roman numerals; a value of a results in lowercase letters; and a value of A results in uppercase letters.
lang	No	This attribute specifies the language used.
letter-value	No	Allows you to choose between alphabetic or other values in determining how the numerals should be represented. If the value is other, the sequence of results is numeric, but if the value is alphabetic, the sequence of results consists of letter characters.
grouping-separator	No	Specifies how digits are separated (some countries use spaces instead of commas for 1,000,000).
grouping-size	No	Denotes the number of digits in a group.

Using the *xsl:decimal-format* Element

Table 12.13 includes xsl:decimal-format attributes that indicate what characters are allowed to appear during the interpretation of format patterns during the process implemented by the format-number() function.

TABLE 12.13: Attributes of the xsl:decimal-format Element

ATTRIBUTE	REQUIRED	CHARACTER SPECIFIED
decimal-separator	No	Decimal sign
grouping-separator	No	Grouping separator
percent	No	Percent sign

Part iv

TABLE 12.13 continued: Attributes of the xsl:decimal-format Element

Attribute	Required	Character Specified
per-mille	No	Per mille sign
zero-digit	No	Zero digit
digit	No	Digit
infinity	No	A string representing infinity
NaN	No	A string representing a value that can't return a number
minus-sign	No	A string representing the default minus sign

Keys and Conditional Processing

One advantage of XSLT is that you can create tests to manage your matches; the match succeeds if it meets a certain condition. In XSLT you manage the way you want matches to be made, but conditional processing makes it possible to offer precise definitions regarding these matches.

Using the *xsl:key* Element

The xsl:key element is similar to the concept of unique identifiers, except that these elements are more generalized in nature. If you've ever searched through a database by keyword, you have an idea of how this element works. The xsl:key element acts similar to a cross-reference. Consider this code line:

```
<xsl:key name="somekeyword"
 match="myElement" use="keyword"/>
```

You could then use a key() or keyref() function with a pattern to search for any elements containing the somekeyword value of the xsl:key element's name attribute. There are no requirements forcing you to make this a unique identifier, so you can create more powerful sorting features with this element. In the code fragment that follows, you can determine that there are 10,000 Red Delicious apples available without directly accessing the information. This is accomplished by using a key reference. Take a look first at the following source:

```
<!-this is a source code fragment ->
<FRUIT>
<APPLES>Red Delicious</APPLES>
<QUANTITY>10,000</QUANTITY>
<AVAILABILITY spring="yes"/>
</FRUIT>
<FRUIT>
<APPLES>Fuji</APPLES>
<QUANTITY>20,000</QUANTITY>
</FRUIT>
```

Now take a look at the following fragment from an imaginary XSLT style sheet:

```
<xsl:key name= "crossRef" match="FRUIT"
 use="APPLES"/>
```

You give the key a name (crossRef) of your choice, then match using XSLT's pattern matching system. The use attribute is an expression that denotes which node of the matched node to use as the value of the key.

To set up a cross-reference, create a template and use a key function to access the quantities of each kind of apple (you'll learn more about functions a bit later in the chapter):

```
<xsl:key name= "crossRef" match="FRUIT"
 use="APPLES"/>
<xsl:template match="/">
   <xsl:apply-templates
    select="key('crossRef', 'Fuji')"/>
      <xsl:text>, </xsl:text>
   <xsl:apply-templates
    select="key('crossRef', 'Red Delicious')"/>
</xsl:template>
```

The result that you get from the previous code looks like this:

```
Fuji20,000, Red Delicious10,000
```

Although a "function" handles this transformation, it is nothing more than an advanced selection process. The xsl:key element tells the processor to use the APPLES element to establish the cross-reference. Then the processor references the key crossRef in the root template. The key takes it from there and selects nodes that match the pattern named in its definition (the FRUIT element). From that information, the processor can tell that the specific APPLES being searched are "Red Delicious" and "Fuji", so it returns each instance of content of the QUANTITY element based on that result. The attributes used by xsl:key are shown in Table 12.14.

TABLE 12.14: Attributes of the xsl:key Element

ATTRIBUTE	REQUIRED	POSSIBLE VALUES	DESCRIPTION
name	Yes	A name token	Specifies the name of the key
match	Yes	Any valid character data	Names the pattern to match against the key
use	Yes	Any valid character data	Node set expression that denotes the set that the key should use

Testing Conditions with the *xsl:if* Element

To see how conditionals work, take a look at Listing 12.14. The root element for the source document in this listing is the advertisement element. This element has an attribute (action) that can take one of several values. The XML document and its style sheets are designed to manage a real-world situation, so one thing the XSLT document allows you to do is decide when and what objects are displayed.

WARNING

You never want to make confidential information publicly available in your XML document, even if you "hide" it using XSLT. If the document is not on a secure server, anyone with something as simple as Telnet can see it.

Listing 12.14: Developing a Style Sheet Based on Conditions

```
<?xml version='1.0'?>
<xsl:stylesheet
 xmlns:xsl="http://www.w3.org/1999/XSL/Transform"
    version="1.0">
<xsl:template match="/">
<html><body>
  <xsl:if test = "advertisement[@action='update']">
    <div style="font-family:sans-serif;
     font-size:18px;
     font-weight:800;
         padding-bottom:14px; color:#333333">
         Classified Advertising Input Form
    </div>
    <div style="color:#FFFFCC;
         font-family:sans-serif;
         border: 3px thin outset;
         background-color:#663300;padding:3px">
        <p><xsl:value-of select=
"advertisement/text/font/center/
➥keyword[@name='empl_category']"/>
        </p>
        <h1><xsl:value-of select=
"advertisement/text/font/center/
➥keyword[@name='empl_title']"/>
        </h1>
        <p><xsl:value-of select=
         "advertisement/text/
           ➥keyword[@name='empl_experience']"/>
        </p>
        <p><xsl:value-of select=
         "advertisement/text/keyword
           ➥[@name='empl_skills']"/>
        </p>
        <p><xsl:value-of select=
         "advertisement/text/center/
           keyword[@name='phone']"/></p>
    </div>
    <div style="padding-top:12px;
     font-family:serif;
     font-weight:800;
         font-size:14px">Update your ad copy in
```

```
              the space below:</div>
        <div style="padding-top:6px">
          <textarea name="adfiller" cols="30"
          rows="8" wrap="VIRTUAL" id="210011">
          </textarea>
        </div>
      </xsl:if>
    </body></html>
    </xsl:template>
  </xsl:stylesheet>
```

In Listing 12.14, the advertisement element's action attribute in the source document helpwanted.xml takes on a value of update. You can find this document online at www.tumeric.net/projects/books/complete/support/Chapter12/helpwanted.xml. According to the DTD, this attribute is allowed several values. For the purposes of this exercise, assume that there are only two options: create or update. Let's also assume the design goal calls for a text area input to be displayed. Thus you would write XSLT choosing the text that labels the text box according to the value of the action attribute. Listing 12.14 shows how this works.

The result of Listing 12.14 is shown in Listing 12.15.

Listing 12.15: The Result Tree from Listing 12.14

```
<html><body>
  <div style="font-family:sans-serif;
   font-size:18px; font-weight:800;
    padding-bottom:14px; color:#333333">Classified
    Advertising Input Form</div>
  <div style="color:#FFFFCC; font-family:sans-serif;
   border: 3px thin outset;
    background-color:#663300;padding:3px">
    <p>Computers </p>
    <h1>Director of Information Technology </h1>
    <p>Modern Communications is seeking a proven
    and dedicated IT professional with at least 5
    years experience in enterprise, systems and
    network management and administration</p>
    <p>Must have experience in COBOL, Y2K, PBX
    systems, Novell, Networking, and be able to
    manage large-scale enterprise systems.</p>
```

```
   <p>no calls please</p>
 </div>
 <div style="padding-top:12px; font-family:serif;
  font-weight:800;
    font-size:14px"> Enter new ad copy in the space
    below:</div>
 <div style="padding-top:6px"><textarea name=
   "adfiller" cols="30" rows="8" wrap="VIRTUAL"
id="210011"></textarea></div>
 </body></html>
```

There are two attributes for the xsl:if element. The required test attribute has a value of the test that should be used for determining whether the process should be implemented. The optional xml:space attribute can be default or preserve to indicate how white space should be treated.

Making Selections with the *xsl:choose* Element

The xsl:when and xsl:otherwise elements are used to help manage the conditional testing of nodes processing. In Listing 12.16, the xsl:choose element is used as the main conditional wrapper. JavaScript and other programming languages use similar conditionals to manage functions. If you compared xsl:choose to a similar JavaScript statement, the xsl:choose element would be equivalent to the if...else statement. Listing 12.15 shows one way this element can be used.

Listing 12.16: Using the *xsl:choose* Element to Choose Output

```
<?xml version='1.0'?>
<xsl:stylesheet
 xmlns:xsl="http://www.w3.org/1999/XSL/Transform"
 version="1.0">
<xsl:template match="/">
  <xsl:apply-templates />
</xsl:template>
<xsl:template match="/">
  <html><body>
    <xsl:choose>
      <xsl:when test="advertisement
      ⑤[@action='create']">
        <div style="font-family:sans-serif;
          font-size:18px; font-weight:800;
```

Part iv

```
                  padding-bottom:14px; color:#333333">
                  Classified Advertising Input Form</div>
        <div style="color:#FFFFCC;
          font-family:sans-serif;
          border: 3px thin outset;
          background-color:#663300;
          padding:3px">

          <p><xsl:value-of select=
"advertisement/text/font/center/
          ➡keyword[@name='empl_category']"/></p>
          <h1><xsl:value-of select=
"advertisement/text/font/center/
          ➡keyword[@name='empl_title']"/></h1>
          <p><xsl:value-of select=
          "advertisement/text/keyword
          ➡ [@name='empl_experience']"/></p>
          <p><xsl:value-of select=
          "advertisement/text/keyword
          ➡ [@name='empl_skills']"/></p>
          <p><xsl:value-of select=
          "advertisement/text/center/keyword
          ➡ [@name='phone']"/></p>
        </div>
        <div style="padding-top:12px;
          font-family:serif;
          font-weight:800;
              font-size:14px">Enter new ad copy in
              the space below:</div>
        <div style="padding-top:6px">
          <textarea name="adfiller" cols="30"
            rows="8" wrap="VIRTUAL"
                  id="210011"></textarea></div>
      </xsl:when>
      <xsl:otherwise>
        <div style="font-family:sans-serif;
          font-size:18px; font-weight:800;
              padding-bottom:14px; color:#333333">
              Classified Advertising Input Form</div>
        <div style="padding-top:12px;
          font-family:serif; font-weight:800;
              font-size:14px">
              To create your ad, enter ad copy in the
```

```
              space below:
          </div>
        <div style="padding-top:6px">
          <textarea name="Newadfiller"
           cols="30" rows="8" wrap="VIRTUAL"
           id="210011"></textarea></div>
      </xsl:otherwise>
    </xsl:choose>
  </body></html>
</xsl:template>
</xsl:stylesheet>
```

The template in Listing 12.16 simply states that when the advertise-ment element has an action attribute value of create, as stated in the xsl:when element, a series of actions should take place.

The attributes for the xsl:choose element are the same as for xsl:if. The required test attribute has a value of the test that should be used for applying, whether or not the process should be implemented. The optional xml:space attribute can be default or preserve to indicate how white space should be treated.

The results of Listing 12.16 are shown in Listing 12.17. Just for grins, change the xsl:when test from 'create' to 'update'. Since the action attribute value in the helpwanted.xml source document is actually update, your XSLT processor will generate a longer document incorporating the elements that appear in the root template.

Listing 12.17: Result Tree from Listing 12.16 Transformation

```
<html><body>
  <div style="font-family:sans-serif;
    font-size:18px; font-weight:800;
    padding-bottom:14px; color:#333333">Classified
    Advertising Input Form</div>
  <div style="color:#FFFFCC; font-family:sans-serif;
   border: 3px thin outset;
    background-color:#663300;padding:3px">
    <p>Computers </p>
    <h1>Director of Information Technology </h1>
    <p>Modern Communications is seeking a proven
    and dedicated IT professional with at least 5
    years experience in enterprise, systems and
    network management and administration</p>
    <p>Must have experience in COBOL, Y2K, PBX
```

```
      systems, Novell, Networking, and be able to
      manage large-scale enterprise systems.</p>
      <p>no calls please<p>
   </div>
   <div style="padding-top:12px; font-family:serif;
    font-weight:800;
      font-size:14px">Enter new ad copy in the space
      below:</div>
   <div style="padding-top:6px"><textarea name=
    "adfiller" cols="30" rows="8"
      wrap="VIRTUAL" id="210011"></textarea></div>
   </body></html>
```

USING VARIABLES IN XSLT

If you're not a programmer, you might assume that introducing variables into a markup language is not fair, but variables in XSLT are not much different than entities in XML. If you can think of them that way, you should have no trouble with them.

Using Variable Elements

There are two kinds of variable elements, xsl:variable and xsl:param. Both are allowed at the top level (a global variable) and in individual templates of the style sheet. An element is considered a top-level element if it is a child of the xsl:stylesheet element. Bear in mind a few general rules when developing style sheet variables:

► There can't be more than one top-level variable with the same name and level of importance. An XSLT processor will either deliver an error message or choose the variable that it deems most important.

► The value of a variable can be any object returned by expressions or the contents of the element that creates the variable (xsl:variable or xsl:param).

► Variables are always called by other elements with a $ symbol. This symbol is not used anywhere else within the XSLT vocabulary, so whenever you see a reference to anything with $ as a leading character, within an expression such as <fo:block font-family ="{$fontFamilyVariable}">, the reference is a variable.

- Unlike programming language variables, variable values cannot be changed dynamically by some function within XSL. This can be disconcerting to programmers accustomed to statements such as "a = if x then b else c," but makes it easier to conditionally change variable values.

- When variables aren't declared in a document's top level, but rather in a template, the variable is available to all siblings and their descendants, not including the xsl:variable or xsl:param elements themselves.

- A variable can be bound to one of the four XPath data types: Boolean, string, number, or node set.

- A variable can be bound to a data type exclusive of variable elements, such as a result tree fragment. You can only perform string operations on result tree fragments, and you can't use the /, //, or [] operators on them. Any action performed on a variable has the same effect as it would on the equivalent node set.

- Result tree fragments can only be returned by variable expressions if the variables are result tree fragments, if they are the results of expression functions that create result tree fragments, or the result of a system property whose result is a result tree fragment.

Binding with the *xsl:variable* Element

The xsl:variable element is the simplest type of variable: it holds a value that can be referenced somewhere else in a document. An xsl:variable element has one required attribute—name—that you can use to name your variable:

```
<xsl:variable name="colorIt">color</xsl:variable>
```

The element content is the value of the variable. You can reference the variable somewhere else in your document, such as within a template, as follows:

```
<xsl:template match="lesPommes">
    <xsl:element name="APPLE">
        <xsl:attribute
         name="{$colorIt}">red</xsl:attribute>
    </xsl:element>
</xsl:template>
```

The preceding example creates a new element, called APPLE, and an attribute for that new element. Note how the attribute takes its name from the value of the previous variable. This creates an attribute—color—that is then assigned a value of red. The value of the variable doesn't involve the content of the attribute, however, and won't change if you maneuver the various conditional elements, as a programmer might do with JavaScript or Java. Rather, the value of the variable is exactly as you assign it, in this case, color. You could name the value of the variable within the element name that was created instead and use the $colorIt variable as the value of the xsl:element element's name attribute. If you're familiar with programming, you might even think that XSLT variables work the opposite of the way programming variables work, in that variables with a constant value are referenced by objects rather than objects with values that vary.

The xsl:variable element also has an optional select attribute, whose value is an expression that provides the value of the variable.

Using the *xsl:param* Element

The xsl:param element works closely with its cousin, the xsl:with-param element, to produce results that come as close to variable value changing as is possible within the XSLT framework. You can use xsl:param the exact same way you use xsl:variable. You can also replace the values of xsl:param elements using the xsl:with-param element, whereas you can't replace the values of the xsl:variables element.

The attributes used with the xsl:param element are the same as those of xsl:variable: a required name (the name of the variable) and an optional select (an expression that provides the variable's value). You can see an example of how the xsl:param element works in the next section.

Using the *xsl:with-param* Element

The xsl:with-param element is used to reference an xsl:param element's value and insert new values as needed within a template. In the following example, an xsl:choose element is used to test whether or not an attribute is equal to a declared variable. Remember that the state of an XSLT variable never changes. Rather, the variable's value is assigned to other elements (or not, depending on whether you end up using it). Listing 12.18 shows variables in action using Listing 12.19 as the source document. The result is Apples are red., but you can change the result easily enough by changing one of the conditional element values in the style sheet or by changing the source document itself.

Listing 12.18: Using Variables

```
<?xml version="1.0" encoding="iso-8859-1" ?>
<xsl:stylesheet
 xmlns:xsl="http://www.w3.org/1999/XSL/Transform"
 version="1.0">
<xsl:output method="text"/>
<xsl:variable name="color"
 select="keys/FRUIT/@color"/>
<xsl:template match="/">
    <xsl:choose>
        <xsl:when test="$color='red'">
            <xsl:call-template name="apples_oranges">
                <xsl:with-param name="fruit"
                select="'apple'"/>
                <xsl:with-param name="season"
                 select="'spring'"/>
            </xsl:call-template>
        </xsl:when>
        <xsl:when test="$color='orange'">
            <xsl:call-template name="apples_oranges">
                <xsl:with-param name="fruit"
                 select="'orange'"/>
                <xsl:with-param name="season"
                select="'winter'"/>
            </xsl:call-template>
        </xsl:when>
        <xsl:otherwise>shucks</xsl:otherwise>
    </xsl:choose>
</xsl:template>
<xsl:template name="apples_oranges">
    <xsl:param name="fruit" select="'nectarines'"/>
    <xsl:param name="season" select="'all'"/>
    Apples are <xsl:value-of select="$color"/>.
</xsl:template>
```

Listing 12.19: The Source Document for Listing 12.18

```
<?xml version="1.0"?>
<keys>
<FRUIT color="red">
<APPLES>Red Delicious</APPLES>
<QUANTITY>10,000</QUANTITY>
<AVAILABILITY spring="yes"/>
```

```
</FRUIT>
<FRUIT>
<APPLES>Fuji</APPLES>
<QUANTITY>20,000</QUANTITY>
</FRUIT>
</keys>
```

In Listing 12.18, the value of the `xsl:variable` element (in the `apples_oranges` template) is extracted from a typical XSLT selection process. The FRUIT element's `color` attribute in the source document being tested will have some color value, and you can't change that color value once you find it in the source document. This is one big difference between XSLT and programming languages. Rather than providing the ability to change the FRUIT element's property, XSLT provides the ability to reference that property and produce more sophisticated result trees based on variable references.

After the `xsl:variable` is declared, two `xsl:param` elements are declared. The value of these won't change, and the value of any objects in memory is unchanged. You're only performing a value switch based on the results of your test. This is a fairly important distinction from a programming standpoint. For our purposes here, it just means that if the value of the FRUIT element's `color` attribute is red, then, using the `xsl:param` element, a new reference is made based on the original `xsl:param` reference. If you look at the `name` attribute of the `xsl:param` element and the `name` attribute of the `xsl:param` element, you'll see that they're the same. That's the reference that makes it possible to insert the new node into the XSLT result tree. You didn't change the variable's (the `xsl:param`) properties as you would in a procedural programming language. Rather, you used that variable's properties to establish a new reference and insert a node into your result tree.

The attributes used with the `xsl:with-param` element are the by-now-familiar pair: a required `name` and an optional `select` (an expression that provides the value of the variable).

Using Attribute Value Templates

One key to using variables involves *attribute value templates*. Simply put, these make it possible for you to use the values of attributes as expressions, as in the following code:

```
<xsl:template match="lesPommes">
  <xsl:element name="APPLE">
```

```
        <xsl:attribute
        name="{$colorIt}">red</xsl:attribute>
    </xsl:element>
</xsl:template>
```

The attribute value assigned to the new element APPLE was assigned through the variable $colorIt. This is an example of an attribute value template in action. An attribute value template is created by an expression in a template. Take a look at the following source document fragment that uses a variable in the attribute value template:

```
<APPLE>
<color>red</color>
</APPLE>
```

If you want to create an attribute value template with color as an attribute rather than a nested element, you could do this:

```
<xsl:template match="APPLE">
    <APPLE color="{color}"/>
</xsl:template>
```

Here you're using a literal result element, which may not help much with automation, so you may instead want to create your elements using the xsl:element and xsl:attribute elements. So taking that same information from that source document fragment, you might end up with this:

```
<xsl:template match="APPLE">
    <xsl:element name="APPLE">
        <xsl:attribute name="{color}">
        red</xsl:attribute>
    </xsl:element>
</xsl:template>
```

The important thing to remember about attribute value templates is that they can use any expression. So they can get just as complex as any expression you are capable of creating.

Learning about Extensions

Microsoft wanted to include some *extensions* to XSLT in the release of IE 5 to make up for features it found lacking in XSL, in particular the handling of data type management. So Microsoft developed elements, like the `xsl:eval` element that is used to evaluate data types and convert them as needed. However, at the time of IE 5's release, there was no way to extend XSL. Microsoft's stated goal was to rework its XSLT support to include extensibility added to the W3C Specification as the various drafts made their way to the W3C Final Recommendation. The specification developers were able to develop syntax for adding extensibility to any language, including Perl, Java, JavaScript, and Python, to name a few.

Extension Functions

Extensions are handled by the `extension-element-available()` and `extension-function-available()` functions. These return `true` when the XSLT processor supports the element or function named in the string parameter, respectively.

The *xsl:fallback* Element

The `xsl:fallback` element contains a template for the XSLT processor to fall back on if it doesn't support the element named in the `extension-element-available()` function. Rather than issue an error, the XSLT processor uses the template named within the `xsl:fallback` element. This is a way to manage backward (and forward) compatibility issues.

The `xsl:fallback` element occurs within an `xsl:template` element; it has no attributes.

Miscellaneous Elements and Attributes

The following elements and attributes are used to perform management of assorted aspects such as versions, attributes, and templates, and to create user messages.

Managing Forward Compatibility with the *version* Attributes

Currently there is no version 2 of XSL, but when there is, you would identify it using the `version` attribute with the `xsl:stylesheet` or `xsl:transform` element and the `xsl:version` attribute with literal result elements. All the `xsl:stylesheet` elements in this book include `version="1.0"` in their definitions.

Using the *xsl:attribute-set* Element

You can group sets of attributes together using the xsl:attribute-set element. When you create this element, you refer to it using the use-attribute-set attribute of the xsl:element, xsl:copy, or xsl:attribute-set element. You can also create a literal result element and add an attribute named xsl:use-attribute-set to call it.

The xsl:attribute-set element requires a name attribute, representing a qualified name for the attribute set. The optional use-attribute-sets attribute is a white space–delimited list of qualified names from other attribute sets that can be used with the current attribute set.

Using the *xsl:call-template* Element

You can call a named template by using the xsl:call-template element. This element shouldn't be confused with xsl:apply-templates. It doesn't return a result, but rather acts as a logic element for managing such issues as recursive, repeatable calls to a template. The only attribute of xsl:call-template is the required name of the called template.

Using the *xsl:message* Element

An XSLT processor can send a message to a user whenever the xsl:message element is invoked. How the message is actually sent to a user depends on the processor. The lone attribute for xsl:message is xml:space, used (as usual) to manage white space through the values default or preserve.

TAKING ADVANTAGE OF XSLT FUNCTIONS

Sets of expressions that return values based on criteria stated within given parameters are known as XSLT *functions*. They provide a means for expanding the way you create selections and allow you to develop very specific criteria for matches as you develop a result tree.

If you're a non-programmer, don't be scared off by programming in XSL. XSLT functions help enhance the transformation process, generally by helping you refine search criteria with patterns. Functions in object-oriented languages, like Java or C++, have a much broader range of capabilities.

XSLT functions use standard *arguments* within their syntax—keywords within parentheses that are passed on as parameters. The function may need some extra information to be processed; arguments give you the chance to pass that information along. In a programming language, a function doesn't necessarily need to contain any specific parameters to work properly, but they do add functionality. The same is true with XSLT functions: Whether a function is required to take an argument depends on the function and its purpose. The functions available through XSLT and XPath are shown in Table 12.15.

TABLE 12.15: XPath and XSLT Functions

FUNCTION	SYNTAX	DESCRIPTION
Boolean()	Boolean (*value*)	Converts *value* to a Boolean. Node lists and result fragments return true if they're not empty; a string returns true if its length is not zero; and a number returns true if it is zero or NaN (stands for "not a number," which is nevertheless a distinct value that is a result of some floating-point calculations, such as dividing by zero).
ceiling()	ceiling (*number*)	Returns the smallest integer greater than or equal to *number*.
concat()	concat (*string1*, *string2*, *string3*...)	Returns a concatenated string from all strings in the argument. (See the note at the end of this section for an explanation of concatenation.)
count()	count (*nodeset*)	Returns the number of nodes in the node set named in the argument.
current()	current()	Returns a node set whose only member is the current node.
document()	document ("object") or document (*nodeset*), where "object" is a string URI and *nodeset* is a string	Permits access of documents outside the original source document by returning either the root node or a document fragment (specified as a string URI in the argument's first parameter, with the second parameter as the base string).

TABLE 12.15 continued: XPath and XSLT Functions

FUNCTION	SYNTAX	DESCRIPTION
element-avail-able()	element-available (*ElementName*)	Returns true if the XSLT processor supports the named element as an extension element.
floor()	floor(*number*)	Returns the largest integer less than or equal to *number*.
function-available()	function-available (*stringFunc-tionName*)	Searches the XSLT patterns for *string-FunctionName*, the function you are testing against; generally used as part of a conditional, such as xsl:test.
generate-id()	generate-id(*string*)	Creates a string to be used as a unique identifier. *string* must consist exclusively of ASCII text and must begin with an alphabetic character.
id()	id(*string*)	Searches for an id whose value matches the argument. Returns a string representing a node set's unique identifier by evaluating the *string* parameter and matching it against any nodes containing that value as an id.
key()	key(*string*, *scalarNodeSet*), where *string* names the key (acquired from the xsl:key element's name attribute) and *scalarNodeSet* is a string value representing the node set to be matched.	Returns a matching node set by retrieving the string value from the name attribute of the xsl:key element named in the first parameter.
last()	last()	Selects the number of nodes in the context node list.
local-name	local-name (*nodeset*)	Returns a string consisting of a first node's local name part.
name()	name (*stringNodeName*)	Returns a string that represents the name of the first node in the argument. The name must be a qualified name as defined by the XML 1 spec. If there is no argument, the function returns the context node.

Part iv

TABLE 12.15 continued: XPath and XSLT Functions

FUNCTION	SYNTAX	DESCRIPTION
namespace-uri()	namespace-uri(*nodeset*)	Selects the namespace in the first node of the argument node set.
number()	number(*value*)	Converts *value* into a number. If *value* is a string, it's converted to a number. If it's a Boolean value of true it is converted to 1; false is converted to 0. If *value* is a node set, it is converted to a string, then converted to a number. If there is no argument, then the context node is returned.
position()	position()	Returns a value based on the position of the context node within the context node list.
round()	round(*number*)	Returns the closest integer to the number contained in the argument. If two numbers can be returned, the even number wins.
starts-with()	nstarts-with()-(*value*, *substring*)	Returns a Boolean true if the tested string (*value*) with the substring specified in the argument (*substring*).
substring()	nsubstring(*string*, *number1*, *number2*), where *string* is the source string; *number1* is the position in the source string of the first character in the string that starts the string fragment; and *number2* is the length of the target string (the substring).	Returns a specified string fragment, determined by a start and end point named in the parameters. Note to JavaScripters: The first position in the string is not 0; it is 1. XSLT does not begin indexing with 0.
substring-before()	substring-before(bigString, littleString)	Returns a substring of *bigString* consisting of everything from the beginning of *bigString* to the first instance of *littleString*'s appearance. Example: substring-before("mySubstring is cool", "cool") would return mySubstring is.

TABLE 12.15 continued: XPath and XSLT Functions

FUNCTION	SYNTAX	DESCRIPTION
substring-after()	substring-after(*bigString*, *littleString*)	Returns a substring of *bigString* consisting of everything from the end of the first instance of *littleString*'s appearance to the end of *bigString*. Example: substring-after("mySubstring is cool and so are you", "cool") would return and so are you.
sum()	sum(*number1*, *number2*, *number3*, ...)	Returns the sum of the numbers (evaluated from strings in a node set to numbers) in the argument.
system-property()	system-property()	Returns a string identifying various aspects of the system, such as the version number of the XSLT transformation used, and information about the XSLT processor's vendor.

Some functions relate specifically to strings. Table 12.16 provides explanations of string functions available to XSLT processors.

TABLE 12.16: String Functions Available to XSLT Processors

FUNCTION NAME	SYNTAX	DESCRIPTION
concat()	concat(*string1*, *string2*, *string3*...)	Returns a concatenated string from the parameters within the argument. (See the note that follows this table for an explanation of concatenation.)
contains()	contains(*string1*, *string2*)	Used to match same strings together: returns true if *string1* is identical to *string2*.
format-number()	format-number(*number*, *formatPattern*, *optionalLocale*)	Converts a number to a string using decimal formatting based on the Java programming language. *formatPattern* is the pattern specified to convert *number* to a string, using a Java-based decimal class. *optionalLocale* is the notation used to describe valid localized characters as defined in JDK 1.1. This means some characters can have a special meaning within your search pattern, but for Java-related reasons these characters can't be either quotes or the currency sign.

TABLE 12.16 continued: String Functions Available to XSLT Processors

FUNCTION NAME	SYNTAX	DESCRIPTION
normalize()	normalize (string)	Normalizes (strips leading and white space from a group of characters) the text contained within the argument.
starts-with()	fstarts-with(string1, string2)	Tests to see whether string1 starts with string2. If the test works, the function returns true; otherwise it returns false.
string()	string(value)	Converts value to a string. If value is a node set, function returns a string value based on the first node in the tree, or an empty string if the node set is empty. If value is a result tree fragment, returns a string of the nodes within the document fragment and automatically concatenates the result as if the fragment were an original source tree node. If value is a number, it's converted to a string and concatenated automatically with a – character if the number is a negative number. If there is no argument, the context node is returned.
substring-before()	substring-before(bigString, littleString)	Returns a substring of bigString consisting of everything from the beginning of bigString to the first instance of littleString's appearance. Example: substring-before("mySubstring is cool", "cool") would return mySubstring is.
substring-after()	substring-after (bigString, littleString)	Returns a substring of bigString consisting of everything from the end of the first instance of littleString's appearance to the end of bigString. Example: substring-after("mySubstring is cool and so are you", "cool") would return and so are you.
translate()	stranslate (string1, string2, string3)	This function looks for a match named in string1, then replaces the characters named in string2 (which is a substring of the first) with those in string3. A common use for this function is for changing between upper- and lowercase.

NOTE

Concatenated strings are built from more than one string, and JavaScript uses this procedure extensively. For example, in JavaScript, if you have two variables, *x* and *y*, each variable might contain the value of a string. If x=this and y=string, you would concatenate these two string variables with x+y and the result would be this string. In XSL, you would use ${x}, ${y}. Concatenation, addition, and the use of the + operator make data typing very important. For example, in a scripting language like JavaScript, you don't want the processing engine to mistake the + for a sum argument and add the values arithmetically. Rather, you want to add the values as strings, so that the result is this string. That's concatenation.

SUMMARY

The best way to really understand how to work with XSLT is to practice, practice, and practice. Open a style sheet in your text editing program and load its associated XML file in a browser, and watch what happens when you save your changes to the style sheet and click the browser's reload button. You'll find that you'll be able to quickly apply the many concepts you learned in this chapter. Among those concepts were:

▶ Transformation, including pattern matching and templates

▶ XML formatting, including how to output to HTML and the basics of using formatting objects to create displayed XML

In the next chapter you'll learn more about how nodes play an important role in XML document management. We'll introduce you to one of the underlying architectures that makes it possible to manipulate XML nodes when we introduce you to modeling with the Document Object Model.

Part iv

Chapter 13

MODELING THE XML DOCUMENT OBJECT

Programming in this day and age usually means working with objects to perform tasks, especially if you work with languages, such as Visual Basic (VB) or Java. Fortunately, XML lends itself well to such object models, in part because its structure is so reminiscent of the notion of nested objects with properties, data types, and encapsulation that make up traditional object-oriented or object-like languages.

In this chapter, I briefly introduce using object models in general. Then I focus on the meatier aspects of the XML Object Model (documents, elements, attributes, nodes, and so forth), showing how you can access them within your own programs.

Adapted from *XML Developer's Handbook*, by Kurt Cagle
ISBN 0-7821-2704-5   619 pages $49.99

NOTE

Editor's note: This chapter on the DOM was written with Microsoft-centric applications in mind. The principles you find here, however, can be ported over to other environments fairly painlessly.

UNDERSTANDING OBJECT-ORIENTED PROGRAMMING

Object-oriented programming (OOP), which has to have one of the most singularly incongruous acronyms ever created, is getting a little long in the tooth. Smalltalk, the predecessor of most of the "visual" languages in use today, has been influencing GUI designers since the late 1970s, while C++ has practically been synonymous with object-oriented programming since the mid-1980s. A quarter-century is a long time in the hyperkinetic world of programming, and in this time OOP has evolved from an interesting (if somewhat incomprehensible) way of simplifying the complicated morass of procedural programming into a central paradigm for designing complex systems.

TIP

In some ways, we have reached the upper threshold of OOP's capabilities and advantages, to the extent that computer historians are beginning to refer to present developments as the emergence of post-OOP design. XML may very well play a big part in this shift.

One consequence of 25 years of experimentation, successes, and failures is that OOP seems to work best when structures are built that model the phenomenon being programmed, breaking down complex objects into interconnected, simpler objects. These object models can take a number of different forms but typically focus on the *properties* that an object has, the actions (or *methods*) that the object can perform, the *events* that the object responds to, and the *relationships* that the object has with other objects within its object space.

The object model for a given object space can get pretty complex. With complex applications such as Microsoft Office, for example, nearly 200 distinct objects are defined with thousands of methods, properties, and events. Java goes one step further in that, with the exception of a few programming primitives, every entity in Java is an object with a distinct object model.

There are currently two major, distinct architectures for manipulating objects: Microsoft's Component Object Model (COM) and the Common Object Request Broker Architecture (CORBA), which is a standard endorsed by the Object Management Group (OMG), a coalition of other software developers and vendors (including Sun, Apple, IBM, and several others). While it is possible to create CORBA objects in Windows, the vast majority of all objects in the Windows 9x and NT categories follow the COM specification, including the XML components described extensively in this book.

THE XML DOCUMENT OBJECT MODEL

In comparison to something like Microsoft Office, the XML Document Object Model (frequently referred to as the XML DOM) is relatively simple, although, if you're not used to working with object models, it can still be a little daunting. There are 23 objects that make up the DOM, although, of those, only half a dozen or so will be used for nearly all of your XML development work. Table 13.1 summarizes what each object's interface does.

TABLE 13.1: The Various Interfaces Contained within the XML Document Object Model (Microsoft's implementation)

OBJECT INTERFACE	DESCRIPTION
DOMDocument	The entry point interface for creating and manipulating XML DOM documents.
DOMFreeThreadedDocument	An apartment-model version of the DOMDocument interface, for use in server environments.
IXMLDOMAttribute	Interface for an XML attribute.
IXMLDOMCDATASection	Interface for a CDATA section, which lets you store tagged, formatted text without having it parsed.
IXMLDOMCharacterData	Base class for several of the other classes, including Text and CDATASection. (Seldom used directly.)

Part iv

TABLE 13.1 continued: The Various Interfaces Contained within the XML Document Object Model (Microsoft's implementation)

Object Interface	Description
IXMLDOMComment	Interface for XML comments.
IXMLDOMDocumentFragment	Interface for document fragments, which are lightweight XML documents for intermediate processing.
IXMLDOMDocumentType	Interface for <DOCType> nodes; it is used to get access to the document type definition (DTD).
IXMLDOMElement	Interface for an XML element. (This is heavily used.)
IXMLDOMEntity	Interface for an Entity object (found within schemas or DTDs).
IXMLDOMEntityReference	Interface for an Entity Reference object (the &xxx; references found within the body of the XML itself).
IXMLDOMImplementation	Interface that lets you determine whether the given version of the DOM document supports a specific feature.
IXMLDOMNamedNodeMap	An extended interface that adds functionality to the Entity and Attribute interfaces.
IXMLDOMNode	The base node interface that most other XML interfaces inherit.
IXMLDOMNodeList	A list structure that contains references to noncontiguous nodes.
IXMLDOMNotation	Interface for supporting Notations, declared within the DTD.
IXMLDOMParseError	Interface for querying the XML object to determine if (and where) specific errors occurred.
IXMLDOMProcessingInstruction	An interface for accessing the processing instructions (PIs) within the document.
IXMLDOMText	An interface for setting or retrieving the text contents of a node.
IXTLRuntime	An interface used extensively by XSL for processing nodes during transformations.
XMLDocument	An interface for dealing with the XML document. It is obsolete (use DOMDocument instead) but is included for backward compatibility.

TABLE 13.1 continued: The Various Interfaces Contained within the XML Document Object Model (Microsoft's implementation)

OBJECT INTERFACE	DESCRIPTION
XMLDSOControl	An interface for using the XML document as a data source.
XMLHTTPRequest	An interface that permits communication across the HTTP protocol.

It is worth defining a few terms here. I've used the expression *object* fairly loosely, but, in fact, an object is technically considered an *instance* of a *class.* That is to say that the class defines what properties, methods, and events are available, while an object holds the actual contents of the properties. An *interface,* in turn, is a description of the class; it specifies which properties are available, for example, but doesn't contain any explicit code to define the behaviors of those properties.

Another frequently used term concerning the interfaces is *node.* Nodes can be considered the most primitive objects within an XML document, and, in fact, nearly all XML objects inherit the node interface. In essence, a node consists of a node name and a connection to one or more other nodes. Thus, an element node might have as children one or more attribute nodes, might have a CDATA (for *character data*) node or a *text node,* and may also have a comment node (among others). (The IXMLDOMNode interface will be discussed in much greater detail in the "Working with Nodes" section later in this chapter.)

EXAMINING THE XML DOCUMENT

In almost every case, one of the first things that you will do when working with XML is to create an XML document object, which, in Microsoft's XML Object Model, is called the DOMDocument. This object is frequently referred to as the *root,* or *top-level,* object in the object model, and it is one of the few objects within the XML DOM that can be created directly; almost everything else, from elements and attributes to node lists and entities, comes from the DOMDocument.

It's fairly easy to instantiate a DOMDocument object from within a scripting language. In the case of either Visual Basic Script (VBScript) or JavaScript, you need to know that the ProgID (a referencing identifier for

Microsoft COM objects) for the XML Document Object Model is MSXML2 .DOMDocument.3.0, and then just instantiate the object using the following object creation command for either language:

VBScript:

```
Dim xmlDoc

Set xmlDoc=createObject("MSXML2.DOMDocument.3.0")

' Note: if you are using MTS, you may want to use

' the server.createObject instead:

' set xmlDoc=server.createObject_

  ("MSXML2.DOMDocument.3.0")
```

JavaScript:

```
Var xmlDoc=new ActiveXObject_

  ("MSXML2.DOMDocument.3.0")
```

In order to use the DOMDocument from Visual Basic, you should first create a reference to the XML parser, as per the following steps:

1. From within Visual Basic, select the Project menu and choose References.

2. From the References list, choose Microsoft XML, Version 3.0 (or select the option for version 3, if that is available).

3. Close the dialog box.

You can now see the XML library in the Object Browser (on the MSXML tab) and can use it within your project.

Once you've created a reference to the XML library, you can declare a variable in VB using the DOMDocument class, as in the following example:

Visual Basic:

```
Dim xmlDoc as DOMDocument

Set xmlDoc=New DOMDocument

' you can also use the createObjects form:

Set xmlDoc=CreateObject("MSXML2.DOMDocument.3.0")
```

You can also use the CreateObject() function within VB, which may be preferable if you are planning on porting routines to VBScript, as in the following example:

Visual Basic:

```
Dim xmlDoc as DOMDocument

Set xmlDoc=CreateObject("MSXML2.DOMDocument.3.0")
```

NOTE

Note that the XML document object sources events. This means that if you want to be able to capture specific XML events within your application, you can (and should) declare the document using WithEvents. See the "Asynchronous XML and Events" section later in this chapter for more information.

WARNING

Some older XML documentation references the MSXML.DOMDocument and/or the Microsoft.XMLDOM ProgID rather than MSXML2.DOMDocument.3.0. These are older, currently unsupported interfaces provided only for backward compatibility. Microsoft has transitioned the release of its XML parser through a versioning system that has allowed different versions of parsers to actually work side by side. You call the appropriate one with a specific ProgID, such as MSXML2.DOMDocument.3.0. You should always use the latest version. You can obtain the latest Microsoft XML parser at http://msdn.microsoft.com.

CREATING A STANDARD XML PROJECT TYPE

If you are trying to use XML in a Visual Basic project (rather than in ASP or DHTML), you will probably find yourself setting the reference attributes for a number of related classes repeatedly. One thing you can do to improve your productivity is to create a couple of new project types.

For example, I typically find that the same applications in which I use XML also tend to require references to the scripting engines, the DHTML type library, and the Active Server Pages library. As a consequence, I created two custom templates: XML Form Project and XML_ASP ActiveX DLL Project.

You can make a custom template yourself by setting up a form or an ActiveX DLL as follows:

1. Open up a new project based on the Standard EXE template (or whatever the project type is that you're attempting to emulate).

2. If setting up a form, resize the form to the dimensions that you ordinarily use, and add components to the toolbar by right-clicking the bar.

CONTINUED ➡

Part iv

3. Add references by selecting Project ➤ References and then selecting the appropriate class references.

4. Save the project in the VB98\Templates\Projects folder and the form in the VB98\Templates\Forms folder.

5. In a similar fashion, you can save commonly used classes, property pages, user controls, and similar resources within the templates folder.

6. Whenever you create a new object of a given type (by selecting File ➤ New for a project or choosing Add from one of the many VB submenus), Visual Basic will automatically look in the template directories and present the items you saved as alternatives to the standard objects.

Loading Documents

Once instantiated, the XML document object exists but is essentially empty: There's no data in it. Before you can do anything meaningful with the document, you need to load in XML data from somewhere—a file, a text string, a data island, or another DOM object. The DOM supports two distinct ways of loading data in:

LoadXML   Lets you pass a string of text formatted as XML into the object.

Load   Lets you pass a filename, URL, or another XML document as a parameter to populate the document.

LoadXML is especially handy for creating short XML documents on the fly. For example, Listing 13.1 presents two listings that demonstrate a way to create a short log message in XML, first in Visual Basic Script (as you might see in Visual InterDev) and then in Visual Basic.

Listing 13.1: Creating a Short XML Document with the LoadXML Method

```
VBScript:
Dim xmlDoc
Dim buf
```

```
Set xmlDoc=createObject("MSXML2.DOMDocument.3.0")
Buf=""
Buf=Buf+"<logMessage>"
Buf=Buf+"<author>Kurt Cagle</author>"
Buf=Buf+"<msg>This is a short message</msg>"
Buf=Buf+"<date>2000-01-12</date>"
Buf=Buf+"</logMessage>"
XmlDoc.LoadXML buf
```

Visual Basic:
```
Dim xmlDoc as DOMDocument
Dim buf as String
Set xmlDoc=new DOMDocument
Buf=""
Buf=Buf+"<logMessage>"
Buf=Buf+"<author>Kurt Cagle</author>"
Buf=Buf+"<msg>This is a short message</msg>"
Buf=Buf+"<date>2000-01-12</date>"
Buf=Buf+"</logMessage>"
XmlDoc.LoadXML buf
```

This code creates an XML-based log message, which may be added into an extended log. LoadXML works best in situations where the XML is generated as text. However, in most cases, you'll probably find that you want to retrieve your XML from a stream of some sort (a file from your local system, an ASP document, the result of a database query that generates XML, etc.). In these cases, you would call the Load function instead, as demonstrated in Listing 13.2.

Listing 13.2: Various Ways of Loading Documents from External Sources through the Load Method

Visual Basic:
```
Dim xmlDoc as DOMDocument
Set xmlDoc=new DOMDocument
```

VBScript:
```
Dim xmlDoc
Set xmlDoc=createObject("MSXML2.DOMDocument.3.0")
' Load from a local file:
XmlDoc.Load "c:\xmlDevHandbook\myData.xml"
' Load from a network drive:
XmlDoc.Load "\\resources\xmlDevHandbook\myData.xml"
```

```
' Load from a URL:
XmlDoc.Load "http://www.xmlDevHandbook/myData.xml"
' Load from a parameterized ASP page:
XmlDoc.Load "http://www.xmlDevHandbook/_
             getNewData.asp?file=myData"
' Load from SQL Query (SQL Server7.5)

xmlDoc.Load "http://www.xmlDevHandbook/data?_
sql=SELECT * FROM MyDataTable WHERE_
Author='Kurt+Cagle', FOR XML AUTO"
```

Typically, when a load is successful, the parser will automatically remove all irrelevant white space from the document; more specifically, the parser throws away the following characters:

- ▶ Leading and trailing spaces in text elements

- ▶ Spaces within elements, except those required to separate items

- ▶ Tabs

- ▶ Carriage returns

- ▶ Line feeds

In many cases, this filtering process has no impact on the content of the document, especially if the document is data-centric. However, for document-centric code, removing white space can make the code especially impenetrable to read or debug.

The preserveWhiteSpace property turns off this filtering mechanism. When this property is set to true, the document will retain the formatting that it had going in, although typically at a cost of adding 20–30 percent to the size of the document. If your XML will likely be read as a text file, or if you have code (such as VBScript) that depends on carriage returns embedded in the XML, then you may want to set this option. This should be set prior to loading the document, by the way; if you set it after loading the document, the white space will already have been stripped.

Another property that should possibly be set before loading the document is async. To understand the purpose of this property, consider that there are two different modes for loading a document: pulling it from a local hard drive, which is generally a very fast operation, or pulling it from a network or the Internet, which ranges from a moderately fast to a glacially slow process, depending on your connection speed.

The async (short for *asynchronous*) property sets an internal flag telling Load to either load the full document at one time before returning to the next line (`async=false`) or to initiate loading and then proceed to the next command without waiting for completion (`async=true`). The parser is relatively intelligent in that it makes local file access synchronous by default while making most other access types asynchronous, but there are situations when you may want alternate behavior. For example, imagine that you need to load a file from the Internet before doing any other action and that you're willing to lock the application until the file is downloaded or it times out.

In general, programming this way isn't recommended, but, at the same time, asynchronous programming generally tends to be much more complex than is worthwhile for simpler applications. Similarly, there are situations when you pull from local data streams that may themselves be asynchronous (such as a SQL query). In either case, you should set `async` to the appropriate Boolean value prior to initiating the load.

NOTE
The "Asynchronous XML and Events" section later in this chapter shows how you can build asynchronous XML programs using the `DOMDocument` methods.

Once you have loaded the XML document, you can retrieve its URL at any time via the `url` property. Note that, internally, the XML document will automatically convert local DOS and network paths to their URL equivalent, as demonstrated in the following example:

```
XmlDoc.load "c:\bin\resources.xml"
Debug.print xmlDoc.url
file:///C|/bin/resources.xml
XmlDoc.load "\\mySystem\bin\resources.xml"
Debug.print xmlDoc.url
file:///mySystem/bin/resources.xml
```

Error Handling with *ParseError*

Suppose something does go wrong with your download. The server may be down. The XML source may be corrupted. You may have mistyped the file location. A DTD may not be valid for the document in question.

A significant proportion of any software project involves handling exceptions to the rules, either as part of the program flow or through some form of error handling. Because XML files can be generated by hand, and due to the large number of things that can go wrong within a document alone (not to mention any of the connections *to* that document), the error mechanism for XML needs to be more robust than simply returning an error code.

Fortunately, the Microsoft XML parser's error-handling mechanism is quite robust; indeed, it's a model that Microsoft itself is beginning to incorporate into some of its more advanced products. Any time an error occurs with the DOM, the parser invalidates the XML structure and then notifies a subordinate class called the `ParseError` object. This object has the properties outlined in Table 13.2 and implements them through the `IXMLDOMParseError` class.

TABLE 13.2: Interface for the `ParseError` Object

PROPERTY	DESCRIPTION
ErrorCode	Comprises the numeric code associated with the error. If no error has occurred, this value will be zero.
Filepos	Gives the character position within the incoming XML stream, establishing where the error occurred. (Zero if no error.)
Line	Identifies the line (carriage return delineated) where the error occurred. (Zero if no error.)
Linepos	Identifies the position, relative to the start of the current line, where the error occurred. (Zero if no error.)
Reason	Provides a description of the error and is usually pretty detailed. (Will be blank if no error occurred.)
SrcText	Retrieves the text of the line where the error occurred.
URL	Identifies the filename or URL where the error took place. (Note that if a file contains an external DTD, this will point to the DTD, not the XML file that was originally retrieved.)

The `ParseError` object can give you detailed information about the nature of any load or validation error and should be used whenever possible to get information about the state of an error. For example, consider a situation where the file being loaded is not completely valid, such as when an opening tag is not matched by a closing tag, as in the following example of the XML document `StatusLog1.xml`:

```
<?xml version="1.0" ?>
<!- StatusLog1.xml ->
<log>
```

```
    <message>
        <author>Kurt Cagle
        <msg>This is a short message</msg>
        <date>2000-01-12</date>
    </message>"
</log>
```

If you attempt to load this document, you will end up generating an error (<author> has no closing tag), and you can trap the error using the code in Listing 13.3.

Listing 13.3: The GetXMLDoc Function Checks the Incoming XML Stream and Displays an Alert Dialog Describing the Error if One Occurs.

```
Visual Basic:
Function GetXMLDoc(srcURL as String) as DOMDocument
    Dim xmlDoc as DOMdocument
    Dim errorMsg as String
    Set xmlDoc=new DOMDocument
    xmlDoc.load srcURL
    If xmlDoc.parseError.errorCode>0 then
        ErrorMsg="An Error occurred (Error "
        ErrorMsg=ErrorMsg+cstr(xmlDoc.parseError_
        .errorCode)
        ErrorMsg=ErrorMsg+")"+vbCRLF
        ErrorMsg=ErrorMsg+ xmlDoc.parseError_
        .reason+vbCRLF
        ErrorMsg=ErrorMsg+" at char"
        ErrorMsg=ErrorMsg"+cstr(xmlDoc.parseError_
        .linePos)
        ErrorMsg=ErrorMsg+" of line "+cstr(xmlDoc._
        parseError.line)
        ErrorMsg=ErrorMsg+" in file "+xmlDoc.parseError_
        .url+vbCRLF
        ErrorMsg=ErrorMsg+"Text of line:"+xmlDoc_
        .parseError.srcText
        Msgbox ErrorMsg
        Set GetXMLDoc=Nothing
        Exit Function
    End if
    Set GetXMLDoc=xmlDoc
```

```
End Function

Dim ErrorDoc as DOMDocument
Set ErrorDoc=GetXMLDoc("StatusLog1.xml")
```

Visual Basic Script:
```
Function GetXMLDoc()
  Dim xmlDoc
  Dim errorMsg
  Set xmlDoc=createObject("MSXML2.DOMDocument.3.0")
  xmlDoc.load srcURL
  If xmlDoc.parseError.errorCode>0 then
     ErrorMsg="An Error occurred (Error "
     ErrorMsg=ErrorMsg+cstr(xmlDoc.parseError_
        .errorCode)+")"+vbCRLF
     ErrorMsg=ErrorMsg+ xmlDoc.parseError_
     .reason+vbCRLF
     ErrorMsg=ErrorMsg+" at char "+cstr(xmlDoc_
     .parseError.linePos)
     ErrorMsg=ErrorMsg+" of line "+cstr(xmlDoc_
     .parseError.line)
     ErrorMsg=ErrorMsg+" in file "+xmlDoc_
     .parseError.url+vbCRLF
     ErrorMsg=ErrorMsg+"Text of line:"+xmlDoc_
     .parseError.srcText
     Msgbox ErrorMsg
     Set GetXMLDoc=Nothing
     Exit Function
  End if
  Set GetXMLDoc=xmlDoc
End Function

Dim ErrorDoc
Set ErrorDoc=GetXMLDoc("StatusLog1.xml")
```

When an error occurs, an alert box will pop up, displaying the details of the error, and then returns the DOMDocument set to the value Nothing. Note that in some cases you may actually want the function to retrieve the error message as an XML document itself; this especially makes sense in client/server systems with the client transmitting data and expecting an XML structure as a return type from the server.

Outputting XML Files

Just as there are two modes for inputting XML, either from a string or from an external resource, the XML DOM parser supports two modes for outputting XML as well: the xml property and the save() method.

The xml property "walks" the XML tree and produces a string representation of the XML. The parser follows this basic set of rules for determining the order that it uses to reconstruct the tree:

▶ The parser proceeds to a child before it processes a sibling.

▶ The parser returns a list of children in the order in which they were entered.

▶ Attributes are parsed before children and are appended to the current node.

▶ If PreserveWhiteSpace is false (the default), then the parser removes any superfluous white space (tabs, carriage returns, etc.) before outputting the result. If the property is true, these things are retained upon output.

▶ Unicode is supported.

▶ Namespace declarations are added for the topmost node.

You will use the xml property in a number of different circumstances, most notably for producing output for ASP pages and for debugging your code, as demonstrated in the following example:

```
XMLDoc.load "http://www.XMLDevHandbook.com/_
resources/summary.xml"
Debug.print XMLDoc.xml
```

While the xml property corresponds to the LoadXML method, the save() method is, of course, the counterpart to the load() method. save()converts the internal XML representation into a string and then saves that string to the location specified.

However, save() has some limitations that load() doesn't. For starters, save() is limited in where it can save information; you must have Write permission for the directory in which you're saving the file, or Save will generate an error. Furthermore, you can't use save() to save files to an HTTP: or an FTP: location, although it is possible to use specific HTTP-based calls to save an XML file (just not by using Save).

The ParseError object only handles errors specifically relating to parsing the data structure, but the save() method generates errors (such as permission locks or providing a nonexistent directory path) that can be trapped through the normal language mechanism. For example, in Visual Basic you can catch the error codes through an On Error statement, as demonstrated in Listing 13.4.

Listing 13.4: The SaveXML Function Demonstrates One Technique for Saving Code to a File.

```
Function SaveXML()
    On Error Goto CannotSave
    XMLDoc.save "c:/invalidDirectory/myXMLFile.xml"
    On Error Goto 0
    Exit Function
CannotSave:
    Select Case Err.Number
        Case -2147024891
            Msgbox "File exists and is read only."
        Case -2147024893
            Msgbox "The System cannot find the path
            specified."
        Case Else
            Err.Raise
    End Select
End Function
```

TIP

Domain boundaries are another problem that you can run into with both loading and saving. Typically, from within a Web page, you will find that you can't load XML files from directories outside of the domain that the page itself comes from. This is a security sandbox issue. Because you can run across domains when working with server code (or within a VB application that's not bound by a Web page's context), the easiest solution to this problem is to load the other domain's XML code onto the server before referencing it on the client.

Scratching the Surface

The DOMDocument interface is fairly rich: There are some 60 methods or properties associated with it, although most of them are tied up with creating or testing elements, attributes, or similar components that make up the document.

While the DOMDocument interface lets you do quite a bit, its primary purpose is acting as a container for those same elements and attributes. In the next section, I take a more detailed look at how you can navigate through an XML structure and work with the basic components: nodes.

WORKING WITH NODES

From the standpoint of the DOM, an XML document is nothing more than a collection of *nodes*. A node is a pretty primitive object, and, in most cases, it is something that you will work with through classes that are derived from it, rather than directly manipulating nodes themselves.

The MSXML DOM defines a node as being an instance of the IXMLDOMNode class and supports the properties and methods described in Table 13.3. However, a node can also be described in simple terms as an object that:

▶ Can be contained by other nodes

▶ Can contain other nodes

▶ Exists in some ordered relationship to its sibling nodes

▶ Can, but doesn't have to, contain a value

▶ Has a text node made up of its own text along with any text that its children have

▶ Serves as the base class for most other XML entities

TABLE 13.3: Properties and Methods of the IXMLDOMNode Class

PROPERTY OR METHOD	DESCRIPTION
AppendChild	Adds a child node to the current node after all other nodes in the childNodes collection.
Attributes	A collection of nodes that retain attribute information.
BaseName	The name of the node without any namespace qualifier.
ChildNodes	The collection of all non-attribute nodes belonging to the current node.
CloneNode	Duplicates the current node and possibly its descendants and returns that node as the result.

Part iv

TABLE 13.3 continued: Properties and Methods of the IXMLDOMNode Class

PROPERTY OR METHOD	DESCRIPTION
DataType	When used with an XML schema, contains the data type of the node's typedValue.
Definition	When used with an XML schema, returns the node in the schema that defines the characteristics of the current node.
FirstChild	Retrieves the first child node in the current node's ChildNodes collection.
HasChildNodes	A Boolean value that returns as true if the node has children, and is false otherwise.
InsertBefore	Lets you insert a new node before an already-existing childNode in the current node's ChildNodes collection.
LastChild	The last child node in the current node's ChildNodes collection.
NamespaceURI	Identifies the XML schema or DTD that defines the node's characteristics.
NextSibling	Returns the current node's next junior sibling node, or nothing if the current node is also the last node in the collection.
NodeName	The name of the node, although the exact meaning changes depending on where the node is used.
NodeType	A numeric value that indexes the type of node used (element, attribute, etc.). (The NodeTypes are contained in Table 13.4.)
NodeTypedValue	Contains the text of the node converted into the type specified in DataType. If no schema is specified (or if a DTD is used), then this will simply return the text of the node as a string.
NodeTypeString	Returns the data type of the node's typed value as a string.
NodeValue	Returns the value of the node, if specified within a DTD. Typically, this property is not used with schemas.
OwnerDocument	Passes a pointer to the DOMDocument object that contains the current node.

TABLE 13.3 continued: Properties and Methods of the
IXMLDOMNode Class

PROPERTY OR METHOD	DESCRIPTION
ParentNode	Returns the containing node of the current node. The root node has no parent node (i.e., `<node.parentNode is Nothing>`).
Parsed	Indicates that the current node has already been parsed upon downloading. (See the "Asynchronous XML and Events" section later in this chapter).
Prefix	Is the namespace designation for the particular node. If no namespace has been declared, this is blank.
PreviousSibling	Is the next senior node in the current node's family or is `Nothing` if the node is the first node.
RemoveChild	Removes the indicated child from the current node's `childNode` list.
ReplaceChild	Replaces one child node with another.
SelectNodes	Lets you select a given collection of nodes by matching a specific criterion.
SelectSingleNode	Lets you select one node from a collection of nodes by matching a specific criterion.
Specified	Indicates whether a definition has been specified for this particular node in the DTD or schema.
Text	Contains the text (i.e., non-tagged) information associated with the current node.
TransformNode	Applies an XSL filter to an XML document to produce a text stream.
TransformNodeToObject	Applies an XSL filter to an XML document to produce another XML document.
Xml	Returns the XML representation of the current node and all its children.

Navigating Nodes

At the node level, navigating an XML document can be likened to tracing a family tree from some distant great-great grandparent to yourself. A node can have children, which can have children in turn. A node can also have siblings, which share the same parent but have a distinct birth order. Finally, all nodes except the root node also have a parent node.

The terminology used for node-level navigation follows this family metaphor. Consider the XML structure given (in part) in Listing 13.5.

Listing 13.5: Part of the Resume.xml File

```xml
<?xml version="1.0"?>
<resume>
    <header>
        <resumeOf>
            <firstName>Kurt</firstName>
            <lastName>Cagle</lastName>
            <middleInitial>A</middleInitial>
        </resumeOf>
        <address>
            <city>Olympia</city>
            <state>Washington</state>
        </address>
    </header>
    <skills>
        <programming>
            <language>
                <title>Visual Basic</title>
                <proficiency>Expert</proficiency>
                <years>8</years>
            </language>
            <architecture>
                <title>Client/Server Programming</title>
                <proficiency>Expert</proficiency>
                <years>4</years>
            </architecture>
            <language>
                <title>Java</title>
                <proficiency>Intermediate</proficiency>
                <years>3</years>
            </language>
            <application>
                <title>Macromedia Director</title>
                <proficiency>Expert</proficiency>
                <years>9</years>
            </application>
```

```
        <language>
            <title>JavaScript</title>
            <proficiency>Expert</proficiency>
            <years>5</years>
        </language>
    </programming>
    <!- There's obviously much more ->
</skills>
    <!- More categories here, too ->
</resume>
```

In the <skills> section, take a look at the second <language> node, associated with Java. This node is well placed to demonstrate all of the navigational properties and methods of the node class. From most nodes, you can navigate to the previous or next node using either the PreviousSibling or the NextSibling property, while the parentNode will return the parent of the current node. The childNodes() property, in turn, returns a collection of all of the children (both elements and other XML objects, such as text nodes, though not attributes) and is zero based. If a node doesn't have a corresponding sibling, parent, or child, then the associated properties return a value of Nothing.

Listing 13.6 illustrates what elements are retrieved with each of these properties, working on the second <language> node in the <skills> section of the resume document.

Listing 13.6: Sample Code That Demonstrates How You Can Navigate from One Node to the Next Using the XML DOM

```
Dim JavaNode as IXMLDOMNode
' Retrieve the 2nd <language> node,
' we don't care how
Set JavaNode=GetJavaLanguageNode()
Debug.Print JavaNode.parentNode.nodeName
"programming"
Debug.Print JavaNode.previousSibling.nodeName
"architecture"
Debug.Print JavaNode.nextSibling.nodeName
"application"
Debug.Print JavaNode.firstChild.nodeName
"title"
Debug.Print JavaNode.lastChild.nodeName
"years"
Debug.Print JavaNode.childNodes(1).nodeName
```

```
"proficiency"
' Note childNodes is a 0 based array.
Debug.Print JavaNode.hasChildNodes
True
Debug.Print JavaNode.childNodes.length
```

Most of these are self evident, although it is worth stressing that the childNodes array, which contains the children of the current node, is a zero-based array: childNodes(0) points to the first child, childNodes(1) to the second child, and so forth.

Technically speaking, childNodes is not a formal array. In fact, it is a structure exclusive to the XML DOM called a *node list*. Node lists are the workhorses of XML navigation, and they play an especially big part when it comes to XML's integration with XSL. Each entry within a node list is a node—specifically a node of the IXMLDOMNode type (this distinction becomes important with elements, covered in the next section)— although you can think of a node list as being a collection of pointers to nodes. One implication of this is that a node list doesn't have to consist of nodes that are all children of the same parent.

One of the advantages of working with a node list is that you can enumerate over the list, just as you would with a collection or a variant array. For example, to enumerate over all of the programming skill types in the preceding resume, you could use the OutputSkills function shown in Listing 13.7.

Listing 13.7: The OutputSkills Function Demonstrates How DOM Can Be Used to Create Output from an XML File.

```
Function OuputSkills()\
```

Visual Basic:

```
Dim xmlDoc as DOMDocument
Dim progNode as IXMLDOMNode
Dim skillNode as IXMLDOMNode
Dim titleNode as IXMLDOMNode
Dim nodeList as IXMLDOMNodeList
Dim buffer as String
Set xmlDoc=new DOMDocument
```

VBScript:

```
Dim xmlDoc
Dim progNode
```

```
        Dim skillNode
        Dim titleNode
        Dim nodeList
        Dim buffer
        Set xmlDoc=createObject("MSXML2.DOMDocument.3.0")

        XmlDoc.load "resume.xml"
        buffer="<ul>"+vbCRLF
        Set progNode=xmlDoc.documentElement._
        childNodes(1). childNodes(0)

        for each skillNode in progNode.childNodes
            buffer=buffer+"<li><b>"+
                strConv(skillNode.nodeName,vbProperCase)_
                +".</b>"
            set titleNode=skillNode.childNodes(0)
            buffer=buffer+"titleNode.text+"</li>"+vbCRLF
        next
        buffer=buffer+"</ul>"+vbCRLF
        OutputSkills=buffer
End Function

Debug.Print OutputSkills()
<ul>
<li><b>Language.</b>Visual Basic</li>
<li><b>Architecture.</b>
        Client/Server Programming
</li>
<li><b>Language.</b>Java</li>
<li><b>Application.</b>Macromedia Director</li>
<li><b>Language.</b>JavaScript</li>
</ul>
```

The output format here is HTML, which renders as:

- ▶ **Language.**Visual Basic

- ▶ **Architecture.**Client/Server Programming

- ▶ **Language.**Java

- ▶ **Application.**Macromedia Director

- ▶ **Language.**JavaScript

A few things should become clear after studying the sample script—perhaps most significantly that referencing nodes by their numeric position within the XML document is guaranteed to bring all sorts of headaches, is nearly unreadable, and seems tailor-made for a better solution. (Don't worry, I'll get to that.)

Beyond that, however, the one thing that stands out is how adding enumeration to the XML structure adds considerably to what can be done with the program. The statement

```
for each skillNode in progNode.childNodes
```

effectively iterates through each of the program node's children and lets you manipulate the subelements (through the nodeName and text properties). To a certain extent, almost all XML programming is based on either searching for a given node or iterating through a selection of nodes.

NOTE
I've also surreptitiously dropped the <documentElement> node into the example. This property of the DOMDocument always points to the root element of the document.

Getting Nodes by Name

Using indexed numbers to retrieve a given node in an XML tree will usually lead to disaster. XML documents change, and if a node is added or removed, that will affect the order of any subsequent node adversely. As a consequence, it makes sense to be able to retrieve elements by their tag name.

Microsoft's XML parser has a very powerful engine, based on the XPath specifications of the W3C (World Wide Web Consortium), for getting nearly any node or possible collection of nodes from an XML tree. This engine underlies all three of the commands that you can use to retrieve specific nodes: getElementsByTagName, selectNodes, and selectSingleNode.

GetElementsByTagName() is a method belonging to the DOMDocument interface and, as such, can only be called at the document level. It works by passing the name of the tag you want to retrieve and returning a node list of all of the tags that match that name. For example, consider the resume sample again, presented in Listing 13.8.

Listing 13.8: The Resume.xml file, Demonstrating the Use of getElementsByTagName

```xml
<resume>
    <header>
        <resumeOf>
            <firstName>Kurt</firstName>
            <lastName>Cagle</lastName>
            <middleInitial>A</middleInitial>
        </resumeOf>
        <homeAddress>
            <city>Olympia</city>
            <state>Washington</state>
        </address>
        <mailingAddress>
            <city>Lacey</city>
            <state>Washington</state>
        </address>
    </header>
    <skills>
        <programming>
            <language>
                <title>Visual Basic</title>
                <proficiency>Expert</proficiency>
                <years>8</years>
            </language>
            <architecture>
                <title>Client/Server Programming</title>
                <proficiency>Expert</proficiency>
                <years>4</years>
            </architecture>
            <language>
                <title>Java</title>
                <proficiency>Intermediate</proficiency>
                <years>3</years>
            </language>
            <application>
                <title>Macromedia Director</title>
                <proficiency>Expert</proficiency>
                <years>9</years>
            </application>
            <language>
```

```
                <title>JavaScript</title>
                <proficiency>Expert</proficiency>
                <years>5</years>
            </language>
        </programming>
        <!- There's obviously much more ->
    </skills>
        <!- More categories here, too ->
</resume>
```

If you wanted to get the last name of the resume's owner, you would call GetElementsByTagname() with the name lastName as a parameter, as demonstrated in the following example:

```
Dim resumeDoc as DOMDocument
Dim nodeList as IXMLDOMNodeList

Set resumeDoc=new DOMDocument
ResumeDoc.load "resume.xml"
Set nodeList=resumeDoc.getElementsByTagname_
("lastName")
```

Note that this function will always return a node list rather than a single node. This means that in order for you to access the node (if it is a singleton) you still need to reference the first element in the node list array:

```
Debug.Print_
    resumeDoc.getElementsByTagName("lastName")_
    (0).text

"Cagle"
```

You can also qualify the element names somewhat. For example, if you wanted to get the city from the above resume, getElementsByTagName would actually return two nodes, one for the home address, the other for the mailing address. However, you can specify that you want the home address city by pre-pending the parent node to the existing node:

```
Debug.Print
resumeDoc.getElementsByTagName_
("homeAddress/city")(0).text
"Lacey"
```

Additionally, you can use the wildcard character to retrieve the collection of all nodes, which you can similarly qualify. For example,

```
Set nodelist=resumeDoc.getElementsByTagName("*")
```

retrieves all of the nodes in the document, while

```
Set nodelist=_
    resumeDoc.getElementsByTagName("programming/*")
```

retrieves all of the immediate children of the <programming> node (the five <language>, <architecture>, <language>, <application>, and <language> nodes, respectively). Similarly,

```
Set nodelist=_
resumeDoc.getElementsByTagName_
("programming/*/title")
```

will retrieve the title nodes of each of these children.

One problem is that getElementsByTagName limits its own utility somewhat. All searches start from the top of the XML tree. Thus, if you have an existing node and you want to retrieve specific child nodes of that node, you have to have an exclusive path to that node before you can perform any query.

The selectNodes function is designed to solve that problem. It works at the node level, not the document level, and it designates the current node as the context for the search. In other words, selectNodes acts (more or less) like getElementsByTagName, with the assumption that the current node is the root node.

To simplify it even more, a singular version called selectSingleNode also exists; this returns the first node that satisfies the search criterion, both of which are more or less the same for either function.

You can see how these functions work well together by rewriting the OutputSkills() function to take advantage of the three functions demonstrated in Listing 13.9.

Listing 13.9: The OutputSkills Function, Rewritten to Use selectNodes, selectSingleNode, and getElementsByTagname

```
Function OuputSkills ()
    Dim xmlDoc as DOMDocument
    Dim skillNode as IXMLDOMNode
    Dim titleNode as IXMLDOMNode
    Dim buffer as String
```

```
XmlDoc.load "resume.xml"
buffer="<ul>"+vbCRLF
for each skillNode in
    xmlDoc.getElementsByTagName("programming/*")
    buffer=buffer+"<li><b>"+_
      strConv(skillNode.nodeName,_
      vbPro    perCase)+".</b>"
    set titleNode=skillNode.selectSingleNode_
    ("title")
    buffer=buffer+"titleNode.text+"</li>"+vbCRLF
next
buffer=buffer+"</ul>"+vbCRLF
OutputSkills=buffer
End Function
```

The structure that the program works on becomes much more obvious, and you don't need to worry about what happens if the element positions are changed.

TIP

Of the two, selectNodes is far more powerful than getElementsByTagName. With selectNodes, you can perform very detailed and selective searches that will cause errors in the other function.

Node Types

The list of properties associated with a node can be a little daunting. In practice, however, you will likely end up using a dozen or so of the properties, especially as certain of the inherited node classes (such as the element node type) simplify some of the more cumbersome aspects of node navigation, creation, and assignment.

Not all nodes are created equal. While most nodes have the same underlying structure, an element node, which would correspond to a standard tag element in an XML structure, can contain both text and other nodes. An attribute can have text but no children, and a text node has no nodeName and, technically, can't contain other elements.

The XML DOM currently defines 13 distinct node types, as displayed in Table 13.4. It also defines a set of globally available constants that begin with NODE_ (left-hand column in the table), which can be used in arguments to test or create new nodes of various types, and which can be queried with the NodeType property. The current version of the MSXML parser also lets you retrieve the type as a string via the NodeTypeString property (right-hand column).

TABLE 13.4: NodeType Constants and Their Values

NodeType CONSTANT NAME	NodeType VALUE	NodeTypeString NAME
NODE_ATTRIBUTE	2	Attribute
NODE_CDATA_SECTION	4	CDATASection
NODE_COMMENT	8	Comment
NODE_DOCUMENT	9	Document
NODE_DOCUMENT_FRAGMENT	11	documentfragment
NODE_DOCUMENT_TYPE	10	documenttype
NODE_ELEMENT	1	Element
NODE_ENTITY	6	Entity
NODE_ENTITY_REFERENCE	5	entityreference
NODE_INVALID	0	Invalid
NODE_NOTATION	12	Notation
NODE_PROCESSING_INSTRUCTION	7	processinginstruction
NODE_TEXT	3	Text

NOTE

Note that the NodeType and NodeTypeString properties are not related to the data type of the text; they indicate whether a node is an element or an attribute, not whether the text it contains is a string or a Boolean value. The relevant text property is the dataType property, and is used in schema development, which is beyond the scope of this chapter. For more information on schema development, refer to Chapter 7 ("An Introduction to XML Schemas") and Chapter 8 ("Writing XML Schemas").

Creating, Adding, and Deleting Nodes

So far, the examples I've given have assumed that, somewhere, you can find a preexisting XML document to use. However, there are numerous times when you want to be able to generate XML documents on the fly (or, at the very least, to add or delete specific nodes from the XML tree). The XML parser provides a sophisticated collection of routines dedicated precisely to this purpose.

A node cannot explicitly create another node. Instead, it has to rely on the document object to create the node for it. Fortunately, one of the properties common to all nodes is ownerDocument, which returns a reference to the document that contains the node.

Once a reference to the document is at hand, the document can call createNode to instantiate a new node based on the node type, as demonstrated in the following example:

```
xmldoc.createNode(type,name as String,_
    namespaceURI as string) as IXMLDOMNode
```

createNode returns a reference to the newly created node. It is especially worth noting at this point that the object just created belongs to the XML document but has not yet been placed *within* the XML document. *This distinction is important.* Essentially, you have created an object but haven't yet specified where the object is to go. If you persist the XML as a string, the newly created node will disappear.

There are two ways of attaching the node: through the appendChild method or the insertBefore method of the prospective parent node. The appendChild method will automatically add the node to the end of the child nodes for the given parent node, while insertBefore will, well, insert the node before a specified child node.

For example, let's say you have an XML document that contains a message log (with <log> root node) and you want to add a new message entry to the log. The log file, StatusLog13.xml, already has one message entry:

```
<?xml version="1.0" ?>
<!- StatusLog13.xml ->
<log>
    <message>
        <author>Kurt Cagle</author>
        <title>First Message</title>
        <date>2000-01-12</date>
        <body>This is a short message</body>
    </message>"
</log>
```

The routine in Listing 13.10 loads the log file, creates a new message from passed arguments, and appends it to the XML log file.

Listing 13.10: `AddMessage1` **Is a First-Cut Pass at Writing a Routine to Append a Message to an XML Message Log.**

Visual Basic:

```
Function AddMessage1(logXML as DOMDocument,_
    Author as string, Title as String,_
    Body as String) as IXMLDOMNode
    Dim MsgNode as IXMLDOMNode
    Dim AuthorNode as IXMLDOMNode
    Dim TitleNode as IXMLDOMNode
    Dim DateNode as IXMLDOMNode
    Dim BodyNode as IXMLDOMNode
```

Replace the preceding header with the following:

VBScript:

```
'Function AddMessage1(logXML,Author,Title)
'    Dim MsgNode
'    Dim AuthorNode
'    Dim TitleNode
'    Dim DateNode
'    Dim BodyNode


    Set msgNode=logXML.createNode(_
    NODE_ELEMENT,"message","")
    LogXML.documentElement.appendChild msgNode
    Set AuthorNode=logXML.createNode(_
        NODE_ELEMENT,"author","")
    AuthorNode.text=Author
    MsgNode.appendChild AuthorNode
    Set TitleNode=logXML.createNode(_
        NODE_ELEMENT,"title","")
    TitleNode.text=Title
    MsgNode.appendChild TitleNode
    Set DateNode=logXML.createNode(_
        NODE_ELEMENT,"date","")
```

```
DateNode.text=Today
MsgNode.appendChild DateNode
Set BodyNode=logXML.createNode(_
    NODE_ELEMENT,"body","")
BodyNode.text=Body
MsgNode.appendChild BodyNode
Set AddMessage1=MsgNode
End Function
```

This is a lot of work to add a fairly simple node, and you might have noticed that there seems to be a certain basic pattern to the code that should be easy to exploit. In general, the code creates a new element node, sets the text for the newly created node, and then appends the node to the prospective parent node. (Note that it's not necessary to attach the node to the tree to set any of the node's properties.)

The XML DOM includes wrapper functions, including the expected `createElement` function, for creating specific types of nodes. For `createElement`, you simply pass the tag name of the element you want to create. The process of assigning an object's text can likewise be handled mechanically, with the implicit assumption that a blank string indicates that no text is passed. Finally, it makes sense to pass the parent node as an argument so that the newly created element gets hooked up automatically, as shown in Listing 13.11.

Listing 13.11: `AddElement` Is a General Worker Function That Will Create a New Element, Assign a String Object to It, and Append It to Its Parent Element.

Visual Basic:
```
Function AddElement(parentNode as IXMLDOMElement,_
    elementName as String,
    optional elementText as String_
    = "") as IXMLDOMNode
    Dim newNode as IXMLDOMNode
```

VBScript:
```
Function AddElement(parentNode,elementName,
elementText)
    Dim newNode
```

```
        Set newNode=parentNode.ownerDocument._
        createElement(_elementName)
        newNode.text=elementText
        parentNode.appendChild newNode
        set AddElement=newNode
    End Function
```

With this function, you can rewrite the AddMessage function in a more simplified fashion, as AddMessage2, as shown in Listing 13.12.

Listing 13.12: AddMessage2 **Encapsulates Some of the Complexity of Creating Elements for the Message Log.**

Visual Basic:
```
Function AddMessage2 (logXML as DOMDocument,_
    Author as string, Title as String, Body as String)_
    as IXMLDOMNode
     Dim MsgNode as IXMLDOMNode
```

VBScript:
```
Function AddMessage2 (logXML,Author,Title,Body)_
    Dim MsgNode

    Set MsgNode=AddElement(logXML.documentElement,"_
    message","")
    AddElement msgNode,"author",Author
    AddElement msgNode,"title",Title
    AddElement msgNode,"date",Today
    AddElement msgNode,"body",Body
    Set AddMessage2=MsgNode
End Function
```

Of course, there may be times when you don't want the item added at the end of the list. For example, you may want to have a stack that grows from top to bottom so that the newest messages are always the first encountered. The insertBefore method handles this particular instance. Because a message list is frequently queued in descending time order, it's easy to create an AddMessageInverted function so that the message element is always inserted first, as demonstrated in Listing 13.13.

Part iv

Listing 13.13: AddMessageInverted **Enters Messages at the Start of the List as They Are Entered.**

```
Visual Basic:
Function AddMessageInverted(logXML as DOMDocument,_
    Author as string, Title as String,_
Body as String)_
    as IXMLDOMNode
    Dim MsgNode as IXMLDOMNode

VBScript:
Function AddMessageInverted(logXML,Author,Title,_
Body) as Dim MsgNode

    'Create the message node
    Set msgNode=logXML.createElement("message")
    'If the log has other messages then
    If logXML.documentElement.length>0 then
        'Insert the message before the first one
    LogXML.documentElement.InsertBefore _
        MsgNode, logXML.documentElement.firstChild
    Else
        'Otherwise,place the message
        'in the empty child set
        LogXML.documentElement.appendChild msgNode
    End If
    'This is identical to AddMessage2
    AddElement msgNode,"author",Author
    AddElement msgNode,"title",Title
    AddElement msgNode,"date",Today
    AddElement msgNode,"body",Body
    Set AddMessage2=MsgNode
End Function
```

Removing a node is simple as well. Using the removeChild method of the node object, you simply pass the reference of the child that you want to remove. When you remove a node, the node in question is disassociated from the tree but doesn't go away. (It's in essentially the same state as a node that has been created but not attached.) You also get a reference to that node and, by extension, all the node's children. removeChild is a handy way of moving a node from one place to another in the XML tree, as demonstrated with MoveNode() in Listing 13.14.

Listing 13.14: MoveNode() Removes a Node from One Point in the Tree and Attaches It to Another.

```
Function MoveNode(sourceNode,targetParentNode as _
    IXMLDOMNode,optional targetNode as IXMLDOMNode =_
        Nothing) as IXMLDOMNode
Dim TempNode as IXMLDOMNode
Function MoveNode(sourceNode,targetParentNode,_
targetNode)
    Dim TempNode

    Set TempNode=sourceNode.parentNode._
removeChild(sourceNode)

    if targetNode is nothing then
        targetParentNode.appendChild TempNode
    else
        targetParentNode.insertBefore_
        TempNode,targetNode
    end if
    set MoveNode=TempNode
End Function
```

Similarly, the ReplaceChild function will take a preexisting node and replace it with a different node. The ReplaceNode() function uses this capability to replace a given node with a new one, as shown in Listing 13.15.

Listing 13.15: ReplaceNode() Removes a Node and Replaces the Same Node with Another One.

```
Visual Basic:
Function ReplaceNode(oldNode as_
    IXMLDOMNode, newNode as
    IXMLDOMnode) as IXMLDOMNode
    Dim tempNode as IXMLDOMNode

VBScript:
Function ReplaceNode(oldNode,newNode)
    Dim tempNode

Set tempNode=oldNode
    OldNode.parentNode.replaceChild oldNode,newNode
    Set ReplaceNode=tempNode
End function
```

Part iv

Finally, to complete the suite of tools that look suspiciously like the Cut, Copy, and Paste functions of traditional editors, the XML DOM supports the ability to clone a node through the `CloneNode()` function. `CloneNode()` actually supports two modes: It includes a deep parameter that indicates whether the function clones just the node and its associated text (`deep=false`) or clones the node and all of its children, grandchildren, etc. (`deep=true`).

Examining Text in Nodes

Text in an XML document has always been somewhat problematic because of XML's origins within SGML. To see why this is this case, it's instructive to look at a sample of XHTML, as in the following lines, which is HTML marked up using the XML grammar.

```
<body>
<h1>Examining Text</h1>
<p><span class="cap">T</span>ext in an XML document
    has always been somewhat <i>problematic</i>.</p>
</body>
```

What should the text of the paragraph attribute be? If you make the call that the text should be only those characters that are in the scope of the paragraph but not of any subelements, then you end up with the following expression:

```
"ext in an XML document has always been somewhat"
```

On the other hand, if you declare that an element contains the text of all of its subelements, then the text of the body tag ends up looking like the following example:

```
"Examining Text Text in an XML document has always
been somewhat problematic"
```

Moreover, things can get a little sticky if you replace the text with a different string of text, because such an action would end up removing all of the subordinate tags as well. The solution that the MSXML parser has taken is to assume that the text of any given node is the text of all subordinate nodes, as well as any text that the node itself currently contains. This text is both read and write; if you change the text of a node, you remove not only the text in that node but also any subordinate tags. This is part of the reason that data-centric XML usually ends up with text found only at the leaf nodes of the tree, since changing the text may well wipe out any existing structure. For example, consider the following structure:

```
<programming>This section contains all of the
programming and related skills.
    <language>Visual Basic</language>
    <architecture>Client/Server Programming
    </architecture>
</programming>
```

Changing the text of the `<programming>` node removes the `<language>` and `<architecture>` nodes from the tree. On the other hand, by encapsulating the description in a separate tag (`<description>`, of course), you avoid the following problem:

```
<programming>
    <description>This section contains all of the
    programming and related skills.</description>
    <language>Visual Basic</language>
    <architecture>Client/Server Programming
    </architecture>
</programming>
```

With the following expression, you could easily change the description for the programming section of your resume:

```
Set progDescrNode=ResumeDoc.GetElementsByTagName(_
    "programming/description")(0)
buffer="This section contains programming_
 and project "
buffer=buffer+"management skills."
progDescrNode.text=buffer
```

One mistake that users new to XML frequently make, however, is believing that you can write XML into a text node and it will automatically convert into the appropriate XML nodes. This *doesn't* work. Instead, the parser will convert any symbol in the text that could be interpreted as being XML into its entity representation. For example, suppose you tried to add a tag into the following program description:

```
ProgDescrNode.text="This <I>section</I> contains
<b>programming</b> and <b>project management
```

```
</b> skills."
Debug.Print ProgDescrNode.text
This &lt;I&gt;section&lt;/I&gt; contains
&lt;b&gt;programming&lt;/b&gt; and &lt;b&gt;
project management&lt;/b&gt; skills.
```

The left and right tag brackets are replaced by their entity representations (< and >, respectively). In some cases, this is desirable; if you are trying to display HTML code as output, for example, this implicit conversion can be a real boon to your programming. Unfortunately, when you are not looking for such a conversion, things get a little more complicated. In general, you will need to use a CDATA section (described in the next section) to store such information.

The text property for a node is actually a little deceptive. Internally, XML treats contiguous blocks of text that are not otherwise within a node as being text nodes. Such a node has the same structure as most other base node types, save that, internally, the node is assumed to have a nodeName of #text, and its value is given as the text contained within. If you look at the underlying structure of the node, you'll discover that an element node can actually contain a separate text node (of the IXMLDOMNodeText type) that holds the actual text data. Moreover, if you have a mixed text element (where text is interspersed with tags), then the node will contain one text node for each separate block of text. For example, consider the following XML structure:

```
<P>This is <I>highlighted</I> text
while this is <B>bold</B> text.</P>
```

The node structure internally can be described as:

```
Element:P
    Text:This is
    Element:I
        Text:highlighted
    EndElement:I
    Text:text while this is
    Element:B
        Text:bold
    EndElement:B
    Text
```

```
    :text.
  EndElement:P
```

In other words, when you make a request for the text property of a given element, it iterates through all of the text nodes contained within the element and concatenates them into a single string, as demonstrated in the following example:

```
'pNode Contains the initial paragraph node
Debug.Print pNode.text
"This is highlighted text while this is bold text."
```

When you assign text, a similar process happens, although the parser protects itself by converting less-than, greater-than, ampersand, and other special XML symbols into their equivalent entity representation (for example, > becomes <). This structure makes mixed nodes possible, although retrieving the text from a node high up in the chain obviously takes considerably longer than retrieving node texts at their point of origin.

Note that because text nodes *are* nodes, they can be created with the DOMDocument CreateNode method as well as with the more specialized CreateTextNode method, as per the following example:

```
Dim textNode as IXMLDOMText
Set textNode=xmlDoc.createNode(NODE_TEXT,textStr,"")
' or
Set textNode=xmlDoc.createText(textStr)
' where textStr contains the text contents
```

TIP

The nodeName of a text node is the hashed name #text. If you are parsing the XML structure at the node level, you can test the node this way or by seeing if the nodeType=3 (NODE_TEXT).

CDATA Nodes

There are times, however, when you may want to save XML like text without converting it into "safe" XML. A prime example of this is with the use of embedded HTML blocks. Unless you use the fairly strict variant XHTML, HTML from versions 4.x and earlier are not generally XML compliant. For example, if you wanted to save the following HTML code within an XML block, you would find that the parser complains that the img tag is not closed:

```
<skill>
    <name>Visual Basic</name>
    <htmlText>
    <div>
        <img src="visualBasic.jpg">
    </div>
    </htmlText>
</skill>
```

Older parsers (Netscape 3 and older, in particular), however, will actually crash if you pass a string that looks like <img src = "visualBasic .jpg"/>, with the terminating slash. Converting it into safe XML doesn't help, however; it will only serve to place the contents of the HTML page up as a code listing.

The only way around this conundrum is to make use of CDATA sections. CDATA can be thought of as "escaped" text; it is explicitly protected from being parsed. CDATA sections always start with the somewhat-cumbersome <![CDATA[notation and terminate with the]]> notation. Thus, the HTML could be safely protected in the preceding sample by enclosing it in a CDATA section, as the following example demonstrates:

```
<skill>
    <name>Visual Basic</name>
    <htmlText><![CDATA[
    <div>
        <img src="visualBasic.jpg">
    </div>]]>
    </htmlText>
</skill>
```

CDATA sections preserve white space as well as XML special characters, so using CDATA makes sense when you want to be able to save script text within an XML document, as in the following example:

```
<resume>
    <script language="VBScript"><![CDATA[
        Function IsNegative(text)
```

```
                    IsNegative=false
              If isNumeric(text) then
                    If clng(text)<0 then
                            IsNegative=true
                    End if
              End if
        End function
    ]]></script>
  </resume>
```

Here, even if line breaks weren't important (they are in VBScript, so this script would be in trouble regardless), the cLng(text)<0 test would end up generating an error because the less-than sign (<) would automatically be interpreted as being the start of an XML tag. With the CDATA section in place, this won't happen.

Reading a CDATA section is easy; it's retrieved using the text property. Thus, if you wanted to get the preceding script (most likely to pass to a scripting object), all you'd need to do is code the following:

```
Dim scriptNode=resumeDoc.getElementsByName_
("script")(0)
    Debug.Print scriptNode.text
    Function IsNegative(text)
          IsNegative=false
          If isNumeric(text) then
                If clng(text)<0 then
                        IsNegative=true
                End if
          End if
    End function
```

Writing CDATA sections is a little more complicated, however. Just as there is a text node type, there is also a CDATA node type. Indeed, when the text property iterates through an element's descendants for text nodes, it also scoops up CDATA sections as it passes through. Creating a CDATA section is also similar, as the following example demonstrates:

```
Dim cdataNode As IXMLDOMCDATASection
Set
```

```
cdataNode=xmlDoc.createNode(NODE_CDATA_SECTION,_
textStr,"")
' or
Set textNode= xmlDoc.createCDATASection(textStr)
' where textStr contains the text contents
```

TIP

The nodeName of a cdata section node is the hashed name #cdata-section. If you are parsing the XML structure at the node level, you can test the node this way or by seeing if the nodeType=4 (NODE_CDATA_SECTION).

I have found, especially with complex data such as scripts, that when I want to add an element I also frequently want to pass a CDATA section rather than text to the element. The final version of AddElement() gives you the option of specifying that the text passed is treated as a CDATA section rather than as normal text, as demonstrated in Listing 13.16.

Listing 13.16: Final Visual Basic Code for the AddElement() Function

```
Visual Basic:
Function AddElement(parentNode as IXMLDOMElement,_
    elementName as String,_
    optional elementText as String = ""_
    optional IsCDATASection as Boolean = False) as
_IXMLDOMNode
    Dim newNode as IXMLDOMNode

VBScript:
Function AddElement(parentNode,_
    elementName,_
    elementText
    IsCDATASection)
    Dim newNode

    Set newNode=parentNode.ownerDocument._
    createElement(_
          elementName)
    if IsCDATASection then
       Dim cdataNode as IXMLDOMCDATASection
       Set cdataNode=parentNode.ownerDocument._
```

```
        createElement(elementText)
                newNode.appendChild cdataNode
    else
        newNode.text=elementText
    end if
    parentNode.appendChild newNode
    set AddElement=newNode
End Function
```

UNDERSTANDING ATTRIBUTES

Elements, text nodes, and CDATA sections provide one way of describing data within an XML document. However, XML supplies another way to describe information: the *attribute node*. *Attributes* are name/value pairs that describe elements in some fashion and are indicated by tokens with associated strings.

NOTE

You can read more about element development in Chapter 3 ("Understanding and Creating Attributes"). You can also find more information on attribute development in Chapter 4 ("Understanding and Creating Entities").

The relationship between elements and attributes is a complex, sometimes-contentious one. Most people are familiar with attributes through their appearance within HTML, where they essentially play the role of modifiers to the HTML objects. For example, the image tag in HTML has a complex set of attributes, as even the following simple example demonstrates:

```
<IMG src="myImage.jpg" lowsrc="myImageLowRes.jpg"
    width=100 height=80 align=left>
```

Here, src, lowsrc, width, height, and align are all attribute names, with their elements indicated by either quoted text or text surrounded by an = sign on one side and a space or close bracket on the other.

XML attributes are similar, although not quite identical. Principally, an XML attribute *will always be quoted*. Always. While this is generally not a problem (especially using the DOM), it does mean that it is a difficult process to convert an HTML document created by many commercial applications straight into XML, although this isn't necessarily a good idea anyway.

The W3C recommendation on XML also makes a few basic recommendations about attributes, namely that they:

- ▶ Cannot appear more than once in any given tag.

- ▶ Should not include explicit line breaks.

- ▶ Should not include XML-specific characters, such as < or >, unless the character is escaped as an entity (i.e., < or >).

- ▶ Should generally be limited in length.

- ▶ Should not include the ampersand character explicitly; instead, it too should be escaped as &.

Attributes versus Elements

If you want to start a religious war at an XML seminar, ask the simple question "When should attributes be used?" Things will get ugly quickly, I assure you. There are as many different views about where attributes should be used as there are XML practitioners.

In general, though, the prevailing views seem to fall into the following camps:

Attributes are unnecessary.   In this approach, attributes simply are not used at all. This approach works well in a data-centric setting where every element has a specific data type, but it is less well suited for situations where the content is mixed.

Attributes provide document-wide characteristics.   Sometimes attributes work well in characterizing metadata about a document. For example, an invoice element may include a *title* attribute that can be used for creating a more meaningful description for a property (*Account Number* instead of *AcctNum*).

Attributes contain element properties.   This is essentially the approach that both XHTML and Internet Explorer 5 (IE 5) behaviors take, where each element tag describes an object and the attributes provide the properties to that object. The image tag described in the previous section demonstrates this model of attribute.

Attributes provide object definition over element metadata. This is the approach that schemas (or the Reduced Data Set that Microsoft employs) use to describe XML structure. In this case, the element information is extremely broad (e.g., <Element name="info">), while the attributes serve to make the element specific to the task at hand. This approach works best as metadata structures.

Attributes identify relations between disconnected information.   In this case, a given element may contain child elements as properties that describe the element, but contain one or more identifiers that either uniquely name that element or create a relationship between the element and another uniquely named element.

So which approach should you use when designing your own data structures? Easy: Whatever works. All five approaches work to solve one problem or another, and once you become proficient with XSL you may find yourself transforming your data from one attribute type to a different one as the need arises. Don't get locked into thinking that only one type of XML structure works in every case; that will make you lose the incredible flexibility that is XML's greatest strength.

TIP

This point will be stressed repeatedly throughout this book: *XML is malleable.* Standards are coming into existence that provide a common language for transmitting data between consumers, but, once at your machine, you should be willing to alter the incoming data into a format that works best for your own application.

TIP

The last approach, where elements contain child elements but unique identifier attributes, works especially well when working with XML as an object description language.

Attributes and Nodes

With respect to the internal representation of an XML document, attributes have a fairly privileged status. In essence, a node actually maintains two sets of nodes: a set pointing to its attributes, and a second set pointing to everything else (other elements, text nodes, CDATA sections, comments—the works).

Part iv

A node accesses its attributes through the `attributes` collection, which is an object of the IXMLDOMNamedNodeMap type. While this may sound a little forbidding, in fact, such a structure is pretty simple and is detailed in Table 13.5.

TABLE 13.5: Properties and Methods of the IXMLDOMNamedNodeMap Interface

PROPERTY OR METHOD	DESCRIPTION
GetNamedItem(name as String)	Returns the node corresponding to the given name
GetQualifiedItem(baseName as String,namespaceURI as String)	Returns the node corresponding to the given name and namespace
Item(index as Long)	Returns the indexed node
Length	Returns the number of items in the map
NextNode	Returns the next node in an iteration
RemoveNamedItem(name as String)	Removes the node specified by the given name
RemoveQualifiedItem(baseName as String,namespaceURL as String)	Removes the node specified by the given name and namespace
Reset()	Sets the iterator back to the first item
SetNamedItem(newItem as IXMLDOMNode)	Appends a node to the current map

All right. So maybe it's not quite as simple as all that. In essence, when you create an attribute using the attributes object, you are working with node objects that are stored in the map. For example, going back to the message log discussed earlier in this chapter, the sample could be modified, as in Listing 13.17, so that each element appearing on output would contain a caption attribute. Furthermore, it would be handy to identify each message uniquely, so this particular element should have an `id` attribute.

Listing 13.17: StatusLog3.xml, Which Now Includes a Set of Standard Attributes

```
<?xml version="1.0" ?>
<!-StatusLog3.xml ->
<log>
```

```xml
<message id="msg_1">
    <author caption="Message From">Kurt Cagle
    </author>
    <title caption="Title">First Message</title>
    <date caption="Date Submitted">2000-01-12
    </date>
    <body caption="Message Body">This is a
      short message
    </body>
</message>
<message id="msg_2">
    <author caption="Message From">Fred Schwartz
    </author>
    <title caption="Title">I need more
    information</title>
    <date caption="Date Submitted">
     2000-01-13</date>
    <body caption="Message Body">I need to find
      out more about XML. What can you tell
      me?</body>
</message>
</log>
```

In order to retrieve the caption from the second author field, you could use the GetNamedItem() function, as in the following example:

```
Dim logXML as DOMDocument
Dim authElNode as IXMLDOMNode
Dim captionNode as IXMLDOMNode

Set logXML=new DOMDocument
LogXML.load "StatusLog3.xml"
Set authElNode=logXML.getElementsByTagName_
("message/author")(1)
Set captionNode=authElNode.attributes._
getNamedItem("caption")
Debug.Print captionNode.nodeName
caption
Debug.Print captionNode.text
Message From
```

GetNamedItem() retrieves the node that matches that attribute name. Once you have this, you can set or get its value through the text property or can retrieve the name of the attribute by using the nodeName property.

> **NOTE**
> Remember here that GetNamedItem() doesn't retrieve a text string; it returns a node instead that you can query to retrieve or set the attribute value.

The GetQualifiedItem() function works in the same manner but lets you specify the namespace of the attribute in addition to the node's base name. (Namespaces are covered at the end of this chapter.)

SetNamedItem() works in a similar fashion. You create a node with the appropriate attribute name and text and then use SetNamedItem() to add this particular item to the map or attribute list. For example, to add an ID to a new message node in the messagelog XML, you could use the function by creating an attribute node (using either CreateNode() or CreateAttribute()—the latter functioning exactly as you would expect) and appending it to the newly created message node, as the following example demonstrates:

```
'Continuing from last example
dim msgNode as IXMLDOMNode
dim attrNode as IXMLDOMNode
set msgNode=logXML.createElement("message")
logXML.documentElement.appendChild msgNode
set attrNode=logXML.createAttribute("id")
attrNode.text="msg_3"
msgNode.attributes.setNamedItem attrNode
```

Similarly, you can remove the attribute using the removeNamedItem() method, or removeQualifiedItem() if you are removing an item that belongs to a different namespace:

```
MsgNode.attributes.removeNamedItem("id")
```

Perhaps the most significant method associated with the NamedNodeMap interface is the iterator, which actually lets you iterate through a set of attributes, touching each attribute node in turn. For example, to return the attributes associated with the HTML image object discussed previously, you could use the code in Listing 13.18. (Note that I've made the image object XML compliant.)

Listing 13.18: The `IterateAttributes` Function Retrieves Each Attribute from a Node and Converts It into a Name/Value Pair String.

```
' From Visual Basic
Function IterateAttributes(Node as IXMLDOMNode)_
 as String
   Dim AttrNode as IXMLDOMNode
   Dim buffer as String


' From VBScript
Function IterateAttributes(Node)
   Dim AttrNode
   Dim buffer

   node.attributes.reset
   Set attrNode=Node.attributes.nextNode
   While not (attrNode is Nothing)
      buffer=buffer+attrNode.nodeName+"='"+_
         attrNode.text+"'"+vbCRLF
      Set attrNode=ImageNode.attributes.nextNode
   Wend
   IterateAttributes=buffer
End Function

ImageDoc.loadXML "<BODY><IMG src='myImage.jpg'_
   lowsrc='myImageLowRes.jpg' width='100'
_height='80' align='left'/></BODY>"
   Debug.Print IterateAttributes(_
ImageDoc.getElementsByTagName("IMG")(0)
```

The iterator's `reset` statement moves the pointer for the NamedNodeMap collection to before the first node, while `nextNode` moves the pointer to the next item (or to the first item if applied immediately after `reset()`) until it runs out of items and returns the VB `Nothing` object. This notation is rather cumbersome in Visual Basic, although in Java or JavaScript it's considerably more compact, as the following example demonstrates:

```
Function IterateAttributesJS(Node){
Node.attributes.reset();
while (!(var attrNode=Node.attributes.nextNode)){
    buffer+=(attrNode.nodeName+"='"_
+attrNode.text+"'\n";
```

```
    }
    return buffer;
    }
```

Because the notation is somewhat cumbersome in Visual Basic or VBScript, the iterator is usually used implicitly within a for each statement rather than using the enumerator format that Java employs. Use of the iterator in Visual Basic is demonstrated in the following example:

```
Visual Basic:
Function IterateAttributes (Node as IXMLDOMNode)_
 as String
   Dim AttrNode as IXMLDOMNode
   Dim buffer as String

   For each attrNode in node.attributes
      buffer=buffer+attrNode.nodeName+"='"+_
        attrNode.text+"'"+vbCRLF
   Next
   IterateAttributes=buffer
End Function
```

TIP

All of the XML collections can be iterated in this same fashion. The enumeration mechanism is typically hidden.

Using Attributes and Elements

The node mechanism is a clean, straightforward mechanism for working with attributes. Well, all right, that's a complete lie: The node mechanism for working with attributes is cumbersome, complex, and, in general, useless for working with attributes in most applications. It *is* worth understanding, however, to help you get a better idea of what happens under the hood within the XML object. Because of the special class that attributes employ, they are frequently faster than the equivalent elements.

Fortunately, in most cases, you don't need to work with this mechanism directly. The IXMLDOMElement interface, which represents elements within the object model, encapsulates the fairly complex attribute handling inside a few easy-to-use functions (see Table 13.6). Indeed, attribute handling is one of the few differences between the `IXMLDOMNode` and `IXMLDOMElement` interfaces.

TABLE 13.6: Attribute-Related Properties and Methods of the `IXMLDOMElement` Interface

PROPERTY OR METHOD	DESCRIPTION
`attributes(index as long)`	Provides a reference to the attributes NamedNodeMap. Same as the node attributes collection.
`getAttribute(name as string)`	Retrieves the value of the attribute as a string.
`GetAttributeNode(name as String) as IXMLDOMAttribute`	Retrieves the named attribute as an attribute node.
`RemoveAttribute(name as String)`	Removes the named attribute from the attribute list.
`RemoveAttributeNode ( DOMAttribute as IXMLDOMAttribute) as IXMLDOMAttribute`	Removes the specified node from the attribute list.
`setAttribute(name as String,value)`	Sets the value of the named attribute (value is a variant).
`SetAttributeNode(DOMAttribute as IXMLDOMAttribute) as IXMLDOMAttribute`	Adds a node of the given name to the attribute list, or replaces the current node if a node of that name already exists.

While you can do all of the same tasks that you can do with the node attribute properties and methods, the element's interface is considerably easier to use. For example, consider the following message log again:

```
<?xml version="1.0" ?>
<!-StatusLog3.xml ->
<log>
<message id="msg_1">
      <author caption="Message From">Kurt Cagle_
      </author>
      <title caption="Title">First Message
      </title>
```

```
    <date caption="Date Submitted">2000-01-12_
    </date>
    <body caption="Message Body">This is a short
     message
    </body>
</message>
<message id="msg_2">
    <author caption="Message From">Fred Schwartz<-
    /author>
    <title caption="Title">I need more information
    </title>
    <date caption="Date Submitted">
     2000-01-13</date>
    <body caption="Message Body">I need to find
     out more about XML. What can you tell
     me?</body>
</message>
</log>
```

In order to retrieve the caption from the second author field with the element attribute, you need to explicitly declare the node of the IXMLDOMElement type (instead of IXMLDOMNode), and then you can use getAttribute() to retrieve the text of the node, as in the following example:

```
Dim logXML as DOMDocument
Dim authElNode as IXMLDOMElement
Dim captionNode as IXMLDOMNode

Set logXML=new DOMDocument
LogXML.load "StatusLog3.xml"
Set authElNode=logXML.getElementsByTagName(_

       "message/author")(1)
Debug.Print authElNode.getAttribute("caption")
Message From
```

Setting it is just as straightforward, using the `SetAttribute()` method, as the following example demonstrates:

```
AuthElNode.setAttribute "caption","This is a message
 from "
Debug.Print authElNode.getAttribute("caption")
This is a message from
```

Removing a node works in the same way:

```
AuthElNode.removeAttribute "caption"
Debug.Print authElNode.getAttribute("caption")
_ Is Nothing
True
```

The iterator for the element is the same as the iterator for the node since, in both cases, you query the attributes' `NamedNodeMap` collection. Thus, the code for iterating through an element's attribute collection is essentially the same as iterating through a node's attributes, as in the following example:

Visual Basic:

```
Function IterateAttributes (Node as IXMLDOMElement)
    as_ String
    Dim AttrNode as IXMLDOMAttribute
    Dim buffer as String
```

VBScript:

```
Function IterateAttributes (Node)
    Dim AttrNode
    Dim buffer

    For each attrNode in node.attributes
    buffer=buffer+attrNode.nodeName+"='"+_
    attrNode.text+"'"+vbCRLF
    Next
    IterateAttributes=buffer
End Function
```

CHANGING INTERFACES

If you work with attributes only sporadically, you may want to keep your variables declared as IXMLDOMNode. (This applies to Visual Basic only; in the scripting language, the specific type mappings are applied transparently.) When you need to work with attributes, you can then declare a variable of the IXMLDOMElement type and set the element variable to the node variable's value, as in the following example:

```
Visual Basic:
dim Node as IXMLDOMNode
dim Elmt as IXMLDOMElement
set Node=GetMyNode() ' This just retrieves a
     ' node from
     ' an unspecified location.
Set Elmt=Node ' This lets node use the attributes
     ' interface
Elmt.setAttribute "comment","This Rocks!"
```

This technique of mapping interfaces works because IXML-DOMElement derives from IXMLDOMNode. You can use a similar technique for getting at the other advanced XML interfaces, such as IXMLDOMComment or IXMLDOMAttribute.

Comments

There are a few other nodes that take on subordinate roles in XML, and while they generally don't have a huge impact on the way most XML gets processed, they can offer a few advantages to the programmer who knows what to do with them.

Comments exist as part of almost every computer language ever written, usually serving the dual role of identifying the purpose of specific pieces of code and removing certain pieces of code from normal execution. XML is no exception.

Unlike elements or attributes, comments aren't required to be within the body of an XML document. They can effectively be anywhere, with the sole exception being that they can't be the first line of text if the XML file contains an xml declaration (i.e., <?xml version="1.0" ?>). Beyond that, comments can go anywhere.

Comments begin with the sequence of characters <!-- and end with the closing characters -->. Comments can contain anything (open or closing brackets, Unicode characters, even binary data), and, as a consequence, the only way that the parser knows that a comment has come to a close is when it encounters the --> characters. One of the most immediate implications of this is that you can't nest comments.

As with text nodes and CDATA sections, comments are stored internally through the use of comment nodes. As a consequence, you can actually associate a comment with a given node; it is a child of the node just as a text or a CDATA section would be. A comment node can be created using the document's `createNode` function or the more specialized `createComment` function, as the following example demonstrates:

```
Dim commentNode As IXMLDOMComment
Dim textStr
textStr="This is a comment."
Set commentNode=xmlDoc.createNode_
(NODE_COMMENT,textStr,"")
' or
Set commentNode= xmlDoc.createComment(textStr)
' where textStr contains the text contents
```

TIP

The nodeName of a comment node is the hashed name #comment. If you are parsing the XML structure at the node level, you can test the node this way or by seeing if the nodeType=8 (NODE_COMMENT).

Comments should generally not be used to store information that is immediately relevant to the data structure (other than documentation). One reason for this is that a number of XML parsers (though not the MSXML parser) will strip comments from the XML structure to reduce memory usage. If you do find that you need to store key information about the data (for example, code that may be specific to a given parser or application), then you should look at processing instructions (PIs) instead.

Processing Instructions

Processing instructions are an artifact of the older SGML specification, and they essentially contain information that may be exclusive to a given application or configuration. Processing instructions were originally designed for use with SGML documents, where they would typically contain information that was not really appropriate to the document but which was needed by the application hosting the document.

A number of vendors (for some reason, database vendors seem to be particularly keen on this) like to add PIs that can be used to retrieve XML data based on SQL queries, as in the following example:

```
<?DatabaseCo-SQL SELECT * FROM MyDataBase
    WHERE sky='Blue'?>
```

When the document parses, the XML is retrieved and inserted into the place where the PI was found.

Although this can certainly be useful, it also sets a troubling precedent by placing proprietary data into the structure that's not a part of the structure. Queries become more complicated, because only applications that know what to do with the PI can return results.

This is a personal opinion, but, in general, unless there isn't any way around it, avoid using processing instructions in favor of some other linking mechanism. They don't have much support in the DOM, and they tend to diminish rather than reinforce the object-oriented nature of XML. (In that context, I would liken processing instructions to global variables, which can also weaken OOP structures.)

There is, however, one important exception. While it is not strictly required for the MSXML parser, a fully well-formed XML document should always start out with an XML declaration, indicating the current version of XML in use along with such things as character set encoding, as in the following example:

```
<?xml version="1.0" encoding="UTF-8" ?>
```

The preceding declaration shows the basic structure of a processing instruction. A PI will always start with the characters <?, followed by the name used to reference the PI. After this, a PI can conceivably have anything, though the standard usage is to follow normal tag naming convention by having the information within the PI contained within attribute name/value pairs, as in the following line:

```
<?devbook system="Windows 2000"?>
```

Finally, a PI is terminated with a closing ?> character set, as shown in the preceding example.

WARNING

The W3C explicitly reserves the right to use *xml* and *xml-* as names for processing instructions, as well as any case permutation of them (e.g, *XML, Xml,* and so forth). If you use a PI, start it with something other than these characters.

The attribute name/value pairs given here are conventional, but you should understand that the contents of a PI—essentially everything after the name—are a complete entity unto themselves. A PI is not parsed and is not considered text; in short, it's ideal for application-specific information.

For example, an XML application could store versioning information into a PI that would be ignored by the parser but would be accessible to a third-party program. If you were to build a product called `ResuméBuilder` that lets you edit r sum s in XML, you could maintain the name of the application, who prepared the r sum , and when—storing this information in processing instructions, as in the following example:

```
<!-- resumé.xml -->
<resumé>
    <?devbook-preparedBy Kurt Cagle ?>
    <?devbook-datePrepared 3/Feb/2000?>
    <?devbook-application ResuméBuilder?>
    <resuméFor>Aleria Sherana</resuméFor>
    <!-- more resumé material -->
</resumé>
```

In order to retrieve these processing instructions, it turns out that you can take advantage of certain XPath properties with the `GetElements-ByTagName()` or `SelectNodes()` functions, as the following example demonstrates. (The output of the `GetPI_Info` function is also included.)

```
Function GetPI_Info(xmlDoc as DOMDocument) as String
    Dim piNode as IXMLDOMProcessingInstruction
    Dim buffer as String
    buffer=""
    For each piNode in GetElementsByTagName("pi()")
        buffer=buffer+"["+piNode.nodeName+"]"+_
        piNode.text+vbCRLF
    Next
    GetPI_Info=buffer
```

```
End Function


Dim ResumeDoc as DOMDocument
ResumeDoc.load "resume.xml"
Debug.Print GetPI_Info(ResumeDoc)
    [devbook-preparedBy]Kurt Cagle
    [devbook-datePrepared]3/Feb/2000
    [devbook-application]ResumeBuilder
```

The pi() function returns a collection of all of the processing instructions contained within the document as processing instruction nodes, which, as you may have guessed, derive from IXMLDOMNode. The nodeName corresponds to the name of the PI, and the text is the text of the PI.

TIP

There are similar query functions for elements (element()), attributes (attribute()), comments (comment()), and so forth. These are covered in Chapter 12, "Transforming XML: Introducing XSLT."

You could use a similar arrangement to retrieve a specific processing instruction or to set the contents of one. The pi() function can take as a string argument the name of the node; if the element exists, then getElementsByTagName() will return a node list with one element. With this node, you can get or set the associated text value, as in Listing 13.19.

Listing 13.19: GetPI and SetPI **Retrieve and Set Processing Instructions within the Passed XML Documents.**

```
Visual Basic:
Function GetPI(xmlDoc as DOMDocument, piName as String) as
String
    Dim piNode as IXMLDOMNode
    Set piNode=xmlDoc.getElementsByTagName(_
      "pi('"+piName+"')")_(0)
    GetPI=piNode.text
End Function
Function SetPI(xmlDoc as DOMDocument,_
    piName aString,piValue as Variant) as IXMLDomNode
    Dim piNode as IXMLDOMProcessingInstruction
    Set piNode=xmlDoc.getElementsByTagName(
```

```
        pi('"+piName+"')")_(0)
    if piNode is Nothing then
        set piNode=xmlDoc.documentElement._
    createProcessingInstruction(piName)
        xmlDoc.documentElement.appendChild piNode
    end if
    piNode.text=cstr(piValue)
Set SetPI=piNode
End Function
```

ASYNCHRONOUS XML AND EVENTS

XML started out as a Web format, and it's still designed around the notion that data is being transferred from one machine or another through some form of Web protocol. When a computer loads in a file from a location on its hard drive, the access time can usually be measured in hundredths, or even thousandths, of a second—a period so small that it usually makes sense to retrieve the entire file at once.

However, on the Internet or a local intranet, file retrieval times (usually called *latency*) are often measured in seconds, minutes, or, in the case of some of today's mega-applications, hours. Any application that fails to take into account the basic latency of distributed systems will find that applications appear to hang while the files are downloaded. There are few things more aggravating than waiting an hour while your application pauses to download a file, only to retrieve a message at the end telling you that the file was unavailable.

Fortunately, the MSXML parser is well equipped to handle latency issues. You can tell the parser to load the file asynchronously (as mentioned in the "Loading Documents" section earlier in this chapter), by setting the document's Async property to true prior to downloading your document. In this section, I focus specifically on what setting that property does and how to handle asynchronous downloads.

When async is true, the nature of the document's Load method changes. Instead of halting the application until the load is complete, Load creates a local input buffer and directs the socket to start filling the buffer in the background while the processing proceeds to the next statement in the code. The parser, in turn, raises the onReadyStateChange event every time a specific level of loading is accomplished and the onDataAvailable event when you can actually start using the data within the document. This function automatically sets another document property, the ReadyState property (as shown in Table 13.7), so that you, as the programmer, can perform an action when the event gets called.

TABLE 13.7: ReadyState Constants and Their Meanings

STATE	NUMERIC VALUE	MEANING
Not yet initialized	0	Document is not yet ready to load file.
Initialized	1	Document is ready to load file.
Loading	2	Document is beginning to load file.
Data available	3	The topmost levels of the document are populated and can be used for processing.
Complete	4	The document has been loaded and is ready to be accessed, or an error occurred and parseError has been notified.

As with any asynchronous event handling, the XML DOM's event handling works by creating an event handle to capture the OnReadyStateChange event whenever the parser fires it. This takes place in a couple of different ways, depending on whether you are using Visual Basic or a scripting language.

For Visual Basic, the XML parser sources events; that is to say, when you declare an XML document, you can use the WithEvents tag in the declaration to indicate to VB that the XML object exposes events, as in the following example:

```
Dim WithEvents xmlDoc as DOMDocument
```

In the Visual Basic IDE, this will automatically add a new object (called xmlDoc) into the left-hand window of the scripting pane and expose the two events, onReadyStateChange and onDataAvailable, in the right-hand pane (see Figure 13.1).

WARNING

Note that sourced declarations can only be placed at a module level (that is, declared as a variable in the General section of a form, module, or class), never within a procedure or method.

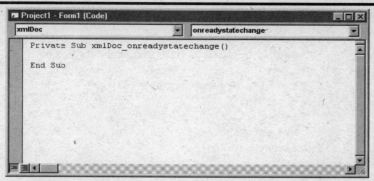

FIGURE 13.1: By sourcing your XML Document object in Visual Basic, using WithEvents, you can write event handlers for asynchronous transfers.

Writing asynchronous loading code requires a little more than writing synchronous code. For starters, the XML documents must be global to the project (though not necessarily public) rather than declared as a local variable. In addition to that, once you make the initial load call, you can't make any assumptions about the state of the document until either the onDataAvailable or the onReadyStateChange event occurs. For example, if you wanted to load an XML document whenever a user selects File ➢ Open in a form, the code would look something like that in Listing 13.20.

Listing 13.20: The Following Code Demonstrates how an XML Document Could Be Loaded into Visual Basic through the Menu Bar.

```
Visual Basic:
Dim WithEvents XmlDoc as DOMDocument
Dim IsDocumentLoading as Boolean

Private Sub mnuFileOpen_Click()
   Dim URL as String
   URL=inputbox("Please Enter a URL","New _
     URL","http://www.xmldevhandbook.com/
_pointers.xml")
   If URL<>"" then
      ' Make the document asynchronous
      XmlDoc.async=True
      ' Load in the URL
      XmlDoc.Load URL
```

```
        ' Not much to do but set the cursor to a
         'wait state
         Screen.mousePointer=vbHourglass
        ' Creating a local variable to keep track of
         ' state
         ' can help prevent actions that are
         ' dependent
         ' on the
         ' xml document.
        IsDocumentLoading=True
    End if
End Sub

Private Sub xmlDoc_onReadyStateChange()
    Dim ErrorMsg as String
    ' Check to see if operation has completed
    If xmlDoc.ReadyState=4 then
        ' restore the cursor
        Screen.mousePointer=vbDefault
        ' clear the document loading flag
        IsDocumentLoading=False
        ' If no error occurred
        If xmlDoc.ParseError.ErrorCode=0 then
            ' then use the xml for display purposes
            Display XMLDoc
        Else
            ' Display an error message in a pop-up
            Msgbox GetErrorMessage(xmlDoc)
        End if
    End if
End Sub

Function GetErrorMessage(xmlDoc as DOMDocument)_
as String
        Dim ErrorMsg as String
        ErrorMsg="An Error occurred (Error "
        ErrorMsg=ErrorMsg+cstr(xmlDoc.parseError._
        errorCode)+_
            ")"+vbCRLF
        ErrorMsg=ErrorMsg+ xmlDoc.parseError._
        reason+vbCRLF
```

```
        ErrorMsg=ErrorMsg+" at char"+_
            cstr(xmlDoc.parseError.linePos)
        ErrorMsg=ErrorMsg+" of line "+_
            cstr(xmlDoc.parseError.line)
        ErrorMsg=ErrorMsg+" in file"+_
            xmlDoc.parseError.url+vbCRLF
        ErrorMsg=ErrorMsg+"Text of line:"+__
            xmlDoc.parseError.srcText
        GetErrorMsg=ErrorMsg
    End Function
```

In many (indeed, most) cases, you will not be concerned about the intermediate states of the load. Rather, you'll just want to know when the XML document is available to start working with. The onDataAvailable event gets fired when the document is complete, and you can use it instead of the onReadyStateChange in most cases, as the following example demonstrates:

```
Private Sub xmlDoc_onDataAvailable()

    Dim ErrorMsg as String

    ' Check to see if operation has completed

    ' restore the cursor

    Screen.mousePointer=vbDefault

    ' If no error occurred

    If xmlDoc.ParseError.ErrorCode=0 then

        ' then use the xml for display purposes

        Display XMLDoc

    Else

        ' Display an error message in a pop-up

        Msgbox GetErrorMessage(xmlDoc)

    End if

End Sub
```

It's worth noting that the Microsoft XML parser is relatively fast and has been optimized as much as possible in the direction of speed. However, when coding, you should look at other possible opportunities to work in an asynchronous mode. You learned about one important alternative in Chapters 7 and 8, which discussed schemas.

SUMMARY

Chapters on APIs are very seldom either fun to read or fun to write, but they do lay the foundation for everything to come. You may have noticed that, despite the complexity of the object model, the vast majority of activities involving the XML Document Object Model revolves around the following points:

▶ The `DOMDocument` object for loading documents, saving documents, and creating nodes

▶ The `IXMLDOMNode` (or its near-identical twin, `IXMLDOMElement`) for manipulating individual elements

▶ The `Attribute` methods for setting or retrieving specific attribute values

▶ The `ParseError` object and the two XML events, `onReadyState-Change` and `onDataAvailable`, for handling asynchronous XML calls

Manipulating the DOM programmatically is certainly important, and the requirements to do it won't go away any time soon. However, XML's strength lies in two related areas: the ability to locate a given piece of information within an XML structure and the ability to transform XML from one format into another. Direct DOM manipulation for either of these two requirements is fairly limited; manually navigating through an XML structure is slow and error prone, and transforming XML with the DOM can prove a challenge to tax the most hierarchically facile minds.

However, the Document Object Model is only one leg of the total XML picture. In Chapter 12, "Transforming XML: Introducing XSLT," you were introduced to the other two legs: the search engine functionality of XPath and the transformative capabilities of Extensible Stylesheet Language Transformations, otherwise known as XSLT.

The next chapter moves into another direction that will be familiar to longtime Web developers. Perl has proven to be quite a resilient programming language for the Web that has weathered a large number of advances that would have eliminated less hardy languages from the mix. XML has marched in, and Perl developers have reacted and made the appropriate adaptations. The next chapter shows you how.

Chapter 14

XML Solutions in Perl

Perl has a history of text processing. In fact, *Perl* is an acronym for Practical Extraction and Report Language, or Practically Eclectic Rubbish Lister, depending on which interpretation you prefer. Because of its heavy text bias, Perl has been involved with Web sites for a long time; it's able to extract and process the information supplied through Web forms and other CGI data streams.

XML is a general utility for marking up content, but it has a strong Internet focus, and so it should be no surprise that Perl has at its disposal a rich selection of XML processors, parsers, generators, and other tools. Most of these tools reside under the XML module tree, and all are available through CPAN.

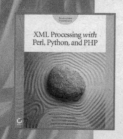

Adapted from *XML Processing with Perl™, Python, and PHP*, by Martin C. Brown

ISBN 0-7821-4021-1   400 pages $49.99

NOTE

CPAN, for you non-Perl programmers, stands for Comprehensive Perl Archive Network and contains a massive compendium of Perl work done over the years by hundreds of people. This includes a huge library of Perl modules, and, of course, the full range of Perl binary and source code distributions. It can be accessed at www.cpan.org/.

Perl evolved over many years and is now probably the best-known and most widely used of the scripting languages available. Nearly everyone has heard of Perl, even if they don't know what it does.

Perl itself was based on some very strong string- and text-processing tools, including awk, sed, and sort, to form a very capable text-processing language. In addition to all of the normal text-processing facilities you would expect, there is an inline regular expression engine and a strong but flexible object-modeling system that is perfect for building the complex information trees that XML documents can develop into.

In this chapter we're going to look at the core modules that make up the Perl XML processing toolset. We'll also examine some of the lesser known tools and modules that, while not vital to your processing, may be useful.

USING *XML::PARSER*

XML::Parser is built on top of the Expat XML processing library written by James Clark. XML::Parser is a vital component of XML processing under Perl because most other modules within Perl use the facilities offered by XML::Parser to support their own processing.

XML::Parser itself is an event-based parser, and because it uses the Expat libraries, it also offers simple validation of your XML documents for well-formedness, although it doesn't validate your documents against a DTD.

The interface to the parser is simple: You create a new XML::Parser object, a suite of functions that are called when the parser determines a start, end, or data portion in your XML document. For example, the code in Listing 14.1 builds a very simple XML parser to output the start and end tags in a document.

Listing 14.1: A Simple XML Parser

```perl
use XML::Parser;

my $parse = new XML::Parser();

$parse->setHandlers(Start => \&handler_start,
                    End => \&handler_end,);

$parse->parsefile($file);

sub handler_start
{
    my ($parser, $element, %attr) = @_;
    print "Start: $element\n";
}

sub handler_end
{
    my ($parser, $element) = @_;
    print "End: $element\n";
}
```

Running this on a simple XML document results in the following output:

```
$ perl exxmlp.pl simple.xml
Start: simple
Start: paragraph
End: paragraph
End: simple
```

As you can see, the sample outputs a list of the start and end tags. Because we "register" the functions that we want to call when different elements are seen, the functions can be called anything we like.

Note as well that the functions are supplied with the name of the tag that was found and the list of attributes for a given tag. We can use this information within the parsing process to be more explicit about the information we pass on.

Using *XML::Parser* to Convert to HTML

Being an event-based parser, the XML::Parser module is ideal in situations where you need to extract or convert those elements into another form. Converting an XML document into an HTML format for display on screen is a good example.

We're going to be looking at a CGI script that I wrote on behalf of a client who wanted to convert an XML document into HTML for displaying on its Web site. The documents themselves were a mixture of XML and some HTML components, and you can see a sample in Listing 14.2.

Listing 14.2: A Sample Review Document

```
<video>
<main>
<title>Alien Resurrection</title>
<para>Sigourney Weaver, Winona Ryder</para>
<title>Witness the Resurrection</title>
<para>The review...</para>
</main>
<panel>
<paneltitle>Purchase</paneltitle>
<para><b>Amazon UK</b></para>
<para><azuk id="B00004CXQ6">Buy Alien Resurrection on
Video</azuk></para>
<para><azuk id="B00004S8GR">Buy Alien Resurrection on
DVD</azuk></para>
<para><azuk id="B00004CXR8">Buy the Alien Box Set on
Video</azuk></para>
<para><azuk id="B00004S8K7">Buy the Alien Box Set on
DVD</azuk></para>
<para><b>Amazon US</b></para>
<para><azus id="787987987">Buy Alien Resurrection on
Video</azus></para>
<para><azus id="787987987">Buy Alien Resurrection on
DVD</azus></para>
<para><azus id="787987987">Buy the Alien Box Set on
Video</azus></para>
<para><azus id="787987987">Buy the Alien Box Set on
DVD</azus></para>
<paneltitle>Related Items</paneltitle>
<para><realref id="video/alien.xml">Alien</realref></para>
<para><realref id="video/aliens.xml">Aliens</realref></para>
<para><realref id="video/alien3.xml">Alien3</realref></para>
<para><realref id="video/alien_boxset.xml">Alien Legacy Box
Set</realref></para>
```

```
<para>
<b>Also see</b>: <keyref id="Sci-Fi">Sci-Fi</keyref>,
<keyref id="Horror">Horror</keyref>,
<keyref id="Action">Action</keyref>
</para>
</panel>
</video>
```

The document contains both traditional XML data and some HTML-specific link information; for example, there are links to other review files and details on the ID and host information required to link to the items available for purchase on Amazon.

The script in Listing 14.3 translates the XML document into HTML. The script works by using a single hash that contains the HTML tags and attributes to output when a specific XML tag is seen. The handler_start() function identifies the tag and then builds the equivalent HTML tag.

Listing 14.3: An XML-to-HTML Converter

```perl
#!/usr/local/bin/perl -w
use strict;
use XML::Parser;

# The %elements hash holds the configuration
# information for the XML tags found by the parser.
# The tags output are HTML.
# Because an individual XML tag can generate
# multiple HTML tags, the base key links to a list
# Within the list are individual hash references for
# each HTML tag, and the hash contains the tag and
# attribute information.
#
# For example, a <title> XML tag produces:
# <tr><td bgcolor="#000094" align="left">
# <font face="Arial, Helvetica" color="#ffffff"><b>

my %elements =
    (
    'video' => [ ],
    'title' => [{ tag => 'tr' },
                { tag => 'td',
                  attr => {
```

```
                                 'bgcolor' => '#000094',
                                 'align' => 'left',
                       },
                  },
                   { tag => 'font',
                     attr => {
                            'face' => 'Arial,Helvetica',
                            'color' => '#ffffff',
                        },
                 },
                   { tag => 'b' },
                   ],
      'paneltitle' => [{ tag => 'tr' },
                     { tag => 'td',
                       attr => {
                              'bgcolor' => '#000094',
                              'align' => 'left',
                          },
                   },
                     { tag => 'font',
                       attr => {
                          'face' => 'Arial,Helvetica',
                          'color' => '#ffffff',
                          },
                   },
                     { tag => 'b' },
                     ],
      'stars' => [{ tag => 'tr' },
                 { tag => 'td' },
                 ],
      'description' => [{ tag => 'tr' },
                     { tag => 'td',
                       attr => {
                              'bgcolor' => '#000094',
                              'align' => 'left',
                          },
                   },
                     { tag => 'font',
                       attr => {
                          'face' => 'Arial,Helvetica',
                          'color' => '#ffffff',
                            },
```

```
                         },
                         { tag => 'b' },
                         ],
         'review' => [{ tag => 'tr' },
                      { tag => 'td' },
                      { tag => 'p' },
                      ],
         'b' => [ { tag => 'b' }
                  ],
         'br' => [ { tag => 'br' }
                   ],
         'main' => [ { tag => 'td',
                       attr => {
                           'width' => '66%',
                           'valign' => 'top',
                       },
                     },
                       { tag => 'table',
                         attr => {
                             'border' => '0',
                             'cellspacing' => '0',
                             'cellpadding' => '2',
                             'width' => '100%',
                         },
                     },
                     ],
         'para' => [ { tag => 'tr' },
                     { tag => 'td' },
                     ],
         'azus' => [ { tag => 'a',
                       href =>
'http://www.amazon.com/exec/obidos/ASIN/%%ID%%
➡/myamzntag' },
                     ],
         'azuk' => [ { tag => 'a',
                       href =>
'http://www.amazon.co.uk/exec/obidos/ASIN/%%ID%%
➡/myamzntag' },
                     ],
         'keyref' => [ { tag => 'a',
                       href =>
                       '/cgi/reviews.cgi?t=k&d=%%ID%%' },
```

```perl
                             ],
        'realref' => [ { tag => 'a',
                           href =>
                     '/cgi/reviews.cgi?t=r&d=%%ID%%' },
                          ],
         'img' => [ { tag => 'img',
                      src => '/img/reviews/',
                      end => 0,},
                  ],
         'panel' => [{ tag => 'td',
                       attr => {
                           'width' => '34%',
                           'valign' => 'top',
                       },
                     },
                        { tag => 'table',
                          attr => {
                              'width' => '100%',
                              'border' => '0',
                              'cellspacing' => '0',
                              'cellpadding' => '2',
                          },
                       },
                        ],
        );

# Because this is a CGI script we output the
# Content-type http header before
# starting the parsing process.

print "Content-type: text/html\n\n";
show_review('alien_r.xml');

# The main show_review() function formats
# a review on screen
sub show_review
{
    my ($title) = @_;

# The review normally forms part of another page,
# so we embed the whole thing into a table
    print <<EOF;
```

```
<table border=0 cellspacing=0 cellpadding=0
 width=100%>
<tr>
EOF

# Create the parser and pass it the XML document
# that we want to process

    my $parse = new XML::Parser();

    $parse->setHandlers(Start => \&handler_start,
                        End => \&handler_end,
                        Char => \&handler_char,);


    $parse->parsefile($title);
# Make sure we close off the table
    print "</tr></table>";

}


# the handler_start() function handles opening
# tags. Because of the %elements structure,
# we need to extract the structure and parse
# %elements to work out the HTML we need to produce

sub handler_start
{
    my ($parser, $element, %attr) = @_;

# First, we check that the XML tag we've just
# recognized has a matching element in the %elements
# hash.
    if (defined($elements{$element}))
    {
# Work through each of the HTML tags in the embedded
# array
        foreach my $tag (@{$elements{$element}})
        {
            print '<',$tag->{'tag'}
                if (exists($tag->{'tag'}));
```

```
# If there are ID attributes in the XML and a
# matching HREF element in %elements
# If we find them then we replace %%ID%% in the HREF
# from %elements with the ID supplied by the XML tag
          if (exists($attr{'id'}) &&
              exists($tag->{'href'}))
          {
              my $url = $tag->{'href'};
              $url =~ s/%%ID%%/$attr{'id'}/;
              print " href=\"$url\"";
              delete($attr{'id'});
          }
# Check if there are any HTML attributes we need to
# generate. If so, work through the attributes
# to build an array of the attribute text, and
# then join them together with spaces to
# make the actual attribute text
          if (exists($tag->{'tag'}) &&
           exists($tag->{'attr'}))
          {
              my @myattrlist = ();
              foreach my $attr (keys %{$tag->
➥{'attr'}})
              {
                  push(@myattrlist,
                      sprintf('%s="%s"',
                          $attr,
                          $tag->{'attr'}->
➥{$attr}));
              }
              print " ", join(' ',@myattrlist);
          }
# Finally, add any other attributes defined in
# the XML to the HTML output.
          foreach my $attr (keys %attr)
          {
              print " $attr=\"$attr{$attr}\"";
          }
# Print the closing tag
          print '>' if (exists($tag->{'tag'}));
# Output any raw elements (which appear as
# normal text) if there are any
```

```
                    print $tag->{'raw'} if (exists
➡($tag->{raw}));
            }
        }
}

# The handler_end() has to output the HTML tags
# from the %elements hash, but in opposite order (to
# produce valid HTML) and as close tags.
#

sub handler_end
{
    my ($parser, $element) = @_;

    if (defined($elements{$element}))
    {
        foreach my $tag (reverse @{$elements
➡{$element}})
        {
            if (exists($tag->{'tag'}))
            {
                print '</',$tag->{'tag'},'>'
                    unless (exists($tag->{end}));
            }
        }
    }
}


# Raw character data is just output verbatim
sub handler_char
{
    my ($parser,$data) = @_;

    print $data;
}
```

In Figure 14.1, you can see the result of running the script on the review document shown in Listing 14.3. Although this was written for a specific solution, you can modify the %elements table to suit your own needs, and it'll convert your own XML documents into HTML.

FIGURE 14.1: An HTML version of an XML movie review document

XML::Parser Traps

The Expat libraries on which XML::Parser is based have a few small traps. Because XML::Parser is used by so many of the other modules within Perl, it's worth mentioning these problems before we go any further:

▶ Errors raise exceptions: Although Expat is non-validating, it still checks the basic layout of your document to ensure that it's well formed. Unfortunately, this means that any error in the basic structure of the document raises an exception. The only way to trap this is to embed your call to the parser within eval(). Luckily, a further call to the parser will allow parsing to continue from the position after the last error.

▶ Expat supplies all data: Everything from the XML document is supplied back through one of the trigger functions you define for XML::Parser to use. This means that whatever function is used for handling character data must make decisions about what to do with characters beyond normal text. Expat supplies linefeed/carriage return characters, spaces, and any other characters to make the XML document more human readable.

▶ Data is returned in UTF-8: Although Expat isn't strictly a Unicode parser, XML::Parser always returns UTF-8 strings. This isn't a problem for most English-sourced documents because UTF-8 and Latin-1 character sets are the same for those first 256 characters. For other Unicode strings, especially foreign languages not supported by the Latin-1 set, you can use Unicode::String for this.

▶ Data portions are supplied in chunks: Because Expat deals with chunks of data, you may find that data portions passed to the data handler function are incomplete. If you want to handle the data portions uniquely, you'll need to cache the information and initiate a separate handler to process a complete data portion. We'll be looking at examples of this throughout the rest of this section.

Beyond these small problems, XML::Parser works pretty much as you would expect.

XML PROCESSING USING SAX

Many of the parser solutions for XML in Perl support a Simple API for XML (SAX) interface to enable us to communicate between different XML processors when reading a document. SAX parsers work in the same basic fashion as XML::Parser; as the document is parsed and different elements within the document are discovered, a function is called to process the entity.

A number of different SAX parsers are available, but the best is probably the XML::Parser::PerlSAX (PerlSAX) module. In fact, that module forms the basis of many other modules, including the XML::Grove module that provides a DOM-like interface for XML documents.

Unlike XML::Parser, which uses references to the functions that handle the entities, with PerlSAX you need to create a new class that defines the methods to use for parsing different XML tags—suitable methods are named according to the tag you want to process. Although this sounds more complex, it does enable you to identify a number of different elements. The full SAX specification covers everything from basic document properties to specific elements.

For example, we can create a simple class to output the start and end tags from an XML document by creating a handler class like the one in Listing 14.4. We inherit from XML::Handler::Sample, which dumps the output for selected entities, and define two functions, start_element()

and end_element(), which will be called when the parser identifies start and end tags in the document.

Listing 14.4: A Simple Handler Class for SAX Parsing

```perl
package MyHandler;

use vars qw/@ISA/;
use XML::Handler::Sample;

@ISA = qw/XML::Handler::Sample/;

sub new
{
    my $self = shift;
    my $class = ref($self) || $self;

    return bless {}, $class;
}

sub start_element
{
    my ($self, $info) = @_;

    print "Start Tag $info->{Name}\n";
}

sub end_element
{
    my ($self, $info) = @_;

    print "End Tag $info->{Name}\n";
}
```

To create the parser, we create a new instance of our handler class and then a new instance of the XML::Handler::PerlSAX class, which will do the actual processing. You can see the final parser script in Listing 14.5.

Listing 14.5: Our PerlSAX Parsing Script

```perl
#!/usr/local/bin/perl -w
use XML::Parser::PerlSAX;
use MyHandler;
```

```
if ($#ARGV != 0) {
    die "You must specify a file to parse";
}
$file = shift @ARGV;

$my_handler = MyHandler->new();

XML::Parser::PerlSAX->new->parse(Source =>
                        { SystemId => $file },
                        Handler => $my_handler);
```

If we run this script on a simple XML document, we get the following output:

```
$ perl perlsax-test.pl simple.xml
start_document
Start Tag simple
characters
Start Tag paragraph
characters
End Tag paragraph
characters
End Tag simple
end_document
```

SAX parsing is great for processing a document in sequence and can be useful for serializing a document into another format. We saw this with the XML::Parser solution earlier in this chapter, which converted our document to HTML.

XML PROCESSING USING DOM

The Document Object Model (DOM) for parsing an XML document is essentially just a method of turning your XML document into an object tree. Because all XML documents are essentially built like a tree, accessing an individual element by its branch seems a logical step.

Lots of different DOM parsers are supported under Perl, including XML::DOM, XML::Simple, and XML::Twig. Of these, my personal favorite is XML::Grove, written by Ken MacLeod. XML::Grove is not strictly a DOM parser—it doesn't adhere to W3C's DOM API, but it does provide a very similar interface. For a genuine DOM parser, use the XML::DOM module.

Part iv

The XML::Grove module provides an easy way to work with an entire XML document by loading an XML document into memory and then converting it into a tree of objects that can be accessed just like any other set of nested references. To demonstrate the tree format offered by XML::Grove, let's look at a sample XML document. We'll use a contact entry within an address book, a structure most people are familiar with. If we think about a single record within a contact database, then the base of the XML document will be the contact. We'll use a fictional version of me for our example, seen in Listing 14.6.

Listing 14.6: A Contact Record Written in XML

```
<contact>
  <name>Martin Brown</name>
  <address>
    <description>Main Address</description>
    <addressline>The House, The Street, The
Town</addressline>
  </address>
  <address>
    <description>Holiday Chalet</description>
    <addressline>The Chalet, The Hillside, The
Forest</addressline>
  </address>
</contact>
```

The grove.pl sample script that comes with the XML::Grove module kit can convert this document into a textual tree. This version has been modified slightly so that it also outputs the array reference numbers of each branch. We'll need this information in a later example. The script itself is shown in Listing 14.7.

Listing 14.7: The grove.pl XML::Grove Sampler

```
#
# Copyright (C) 1998 Ken MacLeod
# See the file COPYING for distribution terms.
#
# $Id: grove.pl,v 1.4 1999/05/06 23:13:02 kmacleod
➡Exp $
#

use XML::Parser::PerlSAX;
use XML::Grove;
```

```perl
use XML::Grove::Builder;

my $builder = XML::Grove::Builder->new;
my $parser = XML::Parser::PerlSAX->new(Handler => $builder);

my $doc;
foreach $doc (@ARGV) {
    my $grove = $parser->parse (Source =>
➥{ SystemId => $doc });

    dump_grove ($grove);
}


sub dump_grove {
    my $grove = shift;
    my @context = ();

    _dump_contents ($grove->{Contents}, \@context);
}

sub _dump_contents {
    my $contents = shift;
    my $context = shift;

    for(my $i=0;$i<@$contents;$i++) {
        $item = $contents->[$i];
        if (ref ($item) =~ /::Element/) {
            push @$context, $item->{Name};
            my @attributes = %{$item->{Attributes}};
            print STDERR "@$context \\\\
➥(@attributes)\n";
            _dump_contents ($item->{Contents},
➥$context);
            print STDERR "@$context //\n";
            pop @$context;
        } elsif (ref ($item) =~ /::PI/) {
            my $target = $item->{Target};
            my $data = $item->{Data};
            print STDERR "@$context ?? $target
➥($data)\n";
        } elsif (ref ($item) =~ /::Characters/) {
            my $data = $item->{Data};
```

```
            $data =~ s/([\x80-\xff])/sprintf "#x%X;"
➥,ord $1/eg;
            $data =~ s/([\t\n])/sprintf "#%d;",
➥ord $1/eg;
        print STDERR "@$context || $data\n";
    } elsif (!ref ($item)) {
        print STDERR "@$context !! SCALAR:
➥$item\n";
    } else {
        print STDERR "@$context !! OTHER:
➥$item\n";
    }
  }
}
```

The script works by recursively calling the _dump_contents() function on each branch of the tree. That function works through every element within a particular branch. Through each iteration, we prefix the output with the location of the current branch. The result of running the script on our sample XML document can be seen in Listing 14.8.

Listing 14.8: A Textual XML Tree of Our Contact Document

```
0: contact \\ ()
0: contact || #10;
0: contact ||
0: contact 2: name \\ ()
0: contact 2: name || Martin Brown
0: contact 2: name //
0: contact || #10;
0: contact ||
0: contact 5: address \\ ()
0: contact 5: address || #10;
0: contact 5: address ||
0: contact 5: address 2: description \\ ()
0: contact 5: address 2: description || Main Address
0: contact 5: address 2: description //
0: contact 5: address || #10;
0: contact 5: address ||
0: contact 5: address 5: addressline \\ ()
0: contact 5: address 5: addressline || The House,
   The Street, The Town
0: contact 5: address 5: addressline //
```

```
0: contact 5: address || #10;
0: contact 5: address ||
0: contact 5: address //
0: contact || #10;
0: contact ||
0: contact 8: address \\ ()
0: contact 8: address || #10;
0: contact 8: address ||
0: contact 8: address 2: description \\ ()
0: contact 8: address 2: description || Holiday
   Chalet
0: contact 8: address 2: description //
0: contact 8: address || #10;
0: contact 8: address ||
0: contact 8: address 5: addressline \\ ()
0: contact 8: address 5: addressline || The Chalet,
   The Hillside, The Forest
0: contact 8: address 5: addressline //
0: contact 8: address || #10;
0: contact 8: address ||
0: contact 8: address //
0: contact || #10;
0: contact //
```

Because we can access individual tags within a DOM-parsed XML document, DOM parsers are particularly useful when we want to update the contents of an XML document. Using SAX to process the document sequentially rather than using the tree model offered by a DOM parser is far from ideal, because it means reading in the content, identifying which bits you want to change as they are triggered, and then regenerating the result.

For example, if we wanted to update my Holiday Chalet address using SAX, we'd have to read in the content, identify first that we were in the address branch, and then that were we in the correct addressline branch. Then we could replace the information in the output.

Using DOM, we parse the entire document, update the address within the branch we want to update, and then dump the XML document back out again. Updating the branch is just a case of referencing the branch's location within the DOM structure.

XML::Grove converts your XML document into a series of nested arrays and hashes. The arrays contain a list of elements within the current branch, and the hashes are used to supply the element type, name, and data (if applicable) for that branch. Because there are different element types, the numbers don't always match what you would normally expect.

In Listing 14.8, you'll notice the array reference numbers required to access each branch. To access the contents of a branch, you access the `Contents` element from the enclosed hash and get the data contained in a branch using the `Data` key. Finally, the `Name` key returns the tag name for a given branch, and the `Attributes` key returns the attributes for the tag.

For example, to get the data from the `name` XML tag, we'd need to access the `Data` key from branch 0 (contact), 2 (name), 0 (the data element):

```
print 'Name: ',$grove->{Contents}[0]->{Contents}
➥[2]->{Contents}->[0]->{Data},"\n";
```

Because it's an object structure, we can update my address using the following:

```
$grove->{Contents}[0]->{Contents}[8]->{Contents}
    ->[5]->{Contents}->[0]->{Data} = 'The Shed,
    The Mountain, The Lakes';
```

We can output the final version of the document using the following:

```
use XML::Grove::AsCanonXML;
print $grove->as_canon_xml();
```

GENERATING XML

The easiest way to generate XML information within Perl is to use `print`, probably in combination with a Here document to make the process easier.

NOTE

A Here document is a feature of Perl that makes it easy to handle long, multi-line strings that use a keyword to identify the end of a string.

Using `print` is an untidy solution, especially since it almost guarantees that you'll introduce errors and inconsistencies into the code that you generate, and debugging the output can be an absolute nightmare.

A much better solution is to output your XML tags by name in a structure format, just as if you were creating the XML tree yourself. We can do this using one of the modules that support DOM parsing, since DOM allows us to build the XML document branch by branch and leaf by leaf.

It would be much better, however, to use a tool such as the XML::Generator module. Instead of having to build the XML tags and objects and structure yourself, XML::Generator enables you to use functions to define the tag. Arguments to the functions create additional branches, leaves, and attributes.

For example, we might populate a contact file using the following:

```perl
use XML::Generator;
my $gen = XML::Generator->new('escape' => 'always',
                              'pretty' => 2);
print $gen->contact($gen->name('Martin C Brown'),
                    $gen->email('mc@mcwords.com'));
```

The functions don't have to be predefined: XML::Generator creates the functions for us on the fly. The previous code generates the following XML document:

```xml
<contact>
  <name>Martin C Brown</name>
  <email>mc@mcwords.com</email>
</contact>
```

The module generates a raw XML document. To generate a DOM tree, which we could then separately parse and process using the techniques we saw earlier in this chapter, we can use the XML::Generator::DOM module:

```perl
use XML::Generator::DOM;
my $gen = XML::Generator::DOM->new();


my $domdoc = $gen->xml($gen->contact(
                         $gen->name
➡('Martin C Brown'),
                         $gen->email
➡('mc@mcwords.com')));


print $domdoc->toString();
```

OTHER XML MODULES

A host of other XML modules are available on CPAN that are too numerous to mention in any detail here. XML and Perl are developing all the time, and if you want more information about any of the modules in Perl, check out the CPAN XML page at `http://www.perl.com/CPAN-local/modules/by-module/XML/`.

DBIx::XML_RDB

Although there are lots of bits of Perl and XML that I really like, the `DBIx::XML_RDB` module is one of my favorites. It simplifies one of the most complicated and often convoluted processes when converting RDBMS information into an XML document.

The `DBIx::XML_RDB` module makes an SQL query submitted to any database accessible through the `DBI` module into an XML document.

Using the module is straightforward—you create a new `DBIx::XML_RDB` object, supplying the data source, driver, user ID, password, and database name:

```
my $sqlxml = DBIx::XML_RDB->new($datasource,
➡$driver,
                                    $userid, $password, $dbname)
        || die "Failed to make new xmlout";
```

Submit an SQL statement:

```
$sqlxml->DoSql("SELECT * FROM $table ORDER BY 1");
```

Then print out the result:

```
print $sqlxml->GetData;
```

It's actually easier to demonstrate the effects using the `sql2xml.pl` and `xml2sql.pl` tools, which are installed when you install the module. These convert an SQL statement into an XML document and vice versa. For example, to dump a table containing ISBN numbers to an XML file, you'd use this code:

```
$ sql2xml.pl -sn books -driver mysql -uid mc
➡-table isbn
 -output hello.xml
```

You can see the resulting XML file in Listing 14.9.

Listing 14.9: The XML Result of an SQL Query Using DBIx::XML_RDB

```
<?xml version="1.0"?>
<DBI driver="bookwatch">
        <RESULTSET statement="SELECT * FROM isbn
        ORDER BY 1">
                <ROW>
                        <isbn>0002570254</isbn>
                        <title>Sony</title>
                        <author>John Nathan</author>
                        <followref>0</followref>
                </ROW>
                <ROW>

                        <isbn>0002570807</isbn>
                        <title>'Tis</title>
                        <author>Frank McCourt</author>
                        <followref>0</followref>
                </ROW>
    ...
</RESULTSET>
</DBI>
```

The xml2sql.pl script obviously does the reverse, converting an XML document following the same format as that in Listing 14.9 back into a series of SQL statements.

XML::RSS

If you use the Web for reading your news and to keep up-to-date with Perl, Python, Apache, and all the other cool stuff that exists out there on the Internet, then you'll know how frustrating it is to have go to 10 or 20 different sites to pick your news.

As a solution to this problem, many sites now export their news and other regularly updated pieces through an RSS (Rich Site Summary) file. RSS files are really just XML documents conforming to a DTD that define the different news stories and how to link to the original items. For example, Listing 14.10 shows a truncated version of the RSS file from CNN.com on June 29, 2001.

Part iv

Listing 14.10: A Sample RSS File from CNN.com

```
<?xml version="1.0"?>

<!DOCTYPE rss PUBLIC "-//Netscape Communications//
➡DTD RSS 0.91//EN"
 "http://my.netscape.com/publish/formats/rss-0.91.
➡dtd">

<rss version="0.91">

<channel>

<title>News from CNN.com</title>
<link>http://cnn.com/index.html</link>
<description>The world's news leader</description>
<language>en-us</language>

<image>
 <title>CNN.com</title>
 <url>http://cnn.com/images/1999/07/cnn.com.logo.
➡gif</url>
 <link>http://CNN.com/index.html</link>
 <width>144</width>
 <height>34</height>
 <description>The world's news leader</description>
 </image>

<item>
  <title>Retired grocery clerk claims $141 million
California lottery
  ➡ jackpot - June 29, 2001</title>
  <link>http://cnn.com/2001/US/06/29/lottery.
➡winner.ap/index.html</link>

  </item>

<item>
  <title>Kmart pulling handgun ammunition from
  shelves in wake of
  ➡ protests - June 29, 2001</title>
  <link>http://cnn.com/2001/US/06/29/kmart.guns.ap/
        index.html</link>
  </item>
...
```

How does RSS make reading news easier?

Once you've downloaded the RSS files from a number of different sites, you can then combine the information in each RSS file in order to aggregate the content into a single Web page. Each item in the RSS file will be a small outline of the full article. If you see something you like, you can go to the full page; otherwise, you can skip to the next story without going to multiple Web sites.

The XML::RSS module enables you to create and update your RSS files, usually from whatever source you use in your news service. Some people use the Slashcode (as used by slashdot.org and many other sites), and in other instances it'll be from the your news database. We can also use RSS to convert an RSS file into HTML.

To get an idea of how RSS works, you might want to try the Meerkat service offered on the O'Reilly Network (http://www.oreillynet .com/meerkat/). If you want to play around with RSS in Perl and reap the benefits of reading all your news from a single Web page, then check out AmphetaDesk. Ironically, AmphetaDesk doesn't use XML::RSS, but it does download, parse, and convert RSS documents into HTML. You can see a sample of AmphetaDesk in action in Figure 14.2. The package is available for Mac, Windows, and Unix.

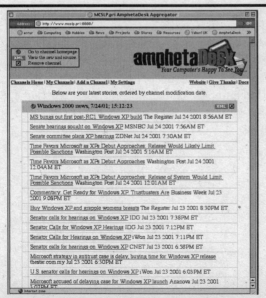

FIGURE 14.2: AmphetaDesk, an RSS aggregator

SUMMARY

As with most problems in Perl, you can generally find a suitable solution in the CPAN archives. XML processing is no exception—there is a whole host of different modules out there for solving your XML processing and parsing problems using Perl.

For basic XML processing in Perl we have the XML::Parser module. It provides a sequential method for calling a specific function when the different elements are identified within an XML document. XML::Parser is an ideal solution for converting the entire content of an XML document into another format such as HTML. We saw a sample of this in this chapter.

For a more structured and ultimately expandable method of processing documents, we have the SAX interface in the form of the XML::Parser::PerlSAX module.

The PerlSAX parser also provides the basis for a number of other modules, including a DOM-like parser in the form of XML::Grove. The XML::Grove module isn't a true DOM parser, but it does enable us to manipulate an XML document as if it were a DOM tree. If you want a full DOM implementation, we also have the XML::DOM and XML::Simple modules.

As if that weren't enough, we also have a host of modules that parse and work with XML documents. The DBIx::XML_RDB module will convert XML documents to and from SQL statements. We can parse RSS documents for news feeds using the XML::RSS module.

The next chapter takes this last concept one step further. We can go beyond news syndication and SQL conversion services to actual application processing over the Web using Perl with SOAP and XML-RPC. You'll learn how to do that next.

Chapter 15

APPLYING SOAP/XML-RPC IN PERL

XML-Remote Procedure Calls (XML-RPC) and Simple Object Access Protocol (SOAP) aren't really XML technologies, nor do we need to know how to parse or extract elements from XML documents to use them.

Instead, XML-RPC and SOAP are XML applications: They convert a function call on a client into a function call on a remote machine by using XML to describe the request to the server. Once the function has been executed, the whole process works in reverse, translating the response by the server into another XML document in order to return the value to the client.

Remote procedures are nothing new; Unix has had RPC capability for years. More recently, many object technologies, such as Common Object Request Broker Architecture (CORBA) and Distributed Common Object Model (DCOM), have also provided remote (or distributed) function calls. The difference is a common standard for making these operations work; both XML-RPC and SOAP are cross-platform and language compatible.

Adapted from *XML Processing with Perl™, Python, and PHP*, by Martin C. Brown

ISBN 0-7821-4021-1   400 pages $49.99

The Perl SOAP::Lite module provides both SOAP and XML-RPC functionality in the same module and hides all of the complexity of the technology behind a set of very simple functions. The Lite in the module's name refers to its ease of use and not its capabilities.

The module itself provides support for HTTP, HTTPS, CGI, TCP, FTP, SMTP, POP3, e-mail parsing, and traditional file-based transport methods for communicating remote requests. The module also provides methods for operating as a stand-alone network service, a CGI interface for providing info through an existing Web server, and a mod_soap module to enable SOAP requests to be handled transparently through Apache and mod_perl extensions.

In this chapter we're going to look at how to use SOAP::Lite to provide a distributed solution, using some of the XML technologies we've already seen elsewhere in this part of the book.

Introducing *SOAP::Lite*

All SOAP systems work on the same basic principle—you have a SOAP server, which replies to requests, mapping the function called by the client to a function within another module. You also have a SOAP client that makes the request in the first place.

With SOAP::Lite, the server side sets up a script that accepts the request over a given transport. That script then calls the function defined within a particular package—either internal or external to the server handler script—before supplying the return value from the function back to the caller.

For example, Listing 15.1 shows a very simple CGI-based server.

Listing 15.1: A Simple SOAP::Lite Server

```
#!/usr/local/bin/perl

use SOAP::Transport::HTTP;

SOAP::Transport::HTTP::CGI
    ->dispatch_to('/export/http/webs/test/',
'SOAP::Demo')
    ->handle();
```

The main line creates a new server handler object. The dispatch_to() method first specifies the location of the module tree that will be used to handle the client requests, and the second argument defines the name of the module that we'll accept and handle from the client. Finally, the handle() method passes off the processing to the module, calling the function requested by the client.

Note the name of the module that we've explicitly defined as being available to clients. The module is SOAP::Demo, and the handler will actually try to load the module/export/http/webs/test/SOAP/Demo.pm.

The client, shown in Listing 15.2, is equally brief.

Listing 15.2: A Simple SOAP::Lite Client

```
use SOAP::Lite;

print SOAP::Lite
    ->uri('http://test.mchome.pri/SOAP/Demo')
    ->proxy('http://test.mchome.pri/SOAP/
➡request.cgi')
    ->getmessage()
    ->result;
```

The client creates a new SOAP::Lite object; calls the uri() method, the proxy() method, and the getmessage() method; and then accesses the result attribute of the object. Because this is part of a call to print, we'll print out the result.

The different components here are important, and we'll look at each item in detail:

▶ The uri() method defines the namespace. The namespace is the location of the module that provides us with the functions that we want to call. In this case, the URI refers to a remote machine (using HTTP) and the SOAP/Demo namespace. Observant readers will have noticed the similarity here with the name of the module defined in the server handler script.

▶ The proxy() method specifies the actual URL that will be used to send the request to the remote server. In this case, we're calling a script called request.cgi in the SOAP directory within the same server as our object.

▶ The getmessage() method is actually the name of the function on the remote server that we want to execute. The function is called within the confines of the remote namespace, which we already know is SOAP/Demo—therefore, the full expansion of the function that is called is SOAP::Demo::getmessage().

▶ The `result` is the return value from the remote function. The `result` attribute is actually an object and includes result and error information (if an error occurred). In this instance, we're going to assume that everything is working okay.

The final part of the puzzle is the module that provides the actual `getmessage()` function. The module is called `Demo`, and it's installed within the SOAP directory on our Web server. You can see the module in Listing 15.3.

Listing 15.3: Our Remote Module

```perl
package SOAP::Demo;

sub getmessage
{
    return "Hello, world!\n";
}

1;
```

The module defines just a single function—the function `getmessage()`, which we know we want to call remotely. The package specification again is important here—it's `SOAP::Demo`, the same as the namespace we requested in the URI we requested in the client and also the same as the name of the module that we specified as available in the request handler.

To install these scripts on your own server:

1. Create a directory on your Web server called SOAP.

2. Copy the request handler (seen in Listing 15.1) into the SOAP directory using the name `request.cgi`. Modify the directory argument to the `dispatch_to()` function to point to the Demo module.

3. Copy the remote module (seen in Listing 15.3) into the SOAP directory using the name `Demo.pm`.

4. Now modify the client (seen in Listing 15.2) to reflect the name of your server in both the `uri()` and `proxy()` methods.

Once you've made all the modifications, you're ready to go. Execute the client and you should get a message:

```
% perl client.pl
Hello, world!
```

Success!

If the script doesn't appear to work, see the "Diagnosing Problems" section later in this chapter.

TIP

I use the .pri domain name extension on my servers to indicate the address is private (for example, the domain mchome.pri is unique to my LAN). The .pri extension is not officially recognized, but it is generally accepted as an alternative for use on internal networks that are not available on the Internet. The host could be public and available on the Internet, on your intranet with an official name, or as I've specified it here.

How *SOAP::Lite* Works

SOAP converts your request to execute a specific function within a specific module into an XML document. The document is then transferred over the transport mechanism to a remote request handler (in our case, a request to a CGI handler on a Web site).

The XML document that is created makes up the SOAP request and contains the namespace, the function to be called, and any supplied parameters. In our case, it turns the request to execute getmessage into the SOAP envelope, shown in Listing 15.4.

Listing 15.4: An XML-Encoded SOAP Envelope

```
<?xml version="1.0" encoding="UTF-8"?>
  <SOAP-ENV:Envelope xmlns:SOAP-ENC =
      "http://schemas.xmlsoap.org/soap/encoding/"
  SOAP-ENV:encodingStyle =
      "http://schemas.xmlsoap.org/soap/encoding/"
  xmlns:xsi="http://www.w3.org/1999/
  ➥XMLSchema-instance"
  xmlns:SOAP-ENV =
      "http://schemas.xmlsoap.org/soap/envelope/"
  xmlns:xsd="http://www.w3.org/1999/XMLSchema">
  <SOAP-ENV:Body>
    <namesp1:getmessage xmlns:namesp1 =
    "http: //test.mchome.pri/SOAP/Demo"/>
  </SOAP-ENV:Body>
</SOAP-ENV:Envelope>
```

Part iv

In this example we were using standard CGI, so SOAP::Lite sends a POST request to the URL specified by the proxy() method in the client script.

The server CGI script extracts the XML document that was sent as part of the POST request and extracts the information it needs to execute the function. The value of the uri() method is encoded in the SOAP envelope body; this tells the request handler which module it should be looking for, along with the name of the function that we want to call.

SOAP::Lite then looks for the module/function (assuming that the request handler has been configured to accept the module and function combination), executes the function, and then serializes the response into another SOAP envelope to send back to the client.

SOAP Client Programming

SOAP is not limited to calling a simple function; you can pass arguments through to the remote function the same as you would call the function within a normal script. For example, we could change our getmessage() function so that we supply the name of the person we are greeting, as shown in this code:

```
my $request = SOAP::Lite
    ->uri('http://foodies.mchome.com/Foodies/
➡Conversion')
    ->proxy('http://foodies.mchome.pri/request.cgi')
    ->greet('Martin');
```

You can also configure the client to automatically pass on calls to functions not identified locally to a remote request handler. In addition, you can use SOAP to access remote objects and their methods.

Explicit Calls

We've already seen examples of explicit calls, such as that in Listing 15.2. The example shows how to access a remote function directly by an explicit name. Explicit calls are great for scripts in which you call only one function.

Automatic Calls

SOAP::Lite also supports a facility called *autodispatch*. This mode uses the autoload mechanism to call a remote procedure automatically when the function name cannot otherwise be resolved. For example, we could change our explicit example from Listing 15.2 into an autodispatching client using the code in Listing 15.5.

Listing 15.5: An Autodispatch Client

```
use SOAP::Lite +autodispatch =>
    uri => 'http://test.mchome.com/SOAP/Demo',
    proxy => 'http://test.mchome.com/SOAP/
➡request.cgi';

print getmessage();
```

The first benefit of autodispatch is that we can call remote functions just as if they were local. The second is that we can obtain their return values just as easily.

Autodispatch is also useful when you want to call a number of different remote functions within your code. The only problem with autodispatch is that if you get the function name wrong, you will be unable to trap that information in the script. See the section "Debugging *SOAP::Lite*" later in this chapter for information on how to find and debug errors in your SOAP code.

Getting Multiple Return Values

When calling a function that returns multiple values, you need to extract the information differently. The result() method returns only the first value returned by the remote function. Further return values are accessible through the paramsout() method.

Because the return values are split across these two method calls, care needs to be taken when extracting the information. For example, the convert_qty() function accepts three arguments: the quantity, the measurement, and the destination measurement group (metric, imperial) that you want the value converted to. The function returns the converted quantity and measurement. You can see a modified client to handle multiple return values in Listing 15.6.

Listing 15.6: A Client to Handle Multiple Return Values

```
use SOAP::Lite;

my $request = SOAP::Lite
    ->uri('http://test.mchome.pri/SOAP/Conversion')
```

```
        ->proxy('http://test.mchome.pri/SOAP/
➥request.cgi')
        ->convert_qty(1.5,'Kg','Imperial');

@res = $request->paramsout;
$result = $request->result;

if ($request->fault)
{
    printf("SOAP Error: %s: %s\n\t%s\n",
            $request->faultcode,
            $request->faultstring,
            $request->faultdetail);
}
else
{
    print "Result is: $result\n";
    print "Params are: ",join(', ',@res), "\n";
}
```

Because of this difference, you might want to standardize on returning a success value in the first argument and then returning the proper argument list in the remaining arguments that are accessible through the paramsout() attribute. That way, you can always check the function/method return status with result() and all the real arguments from paramsout().

The other alternative to handling multiple return values is to return an array or hash reference that then contains all the real values. For example:

```
sub getcontact
{

    # get contact information
    my $result = {'status' => 1,

                    'name' => 'Martin Brown',

                    'email' => 'mc@mcwords.com',

                    ...

                    };

    return $result;

}
```

Now when we get the return value from the result() method call, we have all the information we need without needing to call paramsout().

Using Objects and Methods

SOAP was designed as an object access protocol to replace the many different distributed objects standards out there, so it seems a shame not to mention how we can use it to access objects.

Actually, object access is easy, especially if we use autodispatch. Listing 15.7 shows a request handler (with built-in support module) supporting an accounting system.

Listing 15.7: A SOAP Accounting Server

```perl
#!/usr/local/bin/perl

use SOAP::Transport::HTTP;

SOAP::Transport::HTTP::CGI
    ->dispatch_to('Account')
    ->handle();

package Account;

sub new
{
    my ($self,$name,$balance) = @_;
    my $class = ref($self) || $self;
    bless { balance => $balance,
            name => $name }, $class;
}

sub balance
{
    my $self = shift;

    return $self->{balance};
}

sub deposit
{
    my $self = shift;

    $self->{balance} += shift;
    return $self->{balance};
}
```

```perl
sub withdraw
{
    my $self = shift;

    $self->{balance} -= shift;
    return $self->{balance};
}
```

The client is shown in Listing 15.8. Note that, because we are using autodispatch, execution is identical to what we would normally use in a standard Perl script if using the module locally.

Listing 15.8: A SOAP Object Client

```perl
#!/usr/local/bin/perl
use SOAP::Lite +autodispatch =>
    uri => 'http://test.mchome.pri/Account',
    proxy => 'http://test.mchome.pri/
►accrequest.cgi';

my $current = Account->new('Current',1000);

print $current->deposit(1000);
```

CREATING SOAP SERVERS

The SOAP::Lite module hides all of the complexity of building servers. It handles all of the communication, the serialization of your request into a SOAP envelope, and, in the case of a request handler, the job of deserializing the envelope back into the information required to execute your desired function. As such, the request handlers are limited to controlling the location and/or definition of the module that the client is requesting to execute. However, that doesn't mean we can't be flexible.

Dispatch Methods

The dispatch method passes off control to a function within a given package, but the location of the package does not have to be external, as in the examples we've already seen. You can pass control to an internal package.

The dispatch_to() method controls this interaction between what the client requests and which module is actually loaded and used (if necessary) and also acts as a control mechanism. The dispatch_to() method accepts any number of arguments, which can be in one of three forms:

- ▶ A directory, which is used to populate the @INC variable when importing external modules.

- ▶ A module name, which restricts client requests to any function within the specified module.

- ▶ A module and function definition, which restricts client requests to a specific function in a specific module. Alternatively, you can specify a directory and a module name that restricts the request to a specific module in a specific directory.

All three help to control access to a given module or function as requested by a client. For example, specifying the name of a module limits client requests to functions within that module. In practical terms, it leads to three main dispatch methods: the static internal, the static external, and the dynamic request handler. We can also create a mixture of those solutions by using a combination of those arguments.

Static Internal

The static internal form relies on creating a new package within your request handler. Static internal handlers are useful for stand-alone solutions when you need to support a SOAP service, but within a single file and without reliance on an external module. You can see a modified version of our simple Hello World script in Listing 15.9.

Listing 15.9: A Static Internal SOAP Request Handler

```perl
#!/usr/local/bin/perl

use SOAP::Transport::HTTP;

SOAP::Transport::HTTP::CGI
    ->dispatch_to('SOAP::Demo')
    ->handle();

package SOAP::Demo;

sub getmessage
{
    return "Hello, world!\n";
```

```
    }

    1;
```

Static External

Static external handlers use dispatch_to to pass control to an external but named module that is imported by the request handler explicitly via a normal use statement. An example is shown in Listing 15.10.

Listing 15.10: A Static External SOAP Request Handler

```perl
#!/usr/local/bin/perl

use SOAP::Transport::HTTP;

use SOAP::Demo;

SOAP::Transport::HTTP::CGI
    ->dispatch_to('SOAP::Demo')
    ->handle();
```

Static external request handlers are most useful when you want to restrict access to a particular external module that can be loaded safely from a generic location through the normal @INC array of directories.

Dynamic

The dynamic model enables the client to specify the name of the module to be loaded (through the uri method). It's up to the request handler only to define the location of the modules that can be dynamically loaded to handle the client's requests. This allows a single request handler to support the requests for a number of clients using different modules. We've already seen an example of this; all that's required is to specify the directory location in the dispatch_to method, as shown in Listing 15.11.

Listing 15.11: A Dynamic Request Handler

```perl
#!/usr/local/bin/perl

use SOAP::Transport::HTTP;

SOAP::Transport::HTTP::CGI
    ->dispatch_to('/usr/local/lib/SOAP')
    ->handle();
```

Obviously the dynamic format passes the responsibility of calling the correct module on to the client; it also reduces the security aspect. The request handler has to a large extent been given free reign to the client to request any module available in the directory you configure. This has its advantages because we can use a single request handler to cope with all the requests for a multitude of different modules without ever needing to change the request handler.

NOTE

Dynamic dispatch actually zeros the content of @INC, replacing it entirely with the list of directories that you supply.

Mixed

The mixed format enables you to dynamically load modules from a specific directory and to explicitly preload external modules from the normal @INC variable. For example, the code in Listing 15.12 will dynamically load modules from /usr/local/lib/SOAP while loading the Contacts module from a directory in @INC.

Listing 15.12: Mixed Mode Dispatching

```
#!/usr/local/bin/perl

use SOAP::Transport::HTTP;

SOAP::Transport::HTTP::CGI
    ->dispatch_to('/usr/local/lib/SOAP','Contacts')
    ->handle();
```

SOAP Support Modules

The backend of any SOAP application and request handler is the module or function that it calls. Although writing traditional modules isn't much different, you might need to make a few changes, as well as watch out for some traps along the way:

▶ Modules do not need to export the functions explicitly. You do not need the services of Exporter, nor do you need to populate @EXPORT to provide access to the functions. Calls are made by the dispatcher using the explicit module and function/method name.

► All functions are called with at least one argument—the package (or namespace) used when the request was received from the client. For example, our greet() function is supplied with a single argument: SOAP::Demo.

► All further arguments to a function are supplied just as they are received from the client. For example, from the client call to the module Conversion and the function convert_qty(1.5, 'kg'), the server function receives ('Conversion', 1.5, 'kg').

► Return values from the server-side function remain the same. No additional information is added, but make sure that your client knows how to extract multiple-argument return values (see the section "Getting Multiple Return Values" earlier in this chapter).

In all other respects, any modules that you specifically create for use with SOAP can follow any of the traditional formats and rules that you probably are already using.

Migrating Existing Modules

The majority of modules and functions should be directly compatible with SOAP without too many modifications—after all, we are dealing only with functions that accept arguments and return values. However, therein lies a small trap: Functions called by a SOAP handler accept the class or module in which they were called as their first argument.

This extra initial argument leads to a small problem. If your module is one that you are already using in another local application, then the modifications that you make must be nondestructive.

There are two ways around this. The first is to modify your scripts to silently ignore the first argument if it contains the name of the module from a SOAP client. This is easy for some functions because they accept a specific number of arguments, and you can identify when one too many exists.

A more complex but much more practical solution is to create a glue module that supports the same functions but strips the first element. You use the glue module with the SOAP client. For example, to support an existing module called Conversion that provides a function convert_qty(), you'd create a glue module such as the one shown in Listing 15.13.

Listing 15.13: A Glue Module for Providing Access to an Existing Module

```perl
package SOAP::Conversion;

use Conversion;

sub convert_qty
{
    my $class = shift;
    return Conversion::convert_qty(@_);
}
```

Using a glue module not only solves the problems of that additional function argument, it will also enable you to customize the arguments you accept and the return structure, all without making any modifications to your existing module.

DEBUGGING *SOAP::LITE*

Unfortunately, because of the complexity of the SOAP system, problems are notoriously difficult to diagnose and isolate. The problem could be related to how the function was called or how the server and dispatcher were configured, or it could be a transport problem completely unrelated to the operation of SOAP itself. Something as simple as the wrong hostname could cause your SOAP client to fail.

Avoiding Problems

Prevention is always better than cure, so it's worth taking some time to look at the potential problems (and solutions) that many SOAP::Lite programmers encounter.

With SOAP::Lite, the important elements in the client and server process are

▶ The uri() method (as part of the client initialization), which defines the name of the module (including any parent modules/directories) that contains the function we want to execute.

▶ The proxy() method (as part of the client initialization), which defines the name of the request handler that will actually broker the function call.

► The dispatch_to() function and its arguments (in the request handler), which define the location of the modules to be called and the optional list of modules and functions that the handler is willing to process.

► The location and name of the module that you want to call as defined on the server side.

If any one of these elements is incorrect, your SOAP system will fail. In particular, make sure that you've correctly aligned the URI, the module registration in the request handler, and the name of the module itself.

For example, in our sample system, the URI ends with SOAP/Demo, the package is SOAP::Demo, and the request handler accepts requests for the SOAP::Demo module. Requesting simply Demo in the client would cause the request to fail. If you execute the client program and don't get a valid response from the remote function, then it probably means one of these elements is wrong.

Diagnosing Problems

Two possible solutions are available for diagnosing. The first and most obvious is to use the facilities offered by SOAP::Lite to identify and highlight errors as part of any normal error-checking procedure. By default, all clients will die with a suitable message when an error occurs due to the transport, but they will do nothing if the function and/or module that you have called does not exist.

The second solution is to use the interactive SOAP shell to communicate with your remote proxy handler and submit requests to a remote function interactively.

Adding Error Checking

Error-handling information is held within the return value sent back by the remote function. The return value from the remote function call is actually an object that contains additional information about the success or failure of the result, as well as the result from the remote function. Up to now we've accessed only the actual function result, which is held in the result attribute.

If you change the client script shown in Listing 15.2 so that we access the object rather than the result directly, you can get more information about why the operation failed. You can see a modified version of the script in Listing 15.14.

Listing 15.14: A Client Script with Error Checking

```
use SOAP::Lite;

my $request = SOAP::Lite
    ->uri('http://test.mchome.pri/SOAP/Demo')
    ->proxy('http://test.mchome.pri/SOAP/
request.cgi');

$result = $request->getmessage();

if ($result->fault)
{
    printf("SOAP Error: %s: %s\n\t%s\n",
            $result->faultcode,
            $result->faultstring,
            $result->faultdetail);
}
else
{
    print $result->result,"\n";
}
```

The faultcode always starts with a probable location for the error, such as Client, Server, and so on. The two most common problems are

► Client: Failed to locate method (%s) in class (%s)—You've tried to call a method that the request handler can't find in the module you've requested. This usually points to a typographical error in your client code.

► Client: Failed to access class (%s)—The class you've specified can't be found. Check that the URI the client has requested is valid and that the request handler has the correct directory configured for the class you are trying to access.

Because transport errors are raised by calling die, the only way to trap them reliably is to embed your remote function call in an eval(). The actual error message raised when the problem occurs will be that raised by the transport—when using HTTP or CGI transport, for example, you will have HTTP error codes returned. A full list of the different error codes can usually be found with your Web server.

Examples of error codes include a 404, which indicates that you've probably specified the wrong proxy address, and a 403, which might indicate either a permission problem or incorrect permissions on the request handler. An HTTP error code 500 probably means that there's an error in the request handler—try running the handler locally.

The SOAP Shell

The SOAP shell is installed by SOAP::Lite and provides a shell-like interface to a SOAP request handler. The basic format of the command is

```
SOAPsh.pl proxy [uri [commands...]]
```

For example, we can try using our demo function by using

```
$ SOAPsh.pl http://test.mchome.pri/SOAP/request.cgi
➥http://test.mchome.pri/SOAP/Demo
Usage: method[(parameters)]
> getmessage()
-- SOAP RESULT --
'Hello, world'


>
```

We could deliberately break our request handler by changing the dispatch location:

```
> getmessage
-- SOAP FAULT --
SOAP-ENV:Client
Failed to access class (SOAP::Demo): Can't locate
SOAP/Demo.pm in @INC
➥(@INC contains: /export/http/webs/test/OtherEx)
➥at (eval 5) line 3.
```

USING XML-RPC

The SOAP::Lite package includes support for XML-RPC through the XMLRPC::Lite package. Users familiar with how SOAP::Lite works shouldn't have any difficulties developing XML-RPC–compliant clients and servers. As an example, Listing 15.15 shows an XML-RPC client.

Listing 15.15: An XML-RPC Client

```
use XMLRPC::Lite;

$remote =  XMLRPC::Lite
    -> proxy('http://test.mchome.pri/xml.cgi');

print $remote->call('greet', { username =>
➥'Martin' })
    -> result;

print $remote->call('goodbye', 'Brown')
    -> result;
```

In essence, the mechanics of the two systems are identical. XMLRPC::Lite attempts to hide the complexities of XML-RPC as much as SOAP::Lite tries to hide the complexities of SOAP.

The proxy method specifies the URL that we want to use to send the request. In this instance, we're using a CGI host, but we can also use an HTTP daemon—just remove the reference to the CGI script. Also note that the URL is strictly the location of a server-side handling script—it bears no relation to any module at the receiving end.

Note as well that we use the call() method to specify the function to be called (the first argument, in this case greet) rather than naming the function directly as part of the call. This is less straightforward than the SOAP method, but it may be more practical when you know the function by its name and don't want to use soft references to execute the function.

The server script that will handle the requests is shown in Listing 15.16.

Listing 15.16: An XML-RPC Server Handler

```
#!/usr/local/bin/perl

use XMLRPC::Transport::HTTP;

my $server = XMLRPC::Transport::HTTP::CGI
    -> dispatch_to('methodName')
    -> handle;

BEGIN { @main::ISA = 'XMLRPC::Server::Parameters' }

sub methodName
{
```

```perl
    my $self = shift;
    my $method = $_[-1]->method;

    return $self->$method(@_);
}

sub greet
{
    shift if UNIVERSAL::isa($_[0] => __PACKAGE__);

    my ($params) = shift;

    $username = $params->{username};

    return "Hello $username";
}

sub goodbye
{
    shift if UNIVERSAL::isa($_[0] => __PACKAGE__);

    pop @_;

    return "Goodbye @_";
}
```

The most important point to notice from the server script is that the dispatch() method sends the request to a single, local function. In this case, it's called methodName, but it could be any function. It's up to the methodName function to handle the requests, first extracting the name of the method that was called by the client, which is available in the method attribute of the supplied parameters. We then pass off control to the called function.

The second point to note is that we are not—indirectly or otherwise—passing control to an external module. The Perl SOAP implementation is designed to work with external modules; when a function is called, the handler executes the function from an external module. This is because the SOAP protocol itself was designed to work with classes and objects, which in Perl are better organized in separate modules. XML-RPC, on the other hand, is designed to execute a remote procedure, which could be defined locally or in an external module.

WHERE NEXT WITH *SOAP::LITE* AND XML-RPC

SOAP and XML-RPC are XML applications—they use XML to exchange information between servers and clients about the remote function and arguments and to supply the return values. You can use XML-RPC and SOAP in any situation where you need to communicate with a remote server but don't want to produce your own protocol or rely on the features of another protocol.

We've only scratched the surface just to show you what SOAP and XML-RPC are capable of and, more important, what we can achieve using XML above and beyond the examples that we've already seen.

SOAP and XML-RPC projects and services are popping up all over the Internet right now, and it's easy to see that in a few years we'll be using the distributed offerings of SOAP and XML-RPC in the same way as we use traditional client/server solutions now. It will certainly put an end to incompatibility problems when exchanging data between remote machines—part of the main focus of the XML protocol as a whole.

SUMMARY

We can communicate remotely with a Perl script by hosting it on a Web server and sending and receiving requests. We could also do so through the use of a communications system such as Graham Barr's libnet bundle (http://mysite.directlink.net/gbarr/perl-ldap/). However, neither method provides a simple solution to calling a remote function or object method over a network.

The SOAP and XML-RPC systems provide a more elegant solution to the problem. The SOAP::Lite module is one of the easiest to use of all the solutions we'll see in this book. It provides an almost transparent interface between a remote server and the client. In fact, when using the autodispatch mode, once you've specified in the client what server to communicate with, you'll never have to worry about explicitly executing a remote function again.

On the server side, SOAP::Lite also enables you to support access to all the modules in a directory, specific modules, and even specific functions. The system also supports the creation of objects and calling methods.

A less object-oriented approach, but one that is nonetheless still useful, is the XML-RPC solution supported by the XMLRPC module. The module provides support for both client and server XML-RPC solutions, but it requires much more care when setting up the client and server sides of the solution.

In the next chapter, we'll take a look at XML solutions in Python, which will provide the foundation for yet another SOAP/XML-RPC implementation, which will be covered in Chapter 18, "Applying SOAP/XML-RPC in Python."

Chapter 16

XML Solutions in Python

Although Python has only recently come to people's consciousness, the language has been around almost as long as Perl. Python's background is in all sorts of fields, although it's often used in numerical situations because of its strong long integer and complex number handling. Companies that use Python in a variety of situations include NASA and ILM (Industrial Light & Magic, the people behind the special effects in films such as *Star Wars*).

This is unfortunate, because Python has as good an interface for handling XML as Perl and many other languages. For dedicated Python programmers, the XML parser becomes even easier to use because the object model used by Python for all its objects is often used to model XML documents internally, particularly when using DOM.

Adapted from *XML Processing with Perl™, Python, and PHP*, by Martin C. Brown

ISBN 0-7821-4021-1   400 pages $49.99

Python's XML support is probably one of the most complex of the different solutions available, largely because of the way in which the different XML parsers have been developed. The original XML parsing system provided with Python 1.5.2 is called xmllib, and it comes as standard with all Python distributions. xmllib was developed on the same basis as the sgmllib module, which provides SGML parsing tools.

The xmllib parser is both a simple validation parser and an event-driven data parser that provides the base methods for you to use to parse an XML document. To use it, you need to create a new class that inherits from the xmllib module, providing the necessary methods to trap start and end tags, data sections, and entities.

Python 2.0 introduced a completely new hierarchy of modules and packages for developing with XML. The base xml package now includes xml.dom for processing using the DOM, xml.sax for providing an event-driven parser, and xml.parsers.expat for an interface to the generic Expat parser used by many other languages. In addition, the xmllib module is still available as part of the standard Python library, but its use and support have been deprecated in favor of the superior xml.sax package.

THE *XMLLIB* MODULE

Python has had a long history of supporting parsers for HTML and SGML. Some four years ago a developer I know was using sgmllib in combination with a suite of custom tools to manage the technical documentation for QNX, Inc., a company that develops a real-time Unix-like operating system.

The only problem with Python's SGML support is that it is somewhat limited. In fact, the sgmllib module was designed to support only enough of the SGML standard to be able to handle HTML. This prevented the use of document type definitions (DTDs) and many of the extensions used in SGML that make it attractive. However, it was possible to subclass the sgmllib parser to support the extensions and facilities needed.

The xmllib module is actually quite advanced—it tries to support the entire XML standard and while reading the document performs basic checks on the document structure. These include the basics of checking that the tags balance and that the document is based entirely on a single top-level element.

Unfortunately, xmllib has now been pushed aside in favor of xml.sax, which provides a more standardized event-drive method for parsing XML documents. This doesn't mean that xmllib is now useless, but you should probably avoid using it for production systems because it will no longer be updated in future Python releases.

For us, it's going to form the basis of understanding XML processing with Python before we concentrate on the Expat, SAX, and DOM solutions now recommended. They all work in a largely similar fashion, and xmllib's simplicity will help you understand how the other systems work.

Understanding *XMLParser*

The main part of xmllib is the XMLParser class. The class contains all of the methods required to parse a document, in addition to a series of methods designed to handle different XML content.

To create your own parser, you create a new class based on the XMLParser class, overloading the methods that identify the different elements you want to extract. For example, if you wanted to parse an XML document and identify start and end tags and any raw data, you would overload the unknown_starttag and unknown_endtag methods.

You can see a sample of a basic parser class in Listing 16.1. The resulting script parses the first XML document on the command line. Because we haven't defined any of the other methods, this script merely allows the xmllib parser to check the validity of the XML it's supplied.

Listing 16.1: An Example of *XMLParser*

```
import xmllib,sys

# Create a new class from which we'll
# inherit the base
# methods and parser system we need
class MyParser(xmllib.XMLParser):

    # The instance creator - we need to manually
    # call the initiator for the parent class
    def __init__(self, filename=None):
        xmllib.XMLParser.__init__(self)
        if filename:
            self.loadfile(filename)
```

```
        # Load a file, based on the supplied filename
        # feeding the information to the XML parser
        def loadfile(self, filename):
            xmlfile = open(filename)
            while 1:
                data = xmlfile.read(1024)
                if not data:
                    break
                self.feed(data)
            self.close()

# Get the first argument from the command line
try:
    filename = sys.argv[1]
except IndexError:
    print "You must supply a filename"
    sys.exit(1)

# Create a new MyParser instance and parse the
# file supplied on the command line
# We ignore EOFError's, which just indicate the
# end of file
# The xmllib.Error exception is raised by xmllib's
# parser when an error occurs
try:
    parser = MyParser(sys.argv[1])
except EOFError:
    pass
except xmllib.Error,data:
    print "There was an error in the XML:",data
    sys.exit(1)
except:
    print "Something went wrong"
    sys.exit(1)

# Assuming we haven't trapped an exception, then the
# XML has been validated
print "Everything appears to be fine"
```

The script works very simply: The loadfile() method opens a file and reads the contents, supplying each batch of information to the feed() method defined within the xmllib.XMLParser class. The feed() method passes on information directly to the actual parsing engine. The parsing engine uses regular expressions to extract XML tags and information from the source data stream.

Because we haven't overloaded any of the methods responsible for handling XML tags and data, nothing happens—although they are defined within the XMLParser class, their default operation is to do nothing.

Supply the script with a valid XML document and we get a message to the effect that everything is okay:

```
$ python exxmllib.py alien_r.xml

Everything seems fine
```

However, supply it with a badly formatted XML document and we get an error, trapped through the xmllib.Error exception raised by the parser:

```
$ python exxmllib.py faulty.xml

There was an error in the XML: Syntax error at line 3: missing
end tags
```

Identifying XML Elements

To change the script to identify the different elements, we just need to overload the unknown_starttag() and unknown_endtag() methods for the start and end tags and the handle_data() method to handle the bare text data within the XML document. You can see an example of this in Listing 16.2.

Listing 16.2: A Simple XML Parser Using xmllib

```
import xmllib,sys

# Create a new class from which we'll inherit the
# base methods and parser system we need
class MyParser(xmllib.XMLParser):

    # The instance creator - we need to manually
    # call the initiator for the parent class
    def __init__(self, filename=None):
        xmllib.XMLParser.__init__(self)
        if filename:
            self.loadfile(filename)
```

Part iv

```python
        # Load a file, based on the supplied filename
        # feeding the information to the XML parser
        def loadfile(self, filename):
            xmlfile = open(filename)
            while 1:
                data = xmlfile.read(1024)
                if not data:
                    break
                self.feed(data)
            self.close()

        # Called when a start tag is found
        def unknown_starttag(self, tag, attrs):
            print "Start: ",tag, attrs

        # Called when an end tag is found
        def unknown_endtag(self, tag):
            print "End:    ",tag

        # Called when raw data is found
        def handle_data(self, data):
            print "Data:    ",data

# Get the first argument from the command line
try:
    filename = sys.argv[1]
except IndexError:
    print "You must supply a filename"
    sys.exit(1)


# Create a new MyParser instance and parse the
# file supplied on the command line
# We ignore EOFError's, which just indicate the
# end of file
# The xmllib.Error exception is raised by xmllib's
# parser when an error occurs
try:
    parser = MyParser(sys.argv[1])
except EOFError:
    pass
except xmllib.Error,data:
    print "There was an error in the XML:",data
    sys.exit(1)
```

```
except:
    print "Something went wrong"
    sys.exit(1)

print "Everything seems fine"
```

Now, each time the parser identifies either a start tag, end tag, or raw data, it calls the corresponding method. In our case, the methods just print out the information received (tag, attributes, or data). Now if we execute the script and supply it with an XML document, we get the following:

```
$ python exxmllib2.py simple.xml
Start:  simple {}
Data:

Start:  paragraph {}
Data:   and some data
End:    paragraph
Data:

End:    simple
Everything seems fine
```

Beyond *xmllib*

This concludes our brief look at xmllib. We probably won't be using xmllib again, but the basic principles shown here can also be followed for the Expat and SAX implementations we will be using. Use of xmllib is now deprecated in favor of the other systems.

However, the basics described here apply to the other solutions available in Python because they follow the same basic structure. The xmllib module is also a useful fallback if you need to support XML on production systems currently using Python 1.5.2 or 1.6.

PARSING USING EXPAT

Expat, as we've already seen in Chapter 14, "XML Solutions in Perl," is a non-validating XML parser written in C by James Clark. Like xmllib (and SAX), it's event driven, parsing individual XML constructs and using callbacks to initiate the processing of individual start and end tags and data portions.

Part iv

To use Expat in Python, we need to import the `xml.parsers.expat` module. The module supports one main function, `ParserCreate()`, which creates an instance of the Expat parser that we can use to parse XML documents.

It's probably easiest to create a new class into which you put all the methods you need to use, including those that will be triggered when different XML constructs are seen. It's not a requirement, but it does keep the system nice and tidy. Unlike `xmllib`, however, we don't inherit the methods from the parent class but use them directly. Rather than overloading the methods to handle the different XML elements, we register the functions to the base parser.

For example, Listing 16.3 is a script that mimics our second `xmllib` example.

Listing 16.3: An Expat Version of Our Simple XML Parser

```
import xml.parsers.expat
import sys

# Create a new class to hold all the methods that
# we want to use when parsing an XML document
class MyParser:

    # Instance constructor. We create a
    # new parser instance
    # which we hold locally in parser, then we
    # register the different methods which will
    # handle the XML elements
    def __init__(self, filename):
        self.parser = xml.parsers.expat.
        ➥ParserCreate()
        self.parser.StartElementHandler =
        ➥self.starttag_handler
        self.parser.EndElementHandler =
        ➥self.endtag_handler
        self.parser.CharacterDataHandler =
        ➥self.data_handler
        if filename:
            self.loadfile(filename)

    # Kills off and deletes the parser instance once
    # the processing of a given XML file is complete
```

```python
    # To ensure we get rid of circular references we
    # must delete the parser reference
    def close(self):
        if self.parser:
            self.parser.Parse('',1)
            del self.parser

    # Hand off some data to the parser
    def feed(self, data):
        self.parser.Parse(data, 0)

    # Called when a start tag is found
    def starttag_handler(self, tag, attrs):
        print 'Start: ',repr(tag), attrs

    # Called when an end tag is found
    def endtag_handler(self, tag):
        print 'End:   ',repr(tag)

    # Called when a data portion is found
    def data_handler(self, data):
        print 'Data:  ',repr(data)

    # Load a file and supply the info to the parser
    def loadfile(self, filename):
        xmlfile = open(filename)
        while 1:
            data = xmlfile.read(1024)
            if not data:
                break
            self.feed(data)
        self.close()


try:
    filename = sys.argv[1]
except IndexError:
    print "You must supply a filename"
    sys.exit(1)

try:
    parser = MyParser(sys.argv[1])
```

```
except xml.parsers.expat.ExpatError:
    print "Error in XML"
except:
    print "Some other error occurred"
```

If we use this on our sample document, we should get output similar to that in the xmllib example:

```
$ python exexpat.py simple.xml
Start:  u'simple' {}
Data:   u'\n'
Start:  u'paragraph' {}
Data:   u'and some data'
End:    u'paragraph'
Data:   u'\n'
End:    u'simple'
```

NOTE

The output differs slightly from that given by xmllib; that's because the Expat parser works with Unicode strings, rather than ASCII strings. We'll be looking more closely at how Python works with Unicode and how to encode and decode between Unicode strings and other types in Chapter 17, "Python and Unicode."

PARSING USING SAX

The Simple API for XML (SAX) interface was originally developed under Java, although interfaces now exist under most languages. Python 2 supports SAX version 2 (or more simply SAX2), and the interface is extensive. Python provides the basic interface to the SAX parser, an exception-handling system, a set of base classes for creating SAX handlers, and a low-level interface to the SAX system for building your own low-level SAX-based parsers.

SAX works by accepting a content handler class that you have previously created to handle the different elements. The method is similar in principle to Expat, except that the class you create is entirely devoted to supporting the handler methods for the different elements. SAX handles all of the data reading and feeding of the information to the parser.

Keeping with the basic theme for the moment, Listing 16.4 is a script that uses SAX to output the start and end tags from a sample file.

Listing 16.4: A Simple SAX Parser

```python
from xml.sax import make_parser
from xml.sax.handler import ContentHandler

# Define a new content handler class, the
# defined methods will be triggered when the
# individual elements are found in the XML document
class FindStartEnd(ContentHandler):
    def __init__(self):
        pass
    def startElement(self, name, attrs):
        print 'Start: ', name, attrs
    def endElement(self, name):
        print 'End:   ', name

# Make a new parser
parser = make_parser()

# Create a new handler instance based on our class
sehandler = FindStartEnd()

# Set up the content handler for using our handler
parser.setContentHandler(sehandler)

import sys

try:
    xmlfile = open(sys.argv[1])
except:
    print "You must supply the name of the file
➡to parse"
    sys.exit(1)

# We pass off the name of the file to
# the parsing engine
parser.parse(xmlfile)
```

Aside from not printing out our data sections, the output from this script is identical to the previous examples. Also note that we no longer have to supply the data in discrete segments to the parser: The SAX interface opens a file by name and handles all of the reading internally.

Because of the way SAX works, it's ideally suited to situations where we want to pick out specific elements while processing a document. For example, we can install triggers to identify specific tags and/or data sections in a simpler way than offered by the DOM techniques we'll see in the next portion of this chapter.

SAX can also be a great way of serializing documents into another format because we can act on each element as it's extracted from the original XML source. We'll be looking at some examples of using SAX in this way in Chapter 18, "Applying SOAP/XML-RPC in Python."

Parsing Using DOM

The Document Object Model (DOM) allows you to model an XML document as a tree structure. In fact, the entire document is accessible as a series of objects, and by following the branches of the tree, you can traverse the entire document. Because we are representing the XML document in one piece, we can use DOM both to parse existing documents and to create new documents.

The only problem with using DOM is that it stores the entire document in memory. For the small documents we're working with here, this won't be a problem, but a 512KB document may require up to five times that amount when it's stored internally as a DOM object. Of course, in Python we don't have to worry about allocating the memory, but that also means that we run the risk of using large quantities of memory without realizing it.

Under Python the DOM interface is based on the IDL version of the specification released by W3C. The standard Python 2.x distribution comes with a basic DOM parsing system, called `minidom`, and a more complex `pulldom` system that extracts individual elements from a DOM tree without having to read the entire XML document into memory.

Because of Python's flexible object system, it's very easy to create an equivalent of the tree structure that an XML document mirrors within a Python object. Coupled with the easy object-handling features (especially when working with dictionaries and lists), we have a good platform for handling XML documents.

Using *minidom*

To parse an existing XML document into a DOM object using `minidom`, you need to call either the `parse()` method, which accepts a filename or file object and processes the contents, or `parseString()`, which parses a bare string of information that you may have read separately from a file or network connection. In fact, it's as easy as this:

```python
from xml.dom.minidom import parse, parseString


# Parse a bare string as XML


stringdoc = parseString('<para>Some text</para>')


# Parse a file object


xmlfile1 = open('myfile.xml')
filedoc = parse(xmlfile1)


# Parse a file directly


filedoc = parse('myfile.xml')
```

Once you've converted the XML stream into a DOM object, you can then access the individual tags by name. For example, suppose that we've modeled a client's bank accounts in XML, as shown in Listing 16.5.

Listing 16.5: A Sample Account Record

```xml
<client>
<clientname>Martin Brown</clientname>
<account>
    <accname>Checking</accname>
    <provider>HSBC</provider>
    <balance>$4567.00</balance>
    <transaction>
        <payee>Rent</payee>
        <amount>$280.00</amount>
        <freq>Monthly</freq>
    </transaction>
    <transaction>
```

```
            <payee>Time Subscription</payee>
            <amount>$26.00</amount>
            <freq>Quarterly</freq>
        </transaction>
    </account>

    <account>
        <accname>VISA</accname>
        <provider>Morgan Dean Stanley Witter</provider>
        <balance>$-3485.00</balance>
        <transaction>
            <payee>Supermarket</payee>
            <amount>$-450.00</amount>
        </transaction>
        <transaction>
            <payee>Gas Station</payee>
            <amount>$-18.00</amount>
        </transaction>
    </account>
</client>
```

The document could be represented as a tree structure, as shown in Figure 16.1. We'll be using this diagram to help us understand how Python's DOM implementation works.

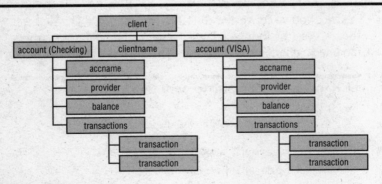

FIGURE 16.1: An XML tree

We could get the name of the client who owns the account information using Listing 16.6.

Listing 16.6: Extracting Content from an XML Document Using `minidom`

```python
from xml.dom.minidom import parse

# Create a function to get the data between
# XML tags. Information is held in nodes
# (discrete blocks) which we'll need to concatenate
# together to get the full picture.
# We only need to add text nodes to the
# string
def getdata(nodes):
    rc = ''
    for node in nodes:
        if node.nodeType == node.TEXT_NODE:
            rc = rc + node.data
    return rc

# Parse the document
client = parse('client.xml')

# Get the first clientname tag from the document
clientname = client.getElementsByTagName
➥("clientname")[0]

# Print out the data contained within the tags
# using getdata to extract the text from the nodes
# defined within the element
print 'Client name is', getdata(clientname.
➥childNodes)
```

The getElementsByTagName() method returns a list of *all* the tag elements with the supplied name. The resulting objects contain the information about the tag, including any attributes if supplied, and a set of nodes that make up the data contained within the tags.

Note that the object returned by getElementsByTagName()is a branch (or leaf) of the tree structure shown in Figure 16.1. The root of the tree is the first (root) tag within the document—so to access all the elements within the XML document, we'd have to access the client branch. From that base, we can then access the other elements. For example, to extract the data from the clientname branch, we must refer to the branch in reference to its parent, the client branch. Further branches and leaves are referenced in the same way, relative to their parent branches.

Had we used this:

```
accounts = client.getElementsByTagName("account")
```

the `accounts` object would now be a list containing the two account branches. Each element would refer to one of the account branches in our diagram. To get a list of the transactions within the checking account, we could have used this:

```
checking = accounts[0]
trans = checking.getElementsByTagName("transaction")
```

Now `trans` would contain the information in the two transactions in our account. Each element would be one of the transaction branches.

DOM in Action

To put all of this into practice, Listing 16.7 is a script that uses DOM to generate a simple list of accounts and transactions for a given client. The script is actually a good example of a tree-based XML parser in Python. Because we're not following the tree sequentially, we can be a little less restrictive about how we extract information: We don't have to worry about recording states or determining whether the output format should change because we've reached a particular end tag.

Listing 16.7: Using `minidom` to Summarize an XML Document

```python
from xml.dom.minidom import parse

def getdata(nodes):
    rc = ''
    for node in nodes:
        if node.nodeType == node.TEXT_NODE:
            rc = rc + node.data
    return rc

def handleclient(client):
    clientname = client.getElementsByTagName
➡("clientname")[0]
    print 'Client:', getdata(clientname.childNodes)
    accounts = client.getElementsByTagName
➡("account")
    handleaccounts(accounts)

def handleaccounts(accounts):
```

```
            print 'Accounts:'
            for account in accounts:
                handleaccount(account)

        def handleaccount(account):
            accname = account.getElementsByTagName
        ➥("accname")[0]
            provider = account.getElementsByTagName
        ➥("provider")[0]
            print ' ' * 4, '%s (%s)' % (getdata
        ➥(accname.childNodes),
                                    . getdata
        ➥(provider.childNodes))
            print ' ' * 4, 'Transactions:'
            trans = account.getElementsByTagName
        ➥("transaction")
            for transaction in trans:
                handletransaction(transaction)
            balance = account.getElementsByTagName
        ➥("balance")[0]
            print ' ' * 9, '%-40s %s' % ('', '======')
            print ' ' * 9, '%-40s %s' % ('',
        ➥getdata(balance.childNodes))
            print ''

        def handletransaction(transaction):
            payee = transaction.getElementsByTagName
        ➥("payee")[0]
            amount = transaction.getElementsByTagName
        ➥("amount")[0]
            print ' ' * 9, '%-40s %s' %
        ➥(getdata(payee.childNodes),

        ➥getdata(amount.childNodes))

        client = parse('client.xml')

        handleclient(client)
```

If we run this script on our client XML document, we get the following output:

```
$ python exdom2.py
Client: Martin Brown
```

```
Accounts:
    Checking (HSBC)
    Transactions:
        Rent                    $280.00
        Time Subscription       $26.00

                                ======

                                $4567.00


    VISA (Morgan Dean Stanley Witter)
    Transactions:
        Supermarket             $-450.00
        Gas Station             $-18.00

                                ======

                                $-3485.00
```

We could have just as easily converted this document into HTML or XHTML or extracted the information easily for writing into the individual tables of a database.

Building XML Documents with DOM

You can write XML documents just by including the necessary print or similar statement in your script, but it relies on generating the tags in the correct order and structure and ensuring that they are matched up. Although this is not an impossible task, it does add extra levels of complexity to the process.

Simple serialization from one format into XML is easy if the information is in sequence and you convert directly into an XML document following the same structure. But what happens if you need to add new branches within the existing structure, or the definition of the XML document requires you to organize the information into a given structure that doesn't match your source material?

The immediately obvious solution is either to separately model the incoming data into a more suitable format before translating it to XML or to cache information into one or more objects and dump them at appropriate times. Neither solution is infallible, and both are entirely reliant on getting the information correctly and in the order you expect in the first place.

A much better solution is at hand, though. The Document Object Model specification is really just a method for modeling XML documents within the confines of a programming language or other system. Up to now, we've used the system only to model an external XML document into an internal tree to extract information.

We can also use DOM to build an XML document by creating the branches and leaves of the document. Because DOM is not a sequential system such as SAX or Expat, we can add new branches and leaves to any part of the document without making modifications to the XML document in its raw text format.

The xml.dom.minidom module supports a very simple interface for adding new XML tags and data to an XML document. For a quick example, see Listing 16.8, which adds both a text block and a tag to a previously parsed XML string.

Listing 16.8: Rebuilding an XML Document

```
from xml.dom.minidom import parseString

dom = parseString('<title></title>')
root = dom.documentElement
nelem = dom.createElement("separator")

root.insertBefore(nelem, None)
cdata = dom.createTextNode("The New Avengers")
root.insertBefore(cdata, nelem)
print root.toxml()
```

The start of the process is to create the equivalent of the blank root document as a DOM object by using the parseString() function to parse a string in XML format into an object.

Then we get the root of the document and create a new element, separator. The insertBefore() method in our document then inserts the element according to its reference location. In this case, we're inserting the element with reference to None, which will insert the tag between the root title tags in our original XML string. The createTextNode() method creates a new block of text that we'll insert before the element we just created.

Part iv

Finally, the `toxml()` method returns the entire DOM structure as an XML string that we print out. Executing the script gives us a very simple document in return:

```
$ python dombuild.py
<title>The New Avengers<separator/></title>
```

Although this is simplistic, it demonstrates how easy it is to insert new tags and text data anywhere within a given DOM tree.

SUMMARY

XML processing in Python is relatively easy. Once you've selected the type of processing that you want to use, it's then a simple case of importing, or in some cases inheriting from, the supporting module. From then on, sequential parsing involves handing off the XML document data and supplying it to the data input of the class we're using.

The `xmllib` module is not the ideal module any longer, but it is the only solution available if you want to guarantee support for older versions of the Python interpreter. For the ultimate in XML parsing in a sequential format, the best solution is the Expat parser, a standard part of the Python distribution since version 2. Expat offers a familiar event-based interface that is supported by a number of different languages.

For more advanced event-based parsing, you should use the SAX parser. Python's SAX module works identically to the Expat and `xmllib` systems, so migration to SAX should not be difficult. The benefit of SAX is that it is a standard agreed upon by the XML standards group, so we can pass information and events both to Python and other language interfaces.

The more flexible option is to use the DOM system. This uses SAX as the base parser to build the DOM object, but once we have the XML document in DOM format, we have more freedom about how to access the tags and data within. We can access elements in the document by name, and if necessary we can also replace and even rebuild parts of the document without having to manipulate any text.

The next chapter, "Python and Unicode" will explore some of Python's capabilities with Unicode, which is an important encoding mechanism in XML and modern programming environments because of its support for global human languages. Then Chapter 18, "Applying SOAP/XML-RPC in Python," will cover Python's role in the emerging world of Web services.

Chapter 17

PYTHON AND UNICODE

As part of the major update that brought much wider support for XML—including a native interface to the Expat parser—Python 2.0 also brought extensive Unicode support. Along with the capability to introduce Unicode and raw Unicode strings, Python now includes facilities for encoding and decoding Unicode and the translation of Unicode characters.

In addition, most of the core modules are also Unicode compliant, so you can execute regular expressions, character manipulations, and other translations using Unicode character strings without needing to resort to a special collection of Unicode functions.

XML Processing with Perl, Python, and PHP

Adapted from *XML Processing with Perl™, Python, and PHP*, by Martin C. Brown

ISBN 0-7821-4021-1   400 pages $49.99

In this chapter, we'll look at how to work with Unicode strings in Python, including creating Unicode and translating it between different formats, as well as methods for looking up Unicode characters and even creating your own Unicode encoder. Armed with this information, you should be able to handle Unicode data within Python and know how to format and encode the information for display or storage.

CREATING UNICODE STRINGS

Rather than supporting Unicode strings natively—as supported by Perl—Python instead supports a new data type: Unicode strings. You can create a new Unicode object by prefixing a string with the letter u, in the same way that you introduce raw strings. For example:

```
>>> u'Hello World'
u'Hello World'
>>> u'Hello\0020World'
u'Hello World'
```

To include special (non-native) characters into the Unicode object, use the Unicode escape, \u. This introduces the character according to the supplied hexadecimal value. In the previous example, we introduced the Unicode character with the hexadecimal value of 20—the space character, which as you can see has been interpreted accordingly in our example. Here's another example, this time inserting a lowercase *o* with a stroke or slash (in other words, ø) into a Unicode string:

```
message = u'J\u00f8rgensen'
```

All other characters are converted according to the Latin-1 encoding. See the section "Translating Unicode" later in this chapter for information on translating a Unicode string to another format. Note that on platforms and systems that support it, the Unicode string conversion will also translate non-ASCII characters into Unicode. For example, on a Mac, introducing accented and other foreign characters is a built-in part of the operating system, so we can insert these characters directly into a u-prefixed string:

```
>>> u'øåé'
u'\xbf\x8c\x8e'
```

To introduce a raw Unicode string, use the `ur` prefix when creating the Unicode object. For example:

```
>>> ur'Rikke\u0020J\u00f8rgensen'
u'Rikke J\u00f8rgensen'
```

Raw Unicode strings work in the same way as their raw string cousins—they exist to enable us to introduce strings that may contain information that we don't want translated or interpreted. As with raw strings, this is especially useful when you're using Unicode strings within regular expressions. In these instances, Unicode escape sequences are interpreted only when there is an off number of backslashes in front of a small u character. You can see this more clearly in the following:

```
>>> ur'\\u0020'
u'\\\\u0020'
>>> ur'\u0020'
u' '
>>> u'\\\u0020'
u'\\\\ '
```

Obviously, as we've already seen, the old `xmllib` module in Python extracts only raw text—it's not Unicode compliant. However, the new SAX, DOM, and Expat interfaces all support Unicode extraction. In the case of Expat and SAX, the information is returned in the form of Unicode objects.

TRANSLATING UNICODE

Most of the time, you'll probably be parsing content in Unicode. It's unlikely that you'll want to deal with Unicode objects all of the time when you're working with data from an XML document.

At the most basic level, you can mix and match Unicode and normal Python string sequences, but the result will always be another Unicode object. For example:

```
>>> 'Hello ' + u'Miss J\u00f8rgensen'
u'Hello Miss J\xf8rgensen'
```

To convert a Unicode object back into a normal ASCII (7-bit) string, use the built-in `str()` function:

```
>>> str(u'Hello World')
'Hello World'
```

Be careful, however, with Unicode strings that are not ASCII compatible. The str() function will raise an error if you try to convert a string that contains non-ASCII characters. For example:

```
>>> greet=u'Miss J\u00f8rgensen'
>>> str(greet)
Traceback (most recent call last):
  File "<stdin>", line 1, in ?
UnicodeError: ASCII encoding error: ordinal
➥not in range(128)
```

Note that this applies however you access the string, even when extracting characters from a Unicode string individually. For example, the following code will still raise an error:

```
for char in u'Miss J\u00f8rgensen':
    print char,
```

NOTE

Errors in encoding and/or decoding strings raise a UnicodeError exception, which can be trapped in the same way as any other exception. The exception supplies the error message as the only argument.

Encoding to Unicode Formats

ASCII is not the most useful of formats. You can translate a Unicode string into one of a number of different using encode(). encode() changes the encoding used to represent the Unicode object directly into another character set, such as Latin-1 or UTF-8. The method takes a single argument—the encoding type that you want to translate the Unicode string to. In fact, the encode() method is what is called when the str() built-in function is used on a Unicode object, supplying the encoding type as ASCII.

Latin-1 encoding, which supports the first 256 characters provided in the 8-bit ASCII table, can be used for most string representations, as in our earlier example:

```
>>> greet = u'Rikke J\u00f8rgensen'
>>> greet.encode('latin-1')
'Rikke Jørgensen'
```

Reproduction of that on screen will of course rely on you having a font, application, and operating system that adhere to the Unicode standard!

A classic example here is the Mac OS, which doesn't directly support the Unicode standard. To get the same effect when writing to a standard Mac document or to the screen, you'll need to use mac-roman encoding.

The encode() method can also be used to encode your Unicode object into one of the native Unicode encoding formats, such as UTF-8 or UTF-16. For example, to encode our sample string, you'd use the following:

```
>>> greet.encode('utf-8')
'Rikke J\xc3\xb8rgensen'
>>> greet.encode('utf-16')
'\xfe\xff\x00R\x00i\x00k\x00k\x00e\x00
➡\x00J\x00\xf8\x00r\x00g\x00e\x00n\x00s\x00e
➡\x00n'
```

Decoding to Unicode Formats

To translate an encoded string back into its Unicode format (that is, to reverse encode()), you need to use the built-in unicode() function. This was introduced with Python 2.0. The function accepts two basic arguments: The first is the bytestream that you want to decode, and the second is the format that you want it decoded into. For example, we can decode Rikke Jørgensen from Mac-Roman format into a Unicode string using the following:

```
>>> unicode('Jørgensen','mac-roman')
u'J\xf8rgensen'
```

The return type is a Unicode object. Be aware that unicode() decodes a string object into its Unicode version using the format you supply—use example, decode Jørgensen, sourced from a Mac document using Latin-1 encoding, and you get a different Unicode string:

```
>>> unicode('Jørgensen','latin-1')
u'J\xbfrgensen'
```

We can also use unicode() to translate directly from one encoding into another. The UTF-8 stream of Jørgensen, for example, can be translated straight into UTF-16 using this:

```
>>> unicode('Miss J\xc3\xb8rgensen','utf-16')
```

The error string is used by the codecs to translate Unicode characters to determine how the encoding and errors should be handled. The actual error strings and their effects are dependent on the codec that you are using, but some standard strings are supported by the translation system.

Using `strict` causes the translation to fail, irrespective of what the problem was. Using `ignore` allows the translation to continue, removing any special characters within encoded string, such as the following:

```
>>> unicode('Jørgensen','utf-8','ignore')
u'Jrgensen'
```

In this case, the ø character cannot be translated from the local character set (`mac-roman` in this case) to `utf-8`. The `'ignore'` tells the Unicode system to ignore any characters that it can't convert, essentially deleting the character from the resulting string.

To replace an unknown character with a character that the codec thinks may be suitable, use an error string of `replace`. Python will use the official \uFFFD replacement character as defined by the codec being used.

Unicode and XML in Python

The most important consideration to make when working with an XML document is that the extracted data will be in Unicode format. The basic `xmllib` module that we've already seen does not support Unicode strings. But the new SAX and DOM interfaces for XML parsing do.

Unicode support in XML affects everything from the tag and attribute names to character data. In particular you'll need to take care when comparing strings hard-coded within your scripts—such as within a dictionary when formatting or translating an XML document—and when used within regular expressions.

For example, when using a dictionary that contains a tag name, make sure that the name is specified as a Unicode string using `u' '`. This will ensure that when a comparison is made, the comparison is between two Unicode strings and not a normal string and the `str()` representation of the Unicode extracted from the XML file.

Also remember if you are displaying XML information on screen that you almost certainly need to convert the string using the `encode()` method into a suitable online version. Most displays support either the Latin-1 or Mac-Roman format. See Appendix A for a list of the different formats.

Remember as well that the process goes both ways—when storing information that has been entered by the user, it'll need to be converted into a UTF-8 or UTF-16 format for storage in an XML file.

Translating Character Numbers

The ord() built-in function will return the number that represents a particular character. The function is Unicode aware, so we can get the Unicode number for a character like this:

```
>>> ord('ø')
191
```

To translate that back into a Unicode character, however, we need to use the unichr() function rather than the chr() function:

```
>>> unichr(191)
u'\xbf'
```

As you can see, this returns a single-character Unicode object.

ACCESSING THE UNICODE DATABASE

Occasionally you may want to access a character in the Unicode database with a description, rather than with a character number. This can be especially useful if you want to introduce a particular character from its on-screen encoding into its Unicode format from within an application.

The unicodedata module provides a direct interface to the Unicode database as defined by the data file released by the Unicode consortium.

To look up a Unicode character by its description, use the lookup() function. For example, to determine the Unicode character for the Greek capital letter pi (∏), use the following:

```
>>> import unicodedata
>>> unicodedata.lookup('Greek capital letter pi')
u'\u03a0'
```

To get the Unicode name for a specific Unicode character, use the name() function:

```
>>> unicodedata.name(u'\u03a0')
'GREEK CAPITAL LETTER PI'
```

Writing Your Own Codec

The unicode() function and the encode() method use the codecs module, which is part of the standard library. The codecs module provides the base classes required to translate between the different formats, but a separate set of modules within the encodings directory in the Python standard library does the actual work.

For example, when you select to translate to Mac-Roman format, it's the mac_roman module within the encodings directory that does the actual work.

Python comes with a standard set of codecs for working with the majority of encoding formats supported by Python. However, there may be times when you want to add an encoding system to support a new language or format. You can also use the encoding system to provide custom encodings, which can be useful if you want to convert specific characters to your own sequences when displaying Unicode strings on screen.

You can write your own codec by creating a new module. It needs to import the codecs module, and you then need to define a Codec class that should inherit from the codecs.Codec class. The Codec class should include two methods: encode() and decode(). The easiest way to implement these two methods is to use the charmap_encode() and charmap_decode() functions within the codecs module.

Both of these accept a character map—a dictionary that maps the character to encode or decode to or from. For example, look at this extract from the mac_roman.py module:

```
{
    0x0080: 0x00c4, # LATIN CAPITAL LETTER A WITH
➥DIAERESIS
    0x0081: 0x00c5, # LATIN CAPITAL LETTER A WITH
➥RING ABOVE
    0x0082: 0x00c7, # LATIN CAPITAL LETTER C WITH
➥CEDILLA
    0x0083: 0x00c9, # LATIN CAPITAL LETTER E WITH
➥ACUTE
    0x0084: 0x00d1, # LATIN CAPITAL LETTER N WITH
➥TILDE
    0x0085: 0x00d6, # LATIN CAPITAL LETTER O WITH
```

➡DIAERESIS

```
    0x0086: 0x00dc, # LATIN CAPITAL LETTER U WITH
```

➡DIAERESIS

```
    0x0087: 0x00e1, # LATIN SMALL LETTER A WITH
```

➡ACUTE

```
...
}
```

If you are updating an existing dictionary, use the `make_identity_dict()` function in the `codecs` module. This creates a base dictionary according to the range you supply. For example, to match the standard 256-character 8-bit ASCII map, you would use this:

```
decoding_map = codecs.make_identity_dict(range(256))
```

You can then merge your updated map dictionary using the `update()` method:

```
decoding_map.update({
    0x0080: 0x00c4, # LATIN CAPITAL LETTER A WITH
```

➡DIAERESIS

```
    0x0081: 0x00c5, # LATIN CAPITAL LETTER A WITH
```

➡RING ABOVE

```
...
})
```

Remember that you'll need two maps: one for the encoding and one for the decoding. Assuming the two translations are opposites of each other (that is, an encode/decode pass on a string should return the original string), then you can create the opposite map using this:

```
encoding_map = {}
for k,v in decoding_map.items():
    encoding_map[v] = k
```

Going back to our `encode()` and `decode()` methods, using the map we've just created, we can define those methods like this:

```
class Codec(codecs.Codec):
    def encode(self,input,errors='strict'):
        return codecs.charmap_encode(input,
                                     errors,
                                     encoding_map)
```

```
    def decode(self,input,errors='strict'):
        return codecs.charmap_decode(input,
                                     errors,
                                     decoding_map)
```

Your codec will also need to define the `StreamWriter` and `StreamReader` classes. These are used by the `codecs` module to read and write specific data stream types and convert them into a suitable character format. You probably won't need this for simple Unicode translations, so we can dummy-define them:

```
class StreamWriter(Codec,codecs.StreamWriter):
    pass


class StreamReader(Codec,codecs.StreamReader):
    pass
```

The final step in creating your codec is to register your code with the `codecs` module, which you do by defining a `getregentry()` function. This should return a four-element tuple containing the `encode()` and `decode()` methods from our class, and the `StreamReader` and `StreamWriter` classes. In our case, this produces a definition like this:

```
def getregentry():
    return (Codec().encode,
            Codec().decode,
            StreamReader,
            StreamWriter)
```

After you've created your codec, drop the module into the `encodings` directory. The codec is ready to use.

Here's a complete codec example that performs the relatively useless operation of translating *a* characters into *e* characters and vice versa:

```
import codecs


# Create our Codec class


class Codec(codecs.Codec):
    def encode(self,input,errors='strict'):
        return codecs.charmap_encode(input,
```

```
                                           errors,
                                           encoding_map)

    def decode(self,input,errors='strict'):
        return codecs.charmap_decode(input,
                                           errors,
                                           decoding_map)

class StreamWriter(Codec,codecs.StreamWriter):
    pass

class StreamReader(Codec,codecs.StreamReader):
    pass

# Register ourselves with the codec module:

def getregentry():
    return (Codec().encode,
            Codec().decode,
            StreamReader,
            StreamWriter)

# Create our decode and encoding maps

decoding_map = codecs.make_identity_dict(range(256))
decoding_map.update({
    0x0041: 0x0045,
    0x0061: 0x0065,
    0x0045: 0x0041,
    0x0065: 0x0061,
})

encoding_map = {}
for k,v in decoding_map.items():
```

```
    encoding_map[v] = k
```

I've called this codec `'mcb'` and put it into the file `mcb.py` in the `encodings` directory within the standard Python library directory. If I start up Python, I can try it out:

```
>>> unicode('ae','mcb')
u'ea'
>>> u'ae'.encode('mcb')
'ea'
```

SUMMARY

Python's Unicode is largely transparent—we can create, merge and manipulate Unicode strings natively within Python without the need for any additional modules or functions. Unicode information can be stored within a special Unicode string; this provides the ability to store Unicode characters and has built-in methods for converting the built-in strings into different Unicode standards, such as UTF-8 and UTF-16.

For more in-depth conversion and translation you use the standard `unicodedata` module, which provides named access to individual characters within the Unicode database. For conversions the built-in `unicode()` function allows you to create strings in different encodings, and to translate strings to different encodings. You can even create your own conversion modules for translating characters.

The next chapter leverages the previous two chapters on Python and XML processing and explores how to develop SOAP applications in Python.

Chapter 18

APPLYING SOAP/XML-RPC IN PYTHON

SOAP and XML-RPC are both applications of the XML language that make use of XML's cross-platform and text format to enable us to call remote functions and object methods. You don't need to know how to parse XML, nor do you need to know anything about XML in order to use either SOAP or XML-RPC. However, an understanding of how the mechanism works and how it relates to XML is useful. SOAP was introduced in Chapter 15, "Applying SOAP/XML-RPC in Perl." You'll also find a SOAP reference in Appendix C.

Support in Python is offered by a number of different modules, all of which do their best to hide the complexities of the SOAP or XML-RPC process. You shouldn't ever have to parse any XML to use these technologies, but you should get a good idea of what's possible with XML.

Adapted from *XML Processing with Perl™, Python, and PHP*, by Martin C. Brown
ISBN 0-7821-4021-1   400 pages $49.99

In this chapter we're going to look at two solutions. The SOAP module is one of a number of SOAP solutions available in Python. Written by Cayce Ullman and Brian Matthews, it provides one of the simplest interfaces to the SOAP system. We'll also look at the xmlrpclib module from Fredrik Lundh, the only solution available at the time of writing.

TIP

For other SOAP and XML-RPC solutions in Python, check out the vaults of Parnassus at www.vex.net/parnassus/.

USING *SOAP*

If you've read Chapter 15, "Applying SOAP/XML-RPC in Perl," you know how easy it is to create clients within Perl. The SOAP.py module in Python actually follows a very similar format, hiding all the complexity of writing SOAP clients and servers from the programmer.

All SOAP services are based on three elements: the client, the server, and an optional support module that provides the functions you want to support over a remote connection.

The client is straightforward to set up. You supply the location of the remote SOAP request handler using an instance of the SOAPProxy class. Individual functions on the remote server are then accessible as methods to the SOAPProxy instance that you have created. You can see how easy this is in Listing 18.1.

Listing 18.1: A Simple Python SOAP Client

```
import SOAP

server = SOAP.SOAPProxy('http://localhost:8081/')
print server.getmessage()
```

If we look at the server in Listing 18.2, you can see that it's similarly brief. In this case, we're setting up a daemon-based server to run on the localhost address on port 8081.

Listing 18.2: A Simple Python Server

```
import SOAP

def getmessage():
```

```
    return 'Hello world!'
```

```
server = SOAP.SOAPServer(('localhost',8081))
server.registerFunction(getmessage)
server.serve_forever()
```

The server actually sets up two elements. First, we set up the configuration of the server itself by supplying the hostname and port on which to serve up your request handler. The SOAP module supports only daemon-based servers at the moment, but more transports are being added all the time.

The next step (and the second element that's required by the server) is to register the functions that we want to provide the client with access to. In this case, we've registered a local `getmessage()` function; we could just as easily have registered a function from an external module.

To actually use the system, first we need to fire up the server so that it can listen for requests from the client. I've deliberately used port 8081, which isn't in use by most machines. Firing up the server is just a case of running the server script:

```
$ pyserver.py
```

If we now run the client, we should get a message back from the server:

```
$ python pyclient.py
```

```
Hello world!
```

It works!

You should also have received some output from the server to indicate that a request had been made. For example, the following shows two requests from the same machine that the server is running on:

```
localhost - - [04/Jul/2001 13:11:06] "POST /
➥HTTP/1.0" 200 -
localhost - - [04/Jul/2001 14:30:45] "POST /
➥HTTP/1.0" 200 -
```

Writing SOAP Clients

SOAP clients are surprisingly easy to write when using the SOAP module. You call a function simply by using it as a method to an open server connection. However, you should be aware of a few tricks and traps when passing arguments and accepting return values.

We'll also take a look at how to access objects—since we're working with the Simple Object Access Protocol—and how to access functions registered in an alternative namespace.

Passing Arguments

You can supply arguments to functions just as you would with any normal function. Strings, numbers, and multiple objects are passed as normal. Arrays and dictionaries can also be passed as normal to a remote function, but they are given special treatment at the server end. We'll look more closely at the mechanics of this process in the next section, "Return Values."

You are limited in the methods in which you can supply arguments to the remote function. Normal function argument passing, such as

```
server.newaccount('Current', 1000, 'MSDW')
```

work as normal, but if you want to supply arguments using the keyword notation, then the supporting function on the server side must be registered using the `registerKWFunction()` method. See the section "Writing SOAP Servers" later in this chapter for more information.

Return Values

A remote function can return any type of value to a client, and you can return multiple objects within a single response just as you would with a local function. The string and numeric types are returned as normal, but arrays and dictionaries are handled slightly differently.

Rather than converting the advanced sequence types to one of the core object types supported internally by Python, the SOAP module creates its own object classes. These are based on the core object types, but they have a few little tricks for the unsuspecting programmer.

Handling Lists and Tuples   If there is a server such as the one in Listing 18.3, you can see that we register a function called `getNames()`, which returns a tuple of names. The SOAP standard doesn't include a tuple type, so the tuple is converted to the SOAP array type during serialization into a SOAP envelope.

Listing 18.3: A Server Supporting Multiple Return Values

```
import SOAP

def getnames():
```

```
            return 'Martin', 'Sharon', 'Wendy', 'Rikke'

    server = SOAP.SOAPServer(('localhost',8081))
    server.registerFunction(getnames)
    server.serve_forever()
```

When accessing the information from the client, you must either use repr(), because str() outputs information about the SOAP module object type, or access the information element by element. You can see the effects of the different access methods by using the client script shown in Listing 18.4.

Listing 18.4: Accessing an Array Returned by a SOAP Server

```
import SOAP

server = SOAP.SOAPProxy('http://localhost:8081/')
result = server.getnames()

print "Direct: ",result
print "Direct: ",str(result)
print "Direct: ",repr(result)
print "Individual: ",
for i in result:
    print i,
```

If you execute the script you get the following output:

```
$ pyclient2.py
Direct:  <SOAP.typedArrayType Result at 135860460>
Direct:  <SOAP.typedArrayType Result at 135860460>
Direct:  ['Martin', 'Sharon', 'Wendy', 'Rikke']
Individual:  Martin Sharon Wendy Rikke
```

Note the output in the third line—the information we returned in the getnames() function was returned as a tuple, but there is no tuple type in the SOAP definition, so what is actually returned is a list, not a tuple. This obviously breaks the usefulness of using a tuple in the first place. We've now listed the immutability of a tuple and ended up with a mutable list. There is no way around this (short of changing the SOAP standard), but if you know that you are expecting a tuple back from a function, you might want to embed the call to the function in tuple().

Handling Dictionaries   Dictionaries are exchanged between server and client as the SOAP structure or compound type. They work in a similar

Part iv

fashion to the array type that we've already seen, except that neither `str()` nor `repr()` will print out a usable version of the object. However, you can access the elements within the returned dictionary just as you would with a normal dictionary.

To access a list of keys, though, you must use the `_keys()` method rather than the normal `keys()` method (note the underscore prefix). You can see an example of accessing information in this way in the fragment below:

```
for i in dict._keys():
    print i,'=>',dict[i]
```

In all ways, `_keys()` works in an identical fashion to `keys()`.

Working with Objects

The SOAP module does not enable us to create remote objects directly, but it does enable us to access remote objects that have been suitably registered by the server. For example, Listing 18.5 shows a SOAP server supporting the Account class, which provides three methods: `balance()`, `withdraw()`, and `deposit()`.

Listing 18.5: An Object-Based SOAP Server

```python
import SOAP

class Account:
    def __init__(self):
        self._account = ''
        self._balance = 0

    def balance(self):
        return self._balance

    def deposit(self, value):
        self._balance += value
        return self._balance

    def withdraw(self, value):
        self._balance -= value
        return self._balance

server = SOAP.SOAPServer(('localhost',8081))
account = Account()
server.registerObject(account)
server.serve_forever()
```

We can now access the methods of the account object that was created in the server, as demonstrated by the script in Listing 18.6.

Listing 18.6: A SOAP Object Client

```
import SOAP

server = SOAP.SOAPProxy('http://localhost:8081/')

print server.deposit(100)
print server.withdraw(50)
```

What we can't do is access the object attributes directly—you must always use a method to obtain or set information. Although this may seem like a limitation, it's actually how the SOAP standard was designed to work. The acronym refers to an object access protocol, so you should expect to access instances of an object and not remote classes.

For new classes that you create specifically to support SOAP servers, this shouldn't be a problem. When developing a SOAP interface to an existing module, you might want to consider creating a separate class that inherits from your original class and then provide additional methods that enable you to set and retrieve attribute information remotely using method calls.

Accessing Namespaces

SOAP servers register and support functions in a number of different namespaces. These can be used to enable a single request handler to support a number of different services to a number of different clients and also as a logical way to divide up the services that you offer.

To use a particular namespace, you can specify the namespace either at the time you create your SOAPProxy, as seen in Listing 18.7, or dynamically during a function call, as shown in Listing 18.8. The former is best used when you are calling functions from a single namespace on a remote server. The latter makes more sense when you are calling functions from multiple namespaces on the same server.

Listing 18.7: A Client Accessing a Namespace Statically

```
import SOAP

server = SOAP.SOAPProxy('http://localhost:8081/',
                        namespace='urn:mySOAPmethods')
print server.getmessage()
```

Listing 18.8: A Client Accessing a Namespace Dynamically

```
import SOAP

server = SOAP.SOAPProxy('http://localhost:8081/')

print server._ns('urn:mySOAPmethods').getmessage()
```

Note in both cases that we prefix the namespace with a `urn:` prefix definition. This is part of the SOAP standard, but it actually isn't required. If you leave out the `urn` declaration, the string will be used as the prefix.

However, be careful. If your prefix contains a colon, the namespace string will be incorrectly split across the colon. For example, we can access the `SOAP::Demo` namespace created for the Perl server that we created in Listing 15.2 in Chapter 15 using the code in Listing 18.9. Here we *must* include the `urn` prefix because the `SOAP::Demo` namespace, which is a Perl module declaration, contains colons.

Listing 18.9: Accessing a Perl Namespace from Python

```
import SOAP

server = SOAP.SOAPProxy('http://test.mchome.pri/
➡SOAP/request.cgi',
                    namespace='urn:SOAP::Demo')
print server.getmessage()
```

Note in Listing 15.5 that the address of the proxy points directly to the CGI request handler, since that's how we configured the server in Chapter 15. We can now run the script and get a reply from our Perl-based server:

```
$ python perl.py
Hello, world
```

Writing SOAP Servers

The SOAP module currently supports only the daemon form of SOAP server. It inherits from the `socket` and `BaseHTTPServer` modules in order to provide an HTTP interface for serving up object and function requests.

The basic process for creating servers using SOAP is first to import the SOAP module and then to register each function that you want to expose to a remote client. For example, in our first sample script, you saw how easy it was to set up a simple server to provide remote access to a local function.

We've already covered in this chapter some of the basics regarding the creation of different servers and the methods that you need to employ to provide an interface to modules—SOAP specific and existing. To finish off our look at the SOAP module and SOAP servers, we'll look at how to register functions and objects in specific namespaces and the different methods for registering functions and objects for providing services. We'll also take a brief look at how to access and use arguments supplied from a client in your SOAP server.

Namespaces

The SOAPServer class provides four registration methods: `register-Function()`, `registerKWFunction()`, `registerObject()`, and `registerKWObject()`. All the methods support the same basic arguments:

```
register*(FUNCTIONNAME|OBJECTNAME [, NAMESPACE])
```

FUNCTIONNAME or OBJECTNAME is the name of the function or object that you want to register. In each case, if NAMESPACE is supplied, then it's registered into the supplied namespace. This should be specified as a raw string—you don't have to prefix the namespace with urn as you do with the client, but you do need to specify the namespace.

We have already seen examples of the two primary methods: `registerFunction()` and `registerObject()`. These register a single function or a single object and all of its methods so that they can be accessed from a remote client.

The `registerKW*()` methods register functions (or methods to an object) that use keyword argument passing instead of straight argument passing.

Using External Modules

If you want to export a function from another module, you can import the module and register the individual functions as usual. Note that importing works either into the module's own namespace, as shown in Listing 18.10, or when imported into the server module's namespace, as shown in Listing 18.11.

Listing 18.10: Exporting a Module's Functions from Its Own Namespace

```
import SOAP
import pyserver3mod
```

Part iv

```
server = SOAP.SOAPServer(('localhost',8081))
server.registerFunction(pyserver3mod.echo)
server.registerFunction(pyserver3mod.strdict)
server.registerFunction(pyserver3mod.getnames)
server.registerFunction(pyserver3mod.getages)
server.serve_forever()
```

Listing 18.11: Exporting a Module's Functions from the Server's Namespace

```
import SOAP
from pyserver3mod import *

server = SOAP.SOAPServer(('localhost',8081))
server.registerFunction(echo)
server.registerFunction(strdict)
server.registerFunction(getnames)
server.registerFunction(getages)
server.serve_forever()
```

Note that the Python namespace has no bearing on or relationship to the SOAP namespace into which the functions are registered.

For objects the process is even easier. Because we are only registering an instance of a class, it makes no difference how we derived the class or instance.

Function/Method Arguments

Server-side functions can accept any form of argument. However, special care needs to be taken when accepting arguments made up of arrays and dictionaries. Just as when we were receiving information back from a server, the way in which you access the contents of the object data supplied as an argument differs from the normal Python object types. In particular, lists need to be accessed individually or output using repr(), and when accessing the individual key/value pairs from a dictionary, you must use _keys(). See "Handling Lists and Tuples" and "Handling Dictionaries" earlier in this chapter for more information and examples of how to extract information from the method/function call.

Debugging

The SOAP module uses the exception system to raise any errors. As you would expect, errors are propagated up from either the socket or HTTP server libraries if there is a problem.

Most problems can be traced either to a transmission fault (a host cannot be found) or to the remote server not responding to connections.

Problems in calling a remote function can be placed into one of two possible categories. Either the remote function does not exist or the call to the function failed because the argument or function implementation didn't work.

In either of these cases, the easiest way to identify any problems is to embed the call in a `try` statement.

XML-RPC SOLUTIONS

If you thought writing SOAP services with Python was easy, then you'll be pleased to hear that supporting XML-RPC is even easier. However, in comparison to the SOAP solutions that are available, the XML-RPC solution written by Python development team member Fredrik Lundh is not quite as mature in its interface.

The `xmlrpclib` package incorporates three files. The main `xmlrpclib` module contains all the core elements need to package up request calls into XML-RPC envelopes and unpackage them back into the method and parameters required to make a call on the server. To install the modules, copy them from the TAR package into the `site-packages` directory in the Python library directory (usually `/usr/local/lib/python2.1`).

XML-RPC Walkthrough

To use `xmlrpclib` from the client side, we need only to specify the location of the request handler when creating a new `server` instance. Once we've created the new instance, just like SOAP, we then access the methods on the remote server by name, as if they were methods to our class instance. You can see this more clearly in Listing 18.12.

Listing 18.12: A Simple XML-RPC Client

```
from xmlrpclib import Server

server = Server("http://localhost:8005/")

print server.echo('Hello')
print server.join(['Rod','Jane','Freddy'])
print server.pprint({'Rod'    : 23,
```

```
                               'Jane'   : 25,
                               'Freddy' : 26})
```

The module enables us to transfer any of the normal object types, using any of the normal methods for supplying data to the remote procedure. You can see from Listing 18.12 that we've supplied a simple string, a list, and a dictionary to the remote functions.

The server side is equally straightforward. To understand how the server side works, look at the xmlrpcserver.py module that comes with the package, included here in Listing 18.13.

Listing 18.13: The Sample XML-RPC Server from *xmlrpclib*

```
#
# XML-RPC SERVER
# $Id$
#
# a simple XML-RPC server for Python
#
# History:
# 1999-02-01 fl  added to xmlrpclib distribution
#
# written by Fredrik Lundh, January 1999.
#
# Copyright (c) 1999 by Secret Labs AB.
# Copyright (c) 1999 by Fredrik Lundh.
#
# fredrik@pythonware.com
# http://www.pythonware.com
#
# ------------------------
# Permission to use, copy, modify, and
# distribute this
# software and its associated documentation for any
# purpose and without fee is hereby granted.  This
# software is provided as is.
# ------------------------
#

import SocketServer, BaseHTTPServer
import xmlrpclib
import sys

class RequestHandler(BaseHTTPServer.
```

```
➥ABaseHTTPRequestHandler):

    def do_POST(self):
        try:
            # get arguments
            data = self.rfile.read(int(self.headers
➥["content-length"]))
            params, method = xmlrpclib.loads(data)

            # generate response
            try:
                response = self.call(method, params)
                if type(response) != type(()):
                    response = (response,)
            except:
                # report exception back to server
                response = xmlrpclib.dumps(
                    xmlrpclib.Fault(1, "%s:%s" %
➥(sys.exc_type, sys.exc_value))
                    )
            else:
                response = xmlrpclib.dumps(
                    response,
                    methodresponse=1
                    )
        except:
            # internal error, report as HTTP
➥server error
            self.send_response(500)
            self.end_headers()
        else:
            # got a valid XML RPC response
            self.send_response(200)
            self.send_header("Content-type",
➥"text/xml")
            self.send_header("Content-length",
                             str(len(response)))
            self.end_headers()
            self.wfile.write(response)

            # shut down the connection (from Skip
Montanaro)
            self.wfile.flush()
```

```
        self.connection.shutdown(1)

    def call(self, method, params):
        # override this method to implement RPC
➥methods
        print "CALL", method, params
        return params

if __name__ == '__main__':
    server = SocketServer.TCPServer(('', 8000),
➥RequestHandler)
    server.serve_forever()
```

As you can see from Listing 18.13, the module creates a new class, RequestHandler, which itself inherits from the BaseHTTPServer class from the Python standard library. The do_POST method then accepts a request from a client, extracts the necessary information, and decodes the XML-RPC envelope to determine the function that has been called. The parameters pass to that function.

The sample also includes a call method that prints out the request and echoes back the parameters to the client. We'll be using the call method later to set up our own server.

Rather than rewrite this module in its entirety, instead we can inherit from the RequestHandler class and override the call method to do something more useful.

The call method that is invoked by RequestHandler must accept two arguments: method, which is the text name of the method that has been called, and params, which is a tuple of the parameters. We need to convert these two pieces of information into a Python function call that will return information that we can pass on to the client.

In the case of the method, we're dealing with a text string, so we'll need to run it through eval in order to convert it into a code object that we can execute. We could pass params on to any function natively, such as this:

```
realmethod = eval(method)
```

```
realmethod(params)
```

We'd have to modify any existing functions to extract a single-element tuple before passing the real arguments supplied to the function. A better solution is to use apply, which accepts a tuple of arguments while actually passing them to the function you are calling as normal parameters.

You can see the final solution in Listing 18.14.

Listing 18.14: A Simple XML-RPC Server Using HTTP

```
import xmlrpcserver
import string

def echo(s):
    return 'Echo: %s' % (s)

def join(list):
    return string.join(list,' ')

def pprint(dict):
    str = ''
    for k in dict.keys():
        str += '%s => %s\n' % (k,dict[k])
    return str

class MyRequestHandler(xmlrpcserver.RequestHandler):
    def call(self, method, params):
        realmethod = eval(method)
        return apply(realmethod,params)

import SocketServer
server = SocketServer.TCPServer(('', 8005),
➡MyRequestHandler)
server.serve_forever()
```

Listing 18.14 shows the versatility of allowing us to call virtually any function. Not only are we accepting the different types supplied by the client in the native formats, but we can also format the information and response. We've even used the information to call an external function (from the `string` module) to handle the request.

The final part to the server process is to create a new socket server on a given port and then supply your request handler class when creating the server instance so that it can handle the requests.

To run the server, just start the script in Listing 18.14. As with all instances of `BaseHTTPServer`, you'll be given a normal Web server–style access log as clients connect, such as this:

```
localhost - - [05/Jul/2001 13:48:27] "POST /RPC2
➡HTTP/1.0" 200 -
localhost - - [05/Jul/2001 13:48:28] "POST /RPC2
➡HTTP/1.0" 200 -
```

```
localhost - - [05/Jul/2001 13:48:28] "POST /RPC2
➥HTTP/1.0" 200 -
```

Note that you'll receive one request for each function call from a call—it doesn't batch requests.

From the client end, we get a nicely formatted set of results:

```
$ python xmlrpcc.py
Echo: Hello
Rod Jane Freddy
Jane => 25
Rod => 23
Freddy => 26
```

As you can see from this walkthrough, XML-RPC is incredibly straight-forward. In fact, once you've resolved the `call` method to handle client requests easily, there's not much more to deal with. We can pass arguments and information to remote functions as we would any other function, and we can get the information back from those functions in the same way.

The only limitation of the `xmlrpclib` is that you cannot handle objects and classes remotely. This is not a limitation of the module at all but a limitation of the XML-RPC standard. If you need object access, use SOAP.

Debugging XML-RPC

As with the SOAP module, the `xmlrpclib` module raises exceptions when an error occurs. Exceptions are actually raised using the `xmlrpclib.Fault` exception, and they are propagated across the network connection.

For example, here's the default exception output when you're trying to call the remote `join` function with the wrong arguments:

```
Traceback (most recent call last):
  File "xmlrpcc.py", line 7, in ?
    print server.join({'Rod' : 23, 'Jane' : 25,
➥'Freddy' : 26})
  File "/usr/local/lib/python2.1/site-packages/
➥xmlrpclib.py", line 547, in __call__
    return self.__send(self.__name, args)
  File "/usr/local/lib/python2.1/site-
➥ packages/xmlrpclib.py", line 630, in __request
    request
```

```
   File "/usr/local/lib/python2.1/site-
➡ packages/xmlrpclib.py", line 585, in request
     return self.parse_response(h.getfile())
   File "/usr/local/lib/python2.1/site-
➡ packages/xmlrpclib.py", line 601, in
➡parse_response
     return u.close()
   File "/usr/local/lib/python2.1/site-
➡ packages/xmlrpclib.py", line 371, in close
     raise apply(Fault, (), self._stack[0])
xmlrpclib.Fault: <Fault 1: 'exceptions.TypeError:
➡sequence
➡ expected, dictionary found'>
```

Unfortunately, the exception system can make identifying the source of an error difficult, because it's almost impossible to determine the actual location of the fault. To give an example, here's the output from a call to the remote join function when calling the function direct, rather than through apply():

```
Traceback (most recent call last):
  File "xmlrpcc.py", line 6, in ?
    print server.join(['Rod','Jane','Freddy'])
  File "/usr/local/lib/python2.1/site-packages/
➡xmlrpclib.py", line 547, in __call__
    return self.__send(self.__name, args)
  File "/usr/local/lib/python2.1/site-
➡ packages/xmlrpclib.py", line 630, in __request
    request
  File "/usr/local/lib/python2.1/site-
➡ packages/xmlrpclib.py", line 585, in request
    return self.parse_response(h.getfile())
  File "/usr/local/lib/python2.1/site-
➡ packages/xmlrpclib.py", line 601,
➡ in parse_response
    return u.close()
  File "/usr/local/lib/python2.1/site-
➡ packages/xmlrpclib.py", line 371, in close
    raise apply(Fault, (), self._stack[0])
```

```
xmlrpclib.Fault: <Fault 1:
➡ 'exceptions.AttributeError:join'>
```

The best advice I can give is to test your functions thoroughly on the server side by using the client module to import the functions it expects to use, rather than calling them remotely. Make sure that you use the same basic process as used by the call() method (see Listing 18.14) in the request handler to invoke the functions.

SUMMARY

Python supports both SOAP and XML-RPC through a number of different modules. The SOAP.py is not the only SOAP solution available for Python, but it does provide one of the easiest and simplest interfaces on both the client side and the server side for setting up the remote server and server-side functions and module access.

The entire SOAP system works through the use of a SOAPProxy class—you create a new instance of the class, supplying the location of the remote server that you want to talk to. From that moment, you can call any remote functions by specifying the remote function name as a method of the SOAPProxy class instance.

When communicating information between the server and the client, you need to be careful because the information is transferred using special objects rather than the base object types; although they work in the same fashion, some of the shortcuts you may have used, such as str(), don't work as advertised on the SOAP data types.

For XML-RPC, one of the solutions is xmlrpclib. It works in a similar fashion as our SOAP module: You create a new instance of the Server class, which simply requires the address of the request handler that you want to talk to. Remote functions are called just as methods to that object; then their request and other information is transferred to the remote server.

Both solutions enable you to access and call functions defined within the handler itself and also those imported from an external module.

The next chapter represents our next foray into XML processing, this time using another popular scripting language that has been around for a long time: Tcl.

Chapter 19

XML AND TCL

Tcl has one of the longest histories of dealing with XML of any of the scripting languages, largely because it was one of the first scripting languages to introduce Unicode support as an integral part of the language. John Ousterhout and the rest of the Tcl development team produced one of the best Unicode-handling systems of any language. Even now, Tcl still provides an excellent base for supporting multiple languages and integrating internationalization into your scripts; it is an ideal base for translating between the different encoding formats supported by Unicode.

Tcl's other advantage is that it provides excellent integration with the Tk GUI development system, making it an ideal language for creating cross-platform–compatible scripts with a consistent GUI whether you are working on Unix, Windows, or Mac OS.

For XML, Tcl provides a single solution called TclXML developed by Zveno Pty Ltd. TclXML is comparable in functionality to Simple API for XML (SAX) in terms of its speed and capability.

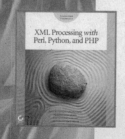

XML Processing *with* Perl, Python, and PHP

Adapted from *XML Processing with Perl™, Python, and PHP*, by Martin C. Brown

ISBN 0-7821-4021-1   400 pages $49.99

TclXML is essentially a suite of tools that provides you with the information you need to parse XML documents. TclXML supports two different parsers: a parser called TclExpat that is based on the now-familiar Expat parser and a native XML parser written entirely in Tcl that is supported directly in the TclXML extension.

Also available is a layer called TclDOM that sits on top of TclXML. It supports the access to and modification of XML documents using the Document Object Model (DOM) API within Tcl. DOM can be a useful way of viewing and manipulating information, especially if you integrate with the capabilities of the Tk interface-building toolkit, which uses an object-like interface.

THE TclXML PARSER

The TclXML parser is based on Expat, which is an event-based parser. In event parsers, different procedures are registered with the parser class when it is created. Then, each time a different entity is identified within the XML file, the command is called and operates on the entity information.

For example, if you register procedures for the start and end tags, then when parsing the XML file

```
<name backref="00120">Martin C Brown</name>
```

the parser would call the registered start command once, supplying the tag name and the attribute list as arguments, and the end procedure once, again supplying the tag name as an argument.

For example, here you can see a simple handler for a start tag:

```
proc Start {name attlist args} {
    puts "Start: $name"

}
```

You create a new instance of the XML parser and register the procedures that you want to use for the different entities using something like the following fragment:

```
set p [xml::parser -elementstartcommand Start \
                   -elementendcommand End \
                   -characterdatacommand CData]
```

You can configure a number of different XML entities to be identified and handled by setting up different commands to handle them and configuring the parser accordingly. See the section "Configuring the Parser" later in this chapter for more information.

Creating the parser is only part of the story, however. You also need to supply the parser with some XML for it to process. You do this by using the `parse` method on the newly created parser object. For example:

```
$p parse "<mytag>mydata</mytag>"
```

You can call this method as many times as necessary in order to supply an entire XML document to the parser. The parser will handle—and if necessary bond together—all of the text in order to build and identify entire entities. Typically, of course, you'll be reading data from an external file as we do in our sample scripts by opening the file and embedding an evaluation of the `read` command on the file.

You can see an example of an XML parser that generates a very simple annotated list of the start, end, and data portions of the XML document in Listing 19.1.

Listing 19.1: A Simple XML Parser

```
#!/bin/sh
# \
exec tclsh8.3 "$0" "$@"

# Import the xml package

package require xml

# set up the handler for opening (start)
# tags. Must accept the tag name, list
# of attributes and a list of additional
# arguments

proc Start {name attlist args} {
    puts "Start: $name"
}

# set up the handler for the closing (end)
# tags. Must accept the tag name and any
# additional arguments

proc End {tag args} {
    puts "End: $tag"
}

# set up the handler for character data
```

```
# we ignore data entirely composed of
# whitespace characters

proc CData {data args} {
    if {![regexp {^[ \t\r\n]+$} $data ]} {
        puts "Data: $data"
    }
}

# Open each file in the argument list

foreach in $argv {
    if {[catch {open $in} ch]} {
        puts stderr "unable to open file \"$in\""
        exit 1
    }

# create a new instance of the XML parser

    set p [xml::parser -elementstartcommand Start \
                       -elementendcommand End \
                       -characterdatacommand CData]

# supply the parser with the test we read from
# the file, catching (and reporting) any errors

    if {[catch {$p parse [read $ch]} err]} {
        puts stderr $err
        exit 1
    }
    catch {close $ch}
}

exit 0
```

The core elements of the script are the procedures that handle the
entities as the XML parser actually sees them. The Start and End procedures are straightforward enough: They get passed the name of the tag
that has just been identified (as well as other information). All we do is
print out the tag with a suitable prefix.

The character data procedure is slightly special. One of the problems
with the way the Expat parser works is that it parses on all information
to the procedures. In the case of tags, the information passed on is what

you would expect. For the character data, this means that the handler may be called a number of times for what appears to you to be a single data block within the XML file.

Furthermore, because it can be called a number of times, on occasion it will be composed merely of white space (spaces, tabs, newline/carriage returns). So that we don't end up outputting useless data, we check the supplied data first by running it past a regular expression. Of course, this is an issue only when using Expat; the TclXML parser doesn't exhibit this problem.

TIP
You can ask the parser to ignore white space by setting the −ignorewhite-space option on the parser.

If we run the script on a simple XML file, we get the following:

```
Start: contact
Start: name
Data: Martin Brown
End: name
Start: address
Start: description
Data: Main Address
End: description
Start: addressline
Data: The House, The Street, The Town
End: addressline
End: address
Start: address
Start: description
Data: Holiday Chalet
End: description
Start: addressline
Data: The Chalet, The Hillside, The Forest
End: addressline
End: address
End: contact
```

Configuring the Parser

You can configure the parser when you create the parser instance, such as the following:

```
set p [xml::parser -characterdatacommand CData]
```

You also can configure it after the parser has been created by using the configure method, like this:

```
$p configure -elementstartcommand Start
```

You can see a full list of the configurable options supported by the parser in Table 19.1. The option is the name of the option that you can configure. Command arguments are the arguments supplied to the command that is evaluated when a particular entity is identified.

TABLE 19.1:   Configurable Options for the TclXML Parser

Option	Command Arguments	Description
-attlistdeclcommand script	name attrname type default value	The command prefix evaluated when an attribute list declaration is encountered within an XML document's DTD.
-baseurl URI		The base URI to use when resolving any relative URIs in the document.
-characterdata- command script	data	The command prefix evaluated when any character data is encountered.
-commentcommand script	data	The command prefix evaluated when a comment is encountered.
-defaultcommand script	data	The command prefix evaluated when an entity not otherwise covered by another configured option is encountered.
-defaultexpand- internalentities Boolean		If True, resolves entities declared in the DTD with the expanded version.
-doctypecommand script	name publicid systemid dtd	The command prefix evaluated when a document type declaration is identified.

TABLE 19.1 continued: Configurable Options for the TclXML Parser

OPTION	COMMAND ARGUMENTS	DESCRIPTION
-elementdecl-command script	name model	The command prefix evaluated when an element markup declaration is encountered.
--elementend-command script	name args	The command prefix evaluated when an end tag is identified.
-elementstart-command script	name attributes args	The command prefix evaluated when a start tag is identified.
-endcdatasection-command script		The command prefix evaluated when the end of a data section is identified.
-enddoctypedecl-command script		The command prefix evaluated when the end of the document type declaration is identified.
-entitydeclcommand script	name args	The command prefix evaluated when the entity declaration is encountered.
-entityreference-command script	name	The command prefix evaluated when an entity reference is identified.
-errorcommand script	errorcode errormessage	The command prefix evaluated when a fatal error is detected. See the "Error Handling" section later in this chapter.
-externalentity-command script	name baseuri uri publicid	The command prefix evaluated when an external entity reference is identified. If the parser is validating the document (see the -validate option), then a default script is supplied that recursively parses the entity's data.

TABLE 19.1 continued: Configurable Options for the TclXML Parser

OPTION	COMMAND ARGUMENTS	DESCRIPTION
-final Boolean		When data is being supplied to the parser in multiple chunks, this should be set to False while there is additional data to be parsed. When you run out of data, set it to True to indicate that the final chunk has been supplied.
-ignorewhitespace Boolean		If set to True, then the parser automatically ignores character data segments in the document that are composed entirely of white space.
-notationdecl-command script	name uri	The command prefix evaluated when a notation declaration is encountered.
-notstandalone-command script		The command prefix evaluated when the parser determines that the XML document requires and/or uses other documents.
-paramentity-parsing Boolean		If set to True, then external parameter entities are parsed.
-parameterentity-declcommand script	name args	The command prefix evaluated when a parameter entity declaration is identified.
-parser name		The name of the parser class to use for this parser object. Only valid when the parser is created.
-processing-instructioncommand script	target data	The command prefix evaluated when a processing instruction is encountered.

TABLE 19.1 continued: Configurable Options for the TclXML Parser

OPTION	COMMAND ARGUMENTS	DESCRIPTION
-reportempty Boolean		If True, then additional arguments are appended to the element start and end callbacks to indicate that the element was empty. Empty elements are ignored otherwise.
-startcdatasection-command script		The command prefix evaluated when the start of the character data section is identified.
-startdoctypedecl-command script		The command prefix evaluated when a document type declaration is identified.
-unknownencoding-command script		The command prefix evaluated when a character using an unknown encoding format is identified.
-unparsedentity-declcommand script	systemid publicid notation	The command prefix evaluated when a declaration is identified for an unparsed entity.
-validate Boolean		If set to True, forces the parser to validate the structure of the XML document.
-warningcommand script	warningcode warningmessage	The command prefix to be evaluated when a warning condition is raised by the parser (see the "Error Handling" section later in this chapter for more information).
-xmldeclcommand script	version encoding standalone	The command prefix evaluated when an XML declaration is encountered.

NOTE

Character data can be handled in two ways. If you want only to output the character data string, then use the -characterdatacommand option. If you want to identify the start and end of any character data sections—useful when converting XML to another format—use the -startcdatasectioncommand and -endcdatasectioncommand options. Note that, when using the latter option, you still need to use -characterdatacommand to obtain the character data.

Error Handling

The simplest way to handle errors is to catch any errors generated during the parsing process using a catch statement. However, you may want to handle the errors a bit more exclusively. The best way of handling errors is to set up a callback to be triggered when an error occurs. To use this method you'll need to set the callback either as part of the options supplied when the parser is created or afterwards using the configure command.

The parser handles two different error conditions:

▶ *Warnings* occur when an XML document has not been created properly, such as when an empty element is used but not declared. The default command for the -warningcommand option silently ignores any problems.

▶ *Errors* are raised when the document is not well formed; that is, when tags do not match (or there is no closing tag) or the nesting is bad. Errors can be trapped by creating a command and setting the -errorcommand option to the parser. The default command set for errors hands back an error response to the caller.

To define a command for either of these options, you must create a command that accepts two arguments, the errorcode (numerical) and the error message (a textual description). How you handle this information is up to you.

If you want your commands to raise an error with the parser, then you can return an error from your handlers. For example, when translating your XML documents into HTML, you may want to raise an error if a tag is identified in the XML document without a matching conversion. The supported return codes and their effects are listed in Table 19.2.

TABLE 19.2: Command Statements for Handlers

CODE	DESCRIPTION
break	Terminates parsing of the XML document, suppressing the invocation of any further entity-handler commands. The parse method returns the TCL_OK return code.
continue	Stops invocation of callback handlers until the current element has finished.
error	Terminates the XML processing immediately. The parse method also returns the TCL_ERROR return code.
default	Any other return code suppresses invocation of all further callback scripts. The parse method returns the same return code.

Tcl and Unicode

The TclXML parser will read Unicode-encoded documents directly, so you need to identify or display either entities or character data. Then you will need to be able to translate between Unicode formats.

Tcl 8.1 and after includes the encoding command, which will convert strings between the different encoding formats for you.

TIP

To determine which encodings are supported by your Tcl installation, use the following: lsort [encoding names]. This will produce a list of the available encodings.

The encoding function supports a number of different options:

```
encoding convertfrom ?encoding? data
```

This converts data to Unicode format from the specified encoding. For example, the following would convert the ASCII string into Unicode format:

```
set s [encoding convertfrom ascii "Hello World"]
```

The convertto option translates a bytestring from Unicode format into the specified encoding:

```
encoding convertto ?encoding? string
```

In both cases, the system encoding is used if the encoding format is not specified. You can set the system encoding using this command:

```
encoding system ?encoding?
```

Part iv

Note that modifying the system encoding may affect the names of commands you evaluate, because the system encoding is used for command names. Using a non-ASCII–compatible system encoding is not recommended.

Viewing XML with Tk

An obvious use of Tcl (in combination with the Tk GUI builder) is to develop an application that enables us to view an XML document marked up so that we can identify start and end tags in the document more easily. We don't really need to do anything clever here—we're not checking the validity of the document in any way. We just need an easier way to view the contents.

You can see a sample of the script in action in Figure 19.1. Start tags are identified by coloring them red; end tags are blue. Character data is left untouched, but all the elements are indented according to the structure, so you can also identify the nesting and document structure.

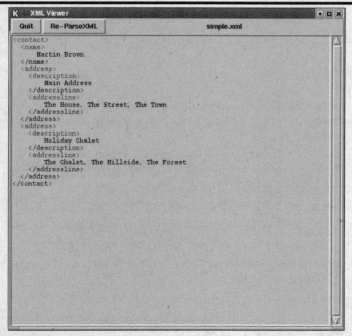

FIGURE 19.1: Viewing an XML document with Tcl/Tk

The code that generated the viewer is shown in Listing 19.2.

Listing 19.2: The Tcl/Tk XML Viewer

```sh
#!/bin/sh
# \
exec wish8.3 "$0" "$@"

# set up our main Tk window

wm title . "XML Viewer"

# Set up our global variables
# indent holds the indentation value
# tagnumber keeps track of the text paragraphs
# input contains the name of the XML file

set indent 0
set tagnumber 0
set input [lindex $argv 0]

# Set up the button bar at the top
# Contains a Quit button and
# a Reparse button to re-read the XML
# and the name of the file

set bf [ frame .menubar ]
pack $bf -fill x
button $bf.quit -text Quit -command exit
button $bf.parse -text Re-ParseXML -command ParseXML
label $bf.label -textvariable input
pack $bf.quit $bf.parse -side left
pack $bf.label -side right -fill x -expand true

# Set up the main textbox to hold our XML

set tf [ frame .text]
pack $tf -side top -fill both -expand true
set t [text $tf.t \
        -setgrid true \
        -wrap word \
        -width 80 \
        -height 40 \
```

```
                      -yscrollcommand "$tf.sy set"]
        scrollbar $tf.sy -orient vert -command "$tf.t yview"
        pack $tf.sy -side right -fill y
        pack $tf.t -side left -fill both -expand true

        # Create two tags to markup the start and end
        # entities without our XML file

        $t tag configure opentag -foreground #ff0000
        $t tag configure closetag -foreground #0000ff

        # Import the XML parser

        package require xml

        # The start handler accepts the XML tag name
        # and outputs the tag, formatted, to the text box

        proc Start {name attlist args} {
            global t indent tagnumber
        # Increment the paragraph number so we can set
        # the tag
            incr tagnumber
        # Add the XML tag to the text box, using the current
        # indentation
            $t insert end [format "%*s%s\n" $indent ""
        ➥"<$name>"]
        # Set the style of the paragraph that we just added
            $t tag add opentag \
                    [eval format "%0.1f" $tagnumber] \
                    [eval format "%d.end" $tagnumber]
        # Now increase the indent so that any nested tag or
        # character data appears to be within this tag
            incr indent 2
        }

        # The end handler accepts the XML tag name
        # and outputs the results to the text box
        # But we mark it with a different text color
        # and decrement the indentation so that
        # tags line up

        proc End {name args} {
```

```
    global t indent tagnumber
# Decrement the indent, to bring the end tag into
# line with the opening tag
    incr indent -2
# Increment the paragraph number
    incr tagnumber
# Add the tag to the text box
    $t insert end [format "%*s%s\n" $indent ""
➥"</$name>"]
# Set the style of the previous paragraph
    $t tag add closetag \
          [eval format "%0.1f" $tagnumber] \
          [eval format "%d.end" $tagnumber]
}


# The character data handler adds the data (except
# whitespace) to the text box

proc CData {data args} {
    global t indent tagnumber
# Check were dealing with a valid text block
    if {![regexp {^[ \t\r\n]+$} $data ]} {
# Increment the indentation
        incr indent 2
# Increment the paragraph number to keep the
# paragraph numbers in check
        incr tagnumber
# Add the text to the text box, using the indent
        $t insert end [format "%*s%s\n" $indent "
➥" $data]
# Decrement the indent
        incr indent -2
    }
}


# Set up the parser. Since this is the same
# procedure called when we click on the Re-ParseXML
# button we also reset the indentation, paragraph
# numbers and the contents of the text box

proc ParseXML {} {
    global input t tagnumber indent
    set tagnumber 0
```

```
set indent 0
$t delete 0.0 end
if {[catch {open $input} ch]} {
    puts stderr "unable to open file \"$input\""
    exit 1
}
set p [xml::parser -elementstartcommand Start \
                   -elementendcommand End \
                   -characterdatacommand CData]
if {[catch {$p parse [read $ch]} err]} {
    puts stderr $err
    exit 1
}
catch {close $ch}
}

# Call the ParseXML procedure and start processing
# the file supplied on the command line

ParseXML
```

The script builds on our simple parser example earlier in this chapter. Before we get to the actual parsing of the XML, we set up a simple window with a few buttons and a main text box to hold the XML.

We then use the text tags feature in a Tk text box to mark up the start and end tags as we see them in the XML document. To ensure that we mark up the right element, we have to keep a count of the paragraphs that we write to the text widget (in the *tagnumber* variable). To aid display, we also indent the structure like a tree (using the *indent* variable). The application was designed as an active viewer for XML documents while editing the XML document in another application. You can reparse the document and redisplay XML by clicking on the Re-ParseXML button. It's not perfect—supply an XML document that has multiple linefeeds/paragraphs in a character data block and the numbering goes awry, but it's a great way to view a basic XML document.

USING XML-RPC

XML-RPC is a solution for executing functions, procedures, and commands on a remote machine using a standard interface. The system is cross-platform and cross-language compatible, and it's all made possible because the request to the remote machine and its response to the client are handled entirely using XML.

When you submit a request, it's packaged into an XML document, which is then sent over your desired transport (TCP/IP and usually HTTP). The whole process is then reversed when sending back the response. Because the request and response are in XML, we can use any XML-capable language.

A few XML-RPC solutions are available for Tcl, but the one with the easiest interface is the XML-RPC Tcl toolkit written by Eric Yeh.

Writing an XML-RPC Client

The client interface for calling a remote procedure is not that different from evaluating a local procedure. In fact, we can dissect the line that performs the call very simply, as in the following line, extracted from our full client sample:

```
[xmlrpc::call "http://localhost:5557" "bond"
➡{{string Cats} {int 101}}]
```

The first part is just the command `xmlrpc::call`, which submits the request to the remote server. The first argument to the call is the URL we want to use to answer queries. In this instance, we're using a server running on port 5557 on the local machine.

The next argument, bond, is the name of the remote function that we want to call. The last argument is a list of the arguments that we want to supply to the remote procedure as part of the call. In this example, we've supplied a string and an integer. Note that you must type these values explicitly so that the XML-RPC package knows how to mark up the values when it builds the request envelope sent to the server.

You can see the full server, which includes error checking and the reporting of the response, in Listing 19.3.

Listing 19.3: A Simple XML-RPC Client in Tcl

```
package require xmlrpc
if {[catch {set res [xmlrpc::call
➡"http://localhost:5557" "bond"
➡ {{string Cats} {int 101}}]}]} {
        puts "xmlrpc call failed"
} else {
        puts "Join: $res."
}
```

```
if {[catch {set res [xmlrpc::call
➡"http://localhost:5557" "circlearea"
➡ {{int 2}}]}]} {
        puts "xmlrpc call failed"
} else {
        puts "Area of circle: $res."
}
```

If you execute this script while running the server—which we'll see shortly—you get the following output:

```
Join: {} Cats101.
Area of circle: {} 12.566370616.
```

Although these seem like fairly simple examples (and they are), the flexibility of XML-RPC cannot be underestimated. We've run a couple of commands on a local machine, but the server could just as easily have been on the other side of the world. In fact, we could have been calling the remote procedures on an embedded system inside a soft drink machine.

Writing an XML-RPC Server

The XML-RPC server handles requests from a given client. The server needs to set up only two pieces of information: the port on which it will accept requests from a client and the one or more functions that you want to support remotely. The XML-RPC toolkit handles the rest of the process; you don't have to register the commands separately that you want to support, as you do with some toolkits.

For example, Listing 19.4 shows a very simple client that supports two commands: bond, which bonds two arguments into a single string, and circlearea, which calculates the area of a circle if given the radius.

Listing 19.4: A Simple XML-RPC Server in Tcl

```
package require xmlrpc

xmlrpc::serve 5557

proc circlearea {r} {
    return [list string [expr 3.141592654 *
➡($r * $r)]]
}

proc bond {a b} {
```

```
        return [list string $a$b]
}
```

```
vwait forever
```

The primary line sets up a daemon-based XML-RPC server on TCP/IP port 5557. Then we define two commands, which will be those supported and accessible by any remote clients.

Arguments to commands are supplied and accessible as normal. However, when returning information, you must ensure that you return a list of items. Each item within the returned list should also be typed explicitly (through int(), double(), or string()) before being returned. For example, you can see in Listing 19.4 that the result of the area calculation is converted explicitly into a double during its calculation and return.

Finally, we set the server to wait for incoming connections forever. The server will handle all connections until either a fatal error or you terminate the process. During execution, the server will display diagnostic information, including the client host and port and the XML-RPC–encoded envelope returned to the client.

For example, the abbreviated snippet that follows is produced when running our client script:

```
in serveOnce: addr: 127.0.0.1
in serveOnce: port: 41179
in doRequest: response:
HTTP/1.1 200 OK
Content-Type: text/xml
Content-length: 142

<?xml version="1.0"?>
<methodResponse>
        <params>
                <param>

<value><string>Cats101</string></value>
                </param>
        </params>
</methodResponse>
...
```

As you can see, both the client and the server are very easy to write. In fact, this is one of the easiest implementations of the XML-RPC system of any of the languages covered in this book.

SUMMARY

Although Tcl is a very useful language in its own right, it really comes into its own when you combine the language with the Tk user interface builder.

The Tcl system supports two main XML parsers: TclXML, which parses documents using an XML parser written entirely in Tcl, and TclExpat, which uses the popular Expat parser system to process the XML document.

In both cases, the system works by passing off the individual elements to a Tcl command. It's up to these commands to process the information, whether it's simply printing out the information or formatting it in a more structured form, such as the Tk XML viewer.

Tcl also supports the XML-RPC system for executing remote procedures. By supporting an HTTP service, a Tcl server script can service requests from a Tcl client, enabling the client to execute commands directly on the server and obtain responses.

Our next chapter explores XML applications using PHP, which is a rapidly growing open source scripting environment for building application servers on Web-based enterprise systems.

Chapter 20

XML AND PHP

P HP4 comes with a built-in suite of functions for parsing and working with XML documents. The parser itself is based on the Expat parser, which is an XML 1.0 parser written by James Clark.

Expat is an event-based parser. This means that the parser processes the document in chunks, accepting parts of the XML document (anything from a byte up to the entire document). As each entity within the document is identified, the parser calls a predefined function whose job it is to handle the entity.

Since PHP is an embedded HTML technology, the most obvious use for an XML parser is to turn an XML document into an embedded part of the HTML document we are producing. Other uses include converting a given Web form into an XML document for storage, either directly or by handing the XML document off to an extension so that it can be translated into a database record.

Written for *XML Complete* by Martin C. Brown

In this chapter, we'll look at the basic mechanics of parsing an XML document within PHP and of converting information to and from the XML format. We'll also take a look at communicating with another function on a remote machine using the XML-RPC technology.

BUILDING A SIMPLE XML PARSER

As we already know, the XML parser available within PHP is based on the Expat library. The Expat library uses callback functions, which are executed when the different entities in the document are identified.

A number of different entities make up an XML document, but the primary components that all XML parsers are capable of handling are the start tag (i.e., <data>), the end tag (</data>) and any character data (any non-tagged element).

The full process for building an XML parser within PHP can be broken down into five steps:

1. Create the handlers that will deal with the different document entities.

2. Create the XML parser.

3. Register the entity handlers with the XML parser.

4. Feed the XML parser with our XML document, probably read from an external file.

5. Close the parser.

You can see a very simple parser in Listing 20.1.

Listing 20.1: A Simple XML Parser

```php
<?php

// set up the function that will handle any opening
// tags. It must accept the tagname and any
// attributes

function startTagHandler($parser,
                         $tagname,
                         $attributes)
{
    echo("START: $tagname<br>");
}
```

```
// set up the function for any end tags
// end tags don't have attributes so we can simply
// accept the tagname for closure

function endTagHandler($parser,
                       $tagname)
{
    echo("END:    $tagname<br>");
}


// set up the function for any character data

function cdataHandler($parser,
                      $data)
{
    echo("DATA:   $data<br>");
}


// create a new XML parser

$parser = xml_parser_create();


// register the tag and data handling functions
// with the parser

xml_set_element_handler($parser,
                        "startTagHandler",
                        "endTagHandler");

xml_set_character_data_handler($parser,
➡"cdataHandler");


// Open the file, here hardcoded,
//that holds the XML

if (!($xmlfile = fopen("simple.xml", "r")))
{
    die("Could not open the file for reading");
}


// Read data from the file in 2K blocks and send it
```

```
    // off to the parser. Any error will trigger a call
    // to die reporting the line and column number that
    // the error occurred within the source XML file
    // !!!NOT!!! the PHP script

    while ($xmldata = fread($xmlfile, 2048))
    {
        if (!xml_parse($parser, $xmldata, feof
➡($xmlfile)))
        {
            die(sprintf("XML error at line %d,
➡column %d",
                        xml_get_current_line_number
➡($parser),
                        xml_get_current_column_number($parser)));
        }
    }

    ?>
```

If you feed the parser a simple XML file, such as the one shown in Listing 20.2, you get the HTML output shown in Listing 20.3. The actual output is probably best demonstrated by Figure 20.1, which shows the HTML in its rendered form.

Listing 20.2: A Simple XML Document to Demonstrate Our PHP Parser

```
<contact>
  <name>Martin Brown</name>
  <address>
    <description>Main Address</description>
    <addressline>The House, The Street, The
Town</addressline>
  </address>
  <address>
    <description>Holiday Chalet</description>
    <addressline>The Chalet, The Hillside, The
    Forest</addressline>
  </address>
</contact>
```

Listing 20.3: The HTML Generated by Our "Simple" XML Parser

```
START: CONTACT<br>
DATA:
<br>
DATA:     <br>
START: NAME<br>
DATA:  Martin Brown<br>
END:   NAME<br>
DATA:
<br>
DATA:     <br>
START: ADDRESS<br>
DATA:
<br>
DATA:      <br>
START: DESCRIPTION<br>
DATA:  Main Address<br>
END:   DESCRIPTION<br>
DATA:
<br>
DATA:       <br>
START: ADDRESSLINE<br>
DATA:  The House, The Street, The Town<br>
END:   ADDRESSLINE<br>
DATA:
<br>
DATA:     <br>
END:   ADDRESS<br>
DATA:
<br>
DATA:     <br>
START: ADDRESS<br>
DATA:
<br>
DATA:       <br>
START: DESCRIPTION<br>
DATA:  Holiday Chalet<br>
END:   DESCRIPTION<br>
DATA:
<br>
DATA:       <br>
START: ADDRESSLINE<br>
```

```
DATA:   The Chalet, The Hillside, The Forest<br>
END:    ADDRESSLINE<br>
DATA:
<br>
DATA:    <br>
END:    ADDRESS<br>
DATA:
<br>
END:    CONTACT<br>
```

FIGURE 20.1: Our Simple XML Document in HTML

You can see a few important aspects of how the Expat parser works by looking in detail at Listing 20.3. Ignoring the formatting for the moment, you can see how each of the different entities in the source are passed off to handler functions that we created.

You'll also notice that the ASCII output of HTML includes several additional spaces and newlines that you might not have expected. These are actually part of the original source file, but they result from the way Expat (rather than PHP) works.

Expat passes on all characters from the source XML file, including spaces, newline, tab, and other characters. You'll also notice that the blocks of character data as they are processed are not consistent with the source file. We know from looking at the XML source that the character data is all in one block; when it's extracted by the Expat parser, it is split into separate chunks.

Both of these issues are unfortunate side effects of the way Expat parses an XML document. In most instances, they are not going to cause a significant problem because these artifacts affect what should be raw data. When converted to HTML, the additional spaces and newlines probably won't seriously affect the output, but you might want to apply a filter to ensure that any blocks of data consisting of any white space are ignored. A simple regular expression will handle this for us—see Listing 20.4 for an updated version of the cdataHandler() function, and see Listing 20.5 for the somewhat cleaner resulting output from our XML file.

Listing 20.4: A Version of the Character Data Handler That Filters White Space

```
function cdataHandler($parser,
                      $data)
{
    if (!ereg("^[ \f\r\t\n]+$",$data))
    {
        echo("DATA:   $data<br>\n");
    }
}
```

Listing 20.5: A Cleaner Version of Our XML File

```
START: CONTACT<br>
START: NAME<br>
DATA:   Martin Brown<br>
END:   NAME<br>
START: ADDRESS<br>
START: DESCRIPTION<br>
DATA:   Main Address<br>
END:   DESCRIPTION<br>
START: ADDRESSLINE<br>
DATA:   The House, The Street, The Town<br>
END:   ADDRESSLINE<br>
END:   ADDRESS<br>
```

```
START:  ADDRESS<br>
START:  DESCRIPTION<br>
DATA:   Holiday Chalet<br>
END:    DESCRIPTION<br>
START:  ADDRESSLINE<br>
DATA:   The Chalet, The Hillside, The Forest<br>
END:    ADDRESSLINE<br>
END:    ADDRESS<br>
END:    CONTACT<br>
```

As you can see from Listing 20.5, the output is now much cleaner, and the resulting rendered HTML page, although not shown here, doesn't look any different.

INSIDE THE XML PARSER

At the risk of repeating myself, the XML parser built into PHP is based on Expat libraries. The standard PHP 4.*x* distributions now include the source for Expat and the extensions for PHP itself to handle the XML processing, and XML should be enabled by default when you configure and build the system.

Information sent to the parser is handled entirely by the parser and the functions that you create to handle the different elements. There's no way to interrupt the flow of parsing and execute another function *unless* it's been triggered by the existence of an entity within the XML file.

In this section we'll look at the specifics of the XML parsing process, the supported XML handlers, and how to debug and trace errors within your XML documents.

Before we get there, here are two more points to note about the PHP XML extensions:

▶ XML documents are encoded using Unicode, which enables you to write documents that include characters beyond the normal 127 ASCII characters you may be used to. Unicode uses multibyte characters to allow you to include accented roman characters as well as Kanji (Chinese/Korean and other Far Eastern languages) and all other native forms, including Indian and Middle-Eastern characters. Check out the sidebar "Unicode Support" for information on how the PHP extensions handle Unicode-encoded XML characters, and remember that the effects are felt by both the character data and entity handlers.

▶ There is no standard for the case within tags in XML documents—in fact, the XML standard deliberately allows lower-, upper-, or mixed-case tags in XML documents. By default, the PHP XML extensions case-fold tags so that when supplied as arguments to the entity handlers they are received as upper case. We can control this through an option—see the section "Getting/Setting Options" later in this chapter for more information.

UNICODE SUPPORT

The PHP XML extensions supports the Unicode character set by using different character encodings for input and output. Input encodings affect how the PHP XML extension interprets incoming characters. The default input encoding is ISO-8859-1, which closely follows the basic roman character set with extensions that are supported by most computer platforms. The ISO-8859-1 set matches the ASCII set for the first 127 characters, so we can parse most ASCII/text-based documents without changing the encoding.

The output encodings are used when transferring information over to the entity handlers that you have configured to parse your XML documents. The output encoding affects all aspects the entities passed on to the entity handling functions, from tag names to character data.

Any errors in handling the input encodings—that is, characters that do not match the set input encoding—raise an error. If the input encoding cannot be translated into the desired output encoding, the character is replaced with a question mark.

Initial Setup

The core function in the PHP XML extensions is xml_parser_create(). This creates a new instance of the XML parser. You can potentially have many such parsers active in your application at one time, but remember that execution and parsing of an XML document is generally uninterrupted from start to finish.

If you want to parse multiple XML documents in sequence, it's a good idea to create a new parser each time, even if you place the resulting parser object into the same variable. The reason for this is that Expat is not a validating parser—that is, it doesn't in any way verify that the content of the XML document follows a given DTD.

What Expat does is check that the document is structured correctly. Start and end tags must match, and any errors that occur during parsing are raised by immediately falling out of the parser with a false return value. See the section "Error Trapping" later in this chapter for information on identifying the location of such errors.

By creating a new parser, you reset the information that the parser has built up regarding the structure of the document.

Creating the Parser

The first step to parsing any XML document is to create the parser itself. The format for the xml_parser_create() function is

```
xml_parser_create([string encoding_format])
```

The optional encoding_format is the character source encoding used when parsing the document. This format can be set only once—if you want to parse another document with a different encoding, you'll have to create a new parser. Accepted values for the input encoding format are ISO-8859-1 (the default), US-ASCII, and UTF-8.

The xml_parser_create() function returns a true value—actually a parser handle—if the parser could be created successfully, or false if an error occurred. You need to catch this return value because you'll need the parser handle when you want to supply the parser with some data. For example:

```
$parser = xml_parser_create("US-ASCII");
```

Supplying Data

Once you've created the parser, you can call the xml_parse() function to start the parsing process. Although nothing will happen when the different entities are identified in the XML document or string that you pass to the function, it will cause the XML to be checked for its structure.

If you want to parse the document and perform different operations according to the different entities, you need to register the entity handlers *before* calling xml_parse().

The format of the xml_parse() function is

```
xml_parse(int parser, string data [, int isFinal])
```

The *parser* argument should be the parser handler that was created when you called xml_parser_create(). The *data* argument is the XML data that you want to supply to the parser. You can supply as much or as little of this information as you like. If you're reading the data from an external file, a figure of 1 or 2 KB is enough for most uses. Remember, though, how Expat deals with character data—if you know that you have large character data elements within your documents, you may want to supply a larger quantity to ensure that the parser identifies the block as one entire unit.

The optional *isFinal* argument specifies whether the block of data that you are supplying is the final block. The parser needs to know this in order to ensure that the structure of the document is valid. When you signify the end of your XML, the parser ensures that the tags match up and don't overlap. If you're reading from an external file, the easiest way to supply this value is to use the return from the `feof()` function on your file's file handle.

Freeing the Parser

Once you've finished parsing an XML document, or if you've trapped an error that means you cannot continue processing the document, you can call the `xml_parser_free()` function. This function clears the parser and any resources it was using from memory. Although this is not a vital part of the process—especially since PHP frees the resources once the script terminates anyway—it is good practice, especially if you expect to be parsing large documents.

Supported Entity Handlers

There are three primary entity handlers: those for the start, end, and data elements of your XML document. We've already seen some examples of these, but to recap, the format of each handler function that you need to create is

```
startTagHandler(int parser, string tagname, array
➥attributes[]);
endTagHandler(int parser, string tagname);
charDataHandler(int parser, string chardata);
```

The names used here are just examples; the handler functions can have any name.

The *parser* argument is the parser handle that invoked the handler. The *tagname* argument is the tag text; for example, the tag <para> would be supplied simply as the string para.

For the start tag handler, the function is also supplied with an associative array of attributes. For example, the tag

```
<ref loc="someotherxml.xml" width=100 height=200>
```

is supplied to the handler function as

```
array("loc"    => "someotherxml.xml",
      "width"  => 100,
      "height" => 200);
```

The chardata argument is the text identified by the parser as character data.

In order for these functions to be accepted as the handlers for the different entities, you need to use one of the xml_set*() functions. The start and end tag handlers are registered using the xml_set_element_ handler() function, while the character data handler is registered by the xml_set_character_data_handler() function. For example:

```
xml_set_element_handler($parser,
                        "startTagHandler",
                        "endTagHandler");


xml_set_character_data_handler($parser,
➥"cdataHandler");
```

Table 20.1 lists other handlers for dealing with different entities that are supported by the XML parser. Note that all entity handlers accept a first argument: the parser handler. Only additional arguments for the handler are listed. Also note that all handler register functions are prefixed by xml_set_ and have a suffix of handler—for example, the processing_ instruction function listed in the first row of the table should be called as xml_set_processing_instruction_handler().

TABLE 20.1: Other Entity Handlers Supported by PHP XML

Handler	Register Function	Handler Arguments	Description
Processing Instruction	processing_ instruction	target, data	Handles processing instructions, which allow an XML document to execute a particular instruction. The target should be the target of the processing instruction (for example, php). The data is the string to be supplied to the target handler. The usual operation is to supply data to the target processor.

TABLE 20.1 continued: Other Entity Handlers Supported by PHP XML

HANDLER	REGISTER FUNCTION	HANDLER ARGUMENTS	DESCRIPTION
Notation Declaration	`notation_decl`	`notation, base, systemid, publicid`	The `notation` is the name of the notation, base the base for resolving `systemId` (currently always a null string), `systemId` the system identifier, and `publicId` the public identifier.
External Entity Reference	`external_entity_ref`	`entityname, base, systemid, publicid`	The `entityname` is the name of the entity that has been identified, base the base for resolving `systemId` (currently always a null string), `systemId` the system identifier (that is, the expansion of the external entity), and `publicId` the public identifier. Most functions should incorporate the contents of `systemId` into the current document.
Unparsed Entity Declaration	`unparsed_entity_decl`	`entityname, base, systemid, publicid, notationname`	Handles entities that are unparsed. See previous handlers for descriptions on how to handle the different arguments.
Default Handler	`default_handler`	Data	The default handler function handles all other entities that do not already have an explicit handler function. The default handler is also called if you have not explicitly registered a handler for a given entity. The data contains the entire entity, including angled brackets.

Getting/Setting Options

The PHP XML parser supports two options that change the way in which the document is parsed and how the information is propagated on to the entity handlers. The two options are:

XML_OPTION_CASE_FOLDING   If this option is set to `true`, tag names are converted to upper case before they are supplied to the start and end tag handlers. Note that this affects only the tag names; attribute names and other elements within the entities remain unchanged. Case folding is on by default; setting the value to `false` disables case folding.

XML_OPTION_TARGET_ENCODING   Sets the type of encoding used when data is parsed on to any of the entity handlers. The default type is the same as the input handler, as defined when the parser was created. If the input and output (target) encodings are different, PHP translates the data to the new encoding format. See the sidebar "Unicode Support" earlier in this chapter for more information.

You can obtain the current value of any option by using the xml_parser_get_option() function. For example, to determine whether case folding is switched on:

```
$casefolding = xml_parser_get_option($parser,
➥XML_OPTION_CASE_FOLDING);
```

To set the value of these options, use the xml_parser_set_option() function. For example, to disable case folding:

```
xml_parser_set_option($parser,
➥XML_OPTION_CASE_FOLDING, false);
```

Other options may be added in the future. Check the documentation for PHP for more information.

Error Trapping

The main xml_parse() function returns an error code if it sees a problem with the XML document that it is parsing. The return code can be matched against one of the predefined XML error codes listed in Table 20.2. Note that nearly all the error codes refer to problems in the XML document that you are parsing and not to problems in the parser or your PHP code.

TABLE 20.2:   XML Error Codes and Descriptions

ERROR CODE CONSTANT	DESCRIPTION
XML_ERROR_NONE	No error.
XML_ERROR_NO_MEMORY	Parser ran out of memory—try supplying the data in smaller chunks.
XML_ERROR_SYNTAX	Syntax error.
XML_ERROR_NO_ELEMENTS	No elements found in the document.
XML_ERROR_INVALID_TOKEN	A tag is not well formed—check for matching <> brackets.
XML_ERROR_UNCLOSED_TOKEN	The tag has not been closed.
XML_ERROR_PARTIAL_CHAR	Unclosed token.

TABLE 20.2 continued: XML Error Codes and Descriptions

Error Code Constant	Description
XML_ERROR_TAG_MISMATCH	Start and end tags do not match.
XML_ERROR_DUPLICATE_ATTRIBUTE	Attributes in a tag have been duplicated.
XML_ERROR_JUNK_AFTER_DOC_ELEMENT	There is junk after a document element or end of the XML document.
XML_ERROR_PARAM_ENTITY_REF	The document references an entity that has not been defined.
XML_ERROR_UNDEFINED_ENTITY	The document uses an entity that has not been defined.
XML_ERROR_RECURSIVE_ENTITY_REF	The entity reference refers back to itself, or to another reference that points back to itself.
XML_ERROR_ASYNC_ENTITY	Asynchronous entity.
XML_ERROR_BAD_CHAR_REF	Document contains a reference to a bad character number.
XML_ERROR_BINARY_ENTITY_REF	Document refers to a binary entity reference (which cannot be handled).
XML_ERROR_ATTRIBUTE_EXTERNAL_ENTITY_REF	Document refers to an external entity reference within a tag attribute.
XML_ERROR_MISPLACED_XML_PI	An XML processing instruction is not in the right place.
XML_ERROR_UNKNOWN_ENCODING	The XML document uses an unknown encoding format (i.e., not UTF-8, US-ASCII, or ISO-8859-1).
XML_ERROR_INCORRECT_ENCODING	The encoding defined in the XML encoding declaration is not supported.
XXML_ERROR_UNCLOSED_CDATA_SECTION	A character data portion has not been terminated properly. If reading from a file, check that the entire file was read properly.
XXML_ERROR_EXTERNAL_ENTITY_HANDLING	There was an error processing an external entity reference.

You can convert any of these error codes into a more meaningful string by using the `xml_error_string()` function. This accepts the error code number, as returned by `xml_parse()`, and returns a string error message. For example:

```
echo xml_error_string(XML_ERROR_NONE);
```

Once an error has occurred, you can also determine your location within the XML document that you were passing using `xml_get_current_line_` number(), xml_get_current_column_number(), and xml_get_current_ byte_index() to determine the line, column, and byte of the location of the error. Note that these functions return the location within the XML document or stream where the parsing error occurred, not the location within your PHP script.

For example, here's a call to the xml_parse() function, which reports an error detailing the line and column number, taken here from our first PHP XML processing example:

```
if (!xml_parse($parser, $xmldata, feof($xmlfile)))
    {
        die(sprintf("XML error %d %d",
                xml_get_current_line_number($parser),

xml_get_current_column_number($parser)));
    }
```

CONVERTING XML TO HTML

Our previous example is not the perfect illustration of what you can do with XML in PHP. Instead, let's have a look at a script, shown in Listing 20.6, that converts an XML document into HTML suitable for display on screen.

Listing 20.6: Converting XML to HTML in PHP

```php
<?php

$file = "alien_r.xml";

// The array which holds the map from XML tag
// to HTML tags and attributes

$xmltohtml = array(
    "TITLE"     => array(array("tag" => "FONT",
                            "attrs" =>
                        array("size" => "+1")),
                        array("tag" => "B"),
                        ),
    "ACTORS"    => array(array("tag" => "FONT",
                            "attrs" =>
                        array("color" => "red")),
                        ),
```

```
            "PARA"        => array(array("tag" => "P")),
            "PANEL"       => array(array("tag" => "table",
                                "attrs" =>
                                array("border" => 0,
                                "cellspacing" => 0,
                                "cellpadding" => 0,))),
            "PANELTITLE" => array(array("tag" => "tr",
                                "attrs" =>
                                array("bgcolor" =>
➥"black",
                                "fgcolor" => "white",)),
                                array("tag" => "td")),

            "PANELBODY" => array(array("tag" => "tr",
                                "attrs" =>
                                array("bgcolor" => "white",
                                "fgcolor" => "black",)),
                                array("tag" => "td")),
            "EXTREF"      => array(array("tag" => "A")),


);


// set up the function that will handle any opening
// tags. This function looks up in the xmltohtml
// associative array and matches an XML tag with an
// equivalent HTML entry for displaying the data


function startTagHandler($parser,
                         $tagname,
                         $attributes)
{
    global $xmltohtml;
    if ($html = $xmltohtml[$tagname])
    {
        for($tagindex = 0; $tagindex <
➥count($html); ++$tagindex)
        {
            $mytagdetails = $html[$tagindex];
            echo "<",$mytagdetails["tag"];
            if ($myattrs = $mytagdetails["attrs"])
```

```
                {
                    while (list($k, $v) =
➥each($myattrs))
                    {
                        echo " $k=\"$v\"";
                    }
                }

                while (list($k, $v) = each($attributes))
                {
                    echo " $k=\"$v\"";
                }

                echo ">";
            }
        }
    }

    // set up the function for any end tags

    function endTagHandler($parser,
                            $tagname)
    {
        global $xmltohtml;
        if ($html = $xmltohtml[$tagname])
        {
            for($tagindex = (count($html)-1);
➥$tagindex >= 0; -$tagindex)
            {
                $mytagdetails = $html[$tagindex];
                echo "</",$mytagdetails["tag"],">";
            }
        }
    }

    // set up the function for any character data

    function cdataHandler($parser,
                            $data)
    {
        if (!ereg("^[ \f\r\t\n]+$",$data))
        {
            echo($data);
```

```
        }
    }

    // Create a new XML parser

    $parser = xml_parser_create();

    // Ensure case folding is switched on

    xml_parser_set_option($parser,
    ➥XML_OPTION_CASE_FOLDING, true);

    // register the tag and data handling functions
    // with the parser

    xml_set_element_handler($parser,
                            "startTagHandler",
                            "endTagHandler");

    xml_set_character_data_handler($parser,
    ➥"cdataHandler");


    if (!($fp = fopen($file, "r"))) {
        die("could not open XML input");
    }

    while ($data = fread($fp, 4096)) {
        if (!xml_parse($parser, $data, feof($fp))) {
            die(sprintf("XML error: %s at line %d",

    xml_error_string(xml_get_error_code($parser)),
            xml_get_current_line_number($parser)));
        }
    }
    xml_parser_free($parser);

    ?>
```

The $xmltohtml variable and the two start and end tag handlers are
the important parts of the script.

The $xmltohtml variable is a nested structure. The top-level structure
is an associative array. The key at this top level is the XML tag that we

want to replace, while the corresponding value is an array of HTML tags that we want to use as the replacement text. Note that we use an array of tags, not an associative array. This is because we need to order the HTML tags correctly in the output.

Each HTML tag is made up of the base tag, and then includes a further associative array of attributes and their values that we want to introduce.

The `startTagHandler()` function identifies the XML tag in the `$xmltohtml` array and then works through the resulting tree to output the corresponding HTML tags that we've configured. Once the HTML tags have been output, we also output any XML tags that we've supplied before closing off each HTML tag.

The `endTagHandler()` function essentially does the same as the `startTagHandler()`, except that it processes the HTML tags in reverse so that they nest properly in the resulting HTML. Now you can see why we have an array of these tags—so that we can sequence and "desequence" in the same order.

We can explain this all better with a sample. Taking the XML code here:

```
<title>Alien Resurrection</title>
```

the tag handlers would generate:

```
<FONT size="+1">
<B><BR>Alien Resurrection</BR></B></FONT>
```

If we supply the script with the whole document, shown in Listing 20.7, we get the HTML output shown in Listing 20.8 (massaged slightly for readability) or the final rendered document shown in Figure 20.2. Note in both cases that I've trimmed the full document (which uses the Lorem Ipsum text) for brevity.

TIP

Lorem Ipsum is a standard piece of text that you can incorporate into a document when you don't yet have the full text.

Listing 20.7: Our Sample XML Document

```
<video>
<main>
<para><title>Alien Resurrection</title></para>
<para><actors>Sigourney Weaver, Winona
Ryder</actors></para>
```

```
<title>Witness the Resurrection</title>
<para>Alien Resurrection is a film...Lorem ipsum dolor sit
amet, consectetuer adipiscing elit, sed diam nonummy nibh
euismod tincidunt ut laoreet dolore magna aliquam erat volut-
pat.
...
It va esser tam simplic quam Occidental: in fact, it va esser
Occidental. A un Angleso it va semblar un simplificat Angles,
quam un skeptic Cambridge amico dit me que Occidental es.
</para>
</main>
<panel>
<paneltitle>Related Items</paneltitle>
<panelbody>
<para><extref href="vhrefeo/alien.xml">Alien</extref></para>
<para><extref
href="vhrefeo/aliens.xml">Aliens</extref></para>
<para><extref
href="vhrefeo/alien3.xml">Alien3</extref></para>
<para><extref href="vhrefeo/alien_boxset.xml">Alien Legacy
Box set</extref></para>
<para><extref href="scifi.php">Sci-Fi</extref>
</para>
<para><extref href="horror.php">Horror</extref>
</para>
<para><extref href="action.php">Action</extref>
</para>
</panelbody>
</panel>
</video>
```

Listing 20.8: The Final HTML Document

```
<P><FONT size="+1"><B>Alien Resurrection</B>
</FONT></P>
<P>
<FONT color="red">Sigourney Weaver, Winona Ryder
</FONT>
</P>
<FONT size="+1"><B>Witness the Resurrection</B>
</FONT>
<P>Alien Resurrection is a film...Lorem ipsum dolor sit
  amet, consectetuer adipiscing elit, sed diam nonummy nibh
```

euismod tincidunt ut laoreet dolore magna aliquam erat
volutpat.
...
It va esser tam simplic quam Occidental: in fact, it va
esser Occidental. A un Angleso it va semblar un simplificat
Angles, quam un skeptic Cambridge amico dit me que
Occidental es.
```
</P><table border="0" cellspacing="0" cellpadding="0">
<tr bgcolor="black" fgcolor="white">
<td>Related Items</td>
</tr>
<tr bgcolor="white" fgcolor="black"><td>
<P><A HREF="vhrefeo/alien.xml">Alien</A></P>
<P><A HREF="vhrefeo/aliens.xml">Aliens</A></P>
<P><A HREF="vhrefeo/alien3.xml">Alien3</A></P>
<P>
<A HREF="vhrefeo/alien_boxset.xml">
Alien Legacy Box set</A>
</P>
<P><A HREF="scifi.php">Sci-Fi</A></P>
<P><A HREF="horror.php">Horror</A></P>
<P><A HREF="action.php">Action</A></P>
</td></tr></table>
<P><FONT size="+1"><B><BR>Alien
Resurrection</BR></B></FONT></P><P><FONT
color="red"><BR>Sigourney Weaver, Winona
Ryder</BR></FONT></P><FONT size="+1"><B><BR>Witness the
Resurrection</BR></B></FONT><P>Alien Resurrection is a
film...Lorem ipsum dolor sit amet, consectetueradipiscing
elit, sed diam nonummy nibh euismod tincidunt ut laoreet
doloremagna aliquam erat volutpat....It va esser tam simplic
quam Occidental: in fact, it va esser Occidental. A unAngleso
it va semblar un simplificat Angles, quam un skeptic
Cambridge amicodit me que Occidental es.</P><table border="0"
cellspacing="0" cellpadding="0"><tr bgcolor="black"
fgcolor="white"><td>Related Items</td></tr><tr
bgcolor="white" fgcolor="black"><td><P><A
HREF="vhrefeo/alien.xml">Alien</A></P><P><A
HREF="vhrefeo/aliens.xml">Aliens</A></P><P><A
HREF="vhrefeo/alien3.xml">Alien3</A></P><P><A
HREF="vhrefeo/alien_boxset.xml">Alien Legacy
Boxset</A></P><P><A HREF="scifi.php">Sci-Fi</A></P><P><A
```

```
HREF="horror.php">Horror</A></P><P><A
HREF="action.php">Action</A></P></td></tr></table>
```

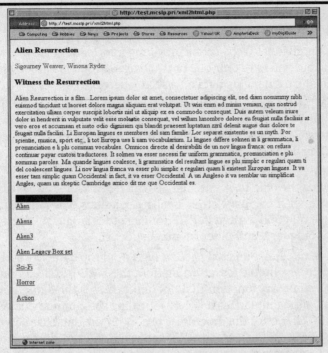

FIGURE 20.2: Our final XML document rendered in HTML

We've only scratched the surface of what we can do. Once you have the XML document working through the parser, you can more or less translate the information however you like. The important elements are the entity handlers, which treat each individual entity as it is seen.

Using XML-RPC

XML-RPC is a technology that uses an XML document transferred over a transport (usually HTTP) that requests a remote function on a machine to be executed. The function called can be any supported function, and you can supply arguments to it just as you would a local function. Also, just like a local function, the results of the function call are sent over the transport link back to the caller.

XML-RPC is useful in those situations when you want to execute a piece of code on a remote machine without resorting to designing your own network protocol and without the need to parcel up information in a CGI request and get it back in HTML format from the server.

It's particularly useful in distributed applications where you may have a number of individual Web servers providing information and services to your clients, but you have only one or two back-end servers processing information and exchanging data on a secure network.

Using XML-RPC, the user requests a document from the server. Then, the server finds that it needs information from one of the data servers, sends the request by XML-RPC to the data server, receives the response back, and then displays that information to the user.

The critical point here is that the remote server is doing much more than simply sending the data back; after all, we can do this already by using MySQL, PostgreSQL, or many other database solutions. The remote server is executing a function written in PHP (or any other language, since XML-RPC is language- and platform-independent).

The server-side function could access data from the database and put it into a structure suitable for returning from the XML-RPC function call. It might be a summary function that not only accesses the data from the database but also summarizes it before returning the summary data to the XML-RPC client. All the processing occurs on the database server, allowing the XML-RPC client (the Web server) to concentrate on process-ing Web requests from the end user.

The XML-RPC solution available with PHP is not quite as easy to use as those we've seen for some other languages. Requests and responses still have to be manually packaged and unpackaged when exchanging data, for example. Although this adds extra complexity to the process, the whole system is still straightforward enough.

As has been explained elsewhere, XML-RPC doesn't require any XML parsing abilities in order to use the system. XML-RPC is just a technology that uses XML to exchange information about functions, arguments, and return values between a server and a client.

The XML-RPC implementation under PHP works using the HTTP/CGI protocol, so the server acts just like any other CGI script on your Web server, and the client communicates with the server by sending a normal POST request. The information is then sent back as if we were dealing with any normal HTTP request, except that the information returned is an XML-RPC envelope, which we decode into the response.

We'll look at both a client and server implementation using PHP. In addition, because XML-RPC is platform- and language-independent, we'll also look at a client that accesses a Perl or Python server.

In order to use XML-RPC, you will need to install the XML-RPC package on your machine. You can find it at `http://xmlrpc.usefulinc.com/php.html`.

Writing an XML-RPC Client

The XML-RPC client communicates from one machine to another, sending a request to execute a specific function, along with the arguments you want to supply to the function, and then extracting and printing or using the returned values in another calculation or operation.

The basic sequence for creating an XML-RPC client in PHP is as follows:

1. Create a request object. This is the object that is "serialized" into XML and sent to the server.

2. Create a client object. This holds the information about the remote handler, its host, and the port on which to communicate.

3. Send the request to the server, using the information we've just built into the client and the request object that we've just created.

4. Decode the response, extracting the elements returned by the remote function into local variables that we can print or use accordingly.

You can see all of this put into a full script in Listing 20.9.

Listing 20.9: A Simple XML-RPC Client in PHP

```php
<html>
<head><title>XML-RPC Client Demo</title></head>
<body>
<?php

// Include the necessary XML-RPC code we need
include("xmlrpc.inc");

// Create a new request, based on the name of the remote
// function, and an array of the arguments that you want
// to supply to the remote function
```

```php
$request = new xmlrpcmsg('remote_echo',
                array(new xmlrpcval("Hello")));

// Create a new XML-RPC client instance using the
// location of the handler that will deal with the request,
// the address of the machine and it's port number
$server = new xmlrpc_client("/xmlrpcs.php",
                              "test.mchome.pri", 80);

// Switch debugging on
$server->setDebug(1);

// Execute the remote function,
// retrieving the response
// from the remote function
$response = $server->send($request);

// Check that the response was received
if (!$response) { die("Couldn't send request"); }

// Make sure that we got a reasonable response from
// the server
if (!$response->faultCode())
{
// Extract the value of the response
    $value = $response->value();

// Print out the value
    print "Remote response: " .
          $value->scalarval() . "<br>\n";
}
else
{
// If we had a fault at the remote end, decode the
// fault response packet and print out the errors
    print "Fault: (" . $response->faultCode() .
        ") " . $response->faultString() . "<BR>";
}

?>
</body>
</html>
```

The important parts are building the request object, which is actually an instance of the xmlrpcmsg class. The arguments to the object's creation are the name of the remote function that we want to call—in this case remote_echo—and the second argument is an array that contains a list of the values we want to supply to the remote function.

The remote function name should be composed of the namespace and the function name. We'll see a Python-compatible version later in this chapter.

You build each argument by using the xmlrpcval class, which accepts the value you want to encode and an optional argument defining how you want it interpreted. For example, we've used a string here that is automatically identified as a string, but you might want to supply a number as an integer or floating-point value. The encoding affects how the information is serialized into the XML-RPC packet sent to the server.

The other vital part is the creation of the client object. The object holds information about the remote host, its address and port number, and the name of the handler (usually the URL of a CGI script) that will process your request. In this example we've used the name of our PHP server, which we'll look at shortly. You could leave it blank, which assumes a direct HTTP connection to a server running in Daemon mode.

If you execute this script, assuming you've modified it to reflect your environment and correctly installed the server sample shown later in this chapter, then you should see something similar to the output shown in Listing 20.10.

Listing 20.10: Sample Output from an XML-RPC Client

```
--GOT--
HTTP/1.1 200 OK
Date: Fri, 06 Jul 2001 14:14:57 GMT
Server: Apache/1.3.20 (Unix) PHP/4.0.6 mod_perl/1.25
X-Powered-By: PHP/4.0.6
Connection: close
Content-Type: text/xml
Content-length: 204

<?xml version="1.0"?>
<!- DEBUG INFO:

0 - new xmlrpcval("Hello", 'string')
```

```
->
<methodResponse>
<params>
<param>
<value><string>Echo: Hello Hello</string></value>
</param>
</params>
</methodResponse>
--END--

--EVALING--[44 chars]--
new xmlrpcval("Echo: Hello Hello", 'string');
--END--
Remote response: Echo: Hello Hello
```

The bulk of the output shown here is debugging information. If debugging was switched off, we'd only see the final line, but you get the idea.

Now let's have a look at a PHP XML-RPC application that talks to a Python XML-RPC server. In this example, we're going to call the `join` function on the Python server, which accepts a list of words and returns a string containing the words joined together by spaces. Listing 20.11 shows the client.

Listing 20.11: Accessing a Python Daemon-based XML-RPC Server

```php
<html>
<head><title>XML-RPC Client Demo (Python)
</title></head>
<body>
<?php

include("xmlrpc.inc");

$myxmlargs=new xmlrpcval(array(
                new xmlrpcval("Tom"),
                new xmlrpcval("Dick"),
                new xmlrpcval("Harry")), "array");

$request = new xmlrpcmsg('join',array($myxmlargs));

$server = new xmlrpc_client("/RPC2",
➥"localhost", 8000);
```

```
$response = $server->send($request);

if (!$response) { die("Couldn't send request"); }

if (!$response->faultCode())
{
    $value = $response->value();
    print "Remote response: " .
➧$value->scalarval() . "<br>\n";
}
else
{
    print "Fault: (" . $response->faultCode() .
        ") " . $response->faultString() . "<BR>";
}

?>
</body>
</html>
```

Let's examine the two critical elements from this script. The first is the arguments that we supply. We need to supply an array as a single argument, so we first build an xmlrpcval array, which in turn contains a list of XML-RPC value objects that include the words we want joined together. We then supply that in the array of arguments that we define when building the request.

Second, because the Python server is daemon based (rather than CGI based) we need to access the server through a different port—in this case 8000—and we specify the hostname rather than a URL to the CGI script that will handle the request. The request handler is the /RPC2 specification. This is defined according to the XML-RPC standards but it's hidden under Perl, Python, and other languages, which automatically append the information when they realize they are communicating directly with an HTTP daemon and not through a CGI service.

Needless to say, the output we get is what we expect:

```
Remote response: Tom Dick Harry<br>
```

Writing an XML-RPC Server

The XML-RPC server is equally straightforward once you understand how to extract the information from the client and then repackage the response to send back to the client. The basic sequence for creating a PHP-based XML-RPC server is as follows:

1. You define the functions that you want to support on your server.

2. Each function extracts the data from the request manually, builds the response, and then returns the response back to the client.

3. You create a new server instance during which you register the functions that you want to support remotely.

You can see the server that supports the function we used in the client in Listing 20.12.

Listing 20.12: A Simple XML-RPC Server in PHP

```php
<?php

// Include the necessary XML-RPC code

include("xmlrpc.inc");
include("xmlrpcs.inc");

// Set up a function to echo back a string

function remote_echo($params)
{
// Get the XML client information
    global $xmlrpcerruser;

// Extract the first parameter from those supplied
    $param = $params->getParam(0);

// Check the parameter is the right type
    if ((isset($param)) && ($param->scalartyp()
==="string"))
    {
// Extract the actual value from the parameter
        $mesg = $param->scalarval();
// Build our response string
        $retval = "Echo: $mesg $mesg";
// Create a new response object and return it
// the contents of the response will be sent back
```

```
// to the client
        return new xmlrpcresp(new xmlrpcval
➥($retval));
    }
    else
    {
// We didn't get the type of argument we were expecting
// So build an error response to be returned to the client
        return new xmlrpcresp(0, $xmlrpcerruser,
                            "Invalid argument");
    }
}


// Create a new instance of an XML-RPC server
// and register our remote_echo function
$s=new xmlrpc_server( array("remote_echo" =>
                        array("function" =>
                            "remote_echo")));

?>
```

The important elements here are the way we get the information from the arguments, how we package the response, and how we register the function(s) that we want to support.

To extract the arguments sent to the remote function from the client, we use the getParam() method, which accepts one argument: the index of the argument that we want to retrieve. In our case, there is only one argument: the string we want to echo back. We then test that the variable and value that we received is the correct type for the rest of the function.

To create a response, whether the return value or an error packet, we create an instance of the xmlrpcresp class. In the case of the return value, we supply a single xmlrpcval object—identical to the one we created when sending the request in the client. If you want to return more than one argument, use the technique we used for the Python XML-RPC client to build an array-based xmlrpcval object.

For an error, we build the response from a false value, the XML user information, and the error message we want to use.

The final part of the process is to register the function within a new instance of the xmlrpc_server class. The class handles all of the communication and extraction for us.

The first argument should be an associative array, where each key is the name of the function as it is exposed to the client. In our case, we've used a value of `remote_echo`, which exists within the standard namespace. You could also prefix the name with the namespace you want to support; for example, `example.remote_echo`.

The value of that element of the associative array is then an embedded array—the `function` key defines the name of the actual function that will respond to the request. By using this two-tier system, we can expose the real `remote_echo` function as `example.echo`, for example.

That's really all there is to it. Obviously you could add more functions to the list, assuming you have definitions. All you need to do to enable the server is to copy it over into your Web server directory.

Summary

The steps to XML processing in PHP are simple. PHP offers an easy-to-use XML syntax to manage these steps:

1. Create an instance of an XML parser. This is a streaming, or event-based, parser.

2. Supply data.

3. Release the parser object.

4. Trap errors.

Then you can manage the XML in a number of ways, as we did it in this chapter when we converted XML to HTML.

To really explore the power of XML in PHP, go ahead and create an XML-RPC server like we showed you in this chapter. You can then use XML-RPC to manage function calls across a wide range of disparate systems.

The next chapter, "Servlets, JSP, and XML," completes our exploration of scripting and processing XML. The newest iterations of Java for the enterprise are making extensive use of XML. This chapter will look at some of the ways this is accomplished.

Chapter 21

SERVLETS, JSP, AND XML

This chapter discusses a combination of the hottest topics in the world of the Internet, XML, and Java. XML (Extensible Markup Language) is the latest incarnation of an idea that has been kicked around for a while, namely, documents that can describe their own contents. The first major attempt to find a way to allow a document to describe itself was SGML (Standard Generalized Markup Language). HTML (Hypertext Markup Language), the language of the Web, is a vastly simplified version of SGML. Programmers' experience with the complexity of SGML and the imprecise and inflexible nature of HTML led to the development of the less complex, but more precise and flexible XML.

Because Java is the ideal medium for portable programs, and XML is the medium for portable data, obviously the Java-XML combination is a marriage made in heaven. In this chapter, I'll cover the basics of using XML-formatted data in Java programs.

Adapted from *Java™ Developer's Guide to Servlets and JSP*, by Bill Brogden
ISBN 0-7821-2809-2   411 pages $49.99

BASIC XML AND JAVA CONFIGURATIONS

Sometimes gathering what you've learned about language syntax and porting it over to a specific environment can be tricky. It might be helpful in this case to review some XML basics and see how they pertain to a particular implementation, in this case a Java server environment. In this section, you'll see the underlying definitions for a dynamic XML document that is generated by a Java-based server.

Starting an XML File

As you know if you've read previous chapters, a well-formed XML document starts with a prolog that declares that this is an XML document and that (optionally) describes the XML version, the character encoding, and whether or not a document type definition (DTD) is provided. The `standalone="no"` in the following example indicates that a DTD will be provided:

```
<?xml version="1.0" encoding="us-ascii"
standalone="no" ?>
<!DOCTYPE BookErrata SYSTEM "BookErrata.dtd">
```

In the example, the `<!DOCTYPE>` tag specifies a few things:

- ► The name of the *root element*, in this case `BookErrata`.

- ► A reference to the DTD. In this case, `SYSTEM` means that the DTD is in a local file. Alternatively, `PUBLIC` would imply that the document follows a publicly available DTD and that the statement includes a name and a URL for that DTD.

- ► If a DTD is specified, a parser may verify that the document conforms to the DTD. Because verification is time consuming, many applications do not actually verify a document against the DTD even if one is specified. Frequently, a program switch is provided to control verification.

The CDATA and PCDATA Content Types

All text in an XML document that is not markup constitutes the character data of the document. An XML processor can treat character data in two ways, as parsed or unparsed, which is indicated in a DTD with #PCDATA and CDATA, respectively.

In a DTD, the element declarations

```
<!ATTLIST Book isbn CDATA #IMPLIED>
<!ELEMENT Title (#PCDATA)* >
```

would be interpreted to mean that the isbn attribute of the Book element consists of unparsed character data, whereas the Title element contents are parsed.

A special form of CDATA can be used to enclose text that will not be interpreted by the XML parser. The start sequence is <![CDATA[, and the end sequence is]]>. The main use for CDATA sections is to enclose text that uses special characters such as < and &, which might otherwise be interpreted as XML markup. Once the start sequence is recognized, the only thing the parser can do is look for the end sequence, ignoring all other text. This is a particularly important consideration when manipulating XML documents in Java and other programming environments.

Namespaces

As more programmers embrace XML, it has become obvious that many tag names, such as *Book*, will be duplicated. The concept of a namespace has been added to XML to provide for unique tag naming. A typical sample tag within the context of this discussion would be <Sybex:Book>, where the ID characters before the colon create the namespace. You can declare a namespace in effect within an element by using an attribute that starts with xmlns: combined with the ID and having as a value a unique identifier such as a corporate URI (Universal Resource Identifier), as in the following example:

```
<Sybex:Book xmlns:Sybex="http://www.sybex.com" >
    <!- various Book elements ->
</Sybex:Book>
```

XML and DTD Examples

We have very handy examples of using an XML document and a DTD in the configuration files used by the Tomcat Web server, the popular Java application server from Apache. The complete files are rather long, so I am showing only sections. Listing 21.1 shows the DTD for the server.xml file.

Listing 21.1: The server.dtd File Used by Tomcat

```
<?xml version="1.0" encoding="ISO-8859-1"?>
<!ELEMENT Server (ContextManager+)>
```

Part iv

```
<!ATTLIST Server adminPort NMTOKEN "-1"
                 workDir CDATA "work">
<!ELEMENT ContextManager (Context+, Interceptor*,
Connector+)>
<!ATTLIST ContextManager port NMTOKEN "8080"
    hostName NMTOKEN ""
    inet NMTOKEN "">
<!ELEMENT Context EMPTY>
<!ATTLIST Context
    path CDATA #REQUIRED
    docBase CDATA #REQUIRED
    defaultSessionTimeOut NMTOKEN "30"
    isWARExpanded (true | false) "true"
    isWARValidated (false | true) "false"
    isInvokerEnabled (true | false) "true"
    isWorkDirPersistent (false | true) "false">
<!ELEMENT Interceptor EMPTY>
<!ATTLIST Interceptor
    className NMTOKEN #REQUIRED
    docBase   CDATA #REQUIRED>
<!ELEMENT Connector (Parameter*)>
<!ATTLIST Connector
    className NMTOKEN #REQUIRED>
<!ELEMENT Parameter EMPTY>
<!ATTLIST Parameter
    name CDATA #REQUIRED
    value CDATA "">
```

Listing 21.2 shows part of a `server.xml` file that controls a Tomcat installation. This example uses the `<Context>` tag to create `/training` as a server alias for a real disk path. Note that not all the attributes listed in the DTD are set in the tag. Although `path` and `docBase` are required, the others have default values.

Listing 21.2: Part of a `server.xml` File

```
<Context path="/training"
  docBase="c:/InetPub/wwwroot/training"
    debug="1" reloadable="true" >
</Context>
```

Listing 21.3 shows part of Tomcat's `web.dtd` file that defines the `<servlet>` element contents. Note that the comment that starts the listing is used to provide extra information.

Listing 21.3: Part of the web.dtd Used by Tomcat

```
<!-- The servlet element contains the declarative data of a
servlet. If a jsp-file is specified and the load-on-startup
element is
present, then the JSP should be precompiled and loaded. -->

<!ELEMENT servlet (icon?, servlet-name,
   display-name?,   description?,
   (servlet-class|jsp-file), init-param*,
    load-on-startup?, security-role-ref*)>



<!-- The servlet-name element contains the canonical name of
the servlet. -->

<!ELEMENT servlet-name (#PCDATA)>

<!-- The servlet-class element contains the fully qualified
class name of the servlet. -->

<!ELEMENT servlet-class (#PCDATA)>
```

An example of configuring a servlet according to the web.dtd is shown in Listing 21.4. The data in the <init-param> .. </init-param> area defines the parameter name and value as passed to the init method in the servlet.

Listing 21.4: Part of the web.xml Configuration File

```
<servlet><servlet-name>saynumb.au</servlet-name>
<servlet-class>com.JSPbook.Chap04.NumberSoundServ</servlet-
class>
  <init-param>
    <param-name>basepath</param-name>
    <param-
value>c:\\tomcat\\webapps\\Root\\JSPbook\\Chap04\\sounds
    </param-value>
  </init-param>
</servlet>
```

THE DOM AND SAX PROGRAMMING MODELS

The orientation of SGML is a complete document, so it is hardly surprising that XML started out thinking in Document Object Model (DOM) terms. All DOM processing assumes that you have read and parsed a complete document into memory so that all parts are equally accessible. This approach is shown symbolically in Figure 21.1.

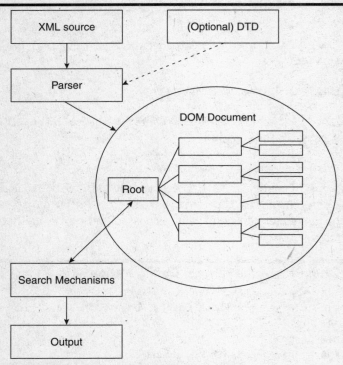

FIGURE 21.1: Document Object Model processing

As people started programming with the DOM, they found it was pretty clumsy if all you wanted to do was pick out a few elements. Furthermore, the memory requirements could get restrictive, if not downright impossible. Thus, the Simplified API for XML (SAX) was born of necessity. Both the DOM and SAX specify application programming interfaces (APIs) that have been implemented in a number of languages in addition to Java.

As shown in Figure 21.2, a SAX parser makes a single pass through an XML file, reporting what it has parsed by calling various methods in the application code. The SAX documentation uses the term *event* for what happens when the parser decides it has identified an element in the XML document, so these methods are called *event handlers*. When the parser reaches the end of the document, the only data in memory is what your application saved.

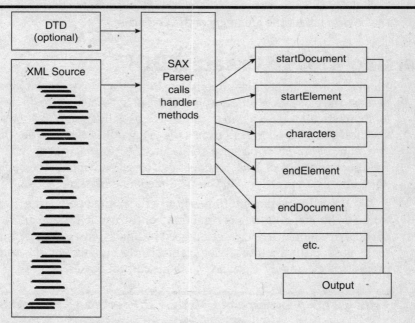

FIGURE 21.2: Simplified API for XML processing

The reason both figures show input from a DTD as optional is that XML is frequently parsed without a DTD. In that case, the parser can determine that the XML is well formed but not whether it is valid.

Both models can be useful for servlet and JavaServer Pages (JSP) programming, as I will demonstrate in the examples. First, however, let's look at the Java tools for both the DOM and SAX. These are tools for the "level 1" DOM and version 1 of the SAX. Just to keep things complicated, version 2.0 of the SAX 2.0 and DOM level 2 are currently in the works.

PROGRAMMING WITH THE DOM

The definitive API for working with the DOM is provided by the org.w3c .dom package, a recommendation of the World Wide Web Consortium (W3C). This API consists entirely of interface definitions plus a single exception class. The basic idea is that an XML document is turned into a DOM consisting of Java objects that implement these interfaces. Every part of the document becomes an object, and the connections between the objects reflect the hierarchy of the document.

Parsing XML to Create a DOM

From the programmer's standpoint, creating a DOM is simplicity itself because the parser does all the work. All the programmer has to do is create an input stream, select a parser, and stand back. Listing 21.5 shows a skeleton of a method to read from a file using utility classes from the com.sun.xml.parser package and return a com.sun.xml.tree .XmlDocument object. The XmlDocument class implements the Document interface as specified in the W3C recommendation.

If you were using parser utilities from a different supplier, the names would be different, but the general flow control would be similar. This particular example uses classes released by Sun as Java Project X and currently used in the Tomcat servlet engine. However, note that the Tomcat project will eventually use whatever Sun's current parser is.

Listing 21.5: A Skeleton of a Method to Create an XML Document

```
public XmlDocument exampleDOM(String src ) {
  File xmlFile = new File( src ) ;
  try {
    InputSource input = Resolver.createInputSource
    ➥( xmlFile );
    // ... the "false" flag says not to validate
    XmlDocument doc = XmlDocument.createXmlDocument
    ➥(input, false);
   return doc ;
  }catch(SAXParseException spe ){
    // handle parse exception here
  }catch( SAXException se ){
    // handle other SAX exceptions here
  }catch( IOException ie ){
```

```
                // handle IO exceptions here
        }
        return null ;
    }
```

Once you have a DOM in memory, you manipulate it using methods provided in the DOM interface recommendation embodied in the `org.w3c.org` package plus additional methods provided by the available toolkit.

The Java Objects in a DOM

In the following discussion, when I speak of objects of various types, you should understand this to mean objects belonging to classes that implement the named interfaces. You don't really need to know the actual class names because they vary from parser to parser.

The primary set of methods for the entire package is provided by the Node interface. There are 13 sub-interfaces derived from Node to represent various parts of a document. Although they all extend Node, certain methods don't make any sense in some sub-interfaces. Table 21.1 summarizes the Node methods. Note that the interpretation of the nodeName and node-Value return values depends on the type of node, as shown in Table 21.2.

TABLE 21.1: The Node Methods

METHOD	RETURNS	VALUE IS USED FOR
getNodeName	nodeName (see Table 21.2)	The string name of the node; interpretation depends on type.
getNodeValue	nodeValue (see Table 21.2)	The string value of the node; depends on type.
setNodeValue	void	
getNodeType	short	A code defined in the Node interface, representing the node type.
getParentNode	a Node reference	The parent of this node in the document hierarchy. Not all types have parents.
getChildNodes	a NodeList reference	NodeList objects provide for accessing an ordered list of Node references.
getFirstChild	a Node reference	The first child of this node, or null if none exists.
getLastChild	a Node reference	The last child of this node, or null if none exists.

TABLE 21.1 continued: The Node Methods

METHOD	RETURNS	VALUE IS USED FOR
previousSibling	a Node reference	The node immediately preceding this one, or null if none exists.
nextSibling	a Node reference	The node immediately following this one, or null if none exists.
getAttributes	a NamedNodeMap reference	NamedNodeMap methods provide for access to attributes by name. Returns null if the node has no attributes.
getOwnerDocument	a Document reference	The document this node belongs to, or null if this node is a document.

Table 21.2 shows how nodeName and nodeValue (refer to Table 21.1) are interpreted. Each Node type is an interface name. Each one also has a unique code defined in the Node interface.

TABLE 21.2: Interpretation of Returned Values

NODE TYPE	NODENAME	NODEVALUE	COMMENTS
Element	tag name	null	Most document objects are elements.
Attr	name of attribute	value of attribute	
Text	#text	text content of node	
CDATASection	#cdata-section	text content	
Entity-Reference	name of the entity referenced	null	
Entity	entity name	null	
Processing-Instruction	target	all other text in the tag	Processing instruction tags start with <? and end with ?>.
Comment	#comment	text content of the comment	Comment tags start with <!— and end with —>.
Document	#document	null	
DocumentType	document type name	null	The name of the document root element from the DTD, if any.

TABLE 21.2 continued: Interpretation of Returned Values

NODE TYPE	NODENAME	NODEVALUE	COMMENTS
Document-Fragment	#document-fragment	null	
Notation	notation name	null	Notations provide information for unparsed entities.

Manipulating the DOM

Given that you have in memory an object having the Document interface, you have several possible ways to search and traverse it. The NodeList interface in the org.w3c.dom package defines ways to manipulate an ordered collection of Node references. Here is how you would obtain a NodeList with all elements named Book in a document:

```
Element E = doc.getDocumentElement();

NodeList vlist = E.getElementsByTagName( "Book" );
```

NodeList provides two methods: length() returns the number of nodes in the collection, and item(int n) returns the nth node in the collection.

Another approach uses the method getFirstChild() to get the first node below the root element of the document. From that node, you can use nextSibling to find the next node at the same level in the document hierarchy.

If, on the other hand, you continued to look for child nodes, you would be conducting a *depth-first* traversal of the DOM. The Sun com.sun.xml.tree package has a TreeWalker class that provides convenient methods for depth-first traversal of any node.

Another convenient interface is NamedNodeMap. This is typically used to manipulate collections of nodes by name, similar to the way you would use a Hashtable. A typical use would be to get the attributes attached to an Element Node. Just as with a Hashtable, there is no particular order in a NamedNodeMap collection.

Although the interfaces of the org.w3c.dom package offer many methods for modifying objects contained in a DOM, the various implementers of XML toolkits in Java typically provide methods of their own. Generally speaking, you can get and set the character contents of any node using getData() and setData(String data).

PROGRAMMING WITH SAX

The following list summarizes the basic steps required to process an XML document with SAX:

▶ Create one or more custom classes to handle the "events" that the SAX parser detects.

▶ Create an object to provide an input stream of characters.

▶ Create a parser from one of the toolkits.

▶ Attach the event-handling classes to the parser.

▶ Attach the input stream to the parser and start parsing.

▶ Handle all the events in your custom classes to capture the data you are interested in, detect errors, and so on.

As you can see, SAX processing of XML involves a programming philosophy that is completely different from using the DOM. Deciding which approach to use for a particular application is your most important design decision. Table 21.3 summarizes the important considerations.

TABLE 21.3: Comparison of DOM and SAX Programming

PROGRAMMING FACTOR	DOM STYLE	SAX STYLE
Memory requirements	May be quite large	Only as large as the items retained in memory
Startup time	Slower because every element is parsed	Faster, especially if the elements of interest are easy to locate
Repeated search time	Faster because everything is in memory	Slower because every search involves a new parsing run
Modification capability	Very flexible	Limited to writing a new XML document with every pass

Interfaces for Event Handlers

Interfaces in the org.xml.sax package define methods that an application writer will typically implement to receive information from the parser about parser decisions. The documentation speaks of these decisions as *events*, but note that these are parser events and are not related to Java Event class objects. Essentially, when the parser decides that it has detected a particular element in the XML data stream, it calls one of these methods.

DocumentHandler Interface

Classes implementing the DocumentHandler interface must provide the following methods. HandlerBase is the utility class that implements all these methods and is typically used as the base for custom classes.

startDocument()   This method is called once when the parser starts. This is a good place to put initialization code.

endDocument()   When this method is called, the parser has finished due to the end of input or an unrecoverable error.

startElement(String name, AttributeList atr)   Called when a starting element and accompanying attributes have been parsed.

endElement(String name)   Called when the parser reaches an end attribute.

characters(char[] buf, int start, int count)   Called with a chunk of character data. This may be only a portion of the data in a character data block, or it may be the entire chunk. The method should read from the buffer only in the range specified.

ignorableWhitespace(char[] buf, int start, int count)   This method lets a parser report nonprinting characters that are not legally part of XML data. Validating parsers are required to call this method, but it is optional for nonvalidating parsers.

processingInstruction(String target, String data)   Called when the parser encounters a processing instruction. The target is the name immediately following the opening <?, and the data string is all of the remaining text.

setDocumentLocator(Locator loc)   Supplies a Locator object reference that the parser will be using. The Locator can be used to obtain additional information about where the parser is in the XML document text. A typical use would be to determine the location that caused an exception.

DTDHandler Interface

This interface defines notationDecl and unparsedEntityDecl methods that report the SAX parser's progress in processing a DTD. To receive these method calls, an application has to register with the parser specifically. If a handler is registered, the parser will call these methods after start-Document has been called but before any calls to startElement.

EntityResolver Interface

This interface defines the `resolveEntity` method. It essentially creates an input stream of characters as a replacement for an entity reference. Your application needs to implement this method only if your XML has external entities that require custom handling.

ErrorHandler Interface

This interface is used if you want to substitute specialized error handling in place of having the SAX parser throw an exception. Your class implementing the interface must register with the parser before it is started. There are three levels of error-handling methods: `warning`, `error`, and `fatalError`. The input to each is a `SAXParseException` reference.

Interfaces for SAX Parsers

To give the maximum freedom to designers of SAX parsers, the specifications define interfaces for classes that a complete parser package must provide.

Locator Interface

A SAX parser may provide an object implementing this interface to assist your application in interpreting events. Parsers are not required to implement this function, but it is strongly suggested.

The methods `getColumnNumber` and `getLineNumber` return an `int` value indicating the column and line in the XML text that the parser read when it generated a particular event.

AttributeList Interface

An object implementing the `AttributeList` interface is used to communicate a list of attributes found in an element to the `startElement` method. Attributes have a name, a value, and a type (all `String` objects), and this interface provides for retrieval both by name and by position in the list.

getLength()   Returns the number of attributes (possibly zero) found in the element.

getName(int i)   Returns the `String` name of an attribute by position in the list.

getType(int i)   Returns the type of an attribute in the list. Possible types are the constants CDATA, ID, IDREF, IDREFS, NMTOKEN, NMTOKENS, ENTITY, ENTITIES, or NOTATION.

`getType(String name)`   Returns the type of an attribute by name.

`getValue(int i)`   Returns the `String` value of an attribute by list position.

`getValue(String name)`   Returns the `String` value by the attribute name.

Classes for Parsers

Most of the elements in the `org.w3c.dom` and `org.xml.sax` packages are specified as interfaces. Presumably this was done to allow parser writers maximum flexibility.

Exception Classes

The `SAXException` class provides the general error-reporting mechanism for XML parsers. Any exception occurring in a SAX parser must be wrapped in a `SAXException` before being thrown to the enclosing application. This design decision means that every exception thrown by a parser will be a `SAXException` or a class derived from `SAXException`.

The `SAXParseException` class provides methods, as in the following list, that can be used as indicators of the location of the cause of a parsing exception. These are the same methods that the `Locator` interface calls for:

▶ The `getColumnNumber` and `getLineNumber` methods return an `int` value indicating the position in the XML document where the parser decided it had an error.

▶ The `getPublicID` method returns a `String` containing the public identifier of the entity the parser was working on when the error occurred.

▶ The `getSystemID` method returns a `String` with the system identifier where the exception occurred. This could be a filename or URL.

A SAX Example

As an example of programming with SAX, I am going to use a practical problem experienced by publishers like my company, LANWrights, Inc. That problem relates to creating, updating, and presenting errata errors in a book that are found after the book is published. We need these errata lists so that subsequent printings can be corrected and so that readers can correct their own copies.

Technical publishing companies vary considerably in their approach to errata. Sometimes you are lucky if a Web page gets updated every six months. We took the approach of creating a Web page on the fly every time a query is made, using a list of errata that can be updated by an online editor. Originally, the list used a simple and compact format that was processed by a Perl script to generate the page, but now we are converting to XML to take advantage of the flexibility it provides.

The XML Document for Errata

A single Web page is provided for all access to errata. The interface lets a user select a book and specify the following criteria:

- ▶ *Seriousness of the error.* The options are major, major plus moderate, or all errors including minor typos.

- ▶ *Printing number the error appears in.* This is needed because errors are frequently corrected in subsequent editions, but new errors may be introduced.

- ▶ *The date after which the error note was created or modified.* With this parameter, a truly methodical user could search for errata that are new or have changed since the last visit.

These criteria are related to the XML elements and attributes as shown in Table 21.4.

TABLE 21.4:   Elements and Attributes of the Errata XML System

ITEM	TYPE	USED FOR
Title	element	Cover title of the book
isbn	attribute	The universally accepted book identification
Errata	element	Encapsulates a single errata report that has identifying attributes plus descriptive text
page	attribute	Identifies the page the error starts on; may be a page number or some other text
printing	attribute	List of printings the error occurs in
significance	attribute	Classification of the error in terms of how serious it is
author	attribute	Identifies the person who put the error in the system
datemod	attribute	When the error was entered or modified

In addition to the elements and attributes described in Table 21.4, the DTD includes HTML formatting codes used to present the text. For example, code listings use the <pre> and <tt> tags, and quotation marks frequently appear in the error text. An alternative to providing for these elements in the DTD would have been to enclose the bulk text in the special <![CDATA[.....]]> tags so it would not be examined for markup characters, as shown in Listing 21.6.

Listing 21.6: The DTD for Errata

```
<!ELEMENT BookErrata (Title|Errata)* >
<!ATTLIST BookErrata isbn CDATA #IMPLIED>
<!ELEMENT Title (#PCDATA)* >
<!ELEMENT Errata (#PCDATA|br|A|TT|B|I|PRE)* >
<!ATTLIST Errata page CDATA #IMPLIED>
<!ATTLIST Errata printing CDATA #IMPLIED>
<!ATTLIST Errata significance CDATA #IMPLIED>
<!ATTLIST Errata author CDATA #IMPLIED>
<!ATTLIST Errata datemod CDATA #IMPLIED>
<!ELEMENT br EMPTY >
 <!ELEMENT A (#PCDATA)* >
<!ATTLIST A HREF CDATA #IMPLIED>
<!ELEMENT TT (#PCDATA|br)* >
<!ELEMENT B (#PCDATA)* >
<!ELEMENT I (#PCDATA)* >
<!ELEMENT PRE (TT)* >
<!ENTITY quot "&quot;" >
```

I chose to implement the code that selects and presents errata as a JavaBean so that the class could be used by a servlet, a JSP page, or an applet. Because queries for errata at our Web site are infrequent, using the SAX model instead of DOM is the best way to minimize memory use by the server. Queries from users may also select only recent additions or the most significant errors so there is no good reason to keep the entire structure in memory.

A single errata entry is shown in Listing 21.7. The page attribute value CS stands for "Cram Sheet," a special book insert.

Listing 21.7: A Single Errata Entry

```
<Errata page="CS" printing="1,2"
significance="1" author="WBB" datemod="990603">
Cram Sheet item 16 should state:
<br/>
```

Part iv

```
Division by zero in floating point arithmetic:
No exception occurs; instead the result is one of
the special values,
<b>NaN, NEGATIVE_INFINITY</b> or
<b>POSITIVE_INFINITY</b> defined in the
<b>Float</b> and <b>Double</b>
wrapper classes.
</Errata>
```

The *ErrataParserBean* Class

The ErrataParserBean class is an extension of the HandlerBase convenience class in the org.xml.sax package. HandlerBase extends java.lang.Object and implements the SAX interfaces EntityResolver, DTDHandler, DocumentHandler, and ErrorHandler. This bean gets search criteria from a form submission and scans the XML file for a particular book, creating formatted output from each entry that matches the criteria.

Listing 21.8 shows the class declaration and the static variables and methods. The parserClass variable is provided in case you decide to experiment with parsers other than the default Sun parser.

Listing 21.8: The Start of the ErrataParserBean Source Code

```
import java.io.* ;
import java.util.* ;
import org.xml.sax.* ;
import org.xml.sax.helpers.ParserFactory ;
import com.sun.xml.parser.Resolver ;

public class ErrataParserBean extends HandlerBase
{
  static public String parserClass =
➡"com.sun.xml.parser.Parser" ;
  static public String crlf = "\r\n" ;
   // these provide default formatting tags
  static public String[] bookTitle =
➡{"<h2>", "</h2>"};
  static public String[] bookISBN =
➡{"<b>ISBN ", "</b>" };

   // these relate the elements that represent
   //xhtml to the output
  static String[] tagnames =
```

```
➡{ "br","tt","b","i","pre"  };
  static String[] startT =
➡{ "<br />", "<tt>","<b>","<i>","<pre>"};
static String[] endT =
➡{  "", "</tt>","</b>","</i>","</pre>" };


  static String[] monthstr = {
 "Jan", "Feb", "Mar", "Apr", "May", "Jun", "Jul", "Aug",
"Sep", "Oct", "Nov", "Dec"};
  static String[] monthnum = {
  "01", "02", "03", "04", "05", "06", "07", "08", "09", "10",
"11", "12" };

  // hashtables providing fast lookup
  //for various functions
  static public Hashtable startHash, endHash,
➡monthHash, signifHash ;
  static { // static initialization block
    startHash  = new Hashtable();
    endHash    = new Hashtable();
    monthHash  = new Hashtable();
    signifHash = new Hashtable();
    for( int i = 0 ; i < tagnames.length ; i++ ){
      startHash.put(tagnames[i], startT[i] );
      endHash.put( tagnames[i], endT[i]   );
    }
    for( int n = 0 ; n < 12 ; n++ ){
      monthHash.put( monthstr[n], monthnum[n] );
    }
    signifHash.put("1","Major errors only");
    signifHash.put("2","Major and moderate errors");
    signifHash.put("3","All errors");
  }
```

Listing 21.9 continues the class with the instance variables that are parsed out of each <Errata> tag by the startElement method and the search criteria variables that are set by a query.

Listing 21.9: The ErrataParserBean Code Continues with Instance Variables

```
// values taken from <Errata tag attributes as they are
parsed
```

Part iv

```
String page ;
String printing ;
String significance ;
String author ;
String datemod ; // yymmdd - 991231 is followed by A00101
boolean match ;
// title and ISBN
String title ;
boolean lookForTitle ;
String isbn ;

String href ; // as found with <A tag elements

// search criteria
String prntSC = "Any" ;
String signifSC = "3" ; // default = all
String datemodSC = "970101" ; // compact format of search
date
String yearSC = "1997" ;
String monSC = "Jan" ;
String daySC = "01" ;
int hitCt = 0 ;
// Input source
String srcFile, srcPath ;
InputSource input ;
StringWriter swrite ;
PrintWriter out ;
```

Next, we have the constructor in Listing 21.10, which must be a no-arguments style constructor because the object will be created as a bean. This is followed by the access methods that follow the bean syntax that permits use of the JSP setProperty tag using the syntax

```
<jsp:setProperty

name="errataParserBean" property="*" />
```

which automatically associates named parameters from a form input with bean variables. For example, the form variable named dtyr will be associated automatically with the setDtyr method to set the yearSC search criteria String. Note that the setWriter method lets the calling JSP or servlet pass an object to receive the bean output.

Listing 21.10: The ErrataParserBean Code Continues

```
// as a Bean, must have a no-args constructor
```

```
public ErrataParserBean(){}

public void setWriter( PrintWriter pw )
{out = pw; }
public void setErrataPath(String s){ srcPath = s ; }

// these set methods correspond to form variable names
public void setErrataFile(String s)
{ srcFile = s ; }
public void setPrver(String s ){ prntSC = s ; }
public void setSignif(String s){ signifSC = s ; }
public void setDtyr( String s ){ yearSC = s ; }
public void setDtmo( String s ){ monSC = s ; }
public void setDtdy( String s ){
   if( s.length() == 1 ) daySC = "0" + s ;
   else daySC = s ;
}
```

In Listing 21.11, we have the checkForMatch method, which compares the attributes of an errata entry with the search criteria values. This is followed by the setDateMod method that converts the year, month, and day search criteria into the compact form used in the XML.

Listing 21.11: The ErrataParserBean Code Continues

```
// return true if this set of parameters match search
// criteria
   boolean checkForMatch(){
      boolean ret = true ; //assume true and disqualify
      int n = datemodSC.compareTo(datemod);
      if( n > 0 ) return false ;
      if( !prntSC.equals("Any")){ // prntSC will be a short
string
         if( printing.indexOf( prntSC ) < 0 ) return false ;
      }
      n = signifSC.compareTo( significance );
      if( n < 0 ) ret = false ;
      return ret ;
   }

// turn search criteria dates into compact format
   void setDateMod(){
      int yr = 1997 ;
      String yrstr = null ;
```

```
        try{ yr = Integer.parseInt( yearSC );
        }catch(NumberFormatException ne){}
        if( yr < 2000 ) yrstr = yearSC.substring( 2 );
        // 97 - 99
        else yrstr = "A" + yearSC.charAt( 3 );
        // A0 - A9
        String mostr = (String) monthHash.get( monSC );
        if( mostr == null ) mostr = "00" ;
        datemodSC = yrstr + mostr + daySC ;
    }
```

The process of scanning an XML file is carried out by the getErrata method as shown in Listing 21.12. I have provided two alternatives for output of formatted text. If the calling JSP or servlet calls setWriter to provide an output stream, it will be used; otherwise, a StringWriter object is created, and the entire formatted output is returned as a string by the getErrata method. Note that the code catching a SAXParseException provides for determining the line and column causing the error.

Listing 21.12: The getErrata Method

```
// This is the main method that
// accomplishes parsing.
// It traps all Exceptions and
// creates an error msg output.
// If out has not been set, it
// creates a StringWriter and
// uses that for output, returning the
// result as a String
public String getErrata(){
    Parser parser ;
    hitCt = 0 ;
    try {
        File f = new File( srcFile );
        input = Resolver.createInputSource( f );
        if( out == null ){
            swrite = new StringWriter( );
            out = new PrintWriter( swrite );
        }
        parser = ParserFactory.makeParser
        ➡( parserClass );
        parser.setDocumentHandler( this );
        System.out.println("Start parse");
        parser.parse( input );
```

```
      }catch(SAXParseException spe){
          StringBuffer sb = new StringBuffer( spe.toString() );
          sb.append("\n  Line number: " + spe.getLineNumber());
          sb.append("\nColumn number: " + spe.getColumnNumber()
);
          sb.append("\n Public ID: " + spe.getPublicId() );
          sb.append("\n System ID: " + spe.getSystemId() +
"\n");
          return sb.toString();
      }catch(Exception e){
          return e.toString();
      }
      if( swrite != null  ){
          return swrite.getBuffer().toString();
      }
      return ""; // out must have been set elsewhere
  }
```

Now we come to the methods that get called as the SAX parser detects various parsing events, starting in Listing 21.13.

Listing 21.13: The Methods Called by the SAX Parser

```
      // the following are required by DocumentHandler interface
      public void startDocument(){
        setDateMod();
        System.out.println("Start Document");
        out.print("<br>"); out.print(crlf);
      }
      public void endDocument(){
        System.out.println("End Document");
        out.print("<br>");
        out.print("Total errata found = ");
        out.print( Integer.toString( hitCt ));
        out.print("<br>"); out.print(crlf);
        out.flush();
      }

      public void startElement
    ➡( String name, AttributeList attrib)
          throws SAXException
      {
        if( "BookErrata".equals( name )){
          isbn = attrib.getValue("isbn");
```

```
            return ;
        }
    if( "Title".equals( name )){
        lookForTitle = true ; return ;
        }
    if( "Errata".equals( name ) ) {
        int ct = attrib.getLength();
        page = attrib.getValue("page");
        printing = attrib.getValue("printing");
        significance = attrib.getValue("significance");
        author = attrib.getValue("author");
        datemod = attrib.getValue("datemod");
        match = checkForMatch() ;  // determine if this matches
criteria
        if( !match ) return ; // not a match
        hitCt++ ;
        out.print( exStartStr() );
        return ;
        }
    if( !match ) return ;
    // if we are in a matching item, need to process special
// tags <b <a etc.
    name = name.toLowerCase();
    String stag = (String) startHash.get( name );
    if( stag == null ){
        if( name.equals("a")){    // A tag gets special handling
            out.print("<a href=\"");
            href = attrib.getValue("HREF");
            if( href == null )
            ➡href = attrib.getValue("href");
            out.print( href );
            out.print("\" >");
        }
    }
    else out.print( stag );
    return ;
    } // end startElement()

    public void endElement(String name ){
        if( "Title".equals( name )){
            outputTitle(); return ;
        }
        if( !match ) return ;
```

```
        if( "Errata".equals( name )) {
            out.print("</p><br>");
            out.print( crlf );
            return ;
        }
        name = name.toLowerCase();
        String etag = (String)endHash.get( name );
        if( etag == null ){
          if( name.equals("a")){
            out.print( "</a>" );
          }
          return ;
        }
        out.print( etag );
    } // end endElement

    // only print if we are in a matching errata item
    public void characters
    ( char[] buf, int start, int count ){
      if( lookForTitle ){
          title = new String( buf, start, count );
          // must be at start, output title and isbn
          lookForTitle = false ;
      }
      if( !match ) return ;
      out.write( buf, start, count );
    }
```

Listing 21.14 gives methods that create HTML formatting for errata entries. Significance is indicated by the color applied.

Listing 21.14: Methods That Supply HTML Formatting of Errata Entries

```
    // the following are formatting methods

    // assumes attributes have been set -
    // displays significance and page
    // in start of <p> paragraph
    private String exStartStr(){
      StringBuffer sb = new StringBuffer(100);
      sb.append("<p><b><FONT COLOR=\"" );
      switch( significance.charAt(0)){
          case '1' : sb.append("red\">"); break ;
```

```
                case '2' : sb.append("blue\">");break ;
                default : sb.append("teal\">"); // case 3 and unknown
            }
            // page can be CS, a roman numeral or a page number
            if( page.equals("CS")){
                sb.append("On Cram Sheet ") ;
            }
            else {
                sb.append("On page "); sb.append( page );
            }
            // superscript printing numbers in angle braces
            sb.append("<sup>");
            StringTokenizer st = new StringTokenizer
➡( printing,",");
            while( st.hasMoreTokens()){
                sb.append("&lt;");
                sb.append( st.nextToken());
                sb.append("&gt;");
            }
            sb.append( "</sup></font></b>, ");
            return sb.toString() ;
        }


        // writes title, isbn and selection criteria
        void outputTitle(){
            out.print(bookTitle[0]);
            out.print(title);out.print(bookTitle[1]);
            out.print(bookISBN[0]);
            out.print( isbn);
            out.print(bookISBN[1] );
            out.print("<br>");
            out.print(crlf);
            out.print("<p>Errata selected for ");
            out.print( signifHash.get( signifSC ));
            out.print("   Printing = ");
            out.print( prntSC );
            out.print(" and errata entered on or after ");
            out.print( yearSC );
            out.print(" ");
            out.print( monSC );
            out.print(" ");
            out.print( daySC );
            out.print("</p>");
```

```
        out.print(crlf);
    }


    // general debug
    public String toString()
    { StringBuffer sb = new StringBuffer
➡("ErrataParserBean ");
        return sb.toString() ;
    }


}
```

The complex environment of a Web server is not the ideal place to debug Java code because so many things can go wrong. It is faster and a lot less frustrating to test as much of your code as possible in a controlled environment. In the case of `ErrataParserBean`, I debugged parsing and formatting functions with a simple graphical user interface (GUI) test rig. This test program, shown in Figure 21.3, was built using `java.awt.Choice` widgets to simulate the HTML form that will be used in an actual Web server. Formatted output goes to a `java.awt.TextArea` so that it can be examined in detail. Figure 21.4 shows formatted output as rendered by a Web browser.

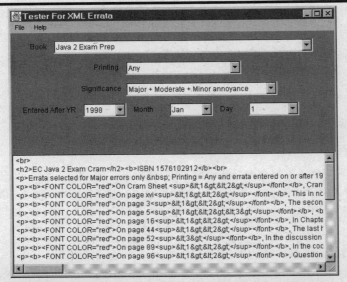

FIGURE 21.3: The program used to test the ErrataParserBean

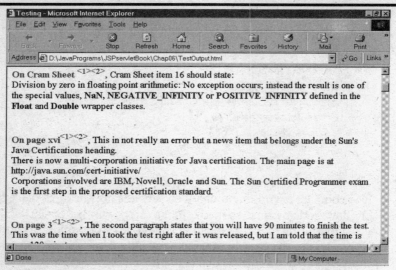

FIGURE 21.4: HTML output from the ErrataParserBean rendered in a Web browser

A DOM EXAMPLE

The example I use to illustrate DOM programming is a requirement on a Web site to display items from a list of publications in a variety of formats. This application is characterized as described here:

▶ The list of publications is accessed frequently.

▶ The total list size is less than 100KB of text.

▶ The XML list is maintained and validated offline.

▶ Several different forms of output are desired.

▶ The ability to search for and sort items must be provided.

▶ New items are added only occasionally.

These requirements are all best met by a DOM approach because that keeps the entire set of entries in the server memory.

The Publications DTD

The DTD devised for this application is shown in Listing 21.15. There are two primary kinds of entry, Book and Article, which have many common attributes. Naturally, there are also some attributes unique to each, such as Cdrom for Book and Pages for Article.

Listing 21.15: The Publications DTD Used in The Example

```
<!ELEMENT Publications (Book|Article)* >
<!ATTLIST Publications date CDATA #IMPLIED>
<!ELEMENT Book
    (Title|Author|Edition|DatePublished|Publisher|Press|
    Series|Size|Topic|Cover|Errata|BriefDescription|Cdrom)* >
<!ATTLIST Book isbn CDATA #IMPLIED>
<!ELEMENT Title (#PCDATA)* >
<!ELEMENT Author (#PCDATA)* >
<!ELEMENT Edition EMPTY >
 <!ATTLIST Edition edition CDATA #IMPLIED>
<!ELEMENT DatePublished EMPTY >
 <!ATTLIST DatePublished year CDATA #IMPLIED>
<!ATTLIST DatePublished month CDATA #IMPLIED>
<!ELEMENT Publisher (#PCDATA)* >
<!ELEMENT Press (#PCDATA)* >
<!ELEMENT Series (#PCDATA)* >
<!ELEMENT Size EMPTY >
 <!ATTLIST Size pp CDATA #IMPLIED>
 <!-- Size is total book length -->
<!ELEMENT Cover EMPTY >
 <!ATTLIST Cover img CDATA #IMPLIED>
<!ELEMENT Topic (#PCDATA)* >
<!ELEMENT Errata EMPTY >
 <!ATTLIST Errata code CDATA #IMPLIED>
<!ELEMENT BriefDescription (#PCDATA)* >
<!ELEMENT Cdrom EMPTY >
 <!ELEMENT Article
 (Title|Author|Publisher|DatePublished|Pages|Topic|
➥BriefDescription)* >
<!ELEMENT Pages EMPTY >
 <!ATTLIST Pages pp CDATA #IMPLIED>
 <!-- Pages is used to give an article page range -->
```

A sample entry for a single book is shown in Listing 21.16. Notice the <Topic> elements, because one of the program examples demonstrates extracting the text from these elements for presentation using a JavaBean.

Listing 21.16: A Single Book Element

```
<Book isbn="1576102912" >
<Title>Java 2 Exam Cram</Title>
<Author>Bill Brogden</Author>
<Edition edition="1" />
<DatePublished year="1999" />
<Publisher>The Coriolis Group</Publisher>
<Press>Certification Insider Press</Press>
<Series>Exam Cram</Series>
<Size pp="388"/>
<Cover img="images/j2ec.gif" />
<Topic>Java</Topic>
<Topic>Certification</Topic>
<Topic>Exam 310-025</Topic>
<Topic>Certified Programmer for the Java 2 Platform</Topic>
<Topic>Study Guide</Topic>
<Errata code="ecj2" />
<BriefDescription>This compact study guide concentrates on
the topics covered in Sun's Java 2 programmer certification
exam.
Numerous questions similar to those on the real exam are pre-
sented and discussed.
</BriefDescription>
</Book>
```

A DOM Library Function

As I suggested in Table 21.3, the DOM approach is ideal if you need access to all the elements of an XML document, as long as the size is reasonable to keep in memory. Given the computational expense involved in creating a DOM, it is wise to keep it in memory if there is a reasonable chance it will be reused. However, keeping track of the uses of a particular DOM object requires some management functions that I have implemented in the DOMlibrary class as an example that you could expand to fit your own situation.

The DOMlibrary class follows the "singleton" design pattern in which static variables and methods are used to ensure that only one instance of the class is created. The reason we want to use an instance rather than all static methods and variables is that the management functions require a separate Thread, so DOMlibrary implements the Runnable interface. Listing 21.17 shows the import statements and the static variable and method that manage the single instance. Note that the getLibrary function is synchronized so that there is no way that multiple instances could be created.

Listing 21.17: A Class to Manage DOM Objects

```
package com.JSPbook.Chap06 ;

import java.io.* ;
import java.util.* ;
import com.sun.xml.tree.* ;
import com.sun.xml.parser.Resolver ;
import org.xml.sax.* ;
import org.w3c.dom.* ;

public class DOMlibrary implements
➡java.lang.Runnable
{
  private static DOMlibrary theLib ;
  public synchronized static DOMlibrary
➡getLibrary(){
    if( theLib == null ) theLib = new DOMlibrary();
    return theLib ;
  }
```

The constructor and instance variables are shown in Listing 21.18. The main instance variables are two Hashtable objects, one to hold Document objects and the other to hold management information. The Thread that is created in the constructor to execute the run method is given minimum priority.

Listing 21.18: The DOMlibrary Instance Variables and Constructor

```
// instance variables below this
private Hashtable domHash, timestampHash ;
boolean running ;
private String lastErr = "none" ;
// private constructor to ensure singleton
private DOMlibrary(){
  domHash = new Hashtable();
  timestampHash = new Hashtable();
  Thread upkeep = new Thread("DOMlibrary upkeep");
  upkeep.setPriority( Thread.MIN_PRIORITY );
  running = true ;
  upkeep.start();
}
```

In this approach, XML documents are located in the `getDOM` method shown in Listing 21.19 by a `String` giving an absolute path to a file. The path is used to retrieve the document object from a `Hashtable` or to read it in if it isn't available in memory.

Probably a better approach would be to have a properties file relating the document title to the file location. That would let you download files via a URL in addition to local files.

Every time a document is retrieved, the current time is stored in the `timestampHash Hashtable` as a `Long` object. This timestamp could be used to choose relatively unused documents to be discarded from memory. An alternative would be to create an object specifically to track usage.

Note that if the `loadXML` method encounters an error, it stores a `String` with error information in the `Hashtable`. When `getDOM` finds a `String` in the `domHash`, it returns null. This means that the library will not repeat an attempt to read a document if it contains an error. It is up to the programmer to fix the error and call `reloadDOM` to recover from this condition.

Listing 21.19: The DOMlibrary Class Listing Continues

```
// either return the doc or null if a problem
public Document getDOM( String src ){
  Object doc = domHash.get( src );
  if( doc == null ){
      loadXML( src );
      doc = domHash.get( src );
  }
  if( doc instanceof Document ) {
      timestampHash.put( src, new Long
( System.currentTimeMillis()));
      return (Document) doc ;
  }
  return null ; // error was encountered
}

// call this to force a reload after src is modified
public Document reloadDOM( String src ){
  if( domHash.get( src ) != null ){
    domHash.remove( src );
  }
  return getDOM( src );
}
```

```
    private synchronized void loadXML(String src ) {
      File xmlFile = new File( src ) ;
      try {
        InputSource input = Resolver.createInputSource
➥( xmlFile );
      // ... the "false" flag says not to validate
        Document doc = XmlDocument.createXmlDocument (input,
false);
        domHash.put( src, doc );
      }catch(SAXParseException spe ){
        StringBuffer sb = new StringBuffer( spe.toString() );
        sb.append("\n  Line number: " +
➥spe.getLineNumber());
        sb.append("\nColumn number: " +
➥spe.getColumnNumber() );
        sb.append("\n Public ID: " +
➥spe.getPublicId() );
        sb.append("\n System ID: " +
➥spe.getSystemId() + "\n");
        lastErr = sb.toString();
        domHash.put( src, lastErr );
        System.out.print( lastErr );
     }catch( SAXException se ){
        lastErr = se.toString();
        System.out.println("loadXML threw " +
➥lastErr );
        domHash.put( src, lastErr );
        se.printStackTrace( System.out );
      }catch( IOException ie ){
        lastErr = ie.toString();
        System.out.println("loadXML threw " +
➥lastErr +
          " trying to read " + src );
        domHash.put( src, lastErr );
      }
    } // end loadXML
```

Because this chapter is already getting pretty long and we have a lot more to cover, I have not included any upkeep functions in the run method shown in Listing 21.20.

Listing 21.20: The run Method and Some Utility Methods

```
    // run is used for upkeep, not reading XML
```

```
public void run()
{ while( running ){
    try{ Thread.sleep( 100000 );
    // place upkeep code here
    }catch(InterruptedException e){
    }
  }// end while
}

public String getLastErr(){ return lastErr ; }

public String toString()
{ StringBuffer sb = new StringBuffer
("DOMlibrary contains ");
  int ct = domHash.size();
  if( ct > 0 ){
      sb.append(Integer.toString( ct ) );
      sb.append( " DOM objects ");
  }
  else { sb.append("no DOM objects");
  }
  sb.append(" Last error: " );
  sb.append( lastErr );
  return sb.toString();
}
}
```

The *BookDOMbean* Class

Now that we have the DOMlibrary class as a general way to create DOM documents in memory, the next thing we need is a class to pull information out of the document for presentation on a Web page. Listing 21.21 shows the import statements, the required no-arguments constructor, and the setSource method that gets a Document read in.

Listing 21.21: Start of the BookDOMbean Class

```
package com.JSPbook.Chap06 ;

import java.io.* ;
import java.util.* ;
import com.sun.xml.tree.* ;
import com.sun.xml.parser.Resolver ;
import org.xml.sax.InputSource;
```

```
import org.xml.sax.SAXException;
import org.xml.sax.SAXParseException;
import org.w3c.dom.* ;

public class BookDOMbean
{
  Document doc ;

  public BookDOMbean(){}

  public void setSource(String src ){
    DOMlibrary lib = DOMlibrary.getLibrary();
    doc = lib.getDOM( src );
  }
```

Now we are ready for some methods to search the document and return data for use in presentation of HTML forms. The first one we will look at can be used to collect all the unique <Topic> text in a publications DTD (refer to Listing 21.15) formatted XML file. The collectValues method shown in Listing 21.22 locates all Elements with the specified name and collects the text associated with the Element. To avoid keeping duplicate String values, we just store them temporarily in a Hashtable. The values from the Hashtable are put in an array and sorted.

Listing 21.22: The collectValues Method in BookDOMbean

```
// object is to collect the text associated
// with elements having s name
// from the entire list and produce an array
// of unique values
public String[] collectValues( String s ){
  Hashtable hash = new Hashtable();
  Element E = doc.getDocumentElement();
  NodeList vlist = E.getElementsByTagName( s );
  String tmp = null ;
  int n, i, ct = vlist.getLength();
  for( i = 0 ; i < ct ; i++ ){
    Node en = vlist.item( i );
    if( en.getNodeType()== Node.ELEMENT_NODE ){
      NodeList clist = en.getChildNodes();
      int nch = clist.getLength();
      if( nch > 0 ){
        for( n = 0 ; n < nch ; n++ ){
          Node cn = clist.item(n);
```

```
                        if( cn.getNodeType() ==
➥Node.TEXT_NODE ){
                  tmp = cn.getNodeValue();
                  hash.put( tmp, tmp );
               }
             }
           }
         }
      } // loop over vlist
      ct = hash.size(); // number of unique values
      String[] ret = new String[ ct ];
      Enumeration e = hash.keys();
      n = 0 ;
      while( e.hasMoreElements() ){
          ret[n++] = (String)e.nextElement();
      }
      if( ct > 1 ) shellSort( ret );
      return ret ;
   }
```

In the publications DTD, International Standard Book Number (ISBN) numbers are an attribute found in the <Book> tag. Getting at attributes by name requires another version of the collectValues method, as shown in Listing 21.23.

Listing 21.23: A Version of collectValues to Collect Attributes

```
// similar except select element el and collect values of
// attribute attrib
// from the entire document
  public String[] collectValues( String el,
➥String attrib ){
    Hashtable hash = new Hashtable();
    Element E = doc.getDocumentElement();
    NodeList nlist = E.getElementsByTagName( el );
    String tmp = null ;
    int n, i, ct = nlist.getLength();
    for( i = 0 ; i < ct ; i++ ){
      Node en = nlist.item( i );
      if( en.getNodeType()== Node.ELEMENT_NODE ){
        tmp = ((Element)en).getAttribute( attrib );
        if( tmp != null && tmp.length() > 0 ){
            hash.put( tmp, tmp );
        }
```

```
        else hash.put("unknown","unknown");
      }
   } // loop over nlist
   ct = hash.size(); // number of unique values
   String[] ret = new String[ ct ];
   Enumeration e = hash.keys();
   n = 0 ;
   while( e.hasMoreElements() ){
        ret[n++] = (String)e.nextElement();
   }
   if( ct > 1 ) shellSort( ret );
   return ret ;
}
```

Listing 21.24 continues the class with some utility methods to retrieve String values from a given Element by name. The getText method is used for elements that have associated text, whereas getAttributeText locates attributes by name.

Listing 21.24: BookDOMbean **Continued**

```
   // from the nd Element
   // get the text associated with child nodes having name
   public String getText(Element nd, String name ){
     StringBuffer sb = new StringBuffer();
     NodeList tlist = nd.getElementsByTagName
( name );
     int ct = tlist.getLength();
     if( tlist.getLength() > 0 ){
        for( int i = 0 ; i < ct ; i++ ){
          Node en = tlist.item(i); // text is a child of
// Element node
          NodeList clist = en.getChildNodes();
          sb.append( clist.item(0).getNodeValue() );
          if( ct > 1 && i < (ct - 1) ){
             sb.append(", ");
          }
        }
     }
     else sb.append("not available");
     return sb.toString();
   }
```

```
    // from the Element nd, get the text from attributes named
attrib
    // from child nodes of type name
    public String getAttributeText(Element nd,
➡String name, String attrib ){
      StringBuffer sb = new StringBuffer();
      NodeList tlist = nd.getElementsByTagName
➡( name );
      int ct = tlist.getLength();
      if( tlist.getLength() > 0 ){
        for( int i = 0 ; i < ct ; i++ ){
          Node en = tlist.item(i); // text is a child of
Element node
          if( en instanceof Element ){
            sb.append(((Element)en).getAttribute
➡( attrib ) );
            if( ct > 1 && i < (ct - 1) ){
              sb.append(", ");
            }
          }
        }
      }
      else sb.append("not available");
      return sb.toString();
    }
```

Listing 21.25 shows a simple method that does a little formatting of the title and ISBN number of a <Book> element.

Listing 21.25: BookDOMbean **Continued**

```
    // shortest output format Title and ISBN
    public String shortTitle(Element nd ){
      StringBuffer sb = new StringBuffer();
      NodeList tlist = nd.getElementsByTagName
➡( "Title" );
      if( tlist.getLength() > 0 ){
        Node en = tlist.item(0); // should have only one title
// per book
        NodeList clist = en.getChildNodes();
        sb.append( clist.item(0).getNodeValue() );
      }
      else sb.append("No Title Available");
      sb.append(" isbn:");
```

```
        String isbn = nd.getAttribute("isbn");
        if( isbn != null ) sb.append( isbn );
        else sb.append( "No ISBN found");
        return sb.toString();
    }
```

Finally, in Listing 21.26, we have some utility methods. The `toString` method returns some information about the state of the object, and the `shellSort` method sorts an array of `String` objects.

Listing 21.26: Utility Methods in BookDOMbean

```
public String toString()
{ StringBuffer sb = new StringBuffer
➡("BookDOMbean ");
    if( doc == null ) sb.append(" DOM not loaded");
    else {
        sb.append("Document: " );
        sb.append( doc.getDoctype().getName() );
    }
    return sb.toString();
}

public  void shellSort ( String[] items ) {
    // h is the separation between items we compare.
    int h = 1;
    while ( h < items.length ) {
        h = 3 * h + 1;
    }
    // now h is optimum
    while ( h > 0 ) {
        h = (h - 1)/3;
        for ( int i = h; i < items.length; ++i ) {
            String item = items[i];
            int j=0;
            for ( j = i - h;
                j >= 0 && item.compareTo( items[j] )
➡< 0;
                j -= h ) {
                items[j+h] = items[j];
            } // end inner for
            items[j+h] = item;
        } // end outer for
    } // end while
```

```
} // end sort
}
```

Using *BookDOMbean* in a JSP Page

To exercise the BookDOMbean, I created the code shown in Listing 21.27.
It uses the two collectValues methods to create forms with selectable
lists of topics and ISBN numbers.

Listing 21.27: The BookTopics.jsp Page

```
<html>
<head>
<title>Topics List</title>
</head>
<body BGCOLOR="#FFFFFF" TEXT="#000000">
<font FACE=VERDANA>
<h2 ALIGN=CENTER>Demonstrating DOM access to Books
</h2><br>
<%@ page language="java" errorPage="/JSPbook/Chapt06
➥/whoops.jsp" %>
<jsp:useBean id="bookBean" scope="page"
      class="com.JSPbook.Chap021.BookDOMbean" >
</jsp:useBean>
<jsp:setProperty name="bookBean" property="source"
   value="c:\\InetPub\\wwwroot\\JSPbook\\
➥pubs.xml" />
<%! String[] topics, isbns ;
%>
<%
  topics = bookBean.collectValues("Topic") ;
  isbns  = bookBean.collectValues("Book", "isbn" );
%>
<center>
<table border="4" bordercolor=gray cellpadding="8" >
<tr><td align="center">
<form METHOD="post" ACTION="/JSPbook/Chap06
➥/ShowBooks.jsp" >
Please select a topic.<br><br>
<select name="topic" >
<%
  for( int i = 0 ; i < topics.length ; i++ ){
    out.print( "<option value=\"" + topics[i] +
➥"\" >" + topics[i] + "\r\n" );
```

```
    }
%>
</select><br><br>
<input TYPE="submit" VALUE="Show" name="seltopic" >
</form></td>
<td align="center">
<form METHOD="post" ACTION="/JSPbook/Chap06/
➥ShowBooks.jsp" >
Please select an ISBN number.<br><br>
<select name="isbn" >
<%
   for( int i = 0 ; i < isbns.length ; i++ ){
      out.print( "<option value=\"" + isbns[i] + "\" >"
➥+ isbns[i] + "\r\n" );
   }
%>
</select><br><br>
<input TYPE="submit" VALUE="Show" name="seltopic" >
</form>
</td></tr>
</table></center>
</body>
</html>
```

The presentation created by this form is shown in Figure 21.5.

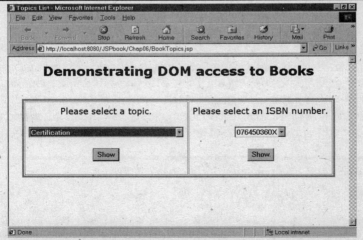

FIGURE 21.5: Displaying the BookTopics.jsp page

ALTERNATIVES TO SAX AND DOM

The perceived complexity of processing XML with the SAX and DOM approaches seems to have set off a flurry of experimentation with alternatives. Some of these approaches have reduced the functionality of parsers to achieve speed while keeping essential functions.

Java Document Object Model (JDOM)

Jason Hunter, co-author of the widely used *Java Servlet Programming* book, maintains a Web site at http://www.servlets.com.

In spite of, or perhaps in consequence of, his familiarity with the DOM and SAX approaches, this Web site contains the following quotation introducing his proposed JDOM API for working with XML.

> *"There is no compelling reason for a Java API to manipulate XML to be complex, tricky, unintuitive, or a pain in the neck. JDOM™ is both Java-centric and Java-optimized. It behaves like Java, it uses Java collections, it is a completely natural API for current Java developers, and it provides a low-cost entry point for using XML."*

Development of the JDOM follows an open-source approach similar to the Apache project. As of this writing, the JDOM code is still beta. For the current status of this project, visit http://jdom.org/.

RELATED TECHNOLOGY

The XML idea has really caught on; various schemes and technologies related to XML are popping up. Table 21.5 presents some technologies that are either currently significant to the world of Java servlets and JSP or are likely to be as soon as the vocabularies become standardized and discovered by large numbers of developers.

TABLE 21.5:   XML-Related Technology

ACRONYM	STANDS FOR	USE
SOAP	Simple Object Access Protocol	Communication between programs.
SVG	Scalable Vector Graphics	A scalable vector graphics format based on XML.

TABLE 21.5 continued: XML-Related Technology

ACRONYM	STANDS FOR	USE
XHTML	Extensible Hypertext Markup Language	A standard resulting from applying XML 1.0 rules to HTML 4.0.
XLink	XML Linking Language (also known as XLL)	The rules for adding hyperlinks to XML documents.
XLL	XML Linking Language (also referred to as XLink)	See XLink.
XMI	XML Metadata Interchange Format	A standard of the OMG for exchanging data about data.
XPath		Rules for addressing internal elements in an XML document.
XQL	Extensible Query Language	Used for addressing and filtering the elements and text of XML documents.
XSL	Extensible Stylesheet Language	A stylesheet format for XML documents.
XSLT	aExtensible Stylesheet Language Transformations	A language used to transform the structure of XML documents.
XUL	Extensible User-Interface Language	A standard for creating the user interface for a cross-platform application. See the Mozilla project at `www.mozilla.org`.

SUMMARY

When you're developing Web pages, what better way is there to manage a group of objects as represented by an XML document than with an object-oriented programming language originally developed for the Web? XML elements are well suited for Java manipulation because they can be de-serialized into Java objects and Java objects can be serialized into XML document fragments. This can all be done dynamically so that the server generates pages based on either a database request or some other input from the user.

Deciding how to manage this kind of dynamic generation will ultimately depend on your comfort level regarding the two main APIs available for such processing: the DOM and SAX. As mentioned in this chapter, the DOM is suitable for those who want fast processing on searches and modification flexibility, but it can have expensive memory requirements and take a long time to load. SAX requires only enough memory to load each item requested because it is an event-based parsing mechanism.

Luckily, there is a growing pool of use cases that should help you decide what is best for you. One example of such a use case, which focuses on the DOM, appears in the next chapter and describes how to develop an online catalog.

PART V

E-Commerce Solutions with XML and JSP

Chapter 22

PRESENTING AN XML CATALOG ONLINE

I n the preceding chapter, you got your feet wet processing XML using servlets and JavaServer Pages (JSP). In this chapter, we survey the APIs for Java servlets, for JavaServer Pages, and for the manipulation of XML elements. These are the essential programming tools for the creation of dynamic Web pages from XML data. Using these APIs, we then explore various approaches for online presentation of catalog items that we'll create using XML.

Adapted from *Java™ Developer's Guide to E-Commerce with XML and JSP*, by William Brogden and Chris Minnick

ISBN 0-7821-2827-0   464 pages $49.99

PRESENTATION TECHNOLOGIES

When creating a commerce-oriented site on the Internet, Java programmers have a tremendous number of options to choose from. All of these options operate within the basic constraints of Web protocols. The most basic of these constraints is that the user's Web browser and the Web server conduct a very simple conversation: A single user request elicits a single server response. This conversation is said to be stateless because there is no requirement in the protocol for the Web server to remember anything about the transaction after the response has been sent.

The HTTP Conversation

The World Wide Web Consortium (W3C) organization (www.w3.org) maintains the current standard for Web servers: HTTP version 1.1. (This is a refinement over the previous HTTP version 1 standard, which has many problems.) The standard defines the required format for browser requests and Web-server responses.

The Browser Request

The request message from browser to Web server starts with a header consisting of one or more ASCII text lines terminated by carriage-return–line-feed (crlf) characters. The first line is required to specify a method, a Uniform Resource Identifier (URI), and an indicator of the HTTP version being used. The standard methods in the HTTP 1.1 protocol are OPTIONS, GET, HEAD, POST, PUT, DELETE, TRACE, and CONNECT, but for commercial sites, GET and POST are the ones we usually have to deal with. A header may or may not be followed by a body of additional data.

A request for a plain HTML page uses the GET method. Simple search requests typically also use GET, whereas form submission requests, such as shopping-cart applications, typically use the POST method. The practical difference is that in GET method requests, parameters (such as search terms) are passed as part of the URI line in the header, but POST method requests pass data in the body of the message.

The header also contains lines that give additional information about the kinds of data the browser will accept, the browser version, and the type of connection desired. Listing 22.1 shows a sample request resulting from clicking the Send button on a simple HTML page with a form using the POST method and having a hidden variable named action and a value of showkeywords.

Listing 22.1: A POST Message from Browser to Web Server

```
POST /servlet/cattest HTTP/1.1
Accept: application/msword, application/
➡vnd.ms-excel, image/gif,
image/x-xbitmap, image/jpeg, image/pjpeg, */*
Referer: http://localhost/XmlEcommBook/
➡CTestSnoop.html
Accept-Language: en-us
Content-Type: application/x-www-form-urlencoded
Accept-Encoding: gzip, deflate
User-Agent: Mozilla/4.0 (compatible; MSIE 5.0;
Windows NT; DigExt)
Host: localhost:9000
Content-Length: 19
Connection: Keep-Alive

action=showkeywords
```

The Web Server Response

The response message from Web server to browser also requires a header. The header always starts with a status line that contains the protocol being used, a numeric status code, and a text version of the status code. Subsequent lines provide additional information in the keyword: value format, followed by a single blank line.

Information passed in the response header typically includes the type and size of the content body of the message. The response header can also contain lines that attempt to set cookie values in the browser. The following is the header received in response to the request shown in Listing 22.1. This was followed by a blank line and then the HTML body of the message.

```
HTTP/1.0 200 OK
Server: Microsoft-PWS/2.0
Date: Mon, 25 Sep 2000 14:15:55 GMT
Content-Type: text/html
```

The body of the server response can be anything, from a standard HTML page to the binary data making up an image (or any number of other specialized data formats). In the preceding header, note that the content type is specified as text/html.

NOTE

For more in-depth coverage of HTML, we recommend *HTML Complete, Second Edition* (Sybex, 2000), or check out www.sybex.com for a detailed listing of related titles.

The API for Java Servlets

Java servlet technology operates at the most basic level of a Web server and is essential to all Java-based server functions. Servlet technology can be used to handle all Web server functions, or servers based on other technologies can be configured to pass certain types of requests to add-on servlet engines.

NOTE

A complete discussion of the servlet API would take a whole book—for example, the *Java Developer's Guide to Servlets and JSP*, by Bill Brogden (Sybex, 2000). This section presents a quick review.

As this chapter is being written, the current API for servlets is version 2.2, with version 2.3 entering the final draft stage. By the time this book is published, the version 2.2 API should be widely supported by stand-alone Web servers and add-ons for existing Web servers. Most likely, version 2.3 will also be production-ready.

In a Web server with an add-on servlet engine, the server has configuration settings that tell it which requests are handled by servlets. Sun Microsystems maintains a list of add-on servlet engines and Web servers at the following site:

```
http://java.sun.com/products/servlet/industry.html
```

Examples of 100% Pure Java Web servers include the following:

Tomcat   An open-source project at the Apache Software Foundation (`http://jakarta.apache.org`).

Enhydra   A low-cost, commercial, Java-based application server (`www.lutris.com`) supporting servlets, JavaServer Pages, and Enterprise JavaBeans.

Orion   A commercial application server (`www.orionserver .com`) but with a free development/noncommercial license. It supports all of the latest Java technology, including E2EE and Enterprise JavaBeans.

Resin   A 100% Pure Java server (www.caucho.com/index.xtp). Designed as an enterprise-scale application server with emphasis on the use of XML and XSL.

In Sun's nomenclature, a Web server handling Java servlets acts as a "servlet container," similar to the way a browser acts as a container for applets. A servlet depends on this container to load and initialize the required classes and to conduct the basic parts of an HTTP transaction. The servlet container creates an HttpServletRequest object, which contains a convenient representation of the user's request, and an HttpServletResponse object, which provides the methods needed for the servlet to send a response.

The servlet container also provides a Thread to execute the servlet code in response to a user request. Each request gets its own Thread that executes the servlet methods independently, but typically only one servlet instance is created. This means that the programmer must be very cautious in using instance variables.

Because a servlet instance typically stays loaded in the Web server memory for extended periods, the response to a request directed to a servlet can be very rapid. This approach is much faster than technologies that have to spawn a new process and load an application each time a request arrives.

Classes and Interfaces for the Java Servlets

The javax.servlet and javax.servlet.http packages contain the classes and interfaces used in servlet creation. The basic classes and interfaces in javax.servlet are generalized, whereas the classes in javax.servlet.http are specialized for working with the HTTP protocol. Table 22.1 summarizes the javax.servlet interfaces.

TABLE 22.1: Interfaces in the javax.servlet Package

INTERFACE	DESCRIPTION
Servlet	This interface defines the methods that all servlets must implement. The GenericServlet class implements the Servlet interface.
ServletRequest	All information about a client request is accessed through an object implementing this interface. Creating a ServletRequest object is the responsibility of the servlet engine.

TABLE 22.1 continued: Interfaces in the `javax.servlet` Package

INTERFACE	DESCRIPTION
ServletResponse	Objects implementing this interface must be created by the servlet engine and passed to the servlet's `service` method to be used for output to the client.
RequestDispatcher	This powerful interface permits you to forward a request from the current servlet to another servlet or a JSP page for additional processing.
ServletConfig	Objects using this interface are used to hold information that helps configure the servlet during servlet initialization.
ServletContext	Objects using this interface let a servlet locate information about the servlet engine the servlet is running in and the servlet's environment.
SingleThreadModel	This interface contains no methods. It is a marker that forces the servlet engine to ensure that only one Thread executes an instance of the servlet at once. The servlet engine can do this either by restricting access to a single instance of the servlet or by creating a separate instance for every Thread.

The classes in the `javax.servlet` package (see Table 22.2) provide basic, bare-minimum functionality. In general, programmers work with classes that extend these for more specific applications.

TABLE 22.2: Classes in the `javax.servlet` Package

CLASS	DESCRIPTION
GenericServlet	A class that provides bare-minimum functionality.
ServletInputStream	A class for reading a stream of binary data from the request.
ServletOutputStream	A class for writing a stream of binary data as part of a response.

Only two exceptions are defined in the `javax.servlet` package. The `ServletException` class is a general-purpose exception used in servlet classes, whereas the `UnavailableException` is to be thrown when a servlet needs to indicate that it is temporarily or permanently unavailable. These classes do not descend from `RuntimeException`, so if a method declares that it throws `ServletException`, a calling method must provide for catching it.

The `javax.servlet.http` package adds the interfaces shown in Table 22.3 and the classes shown in Table 22.4. These are the interfaces and classes you, as a programmer, will be dealing with when creating a Web application with servlets.

TABLE 22.3: Interfaces in the `javax.servlet.http` Package

INTERFACE	DESCRIPTION
HttpServletRequest	This extension of the ServletRequest interface adds methods specific to HTTP requests, such as getting cookie settings.
HttpServletResponse	An extension of the ServletResponse interface, this interface adds methods specific to the HTTP protocol, such as setting cookies and header values.
HttpSession	Objects implementing this interface are an essential part of shopping-cart applications because they allow the programmer to store information about a user between individual page visits or transactions.
HttpSessionBindingListener	Objects implementing this interface can be notified when they are added to or removed from an HttpSession.

TABLE 22.4: Classes in the `javax.servlet.http` Package

CLASS	DESCRIPTION
HttpServlet	This abstract class is the one you will usually extend to create useful Web servlets.
Cookie	These objects are used to manipulate cookie information that is sent by the server to a browser and returned on subsequent requests. Cookie information in a request is turned into Cookie objects by the HttpServletRequest.
HttpUtils	Static methods in this class are useful occasionally.
HttpSessionBindingEvent	The class of events sent to objects implementing HttpSessionBindingListener.

Servlet Request Handling

In a typical commerce application, user requests are processed in the following sequence:

1. The user's request data is used to create an HttpServlet-
   Request object, which contains information from the request
   headers plus any additional data.

   An HttpServletResponse object is also created in prepa-
   ration for the creation of a response.

2. The servlet service method is called with references to these
   two objects. By examining the request type, the service
   method determines which of the request-handling methods
   should be called. Custom servlets typically do not override
   the default service method but instead override the doPost
   and/or doGet methods.

3. The doPost or the doGet method examines the request and
   determines the application function required. For all but the
   simplest application, the servlet class typically makes use of
   other objects to carry out database queries or calculations.

A Simple Servlet Example

A typical servlet application program includes a class that extends Http-
Servlet and implements the methods that will respond to the various
types of requests that the application must handle. The simple example
shown in Listing 22.2 only has to respond to GET requests, so it only
implements the doGet method. Note that the output is written to a
PrintWriter object named out that is obtained from the HttpServlet-
Response object.

Listing 22.2: A Simple Servlet Handling a GET Request (DateDemo.java)

```
import java.io.*;
import java.util.* ;
import javax.servlet.*;
import javax.servlet.http.*;

public class DateDemo extends HttpServlet
{
  public void doGet(HttpServletRequest req,
```

```
                HttpServletResponse resp)
    throws ServletException, IOException
    {
        resp.setContentType("text/html");
        PrintWriter out = resp.getWriter();
        String username = req.getParameter("uname");
        if( username == null ) username =
➥"unknown person" ;
        out.println("<HTML>");
        out.println("<HEAD><TITLE>Date Demo</TITLE>
➥</HEAD>");
        out.println("<BODY>");
        out.println("Hello " + username + "<br>");
        out.println("Date and time now: " + new Date().
➥toString()
                + "<br>");
        out.println("</BODY>");
        out.println("</HTML>");
        out.close();
    }
}
```

In this example, the doGet method attempts to locate a parameter named "uname" in the HttpServletRequest object to be used in the response. Also, note the use of the setContentType method to set the response content type to "text/html".

Servlet Initialization

When a servlet container loads servlet code and creates an instance of the servlet class, the API guarantees that the init method will be the first method called and that it will be executed before any user request is processed. The servlet API provides for passing initialization parameters to the newly created instance using an object of the ServletConfig class.

Prior to the 2.2 version of the servlet API, each vendor had a different approach to configuring these initialization settings. Now that Sun has decided on XML-based configuration nomenclature, we can expect configuration to become standardized.

Listing 22.3 shows the XML used to set initialization parameters for servlets we will be discussing in Chapter 23, "Using Surveys to Know Your Customer."

Listing 22.3: The XML Configuration with Initialization Parameters (web.xml)

```
<web-app>
  <servlet>
    <servlet-name>Questionnaire</servlet-name>
  <servlet-class>com.XmlEcomBook.Chap07.
    ➡QuestionnaireServ</servlet-class>
    <init-param>
      <param-name>homedir</param-name>
      <param-value>e:\\scripts\\questionnaire
      </param-value>
    </init-param>
  </servlet>
  <servlet><servlet-name>Qanalysis</servlet-name>
  <servlet-class>com.XmlEcomBook.Chap07.
➡QanalysisServ
  </servlet-class>
    <init-param>
      <param-name>homedir</param-name>
      <param-value>e:\\scripts\\questionnaire
      </param-value>
    </init-param>
  </servlet>
</web-app>
```

In the init method of the QuestionnaireServ servlet, the parameter named homedir is used to set the value of a String named homedir with the following code, where config is the ServletConfig passed to the init method or acquired from getServletConfig():

```
homedir = config.getInitParameter("homedir") ;
```

Other things that are usually accomplished in the init method include establishing connections to databases and opening logging files.

Servlet Response Generation

All of the resources required to control the response are encapsulated in the ServletResponse and HttpServletResponse interfaces. For example, the following calls to the setHeader method can be used to ensure that the browser will not cache the page that is being sent:

```
response.setHeader("Expires", "Mon, 26 Jul 1990
➡05:00:00 GMT");
```

```
response.setHeader("Cache-Control" ,"no-cache,
➥must-revalidate");
response.setHeader("Pragma", "no-cache");
➥// for HTTP/1.0
```

The ServletResponse object provides an output stream for your servlet program to write the page content. This output stream can be either a PrintWriter type, which can carry out Unicode translation, or a plain binary stream of the ServletOutputStream type that writes bytes without translation.

The Role of JavaBeans

Java has had great success with a simple component architecture called JavaBeans. Although initially planned as an architecture for graphical user interface (GUI) components, it has also been found very useful in nongraphical applications. A *JavaBean* is simply a Java class that meets the following criteria:

- ▶ The class must be public and implement Serializable.

- ▶ The class must have a no-arguments constructor.

- ▶ The class must provide set and get methods to access any variables used by other classes.

By creating classes and naming methods according to these simple JavaBean conventions, you can partially automate many program construction functions, especially in JavaServer Pages. You will also hear the term *Enterprise JavaBeans* used a lot in connection with Web application servers. An Enterprise JavaBean is distinctly different from a JavaBean, and much more complicated.

The API for JavaServer Pages

There have been numerous attempts to develop systems that allow an author to write static HTML content that incorporates dynamic data by means of special tags embedded in the HTML—the idea being that when a page is transmitting, the static file data will be passed through a special processor that recognizes the tags and uses them to insert data dynamically as the page is transmitted. Frequently, the file type is set to a unique name as a clue to the Web server that special processing is required.

Examples of highly successful implementations of special tag processing include the ColdFusion server (www.allaire.com) and Microsoft's Active

Server Pages, ASP (http://msdn.microsoft.com/workshop/server/ default.asp).

Sun's approach to incorporating dynamic Web-page generation is the JavaServer Pages (JSP) API. This standard, at version 1.1 as of the publication of this book, is considered to be an essential part of the Java approach to Web application servers, as embodied in the Java 2 Enterprise Edition platform.

JSP technology is based on servlet technology. Essentially, the JSP processor turns static Web page elements and dynamic elements defined by JSP tags into the Java source code for a servlet class. When a user request that addresses a JSP page comes to the Web server, this class is executed to create a response. As long as the static elements of the JSP page remain unchanged, the response to a request can be very rapid, because the class remains in memory just like servlet classes.

Benchmark tests comparing ASP applications with similar JSP applications have been conducted by one of the major vendors. Recent results have the Orion JSP implementation much faster than ASP. You can see the most recent results at www.orionserver.com/benchmarks/ benchmark.html.

The Language of JSP Tags

In the following JSP page code, the JSP tag starts with <%= and ends with %>. When compiled into a Java class, a request for this page will result in the output of the HTML tags and text plus the String created by the toString method operating on a new Date object.

```
<HTML>
<HEAD><TITLE>JRun Date Demo</TITLE></HEAD>
<BODY>
<H2>Date And Time <%= new java.util.Date().
➡toString() %></H2>
<hr>
</BODY>
</HTML>
```

Because of major changes in the JSP API between early versions and the current version 1.1 API, JSP tags occur in two styles. The old style tags, as shown in Table 22.5, are still available.

TABLE 22.5: JSP Tags Using the <%Style

TAG	USED FOR	EXAMPLE
<%- -%	Comments	<%- this is never shown -%>
<%=%>	Expressions (evaluated as String)	<%= new Date() %>
<%! %>	Declarations	<%! Date myD = new Date() ; %>
<% %>	Code fragments	<% for(int i = 0 ; i < 10 ; i++ { %>
<%@ %>	Directives	<%@ page import="java.util.*" %>

As shown in Table 22.6, the new style tags obey XML tag-formatting rules. In general, Sun is trying to move to an all-XML style for JavaServer Pages.

TABLE 22.6: New JSP Style Tags Use an XML Style

JSP TAG	DESCRIPTION
<jsp:include />	Incorporates bulk text from a file
<jsp:forward />	Forwards the request to a servlet, another JSP, or static Web page
<jsp:param />	Used inside a forward, include, or plugin to add or modify a parameter in the request object
<jsp:getProperty />	Gets the value of a Bean property by name
<jsp:setProperty />	Sets the value of a Bean property
<jsp:useBean />	Locates or creates a Bean with the specific name and scope
<jsp:plugin />	Provides full information for a download of a Java plug-in to the client Web browser

Custom Tag Libraries

An elegant feature of the JSP API is its capability to define a library of custom action tags. This is a very powerful concept that enables you to use specialized toolkits as easily as you use the standard tags.

Custom tags use interfaces and classes in the `javax.servlet.jsp.tagext` package. This capability has great potential for simplifying the authoring of JavaServer Pages.

JSP Request Handling

Here is the sequence of events that occurs when a user request names a JSP page:

1. The request naming a JSP page is directed to the JSP engine by the Web server.

2. The JSP engine looks for the corresponding servlet based on the page name. If the servlet exists and is up to date, the request is passed to the servlet `_jspService` method using `HttpServletRequest` and `HttpServletResponse` objects, just like with a regular servlet.

3. If the source page has been changed or has never been compiled, the page compiler parses the source and creates the equivalent Java source code for a servlet implementing `HttpJspPage`.

4. This code is then compiled, and the new servlet is executed. The servlet object can stay in memory, providing a very fast response to the next request.

The `request` and `response` objects are exactly the same ones used in normal servlets; the difference here is that the creation of the `service` method is accomplished by the JSP engine.

Default Variables in a JSP

Table 22.7 shows the variables that are automatically available in a JSP page.

TABLE 22.7: The Default JSP Page Variables

VARIABLE NAME TYPE		DESCRIPTION
request	An implementation of HttpServletRequest	Represents the user's request

TABLE 22.7 continued: The Default JSP Page Variables

Variable Name	Type	Description
response	An implementation of `HttpServletResponse`	Creates the output response
pageContext	A `javax.servlet.jsp` `.PageContext` object	Contains attributes of this page
session	A `javax.servlet.http` `.HttpSession`	Contains arbitrary variables attached to this user's session
application	A `javax.servlet` `.ServletContext` object	Contains attributes for the entire application and affects the interpretation of several other tags
out	A `javax.servlet.jsp` `.JspWriter` object	Determines the output stream for the response
config	A `javax.servlet` `.ServletConfig` object	Contains servlet initialization parameter name-value pairs and the `ServletContext` object
page	An `Object` reference pointing to `this`	The current servlet object
exception	A `java.lang.Throwable` object	Contains only pages designated as error pages in the page directive

Part V

ORGANIZING THE CATALOG

The catalog of products as created in the XML document has only a sequential organization. However, we want customers to have flexible access to the catalog items, rather than having to page through the entire catalog in the original order to locate products. In this section, we consider Java techniques for organizing access to the elements of the XML catalog.

The W3C Document Object Model API

We will generally be using Sun's JAXP (Java API for XML Parsing) toolkit for XML in this book. The basic API for manipulating parts of XML documents follows the formal Document Object Model (DOM) recommendation by the W3C. This API gives the most complete access to all elements of an XML document at the expense of considerable complexity. There are simpler APIs supporting DOMs, but the W3C version is the most widely accepted and supported.

You can download the current JAXP toolkit from Sun's Web site:

```
http://java.sun.com/xml/xml_jaxp.html
```

Alternatively, you can use the version provided in the Tomcat download from `http://jakarta.apache.org`. The toolkit consists of Java packages that represent the W3C API plus packages that provide implementation of various parsers and utilities.

TIP

You can find a wide (and always growing) range of XML-related Java APIs on the Sun site at `http://java.sun.com/xml/index.html`.

Creating the Catalog DOM

The initial creation of a DOM in Java is very simple because the toolkit parser does all the work. Listing 22.4 shows part of the code for a class to represent the catalog as an `org.w3c.dom.Document` object. The bulk of the constructor code is in catching the various possible parsing errors.

Listing 22.4: An Example of Parsing a Document (TheCatalog.java)

```java
]
import javax.xml.parsers.* ;
import org.xml.sax.* ;
import org.w3c.dom.* ;

public class TheCatalog {

org.w3c.dom.Document catDoc ;

public TheCatalog( File f ){
  try {
    timestamp = f.lastModified();
    DocumentBuilderFactory dbf =
    ➥DocumentBuilderFactory.newInstance();
      // statements to configure the DocumentBuilder would go
here
    DocumentBuilder db = dbf.newDocumentBuilder ();
  }catch(ParserConfigurationException pce){
      lastErr = pce.toString();
      System.out.println("constructor threw " +
➥lastErr );
```

```
      }catch(SAXParseException spe ){
          StringBuffer sb = new StringBuffer
( spe.toString() );
          sb.append("\n Line number: " +
spe.getLineNumber());
          sb.append("\nColumn number: " +
spe.getColumnNumber() );
          sb.append("\n Public ID: " +
spe.getPublicId() );
          sb.append("\n System ID: " +
spe.getSystemId() + "\n");
          lastErr = sb.toString();
          System.out.print( lastErr );
      }catch( SAXException se ){
          lastErr = se.toString();
          System.out.println("constructor
threw " + lastErr );
          se.printStackTrace( System.out );
      }catch( IOException ie ){
          lastErr = ie.toString();
          System.out.println("constructor threw " +
lastErr +
              " trying to read " + f.getAbsolutePath() );
      }
  }
```

The DOM data structure is organized in memory with the same hierarchy as the XML document. Java objects represent the various parts of the XML document and are linked by references to their neighboring elements, as suggested in Figure 22.1.

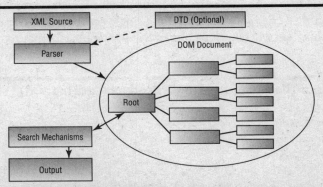

FIGURE 22.1: Document Object Model processing

The programming interfaces for the Java objects that represent the various parts of the document are defined in the `org.w3c.dom` package. Every part of an XML document, including the root element, is represented as an object implementing an interface that is an extension of the fundamental Node interface.

The *Node* Interface

The primary set of methods for the entire `org.w3c.dom` package is provided by the Node interface. There are 13 sub-interfaces in the `org.w3c.dom` package derived from Node to represent various parts of a document. Although they all extend Node, certain methods don't make any sense in some sub-interfaces.

You may want to revisit Table 21.2 of this book, which summarizes the methods in the Node interface. Note that the interpretation of the node-Name and nodeValue return values depends on the type of node.

The type of Node that we will generally be manipulating is called an Element; these objects use the `org.w3c.dom.Element` interface. The Element interface adds a number of methods for dealing with attributes and for dealing with named Nodes contained within an Element.

NOTE

To simplify the discussion, we will be talking about objects implementing the Node, Element, and other interfaces as Node, Element, etc. objects. The actual type of the object implementing the interfaces does not matter because we will be using only interface methods.

Because we don't have space to formally lay out the `org.w3c.dom` API, let's examine how a product entry from the catalog is represented in Java objects. Listing 22.5 shows the XML for a single product; the Element object for this item will contain a hierarchy of Node objects that represent the XML.

Listing 22.5: The XML for a Single Product (`catalog.xml`)

```
<product id="bk0022" keywords="gardening, plants">
  <name>Guide to Plants</name>
  <description>
    <paragraph>
      <italics>Everything</italics>
      you've ever wanted to know about plants.
```

```
      </paragraph>
    </description>
    <price>$12.99</price>
    <quantity_in_stock>4</quantity_in_stock>
    <image format="gif" width="234" height="400"
        src="images/covers/plants.gif">
      <caption>
      <paragraph>This is the cover from the
        first edition.</paragraph>
      </caption>
    </image>
    <onsale_date>
      <month>4</month>
      <day_of_month>4</day_of_month>
      <year>1999</year>
    </onsale_date>
  </product>
```

For example, if you were to execute the getFirstChild method of the product Element you would get a reference to the Node that represents the name Element. The name Element contains a child Node of the Text type; the value of this Node is the String Guide to Plants.

The XML attributes attached to the product Element can be accessed with the getAttribute method, which takes the name of an attribute and returns a String with the attribute value, as in this example:

```
String id = product.getAttribute("id")

String keywords = product.getAttribute("keywords");
```

All of the first level of the hierarchy of Nodes attached to the product Element can be accessed with the getChildNodes method. This returns an object implementing the NodeList interface. A NodeList object differs from other Java collection types in that it holds a dynamic representation of the XML document. This means that if another Node were inserted into the hierarchy of Nodes contained in the product Element it would show up in the NodeList of child nodes automatically.

The *NodeList* Interface

This interface has only the following two methods:

int getLength()   This method returns the current number of Nodes, which may be zero.

Node item(int n)   This returns a reference to the nth Node in the list or null if there is nothing at this position.

The *Document* Interface

The Java object that encapsulates an entire XML document in memory implements the Document interface extension of the Node interface. Most of the methods in this interface are concerned with creating or modifying a DOM in memory. The method we will be using most often simply returns an Element reference for the document, as follows:

```
Element rootE = catDoc.getDocumentElement();
```

For example, to obtain a NodeList of all of the product Elements in the catDoc document, you would use the following:

```
Element rootE = catDoc.getDocumentElement();
NodeList nl = rootE.getElementsByTagName("product");
```

Creating Indexes for Product Lookup

With the preceding quick survey of the Java interfaces for accessing the DOM, we are now ready to look at how to create various indexes that will speed up catalog presentation while still leaving the product information in DOM format. Here are some of the data and functionality we need:

- ▶ A list of the names of the product_line divisions of the catalog
- ▶ A list of all products in a particular product_line
- ▶ A quick lookup of the product Element from the product id
- ▶ A list of all keywords in use so we can present keywords for the user to choose from
- ▶ A quick lookup for products from selected keywords

The scanCatalog method, as shown in Listing 22.6, creates the data structures to fulfill these requirements. These data structures are String arrays named productLineNames, keywords, and Hashtable objects named productLineHT, productHT, and prodByKeyHT. We are using collection classes compatible with both Java 1.1 and Java 1.2 JDKs because, as of this writing, some servlet engines still use Java 1.1 libraries.

The scanCatalog method is called immediately after the XML file is parsed by the constructor for this class (Listing 22.4). Note that in scanCatalog the first method called on the root Element is normalize(). The reason for this is that the Sun parser tends to turn the carriage returns and extra spaces (which XML authors like to use to make the text document easily scanned) into multiple Text nodes. The normalize() method lumps all adjacent Text node content together into a single Text node.

Listing 22.6: The scanCatalog Method Initializes Various Hashtables (TheCatalog.java)

```java
public void scanCatalog(){
  Element rE = catDoc.getDocumentElement();
// the root
  rE.normalize();
  productLineNL = rE.getElementsByTagName(
"product_line");
  productLineHT = new Hashtable();
  productHT = new Hashtable();
  prodByKeyHT = new Hashtable();
  // note that in contrast to other get methods,
getAttributes
  // returns "" if the attribute does not exist
  int i,j, ct = productLineNL.getLength();
  productLineNames = new String[ ct ];
  for( i = 0 ; i < ct ; i++ ){
    Element plE = (Element)productLineNL.item(i);
    productLineNames[i] = plE.getAttribute("name");
    NodeList prodNL = plE.getElementsByTagName
("product");
    productLineHT.put( productLineNames[i],
prodNL );
// node list
    int pct = prodNL.getLength();
    System.out.println( productLineNames[i] +
" ct " + pct );
    for( j = 0 ; j < pct ; j++ ){
      Element prodE = (Element)prodNL.item(j) ;
      String id = prodE.getAttribute("id");
      if( id == null ){
        System.out.println("No id - productLine " +
          productLineNames[i] + " product " + j );
      }
      else { productHT.put( id, prodE );
// product by id
        String keys = prodE.getAttribute
("keywords");
```

```
                if( keys != null ){
                    addProdByKey( keys, prodE );
                }
            }
        }
    }      // end loop over product lines
    ct = prodByKeyHT.size();
    keywords = new String[ ct ];
    i = 0 ;
    Enumeration en = prodByKeyHT.keys();
    while( en.hasMoreElements()){
        keywords[i++] = (String)en.nextElement();
    }
    shellSortStr( keywords );
}
```

Creating the prodByKeyHT is accomplished in the addProdByKey method, as shown in Listing 22.7. This method has to cope with the fact that the keywds String may have more than one word or phrase separated by commas. The StringTokenizer class was designed for this sort of work, but note that we have to use the trim method to trim leading and trailing spaces off the String parsed by the StringTokenizer. The Vector we are storing the Element references in preserves the original order of products in the XML file.

Listing 22.7: The addProdByKey Method (TheCatalog.java)

```
// separate and clean up list, creating/adding to
// Vector in prodByKeyHT
  private void addProdByKey( String keywds,
➡Element pE ){
    StringTokenizer st = new StringTokenizer
➡( keywds, "," );
    while( st.hasMoreTokens() ){
        String key = st.nextToken().trim();
        Vector v = (Vector)prodByKeyHT.get( key );
        if( v == null ){
          v = new Vector();
          prodByKeyHT.put( key, v );
        }
        v.addElement( pE );
    }
}
```

INFORMATION FLOW FOR PRESENTATION GENERATION

Generally speaking, the information that ends up being displayed on the user's browser has gone through several steps to organize the presentation. The basic element of the DOM that is manipulated is an `Element` representing a product. The steps in creating a presentation from the XML catalog follow:

1. Start with the full catalog DOM, represented as a `NodeList` of product elements.

2. Apply selection rules to the `NodeList` of product elements. Possible selection rules include the product `id`, keyword, or product line.

3. Apply sorting to the array of elements, if necessary.

4. For each element, generate the HTML presentation format and add it to the page under construction.

Presenting Choices

Because we have gone to the trouble of coding keywords for each product in the catalog, we certainly want the user to be able to search for products by keyword. Recall from the preceding section that the `scanCatalog` and `addProdByKey` methods create a `String` array of keywords and also maintain a `Hashtable` that keeps a `Vector` of product `Element` references keyed by the keywords.

Rather than having the user type words into a search form to see if certain words are in the keyword list, we can present an HTML form using the `SELECT` input type and having all of the keywords and phrases set in it. The resulting display is shown in Figure 22.2.

The HTML code that created this figure is shown (with only a few of the keywords) in Listing 22.8. Note that in addition to the keyword options we include a hidden variable named `action`, with the value of `keywdsearch`.

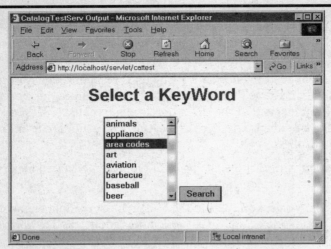

FIGURE 22.2: An input form to select a keyword

Listing 22.8: The HTML to Create the Keyword Selection Form

```html
<center><h2>Select a KeyWord</h2>
<form method="POST" action="http://localhost/servlet
➥/cattest" >
<input type="HIDDEN" name="action"
 value="keywdsearch" >
<select name="keyword" size="8">
<option value="animals" > animals
<option value="appliance" > appliance
<option value="area codes" > area codes
<option value="art" > art
<option value="aviation" > aviation
<option value="barbecue" > barbecue
<option value="baseball" > baseball
<option value="beer" > beer

<option value="writing" > writing
</select>
<input type="SUBMIT" value="Search" >
</form>
</center><hr>
```

To encapsulate catalog-formatting functions in a class that are usable with both servlets and JavaServer Pages, we have written a CatalogBean class. By putting as much as possible of the formatting functions into CatalogBean, we have greatly simplified the servlet code. The following code in the servlet is sufficient to generate the keyword selection form:

```
public void doKeywordSelect( PrintWriter out ){
    CatalogBean cb = new CatalogBean();
    cb.setHidden( "action","keywdsearch");
    out.println("<center><h2>Select a KeyWord
➥</h2>");
    out.print( cb.doKeywordSelect( alias ) );
    out.println("</center><hr>");
}
```

The call to the setHidden method tells the CatalogBean to format all forms with a hidden variable tag. In this case, the result is the following:

```
<input type="HIDDEN" name="action"
 value="keywdsearch" >
```

By having the doKeywordSelect method return a String, as opposed to passing a PrintWriter to the method, we avoid tying the doKeyword-Select method to any particular output stream type. As shown in Listing 22.9, we use a StringBuffer to construct the complete form text. Note that the call to getKeywords gets the String array created by the scanCatalog method (Listing 22.6).

Listing 22.9: A Method to Format a String Array as a Selection Form (CatalogBean.java)

```
public String doKeywordSelect(String alias ){
    StringBuffer sb = new StringBuffer
➥( "<form method=\"POST\" action=\"" );
    sb.append( alias ); sb.append("\" >\r\n");
    String[] kwd = getKeywords();
    int i ;
    int ct = hiddenNames.size();
    if( ct > 0 ){
        for( i = 0; i < ct ; i++ ){
            sb.append("<input type=\"HIDDEN\" name=\"");
            sb.append( hiddenNames.elementAt(i) );
            sb.append("\" value=\"");
            sb.append( hiddenVals.elementAt(i) );
            sb.append( "\" >\r\n");
        }
```

```
    }
    sb.append("<select name=\"keyword\"
➡size=\"8\">" );
    for( i = 0 ; i < kwd.length ; i ++ ){
        sb.append("<option value=\"" );
        sb.append( kwd[i] );
        sb.append( "\" > " );
        sb.append( kwd[i] ); sb.append("\r\n");
    }
    sb.append("</select>\r\n");
    sb.append("<input type=\"SUBMIT\"
➡value=\"Search\" >\r\n" );
    sb.append("</form>\r\n" );
    return sb.toString();
}
```

Formatting Product Descriptions

When trying to decide how to present product descriptions, we determined that our design criteria should emphasize the following:

Flexibility of styles   It is essential to separate considerations of style, such as colors and font sizes, from the code that creates the display.

Flexibility of content   A method is needed that enables the Web page designer to select the content of any part of the XML product description, without requiring a redesign of the Java classes.

Flexibility of Styles

The obvious choice for achieving flexibility of style is to use Cascading Style Sheets (CSS) to set style parameters for the various components of a Web page. CSS is currently the most widely supported standard and is an official part of the HTML 4 specification.

Placing style information in a separate file (called a *style sheet*) greatly reduces the amount of text your servlet has to generate. If the same style sheet is used for all pages on your site, the user's Web browser can cache it, thus reducing the response time for all of your site.

Listing 22.10 shows a simple style sheet that sets styles for the HTML <body>, <h1>, <h2>, and <p> tags and for four named styles that we use in the next example.

TIP

You can find an excellent tutorial on style-sheet usage at www.htmlhelp .com/reference/css.

Listing 22.10: A Sample Style Sheet (`catalog.css`)

```
body{font-family:Arial font-size:10.0pt}
h1{font-size:30pt; font-family:Arial; color:red ;}

h2{font-size:20pt; font-family:Arial; color:navy; }
p {font-size:10pt; font-family:Arial, Helvetica; background-
color:#fef6df ;}

.ch1{font-size:30pt; font-family:Arial; color:red ;}
.ch2{font-size:20pt; font-family:Arial;
➥color:navy ;}
.ch3{font-size:15pt; font-family:Arial;
➥color:purple ;}
.ch4{font-size:10pt; font-family:Arial;
➥color:black ;}
```

A style sheet can be attached to an HTML page with a link tag placed in the <head> area of a page, as in this example:

```
<head><title>Catalog Test Servlet Output</title>
 <link rel="stylesheet"
    href="http://localhost/XmlEcommBook/catalog.css"
➥type="text/css"
    media="screen" >
</head>
```

With the style sheet attached, setting the style for any element can be as simple as adding the style="ch2" attribute to a tag. The style then over-rides the browser's default for that tag. That this is more efficient can be seen by comparing these HTML lines, which accomplish the same thing. Compare the lines (which include style-sheet classes)

```
<a class="ch3" href="http://localhost/servlet/
```

```
➥cattest?
➥action=showproduct">
    Guide to Plants </a><span class="ch4">price
➥ea = $12.99 </span>
```

with the following version (which includes font tags):

```
<font face="Arial" SIZE="15pt" color="purple" >
<a class="ch3" href="http://localhost/servlet/
➥cattest?
➥action=showproduct">
    Guide to Plants </a></font>
<font face="Arial" SIZE="10pt" color="black" >
➥price ea = $12.99 </font>
```

Flexibility of Content

To provide for flexibility of content, we are going to use a formatting class named ProductFormatter. This class will output the data from an XML product Element in a format controlled by a list of field names with a matching list of styles to be applied to the text of the field.

As a simple example, to create a presentation in which the display for each product consists of the product name in the "ch3" format followed by the price in the "ch4" format, we define the following two String arrays:

```
String[] elem = { "prname", "price" };
String[] shortSt = { "ch3", "ch4"
```

We also require that the product name be formatted as a clickable link that will bring up a complete display for the selected product. This is accomplished by setting the alink String to incorporate this value, as in the following line:

```
"http://localhost/servlet/cattest?action=showproduct
```

We also define an int variable named linkN that gives the index of the field that will become the clickable link. In this case, linkN is 0 so that the product name will become the clickable link. With these parameters set, the doOutput method, as shown in Listing 22.11, will format the data for a particular product Element into a String ready for output to an HTML page.

Listing 22.11: The doOutput Method (ProductFormatter.java)

```
public String doOutput( Element el ){
    StringBuffer sb = new StringBuffer( );
```

```
String pid = null ;
if( aLink != null ){
  pid = "id=" + el.getAttribute("id");
}
for( int i = 0 ; i < elem.length ; i++ ){
  if( i == linkN && pid != null ){
    sb.append( "<a class=\"" );
    sb.append( style[i] );
    sb.append("\" href=\"");
    sb.append( aLink );
    sb.append("\">");
    addText( sb, elem[i], el );
    sb.append( " </a>");
  }
  else {
    sb.append( "<span class=\"");
    sb.append( style[i] ); sb.append("\">");
    addText( sb, elem[i], el );
    sb.append( " </span>");
  }
}
return sb.toString();
}
```

For the product Element shown in Listing 22.12, the output of the doOutput method will be as follows:

```
<a class="ch3" href="http://localhost/servlet/
➥cattest?
➥action=showproduct">
Guide to Plants </a>
<span class="ch4">price ea = $12.99 </span>
```

Listing 22.12: A Single product Element from catalog.xml

```
<product id="bk0022" keywords="gardening, plants">
  <name>Guide to Plants</name>
  <description>
    <paragraph>
    <italics>Everything</italics> you've ever wanted to know
about plants.
    </paragraph>
  </description>
  <price>$12.99</price>
```

```xml
<quantity_in_stock>4</quantity_in_stock>
<image format="gif" width="234" height="400"
src="images/covers/plantsv1.gif">
<caption>
<paragraph>This is the cover from the first edition.</para-
graph>
</caption>
</image>
<onsale_date>
<month>4</month>
  <day_of_month>4</day_of_month>
  <year>1999</year>
</onsale_date>
<shipping_info type="UPS" value="1.0" />
</product>
```

That takes care of formatting the data for a single product; now let's look at how to create a list of products. The CatalogBean has an array of Element references named selected. In the setInitialSelect method (Listing 22.13), this array can be set to either the complete list of products or the products in a single product line.

Listing 22.13: The setInitialSelect Method in CatalogBean (CatalogBean.java)

```java
public boolean setInitialSelect(String s){
    boolean ret = false ;
    if( s.equals("all") ){
        selected = cat.getAllProduct(); ret = true ;
    }
    else {
        selected = cat.getProductsByPL( s );
        if( selected != null ) ret = true ;
        else {
            System.out.println("selection problem");
        }
    }
    return ret ;
}
```

CatalogBean also has the doOutput method, which simply calls the ProductFormatter class doOutput method with an Element in the selected array, as follows:

```java
public String doOutput( int n ){
```

```
        return pf.doOutput( selected[n] );
}
```

Now we can put all of these parts together to get a formatted HTML page displaying the complete catalog. Listing 22.14 shows a simplified servlet doPost method. This method sets the response header, then writes the <head> and <title> tags, followed by a String containing the <link> tag pointing to a style sheet, as described earlier. Next, it writes the <body> tag and then calls the completeCatalog method. Finally, it writes the closing tags and closes the PrintWriter.

Listing 22.14: The doPost Method in a Servlet for Display of the Complete Catalog (CatalogTestServ.java)

```
public void doPost(HttpServletRequest req,
➥HttpServletResponse resp)
    throws ServletException, IOException
{
  resp.setContentType("text/html");
  PrintWriter out = new PrintWriter
➥(resp.getOutputStream());
  String action = req.getParameter("action");
  out.println("<html>");
  out.println("<head><title>CatalogTestServ
➥Output</title>");
  out.println( cssLink );
  out.println("</head>\r\n<body>");
  try {
    if( "showcatalog".equals( action )){
      completeCatalog( out );
    }
    else if( "selectkeyword".equals( action )){
      doKeywordSelect( out );
    }
  }catch( Exception e ){
      e.printStackTrace( out );
  }
  out.println("</body>");
  out.println("</html>");
  out.close();
}
```

As shown in Listing 22.15, the completeCatalog method writes the HTML tags to create a table with three columns. Each column is filled with the product information formatted by the doOutput method shown in Listing 22.11.

Listing 22.15: This Method in the Servlet Writes the Complete Catalog (`CatalogTestServ.java`)

```
public void completeCatalog( PrintWriter out ){
  CatalogBean cb = new CatalogBean();
  out.println("<h2>Complete Catalog</h2>");
  out.println("<table width=\"90%\" border=\"3\"
➥align=\"center\" >");
  out.println("<thead><tr><th>Books</th><th>CDs</th>
➥<th>Gadgets</th>"
            + "</tr></thead>");
  out.println("<tbody><tr valign=\"top\"><td>");
  String link = alias + "?action=showproduct" ;
  cb.setInitialSelect("Books");
  int ct = cb.getSelectedCount();
  out.println("We have " + ct + "
➥titles." + brcrlf );
  cb.setOutput("short", link);
  for( int i = 0 ; i < ct ; i++ ){
    out.println( cb.doOutput(i) );
    out.println( brcrlf );out.println( brcrlf );
  }
  out.println("</td><td>");
  cb.setInitialSelect("CDs");
  ct = cb.getSelectedCount();
  out.println("We have " + ct + " CD
➥titles." + brcrlf );
  cb.setOutput("short", link);
  for( int i = 0 ; i < ct ; i++ ){
    out.println( cb.doOutput(i) );
    out.println( brcrlf );out.println( brcrlf );
  }
  out.println("</td><td>");
  cb.setInitialSelect("widgets");
  ct = cb.getSelectedCount();
  out.println("We have " + ct + " kinds." +
➥brcrlf );
  cb.setOutput("short", link );
  for( int i = 0 ; i < ct ; i++ ){
    out.println( cb.doOutput(i) );
```

```
        out.println( brcrlf );out.println( brcrlf );
    }
    out.println("</td></tr></table>");
}
```

Listing 22.16 shows the text of the first part of the resulting HTML page. Note that many of the lines have been wrapped to fit this page. In spite of all of the space-saving use of a style sheet, the full page takes 17,213 bytes.

Listing 22.16: The First Part of the HTML Page Generated by the Servlet

```
<html>
<head><title>CatalogTestServ Output</title>
<link rel="stylesheet"
 href="http://localhost/XmlEcommBook/catalog.css"
    type="text/css" media="screen" >
</head>
<body>
<h2>Complete Catalog</h2>
<table width="90%" border="3" align="center" >
<thead><tr><th>Books</th><th>CDs</th>
<th>Gadgets</th></tr></thead>
<tbody><tr valign="top"><td>
We have 28 titles.<br />

<a class="ch3" href="http://localhost/servlet/cattest?
➥action=showproduct">
    Guide to Plants </a>
<span class="ch4">price ea = $12.99 </span>
<br />


<br />


<a class="ch3" href="http://localhost/servlet/
➥cattest?
➥action=showproduct">
  Guide to Plants, Volume 2 </a>
<span class="ch4">price ea = $12.99 </span>
<br />


<br />
```

```
<a class="ch3" href="http://localhost/servlet/
➥cattest?
➥action=showproduct">
  The Genius's Guide to the 3rd Millennium </a>
➥<span class="ch4">price ea = $59.95 </span>
<br />
```

Now for the end result of all of this effort. Figure 22.3 shows the browser display of the catalog.

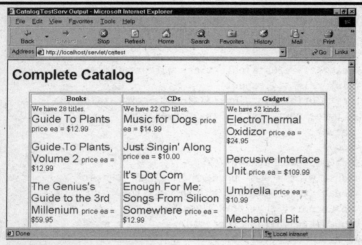

FIGURE 22.3: The complete catalog display

SUMMARY

XML enables you to develop server configurations using an open API that doesn't rely on any one vendor. Even JSP is moving to an all-XML syntax. As you move from the simple catalog example to more complicated endeavors, the advantages of this open approach become more obvious. Over time, developers come and go, but your system remains the same, and accessible to new faces.

In the next chapter, we'll add some complexity to what you've seen so far as we discuss another use case, this one involving customer surveys. Although you'll find this complexity a bit more challenging, the real power of Java's marriage to XML will make itself known.

Chapter 23

USING SURVEYS TO KNOW YOUR CUSTOMER

To be successful, an Internet entrepreneur must be able to understand his or her customers. As that entrepreneur, your starting point will always be the records of sales and of user interactions with your Web site. However, in addition to these records, you have the possibility of getting information directly from the customer by means of online surveys. Most people love to provide their opinions if you can convince them that you won't invade their privacy.

The combination of XML and Java servlets is well suited to the creation of online surveys. In this chapter, we go beyond the simple linear survey and create a system that can alter the questions asked according to the user's input.

Adapted from *Java™ Developer's Guide to E-Commerce with XML and JSP*, by William Brogden and Chris Minnick

ISBN 0-7821-2827-0   464 pages $49.99

Customer Privacy Concerns

The general public and policymakers share a very widespread concern about privacy in this age, focusing on every organization that seems to have a computer database. On one hand, businesses are convinced that knowing as much as possible about their customers is the key to survival in a world of cutthroat competition. On the other hand, people view with dismay the possibility that every detail about their private lives could be open to review. You can make your customers feel more comfortable with using your site if you explicitly explain the privacy standards you follow.

Industry Standards

A desire to address the Internet commerce aspects of this issue without involving government led to the creation of an independent, nonprofit privacy initiative named TRUSTe (www.truste.org). The following is the premise of this group:

▶ Users have a right to informed consent.

▶ No single privacy principle is adequate for all situations.

TRUSTe operates as a privacy branding organization similar to the way the UL (United Laboratories) brand is used with electrical equipment.

Member organizations are entitled to display the TRUSTe logo if their published privacy policies meet the TRUSTe standards, they pay the membership fee, and they pass a privacy statement audit. The fees start at $299 for companies doing less than $1 million in revenue, so membership is really quite reasonable.

NOTE

Sites that may collect information from children under the age of 13 have an even more stringent privacy requirement standard. As this is written, Congress is considering new legislation in this area.

TRUSTe conducts monitoring of member sites to verify that they are adhering to their published privacy standards. This monitoring includes submitting user information for fake users and tracking resulting use of the information. Furthermore, TRUSTe aggressively pursues sites that use the TRUSTe logo without authorization.

For both member and nonmember organizations, the www.truste.org site is an excellent location for catching up on the news affecting privacy considerations, particularly in the United States. TRUSTe also cooperates with other industry groups that are attempting to establish standard practices for ensuring user privacy.

Public Interest Organizations

Many people feel that there is as much danger from government data gathering as from corporate data gathering. Thus, it is no surprise that a number of public interest organizations exist and express their opinions on privacy issues. One such organization is the Electronic Privacy Information Center (EPIC) in Washington, D.C. (www.epic.org/privacy).

EPIC is concerned with civil rights and general privacy rights. It frequently testifies in hearings and actively uses the Freedom of Information Act to uncover government abuses of privacy in the United States.

EPIC is associated with Privacy International (www.privacy.org/pi), an international coalition of groups concerned with privacy issues. This group, founded in 1990, is based in London. Privacy International organizes international conferences on privacy issues. It also frequently gets in the news with its annual Big Brother awards to the government organizations and the corporations it deems to have the most invasive privacy records.

Knowing what your customer wants is essential to any online enterprise. But to avoid any semblance of privacy invasion, it is best to have a clearly stated privacy policy and to always allow your site visitors the chance to opt out of giving nonessential information. If your site caters to children, you also better make sure your information gathering is consistent with the latest legislation.

Creating Your Survey with XML Survey Script

A simple but effective form of information gathering is the online survey. Because XML is all about defining the structure of documents, and a survey is a highly structured document, XML is an ideal tool for our task. The XML-driven survey system discussed in the remainder of this chapter is very flexible. As written, it does not associate a particular user with his or her responses but simply aggregates the results. It could easily be modified to save user responses in a user database, but if you do that you should make sure the user understands what is being done with the data.

In this section, we will be developing a generalized XML structure for creating online surveys. Let's start with the following list of design criteria:

Control of presentation   Ideally, we should be able to present questions within the context of our normal Web-page design.

Flexibility of question design   We need to be able to create a variety of survey methods, from simple yes-or-no questions to a list of multiple-choice options.

Branching capability   A single script should be able to administer different questions to different users depending on their responses to specific questions. For example, if the response to one question indicates that the user never buys music CDs over the Internet, we need to branch away from questions related to music preferences.

Extensibility   If a new form of question presentation needs to be added to the system, it should be possible with minimum alteration to the code.

Recording results   Results from each participant should be recorded completely and independently of other participants. This gives us maximum flexibility in analysis.

Determining the Flow of Questions

Figure 23.1 illustrates possible paths through a question script. Essentially, there are blocks of questions that are always presented without branching, ending in a question that provides branching to determine the next path. A branching question can lead all branches to the same block (blocks C and D in the figure both lead to block E, for example) or to different blocks (block A, for instance, leads to blocks B, C, and D, depending on the answers submitted). Blocks either end with a branching question or are "terminal" and end the questionnaire. On reaching a terminal, the system records all responses in a file. The designer has the option of using a unique file for each terminal.

Translating this diagram into XML entities, we have come up with the following structure. A Questionnaire document has an Intro (introduction) and one or more Block entities at the first level. Each Block has one or more Ques (question) entities and may end with a Terminal entity. A Block has a name attribute that is used to direct branching and a type attribute that has the value "terminal" if the block ends with a Terminal tag. This top-level structure is illustrated schematically in Listing 23.1.

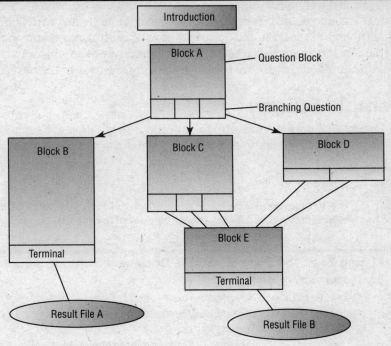

FIGURE 23.1: Potential paths through a script

Listing 23.1: The First and Second Levels of a Questionnaire Hierarchy

```
<Questionnaire>
  <Intro>
  </Intro>
  <Block name="A">
  </Block>
  <Block name="B" type="terminal">
  </Block>
  <Block name="C">
  </Block>
  <Block name="D">
  </Block>
  <Block name="E" type="terminal">
  </Block>
</Questionnaire>
```

Each question in a block is created with the `Ques` tag, which encloses a text statement and two or more selectable options created with `Qopt` tags. Attributes in the `Ques` and `Qopt` tags provide control over branching and the way the question is presented. The easiest way to see this is to look at some questions, which are shown in the sample survey in the next section.

A Sample Survey

Listing 23.2 presents the introduction and first question of a sample survey that you might use to determine new products to stock in your catalog.

NOTE

The first question has the `type` attribute value of `"QMC"`; this style of question is presented so the user can choose only one of the options.

Listing 23.2: The Start of an XML Document Defining a Survey (`customersurvey.xml`)

```xml
<?xml version="1.0" standalone="yes" ?>
<Questionnaire title="Example Customer Survey"
    author="wbb" date="May 30, 2000"
    method="xml" file="e:\scripts\questionnaire\
➥surveyresult.xml"
    >
<Intro><![CDATA[
<h1>Welcome Customers</h1><br>
<p>We here at <i>BuyStuff.com</i> want to meet your every
desire
to buy <b>STUFF</b>. To that end, we are greatly expanding
our online catalog, and we want to concentrate on
<b>STUFF</b>
you will want to buy as soon as you see it. Please help by
completing this simple survey.
</p>]]>
</Intro>
<Block name="intro" type="terminal" >
<Ques id="intro:1" type="QMC" >
   <Qtext>Which of the following are you most interested in
buying online?
   </Qtext>
<Qopt val="a" branch="books" >Books</Qopt>
<Qopt val="b" branch="cds" >Cds</Qopt>
```

```
<Qopt val="c" branch="gadgets">Electronic goodies
</Qopt>
<Qopt val="d" >I am not interested in buying stuff!
</Qopt>
</Ques>
<!-- this terminates the block and the questionnaire -
     could substitute different file for recording -->
<Terminal><![CDATA[<h2>Thanks for looking anyway!</h2>
]]>
</Terminal>
</Block>
```

. . .

The Qopt options with val attributes of "a", "b", and "c" in the first question branch to other blocks, whereas option "d" leads to the terminal message. Only one of these options can be chosen, because the question type is "QMC". In this chapter, we use only two types of question, QMC (Question Multiple Choice) and QMCM (Question Multiple Choice Multiple Answer). The results of the user response to this question are recorded using the question id attribute and the option val attribute values.

Listing 23.3 shows the block (from Listing 23.2) that the branch attribute in the Qopt tag with val="a" leads to. Question "books:1" uses the "QMCM" type, which allows multiple selections to be made. The "cds" and "gadgets" blocks have a similar organization.

Listing 23.3: The "books" Question Block (customersurvey.xml)

```
<Block name="books" type="terminal" >
<Ques id="books:1" type="QMCM" >
  <Qtext>Please select all of the book categories you
  would like to see in our catalog.
  </Qtext>
  <Qopt val="0">Best Sellers of All Types</Qopt>
  <Qopt val="1">Science Fiction</Qopt>
  <Qopt val="2">Fantasy Fiction</Qopt>
  <Qopt val="3">History and Biography</Qopt>
  <Qopt val="4">Computer Technology</Qopt>
  <Qopt val="5">Business Related</Qopt>
</Ques>
<Terminal><![CDATA[<h2>Thanks for answering the
survey!</h2>]]>
</Terminal>
</Block>
```

THE SURVEY ADMINISTERING SERVLET

This section describes the complete code for a Java servlet to administer a survey based on the XML script design we created in the preceding section and to record the results in a form suitable for analysis. We also describe a utility class to manage document objects in a servlet engine, and a servlet for tabulating and reporting survey results.

The Survey Servlet Code

Listing 23.4 shows the import statements, class declaration, and init method for the QuestionnaireServ servlet. The static variable homedir, which can be set from the ServletConfig, is used in the init method to read a properties file in which survey names are related to the system path to the source XML file. The properties file also can be used to set the handler string variable, which is the URL used by the Web server for this servlet.

Listing 23.4: The Start of the QuestionnaireServ Code (QuestionnaireServ.java)

```
package com.XmlEcomBook.Chap07;

import com.XmlEcomBook.DOMlibrary ;
import org.w3c.dom.* ;
import java.io.*;
import java.util.* ;
import javax.servlet.*;
import javax.servlet.http.*;

public class QuestionnaireServ extends HttpServlet
{
    static String brcrlf = "<br>\r\n" ;
    static String homedir = "e:\\scripts\\
questionnaire" ;
    static String handler = "http://localhost/servlet/
Questionnaire" ;
    static String version = "v1.00";
    Properties qProp ;
```

```
    public void init(ServletConfig config) throws
ServletException  {
    super.init(config);
    String tmp = config.getInitParameter("homedir");
    if( tmp != null ) homedir = tmp ;
    System.out.println("Start QuestionnaireServ using " +
homedir );
    File f = new File( homedir, "questionnaire.
➥properties");
    try { qProp = new Properties();
      qProp.load( new FileInputStream(f) );
      tmp = qProp.getProperty("handler");
      if( tmp != null ) handler = tmp ;
      System.out.println("Loaded properties for Questionnaire
handler: "
              + handler );
    }catch(IOException e){
        System.out.println("Error loading " + e );
    }
    }
```

The `QuestionnaireServ` servlet uses sessions to keep track of individual users taking a survey. Initial entry is expected to be a GET from an HTML page with a simple form that sets a qname variable indicating which survey is to be administered. In customizing this servlet for your own application, you could also record a customer id at this point.

The doGet method, as shown in Listing 23.5, tries to get the document object corresponding to qname, using the file path from the properties file and the `DOMlibrary` utility. If it succeeds, it proceeds to get an `HttpSession` and to attach a new `Interpreter` object that holds the document to the session. A new `Recorder` object will also be initialized and attached to the session. Any error will use the `errorMsg` method (see Listing 23.7) to write an error message to the user.

The `Interpreter` object is responsible for creating the HTML forms that will administer the survey, whereas the `Recorder` object is responsible for recording the user's responses. These classes are discussed in the upcoming sections "The `Interpreter` Class" and "The `Recorder` Class."

Output from the doGet method is a page having the text from the `Intro` tag area of the XML document, which is written out by the `Interpreter` object doIntro method and includes a form with a button to start the first question.

Listing 23.5: The doGet Method Code (QuestionnaireServ.java)

```java
    public void doGet(HttpServletRequest req,
HttpServletResponse resp)
        throws ServletException, IOException
    {
      resp.setContentType("text/html");
      PrintWriter out = new PrintWriter(resp.
getOutputStream());
      String qname = req.getParameter("qname") ;
      // System.out.println("Start doGet");
      if( qname == null || qname.length() == 0 ){
          errorMsg( out, "Bad QNAME data", null);
return;
      }
        // MUST have qname = name of xml file
      String src = qProp.getProperty( qname );
      if( src == null ) {
          errorMsg( out, "Bad QNAME lookup", null );
return ;
      }
      String userid = "unknown" ; // customer or student id or
unknown
      String tmp = req.getParameter("userid");
      if( tmp != null ) userid = tmp;
      String usertype = "unknown" ; // "student"
"customer" etc etc
      tmp = req.getParameter("usertype");
      if(tmp != null ) usertype = tmp ;
      DOMlibrary lib = DOMlibrary.getLibrary();
      System.out.println("DOMlibrary initialized, try
for " + src );
      Document doc = lib.getDOM( src );
      if( doc == null ){
          errorMsg( out, "DOM doc failed - unable to
continue", null );
          return ;
      }
      HttpSession session = req.getSession( true );
      // if not new must be re-entering - could recover here
      Interpreter terpret = new Interpreter( doc,
handler );
      // session.putValue( "xmldocument", terpret );
```

```
        session.setAttribute("xmldocument", terpret );
        // the putValue method was used in the 2.1
        // API but is now
        // a deprecated method, you might have to use it if you
are
        // using an older servlet engine such as JRun 2.3
            Recorder rb = new Recorder(userid, usertype,
              session.getId(), src );
        rb.setMethods( doc );
        //session.putValue("recorder", rb );
        session.setAttribute("recorder", rb );
        try { //
          terpret.doIntro( out ); // includes head and Form
          footer( out );
        }catch(Exception e){
            errorMsg( out, "doGet ", e );
        }
    }
```

After the survey introduction, all requests and responses go through the doPost method, as seen in Listing 23.6. After recovering the Interpreter and Recorder objects from the HttpSession, data from the request is gathered and the response is generated by the Interpreter and Recorder objects.

Listing 23.6: The doPost Method of the QuestionnaireServ Class (QuestionnaireServ.java)

```
    public void doPost(HttpServletRequest req,
    ➡HttpServletResponse resp)
        throws ServletException, IOException
    {
      resp.setContentType("text/html");
      PrintWriter out = new PrintWriter(resp.
    ➡getOutputStream());
      //System.out.println("Start doPost");
      HttpSession session = req.getSession(false);
      try {
        if( session == null ){ errorMsg(out, "No
    ➡Session ", null );
            return ;
        }
        Interpreter terpret =
```

```
                    (Interpreter)session.getAttribute("xmldocument");
            Recorder rb =
                 (Recorder) session.getAttribute("recorder");
            if( terpret == null ||
                rb == null ){
                    errorMsg( out, "Data not recovered from
➡Session", null );
                    return;
            }
            terpret.doPostQ( out, req, rb );
            footer( out );
        }catch(Exception e ){
            errorMsg( out, "doPost ", e );
        }
    }
```

Listing 23.7 shows some convenient utility methods in the QuestionnaireServ class. Using the footer method to write the end tags on each page lets you include the servlet version at the bottom. This is very handy during development and can easily be removed for the final version.

Debugging servlets can be very tricky, especially if the bugs show up only occasionally. It is especially hard if the users don't have any clear way of expressing the problem. We like to use the errorMsg method to report errors. If the error involves an exception, it will write a stack trace to the HTML output. It includes an e-mail address for the user to send a message and, hopefully, a copy of the stack trace. Naturally, you should plug in your own e-mail address here.

Listing 23.7: Utility Methods in the Servlet
(QuestionnaireServ.java)

```
    public void footer( PrintWriter out ){
        out.println("<hr> Servlet version: " + version
➡+ "<br>");
        out.println("</BODY>");
        out.println("</HTML>");
        out.close();
    }


        // assumes response has been set to text/html
    private void errorMsg( PrintWriter out, String
➡msg, Exception ex ){
```

```
out.println("<html>");
out.println("<head><title>QuestionnaireServ
Output</title></head>");
out.println("<body>");
out.println("<h2>Error: " ); out.println( msg );
out.println("</h2><br>");
if( ex != null ){
    ex.printStackTrace( out );
}
out.println("<br>");
out.println("<a href=\"mailto:wbrogden@bga.
com\">" +
    "Please mail me the error message.</a><br>");
footer( out );
}

public String getServletInfo()
{
  return "Administers a questionnaire";
}
}
```

The *Interpreter* Class

The work of creating survey form questions from the XML document is encapsulated in the Interpreter class. This class has been designed to be very flexible with respect to presentation of questions. Although only two styles of question are supported in this version, the mechanism can be expanded to provide additional styles.

The import statements and static methods for Interpreter are shown in Listing 23.9. The constants QMC and QMCM stand for the two styles that are provided, QMC meaning a question with multiple choices that allow only a single selection and QMCM a question with multiple choices that allow multiple selections. Consider the XML for a sample question, as shown in Listing 23.8.

Listing 23.8: The Start of a Sample Question Block in XML (customersurvey.xml)

```
<Block name="cds" type="terminal" >
<Ques type="QMCM" id="palm:1">
  <Qtext>Please select all of the CD categories
```

```
        that you would like to see in our catalog.
        </Qtext>
        <Qopt val="0">Classical</Qopt>
        <Qopt val="1">Country and Western</Qopt>
        <Qopt val="2">The Latest Pop Groups</Qopt>
        <Qopt val="3">Current Rock</Qopt>
        <Qopt val="4">Golden Oldies Rock</Qopt>
        <Qopt val="5">Environmental</Qopt>
        <Qopt val="6">Novelty and Humor</Qopt>
    </Ques>
```

The opening Ques tag uses the type attribute to establish that this is a "QMCM" style question. The id attribute is a unique value for this question.

Instead of comparing the type attribute String with the various possible question styles, we use a Hashtable to look up an int value that can be used in a switch statement to select proper handling for the question. The Hashtable is named typeHash and the lookup is performed by the lookUpType method, as shown in Listing 23.9.

To add a new type, you would simply define a new String and int constant in the static variables and in the typeHash Hashtable.

Listing 23.9: Imports and Constants at the Start of the Interpreter Source Code (Interpreter.java)

```java
package com.XmlEcomBook.Chap07;
//
import org.w3c.dom.* ;
import com.sun.xml.tree.* ;
import java.io.*;
import java.util.* ;
import javax.servlet.*;
import javax.servlet.http.*;

public class Interpreter
{
    static final String brcrlf = "<br>\r\n";
    static final int QMC = 1 ;
    static final int QMCM = 2 ;

    static Hashtable typeHash = new Hashtable();
    static { // static initialization block
      typeHash.put("QMC", new Integer( QMC ));
```

```
typeHash.put("QMCM", new Integer( QMCM ));
}

static int lookUpType( String type ){
    Integer N = (Integer)typeHash.get( type );
    if( N == null ) return 0 ;
    return N.intValue();
}
```

Listing 23.10 continues with the instance variables and constructor method of the Interpreter class. Each user session has an instance of Interpreter that stores the document and information about the user's current position in the survey. The nowBlock and nowNode variables are references of the org.w3c.dom.Node interface type.

Listing 23.10: Instance Variables and the Interpreter Class Constructor (Interpreter.java)

```
// instance variables below this
Document theDom ;
Node nowBlock, nowNode ; // nowNode should be
//quest type
boolean terminal = false ; // true if the block
// is terminal
String title ;
String css = "" ; // may change from block to block
String actionStr ;

NodeList blockNodeList ; // Nodes that are <Block> type

// the constructor - doc is the XML script document
public Interpreter( Document doc, String handler )
{
    theDom = doc ; actionStr = handler ;
    Element E = theDom.getDocumentElement(); // the
root
    blockNodeList = E.getElementsByTagName
("Block");
    // note that in contrast to other get methods,
getAttributes
    // returns "" if the attribute does not exist
    title = E.getAttribute("title");
    css = E.getAttribute("css");  // used
```

➡️for \<Intro\>
    }

To provide some flexibility in formatting the questions, there is a provision for specifying a Cascading Style Sheet (CSS) for the overall document and for overriding that default in each block. The writeHead method shown in Listing 23.11 handles the output of the start of an HTML page and includes a style sheet reference if it exists. This listing also shows the startForm and endForm methods. Note that the quesid variable is written into the form as a hidden variable that is later recovered in the doPostQ method (see Listing 23.16).

Listing 23.11: Methods That Write Various Parts of the HTML Page (Interpreter.java)

```java
    // output title and <head> tag area, using css if present
    void writeHead( PrintWriter out ){
        out.println("<html>");
        out.println("<head><title>" + title +
➡️"</title></head>");
        if( css.length() > 0 ){
            out.println("<link href=\"" + css +
                "\" type=\"text/css\"
➡️rel=\"stylesheet\">" );
        }
        out.println("<body>");
    }


    // assumes nowNode is set to the first question
    // output form start and question text
    public void startForm(PrintWriter out ){
        out.print("<form method=\"POST\" action=\"" );
        out.print( actionStr ); out.println("\" >");
    }


    // fills in hidden variable and button
    public void endForm( PrintWriter out, String id )
{
        out.print("<input type=\"hidden\"
➡️name=\"quesid\" value=\""
            + id + "\" ><br>" );
        out.print("<input type=\"submit\" value=\"" );
        out.print("Next" );
```

```
        out.println("\" name=\"action\" ><br>");
        out.println("</form><br>");
    }
```

Creating the Question Display The genQuest method in Listing 23.12 is called after the nowNode variable has been set to the Ques element to be displayed. Note the use of the question type to select the prompt that is displayed. After printing the question text, and the prompt, genQuest creates a form containing the options.

Listing 23.12: The genQuest Method (Interpreter.java)

```
// nowNode known to be a <Quest>
public void genQuest( PrintWriter out ){
    Element E = (Element) nowNode ;
    String qid = E.getAttribute("id") ;
    String type = E.getAttribute("type");
    String lim  = E.getAttribute("limit");
    // out.print("Question id: " + qid + " type: " +
type + brcrlf );
    writeHead( out );
    NodeList nm = E.getElementsByTagName("Qtext");
    out.print( nm.item(0).getFirstChild().
getNodeValue() );
    out.println(brcrlf );
    NodeList opm = E.getElementsByTagName("Qopt");
    int optCt = opm.getLength();
    int typeN = lookUpType( type );
    switch( typeN ){
      case QMC :
        out.print("Choose one"); break ;
      case QMCM :
        if( lim.length() == 0 ){
            out.print("Choose any number");
        }
        else { out.print("Choose up to " + lim );
        }
        break ;
      default :
        out.print("Unknown type");
    }
    out.print( brcrlf );
```

```
        startForm( out ); // creates <form...
        for( int i = 0 ; i < optCt ; i++ ){
            doOption(out, opm.item(i), typeN );
        }
        endForm( out, qid );
    }
```

The genQuest method in the preceding listing calls the doOption method (Listing 23.13) for each <Qopt> element. If you want to add option types, such as a text entry field, this is the method that would have to be modified. This listing also shows the checkBlockType method that is used to locate attributes in a Block element.

Listing 23.13: The doOption Method (Interpreter.java)

```
// opN is from node list of <Qopt> - create output
    // <Qopt val="a" branch="" >Option a.</Qopt>
    private void doOption(PrintWriter out, Node opN,
➥int typeN ){
        Element E = (Element) opN;
        String val = E.getAttribute("val") ;
        String branch = E.getAttribute("branch");
        String content = E.getFirstChild().
➥getNodeValue();
        // what else? type of option display?
        switch( typeN ){ // known valid
          case QMC :
            out.print("<input name=\"opt\"
➥value=\"" + val +
                "\" type=\"RADIO\" >" );
            break ;
          case QMCM :
            out.print("<input name=\"opt\"
➥value=\"" + val +
                "\" type=\"CHECKBOX\" >" );
            break ;
        } // now for the text
        out.println( content );
        out.println( brcrlf );
    }

    // look at the type and css attributes in <Block>
    private void checkBlockType( ){
        Element E = (Element)nowBlock ;
```

```
    String tmp = E.getAttribute("type");
    terminal = tmp.equals("terminal");
    tmp = E.getAttribute("css");
    if( tmp.length() > 0 ) css = tmp ;
    System.out.println("checkBlockType -
➡css:" + css );
    }
```

Creating the Introduction Display Listing 23.14 presents the
doIntro method, which sets up the starting Block element by looking
at the first element in the blockNodeList. With the nowBlock variable
set, a call to setQnodeInBlock sets the nowNode variable to the first
Ques element. Assuming this is accomplished correctly, the Intro text
is output with a simple form that will call up the first question.

**Listing 23.14: The doIntro Method That Outputs Text from the
<Intro> Tag (Interpreter.java)**

```
    // <head> has been set, we are in <body>
    public void doIntro(PrintWriter out ){
        writeHead( out );
        nowBlock = blockNodeList.item(0);
        if( nowBlock == null ){
            out.println("Error 1 setting up first
question.<br>");
            return ;
        }
        if( setQnodeInBlock( 0 )== null ){
            out.println("Error 2 setting up first
question.<br>");
            return ;
        }
        checkBlockType( ); // sets the terminal flag
        out.println( getIntro() );
        out.print("<form method=\"POST\" action=\"" );
        out.print( actionStr ); out.println("\" >");
        endForm( out, "intro" );
    }
```

Handling a Questionnaire Branch Listing 23.15 shows the setBranch
method that is called by doPostQ when a user response that selects a
branch has been found in a question response. This method simply

looks through all of the Block elements for a matching name and sets the nowBlock and nowNode variables accordingly.

Listing 23.15: The setBranch Method (Interpreter.java)

```
    // jump to another block has been detected
  private void setBranch(String block ){
     int ct = blockNodeList.getLength();
     for( int i = 1 ; i < ct ; i++ ){ // block 0 was
  // the start
        nowBlock = blockNodeList.item(i);
        String name = ((Element)nowBlock).
  // getAttribute("name");
        if( name.equals( block )){
           checkBlockType() ; // to set terminal flag
           setQnodeInBlock( 0 ) ; // set nowNode
           return ;
        }
     }
     System.err.println("Interpreter.setBranch
  ➥failed to find " + block );
     nowBlock = nowNode = null ;
  }
```

The doPostQ method starting in Listing 23.16 is called from the servlet doPost method and manages the creation of a new HTML page. Note that the first thing this method does is check to see if the associated Recorder object has recorded the fact that the survey has previously been terminated. This prevents a user from using the browser Back function to return to an earlier page and input data once the end of the survey has been reached and the data recorded.

The next section of code takes care of the special case of the first question by detecting the fact that the quesid equals "intro". In all other cases, the user input must be recorded by comparing the select "opt" values from the form with the <Qopt> tag attributes, using the associated Recorder object.

Listing 23.16: The Start of the doPostQ Method (Interpreter.java)

```
    // req contains user response
  public void doPostQ( PrintWriter out,
  ➥HttpServletRequest req,
```

```
                        Recorder recordB ){
        if( recordB.terminated ){
            writeHead( out );
            out.println("<b>This questionnaire has been
➡terminated.</b>");
            return ;
        }
        String action =  req.getParameter("action");
        String quesid =  req.getParameter("quesid");
        if( !action.equals("Next") ){
            out.println("Unexpected state in Interpreter.
➡doPost<br>");
            return ;
        }
        if( quesid.equals("intro") ){
            // this calls for generating first question
            // doIntro already set nowNode to first
            // <Ques> node
            genQuest( out );
            return ;
        }
        // if here, not generating first question,
        // examine request
        Element E = (Element) nowNode ;
        NodeList oplist = E.getElementsByTagName
➡("Qopt");
        int type = lookUpType( E.getAttribute("type"));
        String lim  = E.getAttribute("limit"); // ?
        String[] optS = req.getParameterValues("opt");
        recordB.record( quesid, type, optS );
```

The next step in the doPostQ method, as seen in Listing 23.17, is to determine whether or not one of the user's responses just recorded causes a branch to be taken. Naturally, a new branch will start at the first question in a block as set by the setBranch method. If a branch is not taken, we have to locate the present question in the current Block element and pick the next question to be displayed. We also have to account for the situation in which the element following the current question is a Terminal, in which case we call genTerminal to handle the output.

Listing 23.17: The doPostQ Method, Continued
(Interpreter.java)

```
        String branch = branchLookUp( oplist, optS );
        if( branch != null ){
            //System.out.println("Taking Branch:" + branch );
            setBranch( branch ); // sets nowBlock and nowNode to
new value
            if( nowNode == null ) genTerminal( out, recordB );
            else genQuest( out );
            return ;
        }

        // branch is null, nowBlock has 1 or more <Ques
        NodeList qlist = ((Element)nowBlock).
getElementsByTagName("Ques");
        int n = 0 ;
        int nct = qlist.getLength();
        while( qlist.item(n) != nowNode &&
                n < nct ) n++ ;
        // n = nowNode
        Node nxtN = qlist.item(n+1);
        if( nxtN != null ){
            nowNode = nxtN ;
            genQuest( out );
            // System.out.println("Found nextQ");
            return ;
        }
        if( terminal ) genTerminal( out, recordB );
        else out.println("nextQ NULL, not
terminal<br>" );
    } // end doPostQ
```

Handling a *Terminal* Element   As shown in Listing 23.18, the
genTerminal method has two main tasks. First, it has to output the
final page of the survey, using either the text associated with the Terminal element or a stock phrase. Next, it has to look for an "altfile"
attribute attached to the Terminal. If present, this value is used by
the Recorder object to save the results to a file; otherwise, Recorder
uses the default file established at the start of the XML document.

Listing 23.18: The genTerminal Method (Interpreter.java)

```
    // we have reached the end of a terminal block
    // note that a <Terminal> tag may have an
    // altfile="filepathandname"
    // that replaces the default established in the file
    // attribute of
    // the <Questionnaire> tag for this particular branch
    private void genTerminal( PrintWriter out,
➥Recorder recordB ){
      NodeList nl = ((Element)nowBlock).
➥getElementsByTagName ("Terminal");
      int ct = nl.getLength();
      String altfile = "" ;
      writeHead( out );
      if( ct == 0 ){
        out.println("Thank you for participating.
➥<br>");
      }
      else { // use text from
            //<Terminal>...</Terminal>
        Element E = (Element)nl.item(0); // only one
            // <Terminal> tag
        out.println( E.getFirstChild().
➥getNodeValue() );
        altfile = E.getAttribute("altfile");
      }
      try {
        recordB.terminal( altfile );
      }catch(IOException e ){
        out.println("Problem recording results; please notify
Webmaster.");
      }
    }
```

Utility Methods in the *Interpreter* Class   Listing 23.19 finishes the
Interpreter class listing with various utility methods.

**Listing 23.19: The Last of the Interpreter Code
(Interpreter.java)**

```
    private Node setQnodeInBlock( int n ){
      Element E = (Element) nowBlock ;
```

```
      NodeList nl = E.getElementsByTagName("Ques");
      nowNode = nl.item( n );
      return nowNode ;
   }

   public String getIntro() {
      Element E = theDom.getDocumentElement(); // the
➥root
      NodeList nl = E.getElementsByTagName("Intro");
      Element I = (Element)nl.item(0);
      nl = I.getChildNodes();
      int ct = nl.getLength();
      if( ct == 0 ) return "Bad Intro Data<br>" ;
      return nl.item(0).getNodeValue();
   }

   // return String if any chosen opt
   // has a branch="", else null
   private String branchLookUp( NodeList oplist,
➥String[] optS ){
      if( optS == null ||
          optS.length == 0 ) return null ;
      Hashtable opHash = new Hashtable();
      int i, ct = oplist.getLength();
      String val, branch ;
      for( i = 0 ; i < ct ;i++ ){
          val = ((Element)oplist.item(i)).
➥getAttribute("val");
          branch = ((Element)oplist.item(i)).
➥getAttribute("branch");
          opHash.put( val, branch ); // branch = ""
➥if no attribute
      }
      if( opHash.size() == 0 ) return null ; // branch not
possible
      for( i = 0 ; i < optS.length ; i++ ){
          branch = (String)opHash.get( optS[i] );
          if( branch != null &&
              branch.length() > 0 ) return branch ;
      }
      return null ;
   }
```

```
   public String toString()
   {
      StringBuffer sb = new StringBuffer
➡("Interpreter ");
      return sb.toString() ;
   }
}
```

The *Recorder* Class

The Recorder class is responsible for storing the user responses to each question and for writing them to a file for later analysis. Each user gets an instance of Recorder that is stored in a session and records only that user's responses.

The root element of the XML document is the Questionnaire tag, which has several attributes used by the Recorder class. As shown in the following sample tag, these attributes are named title, author, date, method, and file:

```
<Questionnaire title="Survey 1" author="WBB"
date="May 19, 2000" method="xml"
file="e:\scripts\questionnaire\testresult.xml">
```

The title, author, and date are simply held by the Recorder for later output, but method and file control the Recorder operation. We have provided the method attribute in case you want to save the data in some format besides XML. For example, if you like to use a spreadsheet analysis program, you could add methods to write a comma-delimited line of text. The output filename established is a default that can be replaced by a filename in a Terminal tag.

In the XML format we are using here, each user's responses are stored within a Qresults tag, with a Ques tag for each question and a Qopt tag for each selected response. This is certainly more bulky than a comma-delimited file, but it is very flexible. The file that is written is not a complete XML document because it does not have a root element. Later, in the "Survey Analysis Options" section, we show how this is handled.

Listing 23.20 shows the import statements, the instance variables, and the single static variable in the Recorder class. The static variable is a String object that is used in a synchronized statement to ensure that only one instance of Recorder is actually writing to a file at any one time.

Listing 23.20: The Start of the Recorder Class Source Code (Recorder.java)

```
package com.XmlEcomBook.Chap07;

import org.w3c.dom.* ;
import com.sun.xml.tree.* ;
import java.io.*;
import java.util.* ;
import javax.servlet.*;
import javax.servlet.http.*;

public class Recorder
{ // this String is used to prevent more than one Recorder
  // from writing anywhere at the "same time"
  static String filelock = "RecorderLock" ;

  // these are instance variables
  String userid, usertype, sessionid ;
  String qresultStr ;
  String source ; // the xml file
  String method, output ; // how and where we save
  Hashtable record ; // one string per response
  public boolean terminated = false ;
```

The Recorder constructor method, shown in Listing 23.21, is called from the doGet method of the servlet. It sets several variables that characterize a particular user. It also creates the Hashtable that will be used to record responses to questions.

Listing 23.21 also shows the setMethods method, which uses the XML document to locate the method and file attributes. It also creates the starting Qresults tag and stores it in the qresultStr variable for later use.

Listing 23.21: The Recorder constructor and setMethods Methods (Recorder.java)

```
public Recorder(String id, String typ, String ses,
➥String src ){
  userid = id ; usertype = typ ; sessionid = ses ;
  source = src ;
```

```
    record = new Hashtable();
}


    // locate method information in the document
    public void setMethods( Document doc  ){
       NamedNodeMap nnm = doc.getDocumentElement().
➥getAttributes();
       method = nnm.getNamedItem("method").
➥getNodeValue();
       output = nnm.getNamedItem("file").
➥getNodeValue();
       // for xml method
       StringBuffer sb = new StringBuffer( 50 );
       sb.append("<Qresults source=\"");
       sb.append( source ); sb.append( "\" date=\"" );
       sb.append( new Date().toString() );
       sb.append( "\" userid=\""); sb.append(userid);
       sb.append( "\" usertype=\"" ) ; sb.append
➥( usertype );
       sb.append( "\" sessionid=\""); sb.append
➥( sessionid );
       sb.append("\">\r\n");
       qresultStr = sb.toString();
    }
```

Listing 23.22 shows the terminal, record, and toString methods.
The terminal method is responsible for writing the collected results
from this user to the designated file. The toString method is provided
to aid in debugging.

The record method is called from the Interpreter doPostQ method
after each question response is received. Note that the record method
provides for switching on the question type in case you want to create
another question type that requires specialized recording. For example, if
you want to accept a text input, it should be saved embedded in a CDATA
section so that the user's accidental entry of characters having XML
meanings will not cause problems.

Each call to record creates a String containing a Ques tag that is
stored in the record Hashtable, using the quesid as a key. Because a
Hashtable does not retain the order of the addition of items, the order in
which Ques tags are later written is not predictable. However, this does
not matter because we can use the XML survey document to determine
the order of questions.

Listing 23.22: The Recorder Class Source, Continued (Recorder.java)

```java
    // called when a <Terminal> block is reached
    // if altdest is not "" this changes the
    // default output
    public void terminal(String altdest ) throws
IOException {
       if( altdest != null &&
           altdest.length() > 4 ) output = altdest ;
       if( output == null || output.length() < 5 ){
           System.out.println("QARG output is: " +
output );
           return ;
       }
       terminated = true ;
       // write in append mode
       synchronized( filelock ){
         FileWriter fw = new FileWriter( output,true );
         PrintWriter pw = new PrintWriter( fw );
         pw.print( qresultStr ); // string constant
         Enumeration e = record.elements();
         while( e.hasMoreElements() ){
           pw.print( (String)e.nextElement() ) ;
         }
         pw.print("</Qresults>\r\n");
         pw.close();
       } // end synchronized block
    }

    public void record( String quesid, int type,
String[] optS ){
       if( terminated ) return ; // prevent backing up
       // from terminal Q
       // System.out.println("Start record: " +
quesid );
       StringBuffer sb = new StringBuffer( 100 );
       sb.append("<Ques id=\"" ); sb.append( quesid );
sb.append("\" >");
       switch( type ){
         case Interpreter.QMC :
         case Interpreter.QMCM :
```

```
          if( optS == null || optS.length == 0 ) break ;
          for(int i =0 ; i < optS.length ; i++ ){
              sb.append("<Qopt val=\"");  sb.append
➡( optS[i] );
              sb.append("\"></Qopt>");
          }
          break ;
        default :
          sb.append("UNKNOWN TYPE");
        }
      sb.append("\r\n</Ques>\r\n");
      String tmp = sb.toString();
      // note this will replace answer if user backed
      // up with browser back
      record.put( quesid, tmp );
      return ;
    }

    public String toString() // for debugging
    { StringBuffer sb = new StringBuffer
➡( "Recorder user: " );
      sb.append( userid ); sb.append(" type: " );
      sb.append( usertype ); sb.append(" session: " );
      sb.append( sessionid );sb.append(" method: ");
      sb.append( method ); sb.append( " output: " );
      sb.append( output ); // how and where we save
      return sb.toString() ;
    }
}
```

Listing 23.23 shows the lines of text written for a single user taking a simple survey. The `source` attribute records the XML file used to create the survey. The `date` attribute records the date and time for the user's initial entry and presentation of the introduction. We have recorded the `sessionid` as an attribute to aid in debugging, but this could probably be eliminated.

Listing 23.23: A Single Survey Results Record in XML

```
<Qresults source="e:\scripts\javatest.xml"
 date="Mon May 22 22:30:20 CDT 2000"
   userid="unknown" usertype="passed"
   sessionid="9590526208594804">
```

```
<Ques id="studying:4" >
    <Qopt val="a"></Qopt><Qopt val="b"></Qopt>
    <Qopt val="d"></Qopt><Qopt val="e"></Qopt>
    <Qopt val="k"></Qopt><Qopt val="l"></Qopt>
    <Qopt val="m"></Qopt>
</Ques>
<Ques id="studying:3" ><Qopt val="1"></Qopt>
</Ques>
<Ques id="studying:2" ><Qopt val="2"></Qopt>
</Ques>
<Ques id="studying:1" >
  <Qopt val="a"></Qopt>
  <Qopt val="f"></Qopt>
</Ques>
</Qresults>
```

Survey Analysis Options

Because the recording format keeps each individual user's input as a single record, there are many options for analysis. For the purposes of this chapter, we present one of the simplest, a simple tabulation that shows a breakdown by question of the number of users selecting each of the options. The tabulation classes are separated from the presentation servlet and could be used to create HTML pages offline.

The first problem we have to solve is converting all of the output files that the `QuestionnaireServ` servlet writes into a form suitable for analysis. Recall that the `Recorder` class simply writes `<Qresults>` tags that accumulate in the output file (or files). We need to create a file that has a root element. This file will essentially be a snapshot of the accumulated questionnaire results. To do this, the analysis program will take these steps:

1. Get the `org.w3c.dom.Document` object containing the survey script.

2. Locate the output-file names.

3. Create a new file for each by combining root elements with the current output-file contents.

The advantages of working with this snapshot of the survey results include the fact that users can continue to take the survey while we are working with analysis.

Part V

A Snapshot-File-Creating Class

Creating snapshot files is done by the `PrepQxml` class, as shown in Listing 23.24 and following listings. The constructor takes an XML Document object and locates the output-file attributes in the `Questionnnaire` and `Terminal` tags. This class is used in the analysis servlet that we present later in this chapter, but it could also be part of other processes.

Listing 23.24: The `PrepQxml` Class Source Code (`PrepQxml.java`)

```java
package com.XmlEcomBook.Chap07;

import com.XmlEcomBook.DOMlibrary ;
import org.w3c.dom.* ;
import com.sun.xml.tree.* ;
import java.io.*;
import java.util.* ;

public class PrepQxml
{
    public int state = 1 ;
    Document doc ;
    public String primaryfile ;
    public String title ;
    public String author ;
    public String date ;
    String[] files ;
    Vector allfiles = new Vector() ;
    Hashtable prepHash = new Hashtable() ;

    PrepQxml( Document d ){
        doc = d ;
        Element E = doc.getDocumentElement();
        primaryfile = E.getAttribute("file");
        allfiles.addElement( primaryfile );
        title = E.getAttribute("title");
        author = E.getAttribute("author");
        date = E.getAttribute("date");
        NodeList terminals = E.getElementsByTagName
➥("Terminal");
        int ct = terminals.getLength();
        // this locates any output files created by <Terminal>
        // tags
```

```
             for( int i = 0 ; i < ct ; i++ ){
               E = (Element)terminals.item(i);
               String tmp = E.getAttribute("file");
               if( tmp.length() > 0 ) allfiles.addElement
➡️( tmp );
             }
          }
          public String[] getFiles(){ return files ; }
```

For each output file from the survey, the createFiles method shown
in Listing 23.25 calls makeXML to create a file that has beginning and ending <QResultSet> tags to create a root element. The name of this file is
created by appending "FMT" to the name of the record file.

Listing 23.25: The createFiles and makeXML Methods
(PrepQxml.java)

```
          // for every file in allfiles, create a temporary with xml
          // root return array of file path/names
          public String[] createFiles() throws IOException {
            files = new String[ allfiles.size() ];
            int n = 0 ;
            Enumeration e = allfiles.elements();
            while( e.hasMoreElements() ){
              String tmp = (String)e.nextElement();
              files[n++] = tmp ;
              System.out.println("Create temporary for " +
➡️tmp );
              prepHash.put( tmp, makeXML( tmp ) );
            }
            return files ;
          }
          // fn is the name of the answers file, return the name of
          // the formatted file with root for creation of DOM
          public String getAnsXml( String fn ){
            return (String) prepHash.get( fn );
          }
          // this creates a complete XML document by adding a root
          // element to the Questionnaire output file contents
          private String makeXML(String fn )throws
➡️IOException {
            File inf = new File( fn );
```

```
    BufferedReader read = new BufferedReader
( new FileReader( inf ));
    int p = fn.lastIndexOf('.');
    String outFN = fn.substring( 0,p ) + "FMT" +
fn.substring(p);
    File outf = new File( outFN );
    BufferedWriter bw = new BufferedWriter( new
FileWriter( outf ), 4096);
    PrintWriter write = new PrintWriter( bw );
    write.println( "<?xml version=\"1.0\"
standalone=\"yes\" ?>");
    write.println( "<!- formatted Questionnaire
results ->");
    write.println( "<QresultSet title=\"" +
title + "\" >");
    String tmp = read.readLine();
    int ct = 1 ;
    while( tmp != null ){
        write.println( tmp );
        tmp = read.readLine();
    }
    read.close();
    write.println("</QresultSet>");
    write.close();
    System.out.println("Created " + outFN );
    return outFN ;
  }

  public String toString()
  { StringBuffer sb = new StringBuffer("PrepQxml
title: ");
    sb.append( title ); sb.append(" author: ");
    sb.append( author ); sb.append(" date: " );
    sb.append( date ); sb.append(" primary
output: ");
    sb.append( primaryfile ); sb.append(" other
files: " );
    sb.append( "none");
    return sb.toString();
  }
}
```

A Survey-Tabulating Class

The TallyQues class uses Simplified API for XML (SAX)-style processing to tabulate the response occurrences in a QResultSet document. SAX processing is the obvious choice because the amount of memory used is independent of the number of total responses in the data.

Listing 23.26 shows the import statements, class declaration, variables, and constructor for the TallyQues class. Note that we base the class on the HandlerBase class in the org.xml.sax package, because it provides default handlers as required by the SAX interfaces. All we have to do is override these handler methods for the events we find interesting.

The operation of TallyQues uses a Hashtable with an entry for each option that appears in the complete set of questions. The entries are instances of the inner class, Counter (Listing 23.30). The key for each entry is the Ques tag id attribute plus the Qopt tag val attribute.

We also keep a Vector named ordered (which holds question information in the order it is presented in the survey) and a Hashtable named qtext (which stores the question Qtext text strings, keyed by the Ques id attribute). The constructor uses the survey Document to create all of these objects.

Listing 23.26: The Start of the TallyQues Source Code (TallyQues.java)

```
package com.XmlEcomBook.Chap07;

import java.io.* ;
import java.util.* ;
import org.w3c.dom.* ;
import org.xml.sax.* ;
import org.xml.sax.helpers.ParserFactory ;
import com.sun.xml.parser.Resolver ;

/* org.xml.sax.HandlerBase is a convenience class that
   extends java.lang.Object and implements the SAX interfaces
   implements EntityResolver, DTDHandler, DocumentHandler,
ErrorHandler */
public class TallyQues extends HandlerBase
{
   static public String parserClass =
➥"com.sun.xml.parser.Parser" ;
  static int counterTextLen = 40 ; // see Counter
```

```
  private Hashtable tally = new Hashtable();  // Counters
  //keyed by
  unique
  // ordered has a Vector of Counters per question
  private Vector ordered  = new Vector();
  private Hashtable qtext = new Hashtable();
// <Qtext> by id

  public String tableStyle = "align=\"center\"
border=\"3\" " ;
  public String lastErr = null ;
  public int resultCt = 0 ;
  String id ; // <Ques> attribute "id" as detected during
parse

  // constructor creates the vectors and hashtables to store
results
  // qd is the questionnaire source XML doc
  public TallyQues( Document qd ){
    Element E = qd.getDocumentElement();
    NodeList qnl = E.getElementsByTagName("Ques");
    int ct = qnl.getLength();
    for( int i = 0; i < ct ; i++ ){
      Vector quesv = new Vector(); // for this
<Ques>
      ordered.addElement( quesv );
      E = (Element)qnl.item(i);  // Element is a
<Ques>
      NodeList txn = E.getElementsByTagName
("Qtext");
      String tx = txn.item(0).getFirstChild().
getNodeValue(); // question text
      String id = E.getAttribute( "id" );
      qtext.put( id, tx );
      quesv.addElement( id ); // first element of
      // quesv is the id
      NodeList opt = E.getElementsByTagName("Qopt");
      int opct =opt.getLength();
      for( int n = 0 ; n < opct ; n++ ){
        Element opE = (Element) opt.item(n);
```

```
                    String val = opE.getAttribute("val");
                    String text = opE.getFirstChild().
➥getNodeValue();
                    Counter cntr = new Counter( id, val, text );
                    quesv.addElement( cntr );
                    tally.put( cntr.unique, cntr );
                }
            }
        }
```

Processing the Survey Snapshot   Actual processing of the survey-results snapshot file is started by the tallyAns method, as shown in Listing 23.27, using the following steps:

1. Open the file as an org.xml.sax.InputSource object.

2. Create a parser as specified by the parserClass String. (We use the parser from the Sun package, but you can substitute any compliant parser.)

3. Attach the TallyQues object to the parser so that it will get the event method calls.

4. Call the parse method to start parsing.

If no error occurs, when the parse method returns, all the tabulating has been done. The tallyAns method returns null to indicate that an error has occurred or returns the ordered variable if all went well.

Listing 23.27: The tallyAns Method (TallyQues.java)

```
    // srcdoc is complete path to a formatted answer set file
    public Vector tallyAns(String srcdoc ){
        Parser parser ;
        InputSource input ;
        try {
            File f = new File( srcdoc );
            input = Resolver.createInputSource( f );
            parser = ParserFactory.makeParser
➥( parserClass );
            parser.setDocumentHandler( this );
            System.out.println("Start parse");
            parser.parse( input );
        }catch(SAXParseException spe){
            StringBuffer sb = new StringBuffer
```

```
➥( spe.toString() );
        sb.append("\n  Line number: " +
➥spe.getLineNumber());
        sb.append("\nColumn number: " +
➥spe.getColumnNumber() );
        sb.append("\n Public ID: " +
➥spe.getPublicId() );
        sb.append("\n System ID: " +
➥spe.getSystemId() + "\n");
        lastErr = sb.toString();
        ordered = null ;
    }catch(Exception e){
        lastErr = e.toString();
        ordered = null ;
    }
    return ordered ;
```

SAX Event Processing   Now let's look at the method that processes the SAX events, as shown in Listing 23.28. Out of all of the SAX interface methods, the only one we need to pay attention to is the startElement method. For every Ques tag, we get the value of the id attribute for use with the Qopt tags that follow in the question. For every Qopt, we create a String that combines the question id value with the option val value, and we use this as a key to get the matching Counter object from the tally Hashtable and to count the occurrence of this user selection.

Listing 23.28: The SAX Event Processing Methods (TallyQues.java)

```
    // this is the SAX specified "callback" called when the
    // parser detects an element
    public void startElement( String name,
➥AttributeList attrib)
        throws SAXException  {
    if( name.equals("Ques") ){
        id = attrib.getValue("id");
    }
    else {
      if( name.equals("Qopt") ){
        String unique = id + ":" + attrib.
➥getValue("val");
        Counter cntr = (Counter)tally.get( unique );
```

```
        if( cntr != null ) cntr.countIt();
    }
    else {
        if( name.equals("Qresults"))resultCt++ ;
    }
   }
 }
```

To recap the collections that the TallyQues class creates, the Vector named ordered has one element for each question in the order of the original XML script. This element is itself a Vector that contains the question id (a String), followed by a Counter object for each of the question options. In the Hashtable named qtext, we have the text for each question keyed by the question id.

Creating the Formatted Tally   Keeping these collections in mind, you can see how the formatTally method shown in Listing 23.29 outputs an HTML table for each question using the original order. Figure 23.2 shows one of these tables from a questionnaire we recently ran at a Web site related to the Java programmer certification exam.

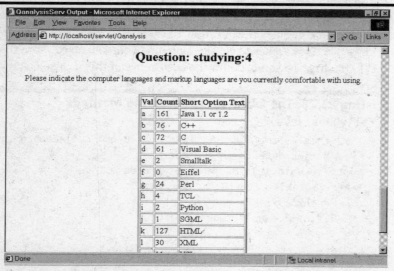

Figure 23.2: A browser display of a table output by formatTally

Listing 23.29: The `formatTally` Method Creates HTML Output (TallyQues.java)

```java
// assumes that tallyAns was just run
public void formatTally(PrintWriter out ){
   out.println("<center><h2>" + ordered.size() + "
Questions "
       + resultCt + " Responses</h2></center>");
   Enumeration e = ordered.elements();
   while( e.hasMoreElements() ){
      Vector v = (Vector) e.nextElement();
      String id = (String)v.firstElement();
      out.println("<center><h2>Question: " + id +
"</h2>");
      out.println("<p>" + qtext.get(id) +
"</p>" ) ;
      out.println("<table cols=\"3\"" +
tableStyle
+ " >");
      out.print("<tr>");
      out.print("<th>Val</th><th>Count</th><th>
Short Option Text</th>");
      out.println("</tr>");
      for( int i = 1 ; i < v.size(); i++ ){
         Counter c = (Counter) v.elementAt(i);
         out.print("<tr><td>" + c.val + "</td>");
         out.print("<td>" + c.count + "</td>" );
         out.println("<td>" + c.text + "</td>
</tr>");
      }
      out.println("</table></center><br><hr>");
   }
}

public String toString()
{ StringBuffer sb = new StringBuffer
("TallyQues ");
   return sb.toString() ;
}
```

The remaining component of the TallyQues class is the inner class named Counter. As shown in Listing 23.30, a Counter object is created with the question id, option val, and option text. The text is limited in length to keep the table compact, but you could easily remove this limitation.

Listing 23.30: The Counter Inner Class (TallyQues.java)

```java
// counter objects represent a single question/option combo
  class Counter {
    public String val ;
    public String unique ; // <Ques id plus
    //":" plus <Qopt val
    public String text ; // the first
    // counterTextLen chars
    public int count = 0 ;

    Counter( String id, String v, String tx ){
      val = v ;
      unique = id + ":" + val ;
      if( tx.length() > counterTextLen ) {
            text = tx.substring(0,
counterTextLen);
      }
      else { text = tx ;
      }
    }
    public void countIt(){ count++ ; }

    public String toString(){
        return "ID: " + unique + " " + count + " "
+ text ;
    }
  }
}
```

The PrepQxml and TallyQues classes discussed in the preceding sections can be used in a variety of ways to create HTML-formatted tabulations. For this chapter, however, we use a servlet described in the next section.

A Reporting-Servlet Example

This section's servlet, QanalysisServ, allows online access to a snapshot of ongoing survey results; this can be called a *reporting servlet*. It uses the questionnaire.properties file to locate all surveys currently being conducted and lets you choose one. It then determines the output files this survey generates and lets you choose one of them for report generation.

Listing 23.31 shows the start of the servlet code with the import statements, variables, and `init` method.

Listing 23.31: The QanalysisServ Servlet (QanalysisServ.java)

```java
package com.XmlEcomBook.Chap07;

import com.XmlEcomBook.DOMlibrary ;
import org.w3c.dom.* ;
import com.sun.xml.tree.* ;
import java.io.*;
import java.util.* ;
import javax.servlet.*;
import javax.servlet.http.*;

public class QanalysisServ extends HttpServlet
{
  static String brcrlf = "<br>\r\n" ;
  static String homedir = "e:\\scripts\\
questionnaire" ;
  static String handler = "http://www.lanw.com/servlet/
Qanalysis" ;
  static String passwd = "lovexml" ;
  static String version = "v1.0 May 28";
  Properties qProp ;

  // note we share properties file with QuestionnaireServ
  public void init(ServletConfig config) throws
ServletException
  {
    super.init(config);
    System.out.println("Start QanalysisServ ");
    homedir = config.getInitParameter("homedir") ;
    File f = new File( homedir, "questionnaire.
properties");
    try { qProp = new Properties();
      qProp.load( new FileInputStream(f) );
      String tmp = qProp.getProperty("analysis");
      if( tmp != null ) handler = tmp ;
      System.out.println("Loaded properties for
```

```
➥Qanalysis: "
                + handler );
    }catch(IOException e){
        System.out.println("QanalysisServ Error
➥loading " + e );
    }
}
```

Initial entry to the servlet is through the doGet method, as shown in Listing 23.32. This would typically be done through a form that requires a user password, just to reduce the chance of a casual user accidentally accessing the servlet. Assuming all goes well, the method generates a page with a form providing for selection among all available surveys. The selected file is passed to the doPost method.

Listing 23.32: The doGet Method of the QanalysisServ Class (QanalysisServ.java)

```java
// entry with password
  public void doGet(HttpServletRequest req,
➥HttpServletResponse resp)
  throws ServletException, IOException
  { System.out.println("Qanalysis doGet");
    resp.setContentType("text/html");
    PrintWriter out = new PrintWriter
➥(resp.getOutputStream());
    String user = req.getParameter("username");
    String tmp = req.getParameter("userpw");
    // Obviously this could be a lot more complex
    if( !passwd.equals( tmp )){
        errorMsg( out, "404 page not found", null );
        return ;
    }
    if( qProp == null ||
        qProp.size() == 0 ){
        errorMsg( out, "Bad Initialization", null );
    return ;
    }
    HttpSession session = req.getSession( true );
    // session.putValue( "username", user );
    // with older servlet engines you will have to use
putValue
    // session.setAttribute( "username", user );
```

```java
    Enumeration e = qProp.keys();
    Vector v = new Vector();
    while( e.hasMoreElements()){
       String key = (String)e.nextElement();
       // everything not "handler" or "analysis" is a XML file
path name
       if( !( key.equals("handler") || key.equals
➥("analysis"))){
          v.addElement( key );
       }
    }
    if( v.size() == 0 ){
       errorMsg( out, "No Questionnaire files
➥found", null );
       return ;
    }
    out.println("<HTML>");
    out.println("<HEAD><TITLE>QanalysisServ Output
➥</TITLE></HEAD>");
    out.println("<BODY>");
    out.println("<h2>Select The Questionnaire XML
➥File</h2>");
    out.println("Found " + v.size() + " XML files" +
➥brcrlf );
    out.println("<form method=\"POST\"" +
       "action=\"http://localhost/servlet/
➥Qanalysis\" >");
    out.println("<select name=\"source\" >");
    for( int i = 0 ; i < v.size() ; i++){
       tmp = (String) v.elementAt( i );
       out.println("<option value=\"" + tmp + "\" >"
➥+ tmp );
    }
    out.println("</select>");
    out.println("<input type=\"hidden\" name=
➥\"username\" value=\""
       + user + "\"><br>" );
    out.println("<input type=\"hidden\"
➥name=\"action\" " +
       "value=\"select\" ><br>");
    out.println("<input type=\"submit\"
➥value=\"Start\" ><br>" );
```

```
    out.println("</form>");
    footer( out );
}
```

The first POST submission will have the value `"select"` for the `action` variable. As shown in Listing 23.33, this causes output of a selection form with all of the possible results files using the `createQList` method.

Listing 23.33: The First Part of the doPost Method (QanalysisServ.java)

```
    public void doPost(HttpServletRequest req,
HttpServletResponse resp)
    throws ServletException, IOException
    {
        resp.setContentType("text/html");
        PrintWriter out = new PrintWriter(resp.
➡getOutputStream());
        String source = req.getParameter( "source");
        String action = req.getParameter( "action");
        String ansfile = req.getParameter("ansfile");
        // select when choosing questionnaire XML file
        // analyze when choosing reformatted result file
        String[] files = null ;
        if( action == null ||
            source == null || source.length() == 0 ){
            errorMsg(out,"Bad source selection", null );
        return ;
        } // source is short name from properties
        String srcfile = qProp.getProperty( source );
        if( srcfile == null ) {
            errorMsg( out, "Bad Source lookup", null );
        return ;
        }
        HttpSession session = req.getSession(false);
        try {
            if( session == null ){ errorMsg(out, "No
➡Session ", null );
                return ;
            }
            DOMlibrary lib = DOMlibrary.getLibrary();
            System.out.println("DOMlibrary ok, try for
➡" + srcfile );
```

```
       Document doc = lib.getDOM( srcfile );
       if( doc == null ){
         errorMsg( out, "DOM doc failed - unable to
➡continue", null );
         return ;
       }
       //PrepQxml pQ = (PrepQxml)session.getValue
➡("prepqxml");
       // you will have to use getValue with older
       // servlet engines
       PrepQxml pQ = (PrepQxml)session.getAttribute
➡("prepqxml");
       header( out );
       if( pQ == null ){  // first pass
         pQ = new PrepQxml( doc );
         files = pQ.createFiles();
         // session.putValue("prepqxml",pQ);
         session.setAttribute("prepqxml",pQ);
}
       else {
         files = pQ.getFiles();
       }
       if( action.equals("select") ){
         out.println("<h1>Test: " + pQ.title
➡+"</h1>" );
         out.println("<p>XML questionnaire file:
➡<i>" + source + "</i></p>");
         out.println("<p>Author: " + pQ.author +
➡" Dated: "
           + pQ.date + "</p>");
         out.println("<p>The primary answer file
➡is: " +
           pQ.primaryfile + "</p>" );
         out.println("<p>There " );
         if( files.length < 2 ) out.println("are no
➡other ");
         if( files.length == 2 ) out.println("is
➡one other ");
         if( files.length > 2 ) out.println(
➡(files.length - 1) + " other ");
         out.println(
           "answer file(s). Select a file and
```

```
➡click <b>Start</b></p>");
      createQList( out, source, files );
   }
```

When the user selects one of the answer files, the value of the `action`
variable will be `"analyze"`. As shown in Listing 23.34, this action causes
the creation of a new `TallyQues` object that is used to create formatted
output.

Listing 23.34: The doPost Method, Continued
(QanalysisServ.java)

```
     if( action.equals("analyze") ){
       out.println("<h1>Analysis</h1>");
       out.println("<p>XML questionnaire file:
➡<i>" + source + "</i></p>");
       String ansXml = pQ.getAnsXml( ansfile );
       out.println("<p>Answer file: " + ansfile +
➡"</p>");
       out.println("<p>Processing file: " + ansXml
➡+ "</p>");
       TallyQues tQ = new TallyQues( doc );//build
       // with questions
       if( tQ.tallyAns( ansXml )== null ){
         out.println("<h2>Error " + tQ.lastErr
➡+ "</h2>") ;
       }
       else {
         tQ.formatTally( out );
       }
     }
     footer( out );
   }catch( Exception ex ){
     errorMsg( out, "QanalysisServ.doPost ", ex );
   }
 }
```

The `createQList` method, as shown in Listing 23.35, creates the
HTML form used to present the possible answer files.

Listing 23.35: The createQList Method (QanalysisServ.java)

```
   // the PrepQxml has located all of the answer files - only
one
   // can be analyzed at a time
```

```
      void createQList( PrintWriter out, String source,
➡String[] files ){
    out.println( "<form method=\"POST\"" +
        "action=\"http://localhost/servlet/
➡Qanalysis\" >");
    out.println("<input type=\"hidden\"
➡name=\"action\"" +
        "value=\"analyze\" ><br>");
    out.println("<input type=\"hidden\"
➡name=\"source\" value=\""
        + source + "\" ><br>");
    out.println("<select name=\"ansfile\" >");
    for( int i = 0 ; i < files.length ; i++){
      String tmp = files[i];
      out.println("<option value=\"" + tmp
➡+ "\" >" + tmp );
    }
    out.println("</select>");
    out.println("<input type=\"submit\"
➡value=\"Start\" ><br>" );
    out.println("</form><br>");
  }
```

We are almost at the end of the QanalysisServ class! Listing 23.36 shows some utility methods required to format the output pages or report errors.

Listing 23.36: Utility Methods in the `QanalysisServ` Class (`QanalysisServ.java`)

```
    public void header( PrintWriter out ){
        out.println("<HTML>");
        out.println("<HEAD><TITLE>QanalysisServ
➡Output</TITLE></HEAD>");
        out.println("<BODY>");
    }
    public void footer( PrintWriter out ){
      out.println("<hr>" + version + "<br>");
      out.println("</BODY>");
      out.println("</HTML>");
      out.close();
    }
    // assumes response has been set to text/html
```

```
      private void errorMsg( PrintWriter out, String
➡msg, Exception ex ){
    out.println("<html>");
    out.println("<head><title>QanalysisServ
➡Output</title></head>");
    out.println("<body>");
    out.println("<h2>" ); out.println( msg );
    out.println("</h2><br>");
    if( ex != null ){
       ex.printStackTrace( out );
    }
    out.println("<br>");
    footer( out );
  }
}
```

XML Document Library Utility

An alternate approach to having each servlet manage its own XML document storage is to use a library utility. That way, the servlet just requests the document from the library and does not have to know where the XML file lives on the disk or whether it is already in memory due to a request in some other transaction.

The DOMlibrary class we have created has the following characteristics:

▶ It uses the *Singleton* design pattern to ensure that only one instance is created. In this pattern, there is no public constructor; instead, a static method controls creation of and access to a single instance of a class.

▶ When XML documents are requested, the DOMlibrary instance checks the timestamp on the document file to ensure that it never serves up an out-of-date document.

▶ It implements the Runnable interface so that it can have a Thread that periodically performs maintenance tasks. A typical task is discarding Document objects that have not been used recently. This way, documents that tend to be used a lot will generally be found in memory, while infrequently used documents will not waste memory capacity.

An alternative to using the Singleton approach would be to implement everything in static methods. However, using the Singleton pattern, we gain considerable flexibility, including the ability to implement Runnable and to use the run method to manage the life cycle of documents in memory. The Singleton design pattern is used in a number of places in the standard Java library.

Listing 23.37 shows the static method, getLibrary, which creates a new DOMlibrary object if necessary. All servlets needing access to an XML document call getLibrary to get a reference to the single library instance, and then they use that reference to request a document. The variable maxAge is used in the run method to determine when a document should be discarded.

Listing 23.37: The DOMlibrary Class Import Statements and Static Method (DOMlibrary.java)

```
package com.XmlEcomBook;

import java.io.* ;
import java.util.* ;
import com.sun.xml.tree.* ;
import com.sun.xml.parser.Resolver ;
import org.xml.sax.* ;
import org.w3c.dom.* ;

public class DOMlibrary implements  Runnable {
   private static DOMlibrary theLib ;
   private static int maxAge = 6000 ;//age in seconds
   public synchronized static DOMlibrary
getLibrary(){
      if( theLib == null ) theLib = new DOMlibrary();
      return theLib ;
   }
   public static void setMaxAge(int t)
{ maxAge = t ;}
```

As shown in Listing 23.38, the only constructor is private to ensure that only the static getLibrary method can create a new object. Resident XML document objects are stored in the domHash Hashtable, using the complete file path as a key. The Hashtable named trackerHash keeps a DomTracker object for each XML document object, using the same key. The DomTracker class is an inner class in DOMlibrary; the code is shown in Listing 23.43. Note that the Thread that executes the run method is given the lowest possible priority.

Listing 23.38: The DOMlibrary Constructor and Instance Variables (DOMlibrary.java)

```java
    private Hashtable domHash, trackerHash ;
    boolean running ;
    private String lastErr = "none" ;

    // private constructor to ensure singleton
    private DOMlibrary(){
      domHash = new Hashtable();
      trackerHash = new Hashtable();
      Thread upkeep = new Thread(this,"DOMlibrary
➡upkeep");
      upkeep.setPriority( Thread.MIN_PRIORITY );
      running = true ;
      upkeep.start();
    }
```

Parsing an XML document in DOMlibrary is done in the loadXML method, as shown in Listing 23.39. In order to avoid repeated attempts to load a document with an incorrect src path, or a document that causes a parse error on loading, this method puts a String containing an error report in the domHash table if any error is encountered. If document parsing succeeds, a matching DomTracker object is saved in the trackerHash table. This is the only method in which parser-specific methods are called; if you were using something besides the Sun parser, some modification of this method would be required.

Listing 23.39: The loadXML Method Handles Parsing (DOMlibrary.java)

```java
    private synchronized void loadXML(File xmlFile,
➡String src ) {
    //File xmlFile = new File( src ) ;
      try {
        long timestamp = xmlFile.lastModified();
        InputSource input = Resolver.createInputSource
➡( xmlFile );
      // ... the "false" flag says not to validate
      // XmlDocument is in the com.sun.xml.tree package
        Document doc = XmlDocument.
➡createXmlDocument
➡(input, false);
```

```
            domHash.put( src, doc );
            trackerHash.put( src, new DomTracker
➡( timestamp ) );
        }catch(SAXParseException spe ){
            StringBuffer sb = new StringBuffer
➡( spe.toString() );
            sb.append("\n  Line number: " +
➡spe.getLineNumber());
            sb.append("\nColumn number: " +
➡spe.getColumnNumber() );
            sb.append("\n Public ID: " +
➡spe.getPublicId() );
            sb.append("\n System ID: " +
➡spe.getSystemId() + "\n");
            lastErr = sb.toString();
            System.out.print( lastErr );
        }catch( SAXException se ){
            lastErr = se.toString();
            System.out.println("loadXML threw " +
➡lastErr );
            domHash.put( src, lastErr );
            se.printStackTrace( System.out );
        }catch( IOException ie ){
            lastErr = ie.toString();
            System.out.println("loadXML threw " +
➡lastErr +
            " trying to read " + src );
            domHash.put( src, lastErr );
        }
    } // end loadXML
```

Servlets call the getDOM method, shown in Listing 23.40, when a document is needed. Any problem with creating the document causes a null to be returned instead of the document reference. Every time a document is found in the Hashtable, the associated DomTracker object is updated with the current time. Note that there are several places where a message is written to System.out for debugging purposes. We suggest you comment these out after you get your system running.

Listing 23.40: The getDOM Method (DOMlibrary.java)

```
    // either return the doc or null if a problem
    public synchronized Document getDOM( String src ){
```

```
        Object doc = domHash.get( src );
        DomTracker dt = (DomTracker) trackerHash.get
( src );
        boolean newflag = false ;
        File f = null ;
        if( doc == null ){
            System.out.println("DOMlibrary.getDOM new "
+ src );
            f = new File( src );
            loadXML( f, src ); // sets trackerHash
            doc = domHash.get( src );
            dt = (DomTracker) trackerHash.get( src );
            newflag = true ;
            System.out.println("DOMlibrary load OK");
        }
        else { // found a document - is it up to date?
          f = new File( src );
          if( dt.changed( f )){
            System.out.println("DOMlibrary reloads " +
src );
            loadXML( f, src ); // sets trackerHash
            newflag = true ;
            doc = domHash.get( src );
            dt = (DomTracker)trackerHash.get( src );
          }
        }
        // if not a document, must be a string due to error
        if( ! (doc instanceof Document )){
            System.out.println("DOMlibrary: " + doc );
            // could try for re-read here
        }
        if( doc instanceof Document ) {
          if( ! newflag ){
            dt = (DomTracker)trackerHash.get( src );
            dt.setLastUse( System.currentTimeMillis());
          }
          return (Document) doc ;
        }
        return null ;
    }
```

Listing 23.41 presents a couple of utility methods that remove or force a reload of a document.

Listing 23.41: Some Utility Methods (DOMlibrary.java)

```java
// use this to force removal of a dom. it
// returns last copy of dom or null if dom not in hash
public Document removeDOM( String src ){
  Document dom = (Document)domHash.get( src );
  if( dom != null ){
    domHash.remove( src );
    trackerHash.remove( src );
  }
  return dom ;
}

// call this to force a reload after src is modified
public Document reloadDOM( String src ){
  if( domHash.get( src ) != null ){
    domHash.remove( src );
    trackerHash.remove( src );
  }
  return getDOM( src );
}
```

The reason for making the DOMlibrary class implement the Runnable interface is so we can have a background Thread that runs at a low priority and can do upkeep chores. The example provided in Listing 23.42 is pretty simpleminded: It just removes any document that has not been recently used. Listing 23.42 also shows the utility methods toString and getLastErr.

Listing 23.42: The run Method and More Utilities (DOMlibrary.java)

```java
// run is used for upkeep, not reading XML
public void run()
{ while( running ){
    try{ Thread.sleep( 60000 );
         // example management code
      Enumeration keys = trackerHash.keys();
      long time = System.currentTimeMillis();
      while( keys.hasMoreElements() ){
        String key = (String) keys.nextElement();
        if(((DomTracker)trackerHash.get(key)).
getAge(time) > maxAge ){
          removeDOM( key );
```

```
            }
          }
      }catch(InterruptedException e){
      }
    }// end while
  }

  public String getLastErr(){ return lastErr ; }

  public String toString()
  { StringBuffer sb = new StringBuffer
➡("DOMlibrary contains ");
    int ct = domHash.size();
    if( ct > 0 ){
        sb.append(Integer.toString( ct ) );
        sb.append( " DOM objects ");
        Enumeration e = domHash.keys();
        while( e.hasMoreElements() ){
          String key = (String)e.nextElement();
          sb.append( key );
          sb.append("   " );
        }
    }
    else { sb.append("no DOM objects");
    }
    sb.append(" Last error: " );
    sb.append( lastErr );
    return sb.toString();
  }
```

An instance of the inner class DomTracker is created every time an XML document is loaded. This instance is managed in parallel with the document object. In the present version, it records two things of interest: the timestamp on the XML file that created the document object and the timestamp of the last request for the document. As shown in Listing 23.43, the getAge method returns the number of seconds since the last use, and the changed method checks the timestamp on the source file.

Listing 23.43: The DomTracker Definition As a Member of DOMlibrary (DOMlibrary.java)

```
    // utility class to aid in tracking memory resident DOM
    class DomTracker {
```

```
    private long lastMod ;
    private long lastUse ;
    DomTracker( long timestamp ){
        lastMod = timestamp ; // from File.
➡lastModified();
        lastUse = System.currentTimeMillis();
    }

    void setLastUse( long ts ){ lastUse = ts ; }
    int getAge( long now ){ // return value in seconds
      return (int)(( now - lastUse)/ 1000) ;
    }

    boolean changed( File f ){
      long n = f.lastModified();
      return !( n == lastMod );
    }
  } // end DomTracker class
} // end DOMlibrary class
```

With the tools described in this chapter, you have a flexible system for gathering information from your current customers and potential customers. Because it uses an XML-driven script that can be changed without restarting the server, you can modify the way you track your customers' interests and opinions on the fly.

SUMMARY

The structure of a survey is perfectly suited for XML. A survey involves a certain level of branching, which can be managed on the fly using Java to produce dynamic customer surveys like the one shown in this chapter. This kind of branching is handled very nicely by XML, which allows you to easily alter the configurations of your survey. XML gives us the ability to properly address several design criteria:

Control of presentation By now, you should be able to see that changing the structure of your survey won't alter the presentation or Web page design.

Flexibility of question design You saw how XML enables you to create a variety of survey methods, such as yes-or-no questions and multiple-choice questions.

Branching capability   The XML document allows you to provide a structure that veers (for example) people who don't buy CDs over the Internet away from music-related questions.

Extensibility   You also saw in this chapter how you can introduce a new form of question presentation with a minimum alteration to the code base.

Recording results   You also discovered how results from each participant can be recorded completely and independently of other participants.

This process of separating content and structure from business logic is similar to what you'll find in the next chapter, which demonstrates how to manage your Web site's news services. Again, the core content is managed by XML, and Java is used to manipulate that content and send it to your users.

Chapter 24

AND NOW FOR THE NEWS

Have you ever visited Web sites of small organizations where their most recent news bulletin was six months old? These enterprises are missing a great opportunity for grabbing the attention of the casual visitor. It may be that the people doing the newsworthy things are not communicating with their respective Webmasters, or maybe it is just too darn much trouble to edit those pages again. Naturally, we have an XML solution in mind, which we detail in this chapter.

Adapted from *Java™ Developer's Guide to E-Commerce with XML and JSP*, by William Brogden and Chris Minnick
ISBN 0-7821-2827-0   464 pages $49.99

DESIGNING A NEWS SYSTEM

We want users who visit our Web site to see the latest company news in a compact and easy-to-scan format. Remember, you have only a few seconds to entice the typical Web surfer to stick around. We want it to be obvious to the user how to find out more information about an item, and then (we hope) enter the catalog system to purchase something.

Consider a news system's desired characteristics and your list will likely include the following:

▶ Flexibility of output

▶ Ease of data entry

▶ Minimum server load

Along with accounting for these characteristics, your primary design decisions are to select the XML elements and attributes to represent the data first, to choose between the SAX and DOM styles of Java processing (the mechanisms for displaying the data to users) next, and to then determine the mechanism for adding new news items.

Flexibility of Output

Because we have already decided to use XML for the primary storage medium, the way to ensure output flexibility is by storing all the data required for the different output formats. Looking around at various commercial Web sites, you see that company news is typically presented to the user in the following three different lengths:

▶ Headlines linked to the full story

▶ Short teasers linked to the full story

▶ Complete news releases

Other news formats include e-mail newsletters, hard-copy newsletters, and corporate reports. The three different lengths (headline, short, and full length) appear to be suitable for these other formats, too. Our first design task is to come up with an XML format that will support all of these formats.

News Text Elements

Although artificial intelligence and computer understanding of language have made great progress, nobody expects a computer to write a great headline by scanning a story, so you have to conclude that news items will need separate headline text created by a human for each presentation length. News items also usually have a date attached that can be a simple date or a dateline, such as *Austin, TX, 1 Jan 2000*, that will have to be generated by a human.

Some news items are greatly enhanced by graphics, sound clips, or off-site links, so consider how the XML format might be designed to accommodate various additional enhancements. For our example in this chapter, we concluded that designing in all possible embellishments would just be too complicated and restrictive. So we decided to store the text for the short and full-length news stories using the XML <[[CDATA ..]]> tag.

Because XML parsers do not attempt to parse text inside a CDATA section, you can store any kind of HTML markup inside the CDATA section without confusing the XML parser.

The elements for holding the date, the headline, and the short and full-length text are illustrated in Listing 24.1.

Listing 24.1: A News Item, Date, and Three Sizes of Text (thenews.xml)

```
<date>Austin, TX, Jun 14 2000</date>
<head>Best Seller at a Great Price</head>
<short><![CDATA[Due to a special deal with the publisher, we
can now offer <i>Dryer Lint Art</i> at 50% off the retail
price.]]></short> <long><![CDATA[This books starts with simple
Dryer Lint projects suitable for the novice and advances
through easy stages to the (literally) <b>monumental</b>
recreation of famous monuments in that most flexible of craft
materials, dryer lint. Even though you may never attempt major
constructions like the Statue of Liberty project documented in
the final chapter, your projects will benefit by a study of
this famous creation. Includes UML diagrams.]]></long>
```

Another aspect of flexibility is the capability to selectively present news items according to topic. Given the wide variety of expected interests of visitors to XMLGifts.com, we want to show each customer the news affecting his or her favorite topic in the spot where the customer is most likely to look. There is bound to be overlap; for example, a book about a musical group would be of interest to both book purchasers and CD purchasers. Therefore, each news item should be tagged with one or more topic categories, and presentation should allow for selecting topics.

We could tag an item with topic information using either an attribute or an element. We've decided to store topic information as an attribute because it is data about content and we expect to restrict the number of topic terms.

News Item Age Representation

The most current news should always be presented first. Because an XML document automatically preserves the order of items, new items must go to the start of the document. Furthermore, it's a good idea to allow the presentation software to select only the most recent items. Therefore, we need a representation of the age of a news item.

After dithering over the many different ways to represent a date so that we can select for recent items, we ended up using a simple integer representing the days since Java's basic timekeeping start. The `long` value returned by `System.currentTimeMillis()` is divided by the number of milliseconds per day to get a `timestamp` attribute value stored in the `Newsitem` tag. Alternatives using the Java `Date` `DateFormat` or `Calendar` classes were rejected because lots of object creation would be involved and we want the news function to have a low load on the server.

News Item Management Information

Because you or your employees will update the news file online, it seems to be a good idea to keep track of who has created a particular item. For instance, you need to know who to blame for a particular error. This is accomplished with an `author` attribute in the `<Newsitem>` element. The news-updating servlet discussed in the "Adding the Latest News" section of this chapter has a simple access control mechanism using an author name and password; it is this author name that becomes the `author` attribute.

To create HTML markup in which headline text is linked to the full-length text of a news item, you must include a unique identifier. For our example, we have taken the simplest approach: a serial number that is attached as the `id` attribute to each `<Newsitem>` as it is added.

The Document Root

We keep track of some parameters used in the entire file in attributes in the document root element, `Newsfile`. The next id attribute is simply `nextid`. It is the responsibility of the item-adding software or, in the case of offline editing, the `Newsitem` author to update the `nextid` attribute.

The root element is also a good place to store attributes related to various display default values. The present example uses only one, called longtemplate, which names an HTML template file as a default value used to format news items.

Listing 24.2 shows an example of all of the XML tags in use.

Listing 24.2: The <Newsfile> Element and One <Newsitem> (thenews.xml)

```
<?xml version="1.0" standalone="yes" ?>
<!- output by NewsUpkeep ->
<Newsfile longtemplate="tmlong.html" nextid="1010" >
<Newsitem timestamp="11045" topic="CDs"
 author="wbrogden" id="1008" >
<head>Your Favorite Music Now Available</head>
<date>Austin, Feb 1, 2000</date>
<short><![CDATA[XMLGifts proudly announces the availability
of the CD that has all the geeks singing, <i>It's Dot Com
Enough for
Me.</i>]]></short>
<long><![CDATA[<p><i>It's Dot Com Enough For Me.</i>
 now in stock!</p>
<p>All those great songs created during breaks in all-night
coding sessions - now recorded by top Silicon Valley garage
bands on our private label. <i>It's Dot Com Enough for Me</i>
will have you singing along - or maybe laughing till the Jolt
cola spurts out your nose. Seventeen songs from geeks at Sun,
Microsoft, Apple, Cisco, and other top tech outfits.
</p>]]></long>
</Newsitem>
</Newsfile>
```

Ease of Data Entry

Because we have opted to use a simple news format as seen in Listing 24.2, data entry can also be very simple. The HTML form- and servlet-based system described in the upcoming "Adding the Latest News" section allows updating with new items over the Internet.

However, making it so easy to enter news items does nothing to control the quality of the writing. To get the best results, management must ensure that both the topics used to classify news items and the styles of writing remain consistent. Management should create guidelines and ensure that they are available to all employees authorized to post news items.

Minimum Server Load

Because we hope to have a lot of traffic on this Web site, we want to make the display of the main pages as simple as possible. We want a page that loads quickly and does not take a lot of server processor power to generate. Consider the following alternatives for displaying news items:

Static news pages   Static pages are fast to serve, and the main pages can be rebuilt from XML sources every time a change is made, but that prevents a custom appearance to each returning customer.

Servlet-generated news pages   Everything can be generated with Java servlets, presumably making use of HTML template files to control many aspects of the site appearance.

JavaServer Pages (JSP)   The advantage of JSP over servlets is that the Web designer does not need to know how to program Java to change the appearance.

The choices to be made in selecting Java processing methods include choosing between Simplified API for XML (SAX) and Document Object Model (DOM) models and validating versus non-validating parsers. The SAX approach would require running a parser for every news-page access. The DOM approach gives rapid access at the expense of keeping the data in memory. Given that the number of news items will probably be in the hundreds, the memory used by keeping a DOM in memory will not have a significant impact on total memory resources, so DOM is the obvious choice.

We can't see any reason to use a validating parser in the online functions. Because we use automated methods to create new entries, there is little chance for a formatting error. Besides, showing the user an error page with validation errors would cause nothing but confusion.

THE NEWS SYSTEM

The final design for the news system is summarized in the block diagram shown in Figure 24.1. Data flow that takes place on the server is shown on the right, whereas offline processing is on the left side of the diagram.

The master XML news file can be updated online or offline, but for normal operation, online is preferred because it automatically maintains the id and timestamp attributes.

The Document Object Model in memory is maintained by the DOMlibrary class that was described in Chapter 23, "Using Surveys to Know Your Customer." Online updating of the master XML file is accomplished by the CompanyNewsServ servlet and NewsUpkeep classes, which are discussed later in this chapter. The formatting of news items into Web-page output by servlets or JavaServer Pages (JSP) depends on the NewsFormatter class, which is discussed in the next section. Other types of formatting for newsletters and print formats should be easy to write, based on the following examples.

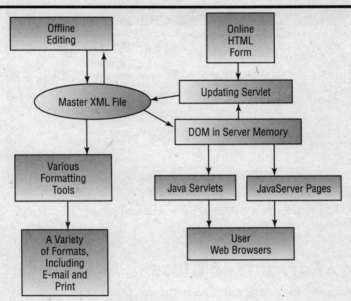

FIGURE 24.1: News-item processing

WEB PAGE PRESENTATION

Before we dive into the code needed for our news system, let's look at an example of the final product. Figure 24.2 shows the framework of a page for news presentation in the context of a larger site. We have left out the various site-navigation tools and other content that a real site would use.

JSP, making use of the NewsFormatter class, which is detailed in the following section, generated this Web-browser display from an XML news file. On the left side of the screen, headlines summarize the most recent news items in all topics. The full news item for the most recent news in the CDs topic appears in the center. And short-format news items in the CDs topic are listed on the right but skip the item that is displayed in full. The headlines and short-format items can be clicked to display the associated full-length news item.

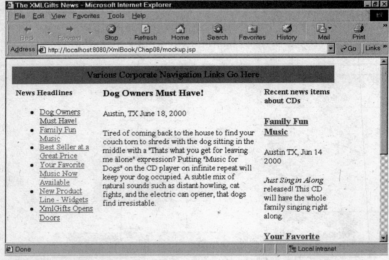

FIGURE 24.2: A news-item Web page generated with JSP

The *NewsFormatter* Class

The key Java class for presentation is the NewsFormatter class. As shown in Listing 24.3 and following listings, a NewsFormatter is created with a File object that points to an XML file. The NewsFormatter class uses the DOMlibrary class that was described in Chapter 23 to get a Document object that holds all the data in a news-item file. The constructor gets a NodeList containing all of the Newsitem nodes and uses this to create an array called itemNodes. This array is used by the various formatting methods.

Listing 24.3: The Start of the NewsFormatter Class
(NewsFormatter.java)

```java
package com.XmlEcomBook.Chap08;

import com.XmlEcomBook.DOMlibrary ;
import java.io.*;
import java.util.* ;
import javax.servlet.*;
import javax.servlet.http.*;
import org.w3c.dom.* ;

public class NewsFormatter
{
  static String handler ; // the servlet for single item
// presentation
  public static void setHandler(String s)
  {handler=s; }

    // instance variables
  File newsFile ;
  String newsFileName ;
  String newsFilePath ;
  String headStr, footStr ;

  Node[] itemNodes ;
  Element docRoot ;
  Hashtable nodeHash ; // <Newsitem Elements keyed by tag
// name

  int maxNitems, skipNitems;
  int itemsCount = 0 ;

  public NewsFormatter( File f ) throws
  IOException {
    newsFile = f ;
    newsFileName = f.getAbsolutePath() ;
    int p = newsFileName.lastIndexOf
  ( File.separatorChar );
    if( p > 0 ){ newsFilePath = newsFileName.
  substring(0,p);
    }
    else { System.out.println("NewsFormatter
```

```
➡path problem");
    }
    DOMlibrary library = DOMlibrary.getLibrary();
    Document doc = library.getDOM( newsFileName );
    if( doc == null ){
        throw new FileNotFoundException
➡( newsFileName );
    }
    docRoot = doc.getDocumentElement();
    NodeList newsItemNodes = doc.getElementsByTagName
➡("Newsitem");
    int ct = newsItemNodes.getLength();
    itemNodes = new Node[ ct ];
    for( int i = 0 ; i < ct ; i++ ){
       itemNodes[i] = newsItemNodes.item( i );
    }
}
```

You will recall from Chapter 23 that the DOMlibrary class reloads an XML file when the timestamp has changed. Because the Document object is not changed by the operation of NewsFormatter, it can be shared by any number of servlets and access to it doesn't have to be synchronized.

There are two versions of the doNews method. The version in Listing 24.4 is used to output multiple news items in headline, short, and long formats. It provides the capability of selecting items by topic and age, and it also can control skipping over items and limiting the total number of items displayed. The hs and fs strings are optional inputs that provide limited additional formatting capabilities.

The doNews method checks for the input of topic- or age-limiting String parameters. If a topstr parameter is not null and not empty, the selectNodes method is called to reduce the full list of news items to those matching the specified topics. Similarly, if an age string is specified, the limitAge method is called. If either call reduces the list of qualifying items to zero, the doNews method exits immediately. Other parameters control the maximum number of items to show and the relative item number to start showing.

Listing 24.4: The doNews Method Selects the Output Method Used (NewsFormatter.java)

```
// hs and fs are head and foot used in short and long display
// you can also specify templates in the <Newsfile element
// PrintWriter, hs, fs, topics, H,S or L, age, mx#
```

```
// skpN is used to skip the first N items that qualify
// presumably printed elsewhere on the page, use 0 to see all
// returns number of news items printed
  public int doNews( PrintWriter out, String hs,
➥String fs,
      String topstr, String sz, String age, int skpN,
➥int mxN ){
    headStr = hs ; footStr = fs ;
    skipNitems = skpN ; maxNitems = mxN ;
    itemsCount = 0 ;
    if( topstr != null && topstr.length() > 0 ){
        if( selectNodes(topstr, out )== 0 )
➥return 0 ;
    }
    if( age != null && age.length() > 0 ){
        if( limitAge( age, out ) == 0 ) return 0 ;
    }
    char szch ;
    if( sz == null || sz.length() == 0 ) szch =
➥'L' ; // default to long form
    else szch = sz.toUpperCase().charAt(0);
    switch( szch ) {
      case 'H' :
        doHeadlineNews( out ); break ;
      case 'S' :
        doShortNews( out ); break ;
      case 'L' :
      default :
        doLongNews(out );
    }
    return itemsCount ;
  }
```

The doNews method shown in Listing 24.5 locates a single news item by the id attribute and formats the long form of the text output. The remaining method in the NewsFormatter class exists to support the two doNews methods.

Listing 24.5: The Version of doNews for a Selected Item
(NewsFormatter.java)

```
// version to do a single item by id - always full length
  public int doNews( PrintWriter out, String hs,
➥String fs, String id ){
```

```
        headStr = hs ; footStr = fs ;
        itemsCount = 0 ;
        Node n = null ; //
        for( int i = 0 ; i < itemNodes.length ; i++ ){
          n = itemNodes[i];   // <Newsitem nodes
          String nid = ((Element)n).getAttribute("id");
          if( id.equals( nid )){
            break ;
          }
        } // if not located by id, will be oldest item
        findNodes((Element) n ); // locates the parts
➡ of <Newsitem
        doNewsItemLong( out ); // with the single id
        return itemsCount ;
      }
```

We have assumed that news-item headlines will always be formatted as HTML "unordered list" lists. This makes the doHeadlineNews method shown in Listing 24.6 very simple.

Listing 24.6: The Method That Formats Headlines (NewsFormatter.java)

```
      // Headline always formatted as <UL> with link
      public void doHeadlineNews(PrintWriter out){
        out.println( "<ul>" );
        for( int i = skipNitems ; i < itemNodes.length;
➡ i++ ){
          if( i >= maxNitems ) break ;
          Node n = itemNodes[i];   // <Newsitem nodes
          String id = ((Element)n).getAttribute("id");
          findNodes((Element) n ); // locates the parts
          //of <Newsitem
          out.print("<li><a href=" + handler + "?id=
➡ " + id + "&size=L >" );
          out.print( nodeHash.get("head") );
          out.println("</a></li>");
        }
        out.println("</ul>");
      }
```

The doShortNews method, as shown in Listing 24.7, checks for the presence of default formatting information and then outputs the short form of news items. Note that the id attribute is extracted from each news item before the doNewsItemShort method is called. This id will be attached to each item as a link to the presentation of the full-length news item.

Listing 24.7: The doShortNews Method (NewsFormatter.java)

```java
public void doShortNews(PrintWriter out){
   NamedNodeMap attrib = docRoot.getAttributes();
   Node n = attrib.getNamedItem( "shorttemplate") ;
   String template = null ;
   if( n != null ) template = n.getNodeValue();
   if( headStr == null &&
       template != null &&
       template.length() > 2 ){
     try {
       setFromTemplate( template );
     }catch(IOException ie ){
       System.out.println("Unable to read " +
➡template );
     }
   }
   out.println( headStr );
   for( int i = skipNitems ; i < itemNodes.length;
➡i++ ){
     if( i >= maxNitems ) break ;
     n = itemNodes[i];  // <Newsitem nodes
     String id = ((Element)n).getAttribute("id");
     findNodes((Element) n ); // locates the parts of
➡<Newsitem
     doNewsItemShort( out, id );
   }
   out.println( footStr );
}
```

As shown in Listing 24.8, the doLongNews method checks for the availability of default formatting information before cycling through the news items in the itemNodes array.

Listing 24.8: The doLongNews Method Outputs the Full-Length News Item (NewsFormatter.java)

```java
public void doLongNews(PrintWriter out){
   NamedNodeMap attrib = docRoot.getAttributes();
   Node n = attrib.getNamedItem( "longtemplate");
   String template = null ;
```

```
         if( n != null ) template = n.getNodeValue();
         if( headStr == null &&
             template != null &&
             template.length() > 2 ){
           try {
             setFromTemplate( template );
             System.out.println("Template set ok " +
➡headStr + footStr );
           }catch(IOException ie ){
             System.out.println("Unable to read " +
➡template );
           }
         }
       out.println( headStr );
       for( int i = skipNitems ; i < itemNodes.length;
➡i++ ){
         if( i >= maxNitems ) break ;
         n = itemNodes[i];
         findNodes((Element) n );
         doNewsItemLong( out );
       }
       out.println( footStr );
     }
```

Listing 24.9 shows the limitAge method that is called whenever a
String giving an age limit is supplied to the doNews method. After
checking for a valid integer number in the age String, it rebuilds the
itemNodes array with the selected news items.

Listing 24.9: The Method That Selects Items by Age
(NewsFormatter.java)

```
// limit to only most recent entries - return number, may be
// zero
  private int limitAge(String age,
➡PrintWriter out ){
    int days = 100 ;
    try {
      days = Integer.parseInt( age );
      if( days <= 0 ) days = 1 ;
    }catch(NumberFormatException nfe){
      return itemNodes.length ; // no change
    }
```

```
    int today =(int)( System.currentTimeMillis()
➥/( 24 * 60 * 60 * 1000));
    int oldest = today - days ;
    Vector v = new Vector( itemNodes.length );
    int nidate = today ; // in case of parse problem
    int i ;
    for( i = 0 ; i < itemNodes.length ; i++ ){
        Node n = itemNodes[i];  // <Newsitem nodes
        String t = ((Element)n).getAttribute
➥("timestamp");
        try { nidate = Integer.parseInt( t );
        }catch(Exception nfe){ // number format or
➥null pointer
            System.out.println( "NewsFormatter.
➥limitAge " + nfe );
        }
    if( nidate >= oldest ){
        v.addElement( n );
    }
    }
    itemNodes = new Node[ v.size() ]; // may be zero
    for( i = 0 ; i < v.size(); i++ ){
        itemNodes[i] = (Node) v.elementAt(i);
    }
    return itemNodes.length ;
    }
```

The reason the selectNodes method is so complex is that both the
topics parameter selecting the output and the topic attribute in the
news items can have a single topic or multiple topics separated by commas. As shown in Listing 24.10, we build a java.util.Hashtable to
speed up recognition of topics.

**Listing 24.10: The Method That Selects Items by Matching Topics
(NewsFormatter.java)**

```
    // topics string has topics separated by commas
    // as does the attribute topics="general,books,java"
    // output capability only used for debugging
    private int selectNodes(String topics, PrintWriter
➥out ){
        Hashtable recognize = new Hashtable();
        StringTokenizer st = new StringTokenizer(
```

```
➥topics.toUpperCase(), ",");
     while( st.hasMoreTokens()){
         String tmp = st.nextToken().trim();
         recognize.put( tmp,tmp );
     }
     // hashtable can now be used to recognize selected
// topics
    Vector v = new Vector( itemNodes.length );
    int i ;
    for( i = 0 ; i < itemNodes.length ; i++ ){
      Node n = itemNodes[i];  // <Newsitem nodes
      String t = ((Element)n).getAttribute("topic");
      st = new StringTokenizer(t.toUpperCase(),",");
      while( st.hasMoreElements()){
          // We just use hashtable get to see if topic is
// present]
          if( recognize.get( st.nextToken().trim() )
➥!= null ){
              v.addElement(n);
              break;
          }
      } // end while over topic list
    } // end loop over all nodes
    // build new array from selected nodes
    itemNodes = new Node[ v.size() ];
    for( i = 0 ; i < v.size(); i++ ){
      itemNodes[i] = (Node) v.elementAt(i);
    }
    return itemNodes.length ;
  }
```

The findNodes method shown in Listing 24.11 is called for each news item to be output. The input Element is a Newsitem node of the XML document. This method creates the nodeHash variable that enables other methods to recover text elements, such as short, from the nodeHash collection by name.

Listing 24.11: The findNodes Method of the NewsFormatter Class (NewsFormatter.java)

```
// locate the nodes that are Elements for text data
private void findNodes( Element ne ){
   NodeList nl = ne.getChildNodes(); // all nodes
```

```
        int ct = nl.getLength();
        nodeHash = new Hashtable( 2 * ct );
        for( int i = 0 ; i < ct ; i++ ){
          Node n = nl.item(i);
          if( n instanceof Element ){
            nodeHash.put( n.getNodeName(), n );
          }
        }
      }
```

Headline and short-form news item output is always formatted with a link that enables display of the full-length item. This link is built into the HTML page by the doNewsItemHead and doNewsItemShort methods, as shown in Listing 24.12.

Listing 24.12: The doNewsItemHead and doNewsItemShort Methods (NewsFormatter.java)

```
// <Newsitem >has been hashed, id is attribute
  private void doNewsItemHead( PrintWriter out,
➡String id ){
    out.print("<a href=" + handler + "?id=" +
➡id + "&size=L >" );
    out.print("<h3>"); out.print(
➡nodeHash.get("head") );
    out.println("</h3></a>");
    out.println();
  }


  // <Newsitem has been hashed, id is attribute
  // output with <p>..</p> formatting
  private void doNewsItemShort( PrintWriter out,
➡String id ){
    // note anchor to full item display
    out.print("<a href=" + handler + "?id=" + id +
➡"&size=L >" );
    out.print("<h3>"); out.print( nodeHash.get
➡("head") );
    out.println("</h3></a>");
    Element de = (Element)nodeHash.get("date");
    out.print( de.getFirstChild() );
    out.println("</p>");
    Element ne = (Element)nodeHash.get("short");
```

```
        String wrk = ne.getFirstChild().getNodeValue().
➡trim() ;
        if( !(wrk.startsWith("<P") || wrk.startsWith
➡("<p")) ){
            out.print("<p>");
        }
        out.print( wrk );
        if( !(wrk.endsWith("/p>") || wrk.endsWith
➡("/P>"))){
            out.print("</p>");
        }
        itemsCount++ ;
        out.println();
    }
```

As shown in Listing 24.13, the doNewsItemLong method formats the headline text with an <h3> tag. A nice improvement for this code would be to allow customizing this sort of formatting. The main long text is formatted as a paragraph using the <p> tag. The item can have any desired HTML formatting tags inside the long text, but the <p> tags will always be used for the entire text.

Listing 24.13: The doNewsItemLong Method Outputs Long-Form News Items (NewsFormatter.java)

```
    //  <Newsitem >elements have been hashed
    // output long form with <p>...</p> formatting
    private void doNewsItemLong( PrintWriter out ){
        out.print("<h3>"); out.print( nodeHash.get
➡("head") );
        out.println("</h3>");
        Element de = (Element)nodeHash.get("date");
        out.print( de.getFirstChild() );
        out.println("</p>");
        Element ne = (Element)nodeHash.get("long");
        String wrk = ne.getFirstChild().getNodeValue().
➡trim() ;
        if( !(wrk.startsWith("<P") || wrk.startsWith
➡("<p")) ){
            out.print("<p>");
        }
        out.print( wrk );
        if( !(wrk.endsWith("/p>") || wrk.endsWith
```

```
➡("/P>"))){
        out.print("</p>");
    }
    itemsCount++ ;
    out.println();
    }
```

Finally, two utility methods are presented in Listing 24.14. The setFromTemplate method locates a file and reads it line by line. It assumes there will be a line starting with the text "<!-INSERT" that separates the HTML markup into two sections that become the headStr and footStr variables. The toString method is provided to assist in debugging.

Listing 24.14: The End of the NewsFormatter Source Code (NewsFormatter.java)

```
    private void setFromTemplate(String template )
➡throws IOException {
        File f = new File( newsFilePath, template );
        FileReader fr = new FileReader( f );
        BufferedReader br = new BufferedReader( fr );
        StringBuffer hsb = new StringBuffer( 100 );
        StringBuffer fsb = new StringBuffer( 100 );
        String tmp = br.readLine(); // strips line
➡terminators
        while( !tmp.startsWith("<!-INSERT" )){
            hsb.append( tmp ); fsb.append("\r\n");
            tmp = br.readLine();
        }
        tmp = br.readLine();
        while( tmp != null ){
            fsb.append( tmp ); fsb.append("\r\n");
            tmp = br.readLine();
        }
        headStr = hsb.toString();
        footStr = fsb.toString();
    }


    public String toString(){
        StringBuffer sb = new StringBuffer("NewsFormatter
➡item ct= ");
```

```
        sb.append( Integer.toString( itemNodes.length ));
        return sb.toString() ;
    }


}
```

Using *NewsFormatter*

This section presents two ways to use the NewsFormatter class: with the general-purpose servlet TheNewsServ and with JavaServer Pages (JSP).

The Code for *TheNewsServ*

This servlet can be used to show a single news item with an id parameter or to present selected items using topic and age parameters. Listing 24.15 shows the import statements and static variables. We have set the static variables to default values for our systems; obviously, you should change them to reflect your own setup.

Listing 24.15: The Start of TheNewsServ Source Code (TheNewsServ.java)

```
package com.XmlEcomBook.Chap08 ;

import java.io.*;
import java.util.* ;
import javax.servlet.*;
import javax.servlet.http.*;

public class TheNewsServ extends HttpServlet
{
  static String workDir = "E:\\scripts\\
➡CompanyNews" ;
  static String newsFile = "thenews.xml" ;
  static String handler = "http://localhost/servlet
➡/thenews" ;
  static String propfile = "conewserv.properties";
  static String version = "v1.0";
  static String pversion = "" ;
  static Properties cnProp ;
  static String brcrlf = "<br />\r\n" ;
  static String defaultHead = "<html>\r\n" +
    "<head><title>Company News Servlet</title>
```

```
➥</head>\r\n" +
   "<body>\r\n" +
   "<h2>Here is the news</h2>\r\n" ;
static String defaultFoot = "</body></html>\r\n";
```

The init method, as shown in Listing 24.16, reads a properties file whose values can be used to replace the default values in the static variables.

Listing 24.16: The init Method of the TheNewsServ Class (TheNewsServ.java)

```
public void init(ServletConfig config) throws
➥ServletException
   super.init(config);
   String tmp = config.getInitParameter("workdir");
   if( tmp != null ) workDir = tmp ;
   tmp = config.getInitParameter("propfile");
   if( tmp != null ) propfile = tmp;
   System.out.println("Start TheNewsServ using " +
➥workDir );
   File f = new File( workDir, propfile );
   try { cnProp = new Properties();
     cnProp.load( new FileInputStream(f) );
     tmp = cnProp.getProperty("thenewshandler");
     if( tmp != null ) handler = tmp ;
     pversion = cnProp.getProperty("version");
     if( pversion != null ){
       defaultFoot = "<hr><br>News Servlet " +
➥version +
           " properties: " + pversion + "<br>
➥\r\n" +
         "</body>\r\n</html>\r\n" ;
     }
     NewsFormatter.setHandler( handler );
     System.out.println( new Date().toString() +
       " Loaded properties for TheNewsServ: "
          + handler );
   }catch(IOException e){
     System.out.println("Error loading " + e );
   }
 }
```

The work of the servlet is performed in the doGet method, as shown in Listing 24.17. Parameter values for topics, the maximum age of news items, the desired size of output, and the news-item id can be passed in the request. Note that a File object that refers to the XML news file is created and passed to the NewsFormatter constructor. Using a File object ensures that the conventions for path separators for the particular system are adhered to; the NewsFormatter does not open this file but uses the name to get a DOM for the file from the DOMlibrary.

Listing 24.17: The doGet Method (TheNewsServ.java)

```
    public void doGet(HttpServletRequest req,
➡HttpServletResponse resp)
    throws ServletException, IOException
    {
        resp.setContentType("text/html");
        PrintWriter out = new PrintWriter(resp.
➡getOutputStream());
        String topics = req.getParameter("topic");
        String ageStr = req.getParameter("days");
        String len = req.getParameter("size" ); //
➡"S","H" or "L"
        String id  = req.getParameter("id"); // a single item is
// requested
        try {
          File f = new File( workDir, newsFile );
          NewsFormatter nf = new NewsFormatter( f );
          if( id != null ){
            nf.doNews( out, defaultHead,defaultFoot,
➡id );
          }.
          else {
            // PrintWriter, head, foot, topics, H,S or
➡L, age, skip#, mx#
            nf.doNews( out, defaultHead, defaultFoot,
➡topics, len, ageStr,0, 10 );
          }
          out.close();
        }catch(Exception e){
          System.err.println("TheNewsServ.doGet " + e );
          errorMsg( out, "TheNewsServ.doGet", e );
        }
    }
```

Note that a try-catch structure in doGet directs all exceptions to the errorMsg method shown in Listing 24.18. Obviously, you should insert your own e-mail address in place of the one here or the message could be a String variable set from the properties file. The header and footer methods simply write standard HTML tags.

Listing 24.18: The errorMsg, header, and footer Methods (TheNewsServ.java)

```java
// assumes response has been set to text/html
  private void errorMsg( PrintWriter out, String msg,
➥Exception ex ){
    header( out );
    out.println("<h2>Error: " ); out.println( msg );
    out.println("</h2><br>");
    if( ex != null ){
        ex.printStackTrace( out );
    }
    out.println("<br>");
    out.println("<a href=\"mailto:wbrogden@bga.com\">
➥Please mail me"
    + " the error message.</a><br>");
    footer( out );
  }

  private void header(PrintWriter out ){
    out.println("<html>");
    out.println("<head><title>Company News Servlet
➥</title></head>");
    out.println("<body>");
  }

  private void footer(PrintWriter out ){
    out.println("<hr><br>Company News Servlet "
➥+ version + " properties: <br>" );
    out.println("</body>");
    out.println("</html>");
    out.close();
  }
}
```

A JavaServer Pages Example

The basic form of the sample page is a table having three columns. To save space in this listing, we cut the example down as much as possible; a real page would, of course, have much more company-related material.

It is the ease of incorporating Java output into HTML markup that makes JavaServer Pages so attractive. Listing 24.19 shows the page source up through the creation of the first row of the table.

Listing 24.19: The First Part of a Simplified JSP News Presentation Page (mockup.jsp)

```
<!DOCTYPE HTML PUBLIC "-//W3C//DTD HTML 4.0
➥Transitional//EN">
<html>
<head>
<title>The XMLGifts News </title>
</head>

<body bgcolor="#FFFFFF">
<%@ page language="java"
   import="com.XmlEcomBook.Chap024.NewsFormatter,
➥java.io.*" %>
<%!
  String newsFilePath = "e:\\scripts\\CompanyNews" ;
  String newsFileName = "thenews.xml" ;
  String newsHandler  = "http://localhost:8080/
➥XMLbook/Chap08/thenews.jsp" ;
  File newsFile = new File( newsFilePath,
➥newsFileName );
  public void jspInit(){
     super.jspInit();
     NewsFormatter.setHandler( newsHandler );
  }
%>
<table width="89%" border="0" align="left"
➥cellpadding="8">
  <tr align="center" bgcolor="cyan">
    <td colspan="3"><font size="4">
 Various Corporate Navigation Links Go Here</font>
    </td>
  </tr>
```

For the purposes of this example, we hard-coded a topic value of "CDs", as shown in Listing 24.20. The first use of the NewsFormatter object is to create the left-hand column of headlines. This is done first because, after the topic selection has been done, the NewsFormatter object will contain only data for news items that match the topics.

Listing 24.20: The JSP Page Continues, with NewsFormatter Output (mockup.jsp)

```
    <!- the nf and pw objects will be used for
➥all three td ->
    <tr valign="TOP" ><font size="3">
        <td><b>News Headlines</b><br>
<%
    // topic could be set from customer records or the
// previous form
    String topic = "CDs" ;
    NewsFormatter nf = new NewsFormatter( newsFile );
    PrintWriter pw = new PrintWriter( out );

/*  Note the doNews signature
    doNews( PrintWriter out, String hs, String fs,
        String topstr, String sz, String age, int
➥skpN, int mxN ) */
    // headlines - all topics
    nf.doNews( pw, "","", "", "H", null, 0, 8 );
%>
    </td>
    <td width="50%">
<%
    nf.doNews( pw, "","", topic, "L", null, 0, 1 );
%>
    </td>
    <!- the short form column ->
    <td width="23%">
<%= "<b>Recent news items about " + topic +
➥"</b><br>" %>
<%
 /*  Note the doNews signature
    doNews( PrintWriter out, String hs, String fs,
        String topstr, String sz, String age, int
➥skpN, int mxN ) */
```

```
          nf.doNews( pw, "","", topic, "S", null, 1, 8 );
       %>
          </td>
          </font>
       </tr>
       <tr align="center" bgcolor="cyan">
          <td colspan="3"><font size="4" >
          Repeat the Navigation links here for
➡convenience<br></font>
          </td>
       </tr>
    <tr>
       <td colspan="3" align='center'>
<font face='arial, helvetica' size='3'>
          &copy;2000 XMLGifts.com<sup>SM</sup>
       <br /></font>
       </td>
     </tr>
    </table>
    </body>
    </html>
```

ADDING THE LATEST NEWS

An important feature of this application is the capability to add new news items without disturbing the normal operation of the Web site. This is the function that appears on the upper-right corner of Figure 24.1. Instead of modifying the DOM in server memory, the CompanyNewsServ servlet writes a modified version of the master XML file to disk storage. This revised news item file will automatically be loaded the next time the DOM is requested from the DOMlibrary.

The *CompanyNewsServ* Servlet

The HTML form for updating is created and managed by the Company-NewsServ servlet. Initial entry to the servlet is through an HTML page that has an ordinary HTML form for inputting an author's name and a password. The servlet looks up the author's name in the properties file to verify that that person is authorized to input news items.

Listing 24.21 shows our properties file for working on the localhost server. Note that the author's name is the property name and the value is the password.

Listing 24.21: The Properties File Used by CompanyNewsServ (conewserv.properties)

```
# properties for CompanyNewsServ
handler=http://localhost/servlet/conewserv
thenewshandler=http://localhost/servlet/thenews
newsfile=thenews.xml
version=June 15, 2000
wbrogden=xmlrules
```

Listing 24.22 shows the import statements, static variables, and init method for the CompanyNewsServ servlet.

Listing 24.22: The Start of the CompanyNewsServ Servlet Code (CompanyNewsServ.java)

```java
package com.XmlEcomBook.Chap08 ;

import com.XmlEcomBook.DOMlibrary ;
import java.io.*;
import java.util.* ;
import javax.servlet.*;
import javax.servlet.http.*;
import org.w3c.dom.* ;

public class CompanyNewsServ extends HttpServlet
{
   static String workDir = "E:\\scripts\\
CompanyNews" ;
   static String propfile = "conewserv.properties" ;
   static String newsFile = "thenews.xml" ;
   static String handler = "http://localhost/servlet/
➥conewserv" ;
   static String version = "v0.12";
   static String pversion = "" ;
   static Properties cnProp ;
   static String brcrlf = "<br />\r\n" ;

   public void init(ServletConfig config) throws
➥ServletException
```

```
    {
      super.init(config);
      String tmp = config.getInitParameter("workdir");
      if( tmp != null ) workDir = tmp ;
      tmp = config.getInitParameter("propfile");
      if( tmp != null ) propfile = tmp ;
      System.out.println("Start CompanyNewsServ using "
➡ + workDir );
      File f = new File( workDir, propfile );
      try { cnProp = new Properties();
        cnProp.load( new FileInputStream(f) );
        tmp = cnProp.getProperty("handler");
        if( tmp != null ) handler = tmp ;
        tmp = cnProp.getProperty("newsfile");
        if( tmp != null ) newsFile = tmp ;
        pversion = cnProp.getProperty("version");
        System.out.println("Loaded properties for
➡CompanyNewsServ: "
                + handler + " file:" + newsFile );
      }catch(IOException e){
          System.out.println("Error loading " + e );
      }
    }
```

The doGet method, as shown in Listing 24.23, checks the input username and password against the properties file loaded when the servlet is initialized. If a name and password match is found, it calls the generateForm
method to create the HTML form for entering a news item.

Listing 24.23: The doGet Method Creates the News Entry Form
(CompanyNewsServ.java)

```
    public void doGet(HttpServletRequest req,
➡HttpServletResponse resp)
    throws ServletException, IOException
    {
      resp.setContentType("text/html");
      PrintWriter out = new PrintWriter(resp
➡.getOutputStream());
      String username = req.getParameter("username");
      String password = req.getParameter("password");
      String action   = req.getParameter("action");
      String tmp = cnProp.getProperty(username);
```

```
        boolean userok = false ;
        if( tmp != null ){
            userok = tmp.equals( password );
        }
        header( out );
        if( userok ){
            generateForm( out, username, password );
        }
        else {
            out.println("<p>User: " + username + "
➡password: " + password +
                " not found.</p>" );
        }
        footer( out );
```

A filled-out form is sent to the doPost method. As shown in Listing 24.24, you extract the various text items and pass them to a new NewsUpkeep object with the addItem method.

Listing 24.24: The doPost Method Captures Data from the Form (CompanyNewsServ.java)

```
    public void doPost(HttpServletRequest req,
➡HttpServletResponse resp)
    throws ServletException, IOException
    {
        resp.setContentType("text/html");
        PrintWriter out = new PrintWriter(resp
➡.getOutputStream());
        String username = req.getParameter("username");
        String password = req.getParameter("password");
        String action   = req.getParameter("action");
        String head = req.getParameter("head");
        String date = req.getParameter("date");
        String topics = req.getParameter("topics");
        String shrtStr = req.getParameter("short")
➡.trim();
        String longStr = req.getParameter("long")
➡.trim();
        DOMlibrary library = DOMlibrary.getLibrary();
        File f = new File( workDir, newsFile );
        try {
         NewsUpkeep nup = new NewsUpkeep( f );
```

```
      nup.addItem( head, date, topics, username,
➡shrtStr, longStr );
      header( out );
      out.println("NewsUpkeep is " + nup + "<br />");
      footer( out );
    } catch( Exception e){
        errorMsg( out, "CompanyNewsServ.doPost
➡", e );
    }
  }
```

The HTML form for news-item input is created by the generateForm method, as shown in Listing 24.25. Note that the username and password are inserted as hidden values in the form.

Listing 24.25: The generateForm Method Creates an Entry Form (CompanyNewsServ.java)

```
    private void generateForm( PrintWriter out,
➡String name, String pw ){
    out.println("<h2>Enter Company News
➡Item Data</h2>");
    out.println("<form method=\"POST\" action=\"" + handler +
"\" >");
    out.println("Headline - 80 char max<br />");
    out.println("<input type=\"text\" maxlength
➡=\"80\" size=\"60\"" +
        " name=\"head\" ><br />" );
    out.println("Dated <br />");
    out.println("<input type=\"text\" maxlength
➡=\"50\" size=\"40\"" +
        " name=\"date\" value=\"" + new Date()
➡.toString() + "\" ><br />" );
    out.println(
    "Topics separated by commas - please stick
➡to the official list.<br />");
    out.println("<input type=\"text\" maxlength
➡=\"80\" size=\"60\"" +
        " name=\"topics\" ><br />" );
    out.println("Short version <br />");
    out.println("<textarea cols=\"60\" rows=\"3\"
➡name=\"short\" >");
    out.println("</textarea><br />");
```

```
    out.println("Long version <br />");
    out.println("<textarea cols=\"60\" rows=\"10\"
➦name=\"long\" >");
    out.println("</textarea><br />");
    out.println("<input type=\"hidden\" name
➦=\"username\" value=\""
        + name + "\"><br>" );
    out.println("<input type=\"hidden\" name
➦=\"password\" value=\""
        + pw + "\" ><br>");
    out.println(
    "<input type=\"submit\" name=\"action\" value
➦=\"Submit\" ><br />" );
    out.println("</form></center>");
  }
```

Finally, we have the typical servlet utility methods, as shown in Listing 24.26. Naturally, you should replace the message with your own address or provide a `String` variable initialized from the properties file.

Listing 24.26: The Utility Methods in CompanyNewsServ (CompanyNewsServ.java)

```
// assumes response has been set to text/html
  private void errorMsg( PrintWriter out, String
➦msg, Exception ex ){
    header( out );
    out.println("<h2>Error: " ); out.println( msg );
    out.println("</h2><br>");
    if( ex != null ){
        ex.printStackTrace( out );
    }
    out.println("<br>");
    out.println("<a href=\"mailto:wbrogden@bga.
➦com\">" +
        "Please mail me the error message.</a><br>");
    footer( out );
  }

  private void header(PrintWriter out ){
    out.println("<html>");
    out.println("<head><title>Company News
Servlet</title></head>");
```

```
        out.println("<body>");
    }

    private void footer(PrintWriter out ){
        out.println("<hr><br>Company News Servlet "
➥+ version +
            " properties: <br>" );
        out.println("</body>");
        out.println("</html>");
        out.close();
    }
}
```

The *NewsUpkeep* Class

The NewsUpkeep class takes an existing <Newsfile> DOM object and the various text strings that make up a new <Newsitem> and rewrites the XML news file. This method is simpler than creating and inserting the <Newsitem> in the memory-resident DOM and ensures that the news file is updated correctly. It also avoids the possibility of one of the display methods encountering a partially changed DOM.

Listing 24.27 shows the start of the NewsUpkeep class source code. The constructor uses the complete filename to get the DOM from the DOMlibrary. Because this DOM is not modified during the rewrite of the XML file, you don't have to worry about interfering with the possibly simultaneous access to this object by NewsFormatter.

Note the creation of the NamedNodeMap variable, rootNNM, which holds the attribute names and values found in the document root, the <Newsfile> tag. The constructor also puts all of the <Newsitem> nodes in the itemNodes array.

Listing 24.27: The Start of the NewsUpkeep Class
(NewsUpkeep.java)

```
package com.XmlEcomBook.Chap08;

import com.XmlEcomBook.DOMlibrary ;
import java.io.*;
import java.util.* ;
import javax.servlet.*;
import javax.servlet.http.*;
import org.w3c.dom.* ;
```

```
public class NewsUpkeep
{
  File newsFile ;
  String newsFileName ;
  Node[] itemNodes ;
  NamedNodeMap rootNNM ; // for root attributes

  public NewsUpkeep( File f) throws IOException {
    newsFile = f ;
    newsFileName = f.getAbsolutePath() ;
    DOMlibrary library = DOMlibrary.getLibrary();
    Document doc = library.getDOM( newsFileName );
    if( doc == null ){
        throw new FileNotFoundException
( newsFileName );
    }
    Element re = doc.getDocumentElement();
    rootNNM = re.getAttributes();
    System.out.println("Root has " +
rootNNM.getLength() + " attributes");
    NodeList newsItemNodes = doc.getElementsBy
TagName("Newsitem");
    int ct = newsItemNodes.getLength();
    itemNodes = new Node[ ct ];
    for( int i = 0 ; i < ct ; i++ ){
      itemNodes[i] = newsItemNodes.item( i );
    }
  }
}
```

Listing 24.28 shows some of the support methods required by
NewsUpkeep. The formatTopics method ensures that the text that
will be written as the topic attribute is correctly formatted.

Listing 24.28: Various Support Functions in NewsUpkeep (NewsUpkeep.java)

```
//ensure there are no leading or trailing spaces on the
// individual topics, comma separated, general, food, etc
private String formatTopics(String s ){
  if( s.indexOf(',') < 0 ) return s.trim();
  // only separator is comma
  StringTokenizer st = new StringTokenizer
( s, "," );
```

```
      StringBuffer sb = new StringBuffer
( s.length() );
      while( st.hasMoreTokens() ){
         sb.append( st.nextToken().trim() );
         if( st.hasMoreTokens() ) sb.append(',');
      }
      return sb.toString();
   }
    // convert system millisecs to days since epoch
   private String timeInDays(){
      long t = System.currentTimeMillis() ;
      int tid = (int)(t / ( 1000 * 60 * 60 * 24 ));
      return Integer.toString( tid );
   }

   // s expected to be decimal number used
in <Newsitem id=
   private String incrementID(String s ){
      try{
         int n = Integer.parseInt( s );
         return Integer.toString( n + 2 );
      }catch(NumberFormatException e){
         return s + "a" ;
      }
   }

   public String toString(){
      StringBuffer sb = new StringBuffer
("NewsUpkeep ");
      sb.append(" Newsitem count: " );
      sb.append( Integer.toString( itemNodes
.length ));
      return sb.toString();
   }
```

Now we come to the main working method, addItem. The first thing this method does is creates a new file with a temporary name and write the standard XML declaration and a comment. Next, the <Newsfile> tag is created by writing the attributes from the rootNNM collection.

As shown in Listing 24.29, the nextid attribute is specially treated. The current value, which becomes the id attribute of the new <Newsitem>, is saved, and the incremented value is written into the <Newsfile> tag.

Part V

Listing 24.29: The Start of the `addItem` Method (`NewsUpkeep.java`)

```java
// items are always added at the top of the file
// so you have to rebuild the start of the root element
public void addItem(
     String head, String date, String topics,
➧String author,
     String shrtStr,
     String longStr ) throws IOException {
   String idVal = "" ;
   String tmpfile = newsFileName + "$$" ;
   File f = new File( tmpfile );
   FileWriter fw = new FileWriter(f);
   PrintWriter out = new PrintWriter( new
➧BufferedWriter( fw ) );
   out.println("<?xml version=\"1.0\" standalone=
➧\"yes\" ?>");
   out.println("<!- output by NewsUpkeep ->");
   int ct = rootNNM.getLength();
   if( ct == 0 ){
     out.println("<Newsfile>");
   }
   else {
     out.print("<Newsfile ");
     for( int i = 0 ; i < ct ; i++ ){
       Node an = rootNNM.item(i);
       String name = an.getNodeName();
       String val  = an.getNodeValue();
       out.print( name + "=\"" );
       if( name.equals("nextid") ){
           idVal = val ;
           val = incrementID( val );
       }
       out.print( val + "\" ");
     }
     out.println(" >");
   }
```

Next, the new <Newsitem> tag is written out, as shown in Listing 24.30, followed by the head, the date, and the short and long text elements. The old <Newsitem> elements are written out by calls to the `writeNewsNode` method. After closing the temporary file, the old XML file is deleted and the temporary file is renamed. The next time this file is requested, the DOMlibrary class will see the changed timestamp and read in the new file.

Listing 24.30: The `addItem` Method, Continued (`NewsUpkeep.java`)

```java
    out.print("<Newsitem timestamp=\"");
    out.print( timeInDays() + "\" topic=\"");
    out.print( formatTopics( topics ) );
    out.println( "\" author=\"" + author + "\"
id=\"" + idVal + "\" >");
    // end of <Newsitem .. >
    out.println("<head>" + head.trim() +
"</head>" );
    out.println("<date>" + date.trim() +
"</date>" );
    out.println("<short><![CDATA[");
    out.println( shrtStr.trim() );
    out.println("]]></short>");
    out.println("<long><![CDATA[");
    out.println( longStr ); out.println("]]>
</long>");
    out.println("</Newsitem>");
    for( int i = 0 ; i < itemNodes.length ; i++ ){
        writeNewsNode(out, (Element)itemNodes[i] );
    }
    out.println("</Newsfile>");
    out.flush(); out.close();
    File forig = new File( newsFileName );
    DOMlibrary library = DOMlibrary.getLibrary();
    // to prevent overlapping XML file operations
    synchronized( library ){
      forig.delete();
      if( !f.renameTo( forig )){
        System.out.println("NewsUpkeep.addItem
rename failed") ;
      }
    }
  }
```

The `writeNewsNode` method, which writes a single `<Newsitem>` element, is shown in Listing 24.31.

Part v

Listing 24.31: The Method That Writes a Single News Item from the DOM (NewsUpkeep.java)

```java
// write a <Newsitem Element duplicating the attributes
public void writeNewsNode(PrintWriter out,
Element e) {
    NamedNodeMap nnm = e.getAttributes();
    out.print("<Newsitem " ) ; //timestamp=\"");
    int i ;     for( i = 0 ; i < nnm.getLength() ;
i++ ){
        Attr na = (Attr) nnm.item(i); //  Attr
extends Node
        String atr = na.getName();
        String val = na.getValue();
        out.print( atr ); out.print("=\"");
        out.print( val ); out.print("\" ");
    }
    out.println(">");
    NodeList nl = e.getChildNodes();
    int ct = nl.getLength();
    for( i = 0 ; i < ct ; i++ ){
      Node nde = nl.item( i );
      if( nde instanceof Element ){
        Element ce = (Element)nde;
        String name = ce.getTagName();
        out.print("<" + name + ">");
        NodeList chnl = ce.getChildNodes() ;
        if( chnl.getLength() == 0 ) continue ;
        Node chn = chnl.item(0);
        if(  name.equals("long") || name.equals
("short") ){
            out.print("<![CDATA[");
            out.println( chn.getNodeValue().
trim() );
            out.print("]]>");
        }
        else { out.print( chn.getNodeValue() );
        }
        out.println("</" + name + ">");
      }
    } // loop over <Newsitem> child nodes
    out.println("</Newsitem>");
```

```
        }

    }
```

Based on our experience with adding news items using the
`CompanyNewsServ` servlet, you should write out a complete news
item in a text editor first. Then, when working with the input form,
you can just cut and paste into the form.

SUMMARY

The last three chapters of this book have focused on specific e-commerce
applications of XML. Each chapter shares one very important tenet:
XML allows you to separate content from business logic. In this chapter,
this separation centered around a simple news server that had three key
characteristics:

Flexibility of output   Our XML format needed to have enough
flexibility to manage a variety of news formats, including the
headline, an abstract or teaser, and the full story.

Ease of data entry   The XML formatting ensures a consistent
structure, even if different users are inputting news stories.
Obviously, this can't negate bad writing, but it at least provides
a structural integrity that helps the news site maintain a consistent look and feel.

Minimum server load   In this case, we chose DOM to manage the business logic, because we only had to worry about a
limited number of news items. Fortunately, because you've read
this book, you are also aware of alternative methods for managing business logic, particularly SAX, which is an event-based
model that puts less stress on the memory requirements but
requires running a parser for every news page access.

You can see how similar the process we've just described is to the
processes described in the previous two chapters. Content is managed
within an XML file, and the business logic is processed through Java
using either JSP or servlets. This makes for very powerful Web applications, but even more important, it makes for powerful applications that
are easy to maintain and change. Often, you can make changes in nothing
but an XML file to initiate a profound change in the application itself.
Such is the nature of XML. It's a content-driven approach that is rapidly
becoming the standard.

Appendix A

EXTENSIBLE MARKUP LANGUAGE (XML) 1.0 (SECOND EDITION)

Adapted from *Mastering™ XML, Premium Edition*,
by Chuck White, Liam Quin, and Linda Burman
ISBN 0-7821-2847-5   1,155 pages $49.99

Whenever you have any doubts about how to apply what you've learned in this book, including whether or not you are concerned about conflicting statements made by its authors, this section provides definitive answers. This section is a reproduction, in its entirety, of the latest edition of the Extensible Markup Language Recommendation from the W3C.

UNDERSTANDING BNF GRAMMAR

Unfortunately, reading through this document can be tedious, and it helps to understand the underlying grammar, called the Backus-Naur Form (BNF).

The XML Recommendation uses the Extended BNF Grammar to help describe its core rules (see "6 Notation"). In addition to adherence to the EBNF rules in the XML specification, in order for documents to be well formed they must also not violate any of the well-formedness constraints outlined by the specification shown on these pages.

Basic Notation

The basic grammar for XML follows the following syntax:

```
symbol ::= expression
```

The `::=` characters simply mean *is defined as*. So to define a symbol *x* to represent a choice of any of four specific digits, you would write:

```
x ::= [0 | 1 | 2 | 3]
```

This simply means, "The symbol *x* is defined as the digits *0* or *1* or *2* or *3*"

You can also refer to *ranges* of sequential characters:

```
x ::= [0-3]
```

This is different, because the OR operator (|) was replaced with a range operator, so it is more inclusive. You could also create a space-delimited list to accomplish the same thing.

The case-sensitivity that applies to XML also applies to the grammar rules found within its specification.

BNF Symbols and Operators

You will encounter several operators and grouping symbols as you read the specification. These are shown in Table A.1.

TABLE A.1: Extended BNF Symbols and Operators

SYMBOL	MEANING
#xN	N is a hexadecimal integer and #xN is the Unicode with the number N)
[a-zA-Z], [#xN-#xN]	Matches any character with a value in the ranges indicated
[^a-zA-Z], [^#xN-#xN]	Matches any character with a value outside the range indicated
[^abc], [^#xN#xN#xN]	Matches any character with a value not among the characters indicated
'text' or "text"	Matches a literal string matching that given inside the single or double quotes
A?	Matches A or nothing; optional A
A B	Matches A followed by B
A|B	Matches A or B but not both
A-B	Matches any string that matches A but does not match B
A+	Matches one or more occurrences of A
A*	Matches zero or more occurrences of A
/* ... */	Comment
[wfc: ...]	Well-formedness constraint
[vc: ...]	A validity constraint

What follows is the official W3C Recommendation for XML, Second Edition, as published by the W3C on October 6, 2000. It is *not* XML 2.0. It is the second edition of XML version 1.0, updated to clean up some errata and for some clarification.

EXTENSIBLE MARKUP LANGUAGE (XML) 1.0 (SECOND EDITION)

W3C Recommendation 6 October 2000

This version (XHTML, XML, PDF, XHTML review version with color-coded revision indicators):

```
http://www.w3.org/TR/2000/REC-xml-20001006
```

Latest version:

    http://www.w3.org/TR/REC-xml

Previous versions:

    http://www.w3.org/TR/2000/WD-xml-2e-20000814

    http://www.w3.org/TR/1998/REC-xml-19980210

Editor	Affiliations	E-mail Address
Tim Bray	Textuality and Netscape	tbray@textuality.com
Jean Paoli	Microsoft	jeanpa@microsoft.com
C. M. Sperberg-McQueen	University of Illinois at Chicago and Text Encoding Initiative	cmsmcq@uic.edu
Eve Maler (Second Edition)	Sun Microsystems, Inc.	eve.maler@east.sun.com

Abstract

The Extensible Markup Language (XML) is a subset of SGML that is completely described in this document. Its goal is to enable generic SGML to be served, received, and processed on the Web in the way that is now possible with HTML. XML has been designed for ease of implementation and for interoperability with both SGML and HTML.

Status of This Document

This document has been reviewed by W3C Members and other interested parties and has been endorsed by the Director as a W3C Recommendation. It is a stable document and may be used as reference material or cited as a normative reference from another document. W3C's role in making the Recommendation is to draw attention to the specification and to promote its widespread deployment. This enhances the functionality and interoperability of the Web.

This document specifies a syntax created by subsetting an existing, widely used international text processing standard (Standard Generalized Markup Language, ISO 8879:1986(E) as amended and corrected) for use on the World Wide Web. It is a product of the W3C XML Activity, details of which can be found at www.w3.org/XML. The English version of this specification is the only normative version. However, for translations of this document, see www.w3.org/XML/#trans. A list of current W3C Recommendations and other technical documents can be found at www.w3.org/TR.

This second edition is *not* a new version of XML (first published 10 February 1998); it merely incorporates the changes dictated by the first-edition errata (available at www.w3.org/XML/xml-19980210-errata) as a convenience to readers. The errata list for this second edition is available at www.w3.org/XML/xml-V10-2e-errata.

Please report errors in this document to xml-editor@w3.org; archives are available.

NOTE

C..M. Sperberg-McQueen's affiliation has changed since the publication of the first edition. He is now at the World Wide Web Consortium and can be contacted at cmsmcq@w3.org.

Table of Contents

1 Introduction

Extensible Markup Language, abbreviated XML, describes a class of data objects called XML documents and partially describes the behavior of computer programs which process them. XML is an application profile or restricted form of SGML, the Standard Generalized Markup Language

(ISO 8879). By construction, XML documents are conforming SGML documents.

XML documents are made up of storage units called entities, which contain either parsed or unparsed data. Parsed data is made up of characters, some of which form character data, and some of which form markup. Markup encodes a description of the document's storage layout and logical structure. XML provides a mechanism to impose constraints on the storage layout and logical structure.

[Definition: A software module called an *XML processor* is used to read XML documents and provide access to their content and structure.] [Definition: It is assumed that an XML processor is doing its work on behalf of another module, called the *application*.] This specification describes the required behavior of an XML processor in terms of how it must read XML data and the information it must provide to the application.

1.1 Origin and Goals

XML was developed by an XML Working Group (originally known as the SGML Editorial Review Board) formed under the auspices of the World Wide Web Consortium (W3C) in 1996. It was chaired by Jon Bosak of Sun Microsystems with the active participation of an XML Special Interest Group (previously known as the SGML Working Group) also organized by the W3C. The membership of the XML Working Group is given in an appendix. Dan Connolly served as the working group's contact with the W3C.

The design goals for XML are:

1. XML shall be straightforwardly usable over the Internet.

2. XML shall support a wide variety of applications.

3. XML shall be compatible with SGML.

4. It shall be easy to write programs which process XML documents.

5. The number of optional features in XML is to be kept to the absolute minimum, ideally zero.

6. XML documents should be human-legible and reasonably clear.

7. The XML design should be prepared quickly.

8. The design of XML shall be formal and concise.

9. XML documents shall be easy to create.

10. Terseness in XML markup is of minimal importance.

This specification, together with associated standards (Unicode and ISO/IEC 10646 for characters, Internet RFC 1766 for language identification tags, ISO 639 for language name codes, and ISO 3166 for country name codes), provides all the information necessary to understand XML Version 1.0 and construct computer programs to process it.

This version of the XML specification may be distributed freely, as long as all text and legal notices remain intact.

1.2 Terminology

The terminology used to describe XML documents is defined in the body of this specification. The terms defined in the following list are used in building those definitions and in describing the actions of an XML processor:

may   [Definition: Conforming documents and XML processors are permitted to but need not behave as described.]

must   [Definition: Conforming documents and XML processors are required to behave as described; otherwise they are in error.]

error   [Definition: A violation of the rules of this specification; results are undefined. Conforming software may detect and report an error and may recover from it.]

fatal error   [Definition: An error which a conforming XML processor must detect and report to the application. After encountering a fatal error, the processor may continue processing the data to search for further errors and may report such errors to the application. In order to support correction of errors, the processor may make unprocessed data from the document (with intermingled character data and markup) available to the application. Once a fatal error is detected, however, the processor must not continue normal processing (i.e., it must not continue to pass character data and information about the document's logical structure to the application in the normal way).]

at user option   [Definition: Conforming software may or must (depending on the modal verb in the sentence) behave as described; if it does, it must provide users a means to enable or disable the behavior described.]

validity constraint   [Definition: A rule which applies to all valid XML documents. Violations of validity constraints are errors; they must, at user option, be reported by validating XML processors.]

well-formedness constraint   [Definition: A rule which applies to all well-formed XML documents. Violations of well-formedness constraints are fatal errors.]

match   [Definition: (Of strings or names:) Two strings or names being compared must be identical. Characters with multiple possible representations in ISO/IEC 10646 (e.g. characters with both precomposed and base+diacritic forms) match only if they have the same representation in both strings. No case folding is performed. (Of strings and rules in the grammar:) A string matches a grammatical production if it belongs to the language generated by that production. (Of content and content models:) An element matches its declaration when it conforms in the fashion described in the constraint "[VC: Element Valid]."]

for compatibility   [Definition: Marks a sentence describing a feature of XML included solely to ensure that XML remains compatible with SGML.]

for interoperability   [Definition: Marks a sentence describing a non-binding recommendation included to increase the chances that XML documents can be processed by the existing installed base of SGML processors which predate the WebSGML Adaptations Annex to ISO 8879.]

2 Documents

[Definition: A data object is an XML *document* if it is well-formed, as defined in this specification. A well-formed XML document may in addition be valid if it meets certain further constraints.]

Each XML document has both a logical and a physical structure. Physically, the document is composed of units called entities. An entity may refer to other entities to cause their inclusion in the document. A document begins in a "root" or document entity. Logically, the document is composed of declarations, elements, comments, character references, and processing instructions, all of which are indicated in the document by explicit markup. The logical and physical structures must nest properly, as described in "4.3.2 Well-Formed Parsed Entities."

2.1 Well-Formed XML Documents

[Definition: A textual object is a *well-formed* XML document if:]

1. Taken as a whole, it matches the production labeled document.

2. It meets all the well-formedness constraints given in this specification.

3. Each of the parsed entities which is referenced directly or indirectly within the document is well-formed.

Document

```
[1]    document   ::=    prolog element Misc*
```

Matching the document production implies that:

1. It contains one or more elements.

2. [Definition: There is exactly one element, called the *root*, or document element, no part of which appears in the content of any other element.] For all other elements, if the start-tag is in the content of another element, the end-tag is in the content of the same element. More simply stated, the elements, delimited by start- and end-tags, nest properly within each other.

[Definition: As a consequence of this, for each non-root element C in the document, there is one other element P in the document such that C is in the content of P, but is not in the content of any other element that is in the content of P. P is referred to as the *parent* of C, and C as a *child* of P.]

2.2 Characters

[Definition: A parsed entity contains *text*, a sequence of characters, which may represent markup or character data.] [Definition: A *character* is an atomic unit of text as specified by ISO/IEC 10646 (see also ISO/IEC 10646-2000). Legal characters are tab, carriage return, line feed, and the legal characters of Unicode and ISO/IEC 10646. The versions of these standards cited in "A.1 Normative References" were current at the time this document was prepared. New characters may be added to these standards by amendments or new editions. Consequently, XML processors must accept any character in the range specified for Char. The use of "compatibility characters", as defined in section 6.8 of Unicode (see also D21 in section 3.6 of Unicode3), is discouraged.]

Character Range

```
[2]    Char  ::=   #x9 | #xA | #xD | [#x20-#xD7FF]
                 | [#xE000-#xFFFD] | [#x10000-#x10FFFF]
/* any Unicode character, excluding the surrogate blocks,
FFFE, and FFFF. */
```

The mechanism for encoding character code points into bit patterns may vary from entity to entity. All XML processors must accept the UTF-8 and UTF-16 encodings of 10646; the mechanisms for signaling which of the two is in use, or for bringing other encodings into play, are discussed later, in "4.3.3 Character Encoding in Entities."

2.3 Common Syntactic Constructs

This section defines some symbols used widely in the grammar.

S (white space) consists of one or more space (#x20) characters, carriage returns, line feeds, or tabs.

White Space

```
[3]    S   ::=   (#x20 | #x9 | #xD | #xA)+
```

Characters are classified for convenience as letters, digits, or other characters. A letter consists of an alphabetic or syllabic base character or an ideographic character. Full definitions of the specific characters in each class are given in "B Character Classes."

[Definition: A *Name* is a token beginning with a letter or one of a few punctuation characters, and continuing with letters, digits, hyphens, underscores, colons, or full stops, together known as name characters.] Names beginning with the string "xml", or any string which would match (('X'|'x') ('M'|'m') ('L'|'l')), are reserved for standardization in this or future versions of this specification.

NOTE

The Namespaces in XML Recommendation (XML Names) assigns a meaning to names containing colon characters. Therefore, authors should not use the colon in XML names except for namespace purposes, but XML processors must accept the colon as a name character.

An Nmtoken (name token) is any mixture of name characters.

Names and Tokens

[4]	NameChar	::=	Letter | Digit | '.' | '-' | '_' | ':'
			| CombiningChar | Extender
[5]	Name	::=	(Letter | '_' | ':') (NameChar)*
[6]	Names	::=	Name (S Name)*
[7]	Nmtoken	::=	(NameChar)+
[8]	Nmtokens	::=	Nmtoken (S Nmtoken)*

Literal data is any quoted string not containing the quotation mark used as a delimiter for that string. Literals are used for specifying the content of internal entities (EntityValue), the values of attributes (AttValue), and external identifiers (SystemLiteral). Note that a SystemLiteral can be parsed without scanning for markup.

Literals

[9]	EntityValue	::=	'"' ([^%&"] | PEReference | Reference)* '"'
			| "'" ([^%&'] | PEReference | Reference)* "'"
[10]	AttValue	::=	'"' ([^<&"] | Reference)* '"'
			| "'" ([^<&'] | Reference)* "'"
[11]	SystemLiteral	::=	('"' [^"]* '"') | ("'" [^']* "'")
[12]	PubidLiteral	::=	'"' PubidChar* '"' | "'" (PubidChar - "'")* "'"
[13]	PubidChar	::=	#x20 | #xD | #xA | [a-zA-Z0-9]
			| [-'()+,./:=?;!*#@$_%]

NOTE

Although the EntityValue production allows the definition of an entity consisting of a single explicit < in the literal (e.g., <!ENTITY mylt "<">), it is strongly advised to avoid this practice since any reference to that entity will cause a well-formedness error.

2.4 Character Data and Markup

Text consists of intermingled character data and markup. [Definition: *Markup* takes the form of start-tags, end-tags, empty-element tags, entity references, character references, comments, CDATA section delimiters, document type declarations, processing instructions, XML declarations, text declarations, and any white space that is at the top level of the document entity (that is, outside the document element and not inside any other markup).]

[Definition: All text that is not markup constitutes the *character data* of the document.]

The ampersand character (&) and the left angle bracket (<) may appear in their literal form only when used as markup delimiters, or within a comment, a processing instruction, or a CDATA section. If they are needed elsewhere, they must be escaped using either numeric character references or the strings "&" and "<" respectively. The right angle bracket (>) may be represented using the string ">", and must, for compatibility, be escaped using ">" or a character reference when it appears in the string "]]>" in content, when that string is not marking the end of a CDATA section.

In the content of elements, character data is any string of characters which does not contain the start-delimiter of any markup. In a CDATA section, character data is any string of characters not including the CDATA-section-close delimiter, "]]>".

To allow attribute values to contain both single and double quotes, the apostrophe or single-quote character (') may be represented as "'", and the double-quote character (") as """.

Character Data

```
[14]    CharData   ::=   [^<&]* - ([^<&]* ']]>' [^<&]*)
```

2.5 Comments

[Definition: *Comments* may appear anywhere in a document outside other markup; in addition, they may appear within the document type declaration at places allowed by the grammar. They are not part of the document's character data; an XML processor may, but need not, make it possible for an application to retrieve the text of comments. For compatibility, the string "--" (double-hyphen) must not occur within comments.] Parameter entity references are not recognized within comments.

Comments

```
[15]    Comment   ::=   '<!--' ((Char - '-') | ('-' (Char - '-
                        ')))* '-->'
```

An example of a comment:

```
<!- declarations for <head> & <body> ->
```

Note that the grammar does not allow a comment ending in --->. The following example is not well-formed.

```
<!- B+, B, or B-->
```

2.6 Processing Instructions

[Definition: *Processing instructions* (PIs) allow documents to contain instructions for applications.]

Processing Instructions

[16]	PI	::=	'<?' PITarget (S (Char* - (Char* '?>' Char*)))? '?>'
[17]	PITarget	::=	Name - (('X' | 'x') ('M' | 'm') ('L' | 'l'))

PIs are not part of the document's character data, but must be passed through to the application. The PI begins with a target (PITarget) used to identify the application to which the instruction is directed. The target names "XML", "xml", and so on are reserved for standardization in this or future versions of this specification. The XML Notation mechanism may be used for formal declaration of PI targets. Parameter entity references are not recognized within processing instructions.

2.7 CDATA Sections

[Definition: *CDATA sections* may occur anywhere character data may occur; they are used to escape blocks of text containing characters which would otherwise be recognized as markup. CDATA sections begin with the string "<![CDATA[" and end with the string "]]>":]

CDATA Sections

[18]	CDSect	::=	CDStart CData CDEnd
[19]	CDStart	::=	'<![CDATA['
[20]	CData	::=	(Char* - (Char* ']]>' Char*))
[21]	CDEnd	::=	']]>'

Within a CDATA section, only the CDEnd string is recognized as markup, so that left angle brackets and ampersands may occur in their literal form; they need not (and cannot) be escaped using "<" and "&". CDATA sections cannot nest.

An example of a CDATA section, in which "<greeting>" and "</greeting>" are recognized as character data, not markup:

```
<![CDATA[<greeting>Hello, world!</greeting>]]>
```

2.8 Prolog and Document Type Declaration

[Definition: XML documents should begin with an *XML declaration* which specifies the version of XML being used.] For example, the following is a complete XML document, well-formed but not valid:

```
<?xml version="1.0"?> <greeting>Hello, world!</greeting>
```

and so is this:

```
<greeting>Hello, world!</greeting>
```

The version number "1.0" should be used to indicate conformance to this version of this specification; it is an error for a document to use the value "1.0" if it does not conform to this version of this specification. It is the intent of the XML working group to give later versions of this specification numbers other than "1.0", but this intent does not indicate a commitment to produce any future versions of XML, nor if any are produced, to use any particular numbering scheme. Since future versions are not ruled out, this construct is provided as a means to allow the possibility of automatic version recognition, should it become necessary. Processors may signal an error if they receive documents labeled with versions they do not support.

The function of the markup in an XML document is to describe its storage and logical structure and to associate attribute-value pairs with its logical structures. XML provides a mechanism, the document type declaration, to define constraints on the logical structure and to support the use of predefined storage units. [Definition: An XML document is *valid* if it has an associated document type declaration and if the document complies with the constraints expressed in it.]

The document type declaration must appear before the first element in the document.

Prolog

[22]	prolog	::=	XMLDecl? Misc* (doctypedecl Misc*)?
[23]	XMLDecl	::=	'<?xml' VersionInfo EncodingDecl? SDDecl? S? '?>'
[24]	VersionInfo	::=	S 'version' Eq ("'" VersionNum "'" | '"' VersionNum '"')/* */
[25]	Eq	::=	S? '=' S?
[26]	VersionNum	::=	([a-zA-Z0-9_.:] | '-')+
[27]	Misc	::=	Comment | PI | S

[Definition: The XML *document type declaration* contains or points to markup declarations that provide a grammar for a class of documents. This grammar is known as a document type definition, or DTD. The document type declaration can point to an external subset (a special kind of external entity) containing markup declarations, or can contain the markup declarations directly in an internal subset, or can do both. The DTD for a document consists of both subsets taken together.]

[Definition: A *markup declaration* is an element type declaration, an attribute-list declaration, an entity declaration, or a notation declaration.] These declarations may be contained in whole or in part within parameter entities, as described in the well-formedness and validity constraints below. For further information, see "4 Physical Structures."

Document Type Definition

```
[28]   doctypedecl   ::=   '<!DOCTYPE' S Name (S ExternalID)?
                           S? ('['
                           (markupdecl | DeclSep)* ']' S?)?
                           '>'
                           [VC: Root Element Type][WFC:
                           External Subset]

[28a]  DeclSep       ::=   PEReference | S
                           [WFC: PE Between Declarations]

[29]   markupdecl    ::=   elementdecl | AttlistDecl |
                           EntityDecl | NotationDecl
                           | PI | Comment [VC: Proper
                           Declaration/PE Nesting]
                           [WFC: PEs in Internal Subset]
```

Note that it is possible to construct a well-formed document containing a doctypedecl that neither points to an external subset nor contains an internal subset.

The markup declarations may be made up in whole or in part of the replacement text of parameter entities. The productions later in this specification for individual nonterminals (elementdecl, AttlistDecl, and so on) describe the declarations *after* all the parameter entities have been included.

Parameter entity references are recognized anywhere in the DTD (internal and external subsets and external parameter entities), except in literals, processing instructions, comments, and the contents of ignored conditional sections (see "3.4 Conditional Sections"). They are also recognized in entity value literals. The use of parameter entities in the internal subset is restricted as described below.

> **Validity constraint: Root Element Type**   The *Name* in the document type declaration must match the element type of the root element.

> **Validity constraint: Proper Declaration/PE Nesting**   Parameter-entity replacement text must be properly nested with markup declarations. That is to say, if either the first character or the last character of a markup declaration (markupdecl above) is contained in the replacement text for a parameter-entity reference, both must be contained in the same replacement text.

> **Well-formedness constraint: PEs in Internal Subset**   In the internal DTD subset, parameter-entity references can occur only where markup declarations can occur, not within markup declarations. (This does not apply to references that occur in external parameter entities or to the external subset.)

> **Well-formedness constraint: External Subset**   The external subset, if any, must match the production for extSubset.

> **Well-formedness constraint: PE Between Declarations**
> The replacement text of a parameter entity reference in a DeclSep must match the production extSubsetDecl.

Like the internal subset, the external subset and any external parameter entities referenced in a DeclSep must consist of a series of complete markup declarations of the types allowed by the non-terminal symbol markupdecl, interspersed with white space or parameter-entity references. However, portions of the contents of the external subset or of these external parameter entities may conditionally be ignored by using the conditional section construct; this is not allowed in the internal subset.

External Subset

```
[30]    extSubset      ::=    TextDecl? extSubsetDecl
[31]    extSubsetDecl  ::=    ( markupdecl |
                               conditionalSect | DeclSep)*
```

The external subset and external parameter entities also differ from the internal subset in that in them, parameter-entity references are permitted *within* markup declarations, not only between markup declarations.

An example of an XML document with a document type declaration:

```
<?xml version="1.0"?>
```

```
<!DOCTYPE greeting SYSTEM "hello.dtd"><greeting>Hello,
world!</greeting>
```

The system identifier `"hello.dtd"` gives the address (a URI reference) of a DTD for the document.

The declarations can also be given locally, as in this example:

```
<?xml version="1.0" encoding="UTF-8" ?>
```

```
<!DOCTYPE greeting [
  <!ELEMENT greeting (#PCDATA)>
]>
```

```
<greeting>Hello, world!</greeting>
```

If both the external and internal subsets are used, the internal subset is considered to occur before the external subset. This has the effect that entity and attribute-list declarations in the internal subset take precedence over those in the external subset.

2.9 Standalone Document Declaration

Markup declarations can affect the content of the document, as passed from an XML processor to an application; examples are attribute defaults and entity declarations. The standalone document declaration, which may appear as a component of the XML declaration, signals whether or not there are such declarations which appear external to the document entity or in parameter entities. [Definition: An *external markup declaration* is defined as a markup declaration occurring in the external subset or in a parameter entity (external or internal, the latter being included because non-validating processors are not required to read them).]

```
Standalone Document Declaration
```

```
[32]   SDDecl   ::=   S 'standalone' Eq (("'" ('yes' | 'no')
                      "'") | ('"'
                      ('yes' | 'no') '"'))
                      [VC: Standalone Document Declaration]
```

In a standalone document declaration, the value "yes" indicates that there are no external markup declarations which affect the information passed from the XML processor to the application. The value "no" indicates that there are or may be such external markup declarations. Note that the standalone document declaration only denotes the presence of external declarations; the presence, in a document, of references to external entities, when those entities are internally declared, does not change its standalone status.

If there are no external markup declarations, the standalone document declaration has no meaning. If there are external markup declarations but there is no standalone document declaration, the value "no" is assumed.

Any XML document for which `standalone="no"` holds can be converted algorithmically to a standalone document, which may be desirable for some network delivery applications.

> **Validity constraint: Standalone Document Declaration**   The standalone document declaration must have the value "no" if any external markup declarations contain declarations of:
>
> ▶ attributes with default values, if elements to which these attributes apply appear in the document without specifications of values for these attributes, or
>
> ▶ entities (other than `amp`, `lt`, `gt`, `apos`, `quot`), if references to those entities appear in the document, or
>
> ▶ attributes with values subject to normalization, where the attribute appears in the document with a value which will change as a result of normalization, or
>
> ▶ element types with element content, if white space occurs directly within any instance of those types.

An example XML declaration with a standalone document declaration:

```
<?xml version="1.0" standalone='yes'?>
```

2.10 White Space Handling

In editing XML documents, it is often convenient to use "white space" (spaces, tabs, and blank lines) to set apart the markup for greater readability. Such white space is typically not intended for inclusion in the delivered version of the document. On the other hand, "significant" white space that should be preserved in the delivered version is common, for example in poetry and source code.

An XML processor must always pass all characters in a document that are not markup through to the application. A validating XML processor must also inform the application which of these characters constitute white space appearing in element content.

A special attribute named xml:space may be attached to an element to signal an intention that in that element, white space should be preserved by applications. In valid documents, this attribute, like any other, must be declared if it is used. When declared, it must be given as an enumerated type whose values are one or both of "default" and "preserve". For example:

```
<!ATTLIST poem  xml:space (default|preserve) 'preserve'>
<!- ->
<!ATTLIST pre xml:space (preserve) #FIXED 'preserve'>
```

The value "default" signals that applications' default white-space processing modes are acceptable for this element; the value "preserve" indicates the intent that applications preserve all the white space. This declared intent is considered to apply to all elements within the content of the element where it is specified, unless overridden with another instance of the xml:space attribute.

The root element of any document is considered to have signaled no intentions as regards application space handling, unless it provides a value for this attribute or the attribute is declared with a default value.

2.11 End-of-Line Handling

XML parsed entities are often stored in computer files which, for editing convenience, are organized into lines. These lines are typically separated by some combination of the characters carriage-return (#xD) and line-feed (#xA).

To simplify the tasks of applications, the characters passed to an application by the XML processor must be as if the XML processor normalized all line breaks in external parsed entities (including the document entity) on input, before parsing, by translating both the two-character sequence #xD #xA and any #xD that is not followed by #xA to a single #xA character.

2.12 Language Identification

In document processing, it is often useful to identify the natural or formal language in which the content is written. A special attribute named xml:lang may be inserted in documents to specify the language used in the contents and attribute values of any element in an XML document. In valid documents, this attribute, like any other, must be declared if it is used. The values of the attribute are language identifiers as defined by IETF RFC 1766, *Tags for the Identification of Languages*, or its successor on the IETF Standards Track.

NOTE

IETF RFC 1766 tags are constructed from two-letter language codes as defined by ISO 639, from two-letter country codes as defined by ISO 3166, or from language identifiers registered with the Internet Assigned Numbers Authority (IANA-LANG-CODES). It is expected that the successor to IETF RFC 1766 will introduce three-letter language codes for languages not presently covered by ISO 639.

NOTE

(Productions 33 through 38 have been removed.)

For example:

```
<p xml:lang="en">The quick brown fox jumps over the lazy
dog.</p>
<p xml:lang="en-GB">What colour is it?</p>
<p xml:lang="en-US">What color is it?</p>
<sp who="Faust" desc='leise' xml:lang="de">
    <l>Habe nun, ach! Philosophie,</l>
    <l>Juristerei, und Medizin</l>
    <l>und leider auch Theologie</l>
    <l>durchaus studiert mit hei em Bem h'n.</l>
</sp>
```

The intent declared with xml:lang is considered to apply to all attributes and content of the element where it is specified, unless overridden with an instance of xml:lang on another element within that content.

A simple declaration for xml:lang might take the form

```
xml:lang NMTOKEN #IMPLIED
```

but specific default values may also be given, if appropriate. In a collection of French poems for English students, with glosses and notes in English, the xml:lang attribute might be declared this way:

```
<!ATTLIST poem   xml:lang NMTOKEN 'fr'>
<!ATTLIST gloss  xml:lang NMTOKEN 'en'>
<!ATTLIST note   xml:lang NMTOKEN 'en'>
```

3 Logical Structures

[Definition: Each XML document contains one or more *elements*, the boundaries of which are either delimited by start-tags and end-tags, or, for empty elements, by an empty-element tag. Each element has a type, identified by name, sometimes called its "generic identifier" (GI), and may have a set of attribute specifications.] Each attribute specification has a name and a value.

Element

```
[39]    element  ::=  EmptyElemTag | STag content ETag
                      [WFC: Element Type Match]
                      [VC: Element Valid]
```

This specification does not constrain the semantics, use, or (beyond syntax) names of the element types and attributes, except that names beginning with a match to (('X'|'x')('M'|'m')('L'|'l')) are reserved for standardization in this or future versions of this specification.

> **Well-formedness constraint: Element Type Match**   The *Name* in an element's end-tag must match the element type in the start-tag.

> **Validity constraint: Element Valid**   An element is valid if there is a declaration matching elementdecl where the *Name* matches the element type, and one of the following holds:

1. The declaration matches EMPTY and the element has no content.

    1. The declaration matches children and the sequence of child elements belongs to the language generated by the regular expression in the content model, with optional white space (characters matching 1. the nonterminal S) between the start-tag and the first child element, between child elements, or between the last child element and the end-tag. Note that a CDATA section containing only white space does not match the nonterminal S, and hence cannot appear in these positions.

    2. The declaration matches Mixed and the content consists of character data and child elements whose types match names in the content model.

    3. The declaration matches ANY, and the types of any child elements have been declared.

3.1 Start-Tags, End-Tags, and Empty-Element Tags

[Definition: The beginning of every non-empty XML element is marked by a *start-tag*.]

```
Start-tag
[40]    STag      ::=   '<' Name (S Attribute)* S? '>'
                        [WFC: Unique Att Spec]
[41]    Attribute  ::=   Name Eq AttValue
                        [VC: Attribute Value Type]
                        [WFC: No External Entity References]
                        [WFC: No < in Attribute Values]
```

The *Name* in the start- and end-tags gives the element's type. [Definition: The *Name-AttValue* pairs are referred to as the *attribute specifications* of the element], [Definition: with the *Name* in each pair referred to as the *attribute name*] and [Definition: the content of the *AttValue* (the text between the ' or " delimiters) as the *attribute value.*] Note that the order of attribute specifications in a start-tag or empty-element tag is not significant.

> **Well-formedness constraint: Unique Att Spec** No attribute name may appear more than once in the same start-tag or empty-element tag.

> **Validity constraint: Attribute Value Type** The attribute must have been declared; the value must be of the type declared for it. (For attribute types, see "3.3 Attribute-List Declarations.")

> **Well-formedness constraint: No External Entity References** Attribute values cannot contain direct or indirect entity references to external entities.

> **Well-formedness constraint: No < in Attribute Values** The replacement text of any entity referred to directly or indirectly in an attribute value must not contain a <.

An example of a start-tag:

```
<termdef id="dt-dog" term="dog">
```

[Definition: The end of every element that begins with a start-tag must be marked by an *end-tag* containing a name that echoes the element's type as given in the start-tag:]

```
End-tag
[42]    ETag    ::=    '</' Name S? '>'
```

An example of an end-tag:

```
</termdef>
```

[Definition: The text between the start-tag and end-tag is called the element's *content*:]

Content of Elements

```
[43]    content   ::=   CharData? ((element | Reference |
                        CDSect | PI | Comment) CharData?)*
```

[Definition: An element with no content is said to be *empty*.] The representation of an empty element is either a start-tag immediately followed by an end-tag, or an empty-element tag. [Definition: An *empty-element tag* takes a special form:]

Tags for Empty Elements

```
[44]    EmptyElemTag  ::=   '<' Name (S Attribute)* S? '/>'
                            [WFC: Unique Att Spec]
```

Empty-element tags may be used for any element which has no content, whether or not it is declared using the keyword EMPTY. For interoperability, the empty-element tag should be used, and should only be used, for elements which are declared EMPTY.

Examples of empty elements:

```
<IMG align="left" src="http://www.w3.org/Icons/WWW/w3c_home"
/>
<br></br>
<br/>
```

3.2 Element Type Declarations

The element structure of an XML document may, for validation purposes, be constrained using element type and attribute-list declarations. An element type declaration constrains the element's content.

Element type declarations often constrain which element types can appear as children of the element. At user option, an XML processor may issue a warning when a declaration mentions an element type for which no declaration is provided, but this is not an error.

[Definition: An *element type declaration* takes the form:]

Element Type Declaration

```
[45]    elementdecl   ::=   '<!ELEMENT' S Name S contentspec
                            S? '>'

                            [VC: Unique Element Type
                            Declaration]

[46]    contentspec   ::=   'EMPTY' | 'ANY' | Mixed | children
```

where the *Name* gives the element type being declared.

Validity constraint: Unique Element Type Declaration   No element type may be declared more than once.

Examples of element type declarations:

```
<!ELEMENT br EMPTY>
<!ELEMENT p (#PCDATA|emph)* >
<!ELEMENT %name.para; %content.para; >
<!ELEMENT container ANY>
```

3.2.1 Element Content

[Definition: An element type has *element content* when elements of that type must contain only child elements (no character data), optionally separated by white space (characters matching the nonterminal S).] [Definition: In this case, the constraint includes a *content model*, a simple grammar governing the allowed types of the child elements and the order in which they are allowed to appear.] The grammar is built on content particles (cps), which consist of names, choice lists of content particles, or sequence lists of content particles:

Element-content Models

[47]	children	::=	(choice | seq) ('?' | '*' | '+')?
[48]	cp	::=	(Name | choice | seq) ('?' | '*' | '+')?
[49]	choice	::=	'(' S? cp (S? '|' S? cp)+ S? ')'
			[VC: Proper Group/PE Nesting]
[50]	seq	::=	'(' S? cp (S? ',' S? cp)* S? ')'
			[VC: Proper Group/PE Nesting]

where each *Name* is the type of an element which may appear as a child. Any content particle in a choice list may appear in the element content at the location where the choice list appears in the grammar; content particles occurring in a sequence list must each appear in the element content in the order given in the list. The optional character following a name or list governs whether the element or the content particles in the list may occur one or more (+), zero or more (*), or zero or one times (?). The absence of such an operator means that the element or content particle must appear exactly once. This syntax and meaning are identical to those used in the productions in this specification.

The content of an element matches a content model if and only if it is possible to trace out a path through the content model, obeying the sequence, choice, and repetition operators and matching each element in the content against an element type in the content model. For compatibility, it is an error if an element in the document can match more than one occurrence of an element type in the content model. For more information, see "E Deterministic Content Models."

> **Validity constraint: Proper Group/PE Nesting**   Parameter-entity replacement text must be properly nested with parenthesized groups. That is to say, if either of the opening or closing parentheses in a `choice`, `seq`, or `Mixed` construct is contained in the replacement text for a parameter entity, both must be contained in the same replacement text.

> For interoperability, if a parameter-entity reference appears in a `choice`, `seq`, or `Mixed` construct, its replacement text should contain at least one non-blank character, and neither the first nor last non-blank character of the replacement text should be a connector (| or ,).

Examples of element-content models:

```
<!ELEMENT spec (front, body, back?)>
<!ELEMENT div1 (head, (p | list | note)*, div2*)>
<!ELEMENT dictionary-body (%div.mix; | %dict.mix;)*>
```

3.2.2 Mixed Content

[Definition: An element type has *mixed content* when elements of that type may contain character data, optionally interspersed with child elements.] In this case, the types of the child elements may be constrained, but not their order or their number of occurrences:

Mixed-content Declaration

```
[51]    Mixed    ::=    '(' S? '#PCDATA' (S? '|' S? Name)* S?
                        ')*'
                   | '(' S? '#PCDATA' S? ')'
                   [VC: Proper Group/PE Nesting]
                   [VC: No Duplicate Types]
```

where the *Name*s give the types of elements that may appear as children. The keyword #PCDATA derives historically from the term "parsed character data."

> **Validity constraint: No Duplicate Types**   The same name must not appear more than once in a single mixed-content declaration.

Examples of mixed content declarations:

```
<!ELEMENT p (#PCDATA|a|ul|b|i|em)*>
```

```
<!ELEMENT p (#PCDATA | %font; | %phrase; | %special; |
%form;)* >
<!ELEMENT b (#PCDATA)>
```

3.3 Attribute-List Declarations

Attributes are used to associate name-value pairs with elements. Attribute specifications may appear only within start-tags and empty-element tags; thus, the productions used to recognize them appear in "3.1 Start-Tags, End-Tags, and Empty-Element Tags." Attribute-list declarations may be used:

- ▶ To define the set of attributes pertaining to a given element type.

- ▶ To establish type constraints for these attributes.

- ▶ To provide default values for attributes.

[Definition: *Attribute-list declarations* specify the name, data type, and default value (if any) of each attribute associated with a given element type:]

Attribute-list Declaration

```
[52]   AttlistDecl   ::=   '<!ATTLIST' S Name AttDef* S? '>'
[53]   AttDef        ::=   S Name S AttType S DefaultDecl
```

The *Name* in the `AttlistDecl` rule is the type of an element. At user option, an XML processor may issue a warning if attributes are declared for an element type not itself declared, but this is not an error. The *Name* in the `AttDef` rule is the name of the attribute.

When more than one `AttlistDecl` is provided for a given element type, the contents of all those provided are merged. When more than one definition is provided for the same attribute of a given element type, the first declaration is binding and later declarations are ignored. For interoperability, writers of DTDs may choose to provide at most one attribute-list declaration for a given element type, at most one attribute definition for a given attribute name in an attribute-list declaration, and at least one attribute definition in each attribute-list declaration. For interoperability, an XML processor may at user option issue a warning when more than one attribute-list declaration is provided for a given element type, or more than one attribute definition is provided for a given attribute, but this is not an error.

3.3.1 Attribute Types   XML attribute types are of three kinds: a string type, a set of tokenized types, and enumerated types. The string type may take any literal string as a value; the tokenized types have varying lexical and semantic constraints. The validity constraints noted in the grammar are applied after the attribute value has been normalized as described in "3.3 Attribute-List Declarations."

Attribute Types

```
[54]    AttType        ::=    StringType | TokenizedType |
                              EnumeratedType

[55]    StringType     ::=    'CDATA'

[56]    TokenizedType  ::=    'ID'                    [VC: ID]
                                                      [VC: One ID
➡per Element Type]

                                                      [VC: ID
➡Attribute Default]

                              | 'IDREF' | 'IDREFS'        [VC:
➡IDREF]

                              | 'ENTITY' | 'ENTITIES'     [VC:
➡Entity Name]

                              | 'NMTOKEN' | 'NMTOKENS'    [VC:
➡Name Token]
```

Validity constraint: ID   Values of type ID must match the Name production. A name must not appear more than once in an XML document as a value of this type; i.e., ID values must uniquely identify the elements which bear them.

Validity constraint: One ID per Element Type   No element type may have more than one ID attribute specified.

Validity constraint: ID Attribute Default   An ID attribute must have a declared default of #IMPLIED or #REQUIRED.

Validity constraint: IDREF   Values of type IDREF must match the Name production, and values of type IDREFS must match Names; each Name must match the value of an ID attribute on some element in the XML document; i.e. IDREF values must match the value of some ID attribute.

Validity constraint: Entity Name   Values of type ENTITY must match the Name production, values of type ENTITIES must match Names; each Name must match the name of an unparsed entity declared in the DTD.

Validity constraint: Name Token   Values of type NMTOKEN must match the Nmtoken production; values of type NMTOKENS must match Nmtokens.

[Definition: *Enumerated attributes* can take one of a list of values provided in the declaration]. There are two kinds of enumerated types:

Enumerated Attribute Types

[57]	EnumeratedType	::=	NotationType | Enumeration
[58]	NotationType	::=	'NOTATION' S '(' S? Name (S? '|' S? Name)* S? ')'
			[VC: Notation Attributes]
			[VC: One Notation Per Element Type]
			[VC: No Notation on Empty Element]
[59]	Enumeration	::=	'(' S? Nmtoken (S? '|' S? Nmtoken)* S? ')'
			[VC: Enumeration]

A NOTATION attribute identifies a notation, declared in the DTD with associated system and/or public identifiers, to be used in interpreting the element to which the attribute is attached.

Validity constraint: Notation Attributes   Values of this type must match one of the notation names included in the declaration; all notation names in the declaration must be declared.

Validity constraint: One Notation Per Element Type   No element type may have more than one NOTATION attribute specified.

Validity constraint: No Notation on Empty Element   For compatibility, an attribute of type NOTATION must not be declared on an element declared EMPTY.

Validity constraint: Enumeration   Values of this type must match one of the Nmtoken tokens in the declaration.

For interoperability, the same Nmtoken should not occur more than once in the enumerated attribute types of a single element type.

3.3.2 Attribute Defaults   An attribute declaration provides information on whether the attribute's presence is required, and if not, how an XML processor should react if a declared attribute is absent in a document.

Attribute Defaults

[60]	DefaultDecl	::=	'#REQUIRED' | '#IMPLIED' | (('#FIXED' S)? AttValue)
			[VC: Required Attribute]
			[VC: Attribute Default Legal]

```
                         [WFC: No < in Attribute Values]
                         [VC: Fixed Attribute Default]
```

In an attribute declaration, #REQUIRED means that the attribute must always be provided, #IMPLIED that no default value is provided. [Definition: If the declaration is neither #REQUIRED nor #IMPLIED, then the *AttValue* value contains the declared *default* value; the #FIXED keyword states that the attribute must always have the default value. If a default value is declared, when an XML processor encounters an omitted attribute, it is to behave as though the attribute were present with the declared default value.]

> **Validity constraint: Required Attribute**   If the default declaration is the keyword #REQUIRED, then the attribute must be specified for all elements of the type in the attribute-list declaration.

> **Validity constraint: Attribute Default Legal**   The declared default value must meet the lexical constraints of the declared attribute type.

> **Validity constraint: Fixed Attribute Default**   If an attribute has a default value declared with the #FIXED keyword, instances of that attribute must match the default value.

Examples of attribute-list declarations:

```
<!ATTLIST termdef
          id      ID       #REQUIRED
          name    CDATA    #IMPLIED>
<!ATTLIST list
          type    (bullets|ordered|glossary)  "ordered">
<!ATTLIST form
          method  CDATA    #FIXED "POST">
```

3.3.3 Attribute-Value Normalization   Before the value of an attribute is passed to the application or checked for validity, the XML processor must normalize the attribute value by applying the algorithm below, or by using some other method such that the value passed to the application is the same as that produced by the algorithm.

1. All line breaks must have been normalized on input to #xA as described in "2.11 End-of-Line Handling," so that the rest of this algorithm operates on text normalized in this way.

2. Begin with a normalized value consisting of the empty string.

3. For each character, entity reference, or character reference in the unnormalized attribute value, beginning with the first and continuing to the last, do the following:

   ▶ For a character reference, append the referenced character to the normalized value.

   ▶ For an entity reference, recursively apply step 3 of this algorithm to the replacement text of the entity.

   ▶ For a white space character (#x20, #xD, #xA, #x9), append a space character (#x20) to the normalized value.

   ▶ For another character, append the character to the normalized value.

If the attribute type is not CDATA, then the XML processor must further process the normalized attribute value by discarding any leading and trailing space (#x20) characters, and by replacing sequences of space (#x20) characters by a single space (#x20) character.

Note that if the unnormalized attribute value contains a character reference to a white space character other than space (#x20), the normalized value contains the referenced character itself (#xD, #xA or #x9). This contrasts with the case where the unnormalized value contains a white space character (not a reference), which is replaced with a space character (#x20) in the normalized value and also contrasts with the case where the unnormalized value contains an entity reference whose replacement text contains a white space character; being recursively processed, the white space character is replaced with a space character (#x20) in the normalized value.

All attributes for which no declaration has been read should be treated by a non-validating processor as if declared CDATA.

Following are examples of attribute normalization. Given the following declarations:

```
<!ENTITY d "&#xD;">
<!ENTITY a "&#xA;">
<!ENTITY da "&#xD;&#xA;">
```

the attribute specifications in the left column below would be normalized to the character sequences of the middle column if the attribute *a* is declared NMTOKENS and to those of the right columns if *a* is declared CDATA.

Note that the last example is invalid (but well-formed) if *a* is declared to be of type NMTOKENS.

Attribute Specification	*a* is NMTOKENS	*a* is CDATA
a=" z xyz"	x y z	#x20 #x20 x y z
a="&d;&d;A&a;&a; B&da;"	A #x20 B	#x20 #x20 A #x20 #x20 B #x20 #x20
a="   A
& #xa;B
"	#xD #xD A #xA #xA B #xD #xA	#xD #xD A #xA #xA B #xD #xD

3.4 Conditional Sections

[Definition: *Conditional sections* are portions of the document type declaration external subset which are included in, or excluded from, the logical structure of the DTD based on the keyword which governs them.]

```
Conditional Section
[61]  conditionalSect    ::=  includeSect | ignoreSect
[62]  includeSect        ::=  '<![' S? 'INCLUDE' S? '['
                               extSubsetDecl ']]>'
                               [VC: Proper Conditional
                               Section/PE Nesting]
[63]  ignoreSect         ::=  '<![' S? 'IGNORE' S? '['
                               ignoreSectContents*
                               ']]>'
                               [VC: Proper Conditional
                               Section/PE Nesting]
[64]  ignoreSectContents ::=  Ignore
                               ('<![' ignoreSectContents
                               ']]>' Ignore)*
[65]  Ignore             ::=  Char* - (Char* ('<![' |
                               ']]>') Char*)
```

Validity constraint: Proper Conditional Section/PE Nesting
If any of the "<![", "[", or "]]>" of a conditional section is contained in the replacement text for a parameter-entity reference, all of them must be contained in the same replacement text.

Like the internal and external DTD subsets, a conditional section may contain one or more complete declarations, comments, processing instructions, or nested conditional sections, intermingled with white space.

If the keyword of the conditional section is INCLUDE, then the contents of the conditional section are part of the DTD. If the keyword of the conditional section is IGNORE, then the contents of the conditional section are not logically part of the DTD. If a conditional section with a keyword of INCLUDE occurs within a larger conditional section with a keyword of IGNORE, both the outer and the inner conditional sections are ignored. The contents of an ignored conditional section are parsed by ignoring all characters after the "[" following the keyword, except conditional section starts "<![" and ends "]]>", until the matching conditional section end is found. Parameter entity references are not recognized in this process.

If the keyword of the conditional section is a parameter-entity reference, the parameter entity must be replaced by its content before the processor decides whether to include or ignore the conditional section.

An example:

```
<!ENTITY % draft 'INCLUDE' >
<!ENTITY % final 'IGNORE' >


<![%draft;[
<!ELEMENT book (comments*, title, body, supplements?)>
]]>
<![%final;[
<!ELEMENT book (title, body, supplements?)>
]]>
```

4 Physical Structures

[Definition: An XML document may consist of one or many storage units. These are called *entities*; they all have *content* and are all (except for the document entity and the external DTD subset) identified by *entity name*.] Each XML document has one entity called the document entity, which serves as the starting point for the XML processor and may contain the whole document.

Entities may be either parsed or unparsed. [Definition: A *parsed entity's* contents are referred to as its replacement text; this text is considered an integral part of the document.]

[Definition: An *unparsed entity* is a resource whose contents may or may not be text, and if text, may be other than XML. Each unparsed entity has an associated notation, identified by name. Beyond a requirement that an XML processor make the identifiers for the entity and notation available to the application, XML places no constraints on the contents of unparsed entities.]

Parsed entities are invoked by name using entity references; unparsed entities by name, given in the value of ENTITY or ENTITIES attributes.

[Definition: *General entities* are entities for use within the document content. In this specification, general entities are sometimes referred to with the unqualified term entity when this leads to no ambiguity.] [Definition: *Parameter entities* are parsed entities for use within the DTD.] These two types of entities use different forms of reference and are recognized in different contexts. Furthermore, they occupy different namespaces; a parameter entity and a general entity with the same name are two distinct entities.

4.1 Character and Entity References

[Definition: A *character reference* refers to a specific character in the ISO/IEC 10646 character set, for example one not directly accessible from available input devices.]

Character Reference

```
[66]   CharRef   ::=   '&#' [0-9]+ ';' | '&#x' [0-9a-fA-F]+
                       ';'

                       [WFC: Legal Character]
```

> **Well-formedness constraint: Legal Character**   Characters referred to using character references must match the production for Char.

If the character reference begins with "&#x", the digits and letters up to the terminating ; provide a hexadecimal representation of the character's code point in ISO/IEC 10646. If it begins just with "&#", the digits up to the terminating ; provide a decimal representation of the character's code point.

[Definition: An *entity reference* refers to the content of a named entity.] [Definition: References to parsed general entities use ampersand (&) and semicolon (;) as delimiters.] [Definition: *Parameter-entity references* use percent-sign (%) and semicolon (;) as delimiters.]

Entity Reference

```
[67]   Reference   ::=   EntityRef | CharRef
```

```
[68]    EntityRef.    ::=    '&' Name ';'
                             [WFC: Entity Declared]
                             [VC: Entity Declared]
                             [WFC: Parsed Entity]
                             [WFC: No Recursion]
[69]    PEReference   ::=    '%' Name ';'
                             [VC: Entity Declared]
                             [WFC: No Recursion]
                             [WFC: In DTD]
```

Well-formedness constraint: Entity Declared   In a document without any DTD, a document with only an internal DTD subset which contains no parameter entity references, or a document with "standalone='yes'", for an entity reference that does not occur within the external subset or a parameter entity, the *Name* given in the entity reference must match that in an entity declaration that does not occur within the external subset or a parameter entity, except that well-formed documents need not declare any of the following entities: amp, lt, gt, apos, quot. The declaration of a general entity must precede any reference to it which appears in a default value in an attribute-list declaration.

Note that if entities are declared in the external subset or in external parameter entities, a non-validating processor is not obligated to read and process their declarations; for such documents, the rule that an entity must be declared is a well-formedness constraint only if standalone='yes'.

Validity constraint: Entity Declared   In a document with an external subset or external parameter entities with "standalone='no'", the *Name* given in the entity reference must match that in an entity declaration. For interoperability, valid documents should declare the entities amp, lt, gt, apos, quot, in the form specified in "4.6 Predefined Entities." The declaration of a parameter entity must precede any reference to it. Similarly, the declaration of a general entity must precede any attribute-list declaration containing a default value with a direct or indirect reference to that general entity.

Well-formedness constraint: Parsed Entity   An entity reference must not contain the name of an unparsed entity. Unparsed entities may be referred to only in attribute values declared to be of type ENTITY or ENTITIES.

Well-formedness constraint: No Recursion   A parsed entity must not contain a recursive reference to itself, either directly or indirectly.

Well-formedness constraint: In DTD   Parameter-entity references may only appear in the DTD.

Examples of character and entity references:

```
Type <key>less-than</key> (&#x3C;) to save options.
```

```
This document was prepared on &docdate; and is classified
&security-level;.
```

Example of a parameter-entity reference:

```
<!- declare the parameter entity "ISOLat2"... ->
<!ENTITY % ISOLat2
         SYSTEM "http://www.xml.com/iso/isolat2-xml.entities"
>
<!- ... now reference it. ->
%ISOLat2;
```

4.2 Entity Declarations

[Definition: Entities are declared thus:]

Entity Declaration

[70]	EntityDecl	::=	GEDecl | PEDecl
[71]	GEDecl	::=	'<!ENTITY' S Name S EntityDef S? '>'
[72]	PEDecl	::=	'<!ENTITY' S '%' S Name S PEDef S? '>'
[73]	EntityDef	::=	EntityValue | (ExternalID NDataDecl?)
[74]	PEDef	::=	EntityValue | ExternalID

The *Name* identifies the entity in an entity reference or, in the case of an unparsed entity, in the value of an ENTITY or ENTITIES attribute. If the same entity is declared more than once, the first declaration encountered is binding; at user option, an XML processor may issue a warning if entities are declared multiple times.

4.2.1 Internal Entities   [Definition: If the entity definition is an `Entity-Value`, the defined entity is called an *internal entity*. There is no separate physical storage object, and the content of the entity is given in the declaration.] Note that some processing of entity and character references in the literal entity value may be required to produce the correct replacement text: see "4.5 Construction of Internal Entity Replacement Text."

An internal entity is a parsed entity.

Example of an internal entity declaration:

```
<!ENTITY Pub-Status "This is a pre-release of the specifica-
tion.">
```

4.2.2 External Entities   [Definition: If the entity is not internal, it is an *external entity*, declared as follows:]

```
External Entity Declaration
[75]   ExternalID   ::=   'SYSTEM' S SystemLiteral
                          | 'PUBLIC' S PubidLiteral S
                          SystemLiteral
[76]   NDataDecl    ::=   S 'NDATA' S Name      [VC: Notation
                          Declared]
```

If the `NDataDecl` is present, this is a general unparsed entity; otherwise it is a parsed entity.

> **Validity constraint: Notation Declared**   The *Name* must match the declared name of a notation.

[Definition: The `SystemLiteral` is called the entity's *system identifier*. It is a URI reference (as defined in IETF RFC 2396, updated by IETF RFC 2732), meant to be dereferenced to obtain input for the XML processor to construct the entity's replacement text.] It is an error for a fragment identifier (beginning with a # character) to be part of a system identifier. Unless otherwise provided by information outside the scope of this specification (e.g. a special XML element type defined by a particular DTD, or a processing instruction defined by a particular application specification), relative URIs are relative to the location of the resource within which the entity declaration occurs. A URI might thus be relative to the document entity, to the entity containing the external DTD subset, or to some other external parameter entity.

URI references require encoding and escaping of certain characters. The disallowed characters include all non-ASCII characters, plus the excluded characters listed in Section 2.4 of IETF RFC 2396, except for the number sign (#) and percent sign (%) characters and the square bracket characters re-allowed in IETF RFC 2732. Disallowed characters must be escaped as follows:

1. Each disallowed character is converted to UTF-8 (IETF RFC 2279) as one or more bytes.

2. Any octets corresponding to a disallowed character are escaped with the URI escaping mechanism (that is, converted to %HH, where *HH* is the hexadecimal notation of the byte value).

3. The original character is replaced by the resulting character sequence.

[Definition: In addition to a system identifier, an external identifier may include a *public identifier*.] An XML processor attempting to retrieve the entity's content may use the public identifier to try to generate an alternative URI reference. If the processor is unable to do so, it must use the URI reference specified in the system literal. Before a match is attempted, all strings of white space in the public identifier must be normalized to single space characters (#x20), and leading and trailing white space must be removed.

Examples of external entity declarations:

```
<!ENTITY open-hatch
        SYSTEM
"http://www.textuality.com/boilerplate/OpenHatch.xml">
<!ENTITY open-hatch
        PUBLIC "-//Textuality//TEXT Standard open-hatch
boilerplate//EN"

"http://www.textuality.com/boilerplate/OpenHatch.xml">
<!ENTITY hatch-pic
        SYSTEM "../grafix/OpenHatch.gif"
        NDATA gif >
```

4.3 Parsed Entities

4.3.1 The Text Declaration
External parsed entities should each begin with a *text declaration*.

Text Declaration

```
[77]    TextDecl    ::=    '<?xml' VersionInfo? EncodingDecl S?
'?>'
```

The text declaration must be provided literally, not by reference to a parsed entity. No text declaration may appear at any position other than the beginning of an external parsed entity. The text declaration in an external parsed entity is not considered part of its replacement text.

4.3.2 Well-Formed Parsed Entities   The document entity is well-formed if it matches the production labeled document. An external general parsed entity is well-formed if it matches the production labeled extParsedEnt. All external parameter entities are well-formed by definition.

```
Well-Formed External Parsed Entity
[78]    extParsedEnt   ::=   TextDecl? content
```

An internal general parsed entity is well-formed if its replacement text matches the production labeled content. All internal parameter entities are well-formed by definition.

A consequence of well-formedness in entities is that the logical and physical structures in an XML document are properly nested; no start-tag, end-tag, empty-element tag, element, comment, processing instruction, character reference, or entity reference can begin in one entity and end in another.

4.3.3 Character Encoding in Entities   Each external parsed entity in an XML document may use a different encoding for its characters. All XML processors must be able to read entities in both the UTF-8 and UTF-16 encodings. The terms "UTF-8" and "UTF-16" in this specification do not apply to character encodings with any other labels, even if the encodings or labels are very similar to UTF-8 or UTF-16.

Entities encoded in UTF-16 must begin with the Byte Order Mark described by Annex F of ISO/IEC 10646, Annex H of ISO/IEC 10646-2000, section 2.4 of Unicode, and section 2.7 of Unicode3 (the ZERO WIDTH NO-BREAK SPACE character, #xFEFF). This is an encoding signature, not part of either the markup or the character data of the XML document. XML processors must be able to use this character to differentiate between UTF-8 and UTF-16 encoded documents.

Although an XML processor is required to read only entities in the UTF-8 and UTF-16 encodings, it is recognized that other encodings are used around the world, and it may be desired for XML processors to read entities that use them. In the absence of external character encoding information (such as MIME headers), parsed entities which are stored in an encoding other than UTF-8 or UTF-16 must begin with a text declaration (see "4.3.1 The Text Declaration") containing an encoding declaration:

Encoding Declaration

```
[80]   EncodingDecl  ::=  S 'encoding' Eq ('"' EncName '"' |
                          "'" EncName "'" )

[81]   EncName       ::=  [A-Za-z] ([A-Za-z0-9._] | '-')
                          */* Encoding name contains only
Latin characters */
```

In the document entity, the encoding declaration is part of the XML declaration. The EncName is the name of the encoding used.

In an encoding declaration, the values "UTF-8", "UTF-16", "ISO-10646-UCS-2", and "ISO-10646-UCS-4" should be used for the various encodings and transformations of Unicode / ISO/IEC 10646, the values "ISO-8859-1", "ISO-8859-2",... "ISO-8859-*n*" (where *n* is the part number) should be used for the parts of ISO 8859, and the values "ISO-2022-JP", "Shift_JIS", and "EUC-JP" should be used for the various encoded forms of JIS X-0208-1997. It is recommended that character encodings registered (as charsets) with the Internet Assigned Numbers Authority (IANA-CHARSETS), other than those just listed, be referred to using their registered names; other encodings should use names starting with an "x-" prefix. XML processors should match character encoding names in a case-insensitive way and should either interpret an IANA-registered name as the encoding registered at IANA for that name or treat it as unknown (processors are, of course, not required to support all IANA-registered encodings).

In the absence of information provided by an external transport protocol (e.g. HTTP or MIME), it is an error for an entity including an encoding declaration to be presented to the XML processor in an encoding other than that named in the declaration, or for an entity which begins with neither a Byte Order Mark nor an encoding declaration to use an encoding other than UTF-8. Note that since ASCII is a subset of UTF-8, ordinary ASCII entities do not strictly need an encoding declaration.

It is a fatal error for a TextDecl to occur other than at the beginning of an external entity.

It is a fatal error when an XML processor encounters an entity with an encoding that it is unable to process. It is a fatal error if an XML entity is determined (via default, encoding declaration, or higher-level protocol) to be in a certain encoding but contains octet sequences that are not legal in that encoding. It is also a fatal error if an XML entity contains no encoding declaration and its content is not legal UTF-8 or UTF-16.

Examples of text declarations containing encoding declarations:

```
<?xml encoding='UTF-8'?>
<?xml encoding='EUC-JP'?>
```

4.4 XML Processor Treatment of Entities and References

The table below summarizes the contexts in which character references, entity references, and invocations of unparsed entities might appear and the required behavior of an XML processor in each case. The labels in the leftmost column describe the recognition context:

		Entity Type			Character
	Parameter	Internal General	External Parsed General	Unparsed	
Reference in Content	Not recognized	Included	Included if validating	Forbidden	Included
Reference in Attribute Value	Not recognized	Included in literal	Forbidden	Forbidden	Included
Occurs as Attribute Value	Not recognized	Forbidden	Forbidden	Notify	Not recognized
Reference in Entity Value	Included in literal	Bypassed	Bypassed	Forbidden	Included
Reference in DTD	Included as PE	Forbidden	Forbidden	Forbidden	Forbidden

Reference in Content   as a reference anywhere after the start-tag and before the end-tag of an element; corresponds to the nonterminal content.

Reference in Attribute Value   as a reference within either the value of an attribute in a start-tag, or a default value in an attribute declaration; corresponds to the nonterminal AttValue.

Occurs as Attribute Value   as a *Name*, not a reference, appearing either as the value of an attribute which has been declared as type ENTITY, or as one of the space-separated tokens in the value of an attribute which has been declared as type ENTITIES.

Reference in Entity Value   as a reference within a parameter or internal entity's literal entity value in the entity's declaration; corresponds to the nonterminal EntityValue.

Reference in DTD   as a reference within either the internal or external subsets of the DTD, but outside of an `EntityValue`, `AttValue`, `PI`, `Comment`, `SystemLiteral`, `PubidLiteral`, or the contents of an ignored conditional section (see "3.4 Conditional Sections").

4.4.1 Not Recognized

Outside the DTD, the % character has no special significance; thus, what would be parameter entity references in the DTD are not recognized as markup in content. Similarly, the names of unparsed entities are not recognized except when they appear in the value of an appropriately declared attribute.

4.4.2 Included

[Definition: An entity is *included* when its replacement text is retrieved and processed, in place of the reference itself, as though it were part of the document at the location the reference was recognized.] The replacement text may contain both character data and (except for parameter entities) markup, which must be recognized in the usual way. (The string "`AT&amp;T;`" expands to "`AT&T;`" and the remaining ampersand is not recognized as an entity-reference delimiter.) A character reference is *included* when the indicated character is processed in place of the reference itself.

4.4.3 Included If Validating

When an XML processor recognizes a reference to a parsed entity, in order to validate the document, the processor must include its replacement text. If the entity is external, and the processor is not attempting to validate the XML document, the processor may, but need not, include the entity's replacement text. If a non-validating processor does not include the replacement text, it must inform the application that it recognized, but did not read, the entity.

This rule is based on the recognition that the automatic inclusion provided by the SGML and XML entity mechanism, primarily designed to support modularity in authoring, is not necessarily appropriate for other applications, in particular document browsing. Browsers, for example, when encountering an external parsed entity reference, might choose to provide a visual indication of the entity's presence and retrieve it for display only on demand.

4.4.4 Forbidden

The following are forbidden, and constitute fatal errors:

▶ the appearance of a reference to an unparsed entity.

▶ the appearance of any character or general-entity reference in the DTD except within an `EntityValue` or `AttValue`.

▶ a reference to an external entity in an attribute value.

4.4.5 Included in Literal   When an entity reference appears in an attribute value, or a parameter entity reference appears in a literal entity value, its replacement text is processed in place of the reference itself as though it were part of the document at the location the reference was recognized, except that a single or double quote character in the replacement text is always treated as a normal data character and will not terminate the literal. For example, this is well-formed:

```
<!- ->
<!ENTITY % YN '"Yes"' >
<!ENTITY WhatHeSaid "He said %YN;" >
```

while this is not:

```
<!ENTITY EndAttr "27'" >
<element attribute='a-&EndAttr;>
```

4.4.6 Notify   When the name of an unparsed entity appears as a token in the value of an attribute of declared type `ENTITY` or `ENTITIES`, a validating processor must inform the application of the system and public (if any) identifiers for both the entity and its associated notation.

4.4.7 Bypassed   When a general entity reference appears in the `Entity-Value` in an entity declaration, it is bypassed and left as is.

4.4.8 Included as PE   Just as with external parsed entities, parameter entities need only be included if validating. When a parameter-entity reference is recognized in the DTD and included, its replacement text is enlarged by the attachment of one leading and one following space (#x20) character; the intent is to constrain the replacement text of parameter entities to contain an integral number of grammatical tokens in the DTD. This behavior does not apply to parameter entity references within entity values; these are described in "4.4.5 Included in Literal."

4.5 Construction of Internal Entity Replacement Text

In discussing the treatment of internal entities, it is useful to distinguish two forms of the entity's value. [Definition: The *literal entity value* is the quoted string actually present in the entity declaration, corresponding to the non-terminal EntityValue.] [Definition: The *replacement text* is the content of the entity, after replacement of character references and parameter-entity references.]

The literal entity value as given in an internal entity declaration (`EntityValue`) may contain character, parameter-entity, and general-entity references. Such references must be contained entirely within the literal entity value. The actual replacement text that is included as described above must contain the replacement text of any parameter entities referred to, and must contain the character referred to, in place of any character references in the literal entity value; however, general-entity references must be left as-is, unexpanded. For example, given the following declarations:

```
<!ENTITY % pub    "&#xc9;ditions Gallimard" >
<!ENTITY   rights "All rights reserved" >
<!ENTITY   book   "La Peste: Albert Camus,
&#xA9; 1947 %pub;. &rights;" >
```

then the replacement text for the entity "book" is:

```
La Peste: Albert Camus,
   1947  ditions Gallimard. &rights;
```

The general-entity reference "`&rights;`" would be expanded should the reference "`&book;`" appear in the document's content or an attribute value.

These simple rules may have complex interactions; for a detailed discussion of a difficult example, see "D Expansion of Entity and Character References."

4.6 Predefined Entities

[Definition: Entity and character references can both be used to *escape* the left angle bracket, ampersand, and other delimiters. A set of general entities (amp, lt, gt, apos, quot) is specified for this purpose. Numeric character references may also be used; they are expanded immediately when recognized and must be treated as character data, so the numeric character references "`&#60;`" and "`&#38;`" may be used to escape < and & when they occur in character data.]

All XML processors must recognize these entities whether they are declared or not. For interoperability, valid XML documents should declare these entities, like any others, before using them. If the entities lt or amp are declared, they must be declared as internal entities whose replacement text is a character reference to the respective character (less-than sign or ampersand) being escaped; the double escaping is required for these entities so that references to them produce a well-formed result. If the entities gt, apos, or quot are declared, they must be declared as internal entities whose replacement text is the single character being escaped (or a character reference to that character; the double escaping here is unnecessary but harmless). For example:

```
<!ENTITY lt     "&#38;#60;">
<!ENTITY gt     "&#62;">
<!ENTITY amp    "&#38;#38;">
<!ENTITY apos   "&#39;">
<!ENTITY quot   "&#34;">
```

4.7 Notation Declarations

[Definition: *Notations* identify by name the format of unparsed entities, the format of elements which bear a notation attribute, or the application to which a processing instruction is addressed.]

[Definition: *Notation declarations* provide a name for the notation, for use in entity and attribute-list declarations and in attribute specifications, and an external identifier for the notation which may allow an XML processor or its client application to locate a helper application capable of processing data in the given notation.]

Notation Declarations

```
[82]   NotationDecl  ::=  '<!NOTATION' S Name S (ExternalID |
                          PublicID) S? '>'
                          [VC: Unique Notation Name]
[83]   PublicID      ::=  'PUBLIC' S PubidLiteral
```

Validity constraint: Unique Notation Name   Only one notation declaration can declare a given *Name*.

XML processors must provide applications with the name and external identifier(s) of any notation declared and referred to in an attribute value, attribute definition, or entity declaration. They may additionally resolve the external identifier into the system identifier, file name, or other information needed to allow the application to call a processor for data in the notation described. (It is not an error, however, for XML documents to declare and refer to notations for which notation-specific applications are not available on the system where the XML processor or application is running.)

4.8 Document Entity

[Definition: The *document entity* serves as the root of the entity tree and a starting-point for an XML processor.] This specification does not specify how the document entity is to be located by an XML processor; unlike other entities, the document entity has no name and might well appear on a processor input stream without any identification at all.

5 Conformance

5.1 Validating and Non-Validating Processors

Conforming XML processors fall into two classes: validating and non-validating.

Validating and non-validating processors alike must report violations of this specification's well-formedness constraints in the content of the document entity and any other parsed entities that they read.

[Definition: *Validating processors* must, at user option, report violations of the constraints expressed by the declarations in the DTD, and failures to fulfill the validity constraints given in this specification.] To accomplish this, validating XML processors must read and process the entire DTD and all external parsed entities referenced in the document.

Non-validating processors are required to check only the document entity, including the entire internal DTD subset, for well-formedness. [Definition: While they are not required to check the document for validity, they are required to *process* all the declarations they read in the internal DTD subset and in any parameter entity that they read, up to the first reference to a parameter entity that they do not read; that is to say, they must use the information in those declarations to normalize attribute values, include the replacement text of internal entities, and supply default attribute values.] Except when standalone="yes", they must not process entity declarations or attribute-list declarations encountered after a reference to a parameter entity that is not read, since the entity may have contained overriding declarations.

5.2 Using XML Processors

The behavior of a validating XML processor is highly predictable; it must read every piece of a document and report all well-formedness and validity violations. Less is required of a non-validating processor; it need not read any part of the document other than the document entity. This has two effects that may be important to users of XML processors.

Certain well-formedness errors, specifically those that require reading external entities, may not be detected by a non-validating processor. Examples include the constraints entitled Entity Declared, Parsed Entity, and No Recursion, as well as some of the cases described as forbidden in "4.4 XML Processor Treatment of Entities and References."

The information passed from the processor to the application may vary, depending on whether the processor reads parameter and external entities. For example, a non-validating processor may not normalize attribute values, include the replacement text of internal entities, or supply default attribute values, where doing so depends on having read declarations in external or parameter entities.

For maximum reliability in interoperating between different XML processors, applications which use non-validating processors should not rely on any behaviors not required of such processors. Applications which require facilities such as the use of default attributes or internal entities which are declared in external entities should use validating XML processors.

6 Notation

The formal grammar of XML is given in this specification using a simple Extended Backus-Naur Form (EBNF) notation. Each rule in the grammar defines one symbol, in the form

```
symbol ::= expression
```

Symbols are written with an initial capital letter if they are the start symbol of a regular language, otherwise with an initial lowercase letter. Literal strings are quoted.

Within the expression on the right-hand side of a rule, the following expressions are used to match strings of one or more characters:

#xN	where N is a hexadecimal integer, the expression matches the character in ISO/IEC 10646 whose canonical (UCS-4) code value, when interpreted as an unsigned binary number, has the value indicated. The number of leading zeros in the #xN form is insignificant; the number of leading zeros in the corresponding code value is governed by the character encoding in use and is not significant for XML.
[a-zA-Z], [#xN-#xN]	Matches any Char with a value in the range(s) indicated (inclusive).
[abc], [#xN#xN#xN]	Matches any Char with a value among the characters enumerated. Enumerations and ranges can be mixed in one set of brackets.
[^a-z], [^#xN-#xN]	Matches any Char with a value outside the range indicated.
[^abc], [^#xN#xN#xN]	Matches any Char with a value not among the characters given. Enumerations and ranges of forbidden values can be mixed in one set of brackets.

`"string"`	Matches a literal string matching that given inside the double quotes.
`'string'`	Matches a literal string matching that given inside the single quotes.

These symbols may be combined to match more complex patterns as follows, where A and B represent simple expressions:

`(expression)`	`expression` is treated as a unit and may be combined as described in this list.
`A?`	Matches A or nothing; optional A.
`A B`	Matches A followed by B. This operator has higher precedence than alternation; thus A B | C D is identical to (A B) | (C D).
`A | B`	Matches A or B but not both.
`A - B`	Matches any string that matches A but does not match B.
`A+`	Matches one or more occurrences of A. Concatenation has higher precedence than alternation; thus A+ | B+ is identical to (A+) | (B+).
`A*`	Matches zero or more occurrences of A. Concatenation has higher precedence than alternation; thus A* | B* is identical to (A*) | (B*).

Other notations used in the productions are:

`/* ... */`	Comment
`[ wfc: ... ]`	Well-formedness constraint; this identifies by name a constraint on well-formed documents associated with a production.
`[ vc: ... ]`	Validity constraint; this identifies by name a constraint on valid documents associated with a production.

A References

A.1 Normative References

IANA-CHARSETS	(Internet Assigned Numbers Authority) *Official Names for Character Sets*, ed. Keld Simonsen et al. See ftp://ftp.isi.edu/in-notes/iana/assignments/character-sets.
IETF RFC 1766	IETF (Internet Engineering Task Force). *RFC 1766: Tags for the Identification of Languages*, ed. H. Alvestrand. 1995. (See http://www.ietf.org/rfc/rfc1766.txt.)
ISO/IEC 10646	ISO (International Organization for Standardization). *ISO/IEC 10646-1993 (E). Information technology—Universal Multiple-Octet Coded Character Set (UCS)—Part 1: Architecture and Basic Multilingual Plane.* [Geneva]: International Organization for Standardization, 1993 (plus amendments AM 1 through AM 7).

ISO/IEC 10646-2000	ISO (International Organization for Standardization). *ISO/IEC 10646-1:2000. Information technology—Universal Multiple-Octet Coded Character Set (UCS)—Part 1: Architecture and Basic Multilingual Plane.* [Geneva]: International Organization for Standardization, 2000.
Unicode	The Unicode Consortium. *The Unicode Standard, Version 2.0.* Reading, Mass.: Addison-Wesley Developers Press, 1996.
Unicode3	The Unicode Consortium. *The Unicode Standard, Version 3.0.* Reading, Mass.: Addison-Wesley Developers Press, 2000. ISBN 0-201-61633-5.

A.2 Other References

Aho/Ullman	Aho, Alfred V., Ravi Sethi, and Jeffrey D. Ullman. *Compilers: Principles, Techniques, and Tools.* Reading: Addison-Wesley, 1986, rpt. corr. 1988.
Berners-Lee et al.	Berners-Lee, T., R. Fielding, and L. Masinter. *Uniform Resource Identifiers (URI): Generic Syntax and Semantics.* 1997. (Work in progress; see updates to RFC1738.)
Brüggemann-Klein	Brüggemann-Klein, Anne. *Formal Models in Document Processing.* Habilitationsschrift. Faculty of Mathematics at the University of Freiburg, 1993. (See ftp://ftp.informatik.uni-freiburg.de/documents/papers/brueggem/habil.ps.)
Brüggemann-Klein and Wood	Brüggemann-Klein, Anne, and Derick Wood. *Deterministic Regular Languages.* Universität Freiburg, Institut für Informatik, Bericht 38, Oktober 1991. Extended abstract in A. Finkel, M. Jantzen, Hrsg., STACS 1992, S. 173–184. Springer-Verlag, Berlin 1992. Lecture Notes in Computer Science 577. Full version titled One-Unambiguous Regular Languages in Information and Computation 140 (2): 229–253, February 1998.
Clark	James Clark. *Comparison of SGML and XML.* See http://www.w3.org/TR/NOTE-sgml-xml-971215.
IANA-LANGCODES	(Internet Assigned Numbers Authority) *Registry of Language Tags,* ed. Keld Simonsen et al. (See http://www.isi.edu/in-notes/iana/assignments/languages/.)
IETF RFC2141	IETF (Internet Engineering Task Force). *RFC 2141: URN Syntax,* ed. R. Moats. 1997. (See http://www.ietf.org/rfc/rfc2141.txt.)
IETF RFC 2279	IETF (Internet Engineering Task Force). *RFC 2279: UTF-8, a Transformation Format of ISO 10646,* ed. F. Yergeau, 1998. (See http://www.ietf.org/rfc/rfc2279.txt.)
IETF RFC 2376	IETF (Internet Engineering Task Force). *RFC 2376: XML Media Types,* ed. E. Whitehead, M. Murata. 1998. (See http://www.ietf.org/rfc/rfc2376.txt.)
IETF RFC 2396	IETF (Internet Engineering Task Force). *RFC 2396: Uniform Resource Identifiers (URI): Generic Syntax.* T. Berners-Lee, R. Fielding, L. Masinter. 1998. (See http://www.ietf.org/rfc/rfc2396.txt.)
IETF RFC 2732	IETF (Internet Engineering Task Force). *RFC 2732: Format for Literal IPv6 Addresses in URL's.* R. Hinden, B. Carpenter, L. Masinter. 1999. (See http://www.ietf.org/rfc/rfc2732.txt.)

IETF RFC 2781	IETF (Internet Engineering Task Force). *RFC 2781: UTF-16, an Encoding of ISO 10646*, ed. P. Hoffman, F. Yergeau. 2000. (See `http://www.ietf.org/rfc/rfc2781.txt`.)
ISO 639	(International Organization for Standardization). *ISO 639:1988 (E). Code for the Representation of Names of Languages*. [Geneva]: International Organization for Standardization, 1988.
ISO 3166	(International Organization for Standardization). *ISO 3166-1:1997 (E). Codes for the Representation of Names of Countries and Their Subdivisions— Part 1: Country codes* [Geneva]: International Organization for Standardization, 1997.
ISO 8879	ISO (International Organization for Standardization). *ISO 8879:1986(E). Information Processing—Text and Office Systems—Standard Generalized Markup Language (SGML). First edition—1986-10-15.* [Geneva]: International Organization for Standardization, 1986.
ISO/IEC 10744	ISO (International Organization for Standardization). *ISO/IEC 10744-1992 (E). Information Technology—Hypermedia/Time-based Structuring Language (HyTime)*. [Geneva]: International Organization for Standardization, 1992. Extended Facilities Annexe. [Geneva]: International Organization for Standardization, 1996.
WEBSGML	ISO (International Organization for Standardization). *ISO 8879:1986 TC2. Information Technology—Document Description and Processing Languages*. [Geneva]: International Organization for Standardization, 1998. (See `http://www.sgmlsource.com/8879rev/n0029.htm`.)
XML Names	Tim Bray, Dave Hollander, and Andrew Layman, editors. *Namespaces in XML*. Textuality, Hewlett-Packard, and Microsoft. World Wide Web Consortium, 1999. (See `http://www.w3.org/TR/REC-xml-names/`.)

B Character Classes

Following the characteristics defined in the Unicode standard, characters are classed as base characters (among others, these contain the alphabetic characters of the Latin alphabet), ideographic characters, and combining characters (among others, this class contains most diacritics). Digits and extenders are also distinguished.

Characters

```
[84]  Letter   ::=  BaseChar | Ideographic
[85]  BaseChar  ::=   [#x0041-#x005A] | [#x0061-#x007A] |
[#x00C0-#x00D6]
    | [#x00D8-#x00F6] | [#x00F8-#x00FF] | [#x0100-#x0131] |
[#x0134-#x013E]
    | [#x0141-#x0148] | [#x014A-#x017E] | [#x0180-#x01C3] |
[#x01CD-#x01F0]
    | [#x01F4-#x01F5] | [#x01FA-#x0217] | [#x0250-#x02A8] |
[#x02BB-#x02C1]
```

| #x0386 | [#x0388-#x038A] | #x038C | [#x038E-#x03A1] | [#x03A3-#x03CE]

| [#x03D0-#x03D6] | #x03DA | #x03DC | #x03DE | #x03E0 | [#x03E2-#x03F3]

| [#x0401-#x040C] | [#x040E-#x044F] | [#x0451-#x045C] | [#x045E-#x0481]

| [#x0490-#x04C4] | [#x04C7-#x04C8] | [#x04CB-#x04CC] | [#x04D0-#x04EB]

| [#x04EE-#x04F5] | [#x04F8-#x04F9] | [#x0531-#x0556] | #x0559

| [#x0561-#x0586] | [#x05D0-#x05EA] | [#x05F0-#x05F2] | [#x0621-#x063A]

| [#x0641-#x064A] | [#x0671-#x06B7] | [#x06BA-#x06BE] | [#x06C0-#x06CE]

| [#x06D0-#x06D3] | #x06D5 | [#x06E5-#x06E6] | [#x0905-#x0939] | #x093D

| [#x0958-#x0961] | [#x0985-#x098C] | [#x098F-#x0990] | [#x0993-#x09A8]

| [#x09AA-#x09B0] | #x09B2 | [#x09B6-#x09B9] | [#x09DC-#x09DD]

| [#x09DF-#x09E1] | [#x09F0-#x09F1] | [#x0A05-#x0A0A] | [#x0A0F-#x0A10]

| [#x0A13-#x0A28] | [#x0A2A-#x0A30] | [#x0A32-#x0A33] | [#x0A35-#x0A36]

| [#x0A38-#x0A39] | [#x0A59-#x0A5C] | #x0A5E | [#x0A72-#x0A74]

| [#x0A85-#x0A8B] | #x0A8D | [#x0A8F-#x0A91] | [#x0A93-#x0AA8]

| [#x0AAA-#x0AB0] | [#x0AB2-#x0AB3] | [#x0AB5-#x0AB9] | #x0ABD | #x0AE0

| [#x0B05-#x0B0C] | [#x0B0F-#x0B10] | [#x0B13-#x0B28] | [#x0B2A-#x0B30]

| [#x0B32-#x0B33] | [#x0B36-#x0B39] | #x0B3D | [#x0B5C-#x0B5D]

| [#x0B5F-#x0B61] | [#x0B85-#x0B8A] | [#x0B8E-#x0B90] | [#x0B92-#x0B95]

| [#x0B99-#x0B9A] | #x0B9C | [#x0B9E-#x0B9F] | [#x0BA3-#x0BA4]

| [#x0BA8-#x0BAA] | [#x0BAE-#x0BB5] | [#x0BB7-#x0BB9] | [#x0C05-#x0C0C]

```
    | [#x0C0E-#x0C10] | [#x0C12-#x0C28] | [#x0C2A-#x0C33] |
[#x0C35-#x0C39]

    | [#x0C60-#x0C61] | [#x0C85-#x0C8C] | [#x0C8E-#x0C90] |
[#x0C92-#x0CA8]

    | [#x0CAA-#x0CB3] | [#x0CB5-#x0CB9] | #x0CDE | [#x0CE0-
#x0CE1]

    | [#x0D05-#x0D0C] | [#x0D0E-#x0D10] | [#x0D12-#x0D28] |
[#x0D2A-#x0D39]

    | [#x0D60-#x0D61] | [#x0E01-#x0E2E] | #x0E30 | [#x0E32-
#x0E33]

    | [#x0E40-#x0E45] | [#x0E81-#x0E82] | #x0E84 | [#x0E87-
#x0E88] | #x0E8A

    | #x0E8D | [#x0E94-#x0E97] | [#x0E99-#x0E9F] | [#x0EA1-
#x0EA3] | #x0EA5

    | #x0EA7 | [#x0EAA-#x0EAB] | [#x0EAD-#x0EAE] | #x0EB0 |
[#x0EB2-#x0EB3]

    | #x0EBD | [#x0EC0-#x0EC4] | [#x0F40-#x0F47] | [#x0F49-
#x0F69]

    | [#x10A0-#x10C5] | [#x10D0-#x10F6] | #x1100 | [#x1102-
#x1103]

    | [#x1105-#x1107] | #x1109 | [#x110B-#x110C] | [#x110E-
#x1112] | #x113C

    | #x113E | #x1140 | #x114C | #x114E | #x1150 | [#x1154-
#x1155] | #x1159

    | [#x115F-#x1161] | #x1163 | #x1165 | #x1167 | #x1169 |
[#x116D-#x116E]

    | [#x1172-#x1173] | #x1175 | #x119E | #x11A8 | #x11AB |
[#x11AE-#x11AF]

    | [#x11B7-#x11B8] | #x11BA | [#x11BC-#x11C2] | #x11EB |
#x11F0 | #x11F9

    | [#x1E00-#x1E9B] | [#x1EA0-#x1EF9] | [#x1F00-#x1F15] |
[#x1F18-#x1F1D]

    | [#x1F20-#x1F45] | [#x1F48-#x1F4D] | [#x1F50-#x1F57] |
#x1F59 | #x1F5B

    | #x1F5D | [#x1F5F-#x1F7D] | [#x1F80-#x1FB4] | [#x1FB6-
#x1FBC] | #x1FBE

    | [#x1FC2-#x1FC4] | [#x1FC6-#x1FCC] | [#x1FD0-#x1FD3] |
[#x1FD6-#x1FDB]

    | [#x1FE0-#x1FEC] | [#x1FF2-#x1FF4] | [#x1FF6-#x1FFC] |
#x2126
```

```
    | [#x212A-#x212B] | #x212E | [#x2180-#x2182] | [#x3041-
#x3094]

    | [#x30A1-#x30FA] | [#x3105-#x312C] | [#xAC00-#xD7A3]
[86]    Ideographic    ::=    [#x4E00-#x9FA5] | #x3007 |
[#x3021-#x3029]

[87]    CombiningChar    ::=    [#x0300-#x0345] | [#x0360-
#x0361]

    | [#x0483-#x0486] | [#x0591-#x05A1] | [#x05A3-#x05B9] |
[#x05BB-#x05BD]

    | #x05BF | [#x05C1-#x05C2] | #x05C4 | [#x064B-#x0652] |
#x0670

    | [#x06D6-#x06DC] | [#x06DD-#x06DF] | [#x06E0-#x06E4] |
[#x06E7-#x06E8]

    | [#x06EA-#x06ED] | [#x0901-#x0903] | #x093C | [#x093E-
#x094C] | #x094D

    | [#x0951-#x0954] | [#x0962-#x0963] | [#x0981-#x0983] |
#x09BC | #x09BE

    | #x09BF | [#x09C0-#x09C4] | [#x09C7-#x09C8] | [#x09CB-
#x09CD] | #x09D7

    | [#x09E2-#x09E3] | #x0A02 | #x0A3C | #x0A3E | #x0A3F |
[#x0A40-#x0A42]

    | [#x0A47-#x0A48] | [#x0A4B-#x0A4D] | [#x0A70-#x0A71] |
[#x0A81-#x0A83]

    | #x0ABC | [#x0ABE-#x0AC5] | [#x0AC7-#x0AC9] | [#x0ACB-
#x0ACD]

    | [#x0B01-#x0B03] | #x0B3C | [#x0B3E-#x0B43] | [#x0B47-
#x0B48]

    | [#x0B4B-#x0B4D] | [#x0B56-#x0B57] | [#x0B82-#x0B83] |
[#x0BBE-#x0BC2]

    | [#x0BC6-#x0BC8] | [#x0BCA-#x0BCD] | #x0BD7 | [#x0C01-
#x0C03]

    | [#x0C3E-#x0C44] | [#x0C46-#x0C48] | [#x0C4A-#x0C4D] |
[#x0C55-#x0C56]

    | [#x0C82-#x0C83] | [#x0CBE-#x0CC4] | [#x0CC6-#x0CC8] |
[#x0CCA-#x0CCD]

    | [#x0CD5-#x0CD6] | [#x0D02-#x0D03] | [#x0D3E-#x0D43] |
[#x0D46-#x0D48]

    | [#x0D4A-#x0D4D] | #x0D57 | #x0E31 | [#x0E34-#x0E3A] |
[#x0E47-#x0E4E]
```

```
    | #x0EB1 | [#x0EB4-#x0EB9] | [#x0EBB-#x0EBC] | [#x0EC8-
#x0ECD]
```

```
    | [#x0F18-#x0F19] | #x0F35 | #x0F37 | #x0F39 | #x0F3E |
#x0F3F
```

```
    | [#x0F71-#x0F84] | [#x0F86-#x0F8B] | [#x0F90-#x0F95] |
#x0F97
```

```
    | [#x0F99-#x0FAD] | [#x0FB1-#x0FB7] | #x0FB9 | [#x20D0-
#x20DC] | #x20E1
```

```
    | [#x302A-#x302F] | #x3099 | #x309A
```

```
[88]    Digit    ::=    [#x0030-#x0039] | [#x0660-#x0669] |
[#x06F0-#x06F9]
```

```
    | [#x0966-#x096F] | [#x09E6-#x09EF] | [#x0A66-#x0A6F] |
[#x0AE6-#x0AEF]
```

```
    | [#x0B66-#x0B6F] | [#x0BE7-#x0BEF] | [#x0C66-#x0C6F] |
[#x0CE6-#x0CEF]
```

```
    | [#x0D66-#x0D6F] | [#x0E50-#x0E59] | [#x0ED0-#x0ED9] |
[#x0F20-#x0F29]
```

```
[89]    Extender    ::=    #x00B7 | #x02D0 | #x02D1 | #x0387 |
#x0640 | #x0E46
```

```
    | #x0EC6 | #x3005 | [#x3031-#x3035] | [#x309D-#x309E] |
[#x30FC-#x30FE]
```

The character classes defined here can be derived from the Unicode 2.0 character database as follows:

- ► Name start characters must have one of the categories Ll, Lu, Lo, Lt, Nl.
- ► Name characters other than Name-start characters must have one of the categories Mc, Me, Mn, Lm, or Nd.
- ► Characters in the compatibility area (i.e. with character code greater than #xF900 and less than #xFFFE) are not allowed in XML names.
- ► Characters which have a font or compatibility decomposition (i.e. those with a "compatibility formatting tag" in field 5 of the database—marked by field 5 beginning with a "<") are not allowed.
- ► The following characters are treated as name-start characters rather than name characters, because the property file classifies them as Alphabetic: [#x02BB-#x02C1], #x0559, #x06E5, #x06E6.
- ► Characters #x20DD-#x20E0 are excluded (in accordance with Unicode 2.0, section 5.14).

▶ Character #x00B7 is classified as an extender, because the property list so identifies it.

▶ Character #x0387 is added as a name character, because #x00B7 is its canonical equivalent.

▶ Characters ':' and '_' are allowed as name-start characters.

▶ Characters '-' and '.' are allowed as name characters.

C XML and SGML (Non-Normative)

XML is designed to be a subset of SGML, in that every XML document should also be a conforming SGML document. For a detailed comparison of the additional restrictions that XML places on documents beyond those of SGML, see Clark.

D Expansion of Entity and Character References (Non-Normative)

This appendix contains some examples illustrating the sequence of entity- and character-reference recognition and expansion, as specified in "4.4 XML Processor Treatment of Entities and References."

If the DTD contains the declaration

```
<!ENTITY example "<p>An ampersand (&#38;#38;) may be escaped
numerically (&#38;#38;#38;) or with a general entity
(&amp;amp;).</p>" >
```

then the XML processor will recognize the character references when it parses the entity declaration, and resolve them before storing the following string as the value of the entity "example":

```
<p>An ampersand (&#38;) may be escaped numerically
(&#38;#38;) or with a general entity (&amp;amp;).</p>
```

A reference in the document to "&example;" will cause the text to be reparsed, at which time the start- and end-tags of the p element will be recognized and the three references will be recognized and expanded, resulting in a p element with the following content (all data, no delimiters or markup):

```
An ampersand (&) may be escaped numerically (&#38;) or with a
general entity (&amp;).
```

A more complex example will illustrate the rules and their effects fully. In the following example, the line numbers are solely for reference.

```
1 <?xml version='1.0'?>
2 <!DOCTYPE test [
3 <!ELEMENT test (#PCDATA) >
4 <!ENTITY % xx '&#37;zz;'>
5 <!ENTITY % zz '&#60;!ENTITY tricky "error-prone" >' >
6 %xx;
7 ]>
8 <test>This sample shows a &tricky; method.</test>
```

This produces the following:

▶ In line 4, the reference to character 37 is expanded immediately, and the parameter entity `"xx"` is stored in the symbol table with the value `"%zz;"`. Since the replacement text is not rescanned, the reference to parameter entity `"zz"` is not recognized. (And it would be an error if it were, since `"zz"` is not yet declared.)

▶ In line 5, the character reference `"&#60;"` is expanded immediately and the parameter entity `"zz"` is stored with the replacement text `"<!ENTITY tricky "error-prone" >"`, which is a well-formed entity declaration.

▶ In line 6, the reference to `"xx"` is recognized, and the replacement text of `"xx"` (namely `"%zz;"`) is parsed. The reference to `"zz"` is recognized in its turn, and its replacement text (`"<!ENTITY tricky "error-prone" >"`) is parsed. The general entity `"tricky"` has now been declared, with the replacement text `"error-prone"`.

▶ In line 8, the reference to the general entity `"tricky"` is recognized, and it is expanded, so the full content of the test element is the self-describing (and ungrammatical) string *This sample shows a error-prone method.*

E Deterministic Content Models (Non-Normative)

As noted in "3.2.1 Element Content," it is required that content models in element type declarations be deterministic. This requirement is for compatibility with SGML (which calls deterministic content models "unambiguous"); XML processors built using SGML systems may flag non-deterministic content models as errors.

For example, the content model ((b, c) | (b, d)) is non-deterministic, because given an initial b the XML processor cannot know which b in the model is being matched without looking ahead to see which element follows the *b*. In this case, the two references to *b* can be collapsed into a single reference, making the model read (b, (c | d)). An initial *b* now clearly matches only a single name in the content model. The processor doesn't need to look ahead to see what follows; either *c* or *d* would be accepted.

More formally: a finite state automaton may be constructed from the content model using the standard algorithms, e.g. algorithm 3.5 in section 3.9 of Aho, Sethi, and Ullman (Aho/Ullman). In many such algorithms, a follow set is constructed for each position in the regular expression (i.e., each leaf node in the syntax tree for the regular expression); if any position has a follow set in which more than one following position is labeled with the same element type name, then the content model is in error and may be reported as an error.

Algorithms exist which allow many but not all non-deterministic content models to be reduced automatically to equivalent deterministic models; see Brüggemann-Klein 1991 (Brüggemann-Klein).

F Autodetection of Character Encodings (Non-Normative)

The XML encoding declaration functions as an internal label on each entity, indicating which character encoding is in use. Before an XML processor can read the internal label, however, it apparently has to know what character encoding is in use—which is what the internal label is trying to indicate. In the general case, this is a hopeless situation. It is not entirely hopeless in XML, however, because XML limits the general case in two ways: each implementation is assumed to support only a finite set of character encodings, and the XML encoding declaration is restricted in position and content in order to make it feasible to autodetect the character encoding in use in each entity in normal cases. Also, in many cases other sources of information are available in addition to the XML data stream itself. Two cases may be distinguished, depending on whether the XML entity is presented to the processor without, or with, any accompanying (external) information. We consider the first case first.

F.1 Detection Without External Encoding Information

Because each XML entity not accompanied by external encoding information and not in UTF-8 or UTF-16 encoding must begin with an XML encoding declaration, in which the first characters must be '<?xml ', any conforming processor can detect, after two to four octets of input, which of the following cases apply. In reading this list, it may help to know that in UCS-4, '<' is "#x0000003C" and '?' is "#x0000003F", and the Byte Order Mark required of UTF-16 data streams is "#xFEFF". The notation ## is used to denote any byte value except that two consecutive ##s cannot be both 00.

With a Byte Order Mark:

00 00 FE FF	UCS-4, big-endian machine (1234 order)
FF FE 00 00	UCS-4, little-endian machine (4321 order)
00 00 FF FE	UCS-4, unusual octet order (2143)
FE FF 00 00	UCS-4, unusual octet order (3412)
FE FF ## ##	UTF-16, big-endian
FF FE ## ##	UTF-16, little-endian
EF BB BF	UTF-8

Without a Byte Order Mark

00 00 00 3C 3C 00 00 00 00 00 3C 00 00 3C 00 00	UCS-4 or other encoding with a 32-bit code unit and ASCII characters encoded as ASCII values, in respectively big-endian (1234), little-endian (4321) and two unusual byte orders (2143 and 3412). The encoding declaration must be read to determine which of UCS-4 or other supported 32-bit encodings applies.
00 3C 00 3F	UTF-16BE or big-endian ISO-10646-UCS-2 or other encoding with a 16-bit code unit in big-endian order and ASCII characters encoded as ASCII values (the encoding declaration must be read to determine which)
3C 00 3F 00	UTF-16LE or little-endian ISO-10646-UCS-2 or other encoding with a 16-bit code unit in little-endian order and ASCII characters encoded as ASCII values (the encoding declaration must be read to determine which)
3C 3F 78 6D	UTF-8, ISO 646, ASCII, some part of ISO 8859, Shift-JIS, EUC, or any other 7-bit, 8-bit, or mixed-width encoding which ensures that the characters of ASCII have their normal positions, width, and values; the actual encoding declaration must be read to detect which of these applies, but since all of these encodings use the same bit patterns for the relevant ASCII characters, the encoding declaration itself may be read reliably

| 4C 6F A7 94 | EBCDIC (in some flavor; the full encoding declaration must be read to tell which code page is in use) |
| Other | UTF-8 without an encoding declaration, or else the data stream is mislabeled (lacking a required encoding declaration), corrupt, fragmentary, or enclosed in a wrapper of some kind |

NOTE

In cases above which do not require reading the encoding declaration to determine the encoding, section 4.3.3 still requires that the encoding declaration, if present, be read and that the encoding name be checked to match the actual encoding of the entity. Also, it is possible that new character encodings will be invented that will make it necessary to use the encoding declaration to determine the encoding, in cases where this is not required at present.

This level of autodetection is enough to read the XML encoding declaration and parse the character-encoding identifier, which is still necessary to distinguish the individual members of each family of encodings (e.g. to tell UTF-8 from 8859, and the parts of 8859 from each other, or to distinguish the specific EBCDIC code page in use, and so on).

Because the contents of the encoding declaration are restricted to characters from the ASCII repertoire (however encoded), a processor can reliably read the entire encoding declaration as soon as it has detected which family of encodings is in use. Since in practice, all widely used character encodings fall into one of the categories above, the XML encoding declaration allows reasonably reliable in-band labeling of character encodings, even when external sources of information at the operating-system or transport-protocol level are unreliable. Character encodings such as UTF-7 that make overloaded usage of ASCIIvalued bytes may fail to be reliably detected.

Once the processor has detected the character encoding in use, it can act appropriately, whether by invoking a separate input routine for each case, or by calling the proper conversion function on each character of input.

Like any self-labeling system, the XML encoding declaration will not work if any software changes the entity's character set or encoding without updating the encoding declaration. Implementors of character-encoding routines should be careful to ensure the accuracy of the internal and external information used to label the entity.

F.2 Priorities in the Presence of External Encoding Information

The second possible case occurs when the XML entity is accompanied by encoding information, as in some file systems and some network protocols.

When multiple sources of information are available, their relative priority and the preferred method of handling conflict should be specified as part of the higher-level protocol used to deliver XML. In particular, please refer to IETF RFC 2376 or its successor, which defines the text/xml and application/xml MIME types and provides some useful guidance. In the interests of interoperability, however, the following rule is recommended.

If an XML entity is in a file, the Byte-Order Mark and encoding declaration are used (if present) to determine the character encoding.

G W3C XML Working Group (Non-Normative)

This specification was prepared and approved for publication by the W3C XML Working Group (WG). WG approval of this specification does not necessarily imply that all WG members voted for its approval. The current and former members of the XML WG are:

Jon Bosak, Sun (Chair)

James Clark (Technical Lead)

Tim Bray, Textuality and Netscape (XML Co-editor)

Jean Paoli, Microsoft (XML Co-editor)

C. M. Sperberg-McQueen, University of Illinois (XML Co-editor)

Dan Connolly, W3C (W3C Liaison)

Paula Angerstein, Texcel

Steve DeRose, INSO

Dave Hollander, HP

Eliot Kimber, ISOGEN

Eve Maler, ArborText

Tom Magliery, NCSA

Murray Maloney, SoftQuad, Grif SA, Muzmo, and Veo Systems

Murata Makoto, Fuji Xerox Information Systems

Joel Nava, Adobe

Conleth O'Connell, Vignette

Peter Sharpe, SoftQuad

John Tigue, DataChannel

H W3C XML Core Group (Non-Normative)

The second edition of this specification was prepared by the W3C XML Core Working Group (WG). The members of the WG at the time of publication of this edition were:

Paula Angerstein, Vignette

Daniel Austin, Ask Jeeves

Tim Boland

Allen Brown, Microsoft

Dan Connolly, W3C (Staff Contact)

John Cowan, Reuters Limited

John Evdemon, XMLSolutions Corporation

Paul Grosso, Arbortext (Co-chair)

Arnaud Le Hors, IBM (Co-chair)

Eve Maler, Sun (Second Edition Editor)

Jonathan Marsh, Microsoft

Murata Makoto, IBM

Mark Needleman, Data Research Associates

David Orchard, Jamcracker

Lew Shannon, NCR

Richard Tobin, University of Edinburgh

Daniel Veillard, W3C

Dan Vint, Lexica

Norman Walsh, Sun

Fran ois Yergeau, Alis Technologies (Errata List Editor)

Kongyi Zhou, Oracle

I Production Notes (Non-Normative)

This Second Edition was encoded in the XMLspec DTD (which has documentation available). The HTML versions were produced with a combination of the `xmlspec.xsl`, `diffspec.xsl`, and `REC-xml-2e.xsl` XSLT stylesheets. The PDF version was produced with the html2ps facility and a distiller program.

Appendix B

XML Schema Elements

Compiled for *XML Complete* by Chuck White

Schemas are now considered by many in the XML community to be the most important validating mechanism available. This is especially true when you're using XML in programming and scripting environments, where data typing is important. DTDs, the other validation mechanism, use very low-level data typing, meaning they don't support validation using such entities as numbers and dates, whereas XML Schema offers a rich data typing validation environment.

The elements included here are derived from XML Schema Part 1: Structures (`www.w3.org/TR/xmlschema-1/`), which is the spec represented by the W3C's May 2, 2001, Recommendation. Data types are covered by the W3C May 2, 2001, Recommendation, XML Schema Part 2: Datatypes (`www.w3.org/TR/xmlschema-2/`).

Most of the examples shown in this reference are derived from the Recommendation document. Most, but not all, element descriptions contain examples.

all

Allows group elements to appear in any order within an element.

Attributes

id   Optional attribute that creates a unique identifier of type ID for an element.

maxOccurs   An integer value, always greater than or equal to a value of one, that indicates the maximum number of allowable occurrences of an element.

minOccurs   An integer value, always greater than or equal to a value of one, that indicates the minimum number of allowable occurrences of an element. Setting this attribute to zero indicates that this element is optional.

Element information

Number of occurrences   Unlimited, unless within a group, where it is allowed one time.

Parent elements   `group, extension, restriction, complexType`

Contents   `(annotation?, element*)`

Example

```xml
<xsd:element name="thing1" type="xsd:string"/>
<xsd:element name="thing2" type="xsd:string"/>
<xsd:element name="thing3" type="xsd:string"/>

<xsd:attribute name="myAttribute"
 type="xsd:decimal"/>

<xsd:complexType name="myComplexType">
 <xsd:all>
  <xsd:element ref="ref_1"/>
  <xsd:element ref="ref_2"/>
  <xsd:element ref="ref_3"/>
 </xsd:all>
 <xsd:attribute ref="myAttribute"/>
</xsd:complexType>
```

annotation

Defines an annotation.

Element information

Number of occurrences   One time in parent element.

Parent elements   Any element.

Contents   (appinfo | documentation)*

Example

```xml
<xsd:simpleType name="northwestStates">
    <xsd:annotation>
        <xsd:documentation>States in the Pacific
        Northwest of US
</xsd:documentation>
    </xsd:annotation>
  <xsd:restriction base="string">
    <xsd:enumeration value='WA'>
      <xsd:annotation>
        <xsd:documentation>Washington
        </xsd:documentation>
      </xsd:annotation>
```

```
    </xsd:enumeration>
    <xsd:enumeration value='OR'/>
      <xsd:annotation>
        <xsd:documentation>Oregon
        </xsd:documentation>
      </xsd:annotation>
    </xsd:enumeration>
    <xsd:enumeration value='ID'/>
      <xsd:annotation>
        <xsd:documentation>Idaho</xsd:documentation>
      </xsd:annotation>
    </xsd:enumeration>
  </xsd:restriction>
</xsd:simpleType>
```

any

Enables any element from the specified namespace(s) to appear in the containing `complexType`, `sequence`, `all`, or `choice` element.

Attributes

id   Optional attribute that creates a unique identifier of type ID for an element.

maxOccurs   An integer value, always greater than or equal to a value of zero, that indicates the maximum number of allowable occurrences of an element. You can use the string unbounded to indicate there is no maximum number.

minOccurs   An integer value, always greater than or equal to a value of zero, that indicates the minimum number of allowable occurrences of an element. Setting this attribute to zero indicates that this "any" group is optional.

namespace   The namespaces containing the elements that can be used. If no namespace is specified, ##any is the default. Specified namespaces must be one of the following:

##any   Elements from any namespace can be present.

##other   Elements from any namespace that is not the target namespace of the parent element containing this element can be present.

##local Elements that are not qualified with a namespace can be present.

##targetNamespace Elements from the target namespace of the parent element containing this element can be present.

List of URI references, ##targetNamespace, ##local Elements from a space-delimited list of the namespaces can be present. The list can contain the following: URI references of namespaces, ##targetNamespace, and ##local.

processContents Allows for finer-grained validation routines for a specified element. If no processContents attribute is specified, the default is strict. If processContents is specified, it must be one of the following:

strict The XML processor is required to search for the schema for the specified namespace and validate any element named by those namespaces.

lax The XML processor searches for a schema according to the namespace but if it doesn't find one, no error occurs.

skip The XML processor skips validation attempts for this element within the specified namespace(s).

Element information

Number of occurrences Unlimited.

Parent elements choice, sequence

Contents (annotation?)

Example

```
<xsd:element name='htmlText'>
  <xsd:complexType>
   <xsd:sequence>
    <xsd:any
      namespace='http://www.w3.org/1999/xhtml'
         minOccurs='1' maxOccurs='unbounded'
         processContents='lax'/>
   </xsd:sequence>
  </xsd:complexType>
</xsd:element>
```

anyAttribute

Enables any attribute from the specified namespace(s) to appear in the containing `complexType` element.

Attributes

id   Optional attribute that creates a unique identifier of type ID for an element.

namespace   The namespaces containing the attributes that can be used. If no namespace is specified, ##any is the default. If the namespace is specified, one of the following values is used:

##any   Attributes from any namespace can be present.

##other   Attributes from any namespace that is not the target namespace of the parent element containing this anyAttribute element can be present.

##local   Attributes that are not qualified with a namespace can be present.

##target   Namespace attributes from the target namespace of the parent element containing this anyAttribute element can be present.

List of URI references, ##targetNamespace, ##local
Attributes from a space-delimited list of the namespaces can be present. The list can contain the following: URI references of namespaces, ##targetNamespace, and ##local.

processContents   Allows for finer-grained validation routines for the specified attribute. If no processContents attribute is specified, the default is strict. If processContents is specified, one of the following values is used:

strict   The XML processor is required to search for the schema for the specified namespace and validate any attribute named by those namespaces.

lax   The XML processor searches for a schema according to the namespace but if it doesn't find one, no error occurs.

skip   The XML processor skips validation attempts for this attribute within the specified namespace(s).

Element information

Number of occurrences   Unlimited.

Parent elements   complexType, extension, restriction, attributeGroup

Contents   (annotation?)

Example

```
<xsd:element name="stringElementWithAnyAttribute">
   <xsd:complexType>
    <xsd:simpleContent>
      <xsd:extension base="string">
      <xsd:anyAttribute
        namespace="##targetNamespace"/>
      </xsd:extension>
    </xsd:simpleContent>
   </xsd:complexType>
</xsd:element>
```

appinfo

Specifies information for processing instructions to be used by applications within an annotation element.

Attributes

source   The application information's source as a URI reference. The source must be a URI reference. Optional.

Element information

Number of occurrences   Unlimited.

Parent elements   annotation

Contents   Any well-formed XML content.

Example

```
<?xml version="1.0"?>
<xsd:schema targetNamespace=""
xmlns="http://www.w3.org/2001/XMLSchema">
  <xsd:element name="State">
```

```
    <xsd:annotation>
      <xsd:documentation>State Name
      </xsd:documentation>
      <xsd:appinfo>Application Information
      </xsd:appinfo>
    </xsd:annotation>
  </xsd:element>
</xsd:schema>
```

attribute

Declares an attribute as a built-in data type or a simple type. Attribute declarations can be child elements of the `schema` element (global scope) or exist within complex type definitions, where attribute declarations can be present as local declarations or references to attributes with global scope. Global attribute declarations always define `simpleType` elements. Attributes can be referenced by `attributeGroup` and `complexType` elements.

Attributes

form   The form for the attribute. The default value is the value of the `attributeFormDefault` attribute of the schema element containing the attribute. The value is either `qualified` (which means this attribute must be qualified with the namespace prefix) or `unqualified` (which means the attribute is not required to be qualified with the namespace prefix).

id   Optional attribute that creates a unique identifier of type ID for an element.

name   An NCName as defined in the XML Namespaces specification.

ref   A qualified name (Q Name) of an attribute declared in this schema (or another schema indicated by the specified namespace).

Default   Attribute has a default value.

If the attribute is not specified on an instance within an XML document, the attribute has the value specified in the value attribute.

If the attribute is specified in an instance within an XML document, the attribute has the value given.

Fixed   Attribute has a fixed value. The value specified in the value attribute must be the value for this attribute.

Required   Attribute must appear once.

If the value attribute is specified, the attribute must have that value.

If the value attribute is not specified, the attribute can have any value.

If the attribute is declared as global (its parent element is schema), this attribute is required on all elements in the schema.

value   The default value or fixed value for the attribute, depending on the use property.

Element information

Number of occurrences   Number of attribute types specified in the schema.

Parent elements   attributeGroup, schema, complexType, restriction, extension

Contents   (annotation?, (simpleType?))

Examples

In the following example, an attribute is declared by reference to a built-in type with a default value of test and used in a complexType element.

```
<xsd:attribute name="mybaseattribute"
 type="string" use="default" value="test"/>
<xsd:complexType name="myComplexType">
  <xsd:attribute ref="mybaseattribute"/>
<xsd:complexType name="myComplexType">
```

In the following example, a required attribute is declared directly within a complexType element.

```
<xsd:complexType name="myComplexType">
  <xsd:attribute name="mybaseattribute"
   type="string" use="required"/>
<xsd:complexType name="myComplexType">
```

In the following example, an attribute is declared by deriving from the built-in integer type (by restriction) and restricting the range of values to between 60 and 95, inclusive.

```
<xsd:attribute name="myHolidayLocationTemperature">
  <xsd:simpleType>
   <xsd:restriction base="integer">
    < xsd:minInclusive value="60"/>
    < xsd:maxInclusive value="95"/>
   </xsd:restriction>
  </xsd:simpleType>
</xsd:attribute>
```

In the following example, an attribute is declared as a list containing decimal values. (This allows an attribute such as shoeSizes="10.5 9 8 11" to contain a list of the values 10.5, 9, 8, and 11).

```
<xsd:attribute name="shoeSizes">
  <xsd:simpleType>
    <xsd:list itemType="decimal"/>
  </xsd:simpleType>
</xsd:attribute>
```

attributeGroup

A child of the schema or attributeGroup or complexType elements that groups a set of attribute declarations into a group of complex type definitions. If a child of the attributeGroup or complexType elements, there must be a ref attribute, and the attributeGroup element must be empty. attributeGroup elements can be nested.

Attributes

id   Optional attribute that creates a unique identifier of type ID for an element.

name   The name of the attribute group. The name must be an NCName as defined in the XML Namespaces specification. Required if the containing element is a schema element; otherwise, the name attribute is prohibited.

ref   The name of the attribute group whose attributes are included in an `attributeGroup` element or `complexType` element.

Element information

Number of occurrences   Unlimited.

Parent elements   `attributeGroup, complexType, schema`

Contents   (annotation?)

Example

The following example shows an attribute group defined (`myAttributeGroup`) and used in a complex type (`myElementType`):

```
<xsd:attributeGroup name="myAttributeGroup">
    <xsd:attribute name="someattribute1"
     type="integer"/>
    <xsd:attribute name="someattribute2"
     type="string"/>
</xsd:attributeGroup>


<xsd:complexType name="myElementType">
    <xsd:attributeGroup ref="myAttributeGroup"/>
</xsd:complexType>
```

The following example shows two attribute groups defined (`myAttributeGroupA` and `myAttributeGroupB`) with one containing the other:

```
<xsd:attributeGroup name="myAttributeGroupA">
    <xsd:attribute name="someattribute10"
     type="integer"/>
    <xsd:attribute name="someattribute11"
     type="string"/>
</xsd:attributeGroup>


<xsd:attributeGroup name="myAttributeGroupB">
    <xsd:attribute name="someattribute20"
```

```
        type="date"/>
    <xsd:attributeGroup ref="myAttributeGroupA"/>
</xsd:attributeGroup>
```

choice

Allows one and only one of the elements contained in the group to be present within the containing element.

Attributes

id   Optional attribute that creates a unique identifier of type ID for an element.

maxOccurs   An integer value, always greater than or equal to a value of zero, that indicates the maximum number of allowable occurrences of an element. You can use the string unbounded to indicate there is no maximum number.

minOccurs   An integer value, always greater than or equal to a value of zero, that indicates the minimum number of allowable occurrences of an element. Specifying a value of zero indicates the choice group is optional.

Element information

Number of occurrences   One within group and complex-Type elements; otherwise, unlimited.

Parent elements   group, choice, sequence, complexType, restriction, extension

Contents   (annotation?, (element | group | choice | sequence | any)*)

Example

```
<xsd:complexType name="chadState">
<xsd:choice minOccurs="1" maxOccurs="1">
 <xsd:element ref="selected"/>
 <xsd:element ref="unselected"/>
 <xsd:element ref="dimpled"/>
 <xsd:element ref="perforated"/>
</xsd:choice>
```

```
    <xsd:attribute name="candidate"
    type="candidateType"/>
</xsd:complexType>
```

complexContent

Contains extensions or restrictions on a complex type that contains mixed content or elements only.

Attributes

id　Optional attribute that creates a unique identifier of type ID for an element.

mixed　Indicates whether character data is allowed to appear between the child elements of this complexType element. The default is false. This mixed attribute can override the mixed attribute value specified on the containing complexType element.

Element information

Number of occurrences　One time.

Parent elements　complexType

Contents　(annotation?, (restriction | extension))

Example

```
<xsd:complexType name="address">
  <xsd:sequence>
    <xsd:element name="name"   type="string"/>
    <xsd:element name="street" type="string"/>
    <xsd:element name="city"   type="string"/>
  </xsd:sequence>
</xsd:complexType>

<xsd:complexType name="USAddress">
  <xsd:complexContent>
    <xsd:extension base="address">
      <xsd:sequence>
        <xsd:element name="state" type="USState"/>
        <xsd:element name="zipcode"
        type="positiveInteger"/>
```

```
    </xsd:sequence>
   </xsd:extension>
  </xsd:complexContent>
 </xsd:complexType>
```

complexType

Determines the set of attributes and content of an element.

Attributes

abstract   Determines whether the complex type can be used in an instance document. If this value is `true`, an element cannot use this complex type directly but must use a complex type derived from this complex type. The default is `false`.

base   A QName that describes a built-in data type, simple type, or complex type.

block   The type of derivation. The `block` attribute prevents a complex type that has the specified type of derivation from being used in place of this complex type. This value can contain `#all` or a list that is a subset of `extension` or `restriction`.

mixed   Indicates whether character data is allowed to appear between the child elements of this complex type. The default is `false`. If the `simpleContent` element is a child element, the `mixed` attribute is not allowed. If the `complexContent` element is a child element, this `mixed` attribute can be overridden by the `mixed` attribute on the `complexContent` element.

final   The type of derivation that prevents the specified type of derivation of this `complexType` element. Possible values are `#all` or a list that is a subset of `extension` or `restriction`.

id   Optional attribute that creates a unique identifier of type ID for an element.

name   The unique, NCName of the type.

Element information

Content   (annotation?, (simpleContent | complex-Content | ((group | all | choice | sequence)?, ((attribute | attributeGroup)*, anyAttribute?))))

`</complexType>`   A complex type can contain one and only one of the following elements:

`simpleContent`   The complex type has character data or a `simpleType` as content and contains no elements.

`complexContent`   The complex type contains only elements.

`group`   The complex type contains the elements defined in the referenced group.

`sequence`   The complex type contains the elements defined in the specified sequence.

`choice`   The complex type allows one of the elements specified in the `choice` element.

`all`   The complex type allows any or all of the elements specified in the all element to appear once   If group, `sequence`, `choice`, or `all` is specified as the child element, the attributes for the `complex-Type` can be declared optionally using the following elements.

`attribute`   The complex type contains the specified attribute.

`attributeGroup`   The complex type contains the attributes defined in the referenced `attributeGroup`.

`anyAttribute`   The complex type can contain any attribute from the specified namespace(s).

If group, `sequence`, `choice`, or `all` is specified, the elements must appear in the following order.

```
group | sequence | choice | all
attribute | attributeGroup
anyAttribute
```

Example

This complex type contains a simple type (decimal) and an attribute and element declaration that uses that complex type.

```
<xsd:complexType name='internationalShoeSize'>
<xsd:extension base='xsd:decimal'>
<xsd:attribute name='sizing'
  type='xsd:string' />
```

```
  </xsd:extension>
 </xsd:complexType>
 <xsd:element name='myShoeSize'
   type='internationalShoeSize'/>
```

The following example shows an instance of the myShoeSize element within an XML document:

```
<myShoeSize sizing='UK'>10.5</myShoeSize>
```

The following example shows the myShoeSize element with the complex type defined anonymously within the element.

```
<xsd:element name='myShoeSize'>
 <xsd:complexType>
  <xsd:extension base='xsd:decimal'>
    <xsd:attribute name='sizing'
     type='xsd:string' />
  </xsd:extension>
 </xsd:complexType>
</xsd:element>
```

documentation

Specifies information to be read or used by users within the annotation element.

Attributes

source   The source of the application information. The source must be a URI reference. Optional.

xml:lang   The indicator of the language used in the contents. Optional.

Element information

Number of occurrences   Unlimited.

Parent elements   annotation

Contents   Any well-formed XML content.

Example

```
<xs:simpleType fn:note="special">
  <xs:annotation>
   <xs:documentation>A type for experts only
   </xs:documentation>
   <xs:appinfo>
    <fn:specialHandling>checkForPrimes
    </fn:specialHandling>
   </xs:appinfo>
  </xs:annotation>
```

element

Declares an element as a built-in data type or a simple type. Element declarations can be child elements of the schema element (global scope) or exist within complex type definitions, where element declarations can be present as local declarations or references to elements with global scope. Global element declarations always define complexType elements. A simpleType or complexType element can only be a child if both the ref and type attributes are not present and can only appear by reference within choice, all, group, sequence, and complexType elements.

Attributes

abstract Indicates whether the element can be used in an instance document. A value of true means the element cannot appear in the instance document and another element whose substitutionGroup attribute contains the qualified name (QName) of this element must appear in this element's place. More than one element can reference this element in its substitutionGroup attribute. The default is false.

block The block attribute prevents an element that has a named type of derivation from being used in place of this element. This value can contain #all or a list that is a subset of extension, restriction, or equivClass:

> **extension** Prevents elements derived by extension from being used in place of this element.

> **restriction** Prevents elements derived by restriction from being used in place of this element.

substitution Prevents elements derived by substitution from being used in place of this element.

#all Prevents all derived elements from being used in place of this element.

default The default value of the element if its content is a simple type or its content is textOnly. The fixed and default attributes are mutually exclusive. If the element contains a simple type, this value must be a valid value of that type.

substitutionGroup The name of an element for which this element can be substituted. This element must have the same type or a type derived from the type of the specified element. This value must be a QName. Prohibited if the containing element is not the schema element.

final Sets the default value of the final attribute on the element element.

extension Prevents elements derived by extension from being used in place of this element.

restriction Prevents elements derived by restriction from being used in place of this element.

#all Prevents all derived elements from being used in place of this element.

fixed A predetermined, unchangeable value of the element if its content is a simple type or its content is textOnly. The fixed and default attributes are mutually exclusive.

form The form for the element. The default value is the value of the elementFormDefault attribute of the schema element containing the attribute. The value is either qualified (which means this attribute must be qualified with the namespace prefix) or unqualified (which means the attribute is not required to be qualified with the namespace prefix.

id Optional attribute that creates a unique identifier of type ID for an element.

maxOccurs An integer value, always greater than or equal to a value of zero, that indicates the maximum number of allowable occurrences of an element. You can use the string unbounded to indicate there is no maximum number. Prohibited if the containing element is the schema element.

minOccurs   The minimum number of times the element can occur within the containing element. The value can be an integer greater than or equal to zero. Setting this attribute to zero indicates that this element is optional. Prohibited if the containing element is the schema element.

name   The name of the element. The name must be an NCName as defined in the XML Namespaces specification. Required if the containing element is the schema element.

nullable   The indicator of whether an explicit null value can be assigned to the element. This applies to element content and not to the attributes of the element. The default is false.

If nullable is true, this enables an instance of the element to have the null attribute set to true. The null attribute is defined as part of the XML Schema namespace for instances.

ref   The name of an element declared in this schema (or another schema indicated by the specified namespace). The ref value must be a QName. The ref can include a namespace prefix. Prohibited if the containing element is the schema element. The type and ref attributes are mutually exclusive. To declare an element using an existing element definition, use the ref attribute to specify the existing element definition.

type   Either the name of a built-in data type, or the name of a simpleType or complexType element defined in this schema (or another schema indicated by the specified namespace). The supplied value must correspond to the name attribute on the simpleType or complexType element that is referenced. The type and ref attributes are mutually exclusive. To declare an element using an existing simple type or complex type definition, use the type attribute to specify the existing type.

Element information

Number of occurrences   Number of elements defined in the schema.

Parent   elements schema, choice, all, sequence, group

Contents (annotation?, ((simpleType | complexType)?,
(unique | key | keyref)*))

Example

```
<xsd:element name="cat" type="string"/>
<xsd:element name="dog" type="string"/>
<xsd:element name="redDog" type="string"
    substitutionGroup="dog" />
<xsd:element name="brownDog" type="string"
    substitutionGroup ="dog" />

<xsd:element name="pets">
  <xsd:complexType>
    <xsd:choice minOccurs="0" maxOccurs="unbounded">
      <xsd:element ref="cat"/>
      <xsd:element ref="dog"/>
    </xsd:choice>
  </xsd:complexType>
</xsd:element>
```

enumeration

Constrains the value space to a specified set of values. Enumeration does
not impose an order relation on the value space it creates; the value of
the ordered property of the derived data type remains that of the data
type from which it is derived. It provides for constraining a value space to
a specified set of values.

Attributes

value   A set of values from the value space of the base type
definition.

annotation   An annotation.

Element information

Content (annotation?)

Example

```
<simpleType name='holidays'>
    <annotation>
```

```
                <documentation>some US holidays
                </documentation>
            </annotation>
            <restriction base='gMonthDay'>
              <enumeration value='-01-01'>
                <annotation>
                    <documentation>New Year's day
                    </documentation>
                </annotation>
              </enumeration>
              <enumeration value='-07-04'>
                <annotation>
                    <documentation>4th of July
                    </documentation>
                </annotation>
              </enumeration>
              <enumeration value='-12-25'>
                <annotation>
                    <documentation>Christmas</documentation>
                </annotation>
              </enumeration>
            </restriction>
        </simpleType>
```

extension

Contains extensions on complex content or simple content, which can also extend a complex type.

Attributes

base   The name of a built-in data type or `simpleType` element. The element containing the `extension` element is derived from the simple type specified by the base value. The base value must be a qualified name (QName).

id   Optional attribute that creates a unique identifier of type ID for an element.

Element information

Number of occurrences   One time.

Parent elements   `simpleContent`, `complexContent`

Contents (simpleContent)   `annotation`, attribute, `attrib-`
`uteGroup`, anyAttribute

Contents (complexContent)   `(annotation?, ((attribute`
`| attributeGroup)*, anyAttribute?))`

Example

For examples, see `simpleContent` Element, `complexContent`
Element, and `complexType` Element.

field

Specifies an XML Path Language (XPath) expression that specifies the
value (or one of the values) used to define an identity constraint (`unique`,
`key`, and `keyref` elements).

Attributes

id   Optional attribute that creates a unique identifier of type
ID for an element.

xpath   An XPath expression that is relative to each element
selected by the selector of the identity constraint. This expression
must identify a single element or attribute whose content or value
is used for the constraint. If the expression identifies an element,
that element must be of a simple type.

Element information

Number of occurrences   One time.

Parent elements   `key`, `keyref`, `unique`

Contents   `(annotation?)`

Example

```
<xsd:field xpath="@myID"/>
```

fractionDigits

The maximum number of digits in the fractional part of values of data
types derived from decimal. The value of `fractionDigits` must be a
nonNegativeInteger.

Attributes

fixed A Boolean value of true or false. If `fixed` is true, then types for which the current type is the base type definition cannot specify a value for `totalDigits` other than value.

value The default value or fixed value for the attribute, depending on the use property. If this attribute is derived from another attribute, this specified value takes precedence over any default or fixed value provided on any inherited attribute.

annotation The annotations corresponding to all the annotation element information items in the children, if any.

Contents (annotation?)

Example

```
<simpleType name='celsiusBodyTemp'>
  <restriction base='decimal'>
    <totalDigits value='4'/>
    <fractionDigits value='1'/>
    <minInclusive value='36.4'/>
    <maxInclusive value='40.5'/>
  </restriction>
</simpleType>
```

group

Groups a set of element declarations so that they can be incorporated as a group into complex type definitions. Any one of the following elements can be a child of the group element:

choice Permits one and only one of the elements contained in the group.

sequence Requires the elements in the group to appear in the specified sequence.

all Allows the elements in the group to appear (or not appear) in any order in the containing element.

The minOccurs and maxOccurs attributes have the default value 1. A group with neither attribute must appear once and only once in the containing element.

Attributes

id   Optional attribute that creates a unique identifier of type ID for an element.

name   The name of the group. The name must be an NCName as defined in the XML Namespaces specification. This attribute is used only when the schema element is the parent of this group element. In this case, the group is a model group to be used by `complexType`, choice, all, and sequence elements.

maxOccurs   The maximum number of times the group can occur. The value can be an integer greater than or equal to zero. You can use the string unbounded to indicate there is no maximum number.

minOccurs   The minimum number of times the group can occur. The value can be an integer greater than or equal to zero. To specify that the group is optional, set this attribute to zero.

ref   The name of a group defined in this schema (or another schema indicated by the specified namespace). The ref value must be a qualified name (QName). The type can include a namespace prefix. To include a group in a `complexType`, use the ref attribute to specify the group to include.

Element information

Number of occurrences   Unlimited.

Parent elements   schema, choice, sequence, `complexType`, `restriction`, `extension`

Contents   `(annotation?, (all | choice | sequence))`

Example

```
<xsd:element name="thing1" type="xsd:string"/>
<xsd:element name="thing2" type="xsd:string"/>
<xsd:element name="thing3" type="xsd:string"/>

<xsd:attribute name="myAttribute"
 type="xsd:decimal"/>

<xsd:group name="myGroupOfThings">
```

```
<xsd:sequence>
 <xsd:element ref="thing1"/>
 <xsd:element ref="thing2"/>
 <xsd:element ref="thing3"/>
</xsd:sequence>
</xsd:group>

<xsd:complexType name="myComplexType">
 <xsd:group ref="myGroupOfThings"/>
 <xsd:attribute ref="myAttribute"/>
</xsd:complexType>
```

import

Identifies a namespace whose schema components are referenced by the containing schema. The difference between the include element and the import element is that the import element allows references to schema components from schema documents with different target namespaces and the include element adds the schema components from other schema documents that have the same target namespace (or no specified target namespace) to the containing schema. In short, the import element allows you to use schema components from any schema; the include element allows you to add all the components of an included schema to the containing schema.

Attributes

id   Optional attribute that creates a unique identifier of type ID for an element.

namespace   The URI reference to the namespace to import. The namespace attribute indicates that the containing schema document may contain qualified references to schema components in that namespace (through one or more prefixes declared with xmlns attributes). If this attribute is absent, the containing schema can contain unqualified references to components in the imported namespace.

schemaLocation   The URI reference to the location of a schema document for the imported namespace. If this attribute is absent, the author is allowing the identification of the schema for the imported namespace to be determined by the XML document that is an instance of the containing schema or the user or application that is processing it.

Element information

Number of occurrences   Unlimited.

Parent elements   schema

Contents   (annotation?)

include

Includes the specified schema document in the target namespace of the containing schema.

Attributes

id   Optional attribute that creates a unique identifier of type ID for an element.

namespace   The URI reference to the namespace to import. The namespace attribute indicates that the containing schema document may contain qualified references to schema components in that namespace (through one or more prefixes declared with xmlns attributes). If this attribute is absent, the containing schema can contain unqualified references to components in the imported namespace.

schemaLocation   The URI reference to the location of a schema document for the imported namespace. If this attribute is absent, the author is allowing the identification of the schema for the imported namespace to be determined by the XML document that is an instance of the containing schema or the user or application that is processing it.

Element information

Number of occurrences   Unlimited.

Parent elements   schema

Contents   (annotation?)

key

Specifies that an attribute or element value (or set of values) must be a key within the specified scope. The key element must contain the following elements in order:

selector   The selector element contains an XML Path Language (XPath) expression specifying the set of elements across which the values specified by field must be unique. There must be one and only one selector element.

field Each field element contains an XPath expression specifying the values (attribute or element values) that must be unique for the set of elements specified by the selector element. If there is more than one field element, the combination of the field elements must be unique. In this case, the values for a single field element may or may not be unique across the selected elements, but the combination of all the fields must be unique. There must be one or more field element(s).

Attributes

id Optional attribute that creates a unique identifier of type ID for an element.

name The name of the key element. The name must be an NCName as defined in the XML Namespaces specification. Required.

The name must be unique within a schema.

Element information

Number of occurrences Unlimited.

Parent elements element

Contents annotation, field, selector

keyref

Specifies that an attribute or element value (or set of values) correspond with those of the specified key or unique element. The keyref element must contain the following elements in order.

selector The selector element contains an XML Path Language (XPath) expression specifying the set of elements across which the values specified by the field element must be unique. There must be one and only one selector element.

field Each field element contains an XPath expression specifying the values (attribute or element values) that must be unique for the set of elements specified by the selector element. If there is more than one field element, the combination of the `field` elements must be unique. In this case, the values for a single `field` element may or may not be unique across the selected elements, but the combination of all the fields must be unique. There must be one or more `field` element(s).

Attributes

id   Optional attribute that creates a unique identifier of type ID for an element.

name   The name of the `keyref` element. The name must be an NCName as defined in the XML Namespaces specification. Required. The name must be unique within a schema.

refer   The name of a key or unique element defined in this schema (or another schema indicated by the specified namespace). The ref value must be a qualified name (QName). The type can include a namespace prefix. Required.

Element information

Number of occurrences   One time.

Parent elements   element

Contents   (annotation?, (selector, field+))

Example

```
<xs:key name="state">
<!- states are keyed by their code ->
  <xs:selector xpath=".//state"/>
  <xs:field xpath="code"/>
</xs:key>

<xs:keyref name="vehicleState" refer="state">
  <!- every vehicle refers to its state ->
  <xs:selector xpath=".//vehicle"/>
  <xs:field xpath="@state"/>
</xs:keyref>
```

length

The number of units of length, where units of length varies depending on the type that is being derived from. The value of `length` must be a non-NegativeInteger.

Attributes

fixed   A Boolean value of true or false.

value   The default value or fixed value for the attribute, depending on the use property. If this attribute is derived from another attribute, this specified value takes precedence over any default or fixed value provided on any inherited attribute.

id   Optional attribute that creates a unique identifier of type ID for an element.

Element information

Contents   (annotation?)

Example

```
<simpleType name='productCode'>
    <restriction base='string'>
        <length value='8' fixed='true'/>
    </restriction>
</simpleType>
```

list

Defines a simpleType element as a list of values of a specified data type. When a data type is derived from a list data type, the following constraining facets can be used: length, maxLength, minLength, enumeration.

The unit of length is measured in the number of list items.

Attributes

itemType   The name of a built-in data type or simpleType element defined in this schema (or another schema indicated by the specified namespace). The simpleType element containing the list element is derived from the simple type specified by the list value. The list value must be a qualified name (QName).

id   Optional attribute that creates a unique identifier of type ID for an element.

Element information

Number of occurrences   One time.

Parent elements   simpleType

Child elements   (annotation?, (simpleType?))

Example

The following example shows a `simpleType` that is a list of integers:

```
<xsd:simpleType name='listOfIntegers'>
  <xsd:list itemType='integer'/>
</xsd:simpleType>
```

The following example shows an instance of an element that has an attribute of type listOfIntegers. Each item in the list is of type integer and is separated by white space—in this case, a space.

```
<myelement listOfIntegers='1 100 9 4000 0'>
```

The following example sets the maxLength to 5, limiting the number of items in an instance of the derivedlistOfIntegers data type to 5.

```
<xsd:simpleType name='derivedlistOfIntegers'>
  <xsd:restriction base='listOfIntegers'>
    <xsd:maxLength value='5'>
  </xsd:restriction>
</xsd:simpleType>
```

maxExclusive

The exclusive upper bound of the value space for a data type with the ordered property. The value of `maxExclusive` must be in the value space of the base type.

Attributes

fixed A Boolean value of true or false.

value The default value or fixed value for the attribute, depending on the use property. If this attribute is derived from another attribute, this specified value takes precedence over any default or fixed value provided on any inherited attribute.

annotation The annotations corresponding to all the annotation element information items in the children, if any.

Element information

Contents (annotation?)

Example

```
<simpleType name='less-than-one-hundred-and-one'>
  <restriction base='integer'>
    <maxExclusive value='101'/>
  </restriction>
</simpleType>
```

maxInclusive

Maximum value. This value must be the same data type as the inherited data type.

Attributes

fixed   A Boolean value of true or false

id   Optional attribute that creates a unique identifier of type ID for an element.

value   The default value or fixed value for the attribute, depending on the use property. If this attribute is derived from another attribute, this specified value takes precedence over any default or fixed value provided on any inherited attribute.

Element information

Contents   (annotation?)

Example

```
<simpleType name='one-hundred-or-less'>
  <restriction base='integer'>
    <maxInclusive value='100'/>
  </restriction>
</simpleType>
```

maxLength

Maximum number of units of length. Units of length depend on the data type. This value must be a nonNegativeInteger.

Attributes

fixed   A Boolean value of true or false

value   The default value or fixed value for the attribute, depending on the **use** property. If this attribute is derived from another attribute, this specified value takes precedence over any default or fixed value provided on any inherited attribute.

id   Optional attribute that creates a unique identifier of type ID for an element.

Element information

Contents   (annotation?)

Example

```
<simpleType name='form-input'>
  <restriction base='string'>
    <maxLength value='50'/>
  </restriction>
</simpleType>
```

minExclusive

The exclusive lower bound of the value space for a data type with the ordered property. The value of minExclusive must be in the value space of the base type.

Attributes

fixed   A Boolean value of true or false.

value   The default value or fixed value for the attribute, depending on the **use** property. If this attribute is derived from another attribute, this specified value takes precedence over any default or fixed value provided on any inherited attribute.

annotation   The annotations corresponding to all the annotation element information items in the children, if any.

Element information

Contents   (annotation?)

Example

```
<simpleType name='more-than-ninety-nine'>
   <restriction base='integer'>
      <minExclusive value='99'/>
   </restriction>
</simpleType>
```

minInclusive

The inclusive lower bound of the value space for a data type with the ordered property. The value of minInclusive must be in the value space of the base type.

Attributes

fixed   A Boolean value of true or false

value   The default value or fixed value for the attribute, depending on the use property. If this attribute is derived from another attribute, this specified value takes precedence over any default or fixed value provided on any inherited attribute.

annotation   The annotations corresponding to all the annotation element information items in the children, if any.

Element information

Contents   (annotation?)

Example

```
<simpleType name='one-hundred-or-more'>
   <restriction base='integer'>
      <minInclusive value='100'/>
   </restriction>
</simpleType>
```

minLength

The minimum number of units of length, where units of length varies depending on the type that is being derived from. The value must be a non-negative integer data type. For string and data types derived from a string, the value of this attribute is measured in units of characters as defined in XML 1.0 (Second Edition). For hexBinary and base64Binary and data types derived from them, `minLength` is measured in octets (8 bits) of binary data. For data types derived by list, `minLength` is measured in number of list items.

Attributes

fixed   A Boolean value of true or false

value   The default value or fixed value for the attribute, depending on the `use` property. If this attribute is derived from another attribute, this specified value takes precedence over any default or fixed value provided on any inherited attribute.

id   Optional attribute that creates a unique identifier of type ID for an element.

Element information

Contents   (`annotation?`)

Example

```
<simpleType name='non-empty-string'>
  <restriction base='string'>
    <minLength value='1'/>
  </restriction>
</simpleType>
```

pattern

Specific pattern that the data type's values must match. This constrains the data type to literals that match the specified pattern. The pattern value must be a regular expression.

value   The default value or fixed value for the attribute, depending on the `use` property. If this attribute is derived from another attribute, this specified value takes precedence over any default or fixed value provided on any inherited attribute.

annotation   The annotations corresponding to all the annotation element information items in the children, if any.

Element information

Contents   (`annotation?`)

Example

```
<simpleType name='better-us-zipcode'>
  <restriction base='string'>
    <pattern value='[0-9]{5}(-[0-9]{4})?'/>
  </restriction>
</simpleType>
```

redefine

Allows simple and complex types, groups, and attribute groups that are obtained from external schema files to be redefined in the current schema.

Attributes

Any valid schema attribute.

Element information

Content   annotation, simpleType, complexType, group, attributeGroup

Example: v1.xsd:

```
<xs:complexType name="personName">
 <xs:sequence>
  <xs:element name="title" minOccurs="0"/>
  <xs:element name="forename" minOccurs="0"
   maxOccurs="unbounded"/>
 </xs:sequence>
</xs:complexType>

<xs:element name="addressee" type="personName"/>
```

Example: v2.xsd:

```
<xs:redefine schemaLocation="v1.xsd">
 <xs:complexType name="personName">
  <xs:complexContent>
   <xs:extension base="personName">
    <xs:sequence>
     <xs:element name="generation"
      minOccurs="0"/>
```

```
            </xs:sequence>
          </xs:extension>
        </xs:complexContent>
      </xs:complexType>
   </xs:redefine>

   <xs:element name="author" type="personName"/>
```

restriction

(XSD) Defines constraints on a `simpleType`, `simpleContent`, or `complexContent` definition.

Attributes

base   The name of a built-in data type or `simpleType` element. The element containing the `extension` element is derived from the simple type specified by the base value. The base value must be a qualified name (QName).

id   Attribute that creates a unique identifier of type ID for an element.

Element information

Content   (annotation?, (simpleType?, (minExclusive | minInclusive | maxExclusive | maxInclusive | totalDigits | fractionDigits | length | minLength | maxLength | enumeration | whiteSpace | pattern)*))

Example

```
<simpleType name='Sku'>
    <restriction base='string'>
      <pattern value='\d{3}-[A-Z]{2}'/>
    </restriction>
</simpleType>
```

schema

Contains the definition of a schema. The `schema` element is the document element (the top-level element) in a schema definition.

The namespaces specified using the xmlns attribute must include the namespace for the schema-defining elements and attributes (schema, element, and so on). Any prefix can be used, but it is convenient to make the Schema namespace the default namespace to avoid having to use a prefix on every XML Schema element.

For XSD, the namespace is the following:

```
http://www.w3.org/2000/10/XMLSchema
```

In addition, the `schema` element should also contain namespace declarations for any other schemas that it uses.

Attributes

`xmlns`   One or more namespaces for use in this schema. The xmlns must be a URI reference. A prefix for the namespace can also be assigned. If no prefix is assigned, the schema components of the namespace can be used with unqualified references.

`attributeFormDefault`   The form for attributes declared in the target namespace of this schema. The value must be one of the following strings: qualified or unqualified. The default is unqualified.

This value is the global default for all attributes declared in the target namespace. Individual attributes can override this setting for their local scope using the `form` attribute.

`elementFormDefault`   The form for elements declared in the target namespace of this schema. The value must be one of the following strings: qualified or unqualified. The default is unqualified.

This value is the global default for all elements declared in the target namespace. Individual elements can override this setting for their local scope using the form attribute.

`id`   Optional attribute that creates a unique identifier of type ID for an element.

`blockDefault`   This attribute sets the default value of the `block` attribute on `element` and `complexType` elements in the target namespace of this schema. Possible values are:

`extension`   Prevents complex types derived by extension from being used in place of this complex type.

`restriction`   Prevents complex types derived by restriction from being used in place of this complex type.

substitution   Prevents substitution of elements.

#all   Prevents all derived complex types from being used in place of this complex type.

finalDefault   An attribute that sets the default value of the final attribute on `element` and `complexType` elements in the target namespace of the schema. Possible values include:

extension   Prevents derivation by extension.

restriction   Prevents derivation by restriction.

#all   Prevents all derivation (both extension and restriction).

targetNamespace   The URI reference of the namespace of this schema.

version   The version of the schema. Optional.

Element information

Number of occurrences   One time.

Parent elements   No parent elements.

Content   `((include | import | redefine | annotation)*, (((simpleType | complexType | group | attributeGroup) | element | attribute | notation), annotation*)*)`

Other   The `include`, `import`, and `redefine` elements must come before the other elements—except for the `annotation` element, which can appear anywhere.

Examples

The following schema uses the XSD namespace as the default namespace, the XSD data types namespace for data type definitions, and defines the schema's target namespace as `http://mynamespace/myschema`.

```
<schema xmlns="http://www.w3.org/2001/XMLSchema"
targetNamespace="http://mynamespace/myschema">
<!-Put schema content here -->
</schema>
```

In the following example, the schema components (element name, type) in the `http://www.w3.org/2001/XMLSchema` namespace are unqualified and those for `http://tempuri.org/myschema` (`mydecimal`) are qualified with the msc prefix:

```
<schema
    xmlns="http://www.w3.org/2001/XMLSchema"
    xmlns:msc="http://tempuri.org/myschema">
<element name="Price" type="msc:mydecimal"/>
</schema>
```

selector

Specifies an XML Path Language (XPath) expression that selects a set of elements for an identity constraint (`unique`, `key`, and `keyref` elements).

Attributes

id   Optional attribute that creates a unique identifier of type ID for an element.

xpath   An XPath expression that is relative to the element being declared. This expression identifies the child elements (of the element being declared) to which the identity constraint applies.

Element information

Number of occurrences   One time.

Parent elements   `key`, `keyref`, `unique`

Contents   (`annotation?`)

Example

```
<selector xpath="//expense[@approved='true']"/>
```

sequence

Requires the elements in the group to appear in the specified sequence within the containing element.

Attributes

id   Optional attribute that creates a unique identifier of type ID for an element.

maxOccurs   A value equal to or greater than zero that represents the maximum number of times a sequence can occur. You can use the string unbounded to indicate there is no maximum number.

minOccurs   A value equal to or greater than zero that represents the minimum number of times the sequence can occur. To specify that this sequence group is optional, set this attribute to zero.

Element information

Number of occurrences   Unlimited, unless within a group, where it is allowed one time.

Parent elements   group, choice, sequence, complexType, restriction, extension

Contents   (annotation?, (element | group | choice | sequence | any)*)

Example

```
<xsd:element name="zooAnimals">
    <xsd:complexType>
        <xsd:sequence minOccurs="0"
        maxOccurs="unbounded">
            <xsd:element name="elephant"/>
            <xsd:element name="bear"/>
            <xsd:element name="giraffe"/>
        </xsd:sequence>
    </xsd:complexType>
</xsd:element>
```

simpleContent

Contains either the extensions or restrictions on a complexType element with character data, or contains a simpleType element as content and contains no elements. The simpleContent element enables you to specify an element as containing a simpleType with no elements but enables you to restrict the value of the element's content or extend the element with attributes.

Attributes

id   Optional attribute that creates a unique identifier of type ID for an element.

Element information

Number of occurrences   One time.

Parent elements   `complexType`

Contents   `(annotation?, (restriction | extension))`

The following element declaration does not allow for adding attributes (such as `sizing`):

```
<xsd:element name="shoeSize" type="decimal"/>
```

Example

Using the `simpleContent` element, the following element declaration contains a `complexType` element that defines the content of the element as a decimal type with a single attribute (`sizing`):

```
<xsd:element name="shoeSize">
  <xsd:complexType>
    <xsd:simpleContent>
      <xsd:extension base="xsd:decimal">
        <xsd:attribute name="sizing">
          <xsd:restriction base="xsd:string">
            <xsd:enumeration value="US"/>
            <xsd:enumeration value="European"/>
            <xsd:enumeration value="UK"/>
            <xsd:enumeration value="Japan"/>
          </xsd:restriction>
        </xsd:attribute>
      </xsd:extension>
    </xsd:simpleContent>
  </xsd:complexType>
</xsd:element>
```

The following example shows an element (`generalPrice`) declared using an anonymous `complexType` (one without a name) with its content defined as a decimal data type and with a `currency` attribute.

```
<xsd:element name="generalPrice">
  <xsd:complexType>
    <xsd:simpleContent>
```

```
        <xsd:extension base="xsd:decimal">
          <xsd:attribute name="currency"
          type="xsd:string" />
        </xsd:extension>
      </xsd:simpleContent>
    </xsd:complexType>
  </xsd:element>
```

ⅉimpleType

Used for text-only content to set the constraints on and provide information about the values of attributes or elements. Simple types are defined by deriving them from existing simple types (built-in data types and derived simple types) and have no attributes or child elements.

Simple types can be defined in one of the following ways.

restriction   Restricts the range of values for the simple type to a subset of those for inherited simple type.

list   Defines a simple type that contains a white space–separated list of values of an inherited simple type.

union   Defines a simple type that contains a union of the values of two or more inherited simple types.

A `simpleType` declaration contained within a `complexType` or `attribute` element has the scope of the `complexType` or `attribute` that contains it. If a `simpleType` declaration has the `schema` element as its parent, it has global scope within that schema.

A simple type can be used in an attribute or element declaration or `complexType` (which, in turn, can be used in an element declaration) definition.

Attributes

id   Optional attribute that creates a unique identifier of type ID for an element.

name   The name of the type. The name must be an NCName as defined in the XML Namespaces specification. Optional.

If specified, the name must be unique among all `simple-Type` and `complexType` elements.

Element information

Number of occurrences   Unlimited.

Parent elements   attribute, element, list, restriction, schema, union

Contents   (annotation?, (restriction | list | union))

Examples

The following examples show simple type definitions using restriction, list, and union elements.

Example: Restriction

```
<xsd:simpleType name="freezeboilrangeInteger">
  <xsd:restriction base="xsd:integer">
    <xsd:minInclusive value="0"/>
    <xsd:maxInclusive value="100"/>
  </xsd:restriction>
</xsd:simpleType>
```

Example: List

```
<xsd:simpleType name="listOfDates">
  <xsd:list itemType="date">
</xsd:simpleType>
```

Example: Union

```
<xsd:attribute name="allframesize">
  <xsd:simpleType>
    <xsd:union>
      <xsd:simpleType>
        <xsd:restriction base="roadbikesize"/>
      </xsd:simpleType>
      <xsd:simpleType>
        <xsd:restriction base="mountainbikesize"/>
      </xsd:simpleType>
    </xsd:union>
  </xsd:simpleType>
</xsd:attribute>
```

```
<xsd:simpleType name="roadbikesize">
  <xsd:restriction base="xsd:positiveInteger">
    <xsd:enumeration="46"/>
    <xsd:enumeration="52"/>
    <xsd:enumeration="55"/>
  </xsd:restriction>
</xsd:simpleType>

<xsd:simpleType name="mountainbikesize">
  <xsd:restriction base="xsd:string">
    <xsd:enumeration value="small"/>
    <xsd:enumeration value="medium"/>
    <xsd:enumeration value="large"/>
  </xsd:restriction>
</xsd:simpleType>
```

totalDigits

The maximum number of digits in values of data types derived from decimal. The value of totalDigits must be a positiveInteger.

Attributes

fixed   A Boolean value of true or false.

value   The default value or fixed value for the attribute, depending on the use property. If this attribute is derived from another attribute, this specified value takes precedence over any default or fixed value provided on any inherited attribute.

annotation   The annotations corresponding to all the annotation element information items in the children, if any.

Contents   (annotation?)

Example

```
<simpleType name='amount'>
  <restriction base='decimal'>
    <totalDigits value='8'/>
    <fractionDigits value='2' fixed='true'/>
  </restriction>
</simpleType>
```

union

Defines a simpletype element as a collection of values from specified simple data types.

Attributes

id   Optional attribute that creates a unique identifier of type ID for an element.

memberTypes   The list of names of built-in data types or simple-Type elements defined in this schema (or another schema indicated by the specified namespace). The simpleType element containing the union element is derived from the simple types specified by the memberTypes value. The values in member-Types must be qualified names (QNames).

Element information

Number of occurrences   One time.

Parent elements   simpleType

Contents   (annotation?, (simpleType*))

Examples

The following example shows a simple type that is a union of two simple types.

```
<xsd:attribute name="fontsize">
  <xsd:simpleType>
    <xsd:union memberTypes="fontbynumber
    fontbystringname" />
  </xsd:simpleType>
</xsd:attribute>


<xsd:simpleType name="fontbynumber">
  <xsd:restriction base="xsd:positiveInteger">
    <xsd:maxInclusive="72"/>
  </xsd:restriction>
</xsd:simpleType>
```

```
<xsd:simpleType name="fontbystringname">
  <xsd:restriction base="xsd:string">
    <xsd:enumeration value="small"/>
    <xsd:enumeration value="medium"/>
    <xsd:enumeration value="large"/>
  </xsd:restriction>
</xsd:simpleType>
```

Example

The following example shows a simple type definition that is a union of all nonnegative integers and the NMTOKEN "unbounded". (This is taken from the schema in the W3C XML Schema Part 1: Structures specification.)

```
<xsd:simpleType name="allNNI">
  <xsd:annotation>
    <xsd:documentation>for maxOccurs</documentation>
  </xsd:annotation>
  <xsd:union memberTypes="nonNegativeInteger">
   <xsd:simpleType>
    <xsd:restriction base="NMTOKEN">
     <xsd:enumeration value="unbounded"/>
    </xsd:restriction>
   </xsd:simpleType>
  </xsd:union>
</xsd:simpleType>
```

unique

Specifies that an attribute or element value (or a combination of attribute or element values) must be unique within the specified scope with the following child elements (in this order of appearance):

selector   A required element whose value is an XML Path Language (XPath) expression specifying a unique set of elements specified by the field elements. Must be unique.

field   A required element containing an XPath expression specifying unique attribute or element values (attribute or element values) named by the selector element.

Attributes

id   Optional attribute that creates a unique identifier of type ID for an element.

name   A required attribute whose value is an NCName of the unique element.

The name must be unique within a schema.

Element information

Number of occurrences   One time.

Parent   `elements` element

Contents   `(annotation?, (selector, field+))`

Example

```
<xsd:schema
targetNamespace="http://tempuri.org/myschema
➥/unique">
<xsd:complexType name="customerOrderType">
 <xsd:sequence>
  <xsd:element name="item" minOccurs="0"
   maxOccurs="unbounded">
    <xsd:complexType>
    <xsd:attribute name="itemID" type="string"/>
    </xsd:complexType>
  </xsd:element>
 </xsd:sequence>
 <xsd:attribute name="CustomerID" type="string"/>
</xsd:complexType>

<xsd:element name="ordersByCustomer">
 <xsd:complexType>
    <xsd:sequence>
     <xsd:element name="customerOrders"
      type="customerOrderType" minOccurs="0"
      maxOccurs="unbounded" />
    </xsd:sequence>
 </xsd:complexType>
 <xsd:unique
  name="oneCustomerOrdersforEachCustomerID">
```

```
    <xsd:selector xpath="customerOrders"/>
    <xsd:field xpath="@customerID"/>
  </xsd:unique>
 </xsd:element>
</xsd:schema>
```

whiteSpace

Constrains the value space of types according to definitions provided by
Attribute Value Normalization in XML 1.0 (Second Edition). Possible
values:

> **preserve**   No normalization.
>
> **replace**   All occurrences of #x9 (tab), #xA (line feed), and
> #xD (carriage return) are replaced with #x20 (space).
>
> **collapse**   After the processing implied by `replace`, contiguous
> sequences of #x20's are collapsed to a single #x20, and leading
> and trailing #x20's are removed.

Attributes

> **fixed**   A Boolean value of true or false.
>
> **value**   The default value or fixed value for the attribute,
> depending on the use property.
>
> **annotation**   The annotations corresponding to all the annota-
> tion element information items in the children, if any.
>
> **Contents**   (annotation?)

Example

```
<simpleType name='token'>
   <restriction base='normalizedString'>
     <whiteSpace value='collapse'/>
   </restriction>
</simpleType>
```

Appendix C

SOAP REFERENCE

SOAP is XML-RPC on steroids. XML-RPC is a process for managing messaging routines between applications in different environments using remote procedure calls (hence the RPC acronym). SOAP is very similar, but it has stronger data typing. Before you automatically develop an application using the SOAP framework, you should check to make sure your needs can't be met with the simpler XML-RPC. You can find more information on XML-RPC at www.xml-rpc.com. You can find more information on SOAP at www.w3.org/TR/SOAP/.

SOAP is a lightweight protocol for exchange of information in a decentralized, distributed environment.

It is an XML-based protocol that consists of three parts: an envelope that defines a framework for describing what is in a message and how to process it, a set of encoding rules for expressing instances of application-defined data types, and a convention for representing remote procedure calls and responses. SOAP can potentially be used in combination with a variety of other protocols; however, the only bindings defined in this document describe how to use SOAP in combination with HTTP and the HTTP Extension Framework.

This reference is adapted from the Zvon SOAP reference developed by Miloslav Nic, which is available under a GNU license at www.zvon.org/xxl/soapReference/Output/index.html.

Body

The SOAP Body element provides a simple mechanism for exchanging mandatory information intended for the ultimate recipient of the message. Typical uses of the Body element include marshalling RPC calls and error reporting. All immediate child elements of the Body element are called body entries, and each body entry is encoded as an independent element within the SOAP Body element.

Attributes

encodingStyle   The SOAP encodingStyle global attribute can be used to indicate the serialization rules used in a SOAP message. This attribute *may* appear on any element, and is scoped to that element's contents and all child elements not containing such an attribute, much as an XML namespace declaration is scoped. There is no default encoding defined for a SOAP message.

Element information

Data types   The following data types are available to SOAP elements:

> array, binary, boolean, byte, century, date, decimal, double, ENTITIES, ENTITY, float, ID, IDREF, IDREFS, int, integer, language, long, month, Name, NCName, negativeInteger, NMTOKEN, NMTOKENS, nonNegativeInteger, nonPositive-Integer, NOTATION, positiveInteger, QName, recurringDate, recurringDay, recurringDuration, short, string, time, time-Duration, timeInstant, timePeriod, unsignedByte, unsigned-Int, unsignedLong, unsignedShort, uriReference, year

Parent elements   None.

Contents   `Fault`

Header

This is an optional child element of the `Envelope` element used to send processing information. All immediate child elements of the SOAP `Header` element *must* be namespace-qualified.

Attributes

`actor`   A URI that names the intended recipient of the header. If omitted, the ultimate recipient of the SOAP message itself is intended.

`mustUnderstand`   A Boolean (0 or 1) that indicates whether the header is mandatory or optional. If mandatory, the header must be understood by the recipient.

Element information

Parent elements   `Envelope`

Contents   User-defined. Attributes are applied to user-defined elements like so:

```
<SOAP-ENV:Header>
    <t:Transaction
        xmlns:t="some-URI"
        SOAP-ENV:mustUnderstand="1">
    5
```

```
      </t:Transaction>
    </SOAP-ENV:Header>
```

detail

The detail element is intended for carrying application-specific error information related to the Body element. It *must* be present if the contents of the Body element could not be successfully processed. It *must not* be used to carry information about error information belonging to header entries. Detailed error information belonging to header entries *must* be carried within header entries. The absence of the detail element in the Fault element indicates that the fault is not related to processing of the Body element. This can be used to distinguish whether or not the Body element was processed in case of a fault situation. All immediate child elements of the detail element are called detail entries, and each detail entry is encoded as an independent element within the detail element.

Attributes

encodingStyle   See Body element.

Element information

Parent elements   Fault

Contents   None.

Envelope

The Envelope is the top element of the XML document representing the message. The element *may* contain namespace declarations as well as additional attributes. If present, such additional attributes *must* be namespace-qualified. Similarly, the element *may* contain additional sub-elements. If present these elements *must* be namespace-qualified and *must* follow the SOAP Body element.

Attributes

encodingStyle   See Body element.

Element information

Parent elements None.

Contents Header, Body

Fault

This element is used to carry error and/or status information within a SOAP message. If present, the SOAP Fault element *must* appear as a body entry and *must not* appear more than once within a Body element.

Element information

Parent elements Body

Contents faultcode, faultstring, faultfactor, detail

faultactor

The faultactor element is intended to provide information about who caused the fault to happen within the message path. It is similar to the SOAP actor attribute, but instead of indicating the destination of the header entry, it indicates the source of the fault. The value of the fault-actor attribute is a URI identifying the source. Applications that do not act as the ultimate destination of the SOAP message *must* include the faultactor element in a SOAP Fault element. The ultimate destination of a message *may* use the faultactor element to indicate explicitly that it generated the fault.

Element information

Parent elements Fault

Contents None.

faultcode

The faultcode element is intended for use by software to provide an algorithmic mechanism for identifying the fault. The faultcode *must* be present in a SOAP Fault element, and the faultcode value *must* be a qualified name. SOAP defines a small set of SOAP fault codes covering basic SOAP faults.

Element information

Parent elements Fault

Contents None.

TABLE C.1: Fault Codes

CODE	DESCRIPTION
VersionMismatch	The processing party found an invalid namespace for the SOAP Envelope element.
MustUnderstand	An immediate child element of the SOAP Header element that was either not understood or not obeyed by the processing party contained a SOAP mustUnderstand attribute with a value of 1.
Client	The Client class of errors indicate that the message was incorrectly formed or did not contain the appropriate information in order to succeed. For example, the message could lack the proper authentication or payment information. It is generally an indication that the message should not be resent without change.
Server	The Server class of errors indicate that the message could not be processed for reasons not directly attributable to the contents of the message itself but rather to the processing of the message. For example, processing could include communicating with an upstream processor, which didn't respond. The message may succeed at a later point in time.

faultstring

The faultstring element is intended to provide a human-readable explanation of the fault and is not intended for algorithmic processing. The faultstring element is similar to the Reason-Phrase defined by HTTP. It *must* be present in a SOAP Fault element and *should* provide at least some information explaining the nature of the fault.

Element information

Parent elements Fault

Contents None.

Sample SOAP Message

```
POST /StockQuote HTTP/1.1
Host: www.stockquoteserver.com
Content-Type: text/xml; charset="utf-8"
Content-Length: nnnn
SOAPAction: "Some-URI"

<SOAP-ENV:Envelope
  xmlns:SOAP-ENV="http://schemas.xmlsoap.
➥org/soap/envelope/"
  SOAP-ENV:encodingStyle="http://schemas.xmlsoap.
➥org/soap/encoding/">
  <SOAP-ENV:Body>
      <m:GetLastTradePrice xmlns:m="Some-URI">
          <symbol>DIS</symbol>
      </m:GetLastTradePrice>
    </SOAP-ENV:Body>
</SOAP-ENV:Envelope>
```

INDEX

Note to the Reader: Throughout this index **boldfaced** page numbers indicate primary discussions of a topic. *Italicized* page numbers indicate illustrations.

B

C

M